CARCERAL LOGICS

Carceral logics permeate our thinking about humans and nonhumans. We imagine that greater punishment will reduce crime and make society safer. We hope that more convictions and policing for animal crimes will keep animals safe and elevate their social status. The dominant approach to human-animal relations is governed by an unjust imbalance of power that subordinates or ignores the interest nonhumans have in freedom. In this volume, Lori Gruen and Justin Marceau invited experts to provide insights into the complicated intersection of issues that arise in thinking about animal law, violence, mass incarceration, and social change. Advocates for enhancing the legal status of animals could learn a great deal from the history of other social movements. Social change lawyers and animal advocates, might learn lessons from each other about the interconnections of oppression as they work to achieve liberation for all. This title is also available as Open Access on Cambridge Core.

Lori Gruen is the William Griffin Professor of Philosophy at Wesleyan University. She is also the founder and coordinator of Wesleyan Animal Studies and the author or editor of over a dozen books, including *Ethics and Animals: An Introduction* (Cambridge, 2021), *Critical Terms for Animal Studies* (2018), and *The Ethics of Captivity* (2014).

Justin Marceau is the Brooks Institute Faculty Research Scholar and Professor of Law at the University of Denver, Research Scholar at the Brooks Institute, and an active animal protection and civil rights litigator. He is the author of *Beyond Cages* (Cambridge, 2019).

Carceral Logics

HUMAN INCARCERATION AND ANIMAL CAPTIVITY

Edited by

LORI GRUEN

Wesleyan University

JUSTIN MARCEAU

University of Denver Sturm College of Law

CAMBRIDGE
UNIVERSITY PRESS

CAMBRIDGE
UNIVERSITY PRESS

University Printing House, Cambridge CB2 8BS, United Kingdom

One Liberty Plaza, 20th Floor, New York, NY 10006, USA

477 Williamstown Road, Port Melbourne, VIC 3207, Australia

314–321, 3rd Floor, Plot 3, Splendor Forum, Jasola District Centre, New Delhi – 110025, India

103 Penang Road, #05–06/07, Visioncrest Commercial, Singapore 238467

Cambridge University Press is part of the University of Cambridge.

It furthers the University's mission by disseminating knowledge in the pursuit of education, learning, and research at the highest international levels of excellence.

www.cambridge.org
Information on this title: www.cambridge.org/9781108843584
DOI: 10.1017/9781108919210

First published 2022

A catalogue record for this publication is available from the British Library.

Library of Congress Cataloging-in-Publication Data
NAMES: Gruen, Lori, editor. | Marceau, Justin, editor.
TITLE: Carceral logics : human incarceration and animal captivity / edited by Lori Gruen, Wesleyan University, Connecticut; Justin Marceau, University of Denver Sturm College of Law.
DESCRIPTION: Cambridge, United Kingdom ; New York, NY : Cambridge University Press, 2022. | Includes bibliographical references and index.
IDENTIFIERS: LCCN 2021051121 (print) | LCCN 2021051122 (ebook) | ISBN 9781108843584 (hardback) | ISBN 9781108825917 (paperback) | ISBN 9781108919210 (epub)
SUBJECTS: LCSH: Animal welfare–Law and legislation–Philosophy. | Imprisonment–Philosophy.
CLASSIFICATION: LCC K3620 .C37 2022 (print) | LCC K3620 (ebook) | DDC 344.04/9–dc23/eng/20220118
LC record available at https://lccn.loc.gov/2021051121
LC ebook record available at https://lccn.loc.gov/2021051122

ISBN 978-1-108-84358-4 Hardback

Contents

Notes on Contributors

Vikram David Amar is Dean and Iwan Foundation Professor of Law at the University of Illinois College of Law.

Ashley N. Beck has been a Deputy District Attorney at the Denver District Attorney's Office in Denver, Colorado, since 2013. During this period, she has held positions in a variety of units within the office, to include county court, the juvenile unit, drug court, district court, and the family violence unit. Since 2018 she has also been the office's primary point of contact for all animal cruelty offenses. In this role, she collaborates with the Denver Police Department and Denver Animal Protection in order to ensure these cases are investigated, filed, and appropriately prosecuted. She routinely provides training opportunities for law enforcement and her peers on the topic of animal cruelty and has partnered with the Humane Society of the United State to conduct webinars and animal cruelty investigations and prosecutions. Outside of the office, Ms. Beck sits on the Board of Directors for the Animal Assistance Foundation and also serves on the Colorado POST Board. She holds a dual BA degree in political science and Spanish from the University of Portland and a Juris Doctor from the University of Colorado Law School.

Marc Bekoff, PhD, is Professor Emeritus of ecology and evolutionary biology at the University of Colorado, Boulder. He has published more than thirty books, the latest being *A Dog's World: Imagining the Lives of Dogs in a World without Humans*, and writes regularly for *Psychology Today* about animal emotions and compassionate conservation. His homepage is marcbekoff.com.

Jennifer M. Chacón is a Professor of Law at the University of California, Berkeley School of Law, and the author of numerous articles, book chapters, and essays on immigration, criminal law, constitutional law, and citizenship issues. She is a past chair of the American Association of Law School's Section on Immigration. She is a member of the American Law Institute, the Ninth Circuit Court of Appeals Rules Committee, and the American Bar Foundation's Board of Directors.

Alan K. Chen is the Thompson G. Marsh Law Alumni Professor at the University of Denver Sturm College of Law, where he teaches and writes about American constitutional law and engages in public interest litigation.

Richard L. Cupp, Jr., serves as the John W. Wade Professor of Law at Caruso Pepperdine School of Law. He is an animal welfare advocate who has published several scholarly articles that address evolving legal protection of animals and animals' appropriate legal status.

Maneesha Deckha is Professor and Lansdowne Chair in Law at the University of Victoria. Her research interests include critical animal law, postcolonial theory, feminist theory, health law, and reproductive law and policy. Her scholarship has appeared in multiple venues and has been supported by the Canadian Institutes of Health Research and the Social Sciences and Humanities Research Council of Canada. She has also held the Fulbright Visiting Chair in Law and Society at New York University. She is the author of *Animals as Legal Beings: Contesting Anthropocentric Legal Orders* (University of Toronto Press), and is a graduate of McGill University, the University of Toronto, and Columbia University.

Jessica Eisen is an Assistant Professor at the University of Alberta Faculty of Law. Her research interests include animal law, constitutional and comparative constitutional law, and feminist and critical legal theory.

Pamela D. Frasch is the Brooks McCormick Jr. Scholar of Animal Law and Policy at Lewis & Clark Law School. She founded the Center for Animal Law Studies at Lewis & Clark in 2008; held the first-ever Animal Law Dean position from 2010 to 2020; and previously served as General Counsel for the Animal Legal Defense Fund. Pamela cowrote the first legal casebook on Animal Law, now in its 6th edition, (*Animal Law Cases & Materials*, Carolina Academic Press, 2019), and *Animal Law in a Nutshell*, now in its 3rd edition (West Academic, 2020). A frequent writer and speaker on animal law and animal law education, she has traveled to multiple countries around the world to provide expertise and support to those seeking to establish animal law in academia. Among other honors, Pamela is the inaugural recipient of the AALS Excellence in Animal Law: Scholarship-Teaching-Service Award.

Aya Gruber is the Ira C. Rothgerber Professor of Constitutional Law and Criminal Justice at the University of Colorado Law School and the author of *The Feminist War on Crime: The Unexpected Role of Women's Liberation in Mass Incarceration*.

Lori Gruen is the William Griffin Professor of Philosophy at Wesleyan University where she also coordinates Wesleyan Animal Studies. She is the author or editor of fifteen books and dozens of chapters and articles. She works at the intersection of practical ethics and political philosophy. She is the inaugural Research Fellow for the Brooks Institute for Animal Law and Policy. Gruen is a founding faculty member of the Center for Prison Education at Wesleyan. She has taught incarcerated students at Bayview Correctional Facility, a women's prison in Chelsea, NY (now closed); the Federal Correctional Institution in Danbury, CT, when it was a women's prison; and Cheshire Correctional Institution in Cheshire, CT, a maximum security men's prison and York Correctional Institution, a woman's prison. Her website is www.lorigruen.com.

Sam Kamin is a Professor of Law at the University of Denver, Sturm College of Law. Holding both a JD and a PhD from the University of California at Berkeley as well as a BA, summa cum laude, from Amherst College, Professor Kamin's research interests include criminal procedure, death penalty jurisprudence, federal courts, and constitutional remedies.

Tamara L. Kuennen is Professor of Law in the Civil Litigation Clinic at the University of Denver Sturm College of Law, where she supervises students who represent survivors of domestic violence and sexual assault in obtaining civil protection orders, low-income tenants in defending against evictions, and immigrant day laborers who are unpaid for their work. She frequently trains judges as a consulting faculty member for the National Judicial Institute on Domestic Violence, a partnership of the US Department of Justice Office on Violence against Women, the National Council of Juvenile and Family Court Judges, and Futures Without Violence. Tamara's scholarship focuses on how the law could more adequately meet the needs of survivors of domestic violence.

Douglas A. Kysar is the Joseph M. Field '55 Professor of Law and Faculty Co-Director of the Law, Ethics, and Animals Program at Yale University.

Benjamin Levin is an Associate Professor of Law at the University of Colorado Law School, where he teaches criminal law and procedure.

Justin Marceau is a Professor of Law, the Brooks Institute Faculty Research Scholar of Animal Law and Policy, the Faculty Director of the Animal Law Program at University of Denver Sturm College of Law. He served as an inaugural member of the Governor's Council for Animal Protection in Colorado, as a member of an oversight committee for the Colorado Bureau of Animal Protection, and on the board of directors for a leading farm sanctuary. He has litigated a variety of animal protection issues, including constitutional challenges to Ag-Gag laws and civil rights cases involving dogs. He is a Fellow of the Oxford Centre for Animal Ethics, and the recipient of numerous awards, including the Justice for Animals Award. He is a member of the American Law Institute, and a frequent peer reviewer for a variety of publications. In 2019 he published his first book, *Beyond Cages*.

Kelly Struthers Montford is Assistant Professor of Criminology at Ryerson University (currently undergoing renaming). She is the coeditor of three volumes spanning colonialism, animality, and the carceral and her work appears in philosophy, legal, law, and animal studies journals.

Karen M. Morin is Professor of Geography at Bucknell University in Lewisburg, Pennsylvania. She is author of *Carceral Space, Prisoners and Animals* (2018), among other books.

David N. Pellow is the Dehlsen Chair and Professor of Environmental Studies and Director of the Global Environmental Justice Project at the University of California, Santa Barbara. His teaching, research, and activism focus on environmental, climate, and multispecies justice in the United States and globally.

Jessica Pierce is a bioethicist and Faculty Affiliate at the Center for Bioethics and Humanities, University of Colorado Anschutz Medical Campus. Her books include *The Last Walk: Reflections on Our Pets at the Ends of Their Lives* and *Run, Spot, Run: The Ethics of Keeping Pets.*

Will Potter is an investigative journalist, author, and leading international voice challenging the erosion of civil liberties in the name of fighting "terrorism." His book, *Green Is the New Red: An Insider's Account of a Social Movement under Siege*, exposed the criminalization of nonviolent protest groups by the FBI, and was awarded a Kirkus Star for "remarkable merit." He has been invited to speak about counterterrorism policies and political repression before the US Congress and meetings of the Australian Parliament and Council of Europe.

Paula Tarankow is a consultant and historian who specializes in nineteenth-century US history, animal studies, and race. Her research explores how the memory of slavery defined the culture of animal protection in post–Civil War America.

Delcianna J. Winders is a Professor at Vermont Law School, where she directs the Animal Law Program.

Acknowledgments

We began discussing plans for this book at a gathering hosted by the Brooks Institute for Animal Law and Policy in 2019. The Brooks Institute has since provided tremendous support for this project, and we are deeply grateful for their commitment to seeing this collaboration through to publication. With Denver Law School, the Brooks Institute cohosted a workshop on early drafts of many of the chapters presented here. We are grateful for that support and to all the discussants at the workshop: Vikram Amar, Amanda Arrington, Frank Ascione, Marc Bekoff, Jennifer Chacon, Gabrielle Chapman, Alan Chen, Maneesha Deckha, Lora Dunn, Jessica Eisen, Pamela Frasch, Aya Gruber, Sam Kamin, Alec Karakatsanis, Tammy Kuennen, Doug Kysar, Benjamin Levin, Shelby McDonald, Karen M. Morin, Timothy Pachirat, Jessica Pierce, Will Potter, David Rosengard, Laura Rovner, Kelly Struthers Montford, Paula Tarankow, Phillip Tedeschi, and Delci Winders. Not every participant was able to complete a chapter, but we are grateful to all of the persons who have helped with this project, either by writing or providing comments or assistance.

Justin is grateful to all of the students who helped edit, revise, or format these chapters, and in particular Nicole King, who helped plan and coordinate the in-person workshop in 2019. I am also thankful to all of the animal advocates who have had the patience and confidence to hear my critiques of the movement with an open mind. Many of the conversations I have had over the past few years have helped me better understand my own thinking on animals and the law. In particular, I am grateful to Amanda Arrington (Pets for Life at HSUS) whose work with communities to help animals is both unique and visionary. I am grateful to Tim Midura and Kristen Stilt for being friends and allies of the sort who support intellectual inquiries, even if they don't agree with all of the conclusions or analysis. Both of these individuals have asked me hard questions about this project over the years, which is a real gift. Most importantly, I would be remiss if I did not say that working with Lori has been the realization of a life goal for me. I have long wanted to collaborate with a philosopher, and I can't imagine one whose work I read (and teach) more regularly, or one who is more incisive and clear in her thinking – I hope we can do it again! Lori is involved in more projects than almost anyone I know, and somehow as generous with her time as any scholar you could meet. And finally, I thank my kids for always asking me hard questions about the intersections of human and animal suffering and for pushing me to imagine a better world for all animals.

Lori would like to thank the students in her "Ethics of Captivity" course at Wesleyan University in the Fall of 2020 for collectively working through issues that are discussed in this volume. I am also deeply indebted to my incarcerated students at both the maximum-security men's prison – Cheshire Correctional Institution – and the only women's prison in Connecticut – York Correctional Institution. I am one of the faculty founders of Wesleyan's Center for Prison Education and have been teaching courses in prison since 2010. What I have learned through my students about the nature of incarceration has deeply informed my thinking about carceral logics. I also want to express my deep respect and appreciation for Justin. He is a brilliant, courageous thinker whom I have learned a great deal from, and he is an absolute delight to work with. I'm so grateful to be able to think and create with him.

Introduction

Lori Gruen and Justin Marceau

The American system of criminal law and punishment is racist, classist, destructive, and ineffective in preventing harm and promoting justice. This isn't an extreme view, nor is it a secret. Indeed, more than half of the country has concluded that aspects of our system of punishment are unfair according to recent polling. Nonetheless, many Americans reflexively seek out punitive interventions in response to vexing social problems. We operate in a realm of dissonance recognizing in the abstract the dysfunction and cruelty of the system, but also endorse criminal interventions in support of the social goals we support. These complicated, contradictory views about the system of law, policing, and imprisonment have been, until quite recently, relatively unexamined. This book encourages reflection on these complex issues of progressive carceralism.

In particular, this book focuses on the connection between our complicated, contradictory views about crime and punishment and our complicated, contradictory views about nonhuman animals. We love dogs, but eat pigs. Birdwatching is a popular pastime, but birdwatching while Black can and has led to police intervention, while eating wild and domesticated birds is simultaneously commonplace. Pitbulls and animal fighting are overwhelmingly associated with urban life and Black men, but killing wild animals for sport is celebrated as a great (primarily white) American pastime. In general, there is also willingness among Americans to overlook, abuse, and cage nonhuman animals. We cage them for our entertainment, because they are deemed a nuisance, or because we plan to eat them or otherwise use their bodies for our human ends. Animal suffering is often invisible under the law or irrelevant as a matter of morality. Leading scholars and activist groups have sought to improve the status of animals in law and society in a variety of ways. Indeed, there is likely more disagreement than agreement about effective legal interventions in animal law. But one of the tactics for promoting justice for animals – perhaps a central focus of animal "law" in the minds of many – is the use of the criminal law as a cudgel to make an example out of certain forms of animal cruelty and abuse. Through prosecution and policing, it is imagined, that animal suffering can achieve an appropriate level of social condemnation.

Strikingly, the law permits most forms of cruelty to evade criminal scrutiny, either through de facto procedures or de jure exemptions. But the forms of individual abuse and neglect that can be prosecuted are the subject of considerable fanfare. It is the injured, abused, or mistreated companion animal (often a dog or cat) that makes its way into TV commercials and mailers about why animal protection matters. An e-mail in April of 2021 from David Rosengard of the Animal Legal Defense Fund to potential donors opens with the following paragraph:

> Franky, a beloved family dog, was stolen from his home in Maine. He was beaten, shot for "target practice," and drowned. Justin Chipman was found guilty of aggravated cruelty to animals for his role in Franky's torture and death. He was sentenced to just one year in prison and ordered to pay only $100 in restitution.

The email goes on to note that because animal cruelty laws are "poorly enforced, the violent criminals responsible all too often get inadequate sentences." The message of this type of communications is twofold: (1) animal abuse is underpoliced, and underprosecuted; and (2) by punishing the individual abuser, the status of animals is improved, and the victimhood of animals finally acknowledged. To engage in this sort of propaganda while pretending that carceral animal law has nothing to do with mass incarceration is an untenable obfuscation.

We live in a world where both humans and nonhumans are suffering because of oppressive carceral logics that rely on scapegoating and othering. This book pulls two seemingly separate concerns – the harmfulness of our system of mass incarceration and the harm that humans do to nonhumans – together. It is an effort to begin an academic dialogue between experts who have more in common than they previously understood. This book puts some of the leading thinkers on human incarceration in discourse with some of the big thinkers on animal confinement. The point is not to equate all carceral conditions, but the hope is to think critically about the role of carceral logics across human and animal spheres. What might those concerned about animals learn from social change and civil right lawyers, and what do animal advocates have to teach us all about social change through policing and prosecution?

The book also lies at the intersection of two emerging fields of study, progressive carceralism and what is loosely called anticarceral veganism. In this vein, the chapters that follow offer some fresh perspectives on the uniquely paradoxical project of incarcerating humans in order to liberate nonhumans, as well as some of the most thoughtful and comprehensive defenses of a carceral approach to animal law written to date.

I.1 ABOUT THE EDITING OF THIS BOOK

We are scholars of philosophy and law, and we are both personally and professionally committed to improving the lives of nonhuman animals. We care about suffering and the oppression of marginalized beings, whether they are human or other-than-human, and we think moral and legal frameworks grievously undervalue the lives of animals. The questions this book seeks to interrogate revolve around the role of carceral logics in catalyzing positive social change. Are animals benefited by the logics of captivity and carcerality, whether the cages are for the animals or reserved for the humans accused of animal abuse or neglect? The chapters that follow take a diverse approach to examining these critical questions. The relationship of human and animal captivity to well-being is a question of defining import for modern animal law. It is also profoundly important for those who are captive.

As editors and authors, we don't approach this topic from a position of detachment or self-proclaimed neutrality. Rather, our own research shapes our view that carceral logics impede more than they advance the project of protecting animals. Our own chapters urge readers to recognize what we view as the futility of a carceral response, and worse, the negative impacts carceral frameworks have on animals. But we recognize this as contested intellectual terrain, and accordingly we have attempted to gather a range of scholars with differing perspectives and varying entry points for this conversation. To this end, we have recruited accomplished and distinguished voices who see policing and prosecution as paths to a promising future for animal law. Indeed, at least one chapter in this volume openly calls for the expansion of the punishment bureaucracy in the form of a new unit at the Department of Justice whose focus would be more vigorous and frequent animal abuse and neglect prosecutions. Other chapters unapologetically and earnestly speak to the role that felony prosecutions might be understood to play in recognizing animals as victims of crime.

This book aims to provide readers with perspectives from persons who possess a variety of backgrounds and beliefs about the criminal system. Some of the authors in this book have only worked on animal protection issues and have very little involvement in the law, or the criminal law. Other chapters are by authors who are field-marking experts on topics of law, such as immigration or domestic violence or drug crimes, who have never previously engaged with the field of animal studies. This array of backgrounds and perspectives is deployed to provide a larger context for examining carceral logics in animal law.

The project is not, however, one of unifying or flattening out differing perspectives. The goal is not to suggest that there is a single, rational response to the devalued status of animals in the law. Rather, our goal is to generate new conversations, making new theoretical connections, and encouraging discourse across disciplinary and ideological lines. There is not a consensus on many of the questions raised in this book, and nothing approaching it.

Historians examine society's legal norms as one of the metrics for gauging fairness and justice. Our view is that history will not look favorably on the practices of carceral animal law – neither our treatment of animals nor our prosecution and policing of persons as a response to animal maltreatment. But we are strong believers that one should confront the strongest version of an argument, and engage with it fully and fairly. And for that reason, the book includes a plurality of perspectives, and we have endeavored to provide the best set of arguments on a variety of topics relating to the intersection of carceral logics and animal protection.

I.2 WHAT DO WE MEAN BY "CARCERAL LOGICS"?

There are two distinct senses of "carceral logics" – one that we might think of as a narrower, internal logic, the logic that orders the legal system, prisons, and other similar institutions; and one that is broader, that shapes our understanding and analyses of social problems and solutions. We can think of the first sort of carceral logic as having its emphasis on the "logic" of carceral systems – the laws, rules, design, and practices of courts, police, and prisons. The second sort or carceral logic emphasizes how the "carceral" and its practices inform, surveil, limit, and constrain our thinking in contexts that go beyond prisons.

That these two senses of carceral logics are distinct, doesn't mean that they don't inform one another, as often they do. One clear example that we briefly mention below is the way in which incarceration as a means of incapacitation to both punish those who have caused harm and prevent them from doing so again shapes thinking about how to respond to people, particularly young people, who harm animals. The carceral logic of the criminal law often justifies lengthy sentences for those who commit violent crimes in part as a way to allow victims, and their communities, to feel protected and safe. Many of those in animal law want to replicate this carceral logic in the context of animal cruelty, suggesting that someone who egregiously harms an animal may very well do so again, and it may not just be nonhumans who are harmed the next time.

Animal protectionists who work to expand carceral responses to harms are not alone in thinking that criminal punishment will elevate the status of the victims and protect others in the future. Indeed, among social justice scholars and activists of all sorts, carceral logics are operating overtly or covertly. So-called carceral feminists seek gender justice and relief from domestic violence by turning to the patriarchal legal system to protect them and punish perpetrators of harm. In the wake of the police killing of George Floyd and Breonna Taylor, and so many other Black men, women, and children, there is usually a large number of people who respond to these murders with a desire to lock the police up. Carceral logics prevent many of those seeking to challenge injustice from seeing how the legal system can perpetuate injustice and from critically imagining less carceral responses to a variety of harms to both humans and to other animals. It has become commonplace to speak of criminal sentences that don't lead to incarceration as noncarceral. Indeed, animal advocates are quick to point to sentences of probation and fines, for example, as useful teaching tools or proactive interventions. It is taken for granted that if an individual is in need of public services such as mental health treatment, the criminal system is an efficient means of connecting individuals with the treatment they need. But this idea that policing, fines, and convictions are a good vehicle for the distribution of civil services is, in fact, a carceral mindset and one that warrants considerably more scrutiny.

I.3 THIS PROJECT IS NOT ANTHROPOCENTRIC

When we talk to people about the problems with a criminal response to animal suffering, a common reaction is to assume that our project is designed at prioritizing human suffering. At least one commentator has concluded that a project concerned with the demonstrated problems inherent in policing and prosecution is a project that is concerned first and foremost with human rights. This is comforting for many animal advocates because it allows them to create a clear distinction between those who are helping primarily humans and those focused on the other-than-human world.

We unequivocally reject this binary. The idea that protecting animals and protecting humans is akin to a zero-sum game in which if one is benefiting humans, for example, by arguing for alternatives to convictions, then animals have to suffer, is maliciously and demonstrably false. There is very little reason for adopting such either/or thinking. We hope this book will generate conversations and lead to research considering the ways that helping humans can help other animals and vice versa.

The chapters that follow provide support for a variety of commitments. We respect the arguments and views expressed in this collection, even though we sometimes don't agree. And we certainly don't purport to have a singular vision of the best path forward for animal advocacy. One thing we reject, however, are claims that we do not sufficiently care about animals, or that we care more about humans who are incarcerated, than we do other nonhuman animals. Our scholarly and practical records show how this is false. Our project here is one of reimagining the discourse about animal law, of opening fields of inquiry about what is possible, and challenging the received wisdom about the role of law in helping animals. We welcome challenges, but it would be a mistake to conflate our view with an effort to deemphasize animal status or undervalue animals. We may disagree with the prevailing wisdom that more prosecutions and investment in the criminal system will lead to "more justice"[1] for animals, but not because we disagree with the idea that animals are grotesquely undervalued in our legal system and in society more broadly.

[1] Jessica Rubin, 34 Harv. L. Rev. F. 263 (2021).

I.4 ANIMAL CRIMES AND THE "LINK" BETWEEN HUMAN AND ANIMAL VIOLENCE

The salience of the so-called link in animal law debates is hard to overstate. It has become nearly impossible to talk about animal cruelty without discussing the presumed threat to humans from animal abusers. Seemingly every piece of carceral animal legislation and nearly every piece of academic commentary defending a criminal response to animal cruelty, including several chapters in this book, take for granted the idea that a criminal response is necessary to protect humans. A prominent animal attorney, Rebeka Breder, was arguing to the media for a longer sentence in an animal abuse case in 2021 and said, because "we know there is a link between animal abuse and human abuse, this should be a sentencing factor." According to this ubiquitous logic, animal abuse is a sort of canary in the coal mine, an early warning for human violence to come, and thus punishments are a necessary intervention to break this link, and protect humans. As one leading organization puts it, "Animal Cruelty Is a Clear Predictor of Future Violence, So Why Are Perpetrators Merely Slapped on the Wrist?"[2]

The appeal to human interest and safety is transparently deployed by animal advocates in their carceral strategies for addressing certain animal harms. The link creates a sort of bogeyman that calls to mind images of serial killers, and is reminiscent of rhetoric like that of so-called superpredators. The public is told that if they want fewer mass shootings, fewer murders, or fewer sexual assaults, than a more aggressive approach to animal policing and prosecution is the answer. The link has become a sort of talisman of carceral animal law, much as superpredators became the poster children of the war-on-crime era at the end of the twentieth century. Judges are told that they need training on the link, and legislators are warned that violent crime rates are intimately linked to violence against animals.

We think it is important to flag our discomfort with the way the link has been used as a justification for carceral interventions in animal law, and though our list of grievances with this line of thought is long, we will focus on just a couple of deep concerns. First, it must be noted that the animal protection movement protests mightily that their calls for tough-on-crime approaches have *anything* to do with mass incarceration – there are not many animal abusers in prison, they often assume. But we have passed the point in history where we can simply engage in hyperbolic discourse about budding psychopaths and would-be mass-shooters without expecting it to grease the gears of the carceral machinery. Promoting a public understanding that warns of lurking criminal monsters and great public dangers because of underenforcement is precisely the type of logic and discourse that made

[2] Steve Wells, *Animal Cruelty Is a Clear Predictor of Future Violence, So Why Are Perpetrators Merely Slapped on the Wrist?* www.all-creatures.org/articles/lit-slap-on-wrist.html (the header on the website reads, "Working for a Peaceful World for Humans, Animals and the Environment").

mass incarceration possible in this country. No one group (not domestic violence advocates, not child protectionists, not anti–drunk driving campaigns, not hate-crime proponents, not anti-drug crusaders) is responsible for shaping the discourse or driving carceral logics on their own. It is a joint project, and one that the animal lawyers – fueled by their moral panic around the link – have participated in consistently. Before turning away from the link, it is worth noting a few other, related objections to the way it is deployed by animal lawyers.

First, the logic of link-think is internally inconsistent. Even if one assumes that persons who harm animals will progress to harming humans (or that animal harm is a strong predictor of such behavior), there is no basis for concluding that a criminal response to the maltreatment of animals will end the presumed cycle of violence. John Dilulio, notorious originator of the falsified theory of superpredators, famously espoused the "thug in prison" theory of crime control, which is fundamentally just a theory of incapacitation: "A thug in prison can't shoot your sister." Presumably the same logic underlies the old mantra, "Abuse an Animal, Go to Jail" – that is, a person in jail cannot hurt animals, or your sister! The problem is that even the most hardline proponents of carceral animal law seem to acknowledge that sentences for years or up to a decade are rather extreme, meaning that the person who is convicted of abusing an animal will be released from prison relatively quickly. It is beyond speculative to imagine that a period of incarceration will stop someone who is intent on harming others. On the contrary, prison conditions don't do anything to help incarcerated people work on their anger issues or inclinations toward violence, and programming on the inside to reflect on one's actions is extremely limited. Just placing one on probation, imposing fines, or placing one on an offender registry, all approaches to carceral animal law that are viewed by movement insiders as progressive reforms, are likely to make one's life harder, and to lead to the sort of stress that might culminate in crime. Creating a bogeyman out of animal abusers and calling for a criminal response to animal crimes simultaneously ignores the possibility for human transformation and reform, and treats criminal punishment as the only protection against downstream human violence.

Another problem with the link's use by advocates is that it rests on a logical fallacy. The fallacy of the converse exists when one infers the truth of a converse of a factual statement. For example, one could say that if the animal is a dog, then she is a mammal. Or if someone uses cocaine tonight, then it is highly likely that he used marijuana in the past. But even assuming the truth of these statements, they do not mean that if an animal is a mammal, then she is a dog, nor does it mean that marijuana use is a good predictor of whether one will subsequently use cocaine. By the same token, it may be assumed (based on existing data) that among persons incarcerated for violent crimes, it is more likely that these persons have previously harmed an animal, but that does not mean that harming an animal is a particularly good predictor of whether one becomes violent toward humans. And yet, commentators frequently deploy this very logic to point out the virtues of all variety of carceral animal law proposals. For example, in Jessica Rubin's 2021 essay about Desmond's Law, she opens by citing a study finding that persons who were incarcerated for violent crimes were about 5.3 times more likely to say they had harmed an animal in the past, and from this concludes, "[t]hose who are cruel to animals are over five times as likely to commit cruelty against humans."[3]

There are a multitude of problems with relying on nonlongitudinal studies of self-reporting among incarcerated persons. But even accepting that persons who have been convicted of violent crimes are more likely to have abused animals than other incarcerated persons does not tell us anything about how good animal abuse is at predicting future violent crime. Such equations only give us half of the fraction – we know the numerator (the number of violent persons who abused an animal), but we have no data about the denominator (the total number of persons who have abused an animal). By the logic of animal advocates, juvenile crime of any sort should be used to predict adult crime because "the vast majority of adult offenders begin offending as juveniles"; however, in reality juvenile crime is a terrible predictor of adult crime because the "majority of juvenile offenders do not continue to offend as adults."[4]

The failure to acknowledge the possibility of human transformation, the bogeyman type thinking that calls for incapacitation, and the logical fallacies at work in this context, all suggest that recourse to the link should be sparing, and certainly not treated as a definitive justification for carceral recourse.

I.5 INTENTIONAL ABUSE IS RELATIVELY LESS COMMON THAN ASSUMED

Animal lawyers tend to focus on the need for criminal responses to the most high-profile acts of sadistic abuse. Think of the e-mail about Franky the dog quoted above. But this is a sort of displacement or distraction, because the research overwhelmingly shows that the vast majority of animal offenses are acts of neglect – that is, crimes of poverty, mental illness, or some combination. In this regard Kendra Coulter and Brittany Campbell's review of animal cruelty statistics for a province in Canada is revealing. They find that for all six of the years they studied, the most common animal cruelty offense (generally more than 50 percent of all animal cruelty) is a violation of a standard of care, such as the provision of adequate food, water, or veterinary care.[5] Other research has tended to confirm this finding that neglect is the most common form of animal cruelty. For example, Lori Donley and

[3] *Id.*
[4] David Skalansky, A Pattern of Violence 174 (2021).
[5] Kendra Coulter & Brittany Campbell, Public Investment in Animal Protection Work: Data from Manitoba, Canada, Animals, 7 (2020).

Gary Patronek found that 62 percent of reported cases of animal maltreatment related to what they called "husbandry," or issues of food, shelter, and the like.[6]

We emphasize this fact not to diminish the importance of addressing neglect, but because it is relevant to conversations about how to respond to animal maltreatment. Rationalizations of carceral animal law often focus attention on mass shooters who supposedly abused an animal in the past or on the graphic details of a high-profile case of animal torture. But these examples do more to stir moral panic than they do to present a clear-eyed look at the realities of animal maltreatment. And once a new felony law is created, based on a story like Franky's, a broadly drafted law can threaten crimes that result from poverty with lengthy, felony prison terms.

It is rather striking to juxtapose the reality of neglect as the dominant form of animal abuse, with the calls by advocacy groups for more and longer sentences for animal crimes. Reflecting on the salience of race and poverty in animal cruelty is a theme of increasing, though still nascent, interest among commentators. For our purposes, though these intersections call to mind the reflections of Dorothy Roberts, who writes about a system that animal lawyers often look to as an inspiration, the child welfare system. It is commonplace to hear animal lawyers aspire to create an animal protection system that is more akin to the child welfare system. But as Roberts explains, "the child welfare system also exacts an onerous price: It requires poor mothers to relinquish custody of their children in exchange for the state support needed to care for them." Roberts continues,

> An African American woman I interviewed in a Black Chicago neighborhood poignantly captured this fundamental problem with U.S. child welfare philosophy: [T]he advertisement [for the child abuse hotline], it just says abuse. If you being abused, this is the number you call, this is the only way you gonna get help. It doesn't say if I'm in need of counseling, or if . . . my children don't have shoes, if I just can't provide groceries. . . . I don't want to lose my children, so I'm not going to call [Department of Children and Family Services] for help because I only see them take away children.[7]

Too often, well-meaning, even loving human companions to animals may not have the funds to properly care for them. Creating solutions that can provide resources, rather than carceral responses, may be the best for animals, their human caretakers, and the communities in which they live.

The chapters that follow invite conversation and debate about whether carceral responses are the best way to protect animals. Looking at the history of carceral responses, as well as other areas in which carceral responses to social problems may

6 Lori Donley and Gary Patronek, *Animal Abuse in Massachusetts: A Summary of Case Reports at the MSPCA and Attitudes of Veterinarians*, 2(1) Journal of Applied Animal Welfare Science, 59 (1999).

7 Dorothy E. Roberts, *Prison, Foster Care, and the Systemic Punishment of Black Mothers*, 59 UCLA L. Rev. 1474, 1485 (2012).

or may not have worked, like cases of domestic violence, the war on drugs, and immigration, the discussion that follows should deepen our thinking about animal protection. There is an abolitionist, anticarceral strand in many projects focused on radical social change. This book contemplates a world in which carceral logics play less of a role in the imagination of law reformers and urges us to think more and harder about a more just world for all animals, human and non.

PART I

Carceral Thinking in Animal Protection: Justifications and Repudiations

Introduction

Lori Gruen and Justin Marceau

This section seeks to tell the contested story about the history and practice of criminal enforcement in the service of animal protection goals. Competing normative and historical accounts are juxtaposed so as to provide a robust background for understanding various concerns about pursuing animal protection through criminal enforcement.

For this section we sought out and are delighted to include some of the most prominent voices in support of policing and prosecution, and their chapters have given us much to think about. Even in the midst of massive societal shifts in attitudes about the value of punitiveness and policing, many voices in the animal protection community continue to view carceral animal law as an important, even indispensable, part of legal advocacy on behalf of animals. In this section we are reminded in striking, visceral terms that animals can be victims of horrific violence, and many readers will likely take comfort in a prosecutor's explanation that she became a prosecutor in order to vindicate the value of "acknowledging right from wrong and enforcing penalties" (Beck). There is an unmistakable instinct to seek accountability, to send a message about the value of animal lives, and to deter future animal maltreatment, and these are the defining goals of the carceral animal law agenda (Beck and Frasch). As Ashley Beck says, in words that one can imagine would resonate with most Americans, she feels an obligation as a prosecutor to "ensure that justice is done, and that those who perpetrate crimes against animals are not given a pass," and this leads her to the conclusion that in serious cases "incarceration may be the only effective way to guarantee . . . the perpetrator cannot victimize another animal."

The history and practice of criminal animal law is often closely associated with a problem that has become well documented - "police bias." But in this context, legal commentators are referring not to the disparate impacts of policing on marginalized communities, but rather the "Oh, it's-just-a-dog response to abuse" (Frasch). There

FIGURE 1.1 Samuel Cousins, print of Sir Edwin Landseer's *Saved!* published by Henry Graves, 1859

nineteenth century, whiteness pervaded humane reasoning in ways that are rendered invisible in animal law (See Figure 1.1).

These sentimental and didactic strains of imperiled white innocence in *Saved!* were all the more potent in post–Civil War America, given the prevailing understandings and expectations of black criminality. Indeed, the pairing of white innocence with nonwhite criminality was mutually reinforcing. Bearing this in mind, the painting conveys not only a white child saved *by* animals, but also the idea that animals needed to be saved *from* criminalized communities of color. Such redemptive humane logics, as I will explore, undergirded carceral logics.

Animal studies scholars have amply demonstrated the extent to which race is forged in the crucible of ideas about animality and nature. In other words, race is a permanent part of the animal question. "Impassionate disputes over the animal practices of racialized others," as political scientist Claire Jean Kim discusses, "open a window onto the synergistic workings of the taxonomies of race and species" – twinned logics that are historically conjoined and mutually constitutive.[2] White reformers who established and retained control of the national leadership of animal anticruelty societies often engaged with cultural debates over the borders of

[2] Claire Jean Kim, Dangerous Crossings: Race, Species, and Nature in a Multicultural Age 25, 283 (2015). *See also* Bénédicte Boisseron, Afro-Dog: Blackness and the Animal Question xx (2018).

humanity – the human/animal boundary as well as the humanity of nonwhite communities – in ways that ultimately shored up white male legal authority and sustained white supremacy.

As a window onto the historical roots of American humane sentiment, *Saved!* nevertheless exemplifies pervasive legal and cultural changes by the mid-nineteenth century that strengthened the association between both childhood and innocence and children and animals as emotional investments and worthy objects of protection based on their shared helplessness.[3] When early animal welfare reformers invited the public to take imaginative, cross-species leaps that could generate sympathetic identification with animal subjectivity, this imagery overwhelmingly showcased scenes of white humanity.[4] In the early visual culture of animal welfare, white innocence was commonly depicted in moments of peaceful repose in pastoral landscapes with nature's animal ambassadors.[5] As historian Robin Berenstein explains, the sentimental white child in the nineteenth century operated "in a busy cultural system linking innocence to whiteness through the body of the child" against which understandings of racial difference were constructed.[6] Sentimentalism in historical context refers to the moral philosophy of a community that is united by a shared recognition of and sympathy with the humanity of others and sustained through social bonds of mutual obligation. As historian Susan Pearson explains, sentimentalism in the nineteenth-century United States was a conduit for channeling affect modeled on the child-centered family that reproduced "hierarchical, vertical relations of benevolence" and reinforced the difference as well as the dependence of the suffering. It was also "more than simply a predecessor or an alternative to legal, institutional, or coercive methods of creating social change."

3 Susan J. Pearson, The Rights of the Defenseless: Protecting Animals and Children in Gilded Age America 8, 23, 29–31, 97 (2011).

4 *See id.* at 116–28, on the roles of sympathy and sentimentalism in humane perspective-taking during the nineteenth century; Cronin, *supra* note 1 (emphasis on chapter 3). *See, e.g.*, Lori Gruen, Entangled Empathy: An Alternative Ethic for Our Relationships with Animals (2015) (emphasis on chapter 2), on the philosophy of empathy in contemporary humane ethics.

5 *See* Pearson, *supra* note 3, at 39–42 (describing the relationship between childhood innocence and didactic humane visual culture in the United States yet neglecting a racial analysis); Cronin, *supra* note 1, at 28, 35, 41, 51, 115, 168, 176, 179, 181 (noting among the fifty-three images featured in J. Keri Cronin's study of early humane visual culture, all of which feature white human subjects when animals are depicted alongside humans, are many scenes exemplifying themes of white innocence that nevertheless do not receive a racial analysis); Paula Tarankow, Loyal Animals, Faithful Slaves: Animal Advocacy, Race, and the Memory of Slavery 145–47 (Ph.D. Dissertation, Indiana University 2019; available through ProQuest database of theses and dissertations), for a racial analysis of two rare images depicting Black child subjects with humane themes, which were featured in the Massachusetts SPCA's organ *Our Dumb Animals*); *See generally* Laura Wexler, Tender Violence: Domestic Visions in an Age of U.S. Imperialism (2000), for an influential study of whiteness through sentimentalism's power in nineteenth-century photography to pacify, naturalize, and shroud violent relations.

6 Robin Berenstein, Racial Innocence: Performing American Childhood from Slavery to Civil Rights 4, 6 (2011).

Anticruelty reformers transformed not only sentimentalism but also the reach of the modern state by yoking the language of sympathy to state power.[7] Consequently, the carceral turn in animal law imbued moralistic judgments of individual behavior with racist and civilizing underpinnings that diverted scrutiny away from structural inequities such as those undergirding human poverty and the related use and treatment of animals, especially by nonwhite individuals.

Such recourse to the legal system to create a more peaceable, kinder society built upon existing frameworks and logics about the perceived rise in crime and newly criminalized human-animal relations after emancipation. In this chapter, I place scholarship on the ideological underpinnings of the animal anticruelty movement into conversation with histories of the construction of race in the United States. In doing so, I recontextualize how white reformers understood and defined the problem of animal cruelty and endeavored to solve it. I also suggest ways in which assumptions of white innocence lay at the core of carceral logics. I begin by charting a new origin story for humane sentiment in the United States rooted in proslavery as well as antislavery sentiment. Here, I provide an inclusive overview of the movement that situates the efforts of African American animal advocates at the turn of the twentieth century within broader debates in the white imagination over black humanity. I then explore how the rise of humane carceral logics, or the rationale that surveillance, policing, prosecution, and incarceration to protect animals through the legal system justified as well as pacified the means, ultimately produced coercive and discriminatory tools that naturalized white reformers' scrutiny of communities of color.

1.2 THE PROSLAVERY AND ANTISLAVERY ROOTS OF HUMANE SENTIMENT

In 1924, Sydney Coleman, who had served on the executive committee of the New York–based American Society for the Prevention of Cruelty to Animals (ASPCA) and as managing editor of the Ohio-based American Humane Association's (AHA) publication, *The National Humane Review*, penned one of the first histories of the animal protection movement. "It is more than a mere coincidence," Coleman pronounced, "that the humane movement in England and America followed so closely upon the abolition of human slavery." As a result of emancipation, he posited, "the rights of the defenseless were established. The conscience of a nation was stirred to its depths, and resulted in the development of an era of humanitarian progress heretofore unknown. . . .Ten years earlier such a movement could not have flourished." Prior to the Civil War, he argued, it was "not difficult to understand the general disregard of animal rights, however, in view of the very general lack of sympathy for the unfortunate members of society." Coleman's overarching narrative

[7] Pearson, *supra* note 3, at 13, 130.

placed humane ethics in lockstep with the march of American progress and described a nation irrevocably changed by four years of "fratricidal struggle." Yet in collapsing nearly three-hundred years of slavery's influence on the structure and development of American institutions and society and positioning the Civil War as the turning point of the movement, his origin story emphasizes instead white national unity through humanitarian sensibilities that stemmed from a collective awakening to "the spirit of mercy" and a recognition of the rights and humanity of the enslaved.[8] Coleman clearly presumes a white northern citizenry who successfully and relatively effortlessly challenged slavery and inequality by embracing abolitionist tenets.

This triumphalist, celebratory, northern- and abolitionist-centered narrative continues to hold sway in public consciousness and dominates scholarly attention given to the movement. Yet early animal advocacy was never a solidly northern and abolitionist movement. Between the 1880s and the 1910s, as the so-called New South systematically dismantled black suffrage and enforced the spatial segregation and violent social control that cemented white supremacy, another movement extended legal protections to the animals laboring in the region. In 1880, elite slaveholding families organized the first southern SPCA in Charleston, the cradle of the Confederacy. The Louisiana State SPCA in New Orleans successfully reorganized in 1885 after prior attempts to form a society in the midst of Reconstruction. By 1889, other states in the former Confederacy with SPCAs included Alabama, Arkansas, Georgia, Mississippi, Virginia, and Tennessee. By 1901, SPCAs expanded within these states, and new anticruelty societies were founded in Florida, North Carolina, and South Carolina.[9] By 1900, all forty-seven states had legislation that delineated and prohibited positive acts of cruelty to animals.[10] American animal advocacy was a cross-racial, cross-regional movement that continued sectional debates over the humaneness of slavery and the humanity of enslaved people. The liberal vision of rights embedded in abolitionist discourses of animal protection could not, and did not, unite all Americans in the cause of humanity.

The post–Civil War marriage between liberalism and sentimentalism nevertheless created essential intellectual common ground for the US movement. A newly forged ideology of sentimental liberalism reconciled dependence with rights and turned cruelty into a social problem to be solved in part by state power.[11] White

[8] Sydney H. Coleman, Humane Society Leaders in America: With a Sketch of the Early History of the Humane Movement in England 14, 33–34 (1924).

[9] Addendum: Directory of Humane Societies in the United States, Report of the Proceedings of the Twenty-fifth Annual Convention of the American Humane Association Held at Buffalo, NY, October 14–17, 1901, at 124–26 (1902). *See also* Tarankow, *supra* note 5, at 15–17.

[10] Pearson, *supra* note 3, at 79 (noting the common-law basis for the crime of cruelty was a pure product of the nineteenth-century state). *See id.* at 78, for a historical overview.

[11] *Id.* at 3–4.

animal protectionists on both sides of the Mason-Dixon line were not united by broad commitments to racial justice. Instead, the emergent culture of animal protection among white animal anticruelty reformers – comprising Union and Confederate veterans and their families, radical and moderate Republicans and southern Democrats, former enslavers and enslaved people as well as former abolitionists – shared common ground in a paternalistic strain of rights that sought to protect as well as preserve animal and human dependencies. They also shared Christian theological views such as humanity's duties toward our "fellow creatures," biblical justifications for dominion that emphasized animals as a species of property and humanity's obligation to serve as good animal stewards, and the belief that acts of animal kindness allowed devout reformers to emulate the supposed boundlessness of God's mercy.[12]

While sentimentalism, liberalism, paternalism, and Christian theology truly matter to the origin story of anticruelty sentiment, ignoring the relationship between white supremacy and the rise of the animal protection movement obscures white supremacy's contributions to the formation of humane carceral logics. Coleman's origin story not only distorts the geographical scope of the movement by profiling only institutions and reformers above the Mason-Dixon line but also contradicts historians' consensus on white America's gradual withdrawal from commitments to equality as the hopeful glow of Reconstruction waned.[13]

The advent of institutionalized animal welfare can be understood as simply the latest in an ongoing sentimental project since the Age of Revolutions to strengthen the moral bonds necessary to sustain a fledgling, egalitarian democracy. Many believed that a commitment to a culture of sensibility, or human sensitivity of perception, especially responsiveness to the pain of others, would help maintain social cohesion and purify society through the encouragement of humanitarian feeling.[14] The Second Great Awakening, an era of Protestant revivalism during the early-nineteenth century, helped crystallize a proactive framework of Christian duty and human perfectibility based on kindness "toward the least among us." It unleashed a surge of humanitarian reform, including abolitionism, child welfare, prison reform, women's rights, temperance, and the fight to end domestic abuse, judicial torture, and corporal as well as capital punishment.[15] Awakening theologians, popular religious literature of the day, novelists, abolitionists, and temperance

[12] Janet M. Davis, The Gospel of Kindness 29–38 (2016); Pearson, *supra* note 3, at 99, 109; Tarankow, *supra* note 5, at 99–105.

[13] For a recent synthesis: *see, e.g.*, Henry Louis Gates, Jr., Stony the Road: Reconstruction, White Supremacy, and the Rise of Jim Crow (2019) (emphasis on chapter 1).

[14] *See generally* Sarah Knott, Sensibility and the American Revolution (2009).

[15] Diane Beers, For the Prevention of Cruelty: The History and Legacy of Animal Rights Activism in the United States 24–29 (2006). *See also* Myra C. Glenn, Campaigns against Corporal Punishment: Prisoners, Sailors, Women, and Children in Antebellum America (1984); Louis P. Mazur, Rites of Execution: Capital Punishment and the Transformation of American Culture, 1776–1865 (1989); Mark

advocates incorporated themes of humanity's moral duty of stewardship over "fellow creatures," linking kindness to animals to their broader advocacy for self-control and denunciations of human impulsivity and proclivity to brutality. American animal advocates who were deeply influenced by antebellum reform movements worked to define a new "gospel of kindness," which, as historian Janet Davis explains, could lay "the foundation of a humane new world rising from the ashes of the Civil War." At once spiritual and secular, this "gospel" soon assumed the trappings of American exceptionalism and evolved into a benchmark for national belonging, assimilation, and readiness for citizenship.[16]

The recent memory of slavery gave postbellum white Americans a cultural context for establishing sympathy with the animal world. The central outcomes of the Civil War – emancipation and Confederate defeat – carved new channels for white sympathetic identification with animals after the war, albeit in unexpected ways. The Second Great Awakening also spread southward and helped shape the ideology of slaveholding paternalism. As a cogent southern defense of slavery coalesced by the 1830s, paternalism drew upon an increasing focus on humanitarianism in sentimental culture in efforts to justify the moral righteousness of slaveholding. According to southern apologists for slavery, the mutual obligations inherent in chattel slavery ennobled both white enslavers and the enslaved people under their care.[17] Whereas northern animal protectionists imported the rhetoric and cultural symbols in abolitionist discourse into their work, as featured in the dominant metaphor of the suffering animal-as-slave, postbellum southern protectionists who engaged in the mythologizing of slavery as benign and benevolent centered humane literature on evidence of animals' gratitude and loyalty and often showcased stories of animals on tranquil plantation landscapes and of humane Confederate leaders. After the war, the highly sentimentalized and nationally resonant Lost Cause mythology celebrating the faithful slave not only helped white southerners manage the devastation of sectional defeat but also left its mark in southern humane literature that gained popularity with white audiences across the nation.[18] In Tennessee, Caroline Meriwether Goodlett, the daughter of a Kentucky slaveowner and cofounder of the United Daughters of the Confederacy, the organization responsible for cementing the Lost Cause on the southern memorial landscape to vindicate the South and its heroes, was fervently remembered as a "most

COLVIN, PENITENTIARIES, REFORMATORIES, AND CHAIN GANGS: SOCIAL THEORY AND THE HISTORY OF PUNISHMENT IN NINETEENTH-CENTURY AMERICA (1997).

[16] DAVIS, *supra* note 12, at 28–29.

[17] JAMIE WARREN, MASTERS OF THE DEAD: SLAVERY, DEATH, AND IDEOLOGY IN THE ANTEBELLUM SOUTH 11, 15, 15 n.16 (2014). *See also* MARGARET ABRUZZO, POLEMICAL PAIN: SLAVERY, CRUELTY, AND THE RISE OF HUMANITARIANISM (2011).

[18] On the national reception of proslavery humane sentiment in Joel Chandler Harris's *Uncle Remus and Brer Rabbit* stories: *see* TARANKOW, *supra* note 5 (emphasis on chapter 4).

humane lady" in her role as vice-president of the Humane Society of Nashville.[19] As we will see, southern animal protectionists did not appear to be conflicted about embracing both humane sensibilities and white supremacy.

In addition to obscuring the proslavery as well as antislavery origins of American humane sentiment, the narrow history offered by Coleman also falls short of capturing the ways in which African American animal advocates after the Civil War, many of whom had been born into slavery, used the treatment of animals to extend their commitments to racial justice. The roots of humane sentiment in America rightly stretch back to the 1619 arrival of the first enslaved Africans in Point Comfort, Virginia. As historian Thomas Andrews convincingly argues, the roots of contemporary animal-rights philosophies originated not with white abolitionists but with their enslaved counterparts, whose testimonies in slave narratives provided evidence of the role of animalization in creating and maintaining the institution of slavery.[20] Some enslaved individuals asserted their personhood in such narratives by staking their claims to humanity on the relationships they nurtured with animals.[21]

African American community leaders who were also animal advocates framed blackness against racist constructions of black animality and critiqued white hypocrisy and apathy toward black suffering that resulted from white supremacist racial violence.[22] Such reformers retooled the discourse of humane sentiment in response to debates among northern white philanthropists and segregationists concerning Black readiness for freedom, progress, and full citizenship – debates encapsulated in the oft-invoked phrases "the Negro problem" and "the Negro question."[23] Coleman's narrative, therefore, not only overstates white America's commitments to liberalism but also invites further scrutiny of the limits of white humane sentiment.

The presence of respectability politics in late-nineteenth century animal welfare discourse suggests further how white humanity served as the benchmark against which black humanity was measured. The politics of respectability emerged as an

[19] S. A. Cunningham, *The President of the N.C.D.C*, 2 Confederate Veteran Magazine, Jan. 1894, at 307; S. A. Cunningham, *Founder of the U.D.C*, 22 Confederate Veteran Mag., Nov. 1914, at 496; Josephine M. Turner, The Courageous Caroline: Founder of the UDC 55 (1965).

[20] Thomas G. Andrews, *Beasts of the Southern Wild: Slaveholders, Slaves, and Other Animals in Charles Ball's* Slavery in the United States, *in* Rendering Nature: Animals, Bodies, Places, Politics 47 (Marguerite S. Shaffer & Phoebe S. K. Young eds., 2015).

[21] Andrews, *supra* note 20, at 46; Jane Spencer, Writing about Animals in the Age of Revolution (2020) (emphasis on chapter 5).

[22] Tarankow, *supra* note 5 (emphasis on chapter 3); Michael Lundblad & Marianne DeKoven, *Archaeology of a Humane Society: Animality, Savagery, Blackness*, in Species Matters: Humane Advocacy and Cultural Theory 77 (Marianne DeKoven & Michael Lundblad eds., 2011).

[23] Natalie Ring, The Problem South: Region, Empire, and the New Liberal State, 1880–1930, at 177 (2012).

identifiable strategy within African American communities for claiming rights and demonstrating black worthiness of respect and national belonging. Humane ethics offered yet another avenue to provide countervailing evidence that African Americans were moral, law-abiding, and self-controlled citizens. Respectability politics provided the tools with which to push back against a constant narrative of deficiency by advocating for the reform of individual attitudes and behavior – here, indifference to animal suffering.[24] Black reformers such as Booker T. Washington who embraced animal welfare and established Bands of Mercy at the Hampton and Tuskegee Institutes saw kindness to animals as a part of larger social justice projects of self-help and self-improvement through racial uplift.[25]

Many elite white southern animal advocates in the Jim Crow South continued to defend slavery by emphasizing that chattel slavery, if paternalistic and hierarchical, was at least benevolent. Kindness to animals was, according to this logic, a natural and moral outgrowth of slaveholding culture. Black animal protectionists, however, fervently believed that the ethic of kindness was essentially antiracist and that animal advocacy and civil rights activism were inseparable. By contrast, many white reformers across the nation continued to view humane ethics and behaviors as a proving ground for individual and community morality and a litmus test for full belonging and inclusion in America.[26]

1.3 THE RISE OF HUMANE CARCERAL LOGICS

The potential of the animal cause to transcend sectionalist sentiments that precipitated the secession crisis energized at least some animal protectionists. Southern reformers in particular hoped their animal welfare organizing would provide countervailing evidence to pervasive northern criticism of a "backwards" and "benighted" region. They promoted southern reintegration by endeavoring to make humane ethics a recognizable signifier of American character.[27] In terms of preventative

[24] Evelyn Brooks Higginbotham, Righteous Discontent: The Women's Movement in the Black Baptist Church, 1880–1920, at 186–87 (1993). *See also* Nikki Lane, The Black Queer Work of Ratchet: Race, Gender, Sexuality, and the (Anti)Politics of Respectability (2019).

[25] Davis, *supra* note 12, at 72–75, 85, 101, 103. Black animal protectionists appear not to have held any executive leadership positions within white-controlled anticruelty societies in either the North or the South, although some Black reformers were affiliated with or employed by the American Humane Education Society under the aegis of the Massachusetts Society for the Prevention of Cruelty to Animals. *See* Paula Tarankow, *Jim Key and Jim Crow: African American Animal Advocacy and Civil War Memory*, in Animal Histories of the Civil War Era (Earl Hess ed., 2022).

[26] On the antiracist work of the Massachusetts SPCA, *see* Janet M. Davis, *Cockfight Nationalism: Blood Sport and the Moral Politics of American Empire and Nation Building*, 65 Am. Q., September 2013, at 554–55.

[27] Tarankow, *supra* note 5, at 106–7. *See* Natalie J. Ring, The Problem South: Region, Empire, and the New Liberal State, 1880–1930 (2012) (discussing the northern criticism of

than people in the third quarter of the nineteenth century.[34] By the late-nineteenth century, emancipation's version of citizenship based on independent, freely contracting individuals remained idealized, even as this ideal no longer reflected the realities of an increasingly complex and interdependent multispecies society.[35]

The merging of sympathy with state power coincided with the dissemination of crime statistics that explained criminal behavior based on racial difference. As historian Khalil Muhammad has shown, a growing link between race and crime calcified following the 1890 census, which was the first to gather statistical data on African Americans born after emancipation. Leading white social scientists, social reformers, journalists, law enforcement officials, and politicians of the day used crime data that bore the marks of police bias and discrimination to conclude that Black citizens posed a particular threat to America. As Muhammad explains, "the collection and dissemination of racial crime data...simplified reality, justified racism, and redistributed political and economic power from black to white."[36] White animal protectionists across the country often elevated the ethical status of animals above that of communities of color by drawing on prevalent understandings of black criminality and scrutinizing immigrants and colonized peoples' fitness for citizenship.

In the nation's capital, the Washington Humane Society's (WHS) uniformed humane agents patrolled city streets on horseback and bicycle alongside the District's police force, confiscated whips, pipes, and other crudely constructed horse bits and clubs involved in "aggravated," "unmerciful," or "brutal" violence, and warned, threatened, and made arrests without warrant. They unharnessed and seized beasts of burden and compelled owners to pay for their temporary lodging, grain, hay, and veterinary attention while detained or ordered to rest. Between the high-water mark years of 1900 and 1917, anywhere from one to ten humane agents employed in a given year shot between 165 and 360 working animals a year, with a median of 230 animals.[37] A recurring theme among US reformers, the Society often accused the city's roughly 600 police officers of being uncooperative, indifferent to animal cruelty, and reluctant to enforce anticruelty statutes. In 1905, the WHS president, Virginia patent lawyer Chester Snow, personally prosecuted a case against

[34] Clay McShane & Joel Tarr, The Horse in the City: Living Machines in the Nineteenth Century 16 (2007).

[35] Pearson, *supra* note 3, at 133–35; Barbara Welke, Recasting American Liberty: Gender, Race, Law, and the Railroad Revolution, 1865–1920 (2001). On the limits of free labor for former slaves, *see, e.g.*, Evelyn Nakano Glenn, Unequal Freedom: How Race and Gender Shaped American Citizenship and Labor (2009); Amy Dru Stanley, From Bondage to Contract: Wage Labor, Marriage and the Market in the Age of Slave Emancipation (1998).

[36] Khalil Gibran Muhammad, The Condemnation of Blackness: Race, Crime, and the Making of Modern Urban America 3 (2010) (and xvii in the 2019 preface edition).

[37] This statistic comes from my data set, which is based on the statistics in the annual WHS reports. All referenced reports are microfilmed in the Washingtoniana Collection, People's Archive, Martin Luther King Jr. Memorial Library, Washington, D.C.

policeman Amos A. Roper for "lashing his horse until blood flowed from its sides and stained the snow."[38] Available records on arrests for animal cruelty indeed reflect a disparity: In 1910, for example, there were 2,017 arrests by humane officers versus 274 (or 13 percent of total arrests) by the police, and in 1916 humane officer arrests outnumbered police arrests 655 to 73 (or 11 percent of total arrests).[39] Over the years, humane agents were required to remain on duty until six-o'clock to look after drivers of teams returning from work at that hour.[40] At the beginning of 1906, the Society divided some seventy square miles of District territory into eight divisions similar to police precincts and each agent was given a division that he was responsible for patrolling constantly. During that year, agents averaged 7 arrests each day for a total of almost 2,000 arrests, and approximately 1,800 complaints of cruelty came directly to the secretary. Agents were required to report in person at the office every morning and by phone at least four times during the day. "By this means," the Society explained, "the Secretary knows approximately the whereabouts of the agents at all times, and can communicate with any agent within a short time."[41] By 1907, each agent was also required to visit all parts of his assigned territory, including slaughterhouses, cattle pens, the markets and commission houses where live poultry and calves were handled, brickyards, sand yards, and construction sites, as well as their regular beat in each division.[42] By 1911, humane agents were on duty during all hours of daylight and oftentimes at night patrolling the entire territory of the District.[43]

In the process of forging new pathways for animal welfare by helping shape a sympathetic and responsive state, reformers' efforts to reduce acts of individual violence were a part of larger conversations about how to solve the nation's problems in the closing decades of the nineteenth century.[44] At that time, most white Americans saw everyday inequalities as a manifestation of a natural social hierarchy among different groups of people in the community.[45] Yet pervasive turn-of-the-century evolutionary theory that linked cruelty with savagery and barbarism and humane behavior to civilization stabilized reformers' assumptions not only that pain and civilization were antithetical to each other but also that sympathy with animal suffering was a marker of racial difference.[46] As scholar Michael Lundblad explains,

38 *Charge Cruelty to Horse*, WASH. POST, Feb. 12, 1905, p. F10.

39 ANNUAL REPORT FOR THE YEAR ENDING, Dec. 31, 1910; ANNUAL REPORT FOR THE YEAR ENDING, Dec. 31, 1916.

40 CONDENSED REPORT OF THE EXECUTIVE COMMITTEE FOR THE YEAR 1905, ANNUAL REPORT FOR THE YEAR ENDING Dec. 31, 1905, at 14.

41 SECRETARY'S REPORT, ANNUAL REPORT FOR THE YEAR ENDING DEC. 31, 1906, at 15.

42 SECRETARY'S REPORT, ANNUAL REPORT FOR THE YEAR ENDING DEC. 31, 1907, at 15.

43 PRESIDENT'S ADDRESS, ANNUAL REPORT FOR THE YEAR ENDING DEC. 31, 1911, at 7.

44 *See* PEARSON, *supra* note 3, at 7, 117.

45 KATE MASUR, AN EXAMPLE FOR ALL THE LAND: EMANCIPATION AND THE STRUGGLE OVER EQUALITY IN WASHINGTON, D.C. 6 (2013).

46 *See* PEARSON, *supra* note 3, at 75–76; DAVIS, *supra* note 12, at 4, 114, 154, 179, 181.

"Humane reform actually became a new and flexible discourse for claiming superiority over various human 'races,' reinforcing the logic that only the more 'civilized' group had evolved enough to treat other groups 'humanely.'" This discourse, he explains, was born "at the same moment that constructions of Black men were also shifting, and, more specifically, while an explosion of lynchings was being justified by the myth of the Back male rapist."[47]

The WHS waned in its sympathy with the growing African American community in the District. In the process of transferring their paternalistic energies onto animals, anticruelty advocates grew increasingly intolerant of impoverished African American day laborers who depended upon animal muscle to achieve a modicum of economic independence. As historian Kate Masur explains, municipal officials in the District "saw freedpeople as an urban problem to be solved" and drew on "long-standing doubts about freedpeople's moral and political capacities to justify racially discriminatory policies" while avoiding blatantly racist language.[48] In the end, reformers chose not to define the problem of animal cruelty as symptomatic of the limited achievements of Reconstruction to help African Americans assume a similar economic standing to white people. Instead, the racialized politics of emancipation informed how reformers demarcated the boundaries of cruel treatment. When it came to prosecuting African Americans who were scraping by below the bottom rung of the economic ladder for violent crimes against equine "wageless workers," the Society's sympathies fell decidedly on the side of animals.

While there is no evidence that African Americans perpetrated the majority of violence against animals according to the aggregate statistical records kept by the Society, the annual reports increasingly highlighted violence by African American men. In 1900, the Society began to identify the race of offenders. Over time, the WHS discussed the crimes committed by Black men as a particular "problem," believing that African Americans' alleged proclivity to commit acts of violence made them prime suspects. Thus, urban animal anticruelty reformers participated in larger trends in the white condemnation of blackness through their evaluations of black inhumanity to animals and black failure to internalize kindness and self-control, which forged a link between race and crime. The abolitionist-centered rhetoric of the Society turned the master-slave relationship on its head, condemning freedmen and other African Americans as whip-wielding "slave drivers," with unchecked power over the bodies of "enslaved" horses.[49]

During the height of American imperialist interventions, conversations about "the white man's burden" hastened discussions among white northern reformers of the imperative to "awaken" Filipinos, Puerto Ricans, and Cubans to the cause of animal

[47] Lundblad & DeKoven, *supra* note 22, at 77–79.

[48] Masur, *supra* note 45, at 52–53, 59.

[49] On the history of the racial politics of the WHS, *see* Tarankow, *supra* note 5 (emphasis on chapter 1); Justin Marceau, Beyond Cages: Animal Law and Criminal Punishment 166–69 (2019).

protection. This "burden" refers to a civilizing imperative tied to American exceptionalism based on the notion that it was the moral duty of white society to rehabilitate and reform "backward" colonial subjects. As moral empire builders, American-sponsored animal protectionists unilaterally banned blood sports such as cockfighting and bullfighting in US-occupied territories and enacted stiff penalties of up to $500 and a prison term of up to six months. As a form of "animal nationalism," as Janet Davis argues, "supporters and opponents alike mapped gendered, raced, and classed ideologies of nation and sovereignty onto the bodies of fighting cocks to stake their divergent political and cultural claims about the rights and responsibilities of citizenship and national belonging." While opponents in the colonies defended their right to preserve their cultural heritage and right to self-determination, white colonial officials who supported cultural assimilation through human-animal relationships "bolstered exceptionalist values of benevolent stewardship."[50] Similarly, in Maneesha Decka's comparative study of animal anticruelty legislation in settler societies within the US and British empires, she finds that such laws reinforced "civilizing missions." The civilizational rationales embedded in anticruelty statutes, Decka argues, contributed to the social construction of various forms of human difference according to attendant hierarchical logics of gender, race, religion, and class, which targeted minoritized practices as "cruel" and normalized colonial practices.[51] Building empires of kindness at home and abroad created new forms of racial knowledge that privileged masculine, white, Protestant, and middle-class perspectives, approaches, and practices. Rationales for instituting carceral animal law policies at home revealed similar race-making processes.

The unregulated sale of horses in American cities often recycled sickly and spavined specimens to an impoverished, underemployed working-class population comprising millions of formerly enslaved men and new immigrants from Southern and Eastern Europe, Mexico, and Asia, who were frequent targets of animal cruelty prosecution on both coasts. In Los Angeles and New York, as Davis explains, "reportage in animal cruelty cases had the power to transform a defendant, already marginalized on the basis of race, class, or immigrant status, into an unassimilable alien." "Newspapers routinely described the accused in racial, ethnic, classed, and gendered language," Davis finds, and "laboring conditions further marginalized people who were dependent on animal muscle."[52] Despite the presence of genuine antiracist sentiment among a segment of the humane movement's executive leadership, day-to-day policing often reinforced existing forms of racial, ethnic, and economic inequality.[53]

[50] Davis, *Cockfight Nationalism,*: *supra* note 26, at 549–74 (emphasis on 555, 549, 551).

[51] Maneesha Decka, *Welfarist and Imperial: The Contributions of Anticruelty Laws to Civilizational Discourse*, 65 American Quarterly, September 2013, at 515–48 (emphasis on 516–17).

[52] Davis, *supra* note 12, at 85–86.

[53] *Id.* at 104.

American reformers who defined cruelty as an aggressive social problem participated in broader conversations about a perceived uptick in crime after emancipation. In 1870, *Our Dumb Animals*, the monthly organ of the Massachusetts SPCA, one of the most dynamic and influential leading animal anticruelty organizations in the United States, declared that the demise of slavery ushered in an "age of humanity." Editor George Angell, the MSPCA's indefatigable founding president and lawyer, believed that the animal cause would attract "the noble-hearted, whole-souled men of the day. . .of whatever creed in religion, politics, or other agitated questions" who could "swear fealty to the cause of humanity."[37] Speaking in 1876 before researchers and reformers at the annual meeting of the American Social Science Association, Angell affirmed that cruelty and criminal behavior were connected logically as well as empirically. Angell reported that out of 2,000 prisoners recently studied in the United States, only 12 had grown up with pets.[54] Affective ties to animals, Angell suggested, transformed children into compassionate citizens. The criminal population, he implied, provided evidence of society's need for the widespread dissemination of humane values that could combat crime rates. In 1889, more than a decade after the end of Reconstruction, Angell felt the waters rising: "There is going on in the United States a steady increase in the number of criminals much greater in proportion than the increase in population. There were 70,000 persons in prison for crime in 1880, and there will be more than 100,000 in prison for great and serious crimes in 1890."[55]

In the South, humane education pioneer Mary Schaffter who edited the weekly humane column in the New Orleans *Daily Picayune*, "Nature's Dumb Nobility," shared Angell's concern with crime prevention. When the Louisiana State SPCA was unable to afford employing a humane agent, she personally performed this work in the streets "rescuing cruelly-treated horses, and saving dogs from the abuses of thoughtless people." In an 1890 speech before delegates to the annual meeting of the American Humane Association (AHA) in Nashville, Tennessee, also the first annual meeting of the AHA held below the Mason-Dixon line, she discussed how humane sentiment could help solve the nation's crime epidemic. "Crime is on the increase," she declared. "How to prevent crime and what to do with our criminals are among the vital questions of the day." Schaffter expressed concern that in "an age of advancement and education," "prison statistics show that by far the greatest number of criminals both read and write." Prevention-focused humane education provided the best answer, she maintained, because "there must be something

[54] *Culture and Progress*, 13 Scribner's Monthly, Dec. 1876, at 277–78 (quoted in Pearson, *supra* note 3, at 87. *See also* George Angell, Ten Lessons on Kindness to Animals 24 (1893).

[55] *Increase in Crime in the United States*, 21 Our Dumb Animals, May 1889, at 140. *See also The Criminals of the Future*, 19 Our Dumb Animals, Nov. 1886, at 49.

radically wrong, then, with the system of education that does not result in self-control."[56]

As a means for constructing humanity through racial difference, southern discussions of cruelty were also a part of the hardening of racial boundaries and maintenance of white supremacy that racial violence served to accomplish.[57] As a regional counterpart to the reforming ideology of sentimental liberalism, a southern logic of humane paternalism built upon proslavery ideology and justified the righteousness of transferring benevolent social obligations from loyal enslaved people onto loyal animals. Commitments to animal welfare ultimately helped white southern animal advocates justify white supremacy and affirm the benevolence of "the white man's burden" in the New South.[58] Southern humane discourse was inextricably linked to powerful conceptions of crime and violence in southern society. As the abolition of slavery fundamentally reordered the South's control of black labor, new legal strategies for the purpose of labor control and racial subordination emerged in the form of labor bondage through contract and criminal justice reforms. White fear of black crime and the anger it generated among white people provided the basis for rebuilding white solidarity by reenslaving Black Americans through convict leasing and chain gangs.[59] In response to criticism that convict labor was unmerciful, cruel, and inhuman, white officials legitimized the outdoor labor on state-controlled plantation-penitentiaries and chain gangs as humane, rehabilitative, and healthful alternatives to incarceration.[60] At the same time, southern reformers steered the passage of animal anticruelty laws through state legislatures.[61] This suggests in part how the discourse of humane reform served as a framework for distinguishing between blackness and whiteness.[62]

56 *Humane Education*, Daily Picayune, Oct. 27, 1890, at 6.

57 Claude A. Clegg, Troubled Ground: A Tale of Murder, Lynching, and Reckoning in the New South xvi, xviii (2010).

58 *E.g.*, Tarankow, *supra* note 5 (emphasis on chapter 2).

59 Colvin, *supra* note 15, at 214–34, 243.

60 *See* David M. Oshinsky, Worse than Slavery: Parchman Farm and the Ordeal of Jim Crow Justice 109–10 (1997); Alex Lichtenstein, Twice the Work of Free Labor: The Political Economy of Convict Labor in the New South 159, 179 (1996). *See also* Douglas A. Blackmon, Slavery by Another Name: The Re-enslavement of Black Americans from the Civil War to World War II (2008).

61 These criminal justice reforms sometimes funneled into one another, as evidenced by records of Black men in Richmond and Charleston who were convicted of animal cruelty and sentenced to the chain gang, although further research is needed to interrogate the extent of the relationship between SPCAs and Jim Crow bureaucracy. Charleston S.C. 21st July 1901 Executive Meeting Minutes (transcript available in South Carolina S.P.C.A. records, 1880–1971, South Carolina Historical Society, Special Collections, Addlestone Library, College of Charleston, Charleston, South Carolina); *Before the Recorder* (Charleston) News & Courier, July 7, 1908, at 5; *Before the Recorder* (Charleston) News & Courier, July 22, 1909, at 3; *Six Months for Beating a Horse*, Charleston Evening Post, June 10, 1919, at 3.

62 Michael Lundblad, Birth of a Jungle 127–28, 138 (2013). *See also* Lundblad & DeKoven, *supra* note 22, at 14.

Leading southern reformers professed that the problem of cruelty facing the South in the age of emancipation was essentially a race problem that could be solved through white paternalism and Jim Crow politics. One prominent southern voice in the chorus was lawyer and Mississippi senator Richard Forman Reed, who was an active leader of the Mississippi Society for the Prevention of Cruelty to Animals and served in the executive committee of the American Humane Association. Reed was also the son of a former slaveholding family who had owned Lachnagan plantation near the river port city of Natchez, which was reportedly home to the greatest number of antebellum millionaires in the South. The Reed family was also related to the wife of Jefferson Davis through his maternal grandmother.[63] Like Schaffter, Reed addressed his fellow delegates at the AHA in Nashville. In his remarks, he suggested that the problem of southern animal cruelty stemmed from white ingratitude toward the services of servants and slaves as well as from emancipation. "It is shocking to realize that in the nineteenth century people for the sake of a simple whim," explained Reed, "should deliberately torment not only a harmless, living creature, but a *servant*." Referring to the fashionable use of the check-rein, a type of rein that held horses' heads unnaturally high, prevented horses' neck muscles from sharing the burden of weight, and often caused serious injuries, Reed likened horses to slaves: "For appearances they torture their defenseless and obedient slaves – How cowardly! How wicked! Such people are without love, without gratitude, without refinement."[64] Here, Reed aligned himself with those in southern society whose experience with enslaved people allegedly taught them gratitude and a sense of moral duty to defend, protect, and cherish those under their immediate care. Given his views on race, he might have also implied that freedmen never had the opportunity or capacity to develop similar values, or perhaps that emancipated people seemed ungrateful for the ministrations of their white masters. Reed might have invoked the horse-as-slave metaphor because he was addressing an audience of primarily northern reformers, but he did so in a way that reflected well on the humaneness in southern culture in connection with the institution of slavery.

Reed discussed the importance of humane education outreach to Black communities for targeting "those who hate law and order" and carrying a "Solid South" for humane work. The late 1880s and early 1890s marked an upsurge in crime and homicide in the South, and many white observers like Reed believed that Black

63 James L. Robertson, Heroes, Rascals, and the Law: Constitutional Encounters in Mississippi History 264 (2019); Oshinsky, *supra* note 60, at 3; Letter from Richard Reed to Burton N. Harrison (March 6, 1895) (on file in folder "1894–1898," box 1 Reed (Thomas) Papers, 1787–1926, Mss. 783, Louisiana and Lower Mississippi Valley Collections, Special Collections, Hill Memorial Library, Louisiana State University, Baton Rouge, LA).

64 Richard F. Reed, *Humane Work in the South*, Light (undated) (on file in folder "Newspaper Clippings – Historical, 1872–1908, n.d.," box 1 Reed [Thomas] Papers, 1786–1926, Louisiana and Lower Mississippi Valley Collections, Special Collections, Hill Memorial Library, Louisiana State University, Baton Rouge, LA).

people committed most of the violence.[65] White perceptions of black proclivity to crime and cruelty offered a psychologically compelling model for interpreting and shaping postwar race relations and anticruelty work.[66] "The majority of the criminals in the Southern States, as it is well known, comes from the colored race," he explained. "And there is no exception to this rule when we consider the violators of the laws for the prevention of cruelty. It seems very difficult to educate the negroes to be gentle and kind in their treatment of animals." He enumerated on the causes:

> They are extremely thoughtless. They neglect to properly care for animals under their control, and then, when because of weakness and ill condition, the poor creature fails to do the work assigned it, the negro driver or rider will abuse it severely. They often punish their own children in an extremely harsh and cruel manner, and generally when they have no excuse to punish the children at all.

He assured his audience that "there are many negroes who are merciful and kind," believing that the majority of Black Americans acted from "uncontrolled passion or thoughtless neglect and seldom from deliberate intent." Yet he maintained that by educating them to be merciful, humane sentiment could "protect both human beings and the lower animals." The majority of southern Black people who lacked self-control, Reed believed, "have to be restrained by active enforcement of the law. They will be merciful because they fear the law; not from any moral motive or principle." He concluded his address with an appeal to noblesse oblige: "We must do our duty toward him, and leave his final destiny to our Divine Father, who cares for even the humblest."[67] While paternalistic notions of "the white man's burden" could be found in northern as well as southern humane sentiment, Reed and others linked freedmen's apparent lack of self-control in human and animal relationships to prevalent understandings of black criminality.[68]

The postbellum civil theology of Redemption shows the extent to which violence became central to white Americans' hopes and concerns about the nation. Many came to believe that black suffering was a "natural" condition of freedom; redemption from slavery required redemption through violence to strip Black bodies of dependency, criminality, and promiscuity.[69] White communities tolerated and even celebrated violence that served to protect white supremacy in defiance of existing laws and procedures.[70] If anything, the introduction of southern animal anticruelty

65 Edward L. Ayers, The Promise of the New South: Life after Reconstruction 153 (1992). *See also* Gilles Vandal, *Black Violence in Post–Civil War Louisiana*, 25 J. Interdisc. Hist. 45–64 (1994).

66 Abruzzo, *supra* note 17, at 233.

67 Reed, *supra* note 64, at 5–7.

68 Davis, *supra* note 12, at 19.

69 Carole Emberton, Beyond Redemption: Race, Violence, and the American South after the Civil War (2013).

70 Many white southerners supported "popular constitutionalism," the idea that the Constitution provided for local communities to determine which crimes could be punished outside the

laws from 1880 onward shows that animals enjoyed more legal protections in the South than the Black community in the midst of an epidemic of extralegal violence. While southern reformers remained silent on how they reconciled violence to animals with racial violence, animal advocacy appeared to offer humane insight on black humanity.

As late as 1924, the president of the Birmingham Humane Society defended her motives and integrity as a humane woman at a meeting of the Society "where women of the Ku-Klux were attempting to reinstate one of their members who had been discharged from the job as 'Humane Officer.'"[71] While the president's speech provided neither reference to nor explanation of the firing of the officer, the controversy provides a rare glimpse at a southern sensibility, however limited or isolated, that racial violence and the prevention of animal cruelty were not incompatible. In their uproar, the female members of the Ku Klux Klan seemed to share an apparent belief that the same hands that could commit acts of violence upon Black bodies could also block the commission of violence upon the bodies of animals. By day, this humane officer might well have kept Black men in check with the power of the law, but under the cover of night, he condoned or even participated in extralegal checks on Black people within the community, including torture and lynching.[72] While the president did not denounce the activities of the Klan, the controversy over the firing ultimately led to the replacement of the presumably local man with a northerner, a highly recommended Ohioan with fourteen years of experience as a humane officer with the Youngstown SPCA who arrived with letters of introduction certifying his integrity and "humane instinct." This striking episode from the extant records of the Society suggests that humane discourse in the New South could be capacious enough to harbor a love of animals alongside racist attitudes toward the African American community. The liberal, abolitionist narrative of animal welfare is simply not sufficiently capacious or historically accurate to capture how white supremacy contributed to the formation of humane carceral logics and molded the conversations of anticruelty reformers across the nation.

1.4 CONCLUSIONS

As animal studies scholar and critical race theorist Aph Ko convincingly argues, white supremacy is "zoological in nature and relies upon notions of the human and

formal rule of law. *See* Christopher Waldrep, The Many Faces of Judge Lynch: Extralegal Violence and Punishment in America (2002).

71 Lizzy S. Whelan, President of Birmingham Humane Society Speech, (1924) (on file in Miscellaneous Records—undated; Birmingham Humane Society Records, Birmingham Public Library, Archives and Manuscripts, Birmingham, AL) at 4.

72 Amy Louise Wood, Lynching and Spectacle: Witnessing Racial Violence in America, 1890–1940, 98–99 (2009).

the animal to maintain its power and order." Racism, Ko explains, "is maintained by the human/animal boundary. Within this setup, white supremacy is both anti-black and anti-animal."[73] In an era before the advent of scientific work on animal cognition and behavior, white animal protectionists conceived of humane sentiment and interpreted animal subjectivity within a complex web of racial beliefs. The recent experience and memory of slavery was the main frame through which many postbellum Americans looked into the eyes of animals and saw reflected what they believed was right and wrong about the world in which they lived. The rhetoric of white southern reformers suggests that the animal welfare movement allowed some animal advocates to retool regional identity after the end of slavery and, at times, confirm their illiberal and antidemocratic racial attitudes toward African Americans. Many white animal advocates in the South argued about the extent to which Black people were equipped to embrace a life of freedom; they believed African Americans required white control and political domination, the heavy hand of the law – both in terms of extralegal or "rough" justice and legal prosecution – and, for the young who could still be saved, reeducation through lessons of mercy to curb violent instincts. While humane sentiment holds the potential to generate broad concern for multispecies injustice, even and especially today these connections often need to be made explicit to be recognized.

In the early movement, humane sentiment often produced racial knowledge that in turn reinforced carceral logics. As we have seen, the logic of saving animals from cruelty through the enforcement of anticruelty statues most often invited racialized scrutiny of nonwhite relationships with animals. Undoing carceral logics and carceral animal law policies necessitates a recognition of discriminatory cultural and legal inheritances from progressive nineteenth-century social reform campaigns led by white reformers.[74] Even as animal anticruelty reformers worked toward systemic solutions through preventative humane education, humane optics centered on affirmations of the humanity of whiteness – both in terms of full social and political belonging and the inherent possession of humane ethics – against presumptive black inhumanity.

Efforts to improve the lives of animals through carceral policies drove inequitable and racist practices. Historical scrutiny of how humane carceral logics bear the racialized markings of American exceptionalism is necessary regardless of whether it leads to full divestment from carceral policies. Efforts to critically interrogate and undo carceral logics can greatly benefit from understanding how white perceptions of the causes of violence to animals forged insidious markers of belonging and

73 Aph Ko, Racism as Zoological Witchcraft: A Guide to Getting Out, xix, 4 (2020).

74 *See* Marceau, *supra* note 49, at 2 n. 5, for a definition of carceral animal law policies.

exclusion. This history need not detract from the measurable successes of the animal protection movement in the post–Civil War era to lessen animal suffering; rather, it contributes to ongoing antiracist and decolonization projects by scrutinizing the extent to which humane sentiment and carceral logics in the United States developed according to a white supremacist frame.

2

Criminal Animal Abuse, Interconnectedness, and Human Morality

Richard L. Cupp Jr.

2.1 INTRODUCTION

Arguing that all oppressions are related, and that to end oppression of humans we must also support ending oppression of animals, is in vogue among many who wish to abolish the property status of nonhuman animals.[1] Professor Justin Marceau's 2019 book, *Beyond Cages*, begins with a quote extolling this argument: "All movements seem to start out with a relatively narrow focus, which then widens in response to the recognition of the interconnectedness of oppression."[2]

Some animal rights activists employ the term "intersectionality" in relation to this argument. For example, while interviewing me in a discussion hosted by the Cambridge Centre for Animal Rights Law in 2020, Professor Raphael Fassel noted:

> There is quite an influential strand in animal rights scholarship that emphasizes the intersectional nature of oppression. . . . [T]he argument is roughly that we shouldn't see animal rights and human rights as a sort of zero sum game, where the more we push for animal rights the more human rights are going to lose out. In fact, different

I owe thanks to Don Buffaloe, Tanner Hendershot & Matan Neuman for their outstanding research assistance, to my Pepperdine Caruso School of Law colleagues who provided helpful feedback on an early draft of the chapter, and to Professors Lori Gruen and Justin Marceau; both for inviting me to contribute a chapter to this deeply interesting book, and for their thoughtful editing insights.

[1] Hereafter "animals." The absence of the commonly employed [in animal rights literature] word "mere" before the word "property" in this sentence is intentional; although we need to evolve toward more thoughtful protection of animals within the property paradigm, sentient animals of course already have some degree of legal protections, and our legal system does not treat them the same as if they are tables, chairs, or other "mere" property.

[2] Justin Marceau, Beyond Cages 1 (2019) (*quoting* pattrice jones, *Afterword to* Sistah Vegan: Black Female Vegans Speak on Food, Identity, Health, and Society 187, 188 [A. Breeze Harper ed., 2010]).

oppressions are related, and we can only achieve more protection for human rights if we also protect animal rights better, and visa-versa.[3]

Marceau also refers to "the intersectionalist perspective on animal protection" in *Beyond Cages*.[4]

The term "intersectionality" is often attributed to Professor Kimberle Crenshaw, who introduced it in highlighting the intersection of race and gender, noting that when one is concerned about the oppression of African Americans, Black women's particular concerns are often overlooked. When one is concerned about the oppression of women, Black women's particular concerns are also overlooked. Black women experience specific forms of oppression at the axis of race and gender, rather than experiencing racial oppression and gender oppression as completely separate and unrelated wrongs.[5]

Appropriately or otherwise, the term has evolved in the usage of many beyond its original meaning. In 2019 a trio of scholars wrote of intersectionality that "[r]arely has one term been asked to do so much. It has been described as a lived experience, an aspiration, a strategy, a way to analyze inequality, and even a movement."[6] Applying intersectionality to mistreatment of animals may represent one of the most ambitious evolutions away from the term's original meaning related to civil rights. Using intersectionality language in relation to animals frequently seems intended to reference simply a broad interconnectedness between different manifestations of oppression, including mistreatment of animals. The original meaning of oppression intersectionality – oppression at the intersection of multiple bases of discrimination – seems inapplicable to many discussions about the mistreatment of nonhuman animals. Thus, to limit any contribution I might otherwise make to overextending intersectionality's meaning, I will henceforth refer to "interconnectedness/intersectionality" regarding oppression and compassion as they relate to how treatment of humans influences treatment of animals, and visa-versa.

Observing that various oppressions are in some manner interconnected has some merit. However, this point is significantly overplayed by many seeking to stretch it into an argument for a "strong" animal rights paradigm, such as applying legal

[3] Raffael Fasel, Cambridge Centre for Animal Rights Law, *Richard Cupp in "Animal Rights Law: For or Against,"* interview, July 8, 2020 (beginning at 21:23, available at https://animalrightslaw.org/).

[4] MARCEAU, *supra* note 2, at 157.

[5] Kimberle Crenshaw, *Mapping the Margins: Intersectionality, Identity Politics, and Violence against Women of Color*, 43 STAN. L. REV. 1241 (1991).

[6] Hajer Al-Faham, Angelique M. Davis, & Rose Ernst, *Intersectionality: From Theory to Practice*, 15 AN. REV. L. & SOC. SCI. 247, 248 (2019). For an interesting discussion of how understanding and uses of the term have evolved from what Professor Crenshaw intended, see Jane Coastan, *The Intersectionality Wars*, VOX (May 28, 2019), https://www.vox.com/the-highlight/2019/5/20/18542843/intersectionality-conservatism-law-race-gender-discrimination.

personhood to animals.[7] In this chapter, I will first focus on some of the agreements, and then disagreements, I have with arguments made by those, such as Justin Marceau, who are critical of pressing for increases in criminal prosecutions and sentencing of humans guilty of animal abuse or neglect. Next, I will address the manner in which attitudes toward humans' moral distinctiveness or the absence of human moral distinctiveness may influence reactions to these sorts of anticarceral arguments. Finally, I will explore challenges for basing animal legal personhood arguments on intelligent animals' cognitive capacities.

2.2 SEEKING AN UNEASY MIDDLE GROUND REGARDING CRIMINAL JUSTICE REFORM RELATED TO ANIMAL ABUSERS

Although multiple scholars have criticized perceived overemphasis by the animal protection movement on criminal punishment to address animal abuse, I will pay special attention to Marceau's groundbreaking *Beyond Cages* book as a recent and prominent illustration. I am intentionally emphasizing the "animal protection" movement as a broader description than the "animal rights" movement; the animal protection movement includes those who advocate for animals from a welfare/ human responsibility perspective, rather than from a "strong" animal rights perspective. I advocate for increasing animal welfare protections, while rejecting animal legal personhood as an unjustified and harmful step too far.[8] Thus, I am an example of someone who supports the broader animal protection movement but not the "strong" animal rights movement.

7 Like intersectionality, the term "animal rights" means different things to different people. Some argue that most or all captive sentient animals in the United States already possess legal rights, because animal welfare laws exist that are designed to provide them at least some degree of protection from suffering. However, some animal rights activists believe that legal rights only exist if the holder of the rights is empowered, directly or through a guardian, to assert them. This "strong" definition of legal rights would require courts and/or legislatures to confer legal personhood on animals before they could truly hold rights. As most animal rights scholars seem to support assigning "strong" legal personhood rights to animals, I will henceforth use the term "animal rights" with this meaning.

8 I elaborate on legal reforms that would enhance animal welfare without creating animal legal personhood in: Richard L. Cupp, Jr., *Considering the Private Animal and Damages*, 98 WASH. U. L. REV. 1313 (2021); Richard L. Cupp, Jr. *Edgy Animal Welfare*, 95 DENVER L. REV. 865 (2018); and Richard L. Cupp, Jr., *Animals as More Than "Mere Things," but Still Property: A Call for Continuing Evolution of the Animal Welfare Paradigm*, 84 CINN. L. REV. 1023 (2016). Some of my concerns about animal legal personhood are addressed in Nonhuman Rights Project, Inc. v. R.W. Commerford & Sons, Inc., 216 A.3d 839, 845 (Conn. App. Ct. 2019), *mot. recons. en banc denied*, AC 192411 (Conn. App. Ct. 2019), *cert. denied*, 217 A.3d 635 (Conn. 2019); Nonhuman Rights Project, Inc. v. Lavery, 152 A.D.3d 73, 78 (1st Dep't 2017), *lv denied*, 31 N.Y.3d 1054 (2018); and People ex rel. Nonhuman Rights Project, Inc. v. Lavery, 124 A.D.3d 148, 151 (3d Dep't 2014), *lv denied*, 26 N.Y.3d 902 (2015). *See also, e.g.*, Richard L. Cupp Jr., *Cognitively Impaired Humans, Intelligent Animals, and Legal Personhood*, 68 FL. L. REV. 465 (2017).

As an animal welfare advocate, I have supported some aspects of enhanced criminalization of animal abusers – for example, I have applauded, and will continue to applaud, the rapid evolution among states to raise animal abuse to a felony-eligible crime in egregious circumstances. Marceau and other critics have not dissuaded me from my view of enhanced sentencing options as a positive development, but they have compelled me to be more thoughtful and concerned about aspects of our criminal justice system's approach to animal abuse and neglect.

In other words, *Beyond Cages* lands some legitimate and heavy blows in its attack on the animal protection movement's obsession with enhanced criminalization of animal abuse and neglect. For example, although it is no great revelation that racial injustice plagues our criminal justice system in general, Marceau convincingly argues that animal protection "is seen as a white thing," and that racial justice is directly in play in our current approach to animal harm prosecutions.[9] I endorse Marceau's condemnation of trying children, whose brains are not fully developed, as adults, either in animal abuse cases or in any other cases.[10] Further, the United States' exceptionally high rate of imprisonment overall is deeply troubling.[11]

But Marceau is vague regarding some specifics, and, at least in tone, the breadth of his condemnation can be read as extreme. He acknowledges that his position is radical, and perhaps that is comforting, in that he may be seeking to jolt our awareness rather than jettison incarceration for animal abuse altogether. This may explain his assertion that incarceration is a form of oppression.[12] Incarceration is doubtless a form of unjust oppression in some circumstances, but certainly in many circumstances it is appropriate rather than unjustly oppressive. Imagine, for example, a sadistic criminal with a long record of torturing animals. An argument that any incarceration of such a person constitutes unjust oppression would be difficult to stomach. Even Sweden, which is often looked to by progressives as a source of enlightened social policies, provides for prison sentences of up to two years for criminal animal abuse.[13]

Similarly, eliminating all felonies for animal abuse, which would make even the most egregious cases of animal abuse misdemeanors, would be misguided. *Beyond Cages* references a "timely" proposal by a criminal law scholar to eliminate all felonies, and Marceau seems to consider the proposal favorably, at least with regard to animal abuse crimes.[14] As a scholarly work intended to raise provocative questions, *Beyond Cages* is effective. But literally moving "beyond cages" – disallowing

[9] See Marceau, *supra* note 2, at 151–92.

[10] *Id.* at 29–30, 60–62.

[11] *Id.* at 27–30.

[12] *Id.* at 273. I am assuming that "oppression" in confinement is viewed as inappropriate confinement.

[13] *See* Animal Protection Index, Sweden, *Laws against Causing Animal Suffering, Enforcement Mechanisms, available at* https://api.worldanimalprotection.org/country/sweden#:~:text=.

[14] Marceau, *supra* note 2, at 38–39.

any incarceration or felony possibilities for animal abusers, regardless of the egregiousness of the abuse – would be deeply problematic.

Focusing on human moral responsibility for mistreatment of animals does not mean we may be unconcerned about substantial flaws in our justice system. These are flaws that must be addressed, rather than necessarily constituting a refutation of any form of criminal justice that entails enhanced prosecution or punishment for certain crimes. Favoring criminal punishment for animal abuse – even favoring the trend toward increasing punishment for severe animal abuse, as I do – is not the same thing as saying throw the book at every criminal and give them the longest sentence possible.

There is no comfortable middle ground regarding our criminal system, only difficult decisions.[15] Ending all imprisonment and the possibility of felony status for animal abuse is a bad idea. Repeat offender sadistic animal torturers, for example, are amply deserving of felony convictions. But Marceau is persuasive in arguing that unmitigated enthusiasm for maximum prosecutions and punishment is also a bad idea.

2.3 HOW ATTITUDES REGARDING HUMANS' MORAL DISTINCTIVENESS OR THE ABSENCE OF HUMAN MORAL DISTINCTIVENESS MAY INFLUENCE REACTIONS TO ANTICARCERAL ANIMAL PROTECTION EFFORTS

An acquaintance who is an ardent animal rights supporter once shared with me that she feels much more compassion for animals than for humans, including human children. Her reasoning: most humans are evil, and all animals are morally innocent. Even if human children are morally innocent, they are likely to become evil as adults. This kind of thinking may not be exceptionally rare among people who are intensely focused on animal rights – I imagine that most readers know multiple people with similar perspectives. In 2020, a celebrity who had just broken up with her fiancé apparently sent a message by wearing a T-shirt bearing the words "Dogs

[15] Another issue Marceau raises that I view as a difficult decision is whether courts should allow volunteer attorneys and law students to serve as advocates in animal abuse and neglect trials. *Id.* at 78–83. Although I respect Marceau's criticism, I have written in cautious support of this potential trend, provided that the advocates are directed to pursue justice rather than the interests of the animal. *See* Cupp, *Edgy Animal Welfare*, *supra* note 8. If the advocates are directed to pursue justice and follow this direction, they should advocate against conviction in appropriate cases. However, I recognize if only particularly egregious animal abuse and neglect cases are prosecuted, or if advocates in fact only focus on animals' interests rather than a broader focus on justice, such occurrences may be merely hypothetical. At present, Marceau's thoughtful arguments on this issue have not persuaded me against appropriately drafted and applied legislation enabling advocates for justice in animal abuse and neglect cases, but I have serious concerns about how bills currently pending in some states are worded, as well as how they might be applied.

over People."[16] The celebrity may well have been employing hyperbole, but likely few people would fail to recognize the sentiment as something they have observed or experienced. Indeed, a Google search of "Dogs over People" reveals a plethora of shirts, coffee mugs, plaques, buttons, bumper stickers, baby clothes, wineglasses and other merchandise with variants of this animals-first message.[17]

Further, much more extreme illustrations, not representative of typical animal rights activists, are also available to emphasize the point that compassion for animals does not necessarily coincide with fondness for humans. Professor Martha Nussbaum reminds us that "[t]he Nazis, we know, were great naturalists and animal lovers. What they appear to have lacked was a sense of the sanctity of human life."[18]

As a criminal justice scholar and an animal law scholar, Marceau is distinctively positioned to recognize the benefits of highlighting interconnectedness/intersectionality in seeking to expand both animal rights and human criminal law reform. However, he is also distinctively positioned to recognize challenges posed by the attitudes of many animal rights activists toward humans – at least toward human criminals who have abused or neglected animals – and perhaps toward other humans as well. *Beyond Cages* exposes and questions the failure of many animal rights activists to care much about lessening perceived oppression of criminals who cause harm to animals. Far from not having much active concern for compassionate treatment of humans who harm animals, many passionate about animal rights doubtless feel – understandably – searing hatred toward such humans. Marceau asserts that animal rights activists need to evolve beyond such hatred, complaining that "it is rather remarkable that a movement predicated on notions of empathy holds the prospect of caging humans in such high regard."[19]

Encouraging an embrace of interconnectedness/intersectionality as applied to animal protection may be viewed as having a "giving" aspect and a "receiving" aspect. The giving aspect is expanding the concern of animal activists such that they provide support for protecting the rights of oppressed humans. The receiving aspect is gaining support from activists who focus primarily on advocating for oppressed humans. In theory, embracing interconnectedness/intersectionality may enhance

[16] Liz Calvario, *Demi Lovato's Ex Max Ehrich Says He Learned Their Relationship Was Over 'Through a Tabloid'*, KVUE ABC Entertainment Tonight (Sept. 26, 2020), https://www.kvue.com/article/entertainment/entertainment-tonight/demi-lovatos-ex-max-ehrich-says-he-learned-their-relationship-was-over-through-a-tabloid/603-0609c4f0-166a-4ac3-898b-b897b113b060.

[17] One particularly creative T-shirt has the message: "DOGS > PEOPLE JOHN 3:30." In the Christian Bible, chapter 3 of the Book of John portrays John the Baptist teaching his followers that they must prioritize Jesus rather than John himself. chapter 3 verse, 30 quotes John as stating regarding Jesus, "He must become greater, I must become less." John 3:30, The Bible, New International Version.

[18] Martha C. Nussbaum, *Animal Rights: The Need for a Theoretical Basis*, 114 Harv. L. Rev. 1506, 1511 (2001).

[19] Marceau, *supra* note 2, at 8.

resources and energy in struggles against all forms of oppression by joining advocates for all oppressed groups together.

The fly in the ointment with this theory is that, as Marceau acknowledges, "[t]here is a stereotype of people concerned with protection of animals as misanthropes."[20] Marceau seems concerned that the movement's general enthusiasm for harsh criminal punishment of humans who are often themselves oppressed encourages this stereotyping as misanthropic. If animal rights activists are perceived as not playing well with others, they are unlikely to generate enthusiastic responses to their pleas for support from other types of rights activists, such as activists pressing for criminal justice reform. Following Claire Jean Kim, Marceau insists that only "mutual avowal" can bring about change, "as opposed to subordination of humans in the service of animals."[21]

Particularly in the context of animal abuse, this is asking a lot of animal rights activists. Perhaps ironically, it seems likely that so many animal rights activists support "throwing the book" at humans who commit crimes harming animals precisely because the activists recognize that humans are dramatically different from other animals. When in 2012 an adult chimpanzee smashed the head of another chimpanzee's baby at the Los Angeles Zoo, killing it, media reports about the incident of course did not include information about the "murderer" chimpanzee being charged with a crime.[22] Most activists would not lose their compassion for the well-being of the murderer chimpanzee, because they would appropriately view the chimpanzee as outside the realm of human moral judgments. Chimpanzees may have a degree of moral agency, but virtually no one would argue today that they have sufficient moral agency to be held justly accountable under our human legal system.

As many animal rights activists implicitly recognize, humans are unique. Our human criminal justice system assumes a norm among human adults and older minors of sufficient moral agency to be held justly accountable for crimes. When we are enraged at humans who abuse animals, we are affirming that they presumably possess sufficient moral accountability to merit our outrage.

The concept of free will – free will in the sense of one bearing ultimate personal moral accountability for an individual human's actions – is important to this analysis.[23] Specifically, the question of how committed we are (or are not) to

[20] *Id.* at 275.

[21] *Id.*, *quoting* Claire Jean Kim, Dangerous Crossings: Race, Species, and Nature in a Multicultural Age 276 (2015).

[22] *Adult Chimpanzee Kills Baby Chimp in Front of Shocked Los Angeles Zoo Visitors*, CBS News (June 27, 2012), http://www.cbsnews.com/news/adult-chimpanzee-kills-baby-chimp-in-front-of-shocked-los-angeles-zoo-visitors/.

[23] Some philosophers may assert that there may be moral accountability without free will, for example if a person makes a moral choice but has no power to effectuate that choice. In this chapter I will use the term "free will" more loosely, assuming that if it exists, humans typically have some power to effectuate their moral decisions regarding personal behavior.

humans generally possessing a strong degree of moral accountability may have a powerful impact on our views regarding criminal punishment of animal abusers.

Marceau implies a view that "free will" is at least nuanced by experiences and other factors.[24] He complains that "[t]he movement balks . . . at the idea that animal abuse might be mitigated or treated as less than an act of utter free will, the defendant's upbringing or culture or other mitigating factors that might militate in favor of a reduced sentence are treated as irrelevant."[25] He also complains that the animal rights movement would have sympathy for an abused dog who is conditioned to violence and who thus engages in violence, but many in the movement would not have empathy for a human conditioned to violence who abuses an animal.[26]

Scientists and philosophers have gone much further in challenging our traditional assumption that humans act with free will.[27] Many neuroscientists are firm determinists who "express deep skepticism about free will."[28] For example, Professor Robert Sapolsky, a primatologist and neuroscientist at Stanford University, opined in 2004 that neuroscience should dramatically transform criminal law by discounting the notion that humans possess free will.[29] He argued that the function of a human brain's prefrontal cortex, which may be damaged or underdeveloped in the brains of many criminals, is a more likely explanation of much criminal behavior than the assumption that such criminals are capable of controlling their behavior.[30] A criminal's brain may be comparable to "a broken car."[31]

If human moral responsibility for criminal behavior is illusory or weak, such that what society has traditionally viewed as "evil" is in actuality closer to a machine malfunction, perhaps one might think that our compassion for a criminal should be as great as our compassion for the being that suffered because of the crime – except that we would have no true choice in any actions we might take in relation to compassion. Stated in a less extreme manner, the less one believes that moral accountability for criminal behavior is generally strong, the more attractive arguments against strong criminal prosecution and punishment for animal abuse may appear.[32] If our decisions are viewed as fully or in large part unavoidable due to some

[24] Of course, perceiving nuances in free will does not imply altogether rejecting human moral accountability.

[25] Marceau, *supra* note 2, at 13.

[26] *Id.* at 26.

[27] See infra notes 28–37 and accompanying text.

[28] *See* Morris B. Hoffman, *Nine Neurolaw Predictions*, 21 New Crim. L. Rev. 212, 222 (2018) (citing sources).

[29] *See* Robert M. Sapolsky, *The Frontal Cortex and the Criminal Justice System*, Philos. Trans. R Soc. Lond. B Biol. Sci. 1787 (2004); *see also* Hoffman, *supra* note 28, at 222.

[30] Sapolsky, *supra* note 29, at 1794.

[31] *Id.* Presumably noncriminals would, under this view, also lack free will, and would perhaps be comparable to acceptably functional cars.

[32] Of course, this does not imply that Marceau or other critics of the animal protection movement's emphasis on criminalization and prosecutions reject human moral accountability.

mix of our genetics and environment, enthusiasm for blaming criminals who abuse or neglect animals is likely to lessen. And if humans are not really to blame, punishment is out of the equation as a goal of criminal law, and we need only to look to deterrence, which is more readily challenged with regard to the effectiveness of incarceration.

However, the hard determinism asserted by many neuroscientists is challenged by many or most legal philosophers. Many philosophers are "soft determinists, also called compatibilists (no free will, but responsibility)."[33] Also, many legal philosophers "reject the proposition that neuroscience will one day prove, or otherwise justify, hard determinism."[34]

Despite scientific advances, the human brain may be too complex to ever fully understand like a machine.[35] In any event, even if ultimate moral accountability does not exist, many believe that it may be necessary for us to act as if it does. Professor Sapolsky acknowledges that "[w]hereas it is true that, at a logical extreme, a neurobiological framework may indeed eliminate blame, it does not eliminate the need for forceful intervention in the face of violence or antisocial behaviour."[36] Completely abandoning human responsibility would wreak havoc on social order. Research indicates that undermining belief in free will leads to increased cheating and aggression, reduced helping behaviors, and less gratitude.[37]

Of course, one need not *completely* reject the assumption of free will to accept the significance of mitigating factors, such as environmental conditioning or neurological limitations. However, relevant to the issue of enhancing compassion, it may be telling that one consequence of lessening emphasis on free will may be a reduction in helping behaviors.

Although I disagree with my acquaintance discussed above who feels more compassion for animals than for humans (even children), she is correct in pointing out the humanity of what we perceive as evil behavior. Regardless of neuroscientists' and academic philosophers' theories, on the ground our society, including the animal protection movement that supports criminal prosecution of abuse, is deeply committed to the belief that humans are responsible for evil actions. In the Abrahamic faiths, Adam and Eve's encounter with the tree of knowledge of good and evil is included in the story of creation,[38] and illuminates the foundational nature of Western society's conviction that humans are distinctive moral beings. Thus, the view that society needs to deter evil human behavior, and that it needs to

[33] Hoffman, *supra* note 28, at 222 (citing sources).

[34] *Id.* (citing sources).

[35] *Id.* at 243–44. Professor Hoffman predicts that courts will never abolish the concept of human responsibility. *Id.*

[36] Sapolsky, *supra* note 29, at 1794.

[37] *See* Peter Gooding, *The Psychology of Believing in Free Will*, THE CONVERSATION (July 2, 2018), https://theconversation.com/the-psychology-of-believing-in-free-will-97193.

[38] *Gen.* 2–3.

punish evil human behavior, cannot be understated; it has the deepest of roots in our history.

Believing in human evil reflects a view that not all incarceration of humans is unjustly oppressive. Given our societal underpinnings, even-handedly imposed societal punishment, including incarceration in particularly serious cases, of people who engage in what is perceived as evil misconduct is likely to be viewed by most as justice rather than as inappropriate oppression. The ubiquitous employment of incarceration systems throughout the world's societies demonstrates how powerfully we believe that incarceration is just in some circumstances. Thus, one may assert that all animals should be freed from their cages – or disagree with that assertion – and still support some form of jail time, and in some cases even felony prosecution, for criminals who engage in sufficiently egregious harm of animals.

2.4 INTERCONNECTEDNESS/INTERSECTIONALITY AND ANIMAL RIGHTS ARGUMENTS BASED ON COGNITIVE CAPACITIES

Critics of the animal protection movement's emphasis on criminal punishment call on the movement to care more about humans, with an apparent hope or assumption that more thoughtfulness and discussion can bring about this change. But arguments such as those presented in *Beyond Cages* seem unlikely to upend the animal protection movement's deep commitment to strong criminal prosecution and imprisonment of criminal animal abusers. It seems reasonable to hope that *Beyond Cages* and other critiques will encourage the animal movement to be more thoughtful and nuanced in its advocacy for enhanced criminalization, but an about-face on encouraging criminal prosecutions is probably not, nor should it be, in the cards.

But there is something else in *Beyond Cages*. The book has the effect – perhaps unintentionally – of illustrating in some depth uncomfortable problems with the caring-for-animal-rights-furthers-caring-about-human-rights argument, at least with regard to arguments that this compassion should lead to legal personhood for animals. In other words, although the book is helpful in calling for change regarding criminal justice, it also shows that passion for animal rights is not always connected to strong compassion for humans. This has significant implications for current animal rights issues. Although many animal rights activists believe that all sentient animals should be legal persons, some activists are focused, at least in the short term, on arguing for legal personhood for particularly intelligent animals based on their cognitive capacities. Under this cognitive capacities approach, a chimpanzee or an elephant might be assigned legal personhood, but less intelligent animals, such as cows and chickens, might remain sentient property. Advocates for the cognitive capacities approach may hope that eventually all sentient animals will become legal persons, and may view an initial focus on cognitive capacities as the best way to steer courts in the direction of breaking down legal barriers between humans and animals.

But disability rights advocates and others have voiced concern that considering a being's cognitive abilities as a measuring tool for determining personhood would be dangerous for the most vulnerable humans.[39] Reliance on the argument from marginal cases to attain personhood for intelligent animals could weaken enthusiasm for strong rights protection of humans who lack strong cognitive abilities. Focusing instead on humans' norm of sufficient capacity to be justly accountable under our legal system protects vulnerable members of the human community – regardless of whether they as individuals meet the norm – because their personhood is anchored in meaningful belonging as part of the human community rather than in individual cognitive abilities).[40]

[39] See. e.g., Joshua Rothman, *Are Disability Rights and Animal Rights Connected?* The New Yorker (June 5, 2017), https://newyorker.com/culture/persons-of-interest/are-disability-rights-and-animal-rights-connected (noting that although disability rights advocate Sunaura Taylor favors a form of animal rights, her book Beasts of Burden is "an extended argument with the philosopher Peter Singer, who bases his case for animal rights in part on the fact that some animals are more cognitively capable than the intellectually disabled people to whom we already extend our empathy"); Gerald V. O'Brien, *People with Cognitive Disabilities: The Argument from Marginal Cases and Social Work Ethics*, 48 Soc. Work 331, 335 (2003) ("[a]s it is described in the writings of animal rights scholars, the [argument from marginal cases] is in opposition to core social work values. . . . The dignity and worth of people living on the margins of society is diminished when we bestow quasi-human status on them or suggest that their moral standing is comparable to animals."); Stephen Drake, *Connecting Disability Rights and Animal Rights – A Really Bad Idea*, Notdeadyet.org, Oct. 11, 2010 ("When disabled people are equated with animals, it never works out well for us."), https://notdeadyet.org/2010/10/connecting-disability-rights-and-animal.html; Carl Cohen & Tom Regan, The Animal Rights Debate 36–37 (2001) (philosopher Carl Cohen asserting that the argument [from marginal cases] deserves "to be permanently set aside"); Douglas MacClean, *Is "Human Being" a Moral Concept?*, 30 Phil. & Pub. Pol'y Q. 16, 20 (2010) (among other concerns, "[a]s life is farther removed from human beings and human society, moral reasons cease to govern our relationships with it"); Richard Posner, *Animal Rights*, in Animal Rights: Legal, Philosophical, and Pragmatic Perspectives 55–59 (Cass R. Sunstein & Martha C. Nussbaum eds., 2004) (among other concerns, an argument for animal rights referencing the moral entitlements of children and humans with cognitive limitations is based on an intuition and does not give a reason for ignoring strongly contrary intuitions); Richard A. Epstein, *The Dangerous Claims of the Animal Rights Movement*, 10 The Responsive Community 28, 33 (2000) ("[t]hese human beings, whatever their impairments, are the fathers, mothers, sisters, and brothers of other human beings in ways that chimpanzees and bonobos are not").

[40] *See* Nonhuman Rights Project, Inc. v. Lavery, 152 A.D.3d 73, 78 (1st Dep't 2017), *lv denied*, 31 N.Y.3d 1054 (2018) (emphasizing that although not all humans are capable of bearing duties or responsibilities, they are still "members of the human community"). This is not irrational speciesism; rather, this is acknowledging connections and characteristics that uniquely exist within the human community. Individuals with significant cognitive limitations are humans first, and no humans are less human due to limitations in abilities. Further, concern for vulnerable humans is serious regardless of whether strong cognitive capacity is viewed as a sufficient but not necessary condition for legal personhood, in that embracing this change

Promoting interconnectedness/intersectionality regarding animal and human rights does not negate concerns about dangers to vulnerable humans created by inventing animal personhood based on cognitive capacities. In 2010, Professor Massimo Filippi, a supporter of "fundamental rights" for animals,[41] and his coauthors performed a functional MRI study of 20 omnivore subjects, 19 vegetarian subjects, and 19 vegan subjects.[42] The subjects' brain activation was measured as the subjects were shown pictures of human beings and animals suffering ("mutilations, murdered people, human/animal threat, tortures, wounds, etc.").[43] According to Filippi's study, the brains of the vegetarians and the vegans reflected greater empathy than the brains of the omnivores.[44] Curiously, although perhaps a bit to the side, a strong preponderance of other studies suggest that vegans and vegetarians are more likely to experience mental health challenges than are omnivores.[45]

These sorts of studies are interesting, but, particularly in light of other evidence and experiences, they are not persuasive regarding capacities-based animal legal personhood. Peter Singer supports animal legal personhood based on cognitive capacities.[46] But rather than being applauded as an interconnected/intersectional ally, he is an ongoing target of protests by disability rights advocates. The advocates are angry that Singer has asserted that parents of babies with significant disabilities should be permitted to euthanize them.[47] This position doubtless does not strike these disability rights advocates as empathetic to vulnerable humans.

The parade of antihuman or insensitive-to-human actions and sentiments by animal rights activists highlighted in *Beyond Cages* should provide a wake-up call

would focus courts' and society's attention on a being's cognitive capacity as a legitimate form of distinction regarding personhood.

41 Massimo Filippi, *Brief Notes on Speciesism and Antispeciesism*, Nov. 27, 2008, *available at* http://serenoregis.org/2008/11/27/brevi-note-su-specismo-e-antispecismo-massimo-filippi/ (English translation).

42 Massimo Filippi et al., *The Brain Functional Networks Associated to Human and Animal Suffering Differ among Omnivores, Vegetarians and Vegans*, PLOS ONE (May 26, 2010), *available at* https://journals.plos.org/plosone/article?id=10.1371/journal.pone.0010847.

43 *Id.*

44 *Id.*

45 *See* Hal Herzog, *The Baffling Connection between Vegetarianism and Depression*, PSYCHOLOGY TODAY (Dec. 4, 2018), *available at* https://www.psychologytoday.com/us/blog/animals-and-us/201812/the-baffling-connection-between-vegetarianism-and-depression. A 2017 study found vegans to be less likely to have a higher educational level compared to meat-eaters, and vegetarians likely to have a higher educational level compared to meat-eaters. Benjamin Allès et al., *Comparison of Sociodemographic and Nutritional Characteristics between Self-Reported Vegetarians, Vegans, and Meat-Eaters from the NutriNet-Santé Study*, 9 NUTRIENTS 1023, 1023 (2017).

46 *See* Peter Singer, *Chimpanzees Are People Too*, N.Y. DAILY NEWS (Oct. 21, 2014).

47 *See, e.g.*, John Pring, *Outrage over Left-Wing Media Website's Singer Interview*, Disability News Service (March 18, 2021), https://www.disabilitynewsservice.com/outrage-over-left-wing-media-websites-singer-interview/; Naaman Zhou, *Peter Singer Event Cancelled in New Zealand after Outcry over Disability Stance*, THE GUARDIAN (Feb. 18, 2020), https://www.theguardian.com/world/2020/feb/19/peter-singer-event-cancelled-in-new-zealand-after-outcry-over-disability-stance.

for any who believe that more compassion for some always leads to more compassion for all. As noted above, Marceau states that animal activists have been stereotyped as misanthropes – not as broadly compassionate people-lovers. He references the *Non-Humans First Declaration*, a document that seeks to govern the behavior and priorities of animal activists.[48] The document captures "the notion that the oppression of humans must be ignored, and everywhere treated as irrelevant."[49] Further, Marceau shares that "it is not hard to find racist comments on the blogs and Facebook pages of leading animal protection groups,"[50] and he provides illustrations of hateful or insensitive racist behavior by animal activists.[51] Marceau appropriately acknowledges that these particularly disturbing views are not representative of most animal activists, but his emphasis on these illustrations demonstrates his broader concern for inadequate human compassion in the movement.

Less extreme manifestations of discounting humans are perhaps representative of a broader cross-section of animal activists. Marceau relates that in 2015, when a wealthy American hunter killed a lion named Cecil in Zimbabwe, widespread outrage led to protests that grabbed headlines across the nation.[52] This led to a backlash in minority communities, as many sensed society expressing much more anger at the killing of a lion than it expresses over the unjustified killing of oppressed humans. Marceau discusses a *New York Times* op-ed written by a Black feminist, in which the author joked [her description] that "I'm personally going to start wearing a lion costume when I leave my house so if I get shot, people will care."[53]

Those who were outraged over Cecil the Lion's killing but who do not fret much over the wrongful deaths of humans are probably, for the most part, not sufficiently sensitive to human suffering rather than misanthropic. Even if animal activists' reputation for misanthropy is mostly undeserved, which I believe is so, comparing intelligent animals with the least cognitively capable humans is fraught with danger.

We have been in a somewhat comparable situation before, with some similarities and some differences, and in that situation our society failed vulnerable people more through insensitivity or apathy regarding their rights than through hatred. In the early-twentieth century, the eugenics movement was viewed by many intellectuals as a cutting-edge concept to better society, supported by enlightened understanding of modern science, rather than simply as a tool to oppress weak humans. Dozens of

[48] Marceau, *supra* note 2, at 157.
[49] *Id.*
[50] *Id.*
[51] *Id.* at 156–66.
[52] *Id.* at 158.
[53] *Id.* (*quoting* Roxanne Gay, *Of Lions and Men: Mourning Samuel DuBose and Cecil the Lion*, N.Y. Times [July 31, 2015]).

balancing human and animal interests. Advocates of an evolving animal welfare paradigm are focused on human responsibility as moral and legal persons for appropriate treatment of animals rather than on animal legal personhood. In practical terms, this may mean that eating meat or allowing biomedical research on animals would be viewed as immoral "oppression" of the animals eaten or experimented upon by many advocates of a strong rights paradigm, whereas animal advocates who support the welfare paradigm would likely utilize the term less broadly while still caring about animal suffering.

Although strong animal rights supporters and animal welfare supporters may have differing views regarding what constitutes unacceptable oppression of animals, both groups embrace cultivating more compassion for animals. This is another answer to those who claim that interconnectedness/intersectionality of compassion should lead to strong animal rights. Interconnectedness regarding compassion may lead people to stronger interest in appropriate animal protections through a welfare paradigm; it need not push them into support of a strong rights paradigm. It may be that seeking to expand the breadth of our compassion is a good fit with a healthy interest in increasing protection of animals as we learn more about their capacities and become more sensitive regarding their suffering. But militant or extreme devotion to an isolated focus of compassion for animals may not be a good recipe for enhanced interconnected/intersectional compassion or rights, and indeed may, as addressed above, in fact create a real (if not short-term) threat to vulnerable humans.

Marceau's deep concern both for animals and for humans is laudable, but, unfortunately, he is not the animal rights everyman. As an advocate for an evolving animal welfare paradigm, I applaud his call for more thoughtfulness and compassion in criminal adjudication in conjunction with more compassion for mistreated animals, but I also view it as illustrating challenges for, rather than providing a path to support for, animal legal personhood – particularly animal legal personhood based on cognitive capacities. Supporting active evolution of animal welfare protections is an uncomfortable but appropriate middle ground balancing of compassion for animals and concern for humans. Similarly, encouraging appropriate reforms of animal abuse prosecutions without completely rejecting incarceration in particularly serious cases is an uncomfortable but appropriate middle ground for enhancing compassion for humans who commit crimes harming animals, while still insisting that these humans are moral beings and subject to justice.

3

Giving a Voice to the Voiceless

A Prosecutor's Efforts to Combat Animal Cruelty

Ashley N. Beck

Animal cruelty ... is not a harmless venting of emotion in a healthy individual; this is a warning sign that this individual is not mentally healthy and needs some sort of intervention. Abusing animals does not dissipate those violent emotions, instead it may fuel them.[1]

3.1 INTRODUCTION

Who are the victims of animal cruelty? There is the short-haired dog shoved outside in below freezing temperatures with no access to shelter, food, or water, and left for hours. There is the ferret sent through the mail in a box who languished for days before chewing his way out. There is the pigeon that was attacked in the local park and hit over and over with a stick until its life drained away. There is the dog bludgeoned to death with a bat for no apparent reason and then put back in his kennel as if he were just peacefully sleeping in a pool of blood. There is the puppy who has suffered more blunt force trauma in her short life than most humans or animals will ever experience. There is the cat thrown against a tree and killed in a fit of anger. And another cat who is repeatedly beaten, kicked, strangled, and left for dead in the dumpster. There is the dog hung from the tree and decapitated. And the dog repeatedly stabbed out of spite. And the dog (or horse) who is sexually abused. Victims of animal cruelty range from companion animals to livestock to wild animals. Unfortunately, no species is safe from human cruelty. Examples are, regrettably, far too many to list, but those are just a few.

Animals are intelligent and sentient beings and, just like human victims, warrant both the protection of our laws as well as the pursuit of justice. Those who abuse

This chapter is dedicated to Sam, who was my exuberant and beloved black lab husky mix; we rescued each other.

[1] 104 CONG. REC. S12,338 (daily ed. Oct. 3, 1996) (statement of Supervisory Special Agent Alan C. Brantley, FBI).

animals should be confronted and held accountable. One way of doing this is through the levying of criminal charges and prosecution.

Prosecutors have a tremendous amount of power, discretion, and responsibility – the intended exercise of which is to advance justice. Fundamentally, justice is defined as the fair and proper administration of laws.[2] Despite a seemingly straightforward definition, the term "justice" has myriad interpretations, and in modern society its applicability has expanded outside the criminal justice system to intertwine with social and economic justice as well. Prosecutors work within the confines of the criminal justice system and the laws that legislators have passed, and a prosecutor's view of justice is thus appropriately tailored to the criminal justice realm. Prosecutors have the responsibility and challenge of pursuing "justice" in every case – striking a balance between the interests of the state (the citizenry they represent) and the accused, fairly and rationally considering what consequences are appropriate, repairing harm done or at least bringing closure to victims, and promoting future adherence to the social contract and laws that govern a cohesive, orderly, and peaceful society.

These are the reasons I became a prosecutor. I believe in the ideals of law and order, in the value of acknowledging right from wrong and in enforcing penalties when an individual's actions harm others. I became a prosecutor to stand up for and give a voice to those who may not have the words, strength, or desire to stand up for themselves; or for those who cannot speak because they have lost their lives at the hands of others. I humbly but proudly serve on behalf of society's most vulnerable members, and that includes animals – intelligent and sentient beings – who cannot speak for themselves. Whoever (or whatever) the victim, I, along with those in my profession, strive for the administration of justice in each and every case. And it is through this work that I try to instill in others that respect for the dignity and life of others – animals included – is necessary for a functioning society and cannot be overlooked.

Animals are everywhere in our lives. It is estimated that at least 67 percent of US households, or about 85 million families, own a pet.[3] And it's no wonder why. Animals – both wild and domesticated – enrich us in so many ways. Pets provide not only companionship, but also encourage us to be more physically active and to get outdoors. They increase opportunities for socialization and can be helpful in managing loneliness and depression. They teach responsibility and other practical skills to kids, provide laughter and entertainment for the whole family, give love unconditionally, are loyal, and will never share your secrets or betray your confidence. Research shows animals can reduce stress, high blood pressure, and anxiety and even make you and your family feel safer at home.

[2] *Justice*, BLACK'S LAW DICTIONARY (9th ed. 2009).

[3] American Pet Products Association, https://www.americanpetproducts.org/press_industrytrends.asp (last visited Sept. 20, 2020).

It is because of these and other attributes that many people consider pets to be part of the family. They really can be a human's best friend. Unfortunately, in addition to being perfect companions, animals are also the "perfect" crime victims. The power dynamic between perpetrator and victim is vast, and animals are usually ill-equipped to defend themselves against human aggression. Additionally, animals lack the ability to report the wrongs done to them, no matter how egregious. Thus, there is a very narrow window of opportunity for holding animal abusers accountable. The prosecution of these crimes relies heavily upon observant citizens coming forward to law enforcement when an act of cruelty is committed in public, the cooperation of friends and family when the cruelty happens within the home, and the keen awareness of veterinarians and other professionals when neither members of the public nor friends or family members are in a position to be able to report the abuse. Animals can't talk – at least not in a language that we speak. Because of this, they are among the most vulnerable and voiceless victims in the criminal justice system.

Holding animal abusers accountable and pursuing justice on behalf of animal victims is a worthwhile and important endeavor. From my perspective, the prosecution of animal cruelty offenders is essential for three primary reasons: (1) the pursuit of criminal charges can be the impetus for the removal of the victim animal from the offender's custody; (2) the levying of criminal charges sends a strong message to both the offender and society as a whole that the proper and humane treatment of animals matters (whether wild, livestock, or pet); and (3) the imposition of a sentence upon conviction – whether it be punitive, rehabilitative, or a combination thereof – aims to ensure that there is an intervention and the offender's conduct is not repeated. Additionally, the victimization of animals often coincides with other crimes, such as intrafamily and intimate partner violence, child abuse, elder abuse, sexual abuse, and organized crime, to name but a few. Accordingly, the prosecution of animal cruelty offenders is beneficial to ensuring that our communities continue to value and respect the lives of animals and humans, and to uncovering other crimes and enhancing community safety as a whole. In this chapter, I do not pretend to speak for all prosecutors. The comments, thoughts, and discussion that follow are based upon my experience and observations, and my personal professional journey.

3.2 THE LEGAL FRAMEWORK: COLORADO ANIMAL CRUELTY LAWS

Prosecutors and members of the law enforcement community who investigate and prosecute acts of animal cruelty have the difficult task of being the voice of these voiceless beings in the courtroom and criminal justice system. Fortunately, Colorado prosecutors have a fairly broad statutory scheme under which we can charge animal cruelty offenses, and thus have many tools at our disposal to try to ensure that animal abusers are held accountable. Conduct constituting cruelty to animals is broadly defined and is not limited to companion animals, but rather extends its protections to "any living dumb creature."[4] An individual can be charged with cruelty to animals, a class one misdemeanor,[5] or aggravated cruelty to animals, a class six felony.[6] In the event that an individual has sustained a prior conviction for either cruelty to animals or aggravated cruelty to animals, the penalty increases and a second or subsequent conviction becomes a class six felony or a class five felony, respectively.

The broadest provision and that which is most widely used in charging these types of offenses prohibits a person from knowingly, recklessly, or with criminal negligence overdriving, overloading, overworking, or tormenting an animal; depriving an animal of necessary sustenance; unnecessarily or cruelly beating an animal; allowing an animal to be housed in a manner that results in chronic or repeated serious physical harm; carrying or confining an animal in or upon any vehicles in a cruel or reckless manner; engaging in a sexual act with an animal; otherwise mistreating (whether by act or omission) or neglecting an animal; or, abandoning an animal.[7] It is also unlawful to intentionally abandon an animal, or to recklessly or with criminal negligence torture, needlessly mutilate, or needlessly kill an animal.[8] In addition, there are also specific provisions under Colorado law that make it a misdemeanor for an individual to commit cruelty to a service animal or a certified police working dog.[9] Any of the above-described conduct results in a class one misdemeanor (assuming it is a first offense). Aggravated cruelty to animals, which is a class six felony offense, prohibits a person from knowingly torturing, needlessly mutilating, or needlessly killing an animal.[10] The difference between misdemeanor and felony acts of cruelty, thus, is the *mens rea* – or mental state – required for the offense, coupled with the degree of harm done to the animal.

In addition to providing a host of theories under which prosecutors can charge individuals for acts of cruelty to animals, Colorado's animal cruelty statute also equips prosecutors with other tools to ensure the safety and continued well-being of the animal victim during the pendency of the criminal case and beyond. Under Colorado law, peace officers who have probable cause to believe an animal is a victim of an act of animal cruelty can lawfully take possession of and impound that animal if the officer believes the animal is or will be endangered if left in the household.[11] In other words, an officer may remove an animal from an abusive situation at the very initial stages of investigation – even before charges are presented to or filed by the district attorney. This provision is paramount to ensuring the

[4] Colo. Rev. Stat. § 18-9-201(2) (2019).
[5] Colo. Rev. Stat. § 18-9-202(2)(a) (2019).
[6] Colo. Rev. Stat. § 18-9-202(2)(c) (2019).
[7] Colo. Rev. Stat. § 18-9-202(1)(a) (2019).
[8] Colo. Rev. Stat. § 18-9-202(1)(b); (1.5)(a) (2019).
[9] Colo. Rev. Stat. § 18-9-202(1)(b); (1.5)(c) (2019).
[10] Colo. Rev. Stat. § 18-9-202(1.5)(b) (2019).
[11] Colo. Rev. Stat. § 18-9-202(1.8) (2019).

animal's well-being, and inherently recognizes and seeks to avoid the harm that can be caused by a slow investigative and filing process. Animal cruelty investigations can take days, weeks, or even several months to complete. By having this statutory authority to seize and impound animals immediately, prosecutors do not have to worry about making a hasty filing decision to ensure that an animal is removed from a dangerous situation. And, in the event that the animal seized and impounded is severely injured, Colorado law goes one step further and allows a licensed veterinarian to care for or, if needed, humanely euthanize an animal that has been seized and impounded if, in the veterinarian's opinion, the animal is experiencing extreme pain or suffering or is severely injured, disabled, or diseased past the point of recovery.[12]

The Colorado criminal code also has a statutory provision that governs impounded animals and the associated costs of care to continue to hold the animal throughout the pendency of a criminal case.[13] The impounding agency (usually animal protection or a local shelter) has the authority to determine the appropriate disposition of an animal in its care if the owner or custodian of the impounded animal either voluntarily relinquishes the animal or if the court finds probable cause for impoundment but the owner or custodian elects not to pay for the animal's care while it is in the shelter. While there are fairly nuanced provisions that govern the cost of care and ensure that the owner or custodian has access to a court hearing and due process on the matter, these provisions provide law enforcement and prosecutors with a legal process to either temporarily or permanently remove animals from harmful situations. The levying of criminal charges and request for payment from the defendant to care for the seized animal often forces the defendant to evaluate whether he or she wants to retain ownership or surrender the animal to the care of the shelter. In the instance where a defendant wishes to retain ownership of the animal, the reality is that the animal will remain in the care and custody of the shelter (though sometimes in a foster placement) until resolution of the case and until a court orders the return or relinquishment of the animal. The wheels of justice often churn slowly, and this may result in the animal being at the shelter for a prolonged period of time. However, in the instance where an animal is surrendered, this means that animal can be cared for by a shelter until it is adopted out to a new family who, ideally, will love and care for the animal and not subject it to further abuse. In either scenario, there is some peace of mind that the animal has at least been removed from harm's way whether temporarily or permanently.

Colorado's fairly strong and comprehensive animal cruelty statutes have led to Colorado routinely ranking in the top tier of states for animal protection laws.[14]

[12] Colo. Rev. Stat. § 18-9-202(1.8) (2019).

[13] Colo. Rev. Stat. § 18-9-202.5 (2019).

[14] In 2019, Colorado was ranked third; in 2020, Colorado was ranked fourth among the fifty states. *Animal Protection: U.S. State Laws Rankings Report*, Animal Legal Def. Fund (2019), https://aldf.org/wp-content/uploads/2020/02/2019-Animal-Protection-US-State-Laws-Rankings-Report

However, despite being a fairly animal-friendly state with a host of favorable statutory provisions and laws that allow prosecutors to pursue justice in these types of cases, the investigation and successful prosecution of animal cruelty cases can be challenging due to resource constraints and sometimes, a lack of investigative know-how.

3.3 RESOURCE CONSTRAINTS

If you ask your typical local prosecutor or friends in law enforcement what constitutes a "serious" crime, the range of responses often includes homicide, sexual assault, aggravated robbery, human trafficking, child abuse, and the like. Most prosecutors are likely concerned, and rightly so, with what we refer to as "victim crimes" and those crimes which are perceived to have the most significant safety risk to the community. These are the cases where *human* lives are lost or changed forever. And they are some of the most gratifying cases to work on and present to a jury. But where does animal cruelty fall on that spectrum? I submit that, unfortunately, in many law enforcement agencies and prosecutor's offices, it has historically fallen toward the bottom of the "severity scale." Fortunately, that is starting to change.

While investigative agencies such as animal protection units, Pet Animal Care Facilities Act (PACFA) inspectors, and specially commissioned agents of the Department of Agriculture exist, many law enforcement agencies don't have units dedicated to the investigation of animal cruelty offenses. In fact, some law enforcement agencies don't have a single detective or officer trained to investigate these offenses. While this certainly varies from jurisdiction to jurisdiction, in Denver, for example, an animal cruelty investigation is usually initiated by an officer with Denver Animal Protection (a division of the Colorado Department of Public Health and Environment), but then must be turned over to the police department to pursue charges at the state level. Once in the hands of the police department, the case is usually assigned to a detective in a general assignment, who has likely never investigated an animal cruelty offense.

While I believe this is changing (thankfully!), the general attitude toward animal cruelty offenses has been that the time and effort needed to investigate or prosecute these offenses are difficult to justify. And from a strict return on investment perspective, that may be true. The "bang for your buck" that you often get with other offenses just doesn't exist with animal cruelty offenses. There will never be a victim who can voice their thanks or appreciation for the work done on their case. No matter how heinous the act, if it is a first offense, the highest chargeable offense is a class six felony, which is a probation-eligible offense and carries a maximum penalty of up to and between twelve months' and eighteen months' incarceration. Animal

.pdf; 2020 U.S. State Animal Protection Laws Rankings, Animal Legal Def. Fund (2020), https://aldf.org/project/us-state-rankings/.

cruelty investigations are unique and can be a challenge to investigate; the more serious cases often require the expenditure of significant resources and energy. It is difficult to justify pulling a criminalist from a homicide or sexual assault scene to assist in the processing of an animal cruelty scene where the stakes (on paper, anyway) are much lower, and frustrating for a case that usually results in a misdemeanor filing, or the lowest level felony, at best.

As with any kind of criminal offense, some cases are easy to solve, and others are quite challenging. Cases that are fairly cut-and-dry take minimal to no resources and thus are easy to get investigative buy-in. For example, in one case, dispatch was made aware that a citizen had observed an individual in a park punching his dog repeatedly in the head and had a cell phone video recording of the incident. In that instance, all that was required was for an officer to respond to the location, interview the witness(es), locate/identify the suspect, and review and collect the cell phone video footage. Similarly, another case involved a security guard at an apartment complex who reviewed security footage in an effort to help locate a tenant's lost cat. In doing so, he uncovered footage of his coworker (also a security guard) punching, kicking, throwing, and strangling the tenant's cat while walking the halls late one evening. The footage then showed the security guard toss the cat in the dumpster and leave it for dead. The security guard who uncovered this footage reported it to law enforcement and identified his colleague in the video. In these circumstances, the evidence is strong and speaks for itself, and the additional investigation required to prove that the criminal act happened is minimal. Most responding officers or detectives will not hesitate to wrap up these kinds of cases and submit them to prosecutors for acceptance of charges.

Oftentimes, however, these cases develop over time and require collaborative action between various agencies and consultation with experts external to the investigation. These more nuanced investigations can be time-consuming and costly, and not every jurisdiction has adequate resources or time to invest into such cases. The following example is a case that took roughly six months to fully investigate and bring to a point where charges could be filed.

A young couple, let's call them Amy and Bob,[15] bought a six-week-old pit bull mix in August, and by the end of October of that same year, the previously perfectly healthy puppy was at an emergency veterinary hospital with numerous broken bones and on the verge of death. The veterinarian astutely called Animal Protection due to concerns of suspected animal cruelty,[16] and law enforcement opened an

[15] Names have been changed.

[16] In Colorado, veterinarians are mandatory reporters of suspected animal cruelty pursuant to Colo. Rev. Stat. §12-315-120 (2019), and must make available veterinary records in their custody to local law enforcement and the Bureau of Animal Protection in the connection with an investigation pursuant to Colo. Rev. Stat. § 12-315-119(2)(c)(II) (2019). Similarly, veterinarians are mandatory reporters of suspected child neglect and abuse pursuant to Colo. Rev. Stat. § 19-3-304 (2020).

investigation. Unlike the previous examples, where we had cooperative witnesses and/or video evidence of the person responsible for the act or acts of cruelty, here we had no readily apparent means to prove at whose hands the animal had suffered.

In this type of case, the first challenge is usually proving ownership and continuity of care for the period of time in which injuries could have been sustained. To do so, we consulted veterinary and shelter records and also looked to see whether Amy or Bob had any prior contact with Animal Protection. Once continuity of care for the months leading up to the veterinary visit had been established, we sought to determine the cause or causes of the puppy's injuries. To do so, we scrutinized the veterinary records and consulted an outside expert.

Reports indicated that upon presentation to the first veterinarian, the puppy was in great distress, cyanotic (bluish in color due to deoxygenation), dyspneic (breathing with great difficulty), and with noticeable petechia on the external pinna of the ears and ecchymoses (discoloration/bruising) on the ventral abdomen. The second veterinarian to see the puppy reported similar observations and through testing learned of additional injuries to include a pneumothorax, at least two acute rib fractures, several older rib fractures, and a fractured left femoral head.

One of the strongest indicators of nonaccidental trauma (i.e., abuse) in animals is the presence of multiple fractures in different stages of healing, which is what we uncovered here. However, to narrow down a suspect, we needed an approximate timeline as to when the injuries occurred. We consulted a forensic veterinarian,[17] who did a comprehensive review of all records associated with the case and confirmed that the puppy had suffered multiple rib, spinal, and leg fractures, all in different stages of healing, which she opined indicated repeated and numerous episodes of blunt force trauma and animal physical abuse. Her findings also revealed that the puppy's blood work – which showed she was mildly anemic, had a very high white blood cell count, low eosinophils, and elevated liver enzymes – was consistent with acute trauma.

Once we determined we could prove that the injuries were consistent with abuse and had an approximate timeline, the next challenge was identifying the individual responsible for the injuries. We caught a break when additional witnesses came forward after the local shelter that was coordinating the treatment of and caring for the puppy posted her story on its social media page as part of a fundraising effort to pay for her surgeries. Three of Amy's coworkers divulged to investigators that a month or so prior, Amy had come into work upset because Bob had been abusing the puppy and had thrown her across the yard after she defecated on him, seemingly stunning or momentarily paralyzing the puppy. This admission to her coworkers and

[17] Veterinary forensics is a fairly new and emerging field. Forensic veterinarians often assist investigators of animal cruelty cases with crime scene investigation as well as the examination of live and deceased victims and provide expert consultation and review of veterinary and other reports. They can be instrumental in an investigation.

the approximate timeframe of disclosure (mid–late September) was corroborated by an anonymous tip that Animal Protection had received in mid-October referencing a September incident of abuse, and aligned with the timeline of injuries we had established.

Despite multiple interviews, neither Amy nor Bob ever provided a full account of what happened to the puppy. Nevertheless, after an extensive and protracted investigation, we ultimately moved forward with charging two counts of misdemeanor animal cruelty (for two distinct incidents we believed we could prove) against Bob.

In many respects, the time and attention required by these more complex animal cruelty cases parallels that of child abuse investigations involving young, nonverbal children. Those cases often require investigators to cast a broader net to eliminate possible suspects before they can identify the actual suspect, and to eliminate explanations of accidental injuries before they can definitively prove abuse. Just as medical experts are able to use their experience to determine whether a child's injuries are consistent with accidental trauma or indicative of physical abuse, so too are veterinarians well situated to assess an animal's injuries and often serve as the first line of defense for these animals. Puppies – just like children – are fairly resilient and heal quickly, and a careful examination of their injuries can tell you a lot about what they have been through even if they can't tell you themselves. While their injuries will rarely tell you exactly how they were sustained (e.g., whether the animal was hit with a bat or golf club, or just kicked), the type and location of injury can often tell you whether it was accidental or nonaccidental trauma.

Given the complexity of these types of cases, they are often difficult to pursue without significant interagency collaboration. Enlisting the assistance of various agencies and experts is time and resource intensive. Regardless of the challenges that these investigations may pose, we should be pursuing these offenses and doing whatever it takes to complete a thorough investigation because, simply put, these cases matter. They matter because animals are sentient beings who very much experience pain and are victims in and of their own right. There is much literature and research surrounding the link between animal cruelty and human violence and other crimes, and in that regard, the public policy argument for pursuing these cases is also strong: when an animal is being abused, human lives and community safety may also be at risk. From my perspective, however, regardless of whether there is a link to other crimes and regardless of whether there is a risk of additional violence, the harm done to an animal, in and of itself, justifies criminal prosecution.

3.4 PURSUING JUSTICE IN THE COURTROOM

Animals are often the smallest and most overlooked victims of intrafamily and intimate-partner violence. Oftentimes abusers intentionally target an intimate partner's animal to exert power and control over them. Sometimes abusers take their rage out on an animal simply because it's there, or they know that hurting the animal will hurt their partner more than anything they could do to them. Other times abusers just go after whoever or whatever is closest. No matter the reason, it is important that we speak not only for the human victim, but also for the animal. Sometimes that means we speak for the animal victim even when the human victim does not desire that we do so. Oftentimes a human victim's desire for justice aligns with getting justice for a harmed animal, but in some cases, for myriad reasons, a human victim may not want the state to pursue charges at all, let alone for an act of animal cruelty. In these instances, prosecutors must exercise compassion and understand the varying dynamics at play and use their discretion in whether or not to pursue charges. From my perspective, it is often most appropriate to pursue animal cruelty charges regardless of what others involved in the case may desire, as we simply cannot ignore violence, whether done to a human or an animal. In other cases, there may not be a secondary victim or witness, but those cases too, remain worthy of our pursuit.

3.4.1 *Case Example 1: The Disgruntled Boyfriend Turned Arsonist and the Cooperative Human Victim*

One case example in which a human victim's desire to pursue charges aligned with the state's interest in pursuing charges involved a couple who had been in a relationship for approximately two years. At one point, the defendant started losing trust in his girlfriend and suspected her of cheating on him. Things came to a head late one evening, and the two started arguing. The defendant began drinking. At first it was just an argument, but the next morning it turned physical as the female attempted to leave for work. The defendant was frustrated that she would not stay to engage in the discussion and so he punched her in the face. Nevertheless, the female victim proceeded to leave her apartment. Shortly after she left for work, the defendant went to a gas station and filled a gas can. He then returned to the victim's apartment, where he broke in and started a fire in the master bedroom. At home at the time were the victim's two cats.

While at work, the female victim received a number of calls and text messages from the defendant, most of which continued to accuse of her cheating. She largely ignored them, but then received a text message from the defendant that stated something along the lines of "the house is burning." She didn't believe him and assumed he was just trying to get her attention. Then she got a call from a friend who told her that her apartment was on fire, and she realized it was true.

She rushed home to find her apartment almost completely destroyed by the fire. Tragically, her two one-and-a-half-year-old cats were unable to escape and died in the fire. Both cats suffered fur and skin burns to their extremities, tongue burns, and significant soot inhalation. When interviewed by police, the girlfriend was extremely emotional when talking about the loss of her cats. The investigating detective went so far as to note that she did not seem to care much at all about the loss of her property or apartment, but rather was most concerned and upset by the loss of her two cats. To her, her abuser killing her cats was far more devastating and far more effective retaliation than the burning of her apartment.

In this instance, the defendant was charged with first-degree arson, two counts of aggravated cruelty to animals, and assault in the third degree. The pursuit of the animal cruelty charges here did not serve the purpose of removing the victim animals from harm's way as they were already deceased and were not the defendant's animals in the first place. However, pursuing two counts of aggravated cruelty to animals presumably sent the message to the defendant that the cats were not simply viewed as collateral damage. Rather, we considered them intentional victims and took into account that he perpetrated a distinct offense by killing each cat. Accordingly, one count of cruelty was charged for each victim cat. Given the human victim's cooperation and the strength of the evidence, this case resolved with a plea bargain that included a plea of guilty to a lesser count of arson, and one count of the aggravated animal cruelty and resulted in the defendant being sentenced to prison.

3.4.2 *Case Example 2: Pursuing Animal Cruelty Charges in the Face of Opposition*

In another case, a mother and son (drunk and angry) were involved in a lengthy and heated argument one evening. At one point, the son went into his mother's room and tried to grab and throw her television across the room. His mother was able to grab on to it and prevent him from throwing it. However, he then moved on to grab something else – something far more meaningful than a television. He grabbed his mother's ten-year-old Chihuahua and threw the animal across the room. He threw the dog with such force that upon striking the wall, the animal suffered a comminuted fracture of the skull and brain hemorrhage. The dog was killed instantly. The police were notified via a call to 911 placed by the defendant's aunt, who had heard the incident unfold and was scared and concerned for her own dogs in the house.

This particular case went to trial, and perhaps not unsurprisingly, the People's primary witnesses – the defendant's mother and his aunt – both became uncooperative as neither wanted to see the defendant, their son and nephew, respectively, "in trouble." Nevertheless, we were able to secure their presence for trial through legal process by having both of them personally served. And when their testimony on the witness stand varied dramatically from what they had originally told officers on scene, we were able to impeach (discredit) their trial testimony with their prior statements captured on body camera.

Despite the mom and aunt's best efforts to testify favorably for the defendant, we were able to secure a conviction. The jury returned a guilty verdict on the sole count of aggravated cruelty to animals. This case is a prime example of where prosecutors have an obligation to recognize that there may be two victims (the mother who lost her beloved pet and the dog who lost his life) and to speak for, and to seek justice for the animal victim even when the human victim is not cooperative with prosecution. Prosecutors don't fault the recanting victim or the scared and uncooperative witness. The judicial process is slow and often unforgiving in the trauma it inflicts on victims and witnesses, who may be compelled to take the stand and talk in front of strangers about some of their worst experiences. And while at times we will respect a victim's wishes not to move forward with a case (for example, few prosecutors will ever force a sexual assault survivor to proceed against their wishes), a prosecutor sometimes has to – or at least should – move forward where there is an independent harm done to another living being. Just because a mother loves her son and has forgiven his transgression, that does not mean that the law should turn a blind eye. My colleague and I pursued this case because it was important; a life was lost, and our aim was to force the defendant to acknowledge his wrongdoing and to seek treatment. As he was unwilling to resolve with a plea offer, the alternative was to move forward with trial. Upon conviction, the defendant was sentenced to ninety days in jail and a term of probation – a forced but necessary intervention.

3.4.3 *Case Example 3: Speaking Up for the Hog-Tied Dog in the Bathtub*

In this case, an apartment manager and maintenance employee entered a tenant's apartment to look for a water leak. They did not locate a leak but were shocked at what they found. When they entered the bathroom, where they suspected they'd find the water leak, they encountered a Labrador-mix dog hog-tied in the bathtub. The dog was positioned partially on its side and back, in a U shape; her front limbs and hind limbs were pulled and tied together with rope at least seven times around, and then her limbs were pulled up and tied to the bathtub faucet such that if the dog moved or yanked hard enough, the cold water would presumably turn on. The dog's mouth was tied shut with rope functioning as a make-shift muzzle, and she was lying in her own feces. The apartment manager and maintenance employee described being able to hear the dog softly moan and whimper. They took photographs of the dog and scene as they found it, and immediately reported it to law enforcement, who then opened an investigation. Investigators were able to put a timeline together and determined that the dog was in that position for over two hours.

The owner was confronted by an animal protection officer later that day and denied doing anything wrong. When confronted with photographic evidence of the position his dog had been found in, the defendant admitted he had tied her up for only a "brief" amount of time while he went out because she had chewed his shoes on a previous occasion, but he still denied any wrongdoing. The dog was seized by the investigating officer and evaluated, and although there were no physical findings of injury, the defendant was charged with one count of aggravated cruelty to animals for needlessly torturing the dog.

In this case, we did not face opposition to pursuing charges, nor did we have any secondary victim or witness who advocated that we pursue the case. Nevertheless, the fact that a living being had been placed in a position that made it difficult to breathe and self-regulate body temperature, and was undoubtedly uncomfortable and in pain for several hours, warranted the levying of criminal charges. Pursuing charges in this case resulted in the removal of the dog from the defendant's custody and took her out of harm's way (the defendant ultimately surrendered the dog and relinquished ownership) and impressed upon the defendant that this type of treatment would not be tolerated. Additionally, once the defendant pleaded guilty, we were able to get the court to order that the defendant not be the primary or sole caretaker for any animals for the duration of his sentence, which also helped to ensure (to the best of our abilities) that the defendant would not victimize another animal in that time frame.

3.5 SENTENCING CONSIDERATIONS

It is our obligation as prosecutors to ensure that justice is done, and that those who perpetrate crimes against animals are not "given a pass" simply because their chosen victims can't talk and aren't considered victims in the truest legal sense (as animals are still considered property under the law). While many prosecutors are aware of and see evidence of the link between violence to animals and violence to humans, we should vigorously pursue animal cruelty crimes not just because a human might be at risk now or later on, but rather do so in recognition that animals are sentient beings who experience pain and suffering. We must pursue these crimes to ensure that the dignity of animals is protected and to reinforce that their lives have value in our communities.

Thus, the question becomes: What constitutes an appropriate sentence for an animal abuser? There is no "one size fits all" answer to this question, and when recommending a sentence, prosecutors typically take a number of different factors into consideration. In my experience, animal cruelty offenders run the gamut. Some offenders are simply uninformed and negligent, others have psychopathic tendencies and are cold, calculated, and intentional in their harm to animals. Others are encumbered with mental health diagnoses, substance abuse issues, or even a dearth of resources that contribute to the act or acts of cruelty. While the criminal justice system may not be fully equipped to address some of these more nuanced and complicated dynamics, it can provide direction and incentive toward more responsible behavior as well as access to resources that can help address these and other criminogenic issues, and thereby assist in protecting the current animal victim and animals in the future. After all, an animal doesn't suffer any less if its abuser has planned to cause it harm or if its abuser has just "snapped" out of anger or because they were under the influence of drugs or alcohol. The harm done doesn't change; the pain an animal feels or the loss of life suffered does not depend on the *mens rea* or intent of its abuser. From my perspective, criminal charges are appropriate where a crime has been committed. It is in the plea-bargaining stage or in the recommendation of a sentence where a particular offender's culpability, needs, and specific characteristics ought to be taken into consideration.

In Colorado, the criminal code clearly sets forth the purposes of sentencing. In doing so, it provides judges, prosecutors, and defense attorneys various points to consider and argue. The purposes of sentencing are multifold and include: punishing a defendant in proportion to the seriousness of the offense; assuring fair and consistent treatment of all convicted offenders; preventing crime and promoting respect for law; deterring others likely to commit similar offenses; and promoting the defendant's rehabilitation.[18] In light of these sentencing purposes, the case-specific facts and circumstances of every defendant must also be taken into consideration.

For most prosecutors, requests for sentences to jail or prison are reserved for the most heinous offenders who we feel cannot be safely managed in a community-based setting or those offenders who continue to offend repeatedly despite numerous prior attempts at intervention and rehabilitation. Animal cruelty can be an indication of mental illness, substance abuse, and other antisocial tendencies. Because of that, treatment-based sentences are often sought in an effort to address the underlying cause(s) of the animal cruelty behavior and interrupt the deviant thought-patterns and, thus, hopefully, rehabilitate the offender before they have the chance to victimize *other* animals or humans. Understanding the reason *why* someone harms an animal can be instrumental in determining the appropriate sentence. To that end, upon conviction at trial or by acceptance of a guilty plea, a court is required to order an evaluation to be conducted prior to sentencing to assist in its determination of an appropriate sentence.[19] If the evaluation results in a recommendation of treatment, and if the court agrees, the person will be ordered to complete an anger-management treatment program and/or any other treatment program that the court deems appropriate. While this provision doesn't explicitly specify an offense-specific evaluation, many prosecutors have taken to requesting a Forensic Animal Maltreatment Evaluation or a similar evaluation. Such an evaluation helps identify behavioral, mental health, and trauma-based issues relevant to the emergence of animal cruelty behavior; provides an estimation of the likelihood and circumstances for continued abusive behavior; identifies community safety concerns; and provides recommendations for intervention, disposition, and supervision of the offender.

If asked in the abstract what sentence is commensurate with intentionally harming society's most vulnerable and truly innocent victims, my answer would almost always be incarceration. Acts of animal cruelty are abhorrent in their own right, and when done knowingly or intentionally, I believe such acts justify our system's most punitive sanction. There are indeed some (and perhaps many) cases of animal cruelty where prosecutors believe that incarceration is more in the interest of

[18] Colo. Rev. Stat. § 18-1-102.5 (2019).
[19] Colo. Rev. Stat. § 18-9-202(2)(a.5)(III) (2019).

justice than a sentence with a purely rehabilitative aim. But we also recognize the bigger picture. We understand that incarceration is finite, and these offenders will be back in the community in short order. Additionally, we understand that these offenders are potentially dangerous and without treatment, can and will likely victimize other animals (and/or humans) in the future. Given that the maximum exposure (under Colorado law) to incarceration for either a first-time misdemeanor or felony animal cruelty offense is eighteen months, it oftentimes makes the most sense to attempt to address the underlying issues that give rise to the offender's violence against animals. That generally means a sentence of probation. If we can address these issues early on – whether substance abuse, mental health, anger management, psychopathic tendencies, and so forth – perhaps we can steer the offender in a different direction and away from the path of continued violence. However, in those circumstances where an animal cruelty offender has already been given a probationary sentence and treatment to address their underlying criminogenic tendencies in prior cases, yet continues to escalate and reoffend, prosecutors often do – and should – request a sentence that is commensurate with their underlying offense and obtains a more appropriate level of justice for the animal victim. To that end, a sentence of incarceration may be the only effective way to guarantee that, for at least a period of time, the perpetrator cannot victimize another animal and perhaps will be more strongly deterred from reoffending.

Whether a sentence is negotiated via plea agreement or open to the court upon conviction at trial, it has been my experience that the majority of first-time animal cruelty offenders receive a sentence of probation, often irrespective of whether they have prior unrelated convictions. Still, there are times where incarceration is certainly appropriate for a first-time offender. At the end of the day, the intent and primary hope of every prosecutor is that whatever sentence is imposed, it will deter future criminal conduct and bring some sense of justice and a measure of closure to the victim and society.

Regardless of whether a defendant receives a sentence of probation or incarceration, prosecutors can negotiate additional terms in a plea agreement or ask the court, in its discretion, to order additional conditions as part of a sentence. Frequently requested additional provisions might include that a defendant agree to ongoing animal welfare checks by the local animal protection agency (if he or she has other animals in the home), or that a defendant not be allowed to own, possess, or care for animals at all for a certain period of time.[20] Negotiating these types of

20 To that end, a provision enacted by the Colorado legislature in the summer of 2020 actually imposes a requirement on courts to enter an order prohibiting an offender convicted of aggravated animal cruelty from owning, possessing, or caring for a pet animal for a period of three to five years, and a juvenile adjudicated a delinquent for animal cruelty from owning a pet animal unless the defendant or juvenile's treatment provider makes a specific recommendation to the court not to impose the ban and the court agrees with the recommendation. COLO. REV. STAT. § 18-9-202(2)(a)(V)(V.5) (2019).

additional terms as part of a plea agreement, or asking the court to order such, is another mechanism by which prosecutors work to ensure a sentence is tailored to limit an offender's immediate and future access to animals to potentially prevent additional crimes.

3.6 CONCLUSION

As George Vest so aptly recognized in his closing argument over a century ago,

> a man's dog stands by him in prosperity and in poverty, in health and in sickness. He will sleep on the cold ground where the wintry winds blow and the snow drives fierce, if only he may be near his master's side. He will kiss the hand that has no food to offer; he will lick the wounds and sores that come from encounter with the roughness of the world. He guards the sleep of his pauper master as if he were a prince. When all other friends desert, he remains. When riches take wing and reputation falls to pieces, he is as constant in his love as the sun in its journey through the heavens.[21]

Do we not owe it to these magnificent creatures (whether companion animals or wild) to learn to reciprocate and to treat them with the respect and dignity? Does not that responsibility extend to prosecutors and law enforcement professionals to uphold the laws that require the appropriate treatment of animals, and to impose appropriate consequences for violations? I submit that the answer to both of these questions is a resounding yes, and that while our criminal justice system may not be perfect (I have yet to find a human-crafted system that is), it is designed to ensure that those who violate laws are held accountable by the imposition of sentences that encourage renewed adherence to the social contract we all bought into when this country was founded with a respect for law and order.

No sentient being deserves to be victimized at the hands of a human, and it is up to us to collaborate with other agencies to do our best to ensure that these crimes are detected and reported and to ensure that animal cruelty offenders are subject to consequences and/or treatment as necessary. To that end, Colorado law provides animal protection agencies, law enforcement, and prosecutors with a significant number of tools to investigate these cases fully and strive to achieve justice for these vulnerable and voiceless victims. Wild animals, livestock, and companion animals alike enrich our lives in so many ways. Prosecutors should continue to advocate for the animals who suffer cruelty at the hands of humans and should encourage their fellow prosecutors and law enforcement colleagues to do the same. If we don't protect our most vulnerable populations, we are failing both the animals and our communities. The criminal justice system is often the last opportunity for intervention and the last chance that society has to encourage behavior to change or to

[21] 148 Cong. Rec. S3,592 (daily ed. May 1, 2002) (citing remarks made in the summation to the jury by George G. Vest, 1870).

remove the dangerous offender from the community. We, as prosecutors, cannot shy away from that responsibility. Most importantly, we must do everything in our power to mitigate the potential for it to happen again and put an end to the abuse of animals. We need to instill within our communities that the well-being and lives of animals matter in their own right, but also that these cases are serious and warrant adequate time, attention, and resources because a perpetrator of animal cruelty has the potential to be a threat to human and community safety.

4

Examining Anticruelty Enhancements

Historical Context and Policy Advances

Pamela D. Frasch

4.1 INTRODUCTION

The criminal justice system can be viewed as a proxy of sorts. A crime's severity – as evidenced, in part, by its maximum possible penalty – is seen by many as a direct reflection of society's values and norms: the higher the maximum possible penalty, the greater the value society places on securing justice for the victim by ensuring that the offender is held accountable for his conduct. There is a reason why armed robbery carries a much higher penalty than theft of the same item – society's disdain for violence is greater than its concern for the simple loss of property. Additionally, the greater the degree of an offender's malice, ill will, or premeditation, the greater the society's interest (as reflected in the exercise of its police power) in holding the offender accountable. This is why an intentional, premeditated homicide is treated far more seriously than a reckless killing.

For years, animal advocates have recognized these dynamics and have worked to reform criminal laws and procedures to elevate the status of animals to reflect more accurately their true standing in society as sentient beings rather than mere property. Many, if not most, of the animal welfare–specific criminal justice system improvements were inspired by, or borrowed from, other areas of the criminal code – such as, child abuse, elder abuse, crime victims' rights, domestic violence, and civil rights/ hate crimes. For example, to overcome police bias in favor of treating domestic violence as a private family matter rather than a crime of violence committed against a true victim, state legislatures enacted mandatory arrest statutes that now require police to investigate and, on probable cause, make an arrest.[1] Similarly, in an effort to overcome widespread police bias in favor of viewing animal cruelty as a low-priority matter not worthy of the officer's time (the "Oh, it's just a dog" response)

[1] *See* E. Buzawa & C. Buzawa, Domestic Violence: The Criminal Justice Response 102 (2d ed. 1996); Thurman v. City of Torrington, 595 F. Supp. 1521 (D. Conn. 1984).

rather than as a serious crime of violence committed against a voiceless victim, state legislatures have enacted mandatory arrest statutes that require an officer with probable cause to arrest an offender in animal abuse cases.[2] Mandatory arrest statutes do more than address police bias. They send a message to prosecutors as well, underscoring that viable cases of animal abuse are deserving of the prosecutor's and court's attention, just as it is now with viable cases of domestic violence.

Despite this work to elevate the status and lessen the suffering of animals, attorneys working in this space are not without their critics. Most commonly, these critics – many of whom seek to suppress and silence us[3] – make their living off of animal suffering, oftentimes on a truly massive scale.[4] Given their deeply rooted economic stake in the issue, these traditional critics are genuinely threatened by the strides animal protection attorneys have made in recent years.[5] More recently, some who work to reform the criminal justice system are also questioning the motives and methodology of animal advocates working to enhance the status of animals in the criminal justice system.[6] These criminal justice reform advocates are rightly seeking to address systemic racism and other ills that have historically and unfairly targeted marginalized people, and in particular Black men.[7] However, there is a danger that the animal welfare progress of the last two decades will be compromised without any workable alternative approaches to take its place. Before taking any action that may unintentionally strip animals of the very few, and hard fought, advances they do enjoy, we must be willing to gather and analyze data to develop thoughtful and effective policy that addresses multiple concerns. We must be willing to understand the importance of criminalizing violence against animals, while simultaneously working to address the inherent problems in our criminal justice system. We must also be willing to make heavy investment in prevention programs and community-based reformation[8] while still recognizing the reality that thoughtful application of

2 *See* A. Ireland Moore, *Defining Animals as Crime Victims*, 1 J. Animal L. 91, 98 (2005).

3 *See* S. French, *The Unaddressed Force of the First Amendment's Petition Clause Underlying Evolving and Expanding Ag-Gag Legislation*, 18 First Amend. L. Rev. 167 (2020).

4 *See, e.g.*, Nat'l Meat Ass'n v. Harris, 132 S. Ct. 965 (2012) (meat producers trade association successfully challenged, on federal preemption grounds, a California statute designed to reduce suffering of animals destined for slaughter). As of 2016, the US meat and poultry industry accounts for $1.02 trillion in total economic output, or 5.6 percent of gross domestic product (GDP). *The United States Meat Industry at a Glance*, North American Meat Institute, https://www.meatinstitute.org/index.php?ht=d/sp/i/47465/pid/47465 (last visited Apr. 21, 2021).

5 *8 Activist Strategies to Dismantle Animal Ag during COVID-19*, Beef Magazine (May 8, 2020), https://www.beefmagazine.com/beef/8-activist-strategies-dismantle-animal-ag-during-covid-19.

6 Justin Marceau, Beyond Cages: Animal Law and Criminal Punishment (2019).

7 *Id.*

8 B. Welsh, D. Farrington, L. Sherman, Costs and Benefits of Preventing Crime (2018); Michael Rempel et al., *NIJ's Multistate Evaluation of Prosecutor-Led Diversion Programs: Strategies, Impacts, and Cost-Effectiveness* (April 2018), https://www.ncjrs.gov/pdffiles1/nij/grants/251665.pdf (prosecutor-led diversion programs within the scope of this study focused on a wide range of goals, not limited to rehabilitation and recidivism reduction, serving a mix of

criminal law remains a valuable and necessary option – never more so than when dealing with those offenders who harm victims who have no legal standing and, thus, no other operable recourse.

In Section 4.2 below, this chapter traces the recent evolution of substantive animal cruelty laws fueled in part by the work of the Animal Legal Defense Fund's (ALDF) Criminal Justice Program (CJP). Section 4.3 examines the historically pervasive nature of animal abuse and argues that the use of the anticruelty laws remains the most viable approach short of a major change in the legal status of animals. Section 4.4 discusses three areas in which some progress is being made for animals: (1) through an innovative project to collect detailed and relevant data on carceral outcome demographics upon which to make informed policy recommendations; (2) by the justice system's recognition of animals as crime victims, which is helping to reshape the status of animals in civil litigation as well as helping animal victims; and (3) through the substantial body of scholarship documenting the link between animal abuse and other forms of violence directed at human victims, which has been and remains important and relevant literature for policy development.

Through these sections, this chapter seeks to provide a historical perspective to a small handful of the issues underlying the arguments both for and against using the criminal justice system to address instances of criminalized animal abuse.

4.2 THE EVOLUTION OF SUBSTANTIVE ANIMAL ANTICRUELTY LAWS

The modern evolution of animal anticruelty statutes has a rich history that is interwoven with the inception and operation of the ALDF's CJP.[9] In the 1980s, state criminal anticruelty laws were woefully lacking. The most heinous conduct was viewed as a minor event, a status offense against the peace and dignity of the state. It was not unheard of for judges, after conviction, to order the return of surviving

target populations – including felonies as well as misdemeanors; many programs allowed defendants with prior criminal records to participate. Diversion participants benefited from a reduced likelihood of conviction and incarceration; and in four of the five programs, pretrial diversion participation led to reduced rearrest rates).

9 Other nonprofit animal protection organizations have, along with ALDF, devoted substantial resources to strengthening anticruelty laws in the fifty states, and have worked closely with prosecutors and investigators on individual cases of animal abuse and neglect. These organizations include but are certainly not limited to: Humane Society of the United States, *Fighting Animal Cruelty and Neglect*, https://www.humanesociety.org/all-our-fights/fighting-animal-cruelty-and-neglect (last visited Apr. 21, 2021); American Society for the Prevention of Cruelty to Animals, *Cruelty Issues*, https://www.aspca.org/animal-cruelty (last visited Apr. 21, 2021); Best Friends Animal Society, *Take Action for Pets and People*, https://bestfriends.org/advocacy (last visited Apr. 21, 2021).

animals (under the guise of releasing the "evidence") to the offender as part of the court's sentence, often with tragic consequences to the animals.[10]

Before 1986, only four states had a felony-level provision within their anticruelty laws.[11] By 1993, six states had adopted some form of a felony anticruelty provision.[12] By 1999, animal advocates had convinced twenty-three states to add at least one form of a felony animal cruelty provision to their laws.[13] In 2014, South Dakota became the last state to adopt a felony anticruelty law, so as of today, all fifty states have at least one form of a felony-level anticruelty law on the books.

There are many practical, positive impacts of sentencing for felony animal cruelty – impacts that profoundly influence the viability of community treatment and genuine reformation of offenders. For example, the duration of probation can be much longer in a felony case than a misdemeanor (but, of course, can be terminated early with judicial approval), giving the state ample time to work with an offender to ensure true reformation without using a prison bed. Equally important in the community-supervision-versus-prison dichotomy is the simple issue of whether an offender will actually have a probation officer to oversee and assist with his reformation at all.[14] In many states, like Oregon, it is all too often the case that misdemeanor convicts are placed on "bench probation" or "case banked," where the offender has no meaningful supervision at all, with the court assigning an actual probation officer only to offenders convicted of a felony offense.[15]

There are two additional and very real procedural benefits, namely: (1) independent review of a prosecutor's charging decision by way of either a preliminary hearing or grand jury; and (2) with the advent of felony sentencing guidelines, a presumptive term of incarceration on a felony conviction can be capped at a much lower term than the misdemeanor in some jurisdictions – for example, in Oregon, aggravated

[10] *See, Judge Orders Animals to Return to Convicted Abuser*, Spectrum News Middletown, New York (March 13, 2015), https://spectrumlocalnews.com/nys/hudson-valley/news/2015/03/12/animals-ordered-to-return-to-convicted-animal-abuser.

[11] *See* D. Campbell, *Animal Abusers Beware: Registry Laws in the Works to Curb Your Abuse*, 48 Val. U.L. Rev. 271, 276 (2013).

[12] Humane Society of the United States, *State Felony Cruelty Laws*, http://www.humanesociety.org/sites/default/files/archive/assets/pdfs/abuse/state-felony-cruelty-laws.pdf (last visited Nov. 6, 2020).

[13] P. Frasch, S. Otto, K. Olsen, & P. Ernest, *State Animal Anti-Cruelty Statutes: An Overview*, 5 Animal L. 69 (1999).

[14] *See* Or. Rev. Stat § 137.630(1)(f) (stating the duties of a probation officer include aiding and encouraging persons under their supervision and to effect improvement in their conduct and condition).

[15] Interview with Benton County District Attorney John M. Haroldson, November 3, 2020, wherein he noted that, in those rare cases where Community Corrections does assign a probation officer to supervise a misdemeanor convict, it is understood by all parties that Community Corrections is doing the court a favor and cannot afford to manage misdemeanor offenders as a general rule. As a result, the vast majority of misdemeanor probationers go unsupervised and lack access to a probation officer who has a statutory duty, as noted above, to aid and encourage them with their reformation.

animal abuse under Oregon Revised Statute section 167.322 has a crime seriousness ranking of "six" under the felony sentencing guidelines with a presumptive maximum possible jail term is ninety days for a first-time offender, far less than the one-year jail term cap for misdemeanors, which are not subject to legislatively imposed sentencing guideline limitations.

While the expansion of felony anticruelty laws marked some evolution in the justice system (by helping to overcome some of the institutional bias against these cases), we found that these felony provisions were nevertheless relegated to the lowest levels for the worst possible type of violence (e.g., torture) within a given jurisdiction and were rarely, if ever, used by prosecutors. More troubling was our observation that police and other agencies tasked with enforcement routinely would ignore animal cruelty cases, even when the most brutal violence against animals was happening.

In my experience working in this space,[16] a number of factors were responsible for this lack of enforcement, including limited resources, a failure to appreciate the level of suffering experienced by animal victims, incomplete or nonexistent police and prosecutor training on how to investigate and prosecute crimes against animals,[17] and simply not caring about animals at a level that would motivate those in the system to take animal abuse seriously.

Compounding the problem is the legal reality that animals are property, do not have legal person status, and thus have no direct legal recourse available to them if they suffer harm.[18] The only meaningful tools available to those working on their behalf were to legislatively prohibit harmful activity against animals, to create a penalty system to change social mores surrounding acceptable treatment of animals, to separate the abuser from the abused for some period of time, which (hopefully) acts as a deterrent.[19]

The principal focus of anticruelty laws is on violence against animals. There are also laws prohibiting neglect, abandonment, and other nondirect harmful activity, but those were, historically, rarely prosecuted. For large-scale hoarding cases in which dozens or even hundreds of animals suffer serious long-term neglect and abuse, the emphasis in some jurisdictions now tends to be more on accessing mental

[16] I was Director of the CJP, and later General Counsel for ALDF between the years 1996 and 2008.

[17] *See* Joshua Marquis, *The Kittles Case and Its Aftermath*, 2 Animal L. 197, 197 (1996) (where the prosecutor of a complex hoarding case admitted he had never heard the term "animal collector" or hoarder prior to filing his case against Ms. Kittles).

[18] Gary Francione, *Animals, Property and Legal Welfarism: "Unnecessary" Suffering and the "Humane" Treatment of Animals*, 46 Rutgers L. Rev. 721 (1994); Erica Tatoian, *Animals in the Law: Occupying a Space between Legal Personhood and Personal Property*, 31 J. Envtl. L. & Litig. 147 (2015).

[19] Megan Boyd & Adam Lamparello, *Vulnerable Victims: Increasing Animal Cruelty Sentences to Reflect Society's Understanding of the Value of Animal Lives*, 45 CONNtemplations 31 (2013).

health support for the defendant, as opposed to jail time for those offenders who are amenable to treatment and reformation.[20]

In these earlier days (and continuing today, although not as prevalently), some laws exhibited nonsensical priorities. For example, prior to 1995, under Oregon law, it was a misdemeanor to torture a dog,[21] but a felony if you stole the dog and treated her better than her owner did.[22] Another example of the grossly misaligned priorities, again using Oregon as an example: it was a felony to record the symphony and sell the recording without permission[23] but a misdemeanor to sexually torture a cat in front of one's child.[24] There needed to be a serious rebalancing of these priorities. Hence, animal protection advocates worked to enact felony laws for the worst offenses, which were and are, even with enhanced penalties, significantly weaker than the laws that apply to the same action if done against a human.[25]

We soon learned that by engaging directly with prosecutors and investigators, we were able to educate the system about what the law says, why taking animal abuse seriously is important, and how to help them figure out appropriate approaches to managing individual cases. Sometimes that involved seeking incarceration, but oftentimes not. Out of this work was born the CJP, which was designed to provide police, animal control officers, and prosecutors with the support necessary to get the best possible outcomes for animals under existing law, which was often to remove the animal from her abuser, as well as to assist states with enacting the necessary statutory improvements to lead us to where we are today. Beyond its legislative work, the CJP embarked on a substantial training campaign, educating humane officers, animal control officers, police investigators, and prosecutors on the full spectrum of issues attendant to an animal cruelty case – from search warrant drafting to pre-conviction bonding/lien foreclosure proceedings designed to avoid revictimizing the

20 Courtney Lee, *Never Enough: Animal Hoarding Law*, 47 U. Balt. L. Rev. 23, 41–42 (2017).

21 Or. Rev. Stat § 167.320 (1993), https://archives.oregonlegislature.gov/ORS_Archives/1993-Chapter-167.pdf (stating first-degree animal abuse was a Class A Misdemeanor).

22 Or. Rev. Stat § 165.055(1)(e) (1993), https://archives.oregonlegislature.gov/ORS_Archives/1993-Chapter-164.pdf (defining theft of a companion animal as a Class C felony).

23 Or. Rev. Stat § 164.869(2) (1993), https://archives.oregonlegislature.gov/ORS_Archives/1993-Chapter-164.pdf (making the unlawful recording of a live performance a Class C felony).

24 Or. Rev. Stat § 167.075(4)(1993), https://archives.oregonlegislature.gov/ORS_Archives/1993-Chapter-167.pdf (making it a Class A misdemeanor to exhibit an "obscene performance" which includes "sexual conduct" between a human and an animal (Or. Rev. Stat § 167.060(10) (1993)); Or. Rev. Stat § 163.575(2) (1993), https://archives.oregonlegislature.gov/ORS_Archives/1993-Chapter-163.pdf (endangering the welfare of a minor when causing a child to witness "sexual conduct" was also only a Class A misdemeanor).

25 Mississippi makes aggravated animal cruelty (i.e., the intentional torture) of a domesticated cat or dog a felony with a maximum possible penalty, on a first offense, of $5,000 fine and not more than three years in prison, *see* Miss. Code Ann § 97-41-16(2)(b), while the same conduct involving a human victim qualifies for the death penalty, *see id.* § 99-19-101(5)(h)(i).

animals.[26] CJP did much of this work and in close collaboration the Association of Prosecuting Attorneys (APA).[27] CJP established grant programs to ensure: (1) that impounding agencies had the money necessary to cover the costs of caring for seized animals; (2) that law enforcement had access to forensic resources otherwise inaccessible to them – including DNA analysis; and (3) that prosecutors could hire the necessary expert witnesses, enabling them to meet their burden of proof at trial. Additionally, CJP embarked on a mission to establish a presence in the appellate courts by filing amicus briefs in support of the state on issues attendant to the prosecution of these cases and in the state legislature by drafting and lobbying new laws.[28]

Finally, ALDF formed a partnership with a state district attorneys association and launched a pilot program to fund a fully sworn, dedicated, independent animal cruelty prosecutor who is available to all elected prosecutors in that state to litigate animal abuse cases that would not otherwise make it to court due to scarce resources.[29]

4.3 ANIMAL ABUSE IS PERVASIVE, AND ENHANCING ANTICRUELTY LAW REMAINS THE BEST OPTION TO PROTECT ANIMALS ABSENT A CHANGE IN LEGAL STATUS OR OTHER SOCIETAL EVOLUTIONS

In American society, the harsh reality for animals is that cruelty and suffering are rampant, pervading every corner of American life, be it:

26 *See* Press Release, ALDF (Oct. 30, 2018), https://aldf.org/article/animal-cruelty-prosecution-conference-aims-to-train-prosecutors-law-enforcement-on-handling-animal-cruelty-cases-louisville-to-host-professionals-from-around-the-country/.

27 ALDF was instrumental in inducing the APA to adopt a statement of principles regarding the prosecution of animal cruelty cases that serves as a recommendation to all prosecutors across the country. October 19, 2020, Letter from CEO David LaBahn (on file with author); *Statement of Principles*, Ass'n of Prosecuting Attorneys, https://www.apainc.org/wp-content/uploads/2017/01/Resolution-regarding-Animal-Cruelty-Crime-Prosecution-2016.pdf.

28 Amicus examples include: Commonwealth v. Duncan, 467 Mass. 746 (2014) (regarding the emergency aid exception to the warrant requirement); State v. Fessenden/Dicke, 333 P.3d 278 (Or. 2014) (finding exigent circumstances to save an animal); State v. Nix, 334 P.3d 437 (Or. 2104), *vacated on procedural grounds*, 345 P.3d 416 (Or. 2015) (finding each animal counts as a victim for purposes of sentencing on separate convictions); State v. Newcomb, 375 P.3d 434 (Or. 2016) (finding a medically necessary blood draw to treat victim animal not a search); People v. Basile, 35 N.E.3d 849 (N.Y. 2015) (involving a jury instruction on culpable mental state); State v. Peterson, 301 P.3d 1060 (WA 2013) (finding animal cruelty statute not unconstitutionally vague); Ortega-Lopez v. Lynch, 834 F.3d 1015 (9th Cir. 2016) (holding that animal fighting qualifies as a crime involving moral turpitude); United States v. Stevens, 559 U.S. 460 (2010) (regarding the constitutionality of federal crime restricting depictions of animal cruelty).

Legislative examples include: S.B. 6, 77th Leg. (Or. 2013) (improving on Oregon's ability to respond to mass neglect cases) and H.B. 2888, 78th Leg. (Or. 2015) (creating a civil option for dealing with animal cruelty by creating a private cause of action for nuisance abatement).

29 Memorandum of Understanding between: Oregon District Attorneys Association, Benton County District Attorney and Animal Legal Defense Fund (Jan. 21, 2013) (on file with author).

- In the family where the husband tries to maintain domination and control of his spouse by threatening, abusing, or killing the family pet. This was the case in *People v. Kovacich*,[30] where a Placer County Sheriff was convicted of murdering his wife based on circumstantial evidence. It was proven that his wife feared her husband for a host of reasons, including the fact that he had previously kicked the family dog to death.
- At the pet shop (or online), where the inventory of designer animals was acquired from cruel, greed-fueled puppy mills[31] as exemplified by the "Puppy World Rescue" store in Tucson, Arizona, whose operator charged $2,000 and up as a so-called adoption fee for purebred "rescue puppies," while failing to reveal the true source of the dogs. This defendant was accused of sourcing from puppy mills and faces enforcement action in Arizona for consumer fraud.[32] Another example comes from Mercer, Tennessee, where puppy mill operators were busted for the mass neglect of over 300 dogs.[33]
- In towns and neighborhoods throughout the United States, where hoarding of animals is uncovered.[34]

Beyond these three tip-of-the-iceberg examples, animal advocates must contend with institutionalized animal abuse, to wit, cruelty carried out by massive meat, dairy, and egg corporations, universities, pharmaceutical companies, colleges, and others, in pursuit of agriculture production, scientific/medical research, as well as hunting, trapping, rodeos, zoos, circuses, and other forms of recreation and entertainment. Institutionalized cruelty serves as stomach-turning examples of how most of our society still accepts a massive amount of animal suffering as either "necessary"

[30] 201 Cal. App. 4th 863 (2011).

[31] "A puppy mill is an inhumane high-volume dog breeding facility that churns out puppies for profit, ignoring the needs of the pups and their mothers. Dogs from puppy mills are often sick and unsocialized." *Stopping Puppy Mills* HUMANE SOCIETY OF THE UNITED STATES, https://www.humanesociety.org/all-our-fights/stopping-puppy-mills

[32] *See* Carol Ann Alaimo, *New Pet Store at Marana Mall under Investigation*, ARIZONA DAILY STAR (Aug. 19, 2020), https://tucson.com/news/local/new-pet-store-at-marana-mall-under-investigation/article_f355853a-ee78–5fad-bb84-b27f82d39fd0.html.

[33] *See* Adam Friedman & Cassandra Stephenson, *Alleged Madison County Animal Abuser Indicted on 338 Counts of Animal Cruelty after June Raid*, JACKSON SUN (Aug. 7, 2020), https://www.jacksonsun.com/story/news/2020/08/07/three-madison-co-residents-indicted-338-counts-animal-cruelty/3321170001/.

[34] *See* Randy Frost et al., *The Hoarding of Animals: An Update*, PSYCHIATRIC TIMES (April 30, 2015), https://www.psychiatrictimes.com/view/hoarding-animals-update (estimating from surveys of animal control agencies and humane societies suggest that there are approximately 3,000 reportable cases of animal hoarding annually in the United States). According to the Anxiety and Depression Association of America, at least 250,000 animals are affected each year. *Animal Hoarding*, ANXIETY & DEPRESSION ASS'N OF AM., https://adaa.org/understanding-anxiety/obsessive-compulsive-disorder-ocd/hoarding-basics/animal-hoarding (last visited November 7, 2020).

or "justifiable" – necessary to keep the price of meat and milk low; justifiable to ensure that our shampoo doesn't burn our eyes; necessary to save more human lives; and justifiable as forms of entertainment operating under the guise of self-reliance. These are huge sectors of our economy that are, as with food production and research, regulated and subsidized by the government.[35] Consequently, to date, these latter categories of conduct are rarely, if ever, prosecuted, regardless of whether the criminal code contains an express exemption or not.

Further, in a consumer-based capitalistic market where "price is paramount," market dynamics have yet to shift away from the production of animals as sources of protein, even though the system in which those animals live and die is inherently cruel and fails to provide even minimum standards of good care and treatment. One avenue to change that dynamic is the emergence of the vegan community, which currently comprises less than 3-percent of the US population.[36] While this segment of American consumers is growing, it has yet to reach a size where it has any true political power in Congress or state legislatures – the power necessary to effectively reduce the actual number of animals suffering. To be fair, there are examples of instances where the vegan community has cause to claim a technical win. For example, California's ban on the production and sale of foie gras produced in the state went into effect in 2012. However, the practical impact of this ban was seriously undermined by a recent ruling that California's ban does not reach sales of foie gras originating from sources and sellers located outside of the state.[37] Despite this discouraging reality, the sheer number of people, nonprofit, and for-profit organizations working on these systemic issues gives us cause to be hopeful, although that road remains very long. In the meantime, while animals continue to remain legal property, and other avenues to address harm done to animals remain elusive, anticruelty laws continue to offer one of the most effective ways to address individual instances of violence against animals.

4.4 MAKING PROGRESS FOR ANIMAL VICTIMS

Some advocates working to reform the criminal justice system argue that the significant racism and bias in many sectors of the system (and in particular drug arrests) exist in the same way and with the same carceral outcomes within the

[35] The US government spends up to $38 billion each year to subsidize the meat and dairy industries. David Robinson Simon, Meatonomics (2013); 7 U.S.C. §§ 1902-1907 (Humane Methods of Livestock Slaughter); 7 U.S.C. §§ 2131-2160 (Animal Welfare Act [AWA]); 9 C.F.R. §§ 1.1-12.1 (regulations under the AWA, including Institutional Animal Care and Use Committee oversight of research animals); 21 U.S.C. §§ 601-695 (Federal Meat inspection Act).

[36] Brandon Kirkwood, *New Study Reveals 9.6 Million Americans Are Vegan Now, A 300% Increase!* Vegan News (March 6, 2020), https://vegannews.press/2020/03/06/vegan-america-study/.

[37] Association des Eleveurs de Canards et d Oies du Quebec et al. v. Harris, No. 12-CV-05735, 2020 WL 5049182, at *5 (C.D. Cal. July 14, 2020).

anticruelty sphere. This overlap of concern may indeed be valid, but the current problem is that the argument is based on anecdotal evidence and (in a few rare instances) incomplete data from small sample populations. Even anticarceral critics acknowledge the lack of data upon which to draw conclusions about the anticruelty laws, let alone upon which to develop legislative priorities or policies that weaken criminal law protections for abused animals. [38]

4.4.1 *Data Collection*

One way this problem is being addressed is through an innovative partnering between The Center for Animal Law Studies at Lewis and Clark Law School (CALS), ALDF, and the Criminal Justice Reform Clinic at Lewis and Clark Law School (CJRC). These organizations (all with unique missions that are not universally aligned as "proprosecution" or "prodefense") have partnered on a first-of-its-kind project to gather detailed data on animal cruelty cases.[39] The goal of this project is to obtain comprehensive data on animal cruelty cases, including demographics of those arrested for and charged with animal cruelty and how cases are typically resolved within the criminal justice system (e.g., incarceration, probation, or diversion). Initially, this project will focus on animal cruelty cases in Oregon, but other states will also be surveyed.

Under the guidance of a neutral and experienced biostatistician, qualitative and quantitative data will be collected in the form of records requests in all Oregon counties and interviews with various stakeholders who have experience with animal cruelty cases, including defense attorneys, district attorneys, and animal control officers. These interviews will supplement the data obtained from the records request and provide background information, including how these stakeholders view animal cruelty (e.g., if it is viewed as a serious, victim crime); whether they have avoided prosecuting or defending these cases in the past and reasons why; and how they overcome the unique challenges animal cruelty cases pose.

Currently, there are two sources of data on animal cruelty cases: (1) attorneys – most often prosecutors – who provide anecdotal information based on their cases,[40] and (2) the FBI's National Incident-Based Reporting System (NIBRS), which began tracking animal cruelty in 2016.[41] While this data is helpful, there are limitations.

38 *Animal Law Podcast #50: Justin Marceau on Animal Law and Criminal Punishment*, Our Hen House (July 24, 2019), www.ourhenhouse.org/2019/07/animal-law-podcast-50-justin-marceau-on-animal-law-and-criminal-punishment/ (at 9:34 and at 24:19 minutes).

39 For the purposes of this project, "animal cruelty" is used as shorthand for any crime committed against an animal, including abuse, aggravated abuse, neglect, and abandonment.

40 Most cruelty cases are resolved at the trial level; thus, the published appellate level decisions do not account for or reflect what happens in the mass of lower-level cruelty proceedings.

41 The FBI collects data on "acts of animal cruelty, including gross neglect, torture, organized abuse, and sexual abuse." Prior to 2016, crimes against animals "were lumped into an 'All Other Offenses' category." *Tracking Animal Cruelty*, Fed. Bureau of Investigation (Feb. 1, 2016).

First, the anecdotal data provided by attorneys is extremely narrow, as it is based on their individual caseloads. In addition, this information is further limited by the attorney's location and does not provide a detailed account of how animal cruelty cases are adjudicated outside of their immediate county or city. Second, the data provided by the FBI also has restrictions because not all jurisdictions report to NIBRS.[42] Further, NIBRS tracks "incidents"[43] and "arrests" of animal cruelty but fails to track cases once they enter the criminal justice system.

Once all of the data is collected, a detailed report will be prepared (and shared widely) that interprets the data and provides policy recommendations, where appropriate.

4.4.2 *Animals as Separate Victims*

Some courts are beginning to recognize each animal as a unique and individual victim, at least as it relates to the issue of merging convictions at sentencing. Merger is a simple statutory concept derivative of the rule against double jeopardy – that is, that a defendant may not be twice punished for the same crime. In essence, convictions for multiple crimes consisting of the same elements committed during the same criminal episode will merge at sentencing, resulting in one punishable offense rather than several. However, when multiple crimes comprising differing elements are committed during the same criminal episode, they qualify as separately punishable offenses, because, by definition, they are not the same offense. An example of this latter dynamic: an offender fires a gun into a crowded bar, killing three patrons within seconds. At sentencing on three homicide convictions committed during the one criminal episode, the defendant would very much like to see just one homicide conviction entered on record. Because there are three separate victims, however, the identity of each victim being a material element of the crime, each count of homicide is not the same as the others. As such, the sentencing court would have the authority to enter separate convictions, one for each victim, and the option (though typically not the obligation) to impose consecutive terms of incarceration.

42 Data collected in 2016 and 2017 represented 31 percent and 32 percent of the US population, respectively. Greg Cima, *FBI Gathers Animal Cruelty Data, but Patterns Have Yet to Emerge*, Am. Veterinary Medical Ass'n (March 27, 2019), https://www.avma.org/javma-news/2019-04-15/fbi-gathers-animal-cruelty-data-patterns-have-yet-emerge.

43 "Under NIBRS, an incident is any report of a suspected offense, either from a citizen or initiated by a law enforcement officer, animal control officer, or humane law enforcement official. To be 'counted,' there does not have to be an investigation or an arrest, simply an incident." Animal Welfare Institute, *Animal Cruelty Reporting Scorecard*, https://awionline.org/content/animal-cruelty-reporting-scorecard (last visited Nov. 7, 2020).

When applying these concepts to animal cruelty cases, Oregon is at the forefront of the issue as evidenced by *State v. Nix*,[44] *State v. Hess*,[45] and *State v. Setere*.[46] These cases make it clear that each animal who is subjected to criminal abuse or neglect is a unique victim and, as such, renders each count a separately punishable crime even when committed during the same criminal episode. Thus, there is no merging of the defendant's convictions in this context. Contrary to what some may assume, these cases do not stand for the proposition that the court must (or even will) impose consecutive (or "stacked") terms of incarceration. But it does honor the unique existence, identity, and intrinsic value of each animal victim.

Recognizing sentient nonhuman animals as victims is a major development in animal rights law that will, over time, necessarily lead to a safer world for animals and a meaningfully improved legal status for animals. ALDF is now building on these foundational cases with a groundbreaking civil lawsuit that is specifically designed to profoundly improve the legal status of animals by, if successful, giving animals legal standing to sue their abusers in civil court for damages in a case pending before the Oregon Court of Appeals.[47]

4.4.3 *The "Link" and Policy Development*

The correlation between those who abuse animals and those who harm humans is the topic of hundreds of studies, reports, books, and papers. Phil Arkow, coordinator of the National Link Coalition and the Chair of the Animal Abuse and Family Violence Prevention Project (funded by the Latham Foundation) maintains the seminal database cataloging this massive body of scholarship.[48] One of the founding attorneys of the animal law movement, Joyce Tischler, provided this perspective in her two-part law review article documenting the history of this movement:

> Through the work of Randall Lockwood, Frank Ascione, Phil Arkow, and others, a body of literature now exists to document "the Link," i.e., the close connection between abuse of animals, abuse of children, and domestic violence. These findings are regularly used to educate prosecutors and law enforcement about the interconnectedness of violence and the importance of prosecuting animal cruelty cases.[49]

44 334 P.3d 437 (Or. 2104), *vacated on procedural grounds*, 345 P.3d 416 (Or. 2015).

45 359 P.3d 288 (Or. Ct. App. 2015).

46 476 P.3d 117 (Or. Ct. App. 2020).

47 *See* Complaint at 2, Justice v. Gwendolyn Vercher, No. 18CV1760, 2018 WL 3997811 (Or. Cir. May 1, 2018), https://aldf.org/article/advocating-for-justice-in-oregon-neglected-horse-sues-former-owner/.

48 Bibliography – The LINK, Therapy Animals, https://www.animaltherapy.net/animal-abuse-human-violence/bibliography-the-link/ (last visited Nov. 7, 2020).

49 Joyce Tischler, *A Brief History of Animal Law, Part II (1985–2011)*, 5 Stan. J. Animal L. & Pol'y 27, 58 (2012) (citations and footnote omitted).

In a 2011 article in the *Journal of the American Veterinary Medical Association* (AVMA), the authors noted the correlation (not causation) – a link – between animal cruelty and violence against humans:

> While this so-called progression thesis has been difficult to substantiate, the belief that violent individuals can harm many victims – both human and animal – is well accepted. Many studies have attempted to verify a link between animal cruelty and human-directed violence. For example, a survey of 38 women entering battered women's shelters found that 71% of the pet-owning women reported that their partner had threatened or actually hurt or killed one or more of their pets. Another study found that people with a history of violence toward animals were at higher risk for exhibiting violence toward people. A retrospective study that examined the histories of incarcerated violent offenders found that these subjects often had long histories of violence toward animals during childhood and adolescence. The authors of that study concluded that violent offenders were significantly more likely than non-violent offenders to have committed acts of cruelty toward animals as children. Although these studies do not prove a causal relationship between childhood violence toward animals and future violence toward humans, they do provide strong evidence that violence toward animals and violence toward people are often concurrent.[50]

These fundamental concepts continue to have great sway with lawmakers. A recent example of this came late in the summer of 2020, when US Senators Sheldon Whitehouse (D-RI), Mike Braun (R-IN), John Kennedy (R-LA), Martha McSally (R-AZ), and Richard Blumenthal (D-CT) introduced the Animal Cruelty Enforcement (ACE) Act (S.4601/H.R.8052).[51] The ACE Act contains some very compelling congressional findings, chief among them:

- There is a significant connection between animal cruelty and violence against humans, domestic violence, child abuse, sexual abuse, homicide, gang activity, drug trafficking, and other crimes.
- There is bipartisan and widespread public support for addressing animal cruelty.
- The lack of a dedicated animal crimes enforcement unit within the Department of Justice has resulted in unacceptable delays in prosecutions, and an overall lack of prosecution of animal crimes.

If passed, the ACE Act will create a dedicated Animal Cruelty Crimes Section within the Environmental and Natural Resources Division of the Department of

[50] Melanie Benetato, Robert Reisman, & Emily McCobb, *The Veterinarian's Role in Animal Cruelty Cases*, 238 J. OF THE AM. VETERINARY MEDICAL ASS'N 31 (2011) (citations and footnote omitted), https://avmajournals.avma.org/doi/full/10.2460/javma.238.1.31.

[51] H.R. 8052, 116TH CONG. (2020), https://www.congress.gov/bill/116th-congress/house-bill/8052/text?r=2&s=1; S.4601, 116TH CONG. (2020), https://www.congress.gov/bill/116th-congress/senate-bill/4601/text?q=%7B%22search%22%3A%5B%22s.4601%22%5D%7D&r=1&s=1.

Justice to help with the investigation, enforcement, and prosecution of animal cruelty crimes. In addition, the act will require the Department of Justice to report the progress made on enforcing animal cruelty statutes on an annual basis. The importance of such federal recognition of the need to better protect animals from cruelty and abuse, as well as the enhancement of their status in our society, should not be glossed over. If animal advocates believe that nonhuman animals are deserving of such protection, we must understand and support the positive impact of such legislation, both practically and symbolically.

In language similar to that found in the ACE Act, Oregon's legislature has made some significantly compelling findings as well. In Oregon Revised Statute section 686.442, the legislature, while debating the merits of requiring veterinarians to report animal abuse, made the following statement:

> The Legislative Assembly finds that there is a direct link between the problems of animal abuse and human abuse and further finds that for the purposes of identifying and prosecuting individuals who have committed crimes against animals, preventing further abuse of animals and preventing animal abuse from escalating to abuse against humans, it is necessary and in the public interest to require mandatory reporting of aggravated animal abuse by veterinarians.[52]

As a general rule, the criminal defense bar's rejection of the key concepts embodied in established link scholarship is understandable, given that their clients are the ones on trial for animal abuse. After all, using this body of research, when a convicted animal offender stands before the court at sentencing, the prosecution is able to illustrate to the court how this person presents a threat to society and, as such, is worthy of more significant state supervision.

Interestingly, however, some critics who argue the Link is not real will, when it suits their needs, cite favorably to the existence of the Link when it will secure a reduced sentence. This dynamic is evident in *State v. Crow*,[53] where defense counsel conceded that the Link findings are valid, sound science and then tried to use them to mitigate his client's sentencing exposure.

The specifics in *Crow* are worthy of review. In *Crow*, the defendant had been previously convicted of multiple acts of animal neglect. Under Oregon's criminal code,[54] by operation of law, Crow was subject upon conviction to a five-year animal possession ban, the violation of which constituted a new misdemeanor crime. Within five years of this prior conviction, Crow was subsequently found to be in the possession of minihorses, cats, and a dog, in direct violation of the statute. Crow was convicted at trial of thirteen counts of unlawful possession of an animal.[55] At sentencing, Crow demanded that the trial court merge her thirteen convictions into

[52] Or. Rev. Stat. § 686.442.
[53] 429 P.3d 1053 (Or. Ct. App. 2018).
[54] Or. Rev. Stat. § 167.332(1)(a).
[55] *Crow*, 429 P.3d at 1054.

one, rather than sentence each crime separately – claiming that the only victim here was society, not the animals whom she had abused. In support of her claim that society was the only victim here, Crow's defense attorney cited the legislature's reliance on the Link between animal abuse and violence against humans when it enacted this statute, section 167.332(1)(a).[56] The court characterized defense counsel's argument this way: "Defendant contends that the link between animal abuse and violence against humans demonstrates that the legislature intended to protect the public when it enacted the provisions of ORS 167.332(1), which prevented a person with convictions for crimes against animals from possessing domestic animals."[57] Of course, the court rejected the defendant Crow's claim, ruling that each individual animal qualifies as a victim and, as such, prevented any merging of convictions. While relevant to the *Nix/Hess* merger issue discussed above, the *Crow* case stands as a clear example of how internally inconsistent critics of state intervention can be. Those who contest the correlation between violence against animals and humans often focus on challenging the Link studies' numbers in an attempt to undermine the nonexistent "finding" of a one-to-one causative effect.[58]

Assume for the sake of argument that these Link critics are right and that only 17 percent (rather than 70 percent) of all animal abusers will also commit (or have committed) violent crimes against humans. Rather than arguing that this finding should be ignored, perhaps a better approach is to recognize that 17 percent is not an inconsequential number[59] of offenders and that the courts, probation officers and

[56] *Id.* at 1057.

[57] *Id.*

[58] *See, e.g.*, MARCEAU, *supra* note 6, at 193 and 224 (stating both that "the link is the theory that violence begets violence, and thus that violence against animals is predictive of violence against humans" and "at the very least, it is clear that the current narrative surrounding the link ['clear predictor of violence'] is incorrect"); Emily Patterson-Kane, *The Relation of Animal Maltreatment to Aggression*, *in* ANIMAL MALTREATMENT: FORENSIC MENTAL HEALTH ISSUES AND EVALUATIONS 140, 143 & 150 (L. Level et al. eds., 2016) (faulting earlier link studies for not using control groups as part of those studies, Patterson-Kain reviewed thirteen link studies that did use control groups and found the prevalence of prior animal abuse in "non-violent" control groups was widely variable—from 0 percent to 72 percent due in part for varying definitions of "animal" with one study including bugs; Patterson-Kane went on to observe that 34 percent of offenders in fifteen other studies who committed acts of violence against a human victim had a history of prior animal abuse; based on this finding, Patterson-Kane used the obvious inverse fact – i.e., that the majority of offenders who committed crimes of violence against a human victim did not have a history of prior animal abuse – to support the view that is no link between the two types of violent conduct, suggesting that nothing short of majority, or perhaps even a one-to-one causal link, will qualify under her paradigm. To her credit, however, Patterson-Kane did concede that, "On the other hand, it may be difficult to accurately detect a prior history of animal abuse in some subjects because it was never detected or disclosed – leading to some underestimation of the real correlation.").

[59] In fact, this is a gross underestimate when compared to findings of studies often cited by those who want to excuse animal abusers from judicial accountability. For example, Patterson-Kane found that 34 percent of all violent offenders have a prior history of animal abuse, Patterson-Kane, *supra* note 58, at 145, while another study documented that 43 percent of school shooters

counselors should factor this very real risk into their calculus when conducting threat assessments of offenders for purposes of sentencing, community supervision, and treatment. Further, the FBI acknowledges the significance of animal abuse in conducting a threat assessment of a suspect, characterizing abusing animals as "novel aggression warning behavior," meaning "an act of violence which appears unrelated to any 'pathway' behavior and which is committed for the first time. The person of concern may be engaging in this behavior in order to test his ability to actually engage in a violent act and it could be thought of as experimental aggression."[60] The risk-correlation embodied in the Link scholarship has repeatedly garnered the attention of, as noted above, lawmakers and the courts.[61]

In sum, the Link documents a relevant correlation between those who abuse animals and the subset of that same population who have previously, or who go on to, abuse humans. Dismissing the correlation between animal abuse and other forms of violence is to ignore an immense body of research (including the conclusion of the FBI's Behavioral Analysis Unit), compelling legislative policy findings, and a growing body of judicial opinions.

4.5 CONCLUSION

While there is still much work to be done, the improvements to the substantive and procedural criminal code as applied to animal cruelty cases have resulted in significant advances for the benefit of animals and have not flooded our prisons and jails with abusers.

Enacting felony anticruelty laws properly elevates violent conduct inflicted upon voiceless victims to a level consistent with societal expectations while, at the same time, affording offenders independent review of the state's charging decisions via grand jury or preliminary hearing – a safety stop that is simply not available in misdemeanor cases. Gathering data to address anecdotal claims of racial bias in the investigation and prosecution of animal cruelty cases will serve to elevate the conversation and provide the basis for sound policy reformation. Pursuing the advancement of the victim-status of animals subjected to abuse will only aid civil practitioners in overcoming standing issues and applying creative causes of action that will further advance the interests of animals in the legal system. Recognizing the

had a history of animal abuse; Arnold Arluke & Eric Madfis, *Animal Abuse as a Warning Sign of School Massacres: A Critique and Refinement*, 18 HOMICIDE STUD. 7, 7–22 (2014).

60 Molly Amman et al., U.S. Dep't of Justice, FBI Behavioral Analysis Unit, *Making Prevention a Reality: Identifying, Assessing, and Managing the Threat of Targeted Attacks* (2015)(endnote omitted), https://www.google.com/url?sa=t&rct=j&q=&esrc=s&source=web&cd=&ved=2ahUKEwjrgMP5087sAhWDq54KHVc8ARoQFjACegQIAxAC&url=http%3A%2F%2Fwww.fbi.gov%2FPreventingTargetedViolence&usg=AOvVaw1V8uSa8_UdTayO7n7CjC9K).

61 *See, e.g.*, People v. Weeks, 369 P.3d 699 (Col. Ct. App. 2015) (relying on link studies in support of court's decision to reject defendant's attempt to exclude prior bad acts evidence of animal abuse in the murder trial involving the death of defendant's three-year-old daughter).

Link for what it truly is – an observation of a correlation between differing classifications of violent conduct with some predictive value (as are a host of other factors, including age, social history, and education level) – is, and remains, a helpful tool for courts and probation officers in assessing the threat an offender represents to society and should help shape outcomes at sentencing and parole hearings.

Underlying the work of anyone concerned about animal abuse should be a clear-headed focus on what is in the animals' best interests; ensuring that those interests are always considered in any case or proceeding; and reducing or eliminating animal abuse in the first instance. As animal advocates, we must never place the animals' needs in a secondary position, no matter how worthy competing interests may be. Animal advocates are the animals' last, and in many cases, only defense against invisibility within our established systems, so it is important to remember our primary obligation to protect animals and establish their legal rights while simultaneously supporting other movements to address the many layers of oppression. It is my hope that these important conversations on how best to serve all marginalized and harmed groups (including animals) will continue in a robust, yet respectful manner as we work together to make progress on these difficult issues.

5

Carceral Progressivism and Animal Victims

Benjamin Levin

Over the course of the past decade, critiques of the criminal system have proliferated in left and progressive circles.[1] Rhetoric and structural critiques once relegated to corners of academia or radical activist circles have been incorporated into popular discourse. Indeed, the last year has seen a shift in the Overton window of criminal policy debates as calls to defund, dismantle, and abolish prisons, police, and other institutions of the prison-industrial complex have entered the mainstream.[2] In short, being anti–mass incarceration has become a veritable requirement of establishing one's left bona fides and being committed to some vision or version of social justice.[3]

But what does it mean to be against mass incarceration, to support criminal justice reform, or even to call for abolition? The uncertainty of each of these positions complicates the current cultural understanding of the left (broadly conceived) as anticarceral. It's easy to oppose criminalization and its abuses in the abstract, particularly when these institutions operate as stand-ins for white supremacy, heteropatriarchy, capital's subjugation of labor, and so forth. It's much harder when confronted with conduct that seems particularly egregious, harm that seems staggering, victims who appear extremely vulnerable, or defendants who appear extremely unsympathetic. In many areas we see a retrenchment. Or, more

[1] In this chapter, I use "criminal system" or "criminal legal system" advisedly – the administration of criminal law in the United States varies dramatically jurisdiction to jurisdiction and hardly represents a "system" in the sense of a single entity driven by a set of unified theories, politics, or principles. *See, e.g.*, Monica Bell et al., *Toward a Demosprudence of Poverty*, 69 DUKE L.J. 1473, 1528 n. 7 (2020); Bernard E. Harcourt, *The Systems Fallacy: A Genealogy and Critique of Public Policy and Cost-Benefit Analysis*, 47 J. LEGAL STUD. 419, 421 (2018); Sara Mayeux, *The Idea of "The Criminal Justice System"*, 45 AM. J. CRIM. L. 55, 65 (2018).

[2] *See, e.g., Introduction*, 132 HARV. L. REV. 1568 (2019); Rachel Kushner, *Is Prison Necessary? Ruth Wilson Gilmore Might Change Your Mind*, N.Y. TIMES, Apr. 17, 2019,https://www.nytimes.com/2019/04/17/magazine/prison-abolition-ruth-wilson-gilmore.html.

[3] *See generally* Benjamin Levin, *The Consensus Myth in Criminal Justice Reform*, 117 MICH. L. REV. 259 (2018).

accurately, we see activists, advocates, and academics who are otherwise critical of prosecutorial politics turn to criminal law and the institutions of the carceral state as the solution or response to a pressing social problem.

In this chapter, I focus on that turn to criminal law and use the criminalization of animal abuse as a case study or window into a phenomenon that I describe as "carceral progressivism."[4] My argument proceeds in two parts. First, I outline my theory of "carceral progressivism," arguing that the link between anticarceral politics and (certain corners of) the left may be more tenuous than it initially appears. Next, I look to the case study of harm to nonhuman animals. Focusing specifically on the language of advocates and its resonance with expressive theories of punishment, I examine the ways in which the criminal turn in this context rests on a vision of the state as speaking for vulnerable victims and sending a message about society's values and social inclusion.[5] I conclude by critiquing this progressive criminalization project and highlighting the limits of criminal law as a vehicle to advance left causes or interests.

5.1 CARCERAL PROGRESSIVISM

Conventional explanations of mass incarceration and the rise of the carceral state tend to lay blame at the feet of the political right.[6] The explosion in prison and jail populations beginning in the 1970s and the dramatic racial disparities in that expansion are described as outgrowths of ideologies explicitly hostile to racial and distributive justice. In these accounts, the criminal system has operated as an engine of social control, and mass incarceration stands as a manifestation or fortification of the dominant social order.

Whether framed in terms of neoliberalism, white supremacy, or social conservatism, these accounts generally downplay the role of the political left (broadly conceived). Maybe we should view mass incarceration as a New Jim Crow – in this account, commentators frame the carceral state as an explicit extension of racist social control; whether exclusively anti-black, a descendant of chattel slavery, or also tied to the marginalization of Native, Latinx, and other populations, this account

[4] *See* Benjamin Levin, *Imagining the Progressive Prosecutor*, 105 MINN. L. REV. 1415 (2021); Benjamin Levin, *Wage Theft Criminalization*, 54 U.C. DAVIS L. REV. 1429 (2021).

[5] Here and throughout, I use "victim" advisedly. As Anna Roberts has argued, "victim" occupies a peculiar place in criminal law and legal discourse, and its use often obscures important political determinations about what is or isn't a crime and whether, or to what extent, someone has committed a crime. *See generally* Anna Roberts, *Victims, Right?* 42 CARDOZO L. REV. 1449 (2021), *available at* https://papers.ssrn.com/sol3/papers.cfm?abstract_id=3569623.

[6] *See, e.g.*, MARY LOUISE FRAMPTON ET AL., EDS., AFTER THE WAR ON CRIME: RACE, DEMOCRACY, AND A NEW RECONSTRUCTION (2008); BRUCE WESTERN, PUNISHMENT AND INEQUALITY IN AMERICA (2007).

suggests that the logic of criminal institutions is one of white supremacy.[7] Alternatively, maybe we should understand mass incarceration as a construction or manifestation of neoliberal penality – in this account, punitive impulses and carceral solutions operate as necessary adjuncts to theories of individual responsibility and free markets; the "weak state" favored by neoliberalism actually rests on a belief in a state with strong carceral dimensions.[8] Or, maybe mass incarceration is a pathology of capitalism – in this account, criminal law operates as a means of managing surplus labor, and the violence of law enforcement serves a necessary function in preserving class hierarchy.[9]

These explanations are compelling and fair as far as they go, particularly if taken together or understood as complementary frames for understanding hierarchy, marginalization, and state violence (rather than as clear, unassailable accounts of causation and intentionality).[10] But what about the left? What about progressives and leftists committed to issues of distributional justice?

One need not conclude that actors on the political left were the primary drivers of mass incarceration in order to recognize that punitive politics are and have been a bipartisan problem in the United States.[11] From hate crimes to intimate partner violence and rape to white-collar crime, activists, academics, and lawmakers on the left have put aside anticarceral commitments when confronted with conduct they viewed as particularly objectionable. Legal scholar Aya Gruber has described this phenomenon as a "carve out" (i.e., the commentator has demonstrated a willingness to "carve out" one area of criminal law as acceptable, if not desirable), while I have described it as "carceral exceptionalism" (i.e., the commentator has demonstrated a willingness to treat one area of criminal law as exceptional and therefore worthy of support).[12] Confronted with a particularly concerning or unforgivable class of conduct, the progressive move remains a return to the state as a solver of problems and a wielder of expressive moral force.

[7] *See, e.g.*, Michelle Alexander, The New Jim Crow: Mass Incarceration in the Age of Colorblindness (2010).

[8] *See, e.g.*, Bernard E. Harcourt, The Illusion of Free Markets: Punishment and the Myth of Natural Order (2011).

[9] *See, e.g.*, Georg Rusche & Otto Kirchheimer, Punishment and Social Structure 5 (Russell & Russell 1968) (1939); Ahmed A. White, *Capitalism, Social Marginality, and the Rule of Law's Uncertain Fate in Modern Society*, 37 Ariz. St. L.J. 759, 790 (2005).

[10] Put differently, any monocausal explanation for mass incarceration always will be unsatisfactory, in part because of the complex politics and institutional structure(s) of US criminal policy.

[11] *See* Naomi Murakawa, The First Civil Right: How Liberals Built Prison America 12–13 (2014).

[12] *See* Aya Gruber, *#metoo and Mass Incarceration*, 17 Ohio St. J. Crim. L. 275, 279 (2020); Benjamin Levin, *Mens Rea Reform and Its Discontents*, 109 J. Crim. L. & Criminology 491, 548–57 (2019).

We might explain this turn as one of political expedience or the result of what Derrick Bell famously described as interest convergence.[13] According to Bell's thesis, marginalized or less powerful groups are more likely to gain legal or political victories when their interests converge with a socially dominant or more powerful group.[14] Applying this reasoning to US criminal policy might help explain bipartisan support for a range of criminal statutes or punitive policies. That is, the realities of US political economy (particularly in an era of neoliberalism) mean that the most realistic regulatory option is criminal law.[15] To get legislation passed, activists on the left might need to find willing partners on the right or among centrists by appealing to common ground; more often than not, that common ground might be an appeal to law-and-order politics.[16] For example, progressive gun control proponents have struggled for decades to pass gun control legislation; however, many of their victories have come in the form of harshly punitive criminal statutes and policies, which have received the backing of conservative politicians and advocates concerned about "the wrong people" getting their hands on guns. Even when forging a liberal or progressive coalition was unsuccessful or insufficient, an appeal to conservative carceral politics allowed for the passage of certain punitive approaches to gun control.[17] That is, "governing through crime" and the use of criminal law as the dominant vehicle for addressing social problems might be the result of convergent interests of proregulation forces and procriminalization forces.[18]

But, pragmatism or interest convergence is just one possible frame through which to view these procriminalization moves by those on the left. It is plausible and at times quite likely that the preference for criminal law as a solution to certain problems reflects not just an acceptance of a least-worst alternative;[19] rather, the selective embrace of criminal law on the part of academics and activists might reflect true enthusiasm for criminalization and the institutions of criminal punishment. That is, the calls for more prosecutions of "white-collar criminals," demands for longer sentences of individuals convicted of sex crimes, or the push to pass more hate crime bills all might represent a belief that those defendants *truly deserve* the full force of state violence. And, relatedly, the failure to punish those defendants or

[13] *See* Derrick A. Bell, Silent Covenants: Brown v. Board of Education and the Unfulfilled Hopes for Racial Reform 165–79 (2004).

[14] *See id.*

[15] *See generally* Lisa L. Miller, The Myth of Mob Rule: Violent Crime & Democratic Politics (2016).

[16] *See* Aya Gruber, *Equal Protection under the Carceral State*, 112 Nw. U. L. Rev. 1337, 1365 (2018).

[17] I have made this argument at length elsewhere. *See generally* Benjamin Levin, *Guns and Drugs*, 84 Fordham L. Rev. 2173 (2016).

[18] On governing through crime, *see generally* Jonathan Simon, Governing through Crime: How the War on Crime Transformed American Democracy and Created a Culture of Fear (2007).

[19] In such a view, the state failing to address the problem altogether presumably would represent the greater evil.

criminalize their conduct might represent a failure by society not only to hold them accountable but to signal its resistance to taking the underlying issues (economic inequality, gender subordination, and bigotry) seriously.

In other words, the carceral turn might be explained (at least in part) by the same impulse that leads progressives to the state in other noncriminal contexts: a desire to see the state definitively address social problems. To the extent that the United States has representative democracy and a state apparatus, shouldn't those institutions be there to protect the powerless? To the extent that criminal law and punishment represent (or purport to represent) public morality and public values, shouldn't they reflect the right values?[20] To the extent that the criminal system might serve a distributive function, shouldn't it advance the distributive ends that we (whoever "we" may be) favor?[21]

Those are questions that might – in both theoretical and practical terms – lead many to embrace criminal law as a suitable regulatory tool to address inequality, injustice, and a host of social problems. But, to be clear, this answer is an answer that suggests the evil of the carceral state is not the violence it does or the fundamental cruelty of cages, surveillance, and social control. Rather, it is one of scale, of choosing the deserving worst of the worst, and of the right distributive values that institutions of state violence should enhance.[22] It rests on a belief that the institutions of mass imprisonment and policing might be repurposed for good and might be a means to a more desirable end. Or, more pointedly, it suggests that incarceration and institutions of state violence are not incompatible with egalitarian ends; rather, they are important and at-times-necessary vehicles for achieving those ends.

5.2 HARM TO NONHUMAN ANIMALS

Which brings us to nonhuman animals and the common preference for using criminal law to address abuse by humans. As legal scholar Justin Marceau recounts, criminal law took on a greater role in the animal rights advocate's toolkit in the 1990s when "the movement hitched its wagon . . . to the star of mass criminalization."[23] By the midnineties, activists had "declared war on cruelty . . . by launching a nationwide campaign for stiffer laws [and] more vigorous prosecution of animal abusers, and [by] making available the tools to win convictions."[24] Indeed, a ubiquitous

[20] On criminal law as reflective (or constitutive) of public values, *see, e.g.*, ÉMILE DURKHEIM, THE DIVISION OF LABOR IN SOCIETY 102 (W.D. Halls trans., 2014) (1893); MICHEL FOUCAULT, DISCIPLINE & PUNISHISMENT 138 (Alan Sheridan trans., 2d ed. 1995).

[21] On criminal law as redistributive, *see, e.g.*, Aya Gruber, *A Distributive Theory of Criminal Law*, 52 WM. & MARY L. REV. 1, 1 (2010); Kate Levine & Benjamin Levin, *Redistributing Justice* (manuscript on file with author).

[22] *See generally* Levin, *The Consensus Myth*, *supra* note 3 (describing and critiquing this position).

[23] JUSTIN MARCEAU, BEYOND CAGES: ANIMAL LAW AND CRIMINAL PUNISHMENT 22-23 (2019).

[24] *Id.* at 14.

bumper sticker produced by the Animal Legal Defense Fund reads, "Abuse an Animal, Go to Jail!"[25] And Marceau describes this slogan as "fairly representative as a motto for the entire disparate [animal protection] movement."[26]

All fifty states criminalize animal abuse in some form or other.[27] Over the past twenty years, at least twenty-one states have increased criminal penalties for individuals convicted of abusing nonhuman animals or have redefined conduct as felonious that previously constituted only a misdemeanor.[28] Additionally, numerous states have passed new criminal statutes addressing animals left or tethered in hot cars or sexually abused.[29] And, in November 2019, President Donald Trump signed into law the Preventing Animal Cruelty and Torture Act ("PACT Act"), a statute passed *unanimously* by Congress that made certain acts of animal abuse federal crimes punishable by up to seven years in prison.[30] Put simply, criminal responses to animal abuse and neglect aren't new, but they appear to have gained significant traction.

Without wading too deeply into the legal architecture or advocacy ecosystem of animal protection's criminal turn,[31] I suggest that this turn reflects the sort of "carceral progressivism" described above. Importantly, many of the activists and advocates supporting criminal law and criminal legal institutions in this area have articulated positions generally hostile to the use of cages and inhumane punishment. Indeed, many of the specific targets of critique from the animal advocacy community are well-documented features of the US penal system, from denial of self-determination to confinement in cages to failure to provide necessary food and medical care. In short, the case of criminalizing mistreatment of animals represents the exact sort of carve-out or carceral exceptionalism that recurs in various corners of the US left (broadly defined). A general condemnation of society's inhumane institutions somehow comes to excuse, or perhaps justify, the much-maligned

25 *See, e.g.*, Stephen Wells, *Letter from the Executive Director: Putting Animals behind Bars*, Animals' Advoc., Spring 2013, p. 2.

26 Marceau, *supra* note 23, at 2.

27 *See* L.S. Stegman, *Do We Need to Make a Federal Case Out of It? The Preventing Animal Cruelty and Torture Act as Over-federalization of Criminal Law*, 57 Am. Crim. L. Rev. Online 135, 137 (2020).

28 *See, e.g.*, 72 Del. Laws 417 (West); Ga. Code Ann. § 4-11-16 (West); NY CLS Agr & M § 353-a; Tex. Penal Code § 42.092 (West); Or. Rev. Stat. Ann. § 167.320 (West); Md. Code Ann., Crim. Law § 10-606 (West); W. Va. Code § 61-8-19 (West); Tenn. Code Ann. § 39-14-202 (West); R.R.S. Neb. § 28-1009 (West); Wyo. Stat. Ann. § 6-3-203 (West); A.C.A. § 5-62-103 (West); Miss. Code Ann. § 97-41-16 (West); Utah Code Ann. § 76-9-301.7 (West); H R S § 711-1109 (West); SDCL § 40-1-2.4 (West); 3 Pa. Stat. Ann. § 459-602 (West); N.D. Cent. Code Ann. § 36-21.2-01 (West).

29 *See, e.g.*, 2006 Cal Stats. ch. 489 (West); 510 I.L.C.S. 70/3.01 (West); 11 Del.C. § 1325 (West); Wash. Rev. Code Ann. § 16.52.205 (West); Fla. Stat. Ann. § 828.126 (West); Or. Rev. Stat. Ann. § 167.333 (West); Tex. Penal Code Ann. § 21.09 (West); Mass. Gen. Laws Ann. ch. 272, § 77C (West).

30 *See* Mihir Zaveri, *President Trump Signs Federal Animal Cruelty Bill into Law*, N.Y. Times, Nov. 25, 2019, https://www.nytimes.com/2019/11/25/us/politics/trump-animal-cruelty-bill.html.

31 Other chapters and authors provide much richer interventions than I could offer here.

institutions of mass incarceration and the carceral state. Or, as one commentator puts it in advocating for sweeping criminal punishment for defendants convicted of animal abuse, "attitudes about animal cruelty and neglect are changing, and society is moving slowly toward realizing that a truly civilized community must care for all of its vulnerable members, including the impoverished, the elderly, children, and domesticated animals."[32] Put differently, caging abusers is the way that society signals its status as "truly civilized."

The story of the animal protection movement's embrace of criminal law has been told elsewhere,[33] and it (or aspects of it) certainly might reflect interest convergence and a grudging acceptance of the criminal system as the appropriate regulatory framework. But here I suggest that it also reflects the sort of enthusiasm for or embrace of criminal legal institutions that characterizes carceral progressivism and the turn to criminal law to advance left, redistributive, or egalitarian ends elsewhere. We might identify a host of common strands, themes, or arguments in any of these progressive criminalization projects.[34] In the context of carceral animal law, though, two familiar justifications or points of rhetorical emphasis stand out: (1) the presence of a particularly vulnerable class of victims; and (2) the claim that criminal law can send a message about society's respect for that class of victims and condemnation of harm done to them. In this part, I take those two features in turn as a means of illustrating the troubling (and potentially unbounded) carceral logic that underpins the turn to criminal law as regulatory paradigm for advancing animal welfare.

5.2.1 *Vulnerable Victims*

Progressive proponents of criminal law tend to emphasize victims' vulnerability and the role of the prosecution in vindicating the rights and interests of those victims. The victim of a hate crime is presumably more sympathetic and more in need of the state's protection because she belongs to a historically marginalized group. The victim of rape, intimate partner violence, or some other form of gender-based harm requires additional assistance in overcoming the structures of heteropatriarchy and gender subordination that might make noncriminal alternatives insufficient. And, the victim of wage theft might be precariously employed, an undocumented immigrant, or lacking the legal, political, and economic status to hold her boss accountable in civil or administrative proceedings.

32 Margit Livingston, *Desecrating the Ark: Animal Abuse and the Law's Role in Prevention*, 87 IOWA L. REV. 1, 72 (2001).

33 *See generally* MARCEAU, *supra* note 23.

34 For various characterizations of such arguments *see, e.g.*, Ely Aharonson, *"Pro-Minority" Criminalization and the Transformation of Visions of Citizenship in Contemporary Liberal Democracies: A Critique*, 13 NEW CRIM. L. REV. 286, 287 (2010); Hadar Aviram, *Progressive Punitivism: Notes on the Use of Punitive Social Control to Advance Social Justice Ends*, 68 BUFF. L. REV. 199, 199 (2020); Levin, *Wage Theft Criminalization*, *supra* note 4.

Often in these accounts, the vulnerable victims are particularly deserving of or in need of state (criminal) assistance because they have been harmed by the state's long-standing failure to protect them.[35] This claim is a particularly powerful theme in the literature and advocacy regarding gender-based violence, but it also recurs in work around hate crimes and violence against racial, religious, and sexual minorities.[36] If freedom from violence represents the "first civil right," then the prosecution of individuals who use violence to subordinate marginalized communities can be seen as a means of vindicating rights and leveling the societal playing field.[37]

In some sense, the nonhuman animal stands as the apotheosis of the progressive's ideal victim: nonhuman animals lack a host of civil and political rights and, outside of human allies and advocates, have no meaningful vehicle to advance their interests via the legal system or political process. As a result, it should come as no surprise that the same rhetoric of helpless or vulnerable victims and crusading and protective prosecutors takes center stage in this context. For example, in celebrating the passage of the PACT Act, the vice president of field services at the Humane Rescue Alliance argued that absent a federal criminal statute (to reach conduct already criminalized in most jurisdictions), his organization had "been unable to truly bring justice for the animals in instances when the cruelty occurs across multiple jurisdictions."[38]

There's something intuitively appealing about this logic. Indeed, that's probably why it is so ubiquitous in mass cultural representations of prosecutors and in the advocacy supporting harsh criminal policies. But that ubiquity is part of the problem: if prosecutors are so good at vindicating the interests of victims and if criminal law and punishment are the ways to advance the interests of victims, why embrace critiques of the criminal system in the first place? There appears to be an implicit assumption that drives the carceral progressive carve-out for vulnerable victims – some assumption that most crimes (or most crimes committed by defendants worthy of sympathy) are victimless or involve victims who aren't vulnerable. That assumption would be consistent with a narrative in certain liberal or progressive circles that the War on Drugs and nonviolent or victimless crimes have been the drivers of mass incarceration. But that narrative gets it wrong;[39] the majority of people are incarcerated for crimes categorized as "violent," and victims are often from marginalized

[35] *See, e.g.*, Mari J. Matsuda, *Public Response to Racist Speech: Considering the Victim's Story*, 87 MICH. L. REV. 2320, 2328 (1989).

[36] *See, e.g.*, RANDALL KENNEDY, RACE, CRIME AND THE LAW (1997); Alexandra Natapoff, *Underenforcement*, 75 FORDHAM L. REV. 1715, 1717 (2006).

[37] *See generally* MURAKAWA, *supra* note 11.

[38] Caitlin O'Kane, *Trump Signs Bill Making Animal Cruelty a Federal Felony*, CBS NEWS. Nov. 25, 2019, https://www.cbsnews.com/news/animal-cruelty-felony-president-trump-signs-animal-cruelty-pact-act-bill-making-it-a-federal-felony-2019-11-25/.

[39] *See, e.g.*, MARIE GOTTSCHALK, CAUGHT: THE PRISON STATE AND THE LOCKDOWN OF AMERICAN POLITICS (2014); JOHN F. PFAFF, LOCKED IN: THE TRUE CAUSES OF MASS INCARCERATION AND HOW TO ACHIEVE REAL REFORM (2017).

communities.[40] In other words, if we need criminal law whenever a vulnerable or marginalized victim is harmed, we need a lot of criminal law, and decarceration is hardly an achievable goal.

Much contemporary anticarceral and abolitionist scholarship and advocacy focuses on critiquing those assumptions (i.e., that prosecutors serve victims' interests and that criminal punishment is the best way to make victims whole). Further, the assumption that prosecutors serve to shield the powerless victim from the powerful defendant is undercut by an extensive literature that deconstructs the victim/offender binary, stressing that people charged with crimes are themselves often victims of state and/or interpersonal violence. And, to the extent that the criminal system is embedded in a culture wracked with deep structural and institutional biases, there's good reason to think that the defendants selected for prosecution and punishment are themselves often relatively powerless or marginalized, even if they enjoy some power or advantage over a given victim. Maybe that's still an acceptable or desirable outcome for animal welfare advocates – maybe prosecuting and incarcerating the poor person of color who has harmed a nonhuman animal reflects the state at its protective and progressive best. But it's important to recognize that the progressive goal is being advanced on the backs of relatively powerless actors. And, the procarceral logic advanced by animal welfare advocates in this context would justify much of what goes on in the criminal system: the poor person with a gun may have relatively more power than the unarmed poor person, but does prosecuting the former really constitute a redistribution of power and a move to shield the weak? And, even if it does, at what cost?

So much of the activism and scholarship that have led to the contemporary moment of reckoning with mass incarceration has stressed the tremendous social cost and harms associated with arrest, prosecution, and incarceration. That is, even if it's fair to say that the human who has harmed a nonhuman animal has done something bad (even extremely bad) and has done it to a relatively powerless victim, turning to criminal law and institutions of state violence should require a reckoning with how much additional harm will be done and to what end. Those questions have become essential components of the discussion about dismantling the carceral state. Thus, they should be a part of any conversation about criminal law, even if that conversation is focused on conduct or defendants that progressives or leftists find particularly objectionable.

5.2.2 *Sending a Message*

Progressive criminalization projects often rely on an expressive theory of punishment or an account of criminal law as sending a message about society's values. That

[40] *See* Wendy Sawyer & Peter Wagner, *Mass Incarceration: The Whole Pie 2019*, Prison Pol'y Initiative, Mar. 19, 2019, https://www.prisonpolicy.org/reports/pie2019.html.

is, prosecuting the boss who steals her workers' wages or the racist who hurts a neighbor because of her race sends a message about what society should look like: work is valued, and greedy bosses are unacceptable; communities should welcome diversity, and racism is anathema to multicultural values.[41] Criminal law, in this frame, serves to signal inclusion of the victim in the polity by signaling deep disapproval of the harm done to that victim (or class of victims).[42] Or, as criminologist Dario Melossi describes it, "[p]unishment functions as a sort of 'gazette of morality[,]' announcing what is allowed and what is forbidden at a specific place at a specific time."[43]

This rhetoric of criminalization, prosecution, and punishment "sending a message" recurs throughout the advocacy and literature on animal welfare. For example, in 2010 when Suffolk County, New York, moved to create a registry of people convicted of crimes against animals, the bill's Democratic sponsor argued that "[a] society is judged by the way it treats those who are most vulnerable, and the creation of this registry sends a strong message that all of God's creatures deserve protection from torture and abuse."[44] Similarly, the lead prosecutor in the animal protection unit of Atlanta's District Attorney's office has argued that "[a]llowing animal cruelty to go uncharged, uninvestigated and unprosecuted sends a message ... that violence is acceptable so long as it's not to a human."[45]

Notably, the passage of the PACT Act was accompanied by much fanfare highlighting its expressive value. Kitty Block, the president and chief executive of the Humane Society of the United States, argued that the announcement of federal penalties for conduct already criminal under state law "makes a statement about American values."[46] Further, the Humane Society put out a press release stating that "PACT makes a statement about American values. Animals are deserving of protection at the highest level."[47]

41 *See, e.g.*, Avlana Eisenberg, *Expressive Enforcement*, 61 UCLA L. Rev. 858, 860 (2014); Angela P. Harris, *Heteropatriarchy Kills: Challenging Gender Violence in a Prison Nation*, 37 Wash. U. J.L. & Pol'y 13, 34 (2011).

42 *See, e.g.*, Sara Sun Beale, *Federalizing Hate Crimes: Symbolic Politics, Expressive Law, or Tool for Criminal Enforcement?*, 80 B.U. L. Rev. 1227, 1265 (2000).

43 Dario Melossi, *Gazette of Morality and Social Whip: Punishment, Hegemony and the Case of the USA*, 1970–92, 2 Soc. & Legal Stud. 259, 262 (1993).

44 *Historic Vote in Suffolk County, New York Creates Nation's First Registry for Animal Abusers*, Animal Legal Def. Fund (Oct. 12, 2010), http://aldf.org/press-room/press-releases/historic-vote-in-suffolk-county-new-yorkcreates-nations-first-registry-for-animal-abusers-2/; *see also* Danielle K. Campbell, *Animal Abusers Beware: Registry Laws in the Works to Curb Your Abuse*, 48 Val. U. L. Rev. 271, 328 (2013).

45 Allie Phillips, *The Few and the Proud: Prosecutors Who Vigorously Pursue Animal Cruelty Cases*, Prosecutor, July/Aug./Sept. 2008, at 20, 26.

46 Zaveri, *supra* note 30.

47 Press Release, The Humane Society of the United States, Extreme Animal Cruelty Can Now Be Prosecuted as a Federal Crime (Nov. 25, 2019), https://www.humanesociety.org/news/extreme-animal-cruelty-can-now-be-prosecuted-federal-crime.

As a general matter, there is good reason to be skeptical about claims of criminal law's expressive force or justification. To whom does criminal law speak and how does it speak? Why should we believe that people are aware of every criminal statute, of every prosecution, or of every punishment? Further, even if criminal law is properly understood as advancing expressive ends, how exactly can or should we judge its success? If few defendants are prosecuted for harming animals, does that send a message that nonhuman animals don't really matter or that harm to them isn't a serious problem? It's well documented that the federal government has not been particularly aggressive in prosecuting crimes defined by explicitly expressive statutes (e.g., hate crimes and gender-based violence), which raises the question of whether the expressive function relies on a certain optimal rate of enforcement. And how much punishment sends the right message? As noted above, much recent advocacy involves amping up punishment for already-criminal conduct, which suggests that the existent punishments are insufficient to satisfy advocates.

All of which is to say that once we start down the road of expressive justifications, it seems hard to step off the gas. The logic appears to demand more prosecutions and more punishment, or else the expressive function withers away. And, if that's an acceptable approach, why should we stop with crimes against animal victims? There are many other values that progressives and leftists believe that the state should advance. Why isn't it acceptable to use criminal law to advance each of those values? I hope it's clear that such a line of reasoning opens the door to (or preserves) a massive criminal and prosecutorial apparatus. Additionally, there's something striking about celebrating the PACT Act at the same time that the Trump administration has been widely criticized for incarcerating immigrant children and supporting police violence against protestors demanding racial justice. The logic of expressivism and community values presumes that the state and, particularly, its prosecutorial arm(s) have a certain moral legitimacy and high ground from which to dispense public justice. That may be a view that some commentators hold. But it's fundamentally at odds with left and progressive critiques of the carceral state. And, even if one doesn't share those sweeping critiques of carceral institutions, there's something deeply problematic about suggesting that the way the state signals that society believes caging and abusing animals is wrong is by caging and abusing people.[48]

5.3 CONCLUSION: THINKING BEYOND CAGES AND CARCERAL LOGICS

Marceau ends his book on the problems with a carceral approach to animal protection with a quotation from critical theorist Audre Lorde: "there is no such

[48] *Cf.* Chad Flanders, *Shame and the Meanings of Punishment*, 54 CLEV. ST. L. REV. 609, 622 (2006) ("Although imprisonment can be equated with putting people in small boxes with bars, it is closer to the truth if it is equated with putting people in cages like animals.").

thing as a single issue struggle."[49] That is, cordoning off discussions of animal protection and liberation from conversations about mass incarceration would be a mistake. Lorde is also widely cited for her observation that "the master's tools will never dismantle the master's house."[50] This claim is reflected and embodied in a growing abolitionist discourse and praxis that treat carceral institutions as fundamentally at odds with egalitarian, redistributive projects. Cages, criminal punishment, surveillance, and social control are markers of an inegalitarian state or society. In other words, the institutions of the US criminal system are inherently regressive and cruel, regardless of the goals they are used to achieve. And, more pointedly, it is a mistake to think they ever could achieve those ends, because they will always entrench, legitimate, and reify the same troubling hierarchies, inequalities, and injustices.[51]

Despite the appeal of that radical frame, despite the fact that it resonates with many who advocate for left and progressive causes, and despite the increasing prevalence of the rhetoric of abolition, I see the case study of animal victims as revealing a selective application of that principle.

The carceral state and the structures of mass incarceration have resulted from "a series of small decisions, made over time, by a disparate group of actors."[52] And, the suggestion that one area of criminal policy might be distinguished easily from another area of criminal policy would be a mistake. Legal and policy arguments migrate; that is, once raised or introduced, procarceral rhetoric may take root in the cultural consciousness(es) and may be mobilized by different thinkers and advocates

49 Audre Lord, Sister Outsider 130 (2020) (1984) (quoted in Marceau, *supra* note 27, at 283).

50 Audre Lorde, *The Master's Tools Will Never Dismantle the Master's House*, in Sister Outsider: Essays and Speeches by Audre Lorde 110, 112 (1984); *see also* I. Bennett Capers, *Reading* Michigan v. Bryant, *"Reading" Justice Sotomayor*, 123 Yale L.J. Forum 427, 445 (2014) (collecting uses of the "master's tools" adage in Critical Race Theory scholarship).

51 To be clear, I see this sort of abolitionist critique as reflecting (at least) two different impulses or concerns. On the one hand, perhaps the problem with the carceral state and the institutions of the prison industrial complex are their distributive consequences – they serve to harm or marginalize already-marginalized communities. *See, e.g.*, Paul Butler, *The System Is Working the Way It Is Supposed To: The Limits of Criminal Justice Reform*, 104 Geo. L.J. 1419 (2016); Dorothy E. Roberts, *Foreword: Abolition Constitutionalism*, 133 Harv. L. Rev. 1 (2019). On the other hand, perhaps the problems would exist regardless of the distributive realities – the institutions fall afoul of some set of first-principles or deontological concerns, whether rooted in humanitarian, religious, or ethical commitments, etc. *See, e.g.*, Thomas Mathiesen, The Politics of Abolition Revisited (2015); Máximo Langer, *Penal Abolitionism and Criminal Law Minimalism: Here and There, Now and Then*, 134 Harv. L. Rev. F. 42 (2020). In discussions of the US criminal system, the turn to abolitionism (at least in activist and legal policy and academic circles) appears to reflect the first or distributive frame. While a discussion of these alternate strands of abolitionist theory and praxis falls largely outside of the scope of this chapter, this distinction might ultimately be significant in assessing the limits of abolitionism and in understanding the continuing allure of criminal law to at least some radical commentators.

52 James Forman, Jr., Locking Up Our Own: Crime and Punishment in Black America 229 (2017).

in very different realms.[53] The turn to criminal law as acceptable in one "exceptional" context is not necessarily exceptional; instead, it risks normalizing and legitimating the same moves and institutions in other contexts. In this chapter, I haven't offered a solution to wide scale mistreatment of nonhuman animals. Instead, I have stressed the ways in which a criminal turn here legitimates a host of deeply objectionable institutions and arguments. Protecting vulnerable victims and sending a message about the way that society should value the lives and dignity of nonhuman animals are worthwhile goals. That said, by turning to the institutions of the criminal system to achieve those goals, activists and academics risk falling into the trap of carceral progressivism and excusing state violence, its inequities, and its inhumanities in the name of the "right" politics, causes, or victims.

[53] *See* Jeannie Suk, *The Trajectory of Trauma: Bodies and Minds of Abortion Discourse*, 110 COLUM. L. REV. 1193 (2010).

PART II

Animal Law in Context: The Limits of Carceral Strategies

Introduction

Lori Gruen and Justin Marceau

Animals have long been undervalued in both society and in the law. Animal advocates seeking legal recognition of the capacity of animals to suffer have frequently turned to the criminal law in recent decades. More convictions and longer sentences for animal abusers have been treated as markers of success in the battle for the social recognition of animals. For his role in a dogfighting enterprise, a Black man in Virginia, Eldridge Freeman, Jr., was recently sentenced to 108 years of incarceration, with 98 of the years suspended (meaning that he will serve at least 10 years, followed by probation and the threat of an additional 98 year sentence), and a fundraising email from a national group lauded the case, explaining that "the successful prosecution and appropriate sentencing in this case demonstrates what is possible when state laws are strong and animal cruelty is taken seriously."[1]

No one can doubt the good faith efforts of these advocates to protect animals. But the notion that animals are safer because of more vigorous prosecution, or that anthropocentrism is reduced by this sort of legal intervention, is speculative, to say the least. In the past, victims of hate crimes and domestic violence, among others, have also sought to use law, in particular criminal law, to advance their social change objectives. Among other goals, Part II seeks to understand the effectiveness of carceral social change projects outside of the animal law, so that animal lawyers might learn from these histories.

For example, advocates and scholars observe that there is reason to doubt "the hopefulness with which . . . largely white, activists in the…movement imbued [criminal] law" (Kuennen). There is a reflexive urge to assume, for example, that mandatory arrest, felony laws, no-drop policies, and other tough-on-crime innovations will yield progressive social change. But "any expectation of a reliable, protective response by police is a product of not merely white, but also

[1] Email from Lora Dunn, *26 Dogfighting Victims* (May 25, 2021), https://www.wric.com/news/crime/dinwiddie-man-to-serve-10-years-for-dogfighting-animal-cruelty-charges/.

heteronormative privilege," and the effect of investment in criminal solutions is not merely neutral; rather, the focus on carceral strategies has been shown to be "crowding out" systemic solutions (Kuennen). Scholars from outside of animal law, such as those who study domestic violence, offer lessons about the way that top-down strategies that focus on convictions and incarceration risk alienating grassroots activists, feed the mass-incarceration system, and often fail to reduce the types of conduct they hope to end.

Drawing on lessons from the war on drugs and domestic violence, the chapters in this section can help animal lawyers by highlighting the mistakes of other movements. The chapters discuss some of the unintended consequences and limitations of carceral strategies. Animal lawyers seem to imagine that their carceral advocacy occurs in a vacuum, considerably distanced from the unseemly aspects of the criminal system. The race and unfairness problems that plague the criminal system don't have much application in the animal prosecution realm, advocates have long assumed. But scholars of criminal law find such claims of animal law exceptionalism striking: "there is no reason to think that the enforcement of laws forbidding animal abuse is likely to be more equitable than any other sort of criminal law enforcement" (Kamin). Even if the expansion of animal crime laws and policing is genuinely motivated in every state by race- and class-neutral goals, the enforcement of an expanding web of criminality will have predictably disparate impacts. For some, traffic stops might seem like quintessentially race-neutral offenses; after all, one's guilt has nothing to do with one's race. Yet, experts in the field have long noted that as the substantive criminal law expands (more offenses and broader definitions of crimes), the protections of the Fourth Amendment diminish proportionately. So if it is a crime to stop a car with an air freshener, then law enforcement seeking to engage in pretextual stops can (and have been documented to) use the air freshner as a justification for stopping the car of persons who look out of place or whom the officer suspects of other crimes. And when an officer approaches a car or a home, the smell of drugs inside might produce the sort of probable cause that justifies entry. Expansions in the criminal law have predictable, and proven, impacts on marginalized communities. Thus, one author makes a poignant comparison between animal law and the war on drugs: "There is genuine risk that the barking dog will become the new smell of marijuana" (Kamin).

More generally, these chapters raise challenges to carceral animal law and their pursuit of tough-on-crime legislation. Is it truly helpful for animal advocates to team up with conservative republican lawmakers to pass new felony laws that are heralded as groundbreaking? Is it appropriate to support the firing of animal control officers and prosecutors who are deemed "too soft" on animal crime and to deride "slap on the wrist" punishments in cases of neglect (Gruber)? Important parts of the animal law movement have become a caricature of 1990s style tough-on-crime rhetoric, and this message has been reinforced by the leading groups in this country for decades (Gruber). These chapters also challenge the claim that animal cruelty enforcements are relatively rare, and mostly for affirmative abuse: "Since Libre's Law 2017 passage, the state has prosecuted thousands of human animals – 21,206 to be exact. In 2017, the number was 967 cases, which spiked to 11,836 filings in 2018, and 8,405 in 2019. The majority of the cases (52 percent) were for neglect" (Gruber). Are these dramatic case increases a sign of animal rights on the rise or just another chapter in the nation's mass incarceration story?

Likewise, the movement's recent celebration of noncustodial sentences as a kinder and gentler approach to animal law is much less than it seems. "[A]nimal law is still far too carceral in its rhetoric and approach to law reform, and the pivot towards fines, fees, and probation is not nearly as salutary as the animal protection lawyers imagine" (Marceau). Simply put, "a critique of incarceration alone would actually let the movement off too easy" (Marceau).

Beyond carceral animal law and the efforts to acknowledge animal suffering through incarceration, Part II also considers the carceral logics inherent to "spectacular immigration enforcement" efforts at meat production plants (Chacon). The entanglements of meat production, poverty, and carceral strategies collide to produce a type of "violence" that is an oft-ignored feature of American meat consumption, and highlight the complex webs of carcerality that define our relations with animals (Chacon). The very prosecutors championed for bringing justice to animal victims are quick to point out that persons working in meatpacking plants without authorization "deserve prosecution," or as the Trump Administration candidly put it, "the cruelty is the point." Finally, another aspect of carceral thinking explored in Part II is the connection between caging humans (in prison) and caging animals. The cruel caging of monkeys for maternal deprivation studies helped fuel a "nascent animal rights movement," and simultaneously "bolstered opposition to solitary confinement of human prisoners" (Winders). And the United States is the world leader in the solitary confinement of both humans and animals. But as this section shows, facile efforts to equate human and animal caging should be avoided, both because they are inaccurate and tend toward exaggeration (e.g., we treat humans worse than animals), and also because the comparisons inevitably result in a compassion competition that pits the interests of humans and nonhumans against each other (Winders).

This section complicates the conventional narratives about carceral strategies. Law reform in this area may not be as beneficial for animals nor as enlightened and progressive for humans as prior discourse assumes. Likewise, the perils of human incarceration and meat production should not be underestimated, but the unimaginative and anthropocentric framing of the problem as one of treating humans like animals obscures more than it illuminates. Carceral logics are everywhere in law and are increasingly saturating social consciousness. They represent a hope for simple narratives (and solutions) to complicated social problems, and Part II confronts this dilemma directly.

6

Spectacular Immigration Enforcement in Hidden Spaces

Jennifer M. Chacón

6.1 INTRODUCTION

This chapter analyzes recent, spectacular immigration enforcement efforts at the paradigmatic sites of animal caging and killing: meatpacking and poultry processing plants. Over the last four decades, the growing role of immigrant workers in these industries has paralleled the rise of a massive immigration enforcement machine in the United States. Though the US government now expends more than $18 billion on immigration enforcement every year, immigration enforcement at these sites is selective and sporadic.

This is by design. The infrequent but highly visible nature of immigration enforcement at meatpacking and poultry processing plants ensures that workers live and work in fear of the possibility of deportation. Employers generally can count on the continued existence of a sizable, yet legally vulnerable, immigrant workforce. Immigration enforcement is an essential ingredient in the making of meat and poultry in the United States, not only because it produces the material conditions for workplace exploitation, but also because it is performed in ways that contribute to social structures of racial inequality and domination at the heart of the workplace exploitation that produces cheap food.

Spectacular immigration enforcement – large-scale, highly publicized immigration enforcement efforts in concentrated geographic spaces – plays an important role in the maintenance of the racial order of the United States and of the global region that it dominates. These enforcement efforts, like prison walls and border walls, act as high-visibility markers of sociopolitical exclusion and inclusion. Spectacular immigration enforcement has a direct, material effect: through these efforts, officials signal the condition of deportability to immigrant workers without significantly undercutting the industry's labor supply. But they also have a more diffuse effect on the structure and understanding of power and of belonging.

By focusing on spectacular immigration enforcement efforts at sites of animal slaughter, this chapter sheds light on how immigrant deportability is facilitated by and reinforces structural racism. It also underscores the salience of race in shaping how people see – or fail to see – the exercise of state and private violence. This is not, of course, the only place where spectacular immigration enforcement occurs, but this analysis of one exemplary site helps limn particular elements of the role of racial spectacle in immigration enforcement choices.

The chapter proceeds in four parts. Section 6.2 briefly summarizes the changes in industrial meat and poultry processing over the past forty years, as the workforce makeup of the industry has shifted from predominantly white to predominantly Black, Asian and Latinx, with a sizable undocumented workforce. Section 6.3 discusses how the confluence of labor recruitment and immigration regulation at these sites (and elsewhere) has generated a "deportable" workforce. Section 6.4 describes several recent examples of spectacular immigration enforcement at meat-packing and poultry processing sites, with attention to the mechanism through which these enforcement efforts contribute to the illegalization and criminalization of Latinx workers in particular. Section 6.5 analyzes the ways that spectacular immigration enforcement is publicized and explores how this messaging both draws from and reinforces racism.

Sites of animal slaughter are designed to stay out of sight. They come into focus only when light is shined deliberately upon them. Spectacular immigration enforcement focuses an intense light on certain aspects of meat and poultry processing, but does so in a deliberately deceptive way – one that offers a biased and incomplete vision of work in the US heartland. These efforts conceal as much as they reveal, reaffirming racial scripts even as they obscure recurring patterns of cruelty and transnational capitalist exploitation.

6.2 CHANGING INDUSTRY, CHANGING WORKERS

Most people are familiar with the horrors of early-twentieth -century meatpacking, exposed by Upton Sinclair in his watershed 1906 book, *The Jungle*.[1] The abusive working conditions, the endemic mistreatment of nonhuman animals, and the unsanitary production processes that Sinclair documented helped to galvanize a push for greater regulation – of a piece with similar efforts in other industries. This progressive regulatory impulse, running alongside the economic collapse of the Great Depression, ushered in the demise of the *Lochner* era,[2] and generated a

[1] Upton Sinclair, The Jungle (2001).

[2] *See* Lochner v. New York, 198 U.S. 45 (1905) (striking down a New York maximum hour law for bakers, reasoning that "the freedom of master and employees to contract with each other in relation to their employment, and in defining the same, cannot be prohibited or interfered with, without violating the Federal Constitution."); *see also* Howard Gillman, The

new wave of judicial tolerance for the increased regulation of meatpacking and other industries.[3]

In the years that followed, the meatpacking industry became a somewhat better place for humans to work, even as the growing size and productivity of the industry increased the scale of immiseration of nonhuman animals. A great deal of animal slaughter and processing occurred in urban centers, often overseen by a unionized workforce.[4] The work was difficult and dangerous, but relatively well compensated. Increasing regulation of the industry resulted in improved working conditions for humans as well as some improvements in the treatment of nonhuman animals.[5] But in the 1960s, things began to change.[6]

First, as was the case in the manufacturing sector more broadly, the meat processing industry consolidated. In 1970, the four largest meatpacking companies controlled 21 percent of the beef market; today four companies control more than 80 percent of the market.[7] Second, the site of processing shifted. Previously, animals were shipped from the rural areas to cities, where they were butchered and distributed. But in the 1970s and 1980s, the industry relocated the packinghouses to the areas where livestock was raised, transitioning to a system in which meatpackers do most butchering at the site of animal husbandry and slaughter.[8] These new sites of butchering are largely – and not coincidentally – situated where unionized work forces are rare.[9]

Newly consolidated companies staunchly opposed unionization at these worksites, and the unionization of the workforce in meatpacking facilities entered a period of steep decline, making it more difficult for workers to negotiate for better wages and working conditions.[10] In the early 1960s, 95 percent of meatpacking

CONSTITUTION BESIEGED: THE RISE AND DEMISE OF LOCHNER ERA POLICE POWERS JURISPRUDENCE (1993).

3 *See, e.g.*, United States v. Caroline Products 304 U.S. 144 (1938) ("the question is at least debatable whether commerce in filled milk should be left unregulated, or in some measure restricted, or wholly prohibited. As that decision was for Congress, neither the finding of a court arrived at by weighing the evidence, nor the verdict of a jury can be substituted for it."); West Coast Hotel v. Parrish 300 U.S. 379 (1937) ("regulation which is reasonable in relation to its subject and is adopted in the interests of the community is due process.").

4 RUTH MILKMAN, IMMIGRANT LABOR AND THE NEW PRECARIAT 85 (2020).

5 *Id.*

6 *Id.*

7 TIMOTHY PACHIRAT, EVERY TWELVE SECONDS: INDUSTRIALIZED SLAUGHTER AND THE POLITICS OF SIGHT 275, n.2 (2011).

8 *Id.* at 276; *see also* MILKMAN, *supra* note 4, at 86; Roger Horowitz, *The Decline of Unionism in America's Meatpacking Industry*, 32 SOC. POL'Y 32–36 (2002); William Kandel & Emilio A. Parrado, *Restructuring of the U.S. Meat Processing Industry and the New Hispanic Migrant Destinations*, 31 POPULATION DEV. REV. 447, 447–71 (2005).

9 Kandel & Parrado, *supra* note 8.

10 MILKMAN, *supra* note 4, at 85–88.

workers outside the South belonged to one of two unions.[11] By the late 1960s, these unions experienced significant declines in membership.[12] In the 1980s the final straw for unions in the industry came in the form of nonunion plants overtaking unionized ones.[13] Wages plummeted.[14]

The decline of worker bargaining power coincided with a steady increase in demand for beef, chicken, and pork – not only nationally, but globally. The resulting managerial insistence on speed in the slaughtering and processing of animals made the workplace increasingly dangerous, as workers were asked to meet rising productivity quotas.[15] With declining relative wages and working conditions, the industry experienced a white flight. The white working-class men who had largely staffed meatpacking plants left these jobs in droves. Plant operators tried to meet their labor needs by hiring white women – some plants even experimented with daycare centers – but this also proved inadequate to the needs of the industry.[16] So meat processing companies began to recruit nonwhite workers, investing heavily in the recruitment of Latino workers.[17] They initially targeted workers in large urban centers like Los Angeles and Chicago. Finding those labor sources inadequate, recruiters expanded their efforts to target incoming refugees from Asia and Africa, as well as workers willing to move from Mexico and Central America.[18] Ruth Milkman notes that these workers are often blamed for displacing US workers, though in fact, the changing nature of the industry drove US workers away before immigrant workers were recruited to fill these jobs.[19] These workers actually saved many industry-adjacent jobs.[20]

Comparable shifts were under way in the poultry industry, though on a slightly different timetable. That industry also experienced corporatization and centralization after the 1970s.[21] Tyson Foods, Pilgrim's, Perdue, and Sanderson Farms, the

[11] Daniel Calamuci, *Return to the Jungle: The Rise and Fall of Meatpacking Work*, 17 New Lab. Forum 66, 70 (2008); John Brueggemann & Cliff Brown, *The Decline of Industrial Unionism in the Meatpacking Industry: Event-Structure Analyses of Labor Unrest, 1946–1987*, 30 Work & Occupations 327, 333 (2003).

[12] Calamuci, *supra* note 11, at 72.

[13] Horowitz, *supra* note 4, at 32, 35.

[14] Milkman, *supra* note 4.

[15] *Id.* at 88 ("By 1991, meatpacking was the most dangerous industry for workers in America."); *see also* Donald D. Stull & Michael J. Broadway, Slaughterhouse Blues: The Meat and Poultry Industry in North America 75 (2012).

[16] Milkman, *supra* note 4, at 90.

[17] *Id.* at 93; see also Stull & Broadway, *supra* note 15, at 16.

[18] Milkman, *supra* note 4, at 93.

[19] *Id.* at 31; *see also* Giovanni Peri & Chad Sparber, *Task Specialization, Immigration, and Wages*, 1 Am. Econ. J.: Applied Econs. 135–69 (2009) (documenting and discussing this worker complementarity).

[20] Peri & Sparber, *supra* note 19.

[21] Angela Stuesse, Scratching Out a Living: Latinos, Race, and Work in the Deep South 70 (2016).

four largest poultry companies, today employ more than 100,000 poultry processing workers and control almost 60 percent of the market.[22]

As with the slaughterhouses that process the meat of cows and pigs, poultry plants were also concentrated in states with legal regimes hostile to unionization. Anti-black racism has functioned as an effective tool for frustrating unionization efforts, pitting white workers against the Black workers who were increasingly entering the business in the 1960s after a long period of racial exclusion.[23] White workers with better job options than their Black coworkers (who confronted widespread racism) increasingly left the industry, and industry elites successfully discouraged efforts by the remaining workers to unionize.[24] Wages continued to stagnate; working conditions continued to be terrible.[25] Since the 1990s, following the trend set by the meatpacking plants of the Midwest, companies sought to fill their labor through the recruitment of refugees in the United States and foreign labor.[26] "By 2000, over half of the country's quarter-million poultry workers were immigrants, the vast majority of these foreign-born Hispanics."[27]

The changing labor needs of increasingly corporatized meat and poultry production in states politically hostile to unionization coincided with changes to immigration law that, for the first time, imposed numerical quotas on workers from Mexico

[22] *No Relief: Denial of Bathroom Breaks in the Poultry Industry*, Oxfam Am. Pol'y and Advoc. (2016) https://www.oxfamamerica.org/static/media/files/No_Relief_Embargo.pdf.

[23] Stuesse, *supra* note 21, at 62-64.

[24] *Id.* at 44–67; *see also* Angela Stuesse, *The Poultry Industry Recruited Them. Now ICE Raids Are Devastating Their Communities*, Wash. Post (Aug. 9, 2019), https://www.washingtonpost.com/outlook/2019/08/09/poultry-industry-recruited-them-now-ice-raids-are-devastating-their-communities/.

[25] Tom Fritzsche, *Unsafe at These Speeds: Alabama's Poultry Industry and Its Disposable Workers*, S. L. Poverty Ctr. (2013), https://www.splcenter.org/sites/default/files/Unsafe_at_These_Speeds_web.pdf; Michael Grabell, *Exploitation and Abuse at the Chicken Plant*, The New Yorker (May 8, 2017), https://www.newyorker.com/magazine/2017/05/08/exploitation-and-abuse-at-the-chicken-plant (describing abuses at Case Farms, and noting that in "2015 alone, federal workplace-safety inspectors fined the company nearly two million dollars, and in the past seven years it has been cited for two hundred and forty violations. That's more than any other company in the poultry industry except Tyson Foods, which has more than thirty times as many employees."); Stuesse, *supra* note 21, at 76; *see also* Jessica Ramsey et al., *Evaluation of Carpal Tunnel Syndrome and Other Musculoskeletal Disorders among Employees at a Poultry Processing Plant*, Health Hazard Evaluation Program (March 2015) (https://www.cdc.gov/niosh/hhe/reports/pdfs/2014-0040-3232.pdf); *No Relief*, *supra* note 22 (discussing the egregious working conditions in poultry processing plants); *Wages and Working Conditions in Arkansas Poultry Plants*, The Nw. Ark. Workers' Just. Ctr. (February 1, 2016), https://www.uusc.org/sites/default/files/wages_and_working_conditions_in_arkansas_poultry_plants.pdf.

[26] Stuesse, *supra* note 21, at 78–91.

[27] *Id.* at 10; *see also* Anna Williams Shavers, *Welcome to the Jungle: New Immigrants in the Meatpacking and Poultry Processing Industry*, 5 J. L. Econ. & Pol'y 31, 63–64 (2009) (recording that "non-Hispanic whites" made up 75 percent of slaughterhouse workers in 1990, but only 40 percent in 2000, with Latino workers making up most of the difference).

and Central America.[28] Unable to fit within the immigration quota categories designed for workers with high levels of formal education, and lacking the familial networks that would allow for lawful family-based immigration, these workers often came to the United States outside legal channels.[29] Mexican nationals constituted the overwhelming majority of these workers in the 1970s and 1980s,[30] though recruiters have increasingly focused on Central America as a site for worker recruitment in more recent years.[31]

Unsurprisingly, then, many of the people who work in meat and poultry processing today are undocumented.[32] The prevalence of undocumented workers in the industry is widely known and unofficially tolerated. Indeed, these industries extract profits from workers through the exploitation of the deportability of large segments of the workforce. The precarity of the undocumented immigrant workforce is echoed to some degree throughout the workforce. Immigrants present on temporary work visas are also quite vulnerable to industry exploitation, even though they are legally

[28] Until the mid-1960s, US agricultural and ranching employers actively recruited workers from Mexico under the auspices of a guest worker program known as the *Bracero* program. Congress ended the program in 1964. Kitty Calavita, Inside the State: The Bracero Program, Immigration, and the I.N.S. (1992). In 1965, Congress added the first-ever numeric cap on immigration from the Western Hemisphere. Act of Oct. 3, 1965, Pub. L. 89-236, 79 Stat. 911 (codified as amended at 18 U.S.C. §§ 1101–1537). These two legal changes did not end labor migration from south of the US border, but they did make that migration illegal. Muzaffar Chishti, Faye Hipsman, & Isabel Ball, *Fifty Years On, the 1965 Immigration and Nationality Act Continues to Reshape the United States*, Migration Pol'y Inst. (October 15, 2015), https://www.migrationpolicy.org/article/fifty-years-1965-immigration-and-nationality-act-continues-reshape-united-states.

[29] *Cf.* Hiroshi Motomura, Immigration outside the Law 38–41 (2014) (describing the forces that drive unauthorized migration into the United States and that structured the legal treatment of these immigrants after arrival).

[30] Mae Ngai, Impossible Subjects: Illegal Aliens and the Making of Modern America 58 (2004); *see also* Nicholas de Genova, *Migrant "Illegality" and Deportability in Everyday Life*, 31 Ann. Rev. Anthro. 419 (2002) (positing migrant "illegality" as a product of a sociolegal process of "illegalization," in addition to a consequential status designation).

[31] Central American workers of indigenous descent constituted the majority of the arrestees in both the Postville raid of 2007 and the Mississippi poultry plant raids of 2019. See Section 6.4. For a discussion of the role of Central American workers – largely from Indigenous communities– in the poultry industry, and the tensions between them and other immigrant workers from Mexico, Central and South America, *see, e.g.* Stuesse, *supra* note 21, at 151–53.

[32] The statistics are hard to come by and vary. But a 1998 GAO federal study estimated that 25 percent of meatpacking workers in Iowa and Nebraska were undocumented, and that trend continued into the next decade. See *Workplace Safety and Health: Safety in the Meat and Poultry Industry, While Improving, Could Be Further Strengthened*, GAO-05-96 (Jan. 12, 2005), https://www.govinfo.gov/content/pkg/GAOREPORTS-GAO-05-96/html/GAOREPORTS-GAO-05-96.htm ("we reported in 1998 that the U.S. Immigration and Naturalization Service [now the Citizenship and Immigration Services] had often found [unauthorized immigrants] employed in meatpacking plants; one agency official estimated that up to 25 percent of workers in meatpacking plants in Nebraska and Iowa were illegal aliens. As recently as March 2004, as the result of an internal audit, one large meatpacking company found 350 undocumented workers employed in one of its plants in the Midwest."); see also Shavers, *supra* note 27, at 63–64 (2009) (citing GAO reports and discussing implications).

authorized to work.[33] Refugees who have not yet become lawful permanent residents are also extremely vulnerable.[34] And lawful permanent residents and citizens experience the lack of bargaining power that comes with working in a heavily deportable workplace.[35] In other words, the precarity of the workforce extends far beyond and is amplified by the precarity of the undocumented workers in that workforce.

6.3 DEPORTABILITY AND RACE IN THE REALM OF INDUSTRIALIZED SLAUGHTER

An extensive literature documents the gap between the size of the unauthorized workforce in the United States and the scale of the governmental enforcement efforts that would be needed to achieve anything nearing perfect enforcement of the immigration laws as they are written. Public resources are insufficient to accomplish even a fraction of this goal. And that is true even looking only to the undocumented population, before one even considers the many immigrants authorized to live and work in the country, but potentially removable for other reasons. These resource choices reveal that the removal of all "deportable" workers is not now and has never been the goal of the federal government.

The threat of deportation,[36] often unrealized but omnipresent, in combination with the increasingly ubiquitous enforcement technologies of both governmental

[33] The H-2 visas for agricultural workers notoriously facilitate worker exploitation. *See, e.g.*, David Bacon, *Be Our Guest*, THE NATION, September 27, 2004.

[34] For an assessment of some of these vulnerabilities, *see, e.g.*, Donald Kerwin, *Faltering U.S. Refugee Protection System*, 31 REFUGEE SURV. Q. 1, 16–17 (noting that lawful permanent resident status is not automatic for refugees, but requires application after a year, creating vulnerability to removal in the period prior to obtaining LPR status.)

[35] Leticia Saucedo, *The Employer Preference for the Subservient Worker and the Making of the Brown Collar Workplace*, 67 OHIO ST. L.J. 961 (2006) (explaining that working conditions degenerate in workplaces largely made up of legally vulnerable workers); *see also* Jennifer Gordon & R.A. Lenhardt, *Rethinking Work and Citizenship*, 55 UCLA L. REV. 1161 (2008) (discussing the precarity of undocumented workers and the challenges this poses for coalition-building among workers); de Genova, *supra* note 30 (demonstrating how the deportability of workers renders them susceptible to workplace exploitation).

[36] In immigration law, "deportation" is a term of art, referring to the removal of an individual who has previously been inspected and admitted. Individuals who have not yet been admitted, including those who entered the country without inspection, are technically subject to grounds of inadmissibility, not grounds of deportation, and their removal from the country is legally treated as an exclusion, not a deportation. This is true no matter how long they reside in the country. Both deportation and exclusion are "removals."

Prior to 1996, anyone who had entered the country would have been placed in deportation proceedings, and those seeking to enter would be subject to exclusion. But Congress moved the line in 1996, making "admission," rather than entry the critical legal touchstone. Consequently, the proper legal term for the legal expulsion experienced by many undocumented workers is "removal" and not "deportation," because many were never formally admitted to the country. I nevertheless use the term "deportation" throughout this chapter to the legal removal of residents of the United States whether or not they have been formally

and private actors, instead operates as a mechanism of exploitative labor extraction. Nicolas de Genova has used the concept of "deportability" to explain the precarious and designedly exploitable condition of undocumented workers in the United States. Deportability is generated through a process of "illegalization" – official acts and policies instantiated by public and private actors that define certain segments of the population as existing outside of and in violation of the law, thereby exposing them to a constant threat of deportation. De Genova explains:

> It is precisely because of their distinctive legal vulnerability, their putative "illegality" and official "exclusion," that inflames the irrepressible desire and demand for undocumented migrants as a highly exploitable workforce – and thus ensures their enthusiastic importation and subordinate incorporation. And this is above all true because of the discipline imposed by their ultimate susceptibility to deportability.[37]

Deportability is a state-created condition that is leveraged by public and private actors to maximize labor extraction from a precarious group. In the United States, the exploitation of "deportable" workers is facilitated by the fact that many of these workers are barred from formal political participation. Their efforts to reshape policies to take into account their needs and reward their efforts are often thwarted by their political exclusion.[38] Political exclusion, in turn, is compounded by the language barriers encountered by those residents with limited ability to speak English.

> The exquisitely refined legal vulnerability of undocumented migrant labor – above all, materialized in its deportability – plainly serves to radically enhance the preconditions for its routinized subordination within the inherently despotic regime of the workplace...But this deportability likewise emerges as a telltale site where the totalizing procedures of otherwise partitioned "politics" and "economy" enter a zone of indistinction.[39]

This account of "deportability," which has been extensively redeployed throughout the literature on migration, offers a materially grounded account of contemporary migration management in which deportability is both a mechanism of political exclusion and a tool of labor exploitation, with the former reenforcing and facilitating the latter.

admitted. This term evokes a common understanding, and the violence of deportation is understood. It is worth noting, however, the ironic echoes of nineteenth-century "Indian removal," in the current legal use of the term "removal" to describe the displacement of hundreds of immigrant workers, many of whom belong to indigenous communities in their home countries.

[37] Nicholas de Genova, *The Deportation Regime: Sovereignty, Space and the Freedom of Movement*, in The Deportation Machine 47 (Nicholas de Genova & Nathalie Peutz, eds., 2010).

[38] This is not to discount the many ways in which noncitizens in the United States have actively and successfully pressed for policy changes.

[39] De Genova, *supra* note 30, at 47.

What is missing in the story of deportability recounted thus far, but readily evident in the history of the slaughterhouse and poultry processing industry, is the role of race in the production of deportability and the relationship between deportability and racism. Though the "illegalization" that generates deportability is a racialized practice, in many discussions of deportability, issues of race and racism are sidelined. Generally, race is treated as an epiphenomenon, notable to the extent that social constructions of race facilitate the targeting of the mechanisms of illegalization. But race is central to, constituted by, and productive of this set of material arrangements. The dual economic and political marginalization of racialized immigrant workers flows out of and reinforces US racism.

Racism is ideological, but it is not simply ideology. It has structural manifestations. As Moon-Kie Jung explains, racism includes "the structures of racial inequality and domination, not only the ideological component. Like other structures, racism is the reiterative articulation of schemas and resources through practices."[40] An analysis of immigration enforcement in the places where animals are killed to create meat and poultry reveals the racial project that undergirds and is fueled by the social construction of deportability.

As previously noted, the vulnerable immigration status of many line workers exists in a context of workforces that are now predominantly nonwhite. Jobs in meatpacking were shaped into less desirable positions as a result of deunionization, deregulation, and corporate restructuring at the very time that those jobs became a part of a whole new category of low-wage work stereotyped as "brown-collar" work in which Latinx workers dominate the industry.[41] Immigrant workers lacking formal education have increasingly filled the least desirable jobs in these undesirable workplaces, jobs that do not require English language skills.[42] English-speaking US workers typically work in other sectors, where English is required. Because English language ability is a key component of labor-market segregation, labor-market mobility is possible for some immigrant and Latinx workers who have work authorization and English proficiency.[43] Undocumented workers and non-English speakers, however, continue to fill the dirty and dangerous jobs that "are shunned by even the least educated U.S.-born workers."[44] And ultimately, even those workers who are lawful permanent residents or citizens experience the vulnerability produced by racial

[40] Moon-kie Jung, Beneath the Surface of White Supremacy: Denaturalizing U.S. Racisms Past and Present 31, 49 (2015). Jung borrows from and builds upon Eduardo Bonilla-Silva's structural theory of racism and the theory of structure developed by William Sewell, Jr. *Id.* at 21–48.

[41] Lisa Catanzarite, *Dynamics of Segregation and Earnings in Brown-Collar Occupations*, 29 Work and Occupations 300 (2002).

[42] Milkman, *supra* note 4, at 30 (citing David S. Massey and Magaly Sánchez R., Brokered Boundaries: Creating Immigrant Identity in Anti-Immigrant Times [2010]).

[43] *Id.*

[44] *Id.* at 26 (citing Giovanni Peri & C. Sparber, *Task Specialization, Immigration, and Wages*, 1 Am. Econ. J.: Applied Econs. 135 (2009)).

exclusion and overcriminalization. This is true in the narrow sense that vulnerable workers can sometimes make unionization and other worker-protective moves more difficult within a given workplace.[45] But it is also true in a broader sense, insofar as the tools for surveilling and controlling unauthorized workers are often turned against citizens. [46]

Slaughterhouses and poultry processing plants are far from the blue-state cities that are often the epicenter of analyses of deportability, illegalization, and securitization.[47] But as the historical account in the previous section makes clear, they operate in intimate and complex symbioses with those urban centers, and have histories deeply intertwined with them. At the same time, these sites are very different from the urban spaces where many recent studies of "deportable" workers are situated. One of the key features of the contemporary slaughterhouse or poultry processing plant is its relative social invisibility. As Tim Pachirat has argued, even when slaughterhouses are located within the bounds of relatively populous cities, they are designed to be low-visibility. "Facing outward, th[e] industrialized slaughterhouse blends seamlessly into the landscape of generic business parks ubiquitous in Everyplace, U.S.A., in the early twenty-first century."[48]

Patterns of immigration enforcement at these sites disrupt their near invisibility. Given the relatively high percentage of unauthorized workers in these spaces who lack official authorization to live and work in the United States, one might imagine that these workplaces would be prime targets for immigration enforcement. But that is not the case. Agribusinesses, slaughterhouses, and poultry plants are seldom sites of immigration enforcement. When enforcement actions do occur, they are usually low-visibility affairs, often initiated at the behest of managers and owners seeking to quell labor organizing efforts or complaints about working conditions.[49] But occasionally, the federal government leads highly-publicized immigration enforcement efforts at these sites. These efforts shine a bright, but selective, spotlight on spaces that are generally hiding in plain view. These spectacular immigration enforcement

45 *See* Gordon & Lenhardt, *supra* note 35; see also Saucedo, *supra* note 35.

46 *See, e.g.*, Jennifer M. Chacón et al., *Citizenship Matters: Conceptualizing Belonging in an Era of Fragile Inclusions*, 52 U.C. Davis L. Rev. 1 (2018) (describing how the policing of immigration status has an adverse effect on Latinos regardless of citizenship status). Indeed, the very existence and framing of trope of the "illegal migrant" functions to control citizens. Nicholas de Genova & Ananya Roy, *Practices of Illegalization*, 52 Antipode: A Radical J. of Geography 352 (2020) (exploring how "the denigration and castigation of the figure of the 'illegal migrant' has increasingly come to be pressed into service for the subjugation of citizens.").

47 Susan Bibler Coutin, *Confined Within: National Territories as Zones of Confinement*, 29 Pol. Geography 200–208 (2010). Coutin has argued that the securitization of immigration "entails both extraterritoriality, that is the extension of U.S. legal regimes into foreign territories, and intraterritoriality, or the operation of different legal regimes within national territories." *Id.*

48 Pachirat, *supra* note 7, at 23.

49 Michael J. Wishnie, *Prohibiting the Employment of Unauthorized Immigrants: The Experiment Fails*, 2007 U. Chi. Legal F. 193 (2007).

efforts are not only designed to serve as a reminder to immigrant workers of the threat of deportation, but also to validate and reinforce broader racial messages of belonging and exclusion. These enforcement efforts tap into and reproduce existing racial narratives of belonging and worth, and they directly contribute to material arrangements that reinscribe racial hierarchy.

6.4 SPECTACULAR IMMIGRATION ENFORCEMENT AT SITES OF INDUSTRIALIZED SLAUGHTER

Spectacular immigration enforcement is distinct from the immigration enforcement that occurs when government agents execute a few warrants, sometimes taking in a few, additional, "collateral" arrestees. Spectacular immigration enforcement involves planned, coordinated, high-visibility, high-publicity enforcement efforts. In the workplace, these efforts involve large numbers of heavily armed federal, state and local law-enforcement officials. They result in the arrest, sometimes the prosecution, and always the removal, of hundreds of people at affected sites. In instances of spectacular enforcement, the federal government generally has a small number of warrants targeting a handful of managers, or even owners, of a plant, usually for violations of tax laws or of the 1986 Immigration Reform and Control Act's requirement of employer verification of worker authorization. But these enforcement efforts unfold through the large-scale, on-site arrests of hundreds of employees – for whom no warrants exist – on the grounds that those workers are unable to demonstrate at the time of the raid that they are legally authorized to live and work in the United States. Though punishment may ultimately be imposed on the midlevel managers or relatively small-time business owners that are the purported target of the precipitating warrants, the mass removal of immigrant workers from subordinated racial groups is the most significant and visible fruit of these raids.[50]

The enforcement is "spectacular" in that government officials seek to create a spectacle through their efforts. With heavy armaments brought to bear against hundreds of unarmed civilians, these enforcement efforts prop up a narrative that immigrant workers are "dangerous" to the public. As litigation documents at the site of these efforts make clear, officials target only those workers who fit the preexisting

[50] An ICE report in 2013 revealed, for example, that even at the height of the Obama Administration's efforts to shift the focus of enforcement efforts from workers to employers, of the 452 worksite *criminal* arrests they made in fiscal year 2013, only 179 of those arrests were of managers or employers. U.S. Immigration and Customs Enforcement, *Worksite Enforcement*, Dep't of Homeland Sec. (Apr. 1, 2013), https://www.ice.gov/factsheets/worksite. The pattern in high-profile raids would suggest that most of those arrests are for low- and mid-level managers. The majority of criminal arrests are of immigrant workers. And the arrest numbers do not even take into account the number of immigrant workers removed on civil immigration grounds. *See, e.g.*, Complaint, Zelaya v. Hammer, No. 19-cv-00062, 2019 WL 5883130 (E.D. Tenn. Feb. 21, 2019) (alleging that only 11 of 100 arrested workers were charged with a crime in a mass roundup of immigrant workers at a Bean, Tennessee, meatpacking plant).

racial script of criminalized immigration enforcement – those who are deemed to be "foreign."[51] This often means that they single out Latinx workers, notwithstanding the fact that many of those workers are, in fact, legally authorized to work. By sorting workers into the presumptively "legal" and the presumptively "illegal," using race as a sorting device, officials participating in these enforcement efforts not only draw from, but also reinforce, narratives of belonging and exclusion.

The racial spectacle of enforcement is enhanced through the extraordinary efforts undertaken to secure the rapid, mass prosecution and removal of as many workers as possible. Judges and prosecutors, who are largely white, preside over improvised spaces where nonwhite workers are brought before them in streamlined fashion – and sometimes only via videoconference – so that they can plead guilty to criminal charges or engage in largely futile efforts to challenge their deportation. Government officials deliberately make examples of these workers, citing their violations of civil immigration law and their use of borrowed social security numbers as moral wrongs that justify the separation of their families and upending of whole communities.

Spectacular immigration enforcement is nothing new. The efforts of US states and the federal government to exclude Chinese immigrants – and to banish long-term Chinese residents – at the end of the nineteenth century included clear, early examples of such efforts. The Palmer raids of the 1920s, the so-called Mexican repatriation of the 1930s, and "Operation Wetback" and accompanying enforcement efforts in the 1950s all epitomize spectacular immigration enforcement. The racial motivations and effects of these earlier examples are clear, and official efforts were often accompanied by massive private violence against the targets of enforcement.[52]

In the post–Civil Rights era, express targeting of individuals on account of their race ended. There was no more "Chinese Exclusion" or "Mexican repatriation." But immigration status facilitated the targeting of workers in ways that reproduced expressly racist immigration policies. In the 1970s and 1980s, enforcement patterns settled into regular, disruptive factory raids, like the one that the Supreme Court endorsed in the 1984 case of *INS v. Delgado*, where racial profiling served as the key to both site selection and the selection of workers to target within sites.[53] The passage

[51] *See, e.g.*, Complaint, Zelaya v. Hammer, No. 19-cv-00062, 2019 WL 5883130 (E.D. Tenn. Feb. 21, 2019) (alleging that only Latino workers were arrested in a plant raid where 100 workers were subjected to warrantless arrests on-site).

[52] *See, e.g.*, Francisco Baldarrama & Raymond Rodríguez, Decade of Betrayal: Mexican Repatriation in the 1930s (2006); Kelly Lytle Hernández, City of Inmates: Conquest, Rebellion, and the Rise of Human Caging in Los Angeles, 1771–1965 73–91 (2017) (describing the horrific violence targeting Chinese immigrants in California as officials worked to enforce the Chinese Exclusion Act); *see also* K-Sue Park, *Self-Deportation Nation*, 132 Harv. L. Rev. 1878 (discussing the role of private violence in effectuating deportation).

[53] 466 U.S. 210 (1984).

of the Immigration Reform and Control Act of 1986,[54] which for the first time penalized (and, in some instances, criminalized) the hiring of unauthorized workers, did little to change prevailing patterns of enforcement. Wealthy farmers, ranchers, and business owners continued to use their political power to oppose unwanted enforcement actions in their jurisdictions. Enforcement functioned selectively and sporadically, much more as a tool for labor control than a means of regulating migration.[55] Mexican workers were the primary target of these efforts. These enforcement efforts took advantage of the Supreme Court's prior legitimation of extraordinary policing practices targeting of people perceived as "Mexican" in immigration enforcement and related criminal legal investigations.[56]

When the September 11, 2001, attacks on the United States prompted a reorganization and massive expansion of the immigration enforcement bureaucracy, new purposes had to be found for new resources. In addition to substantial border militarization, the expansion of detention capacity, and the further externalization of US border-control efforts, this also meant new forms of interior enforcement.[57] The resulting, invigorated interior enforcement included the creation and national implementation of the Secure Communities program. Under Secure Communities, every state and local arrest is now checked against a federal immigration enforcement database, allowing federal officials to request that targets of interest be held by state or local officials pending transfer to federal custody.[58] The Secure Communities program is the point of origin for the majority of deportations from within the United States today.[59]

Interior enforcement also expanded in the form of increased direct enforcement efforts by federal immigration officials, largely in the workplace. Though direct

54 Act of Nov. 6, 1986, Pub. L. 99-603, 100 Stat. 3359 (codified as amended at 18 U.S.C. §§ 1101 *et seq.*).

55 Wishnie, *supra* note 49.

56 *See, e.g.*, United States v. Brignoni-Ponce, 422 U.S. 873 (1975) (finding that "the public interest demands effective measures to prevent the illegal entry of aliens at the Mexican border," and that this justified stopping vehicles on the basis of the occupants "apparent Mexican ancestry" taken together with factors like "proximity to the border" or "haircut"); United States v. Martinez-Fuerte, 428 U.S. 543, 551, 556, 564 & n.17, n.18 (1976) (noting "the substantiality of the public interest in the practice of routine stops for inquiry at permanent checkpoints" to prevent the entry of immigrants seeking work in the United States, sufficient to justify random vehicle stops at checkpoints on the basis of "apparent Mexican ancestry"); INS v. Lopez-Mendoza, 468 U.S. 1032, 1046, 1049 (1984) (noting the "staggering dimensions" of the problem of unauthorized migrant workers, and analogizing the harm of the continuing presence of unauthorized immigrants to a "leaking hazardous waste dump" in rejecting the application of the exclusionary rule to workplace raid search and seizure practices that violate the Fourth Amendment).

57 Doris Meissner et al., Migration Policy Inst., Immigration Enforcement in the United States: The Rise of a Formidable Machinery (2013).

58 *Id.*

59 See Randy Capps et al., *Revving up the Deportation Machinery: Enforcment under Trump and the Pushback*, Migration Policy Inst. (2018), – https://www.migrationpolicy.org/research/revving-deportation-machinery-under-trump-and-pushback.

enforcement results in far fewer removals than the less visible Secure Communities program, these direct enforcement efforts are significant precisely because of their visibility. In contrast to Secure Communities, which works in quiet, technocratic fashion in the jail spaces that already operate on the edges of public consciousness, direct enforcement efforts aim to bring less-visible social spaces into the light. Here again, race operates to sort the targets of enforcement.

One of the most significant example of spectacular immigration enforcement during the presidential administration of George W. Bush took place on May 12, 2008. On that day, government officials orchestrated a massive raid on a meatpacking plant in Postville, Iowa. The raid resulted in the arrest, criminal prosecution, and removal of hundreds of immigrant workers and drew significant media and scholarly attention.[60]

The raid was described vividly by Erik Camayd-Freixas, who went to Postville to serve as a translator in administrative proceedings. He writes:

> On May 12, 2008, this tiny Heartland farm town, secluded amid the rolling hills and cornfields of northern Iowa, became the site of the largest immigration raid in U.S. history. Of the 389 people arrested, three-quarters were Kaq'chikel ethnic Mayans from the hills of Chimaltenango, Guatemala. Only five (1.2%) had minor criminal records. Yet they were all arraigned on felony charges of identity theft, making this an unprecedented criminalization of migrant workers. Despite begging to be deported, these Agriprocessors employees were jailed for 5 to 12 months while their families suffered severe hardship. A decision made in Washington, D.C. destroyed the livelihoods and hopes of hundreds of working families and sank well over a thousand children, from Iowa to Guatemala, deeper into poverty and malnutrition, while serving to perpetuate the generational cycle of labor migration.
>
> The direct cost of this raid to taxpayers, including prosecution and detention, is close to $10 million. But government expense was dwarfed in comparison to the economic impact on the tri-state region. Unable to replace its workforce and facing mounting civil and criminal penalties, the employer, Agriprocessors kosher slaughterhouse, was forced into bankruptcy. This yielded a projected $300 million a year in regional loss of business for family farms and ordinary Americans, as well as an additional estimated annual loss of $7 million in remittances to some of the poorest families in Mexico and Guatemala. The raid will have lasting economic, social and political impacts at local, regional, national and international levels. It is a landmark case.[61]

[60] For media reports and analysis, *see, e.g.*, Editorial, *The Shame of Postville*, N.Y. TIMES (July 13, 2008); Nigel Duara, Grant Schulte & William Petroski, *ID Fraud Claims Bring State's Largest Raid*, DES MOINES REG. (May 13, 2008), at 1A; Editorial, *Raid a Reminder of Need for Reform*, DES MOINES REG. (May 14, 2008), at 12A; for scholarly commentary, *see, e.g.*, Sioban Albiol, R. Linus Chan & Sarah J. Diaz, *Re-interpreting Postville: A Legal Perspective*, 2 DEPAUL J. FOR SOC. JUST. 31 (2008); *see also* notes 61-62, *infra*.

[61] Erik Camayd-Freixas, *Raids, Rights and Reform: The Postville Case and the Immigration Crisis*, 2 DEPAUL J. FOR SOC. JUST. 1, 1–2 (2008).

Bill Ong Hing situates this raid in the broader context of agricultural workplace raids undertaken by the George W. Bush administration in the period leading up to and including the Postville raid. ICE conducted several major raids at meatpacking plants in the period from 2004 to 2008, perpetuating "racial profiling,... trauma to children and families, [and] damage to communities."[62] At the meatpacking and poultry processing raids he describes, the workers targeted were exclusively Latino. For example, Hing describes the Swift raids of 2006, in which numerous ICE agents executing warrants for fewer than 1 percent of the company's employees rounded up and detained some 13,000 workers in Swift plants across Iowa.

> The sheer number of ICE agents on the scene and the manner in which the operation was conducted made clear that the execution of those warrants was not the government's real purpose. Rather, the raids seemed designed to ramp up the number of arrests and capture the headlines on the evening news.[63]

Hing also documents an evening raid on a community of Latino workers at a poultry processing plant in Stillman, Georgia, in 2006, in which 125 workers were arrested, and a 2007 raid in New Bedford, Massachusetts, where 500 ICE agents descended on a leather goods factory and detained hundreds of workers, primarily from Central America.[64] Although significant immigration enforcement efforts occurred elsewhere,[65] sites of animal slaughter and processing were the staging grounds for many of the largest and most spectacular immigration raids orchestrated by the new Department of Homeland Security under President George W. Bush.

President Obama's administration largely backed away from this kind of large-scale, spectacular raid. The workplace enforcement efforts of Postville and New Bedford made way for "silent raids" – in which government inspectors examined workplace documentation at many different kinds of businesses for paperwork irregularities around employee work authorization. Indeed, rather than engaging in spectacular raids of agrobusinesses, meatpacking plants, and poultry processing facilities, the Obama Administration sometimes opted for strategies that strengthened the protections of workers in those workplaces, including by allowing the Department of Labor to provide law enforcement certifications to enable workers alleging wage, hour, and conditions violations by their employer to access U visas.[66] Immigration enforcement shifted, for a time, from a tool of pure labor

[62] Bill Ong Hing, *Institutional Racism, ICE Raids, and Immigration Reform*, 44 U.S.F. L. Rev. 307, 308 (2009).

[63] *Id.* at 311.

[64] *Id.* at 315–17.

[65] Shortly after the Postville raids, for example, the government staged a massive raid of the Howard Industries factory in Mississippi that exceeded even the Postville raid in its scale. Associated Press, *Feds Detain Nearly 600 in Miss. Plant Raid*, NBC News (Aug. 26, 2008), https://www.nbcnews.com/id/wbna26410407.

[66] *See* Stephen Lee, *Monitoring Immigration Enforcement*, 53 Ariz. L. Rev. 1089, 1126 & n.144 (noting the Department of Labor's decision under President Obama to certify U visa

subjugation to a tool that, at the margins, could occasionally empower a small number of workers in the workplace.

The broader enforcement strategy of the Obama Administration, however, increasingly *criminalized* immigrant workers, particularly through heavy reliance on state and federal criminal law as an immigration enforcement sorting mechanism after the widespread implementation of the inaptly named Secure Communities program.[67] Consequently, the administration's ameliorative shifts in workplace enforcement strategies were eclipsed by the effects of an immigration enforcement strategy that parroted and amplified racialized tropes of migrant criminality specifically, and the criminality of Black and Latinx individuals more generally. Obama-era policies may have disfavored the racial theater of spectacular enforcement, but the administration's more technocratic and automated enforcement efforts, coupled with its strategy of detaining families to deter Central American asylum seekers at the southern border, relied upon and continued fueling the underlying racial narrative of immigration enforcement. Immigrants from south of the US-Mexico border were treated as dangerous risks to be managed, and the task of risk management was delegated largely to the criminal justice infrastructure that the administration, ironically, was simultaneously critiquing on the grounds of its racial disproportionality.

When the Trump Administration came into office, the federal government abandoned any pretense of seeking to protect unauthorized immigrant workers.[68] The administration's enforcement strategies shifted back into full alignment with corporate interests and away from any form of workplace protection. The Trump Administration brought back the spectacular raids of the George W. Bush era, and combined these efforts with an overtly racist rhetoric that made no effort to hide the objective of these raids: to degrade, demean, and criminalize immigrant workers, particular Black and Latinx immigrant workers, around the country.[69] At the same time, most companies and company executives that employed unauthorized workers continued to thrive. Indeed, President Trump even pardoned Sholom Rubashkin, the highest-ranking official to be prosecuted in connection with the Postville raids, whose twenty-seven-year prison sentence had, in fact, been an extraordinary deviation in a world where executives generally receive no criminal penalties for their

applicants); *see also* Leticia Saucedo, *A New "U": Organizing Victims and Protecting Immigrant Workers*, 42 U. RICH. L. REV. 891 (2008) (advocating for government use of U visas to advance workplace protections).

67 There is no evidence that Secure Communities actually increased the security of any communities. *See* Thomas J. Miles & Adam Cox, *Does Immigration Enforcement Reduce Crime? Evidence from Secure Communities*, 57 J. L. & ECON. 937 (concluding that the Secure Communities program has had no observable effect on the overall crime rate).

68 *Immigration and the Bully Pulpit*, 130 HARV. L. REV. F. 243 (2017).

69 *See, e.g.*, Daniel Alvord, Cecilia Menjívar & Andrea Gómez Cervantes, *The Legal Violence in the 2017 Executive Orders: The Expansion of Immigrant Criminalization in Kansas*, 5 SOC. CURRENTS 411 (2018).

employment of unauthorized workers.[70] Unsurprisingly, none of the hundreds of immigrant workers convicted of charges like identity theft received pardons.

Three examples of immigration raids that took place under President Donald J. Trump – an April 2018 raid of a meatpacking plant in Bean Station, Tennessee; a June 2018 raid at a meatpacking plant in Salem, Ohio; and a massive, seven-site raid of poultry processing plants in Mississippi in August 2019 – illustrate the Trump Administration's elevation of spectacular enforcement to new prominence.

On April 5, 2018, federal immigration enforcement officials raided a meatpacking plant in Bean Station, Tennessee, in which they arrested and placed ninety-seven workers into removal proceedings. The pretext for the raid was the service of warrants on the owners of the facility for tax violations, yet workers were rounded up en masse by the agents at the facility. A lawsuit filed in federal court, *Zelaya v. Hammer*, offers detailed assertions that only the Latino workers at the meatpacking plant were detained, and that they were detained regardless of their immigration status.[71] Some were allegedly assaulted by ICE officers.[72]

When it occurred, the Bean Station raid was the immigration service's largest raid since 2008,[73] but this record did not last long. On June 19, 2018, more than 146 workers were arrested by ICE agents at four northern Ohio locations of the Fresh Mark pork processing company. "ICE agents arrived at the meat plant with federal and state search warrants, but without providing any notice to the owners. The ICE agents descended upon Fresh Mark in helicopters with attack dogs and assault rifles, giving the impression that employees of the meat supplier were not free to leave."[74] In addition to placing the workers in removal proceedings, the federal government filed criminal charges against thirteen people for making false claims of citizenship and using the identity documents of another person.[75]

Both of these raids were subsequently dwarfed on August 7, 2019, when federal agents arrested 680 immigrant workers from seven chicken processing plants in Central Mississippi.[76] Although ICE purported to be executing warrants for a handful of middle managers, those individuals were not even arrested on the day

[70] Mitch Smith, *President Commutes Sentence of Iowa Meatpacking Executive*, N.Y. TIMES, (Dec. 20, 2017), at A21.

[71] Zelaya v. Hammer, No. 19-cv-00062, 2019 WL 5883130, at *3 (E.D. Tenn. Feb. 21, 2019).

[72] *Id.* at *32.

[73] Meredith Hoffman, *Inside ICE's Biggest, Most Aggressive Raid under Trump*, VICE (Apr. 9, 2018), https://www.vice.com/en_us/article/d354mw/inside-ices-biggest-most-aggressive-raid-under-trump.

[74] G. Piantini, *Welcome to Trump's Ice Age: Violations of Undocumented Immigrants' Fourth Amendment Rights during Workplace Raids*, 32 ST. THOMAS L. REV. 77, 77–78 (2019).

[75] UNITED STATES ATTORNEY'S OFFICE, NORTHERN DISTRICT OF OHIO, PRESS RELEASE: THIRTEEN PEOPLE INDICTED FOR IMMIGRATION-RELATED OFFENSES FOLLOWING DETENTION NEAR SALEM (2018), https://www.justice.gov/usao-ndoh/pr/thirteen-people-indicted-immigration-related-offenses-following-detention-near-salem.

[76] Alissa Zhu, *ICE Raids: 4 Poultry Execs Indicted*, CLARION-LEDGER (Aug. 7, 2020).

of the raids.[77] And while four of these managers were eventually indicted for immigration related crimes, it was the workers who bore virtually all of the civil and immigration consequences of the raids.[78]

Workers arrested in the Mississippi raids were bused to a local Mississippi National Guard hangar to be interviewed about their immigration status.[79] During the 2008 Postville raid, hundreds of people had been criminally tried and subjected to civil removal orders at the plant site.[80] The 2019 Mississippi raids replicated this use of improvised courts in unusual spaces to assure quick case processing. US Immigration and Customs Enforcement Deputy Director Matthew Albence reported that on the same day as the raid itself that the federal government had already issued 126 indictments and obtained 73 convictions.[81]

Thus, in the course of just over a year, the federal government deployed significant personal, weaponry, and fiscal resources to secure the arrest of more than a thousand, and the removal of hundreds of immigrant workers – mostly Mexican and Central American – in a highly visible series of workplace raids at meatpacking and poultry processing plants.

The violence that these raids inflicted on immigrant workers is undeniable. For example, after the initial, stunning arrest of 680 workers in Mississippi, about 300 were released over the course of the day that followed on "humanitarian grounds," so that they could go home while awaiting their removal proceedings. But

> the Clarion Ledger and USA Today found that in some instances, breastfeeding mothers and single parents were kept in detention. Care of the children sometimes fell to extended family, friends or a neighbor. After the raids, chicken plants laid workers off. Hundreds of families were left without a source of income and had to rely on donations collected by local religious organizations and nonprofits to pay their bills and put food on the table.[82]

And, of course, hundreds of families were sundered and displaced as a result of the raid. Professor Camayd-Freixas's assessment of the economic and social devastation wrought by the Postville raids has been replicated in the aftermath of these other raids as well: the increased impoverishment and immiseration of working families already living on the edge; lost remittances in countries suffering from the ongoing harms of neocolonial exploitation and climate change; and lost jobs due to declining productivity of the processing facilities.

[77] *Id.*
[78] *Id.*
[79] Richard Gonzalez, *Mississippi Immigration Raids Lead to Arrests of Hundreds of Workers*, NPR (Aug. 7, 2019), https://www.npr.org/2019/08/07/749243985/mississippi-immigration-raids-net-hundreds-of-workers.
[80] Freixas, *supra* note 61, at 1–2.
[81] Zhu, *supra* note 76.
[82] *Id.*

6.5 RACIALIZED DEPORTABILITY

What justifies the imposition of such large-scale harm on communities of workers? Local reporting on these raids captures how government employees construct a narrative of harm and criminal wrongdoing to justify their own violent acts. A year after the coordinated Mississippi raids, on August 7, 2020, federal officials hosted a high-profile press conference in Jackson, Mississippi, to announce the resulting criminal prosecutions. These officials staged the press conference in a way that drew upon and reinforced the racial logics of the broader immigration enforcement narrative.

At the press conference, seven middle-aged white men flank a middle-aged white male prosecutor, Michael Hurst, who stands at a podium outside the federal courthouse announcing the indictment of four middle managers at the poultry plants, and more than one hundred immigrant workers charged with document-related criminal offenses, but no indictments for corporate executives. All of the men are masked for COVID protection, even as many of the targets of their enforcement efforts languish in COVID-ridden detention facilities.[83] Midway through a thirty-eight-minute press conference, Hurst swaps places with Matt Albence, another middle-aged white man and the Acting Director of ICE. The two men then exchange places at the podium while taking questions from the press.

The men at the podium stress the criminality of their targets and posit that "American citizens" were their victims. US Attorney Mike Hurst claims that he is "pro-legal immigration all day long" while citing the need to prosecute those who immigrate without legal authorization.[84] He criticizes the "sensational" new stories that focused on the disruption of the lives of hundreds of families and the surrounding communities, and suggests that the true harm was experienced by "American citizens victimized by identity fraud," including "an 8-year-old boy, a teen who was trying to enter the U.S. Navy and a woman with mental health issues who lost her social security benefits and medicine because of the fraud."[85] Albence, the Acting ICE director, emphasizes the fact that "illegal immigration. . .feeds criminality" by funneling money to human traffickers who smuggle people across the border.[86] Neither Hurst nor Albence acknowledge the fact that neither document fraud nor smuggling would be necessary but for arbitrary limits on immigration. Restrictive

[83] As of March 2021, the UCLA COVID Behind Bars project had documented 112 reported COVID cases in ICE detention facilities in Mississippi. *See COVID-19 Behind Bars Data Project*, UCLA LAW https://uclacovidbehindbars.org/. The actual numbers are probably much higher. See Dennis Kuo et al., *The Hidden Curve: Estimating the Spread of* COVID-19 *among People in ICE Detention*, VERA (June 2020), https://www.vera.org/the-hidden-curve-covid-19-in-ice-detention (concluding that "there is no scenario in which the data ICE has reported to the public reflects the true scope of the spread of COVID-19 in [immigration] detention.").

[84] Zhu, *supra* note 76.

[85] *Id.*

[86] *Id.*

US immigration laws illegalize migrants. By criminalizing people for lacking access to documents that are not available to them, federal and (increasingly) state governments engage in what Amada Armenta describes as making lawbreakers.[87]

Acting ICE Director Albence goes on to analogize the poultry plant workers' borrowing of other people's social security numbers – numbers used to secure difficult, dirty, and dangerous work – to stealing a high-end car. The *Clarion-Ledger* reported his words:

> "I may want to go out and buy a Jaguar tomorrow," Albence said. "I don't have the money to buy a Jaguar. Does that mean I can go out and steal money, because I don't feel like waiting until I earn enough money to go buy a Jaguar? You just can't commit crime because you don't have the ability. There's a legal way to do it."

Albence's analogy is revealing. First, it equates the act of securing work to fulfill human needs for food, shelter, and physical security with the purchase of a luxury car. In this way, Albence positions basic human needs as undeserved luxuries for these workers. He simultaneously promotes what he, as ICE director, must know to be a falsehood when he suggests that these workers *could have* legally immigrated if they had so chosen. In fact, for most of these workers there was and still is no "legal way" to immigrate and obtain status to work. This rhetorical move is important because it presents the workers as line jumpers and usurpers,[88] and therefore entirely undeserving of these jobs, while masking another well-known fact: the industry deliberately recruits them to perform this work in spite of, or perhaps more properly because of, their immigration status.[89] Indeed, many of the workers initially arrested in the Mississippi raids actually were allowed by their employers to return to work with new sets of false documents when the COVID-19 pandemic resulted in worker shortages, illustrating the primacy of the labor management function of these raids over their immigration control function.[90] Albence never acknowledges this fact.

Albence also glosses over the reality that in the vast majority of these document offense cases, a worker's act of borrowing identity documents generates no actual harm or loss to the person whose identity is borrowed, and the worker intends no such harm or loss. While some people occasionally engage in acts of identity theft for monetary gain, that is not what is happening in the overwhelming majority of

87 Amada Armenta, Protect, Serve and Deport: The Rise of Policing as Immigration Regulation 3 (2017) (describing how the Tennessee legislature made people into lawbreakers by prohibiting them from obtaining a driver's license).

88 On the significance of the line metaphor in contemporary understandings of fairness, see Arlie Russell Hochschild, Strangers in Their Own Land: Anger and Mourning on the American Right 260 (2016). Though she never adequately grapples with the point, Hochschild's interviews reveal the extent to which white racial entitlement structures social understandings of the proper order of the line.

89 *See, e.g.*, Milkman, *supra* note 4, at 93.

90 Maria Hinojosa & Reynaldo Leaños, Jr., Mississippi Rising, Latino USA Podcast, October 15, 2021.https://www.latinousa.org/2021/10/15/mississippirising//.

these cases. In fact, Albence's analogy actually would be more apt if applied to the corporate executives who knowingly recruit and rely upon an unauthorized workforce in order to increase their profit margins. The analogy even works for the consumers of beef and poultry (presumably including Hurst and Albence) who can save money for their own new cars because the work of unauthorized immigrants makes their food cheaper. There is plenty of wrongdoing to go around. But with few exceptions, it is the Latino worker that bears the brunt of the punishment, with significant spillover effects upon the lives of their coworkers and community members.

The Jaguar theft analogy, in all of its flaws, brilliantly limns what is actually going on in cases of spectacular immigration enforcement. The racialized deportability that is reconstructed in every instance of spectacular immigration enforcement is an important element of broader racial schema. US Attorney Hurst speaks about how people who immigrate to work without authorization "deserve prosecution," and he clearly holds out the mass raids and the ensuing prosecutions as sending a signal designed to deter these types of legal violation. But the workers are not really the intended audience for this press conference, and the messages telegraphed by the press conference are different from those that Hurst explicitly conveys. At every level, the press conference seeks to legitimate the racial violence that unfolded on the day of the raids – in which a white power structure engages in a massive deployment of force, caging, and family separation aimed exclusively at nonwhite workers. The intended recipients of this message are not just the workers in meatpacking plants and processing facilities; this message is intended for white Americans anxious about their racial status.

Of Trump's enforcement policies, Adam Serwer once famously wrote that "the cruelty is the point."[91] He observed the ways that white US citizens often have had the opportunity to bond around racialized spectacles of cruelty. Using the example of white mobs leering joyously at the sight of the lynching of Black people, he posits that Trump's policies operate as a continuation of such efforts – allowing racial in-groups to bond over the violent subjugation of racial outsiders.[92] The mass mobilization of enforcement agents and the high-profile press conferences that accompany these spectacular immigration enforcement efforts benefit those members of the community who derive psychic benefit from the humiliation of members of other racial groups. Enforcement efforts at slaughterhouses tend to be quite costly for communities, and they do not lead to significant new jobs for authorized workers. But they do important work to shore up the same exclusionary narrative that is threaded through the fabric of life in the United States. Without undercutting the availability of a precarious workforce, these sporadic, spectacular, and performative

[91] Adam Serwer, *The Cruelty Is the Point*, The Atl. (Oct. 3, 2018), https://www.theatlantic.com/ideas/archive/2018/10/the-cruelty-is-the-point/572104/.

[92] *Id.*

enforcement efforts operate as an important form of racial theater, and in so doing, reify foundational racial scripts.

The Jaguar story, as told by Albence on the steps of the Jackson courthouse, is perfectly crafted to reaffirm the power of the dominant racial group, and to justify that group's ongoing, racialized acts of violence. This is not simply about the generation of a deportable class of immigrant workers, but about reinscribing a broader social narrative about who is worthy, and who belongs. The whiteness of the press conference is an important background fact that cements the perfection of the racial spectacle. Jackson, Mississippi, is a city of 160,000 people, and 82 percent of the city's residents are Black. But not a single Black person stands in front of the federal courthouse at this press conference. The workers targeted for prosecution – invisible at the press conference – are all Latino, many of them indigenous. On land seized from the Choctow people two hundred years ago, racial removal remains a constitutive force of both state and nation.

6.6 CONCLUSION

Against the backdrop of an industry that works extraordinarily hard to stay out of sight, the splashy press conference in Jackson, Mississippi, makes plain that there is a broad audience for spectacular enforcement. These efforts communicate a story about who belongs and who does not. Belonging is coded, and not subtly, in racial terms. The logic of immigration and criminal law enforcement are offered up to justify the unequal distribution of material wealth toward white workers and away from the Latino workforce, and away from all workers in favor of a largely white economic elite. The actual labor of the workforce – and the centrality of their work to the sanitization of global consumption of nonhuman animals – is meticulously concealed, even as their purported transgressions against "Americans," are highlighted and exaggerated.

The literature on deportability focuses (rightly) on the ways that the racialized practice of immigration policing sends a signal to vulnerable workers that they are the targets of ongoing surveillance and enforcement efforts. But a focus on spectacular enforcement reveals how the signaling function of immigration enforcement is aimed not only, and perhaps not even primarily, at workers and their employers. By targeting certain people for treatment that is demeaning by design, spectacular immigration enforcement efforts naturalize racial violence.

Spectacular immigration enforcement illustrates with extraordinary clarity the need for "a context-sensitive politics of sight."[93] Read one way, these highly visible enforcement efforts "shine a light" on the labor practices in meatpacking and poultry processing plants, revealing these industries' deep reliance on unauthorized

[93] Pachirat, *supra* note 7, at 255.

immigrant labor. But these moments of illumination conceal as much as they reveal. Like the design of the meatpacking plants themselves, they allow for "sequestration. . .even under conditions of total visibility."[94] Press conference consumers confront images of criminalized, foreign workers without seeing historical and contemporary forces that have set the stage for this particular show.

[94] *Id.*

7

Against a "War on Animal Cruelty"

Lessons from the War on Drugs and Mass Incarceration

Sam Kamin

7.1 INTRODUCTION

On November 25, 2019, President Trump signed into law the Preventing Animal Cruelty and Torture Act (PACT), the first federal law punishing animal cruelty. PACT makes it a crime, punishable by up to seven years in prison, to engage in "conduct in which one or more living nonhuman mammals, birds, reptiles, or amphibians is purposely crushed, burned, drowned, suffocated, impaled, or otherwise subjected to serious bodily injury."[1]

While PACT is the first federal law on the topic, it is part of a broader move to criminalize harm to nonhuman animals throughout the nation. Often spurred on by animal advocacy groups, states are increasingly using their own criminal justice systems as a tool in combating the abuse of nonhuman animals. In fact, it is fair to say that an arms race has developed among the states, with organizations like the Animal Legal Defense Fund (ALDF) annually rating various state law regimes on their punitiveness toward animal abuse. For example, the ALDF gives higher rankings to states that criminalize the possession of animal-fighting paraphernalia than those that merely permit the seizure of such items, rewards states for imposing lifetime bans on pet ownership following an animal cruelty conviction, and credits mandatory reporting of abuse by veterinarians.[2] To qualify as a top-five state under the ALDF's ranking, a state must not just criminalize, but impose felony punishments for cruelty, neglect, fighting, abandonment, and sexual assault.[3] In other words, the more punitively a state deals with the problem of animal cruelty, the higher it will rate in the ALDF's rubric.

1 18 U.S.C. § 48(f)(1).

2 Animal Legal Defense Fund, Animal Protection US State Laws Ranking Report, 2019 at 14–18.

3 *Id.* at 20.

Upon the passage of PACT, Kitty Block, the president and CEO of the Humane Society of the United States, praised the law, stating that "PACT makes a statement about American values."[4] Unfortunately, that statement may be far truer than Ms. Block intended – for PACT and its sister laws in the states are emblematic of America's embrace of the criminal justice system as the principal means of addressing myriad societal harms. In this chapter I argue that the embrace of a punitive system of animal protection at both the state and federal levels will have unintended, but certainly foreseeable, negative consequences in the years to come.

Drawing on the related but distinct phenomena of mass incarceration, America's fifty-year War on Drugs, this chapter warns that a carceral approach to animal cruelty will result in a net-widening effect whereby the criminal justice system extends its reach into the daily lives of more and more Americans. Perhaps more perniciously, the criminalization of animal cruelty is very likely to have a disproportionate impact on the poor and people of color, an impact that will go far beyond the number of people actually prosecuted or convicted under the raft of new state and federal criminal laws going into effect.

7.2 FACTS AND MYTHS ABOUT MASS INCARCERATION IN THE UNITED STATES

America's mass incarceration problem is well documented. As of last count, more than 2 million people were currently being held in America's prisons and jails.[5] But while this number is a matter of public record, myths and misinformation about mass incarceration continue to persist. To understand this phenomenon properly, it is important to understand its relatively recent vintage. Between 1925 and 1975, the incarceration rate per 100,000 people in the United States was surprising flat, even as the country boomed and busted and its population exploded.[6] From a low of 79 per

4 Richard Gonzales, *Trump Signs Law Making Cruelty to Animals a Federal Crime*, National Public Radio (November 25, 2019), https://www.npr.org/2019/11/25/782842651/trump-signs-law-making-cruelty-to-animals-a-federal-crime.

5 *See, e.g.*, U.S. Department of Justice, Bureau of Justice Statistics, Correctional Populations in the United States (2017–2018), https://www.bjs.gov/content/pub/pdf/cpus1718.pdf. The release of information at the federal level has slowed significantly in recent years, meaning that most published data is now almost two years out of date. For example, the 2017–18 report just cited was not released until August 2020. *See Mass Incarceration: The Whole Pie*, The Prison Policy Initiative, 2020, https://www.prisonpolicy.org/reports/pie2020.html ("since 2017, government data releases have been delayed by many months - even years - compared to past publication schedules, and the data collected over two years ago have yet to be made public."). Throughout I attempt to use the most recent data available in each category.

6 U.S. Department of Justice, Bureau of Justice Statistics Bulletin: Prisoners 1925-81 at Table 1, https://www.bjs.gov/content/pub/pdf/p2581.pdf. Because the method of counting changed in 1977, it is difficult to compare years prior to 1977 with those after. However, the relative changes in each period are quite reliable. *See id.* at note 5.

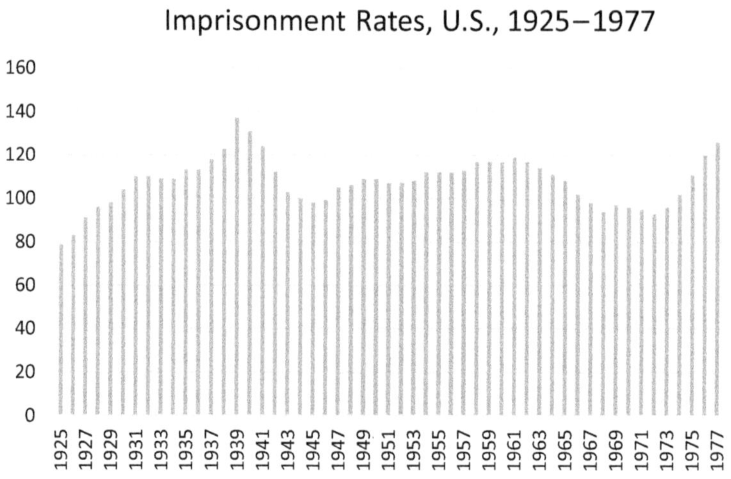

FIGURE 7.1 Imprisonment Rates, United States., 1925–1977.
Source: Bureau of Justice Statistics, Bulletin: Prisoners, 1925–1980

100,000 in 1925 to a high of 139 per 100,000 in the depression year of 1939, the national imprisonment rate oscillated around 100 people per 100,000 (0.1% of the population) for half a century (see Figure 7.1).[7]

Beginning in the late 1970s, however, the share of incarcerated Americans began to skyrocket. By its peak in 2007, 527 of every 100,000 people in the United States (more than one-half of one percent of the total population) were incarcerated.[8] That is, on a percentage basis, approximately five times as many americans were incarcerated in 2007 as were incarcerated on average during the middle fifty years of the twentieth century. And while that rate has shrunk slightly over the last several years, it is still at historically high numbers. Like a coronavirus curve that rises steeply and then declines gradually, the ascent of incarceration in America was swift and prolonged while the descent has been grudgingly slow (see Figure 7.2).

Sadly, this overall picture only tells part of the story of America's use of prisons, for it is impossible to separate mass incarceration in the United States from America's entrenched racial divide. As high as the American incarceration rate is overall, it is far higher for men, for ethnic minorities, and for those under forty. That is, the overall incarceration rate of 419 per 100,000 at the end of 2019 vastly understates the

[7] I use imprisonment rates rather than prison populations throughout to control for changes in population over time and to be able to compare the extent of incarceration across different jurisdictions with differing populations. However, this choice obscures another aspect of prison growth. Because population has been growing as incarceration rates have, the total *number* of people incarcerated – and the number of prisons, the number of carceral employees, etc – have all gone up.

[8] Bureau of Justice Statistics, Data Analysis Tool – Corrections (2021), https://www.bjs.gov/index.cfm?ty=daa.

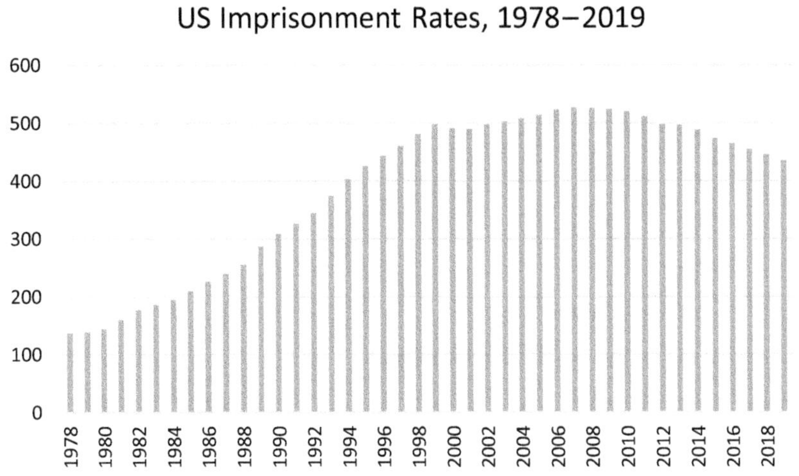

FIGURE 7.2 US imprisonment rates, 1978–2019.
Source: BJS, DATA ANALYSIS TOOL, TOTAL PRISON POPULATION RATES

impact that mass incarceration has on subgroups of the population.[9] For Black men the rate was five times that figure; nearly 2.2 percent of Black men were incarcerated as of December 31, 2019, and nearly 4.5 percent of all Black men between the ages of 35 and 39 were in prison as of that date.[10] What is more, mass incarceration, while widespread in the United States continues to have a strong regional valence as well. States in the American South and Southwest account for the eight highest incarceration rates in the nation;[11] those in the upper Midwest and Northeast are consistently among the lowest.[12] For example, the incarceration rate in Louisiana in 2019 was 680 per 100,000 while in Massachusetts it was "just" 133 per 100,000, less than one-fifth the rate in Louisiana.[13] As with many things about mass incarceration, the overall picture, frightening though it may be, greatly understates the realities for many Americans.

It is also important to note that the explosion in America's use of prisons is unparalleled among the nations to which the United States generally likes to compare itself.[14] The Institute for Crime and Justice Policy Research at the

9 BUREAU OF JUSTICE STATISTICS, PRISONERS IN 2019, Table 10, https://bjs.ojp.gov/content/pub/pdf/p19.pdf.

10 *Id.*

11 The eight most incarcerating states are, in order: Louisiana, Oklahoma, Mississippi, Arkansas, Arizona, Texas, Kentucky, and Georgia. Prisoners in the United States, 2019, Table 7.

12 The six states with the lowest incarceration rates are, in order: Massachusetts, Maine, Rhode Island, Minnesota, Vermont, and New Hampshire. *Id.*

13 *Id.* Because these figures include both state and federal prisoners, they actually understate the effect of different state policies on incarceration rates.

14 It is worth noting that in this and other ways, mass incarceration resembles America's continuing use of the death penalty. The death penalty is also a uniquely American practice among

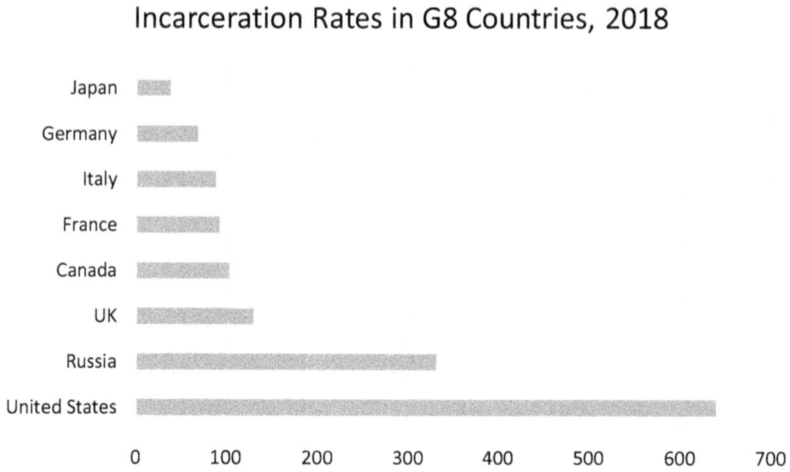

FIGURE 7.3 Incarceration rates in G8 countries, 2018.

Birkbeck, University of London, compiles statistics on prison populations around the world. It lists the United States as having the highest incarceration rate among the 223 nations surveyed, with an incarceration rate more than 10 percent greater than second-place El Salvador. Of the G8 nations, the United States stands alone – no other industrialized democracy uses incarceration even remotely akin to the way the United States does (see Figure 7.3).[15]

All of this is to say that mass incarceration is neither a necessary fact of life in either the United States or elsewhere in the world. Throughout modern American history, mass incarceration was not deemed a necessary fact of life and it is not seen as prerequisite to safety and security in any other industrialized democracy. Rather, it is rightly viewed as a uniquely American policy choice.

Western Democracy (with the lone exception of Japan) and is carried out largely in countries from which the United States generally tries to distance itself; the top countries carrying out executions since 2018 include China, Iran, Saudi Arabia, Iraq, Egypt, the United States, Pakistan, and Somalia. See DPIC, EXECUTIONS AROUND THE WORLD, https://deathpenaltyinfo.org/policy-issues/international/executions-around-the-world. For a discussion of the low-visibility use of the death penalty in Japan see DAVID T. JOHNSON, THE CULTURE OF CAPITAL PUNISHMENT IN JAPAN (2020). Like mass incarceration, the death penalty has disproportionate impact on people of color and is marked by strong regional differences. *See, e.g.*, FRANKLIN ZIMRING, THE CONTRADICTIONS OF AMERICAN CAPITAL PUNISHMENT (2003) (demonstrating that states using the death penalty at the turn of the twentieth century were the states most likely to have experienced lynching at the turn of the nineteenth century).

15 Source, WORLD PRISON BRIEF, PRISON POPULATION TOTAL, https://www.prisonstudies.org/highest-to-lowest/prison-population-total. It should be noted that the World Prison Brief counts all people sentenced to prisons and jails, so the incarceration rate it reports for the United States is higher than that reported in charts 1 and 2, above. *See* WORLD PRISON BRIEF, UNITED STATES OF AMERICA, https://www.prisonstudies.org/country/united-states-america (last visited May 31, 2021) (reporting both prison and jail populations).

That said, it is often difficult to identify exactly which decisions were made or which actors were responsible for the decisions that led to mass incarceration. That is, no one policy maker decided in 1977 or 1978 that the proportion of Americans in prisons and jails should increase five-fold over the next twenty years. In fact there is no single person or entity that *could* have decided to achieve such a result; the American criminal justice system is diffuse, with millions of low-profile decisions made at the federal but primarily at the state and local levels. David W. Ball has identified as one of the fundamental drivers of mass incarceration what Franklin E. Zimring and Gordon Hawkins originally referred to as the prosecutor's free lunch:[16] local prosecutors can afford to be tough on crime by imposing long spells of imprisonment because prisons (as opposed to jails where shorter sentences are served) are paid for at the state rather than county level.

> Even though counties use state prison resources at different rates, they do not typically pay the state based on this usage. State prisons are paid for out of general revenues: counties are not charged for heavy usage, nor are they reimbursed for light usage. Counties that choose to use state prison to address crime are, in essence, subsidized by counties that choose local programs such as probation and treatment instead, since the state typically pays for prison and the county pays for local dispositions…[U]nless the case could be made for the superiority of prison over other dispositions, the state should not subsidize prisons without subsidizing other responses to crime.[17]

Multiplying this perverse incentive structure over thousands of local prosecutors' offices around the country helps us understand how mass incarceration happened without any prior planning.[18]

Two final, related points sum up the almost incalculable scale of the criminal justice system in the United States. First it is important to recognize that even this enormous prison and jail system in this country is swamped by those on probation and parole; nearly 4.4 million people are on probation or parole in this country, nearly twice as many people as are currently incarcerated.[19] And though they are not incarcerated, those on probation and parole are subject to significant

[16] Franklin E. Zimring and Gordon Hawkins, The Scale of Imprisonment 140 (1991).

[17] David W. Ball, *Defunding State Prisons*, 50 Crim. L. Bull. 5 (2014).

[18] See John Pfaff, Locked In: The True Causes of Mass Incarceration and How to Achieve Real Reform 142 (2017)

> Prosecutors exploit, perhaps not even always intentionally, a gigantic moral hazard problem that arises from the way legal authority and financial responsibility are (poorly) allocated in the criminal justice system. Like jails and probation, prosecutor offices are either entirely or predominantly funded out of county budgets – unlike prisons, which are paid for by the state…[p]rosecutors get all the tough-on-crime political benefit of sending someone to prison, but the costs of the incarceration are foisted onto the state as a whole.

[19] U.S. Department of Justice, Bureau of Justice Statistics, Probation and Parole in the United States, 2017–2018, https://www.bjs.gov/content/pub/pdf/ppus1718.pdf.

curtailments of their liberty and are at risk for being quickly committed to prison or jail if they fail to live up to the terms of their supervised release.[20] Because the costs of such surveillance are generally borne by those subject to it, the risk of failure (and of the resulting incarceration) is more profound for the poor than the well-off.[21]

Second, the 2.3 million people incarcerated in the United States at any one time are themselves only a small fraction of those impacted by mass incarceration each year. While the average jail population during the year 2018 was 738,000, more than *10 million people* were admitted to jails throughout the country during that year.[22] That is, almost 5 percent of Americans are brought into the carceral system every single year, and the total number of Americans passing through jails and prisons is more than *four times* the number inside the system at any one time.[23] Thus, it is the "churn" – the number of those processed through America's jails after arrest – rather than the average population of county jails at any particular time that tells the true story of how vast America's prison and jail system truly is. And once again, these costs are overwhelmingly borne by the poor. The American cash bail system means that our jails are mostly full of people who have been convicted of no crime, and who are incarcerated simply because they are unable to pay for their freedom.[24]

In sum, the American criminal justice system – not just its prisons and jails, but its web of surveillance and supervision – is without parallel fantastically large. Ironically, the presence of more than 2 million people in our prisons and jails actually understates the scope of the problem. As I argue in the next section, the War on Drugs – which provides a cautionary tale for the criminalization of animal abuse – has been an important, though perhaps overestimated, ingredient in this phenomenon.

7.3 THE WAR ON DRUGS

Though the two are often conflated, the War on Drugs is a separate and distinct phenomenon from mass incarceration. And, though the two have overlapped and

[20] See generally MALCOLM M. FEELEY & JONATHAN SIMON, *New Penology: Notes on the Emerging Strategy of Corrections and Its Implications*, 30 CRIMINOLOGY 449, 456 (1992)

> Instead of treating revocation of parole and probation as a mechanism to short-circuit the supervision process when the risks to public safety become unacceptable, the system now treats revocation as a cost-effective way to police and sanction a chronically troublesome population. In such an operation, recidivism is either irrelevant or. . . is stood on its head and transformed into an indicator of success in a new form of law enforcement.

[21] *See, e.g.*, MICHELLE PHELPS, *The Paradox of Probation: Community Supervision in the Age of Mass Incarceration*, 35 L. & POL'Y. 51, 56 (2013) (arguing that the well-off are able to negotiate the complicated demands of supervised release better than are the poor).

[22] U.S. DEPARTMENT OF JUSTICE, BUREAU OF JUSTICE STATISTICS, JAIL INMATES, 2018 Table 1 (2020), https://www.bjs.gov/content/pub/pdf/ji18.pdf.

[23] *Id.*

[24] *See, e.g.*, *The Whole Pie*, *supra* note 5 (Reporting that only 161,000 of the 631,000 people in America's jails had been convicted of any crime).

fed on each other over the last fifty years, the relationship between them has often been shrouded with confusion.

The modern history of the drug war probably begins with the passage of the Controlled Substances Act (CSA) in 1970. Although the phrase "controlled substance" wouldn't be used for the first time until President Richard Nixon coined it the following year, the CSA was designed to be a blow against the counterculture that had largely defined the previous decade. More than that, the War on Drugs was both racialized and partisan from the start.[25] The War on Drugs was a means to get back at the president's enemies and to use the criminal law to target political opponents.

But it is important not to overstate the importance of the CSA or any other federal law – such as the infamous crack-to-powder-cocaine sentencing disparity[26] – in the day-to-day implementation of the War on Drugs. The role of the federal government in setting national criminal justice policy is far more symbolic than practical. More than 90 percent of those serving time in prisons and jails in the United States are under state and local rather than federal supervision. While the federal government plays a larger role in the prosecution of drug crimes – most of the crimes of violence that lead to long prison terms in the United States lack a federal nexus and are thus prosecuted almost exclusively at the state level – it remains true that even the vast majority of drug law enforcement is done at the state and local level. The importance of federal criminal justice policy serves primarily as an announcement of values to the states coupled in many instances with the provision of federal and

[25] *See, e.g.*, Dan Baum, *Legalize It All: How to Win the War on Drugs*, HARPERS (June 2013), https://harpers.org/archive/2016/04/legalize-it-all/. Baum quotes John Ehrlichman, Nixon's former domestic policy adviser as explaining the origins of the war on drugs:

> The Nixon campaign in 1968, and the Nixon White House after that, had two enemies: the antiwar left and black people. You understand what I'm saying? We knew we couldn't make it illegal to be either against the war or black, but by getting the public to associate the hippies with marijuana and blacks with heroin, and then criminalizing both heavily, we could disrupt those communities. We could arrest their leaders, raid their homes, break up their meetings, and vilify them night after night on the evening news. Did we know we were lying about the drugs? Of course we did.

The racist history of the war on drugs, particularly marijuana, is extensive. *See, e.g.*, RICHARD J. BONNIE AND CHARLES H. WHITEBREAD II, THE MARIJUANA CONVICTION 40–52 (1999) (discussing the ways in which early efforts to eradicate marijuana use were motivated by antipathy toward African Americans and Mexican immigrants). Anti-immigrant bias was also a motivation for the national alcohol prohibition occurring at approximately the same time. *See* generally LISA MCGIRR, THE WAR ON ALCOHOL: PROHIBITION AND THE RISE OF THE AMERICAN STATES (2016).

[26] See Pub. L. No. 99–570 (1986) (creating mandatory minimums for crack and powder cocaine); U.S. SENTENCING COMMISSION, REPORT TO THE CONGRESS: IMPACT OF THE FAIR SENTENCING ACT OF 2010 (Aug. 2015), https://www.ussc.gov/sites/default/files/pdf/news/congressional-testimony-and-reports/drug-topics/201507_RtC_Fair-Sentencing-Act.pdf (reporting on the history and impact of the 100-to-1 crack to powder cocaine ratio).

assistance to states for their cooperation in federal initiatives.[27] Much as we saw that mass incarceration is largely attributable to individual decisions made by thousands of prosecutors in millions of cases around the country, so the War on Drugs was carried out primarily by the state legislatures and local law enforcement officials and prosecutors within those states.[28]

In her groundbreaking and discussion-moving book on mass incarceration in the United States, Michelle Alexander makes the connection between mass incarceration and the War on Drugs explicit. "In less than thirty years, the US penal population exploded from around 300,000 to more than 2 million, with drug convictions accounting for the majority of the increase."[29] The reality is, to say the least, more complicated. In his book *Locked In*, John Pfaff takes on the connection between these phenomena, arguing that the War on Drugs actually played a relatively minor role in the rise of mass incarceration.

> When we look at the data more closely, it becomes increasingly difficult to defend the claim that the war on drugs is the main driver of prison growth. This is true for pretty much any definition of the "war on drugs," from one that refers to just the incarceration of those convicted of drug offenses to broader perspectives that include anyone who would not have been in prison if the United States had not prohibited certain drugs or enforced their prohibition. No matter how we define the war on drugs, its impact appears to be important, but unequivocally secondary to other factors.[30]

In fact, when we look at the state and federal prison system as a whole, we see that most people serving felony sentences are imprisoned for crimes of violence, while those convicted of drug crimes constitute only a tiny fraction of the overall prison population. According to the Bureau of Justice Statistics, 55.5 percent of all prisoners in state and federal custody were there for violent crimes,[31] while only 14.1 percent of all prisoners in the United States were there for drug offenses, with just 3.7 percent imprisoned for possession alone. Thus, any political solution to mass incarceration that focuses primarily on so-called low-level or nonviolent drug offenders will

[27] See, e.g., Pfaff, *supra* note 18, at 30 ("[T]here is no single 'war on drugs," but rather somewhere between 50 and 33,300 wars on drugs, fought with varying degrees of intensity at different times, in different jurisdictions, and in different ways.").

[28] While it is true that marijuana (and other drug) law reform in the states has shaken the consensus between state and federal priorities in this area, it remains true that state and local law enforcement officials continue to make an enormous number of arrests for relatively minor drug offenses. The War on Drugs, in other words, did not stop with the legalization of marijuana, paradoxically, even in those states that chose to legalize the drug. Marijuana production and sale remains illegal outside of the taxed and licensed regulatory regime, and possession by minors and use in public remain illegal as well. Ironically, states that have "legalized" marijuana continue to see disparities in how those laws are enforced.

[29] Michelle Alexander, The New Jim Crow 6 (2012).

[30] Pfaff, *supra* note 18, at 23.

[31] Prisoners in 2019, Table 13.

produce no more than baby steps toward solving America's mass incarceration problem. Even if we were to release everyone whose most serious offense is a drug crime – including both large-scale drug dealers and those convicted of providing drugs to minors, for example – it would make only a small dent in America's mass incarceration problem.[32] Any meaningful reform will require us to confront the long prison sentences that we apply to violent crimes such as murder, robbery, and rape.

This is decidedly not to say, however, that the War on Drugs plays only an insignificant part in the American carceral state. We have seen, for example, that prison and jail populations in the United States – enormous though they are – vastly *understate* the size of the carceral state in America. For example, there were more than 10 million arrests in the United States in 2017 and nearly one in six of them was for what the FBI calls a drug-abuse offense.[33] In fact, there were almost as many arrests for drug crimes as for the eight major index crimes – murder, robbery, rape, aggravated assault, burglary, theft, auto theft, and arson – combined.[34] What is more, 85 percent of those arrested on drug offenses were arrested for possession rather than the more serious offenses of manufacturing or distributing drugs; while possession, sensibly, accounts for only a small percentage of the prison population, it makes up an outsized fraction of those arrested. And though few of these arrests lead to long prison terms, they are far from costless for those they sweep into the system. The fact of even a minor conviction (or even just an arrest) can have a profound negative impact on one's life prospects. Criminal justice scholars have devoted great attention in recent years to the so-called collateral consequences of involvement in the criminal justice system, documenting how arrest and conviction can lead to deprivation of everything from voting rights to gun rights to access to federal benefits.[35] And of course, the burdens of the War on Drugs, like those of mass incarceration, have fallen disproportionately on Black and brown people. A report produced by ACLU found that although they use marijuana at similar rates, Black people were nearly four times more likely to be arrested for the use of that drug than were white people.[36] Studies in other jurisdictions, even those that have liberalized their marijuana

[32] In fact, if we wanted to reduce mass incarceration by more than 50 percent, it would be necessary to begin releasing people convicted of violent crimes – homicide, rape, robbery, and assault – as they make up more than half of those incarcerated. In other words, even releasing *every* nonviolent criminal from prison would still not reduce America's imprisonment rate to the same level as that in other Western democracies.

[33] See Federal Bureau of Investigations, Crime in the United States 2019 Table 29.

[34] *Id.*

[35] Margaret Love & David Schlussel, The Many Roads to Reintegration: A 50-State Report on Laws Restoring Rights and Opportunities after Arrest or Conviction (2020).

[36] ACLU, A *Tale of Two Countries: Racially Targeted Arrests in the Era of Marijuana Reform* 5 (2018), https://www.aclu.org/report/tale-two-countries-racially-targeted-arrests-era-marijuana-reform ("On average, a Black person is 3.64 times more likely to be arrested for marijuana possession than a white person, even though Black and white people use marijuana at similar rates.").

laws, continue to report disparities in the rate at which Black people and white people are arrested.[37]

7.4 IMPLICATIONS FOR ANIMAL LAW

What I hoped to show in the previous section is that the War on Drugs is both under- and overappreciated as a driver of the growth of the carceral state in this country. It is not responsible for the fact that more than 2 million people are in prisons and jails in this country, but it does adversely impact the lives of literally millions of Americans each year – disproportionately people of color – limiting both their liberty and their life choices in wide-ranging and significant ways. In this section, I argue that the War on Drugs has a lot to tell us about the trend toward criminalizing animal abuse in this country.

First, there is no reason to think that the enforcement of laws forbidding animal abuse is likely to be more equitable than any other sort of criminal law enforcement. In fact, the most prominent prosecution for animal cruelty is something of a cautionary tale for the racialized policing that may come with the criminal enforcement of PACT. Take, for example, the most high-profile animal cruelty prosecution of the last fifty years – that of Atlanta Falcons quarterback Michael Vick for running a dogfighting ring. Vick's prosecution by both state and federal authorities was fraught with racist overtones. My colleague Justin Marceau, noting the fact that dog breeding and fighting had historically been associated with upper-class white people, wrote of the Vick prosecution: "It is notable that the most high-profile animal cruelty prosecution in decades turns on the prosecution of an African American for the very practice that was flaunted as a symbol of his racial inferiority during his grandparents' lives." The comedian Chris Rock put things more pithily on the David Letterman show in 2008 when Alaska governor Sarah Palin was running as John McCain's running mate on the Republican presidential ticket. Rock imagined Michael Vick in his prison cell studying the widely circulated photo of Palin posing with a bloody moose she and her son had shot, wondering to himself "Why am I in jail? You let a white lady shoot a moose; Black man wanna kill a dog, that's a crime."[38] Behind the laugh line is a grim reality: the criminal enforcement of animal cruelty laws, like the enforcement of drug laws before them, and alcohol laws before those, will necessarily be filtered through a racial lens which defines which sorts of animal cruelty merit law enforcement intervention.

[37] See, e.g., Colorado Division of Criminal Justice, Impacts of Marijuana Legalization in Colorado, Table 3 (Oct. 2018), https://cdpsdocs.state.co.us/ors/docs/reports/2018-SB13-283_Rpt.pdf (showing that five years after the legalization of marijuana in Colorado, Black people were still twice as likely to be arrested for marijuana offenses as were white people).

[38] Chris Rock Letterman Palin vs Nick, YouTube (Sep. 23, 2008), https://www.youtube.com/watch?v=OrxpOxkiOms&ab_channel=1CrazyUncle.

What is more, there is good reason to fear that the enforcement of animal cruelty laws will pose a deadly threat to all citizens (and particularly Black and brown ones) much as the enforcement of drug prohibition has long been a driver of police killings. Breonna Taylor was killed when police officers executed a warrant at her home in the middle of the night, believing that she was holding either cash or drugs for an ex-boyfriend. When the officers failed to identify themselves with sufficient clarity, Taylor's current boyfriend opened fire and Taylor was killed in the violent police response. Cases such as Taylor's are sadly common; given the judicially accepted presumption that drug trafficking involves the use of weapons;[39] nonviolent drug offenses are often treated by law enforcement as life-threatening. The vision, perpetrated by cases like Vick's, of the fighting dog trainer as a violent, almost subhuman predator is likely to mean that warrants enforced against those suspected of animal cruelty will present the same kind of dangers we too often see with the enforcement of drug laws.[40]

Another concern is the way that expansion of substantive criminal law impacts constitutional criminal procedure. The Supreme Court's early Fourth Amendment cases – dealing with wiretaps[41] and automobile searches[42] – arose in the context of the nation's failed experiment with alcohol prohibition. Prohibition made alcohol smuggling profitable, and the new federal bureaucracy that arose to enforce it required the Court to consider, often for the first time, the permissible means of criminal investigation and prosecution.[43] After Prohibition was repealed, other criminal statutes operated as a lever for law enforcement officers to access citizens' persons, houses, papers, and effects. In this context, the prohibition of drugs has played a large part, influencing everything from the constitutionality of technological surveillance[44] to the use of dogs to detect controlled substances[45] to random checkpoints targeting the transportation of illicit drugs.[46] As noted above, the enforcement of drug laws impacts not just those who are investigated and prosecuted

39 *See, e.g.*, Illinois v. Wardlow, 528 U.S. 119, 122 (2000) (validating the search of a young man who ran at the sight of police because in the officer's "experience it was common for there to be weapons in the near vicinity of narcotics transactions.").

40 *See, e.g.*, Commonwealth v. Santiago, 452 Mass. 573 (2008) (holding that, while the mere presence of a dog in the home, even of a pit bull, was insufficient to justify a "no knock" warrant, that same warrant could be justified, at least in part by the fact that "the magistrate knew that the defendant possessed a type of dog which, in the officer's experience, was known to be dangerous and aggressive, and could be used to confront the officers.").

41 Olmstead v. U.S., 277 U.S. 438 (1928).

42 Carroll v. U.S., 267 U.S. 132 (1925).

43 *See, e.g.*, Robert Post, *Federalism, Positive Law, and the Emergence of the American Administrative State: Prohbition in the Taft Court Era*, 48 Wm. & Mary L. Rev. 1, 117 (2006) ("prohibition sparked a virtual 'doctrinal explosion' of Fourth Amendment jurisprudence.").

44 U.S. v. Jones, 565 U.S. 400 (2012).

45 Illinois v. Caballes, 543 U.S. 405 (2005).

46 Indianapolis v. Edmond, 531 U.S. 32 (2000).

for trafficking drugs; the constitutional law made in drug trafficking prosecutions affects the rights of the law-abiding and the law-defying alike.[47]

Those of us who teach criminal procedure or practice criminal defense are all too familiar with the almost mythical role that the odor of marijuana plays in the enforcement of criminal law in this country; the smell of marijuana is a kind of Fourth Amendment shibboleth, opening doors to officers who can assert that they have encountered it.[48] For example, in *U.S. v. Kizart*,[49] the defendant's car was pulled over for speeding and the officer testified that he smelled the unmistakable odor of burnt marijuana emanating from the passenger compartment of Kizart's car. The officer searched both Kizart and the passenger compartment but found no contraband. The officer then opened the trunk of the sedan and found both marijuana and methamphetamine wrapped in packages inside a trash bag, which was inside a backpack, inside the trunk. Although Kizart argued that the smell of burnt marijuana was consistent only with personal use of the drug and that therefore the officer had no probable cause to believe that bulk marijuana would be found in the trunk, the appellate court disagreed. The smell of marijuana, coupled with Kizart's anxiety when questioned by the police, the court concluded, justified a full search of the entire car as well as any closed containers therein. Similar examples are almost too numerous to choose from.[50]

There is genuine risk that the barking dog will become the new smell of marijuana, the unquestionable evidence that entitles police officers to make a warrantless entry or search. This is not speculation; we have already seen cases litigated in which the government has argued that its interest in public safety includes concern for nonhuman animals as well as for human well-being. In one such case, *Commonwealth v. Duncan*,[51] the Massachusetts high court extended the

[47] More recently, the prohibition of child pornography has allowed law enforcement to intrude into virtual spaces in much the same way prior prohibitions permitted searches and seizures of cars, persons, and packages. See, e.g., Thomas K. Clancy, *Digital Child Pornography and the Fourth Amendment*, 49 No. 3 JUDGES' J. 26, 26 (2010) ("Almost 70 percent of all reported appellate decisions involving the search or seizure of digital evidence are concerned with the recovery of child pornography.").

[48] The move to legalize marijuana for personal use has begun to chip away at the magical powers of the marijuana odor, however. Consider the Colorado case of People v. Zuniga, 372 P.3d 1052 (Co. 2016) decided after Colorado passed Amendment 64, authorizing the possession and use (as well as licensed production and sale) of marijuana by adults. Zuniga was stopped by Colorado highway patrol and a trained narcotics dog "alerted" on his car. The dog had been trained to detect the presence of a number of illicit substances, including both methamphetamine and marijuana. The Colorado Supreme Court concluded that because the dog was trained to detect marijuana, and because marijuana is a substance with both legal and illegal uses, the dog's alert could not be the basis of probable cause to search.

[49] 967 F.3d 693 (7th Cir. 2020).

[50] To name just a few, the Supreme Court has decided: District of Columbia v. Wesby, 138 S.Ct. 577 (2018) (smell of burnt marijuana); Florida v. Jardines, 569 U.S. 1 (2013) (dog trained to detect the odor of marijuana); Kentucky v. King, 563 U.S. 452 (2011) (odor of burnt marijuana outside defendant's apartment); U.S. v. Sharpe, 470 U.S. 675 (1985) (odor of raw marijuana during an automobile stop); United States v. Johns (odor of marijuana giving rise to probable cause).

[51] 467 Mass. 746 (2014).

"emergency aid" exception to both the warrant and probable cause requirements to the protection of nonhuman animals, validating officers' decision to enter Duncan's property without a warrant after hearing feeble whimpering and barking from an animal apparently in distress on Duncan's property. In reaching this conclusion, the court was supported by amici, including the ALDF, ASPCA, Humane Society, and Animal Rescue League, and law enforcement agencies who argued that Massachusetts' decision to treat animal abuse as a serious crime justified the warrantless entry onto Duncan's property:

> The Commonwealth's broad and comprehensive animal protection statutes reflect its citizens' strong interest in the humane treatment of animals and the growing recognition that the prevention of animal suffering is both a moral imperative and in the public's interest. Application of the emergency exception to the warrant requirement to the protection of animals in peril logically and necessarily flows from this statutory scheme and the community values it embodies. A contrary result would be anathema to the spirit of the Commonwealth's existing animal protection laws and at odds with prevailing public sentiment.[52]

The Duncan case has been cited favorably in Kentucky,[53] Ohio,[54] and Vermont.[55]

Notice the connection between where we began and the holding in *Duncan*. This chapter started with a description of how ALDF and other advocacy groups reward states for making various animal abuse offenses felonious. Many of these same advocacy groups then argue that because a state has chosen to treat animal abuse as a serious felony, the state necessarily has a strong interest in the protection of animals sufficient to overcome a homeowner's interest in avoiding warrantless searches and seizures.

7.5 CONCLUSION

It is easy enough to dismiss the failed alcohol prohibition of the last century as a moral panic, a moment of hysteria from the distant past. But this account overlooks the fact that Prohibition, for all its faults, was part of a broad progressive movement

52 Brief of Amicus Curiae the American Society for the Prevention of Cruelty to Animals, Commonwealth v. Duncan (Oct. 24, 2013), 2013 WL6051368, at *9.

53 Lawton v. Commonwealth, No. 2019-CA-001282, 2020 WL 5083460, *5 (Ky. Ct. App. Aug. 28, 2020) ("[The officers] did not know there was a dog in need of aid until they observed her lying under the house. Under different circumstances, we would be inclined to extend the emergency aid exception to animals. Courts in other jurisdictions have extended this exception to render aid to animals in true emergency situations and further promote the public policy of the humane treatment of animals.").

54 State v. Glowney, Nos. 27896 & 27897, 2019 WL 3986353, *7 (Ohio Ct. App. Aug. 23, 2019)

> Officer Davis's entry into the backyard of 636 Cushing reasonably addressed the concerns raised by a loose dog, particularly one whose ownership was then unknown. In short, Officer Davis's actions were reasonably necessary for the safety of both the public and Dyson. Her seizure of Dyson was thus a reasonable exercise of her community caretaking duties, and her actions did not violate the Fourth Amendment.

55 State v. Sheperd, 170 A.3d 616, 624 (Vt. 2017) ("[W]e must take the animals' welfare into consideration when determining the legality of a search or seizure.").

that encompassed slavery prohibition and women's suffrage. Freeing men from the bondage of addiction was seen by many of Prohibition's proponents as the last great emancipation project of the period. In founding the Prohibition Party, the slavery abolitionist Gerrit Smith made the connection plain:

> He suggested that this continuing form of bondage might be more miserable, and more dangerous, than the one recently abolished. "No outward advantages can bring happiness to the victim of alcohol – to him who has killed his own soul," Smith said. "The literal slave does harm to no one, whilst the self-made slave of whom we speak is a curse to his kindred, a burden upon all, and, in no small share of the cases, a terror to all."[56]

One hundred years after Prohibition began, however, its progressive roots are largely forgotten. When Americans think of the period from 1920 to 1933, what they generally remember is failure, corruption, and discrimination. Prohibition gave rise not just to organized crime, but to a federal police force that enforced the law unevenly, singling out disfavored groups for sanction.

> Prohibition policing differed by region, by rural or urban setting, and most especially by race, ethnicity and class. An unprecedented campaign of selective enforcement lurked beneath the surface glamor of the roaring twenties that left the urban elite sipping cocktails in swank, protected nightclubs, while [other men] died over a jug of whiskey.[57]

The analogy from prohibitions – of alcohol and drugs – to the increasing punishment of animal abuse is obviously an imperfect one. The desire to alter one's consciousness is near universal, whereas the instinct to abuse animals is aberrational; prohibiting substances creates an illicit market for them in a way without a clear parallel to criminalizing animal abuse. But the prohibitions of alcohol and drugs can show us the dangers of relying on the criminal justice system to solve the nation's perceived ills. Prohibition didn't just fail. It created much of the infrastructure that supported mass incarceration.[58]

The move to criminalize animal abuse is unlikely to so radically change society; the edifice of state power and control is already in place. But both Prohibition and

[56] Kelefa Sanneh, *Drunk with Power*, THE NEW YORKER (December 21 & 28, 2015). During this time, Americans were notorious for their drinking. One study indicated that Americans in the early-nineteenth century drank nearly three times as much as Americans do today. See Michael A. Lerner, *Going Dry: The Coming of Prohibition*, 32 HUMANITIES 5 (2011).

[57] LISA MCGIRR, THE WAR ON ALCOHOL 71 (2016).

[58] *Id.* at 192.

> Overshadowed by high-profile art, literature, and public works agencies, and social provisioning projects from social security to labor rights, the unprecedented development of the federal government's law enforcement and punitive capacities contributed to the bone and sinew of the twentieth-century American state. Nothing did more than the nation's Prohibition war to build this less-examined side of state building in the first half of the twentieth century.

the War on Drugs teach us that the desire to use the criminal justice system to achieve even beneficent goals often harms the very communities they are ostensibly intended to protect. The negative effects of a carceral approach to animal protection, foretold by previous spasms of criminalization, are likely to be both far-ranging and unevenly distributed. To avoid these harms, it is not enough merely to moderate the impulse to create new categories of crime – to create misdemeanors rather than felonies. As Alexandra Natapoff has written, so-called decriminalization is often a trap that does the opposite of what it promises:

> [D]ecriminalization represents the next generation of the "net-widening" phenomenon. Net-widening refers to reforms that make it easier to sweep individuals into the criminal process, and decriminalization does so in sophisticated ways. Primarily, it makes it possible to reach more offenders by simplifying the charging process and eliminating counsel, along with other forms of due process. But it also heightens the impact of the net by turning to supervision and fines as indirect, long-term constraints on defendant behavior, and by extending the informal consequences of a citation or conviction deep into offenders' social and economic lives. The widening net, moreover, is not colorblind: decriminalization risks further racializing the selection process as police are empowered to stop and cite young Black men more freely without the constraints of criminal adjudication or the threat of defense counsel.[59]

Only what she calls true decriminalization – not just decreasing criminal penalties but moving conduct entirely outside the criminal justice system – is likely to avoid the harms that system imposes.

59 Alexandra Natapoff, *Misdemeanor Decriminalization*, 68 VAND. L. REV. 1055, 1059 (2015).

8

Criminalization as a Solution to Abuse

A Cautionary Tale

Tamara L. Kuennen

8.1 INTRODUCTION

The Battered Women's Movement and I were born in the late 1960s. In its infancy, the movement coalesced around the grassroots goals of sheltering women and raising political consciousness about the connection between domestic violence and gender subordination. Later, it looked to law as a tool to effect the social change it envisioned – gender equality. Activists first lobbied for civil legal relief in the form of civil restraining orders, then turned to enforcement of the criminal law. Between 1984 and 2000, the criminal law of domestic violence exploded.[1]

Amid this explosion, in 1992, I worked in a domestic violence shelter. It was my first real job after college. I worked all my hours for the week in a single shift, living in the shelter from Friday at 5:00 p.m. through Sunday at 5:00 p.m. On these weekends, I heard from residents about their appointments during the week with the local legal aid attorney, who promised safety and freedom through civil protection orders and cooperation with aggressive prosecutors. Feeling the same sense of optimism that many residents felt about law, and the same growing sense of pessimism about shelters in creating meaningful social change, I decided to go to law school. Sending the message to would-be batterers that they could be arrested, prosecuted and court-ordered to move out of their own homes (rather than victims needing to do so) seemed a much more proactive, empowering, and effective solution than providing victims a place to stay, after the fact of abuse.

It may not come as a shock to the reader to learn that I am a middle-class white woman. This chapter reflects on the hopefulness with which I and other, largely white, activists in the anti–domestic violence (DV) movement imbued law – a hopefulness that is not uncommon in social movement work and is a product of

[1] Leigh Goodmark, A Troubled Marriage: Domestic Violence and the Legal System 16–28 (2012) (providing a comprehensive overview of the development of the legal response to DV in the United States from the 1970s to 2012).

white privilege. Because leaders of the animal rights movement are overwhelmingly white[2] and because the trajectory of the animal rights movement appears, at least currently, to track the same reliance on criminal law to effect social change, it is my hope that the reflections offered in this chapter provide reasons for pause.

As a solution to the problem of DV, we (activists) placed most of our chips in the pot of criminal law. Then we went all in, on this criminalization strategy, also known as "crime logics"[3] and "carceral feminism,"[4] with mandates: mandatory reporting of DV to law enforcement by professionals in the community; mandatory arrest of DV perpetrators at the scene of a crime; and mandatory prosecution of charges involving DV. As this chapter will discuss, the mandatory (versus discretionary) arrest of suspected perpetrators, tough-on-crime "no-drop" prosecution policies, and "zero-tolerance" attitudes did *not* create the meaningful social change hoped for. By some accounts, the criminalization strategy has made but a dent in the prevalence or acceptability of DV, and in many ways (discussed herein) it has harmed rather than helped those it was intended to protect. Worse, these policies have contributed to the disproportionate incarceration of people of color and other marginalized individuals. Indeed, a critical and shameful mistake in the anti-DV movement has been its racist indifference to the treatment of people of color by law enforcement. Starting from the position that any expectation of a reliable, protective response by police is a product of not merely white, but also heteronormative, privilege, it is clear that privilege must be reckoned with. This reckoning is particularly critical for movements centered on equality and dignity, as are both the anti-DV and animal rights movements.

The chapter begins with a thumbnail sketch of laws promulgated to protect victims of domestic violence, pointing out parallel law reform efforts in the animal rights movement. Although there were many unintended consequences of an overly optimistic reliance on law to combat DV, I focus on four: the crowding out of other potential solutions; the increased arrest of women and other problems with mandating arrest at the scene of a domestic disturbance; the problem of police as perpetrators of both partner and animal abuse; and the loss of activists' initial vision and goals. The chapter concludes with personal reflections. For twenty-five years, I have represented people who experience abuse to obtain civil protection orders, child custody, divorce, and lawful immigrant status. I went to law school because I thought that enforcing the law, rather than providing services like shelter, was a more effective way to address DV. Now I wish that the millions of federal dollars spent each year on policing and prosecuting could instead be funneled into housing, childcare, and other resources that the victims we are trying to help

[2] Justin Marceau, Beyond Cages: Animal Law and Criminal Punishment 159 (2019).

[3] Donna Coker, *Crime Logic, Campus Sexual Assault, and Restorative Justice*, 49 Tex. Tech. L. Rev. 147, 155–61 (2016).

[4] Elizabeth Bernstein, Brokered Subjects: Sex, Trafficking, and the Politics of Freedom 37 (2019).

actually need. Ironically, the shelter I worked at before attending law school provided precisely these resources.

8.2 THUMBNAIL SKETCH OF CRIMINAL AND CIVIL REMEDIES FOR DOMESTIC VIOLENCE

Fifty years ago, there was no criminal or civil justice system response to the problem of DV. In fact, the concept of "domestic violence" as opposed to stranger violence, at least as far as the law was concerned, did not exist. Today, sending a harassing text message to an ex who lives across state lines is punishable as a federal crime, a state crime (potentially a couple of different state crimes), and often contempt of court.[5]

The seriousness with which the justice system now treats DV is the result of a number of reforms anti-DV activists lobbied for in response to, in their view, the state's history of indifference.[6] Much like animal rights activists,[7] anti-DV activists in the 1970s and 1980s believed that laws on the books were underenforced, or simply not applied, in cases of abuse.[8] They observed that police avoided responding to calls for help from victims of DV, and when they did respond, it was with reluctance to interfere in a "private family matter" and might end with (if the "squabble" was sufficiently serious) a walk around the block for the perpetrator to cool down.[9] To address this problem with police discretion, feminist activists and victim advocates fought for reform of the law to *require* police to arrest alleged perpetrators at the scene of a DV disturbance. These are referred to as "mandatory arrest" policies. Advocates for animal rights have urged similar mandatory arrest laws for animal cruelty and have done so for similar reasons.[10] Indeed, all fifty states have adopted a felony animal abuse statute.[11]

It is important to note that not all anti-DV activists agreed with the criminalization strategy. In fact, activists of color were – and remain – deeply skeptical.[12] For communities of color, increased police presence had never been a means of achieving

[5] 18 U.S.C. § 2262(a)(1), (2) (federal crime of interstate stalking). In most states, harassment when aimed at an intimate or formerly intimate partner qualifies as domestic violence, and in most states, contempt of court for such conduct is a remedy available to victims who have civil or criminal protection orders, in addition to, in most states, a separate crime of violating such an order.

[6] *Cf.* Aya Gruber, The Feminist War on Crime 72 (2020) (noting that this was the "conventional feminist narrative" of police responsiveness and arguing that this was revisionist history).

[7] Marceau, *supra* note 2, at 111.

[8] Leigh Goodmark, Decriminalizing Domestic Violence 4 (Claire M. Renzetti ed., 2018).

[9] *See* Deborah Epstein, *Procedural Justice: Tempering the State's Response to DV*, 43 Wm. & Mary L. Rev. 1843, 1851–53 (2002).

[10] Marceau, *supra* note 2, at 111.

[11] *Id.* at 102.

[12] Beth E. Richie, *A Black Feminist Reflection on the Antiviolence Movement*, 25 Signs 1133, 1136 (2000).

safety. Activists of color therefore warned against partnering with the state and particularly the criminal justice system. Their protests were unheeded.[13]

Interestingly, mandatory arrest laws proliferated in the 1980s, around the time of the alleged murder of a white woman by her ex-husband, who is Black: the murder of Nicole Brown Simpson by O. J. Simpson. As noted by Professor G. Kristian Miccio,

> Soon after [the murder of Nicole Brown Simpson], New York joined a majority of states in passing mandatory arrest laws in cases involving DV. Most of the legislation passed that day had languished for years in state legislatures. With the death of Nicole Brown, politicians raced to the state house to invoke DV laws, jumping on the "zero tolerance" bandwagon.[14]

Rates of arrest increased dramatically. To be certain that arrests paid off, activists advocated that states and municipalities require district attorneys to prosecute DV aggressively, with "no drop" prosecution policies aimed at curtailing prosecutor discretion to dismiss criminal charges in DV cases.[15] By 1996, two-thirds of prosecutors' offices had adopted some variation of a "no-drop" prosecution policy.[16] Advocates for animal rights have urged similar mandatory arrest laws and aggressive prosecution policies for animal cruelty, and have done so for similar reasons.[17]

At about the same time as states engaged in criminalization tactics, Congress passed in 1994 the first federal law prohibiting DV, the Violence Against Women Act ("VAWA"). VAWA made it a federal crime to cross state lines to abuse or stalk an intimate partner or to possess a gun if convicted of even a misdemeanor crime of DV. Women's advocates and activists played a major role in crafting the VAWA and in shaping federal funding priorities under that act. "Their priority was using federal funds to reinvent the legal system to make police, prosecutors and judges more responsive."[18] The first iteration of VAWA required states to pass mandatory arrest laws to receive federal funding, and the single largest pool of money under VAWA was the Services for Training Officers and Prosecutors grant, specifically intended to increase the apprehension, prosecution, and adjudication of persons perpetrating

13 Goodmark, *supra* note 8, at 4; Gruber, *supra* note 6, at 87.

14 G. Kristian Miccio, *A House Divided: Mandatory Arrest, DV, and the Conservatization of the Battered Women's Movement*, 42 Hous. L. Rev. 237, 238 (2005).

15 *See generally* Cheryl Hanna, *No Right to Choose: Mandated Victim Participation in DV Prosecutions*, 109 Harv. L. Rev. 1849 (1996) (describing, and supporting, aggressive prosecution policies in DV cases). For a compilation of representative aggressive or "no-drop" prosecution policies, *see* Tamara L. Kuennen, *Private Relationships and Public Problems: Applying Principles of Relational Contract Theory to DV*, 2010 BYU L. Rev. 515, 592–95 (documenting local policies in thirty-five states).

16 Goodmark, *supra* note 8, at 15.

17 Marceau, *supra* note 2, at 111.

18 Goodmark, *supra* note 1, at 19.

violent crimes against women.[19] Advocates for animal rights have urged similar federal legislation.[20]

On the civil side of domestic violence rulemaking, civil protection orders (or restraining orders) became available to victims in the late 1970s and throughout the 1980s. By 1989, every state provided for this emergency civil remedy that restrains the perpetrator from coming near or contacting the victim, amongst other forms of relief.[21] The VAWA provided an array of protections in the civil justice system as well. These range from remedies for immigrant victims to gain lawful immigrant status to prohibitions on landlords for discriminating against victims who apply for housing.[22] Advocates for animal rights have urged similar federal policy and legislation.[23]

In short, in the last half century, US law and policy reforms have caused a sea change in how the civil and criminal justice systems respond to DV. While there have been benefits for those victims who are able and who desire to use the justice systems for help, feminist activists who advocated for these landmark reforms, on reflection, have questioned their effectiveness in ending DV and meaningfully advancing the rights and safety of victims.[24] Their questions flow from several of the unforeseen consequences of the reforms, discussed below.

[19] Garrine P. Laney, Cong. Rsch. Serv., RL30871, Violence against Women Act: History and Federal Funding 4 (2005).

[20] Marceau, *supra* note 2, at 205 ("Legislators are contemplating animal abuse registries, and the FBI recently announced that it will track statistics for animal abuse, just as it does with other serious crimes. All of these reforms are endorsed by the animal protection community").

[21] Goodmark, *supra* note 1, at 17.

[22] Violence against Women and Department of Justice Reauthorization Act of 2005 (VAWA III), Pub. L. No. 109-162, 119 Stat. 2960 (2005).

[23] Marceau, *supra* note 2, at 205 (discussing how the FBI is tracking statistics for animal abuse akin to other serious crimes).

[24] Gruber, *supra* note 6, at 88; Elizabeth M. Schneider, Battered Women & Feminist Lawmaking 52 (2000).

> The promise of "legal liberalism" is disconnected from the realities of women's lives. Legal intervention alone cannot do the job. Legal intervention may provide women certain protection from battering, but it does not provide women housing, support, childcare, employment, community acceptance, or love...The contradiction is profound.

See also Goodmark, *supra* note 1, at 28.

> [T]he movement fought for and won legislative victories that allowed it to reconstruct the legal landscape, creating criminal and civil justice remedies and funding the development of those systems. But those victories came at a price. The movement went from being woman-centered to victim-centered, from self-help to saving, from working with women to generate the options that best met their needs to preferring one option, separation, facilitated by the intervention of the legal system, from being suspicious of and cautious about state intervention to mandating such intervention. The question is whether, for women subjected to abuse, that price has been worth paying.

8.3 PROBLEMS WITH OVERRELIANCE ON THE CRIMINAL JUSTICE SYSTEM

8.3.1 *Crowding Out of Other Solutions*

Massive federal funding continues to be diverted to the enforcement of the criminal law as a primary solution to the problem of DV.[25] The problem, stated succinctly by Professor Leigh Goodmark, is that "in the zero-sum game of funding, monies spent on law enforcement are not spent on other crucial services like housing, job training, education or economic development."[26] Housing is the number-one need of people experiencing abuse.[27] Unemployment and poverty have for years been known to be not merely risk factors associated with increased danger and lethality, but structural causes of DV.[28] One study showed that women who experience abuse have benefited as much from having help with child care, laundry, and errands as from legal advocacy.[29] Outsourcing the problem of DV to the justice system has precluded community-driven solutions and drained commitment to social and mental health services for both those who perpetrate and those who experience abuse. It has also decreased the available emergency shelter beds for women, children and their pets, which is important not only practically but symbolically, given that the battered women's movement began as a shelter movement.

The continued faith in the efficacy of law, and particularly criminal law, to redress DV is therefore puzzling for several reasons. First, it ignores the explicitly stated needs of people who experience abuse – this, despite that the concept of listening to women's voices and to their lived experience is a central tenet of the battered women's movement. Second, it comes at the high price of racial injustice, not merely in the overincarceration of Black men and the deportation of brown men, though these phenomena are well documented. But with the funneling of money toward punitive criminal and immigration law enforcement, and the decrease in funding for housing, there has been an increase in the eviction of women of color from their homes. As Mathew Desmond succinctly observed in his Pulitzer Prize–winning book, *Evicted: Poverty and Profit in the American City*, "If incarceration had come to define the lives of men from impoverished Black

[25] Goodmark, *supra* note 8, at 3.
[26] Goodmark, *supra* note 1, at 22.
[27] Goodmark, *supra* note 8, at 3.
[28] *Intimate Partner Violence: Risk and Protective Factors for Perpetration*, CDC: Violence Prevention, www.cdc.gov/violenceprevention/intimatepartnerviolence/riskprotectivefactors.html (last updated Oct. 9, 2020).
[29] Lisa Goodman & Deborah Epstein, Listening to Battered Women, A Survivor-Centered Approach to Advocacy, Mental Health and Justice 24-25 (American Psychological Association 2008).

neighborhoods, eviction was shaping the lives of women. Poor Black men were locked up. Poor Black women were locked out."[30]

What is worse is that increased criminalization has not made the impact hoped for by activists regarding the prevalence of DV. Although there has been some evidence of a decrease in rates of DV beginning about a decade after the VAWA first passed, this decline has not been substantial. Between 2004 and 2010, rates of DV fell, but they fell less than the overall crime rate.[31] Between 2012 and 2019, rates of DV have not fallen, but stagnated.[32] Given the hundreds of millions of dollars specifically directed to criminal law enforcement since 1994, this trend is deeply problematic.[33] Worse, though, is that funding for criminal law enforcement has increased – and funding for housing and social services decreased – in *every* reauthorization of the Violence Against Women Act since 1994.[34]

8.3.2 *Detrimental Consequences of Mandating Arrest*

Most striking is that in states with mandatory arrest laws, there has been evidence of an *increase* in serious violence against women; for example, a 2005 study found a 54 percent increase in intimate partner *homicides*.[35] Dialing back mandatory arrest, even without other changes, may benefit women, especially women in low-income communities of color.[36] The increase in homicide rates, combined with victims' increasing reluctance – since the promulgation of aggressive arrest and prosecution policies – to call the police for help should give animal rights activists pause.[37]

[30] Matthew Desmond, Evicted: Poverty and Profit in the American City 98 (2016).

[31] *See* Shannan Catalano, Intimate Partner Violence 1993–2010, Bureau of Justice Statistics, U.S. Dep't of Justice 1 (Nov. 2012), www.bjs.gov/content/pub/pdf/ipvus.pdf.

[32] Number of Violent Victimizations by Victim-Offender Relationship and Sex, 1993–2019, Bureau of Justice Statistics, U.S. Dep't of Justice. (Generated using the NCVS Victimization Analysis Tool, www.bjs.gov, Dec. 16, 2020.).

[33] Professor Leigh Goodmark has repeatedly argued this point. Most recently, *see* Alisha Haridasani Gupta, *Is the Legal System an Effective Solution to Domestic Violence?* N.Y. Times (Dec. 16, 2020), www.nytimes.com/2020/12/15/us/domestic-violence-fka-twigs-shia-labeouf.html.

[34] As of this writing, the Violence Against Women Act is on the cusp of being reauthorized for the fifth time; there is reason to hope that it *may* provide funding to noncriminal solutions such as community education regarding cultural messages about the acceptability of DV. *See* H.R. 1620, 117th Cong. (as passed by House, March 17, 2021), /www.congress.gov/bill/117th-congress/house-bill/1620/text.

[35] Radha Iyengar, *Does the Certainty of Arrest Reduce Domestic Violence? Evidence from Mandatory and Recommended Arrest Laws*, 93 J. of Pub. Econ. 85, 89 (2009).

[36] Aya Gruber, *How Police Became the Go-to Response to Domestic Violence*, SLATE (July 07, 2020), https://slate.com/news-and-politics/2020/07/policing-domestic-violence-history.html.

[37] *See* Donna Coker et al., *Responses from the Field: Sexual Assault, Domestic Violence and Policing*, ACLU 1, 1 (Oct. 20, 2015) (An overwhelming majority of the respondents, 88 percent, reported that police "sometimes" or "often" do not believe victims or blamed victims for the violence); T.K. Logan & Rob Valente, *Who Will Help Me? Domestic Violence Survivors Speak Out about Law Enforcement Responses*, The Nat'l Domestic Violence Hotline 1, 2 (2015)

Another unforeseen consequence of mandatory arrest has been the increased arrest of women for abusing their male partners.[38] Though more women are being arrested, there has been no empirical data suggesting that women's use of violence in their relationships has dramatically increased.[39] As a result, it is difficult not to wonder whether the increase in arrest of women is directly attributable to the implementation of mandatory arrest laws. Mandatory arrest laws compel police to make *an* arrest, one way or another, if they have probable cause to believe that DV occurred. Perhaps for this reason, and in hindsight, it makes sense that arrest rates of women increased with the promulgation of mandates; after all, it is beyond empirical doubt that women can, and do, use physical violence in their relationships, whether they be relationships with other women or with men.[40]

But "[w]omen typically do not control, intimidate, or cause fear in their partner when they use violence, which is the opposite of the goals that most male abusers try to accomplish through their use of force against their female partners."[41] The question then is whether the police can, or should, at the scene of a domestic disturbance, attempt to understand the context and history of the parties. Given that police are resistant even to determining who physically attacked whom first (or who was the primary aggressor), asking police to complete a contextual analysis is unrealistic. More problematic generally, though, is that many police do not appreciate that their discretion to arrest has been taken away with "bullshit laws" like mandatory arrest laws.[42]

Another type of violence in intimate relationships is "violent resistance."[43] This occurs when people who've been systematically abused anticipate an incident of physical abuse and so they, the victims, provoke it by attacking first. This type of violence in intimate partnerships is different in kind from the type that anti-DV advocates wanted to prevent; they wanted to prevent the ongoing pattern of coercion and/or physical violence for the specific purpose of controlling a partner. Violent

(More than half of the participants said calling the police would make things worse, and two-thirds or more said they were afraid police would not believe them or do nothing).

38 *See, e.g.*, Shamita Das Dasgupta, *A Framework for Understanding Women's Use of Nonlethal Violence in Intimate Heterosexual Relationships*, 8 VIOLENCE AGAINST WOMEN 1364, 1365 (2002); Lisa Y. Larance et al., *When She Hits Him: Why the Institutional Response Deserves Reconsideration*, 5 VIOLENCE AGAINST WOMEN NEWSLETTER, 2005, at 10–18; Martha McMahon & Ellen Pence, *Making Social Change, Reflections on Individual and Institutional Advocacy with Women Arrested for Domestic Violence*, 9 VIOLENCE AGAINST WOMEN 47, 47–74 (Jan. 2003).

39 Alesha Durfee, *Situational Ambiguity and Gendered Patterns of Arrest for Intimate Partner Violence*, 18 VIOLENCE AGAINST WOMEN 64, 75 (2012).

40 SUSAN L. MILLER, VICTIMS AS OFFENDERS: THE PARADOX OF WOMEN'S VIOLENCE IN RELATIONSHIPS ix (2005).

41 *Id.* at x.

42 *Id.* at 58–59.

43 This term was coined by sociologist Michael Johnson. *See* Joan B. Kelly & Michael P. Johnson, *Differentiation among Types of Intimate Partner Violence: Research Update and Implications for Interventions*, 46 FAM. CT. REV. 476, 479 (2008).

resistance is nonetheless "domestic violence" under many states' criminal laws. Or it could be that at the scene of a domestic disturbance, it is simply too difficult to determine whether an act of violence is one of self-defense versus proactive aggression.

For all these reasons, given no, or little, discretion about making *an* arrest at the scene of a domestic disturbance, police may err on the side of being safe rather than sorry by arresting both parties at the scene, a phenomenon known as dual arrest. Whatever the cause, mandatory arrest laws that take away police discretion have proven not to be as effective as anti-DV activists had hoped and, in fact, have in many cases hurt the people that they were intended to protect. Why should any of this matter to animal rights activists? Put simply, if criminal law hurts rather than helps, it may not be easy to amend, let alone repeal. Particularly in this day and age, when laws that ratchet up, rather than down, carceral solutions are sticky.

8.3.3 *Police as Perpetrators of DV*

One group of people who have never borne the risk of overarrest are police themselves. Yet rates of DV are higher amongst police than in the general population.[44] Little attention has been paid to this issue by anti-DV and by animal rights activists.

In his 2014 article in the *Atlantic*, entitled *Police Have a Much Bigger Domestic-Abuse Problem Than the NFL Does*, journalist Connor Friedersdorf noted the dearth of empirical data available. He relied upon the only sources he could find: a fact sheet created by the National Center for Women and Policing,[45] finding that "[t]wo studies have found that at least forty percent of police officer families experience DV, in contrast to ten percent of families in the general population. A third study of older and more experienced officers found a rate of twenty-four percent, indicating that DV is two to four times more common among police families than American families in general."[46]

Friedersdorf also cited a 2013 investigative article in the *New York Times*, finding "In some cases, researchers have resorted to asking officers to confess how often they had committed abuse. One such study, published in 2000, said one in 10 officers at seven police agencies admitted that they had 'slapped, punched or otherwise

[44] *See generally* Leigh Goodmark, *Hands Up at Home: Militarized Masculinity and Police Officers Who Commit Intimate Partner Abuse*, 2015 BYU L. Rev. 118 (2015).

[45] When I started research for this chapter in July 2020, I visited the National Center for Women and Policing website and found the fact sheet to which Friedersdorf refers, which I copied and pasted into a word document. The link no longer works but the fact sheet is on file with the author.

[46] Conor Friedersdorf, *Police Have a Much Bigger Domestic-Abuse Problem Than the NFL Does*, The Atl. (Sept. 19, 2014), www.theatlantic.com/national/archive/2014/09/police-officers-who-hit-their-wives-or-girlfriends/380329/.

injured' a spouse or domestic partner."[47] After reporting requirements were tightened in 2007, requiring fingerprints of arrested officers to be automatically reported to the agency that licenses them, the number of domestic abuse cases more than doubled – from 293 in the previous five years to 775 over the next five.

Advocates for animal rights should care about higher rates of abuse amongst police because of the correlation between the abuse of intimate partners and the abuse of the partner's animals.[48] In domestic violence cases, perpetrators often threaten to, or actually do, cause harm to animals as a means of coercing or causing psychological injury to their intimate partners. If police are more likely than people in the general population to abuse their partners, and a form of abuse of partners is harming that partner's animals, police may as a group be more likely to abuse animals. Before relying on police as first responders to the problem of abuse of animals, activists must investigate carefully their rates of abuse of animals lest they find themselves in the same conundrum as anti-DV activists: relying on perpetrators to protect victims.

But there is a more troubling issue lurking here. Many animal rights advocates vehemently argue that there is a link between violence against animals and the proclivity to use violence against people. This link is one justification that animal rights activists use in support of more officers enforcing animal crimes. In other words, more police, if animal activists are correct about the link, should reduce domestic violence. Alas, the *opposite* is true in the context of DV. More police enforcing animal laws yields more, not less, abuse of people.

8.3.4 *Co-option of the Definition of DV*

Overreliance on the criminal justice system response had another unintended consequence in the broader social context. The definition of DV changed from what activists in the early battered women's movement intended. This movement grew out of the women's liberation movement of the 1960s and 1970s. At its inception, the "battered wives' movement," as it was first called, was about ensuring that women not only had the right to be safe in their own homes, but the right to be equal. Physical violence against women was just one manifestation of a larger pattern of subordination that included many other forms of control – over money, jobs, education, relationships outside of the home, to name a few. The goal of early

47 *Id.* (quoting from Sarah Cohen et al., *Departments Are Slow to Police Their Own Abusers*, N.Y. Times (Nov. 23, 2013) www.nytimes.com/projects/2013/police-domestic-abuse/index.html).

48 *See generally* Sharon L. Nelson, *The Connection between Animal Abuse and Family Violence: A Selected Annotated Bibliography*, 17 Animal L. 369 (2011); Frank. R. Ascione *et al.*, *Battered Pets and Domestic Violence: Animal Abuse Reported by Women Experiencing Intimate Violence and by Nonabused Women*, 13 Violence against Women 354 (2007); Jeff Fink, *The Link: Domestic Violence and Animal Abuse*, Off. of Women's Health Blog (Nov. 7, 2017), www.womenshealth.gov/blog/domestic-violence-animal-abuse.

activists was to win autonomy – the ability to be full and equal citizens in society – not merely to win the right to be physically safe.

The criminal law definition focuses – as it does in cases of assaults perpetrated by a stranger – on a discrete, physical incident of violence.[49] It is the criminal definition, and not control over money or access to education or jobs, that people commonly think of when they think of DV. Think for a moment of the ads we see during the Super Bowl, or the images of women with black eyes on billboards. None captures the underlying causes of DV; all capitalize on the physical injury that matters to the criminal definition of DV.

There is thus a mismatch between the conduct for which offenders are arrested, restrained, and prosecuted, and the construct of DV as many activists understand it. The VAWA defines DV as "any felony or misdemeanor crime" perpetrated by one person against another in an intimate or familial relationship.[50] The felony or misdemeanor is set forth in states' criminal codes. No state statute criminalizes a "pattern of behavior for the purpose of gaining power and control" in a relationship. Indeed, few states have codified a standalone offense of "DV." Instead, states label, categorize, or enhance the penalties for numerous crimes such as assault, battery, and kidnapping in one circumstance: when perpetrated in a relationship.[51] Few state statutes mention, let alone require proof of, any motive.[52] Nor does any state statute require that criminal acts of violence within an intimate relationship be part of a

[49] Evan Stark, *Re-presenting Battered Women: From Battered Woman Syndrome to Coercive Control*, 58 ALA. L. REV. 973, 980 (1995).

[50] 34 U.S.C.A. § 12291(a)(8) (2017).

[51] ALA. CODE § 13A-6-130 *et seq*., § 13A-6-138, § 13A-6-139.1 (1975); ARIZ. REV. STAT. ANN. § 13-3601 (A), § 13-3601.02 (2007); ARK. CODE ANN. § 5-26-303 *et seq*., § 5-26-306 et seq. (2017); GA. CODE ANN. § 16-5-23(f) *et seq*. (2015); HAW. REV. STAT. ANN. § 709-906(1); IDAHO CODE ANN. § 18-918 (2018); 720 Ill. COMP. STAT. ANN. 5/12-3.2 et seq. (2015); IND. CODE ANN. § 35-31.5-2-76, et seq. (2016); IOWA CODE ANN. § 708.2A (2017); KAN. STAT. ANN. § 21-5414 (2018); KY. REV. STAT. ANN. § 508.032; LA. STAT. ANN. § 14:35.3, § 14:37.7 (2018); ME. REV. STAT. tit. 17-A, § 207-A, § 209-A, § 210-B, § 210-C, § 211-A (2018); MICH. COMP. LAWS ANN. § 750.81(2) (2016); MINN. STAT. ANN. § 609.2242, § 609.2247; MISS. CODE. ANN. § 97-3-7(3)(a), § 99-3-7(5); MO. ANN. STAT. § 565.072, et seq. (2017); MONT. CODE ANN. § 45-5-206; NEB. REV. STAT. ANN. § 28-323; NEV. REV. STAT. ANN. § 33.018, § 200.485 (2018); N.H. REV. STAT. ANN. § 631:2-b; N.J. STAT. ANN. § 2C:25-19 (2016); N.M. STAT. ANN. § 30-3-12, *et seq*.; N.C. GEN. STAT. ANN. § 50B-1 (2015); OHIO REV. CODE ANN. § 2919.25 (2019); OKLA. STAT. ANN. tit. 21, § 644, *et seq*.; 12 R.I. GEN. LAWS ANN. § 12-29-2; S.C. CODE ANN. § 16-25-20, § 16-25-65 (2015); TENN. CODE ANN. § 39-13-111 (2018); UTAH CODE ANN. § 77-36-1(4) (2018); VT. STAT. ANN. tit. 13, § 1042; VA. CODE ANN. § 18.2-57.2 (2014); WASH. REV. CODE ANN. § 10.99.020; W. VA. CODE ANN. § 61-2-28 (2017); WIS. STAT. ANN. § 968.075 (2016); WYO. STAT. ANN. § 6-2-510, *et seq*. (2018).

[52] No state statute mentions "power and control," but some mention "coercion" and "control." *See, e.g.*, COLO. REV. S. § 18-6-800.3, which defines DV for the purposes of sentence enhancement as "an act or threatened act of violence upon a person with whom the actor is or has been involved in an intimate relationship," and as "any other crime against a person. . .- when used as a method of coercion, control, punishment, intimidation, or revenge directed against a person with whom the actor is or has been involved in an intimate relationship."

pattern, though repeated acts against the same partner might warrant enhanced penalties.[53]

Thus, *any* single criminal act committed by one partner against another, for *any* reason, can qualify as a crime subjecting the perpetrator to mandatory arrest, aggressive prosecution, and restraint. This treatment bears little resemblance to the definition of DV that anti-DV activists most wanted, and indeed still do want, to target: a pattern of acts, not necessarily including physical violence, in which one partner seeks to control the liberty and autonomy of the other.

In short, the criminalization strategy usurped the very definition of the problem, as conceived of by anti-DV movement leaders. In 2006, pioneering activist Ellen Pence wrote:

> the new laws as well as procedures and public policies that were crafted to confront such abuse, lumped all acts of domestic violence into a unitary category. For example, the phrase "zero tolerance" was coined to emphasize the struggle to end intimate partner battering. However, over the years, its target has been extended to include all violence and any potential violence. That is, the single focus of stopping the ongoing use of violence and coercion against women by their partners became a diffused goal of confronting all acts of violence between couples under the rubric of "zero tolerance." We differ with this over-generalization and believe that it would lead to a "one-size-fits-all" intervention approach, which would meet neither the goals of fairness nor public safety.[54]

Overreliance on law's definition of DV draws attention away from, rather than toward, systemic violence, risking that we lose the war to win only small battles. At the beginning of the second wave of feminism in the early 1970s, activists made connections between abusive tactics within relationships and the larger institutions that supported those individual tactics. After naming specific tactics of an individual abusive partner, a second inquiry always followed. Women in shelters and in community support groups were asked to name, explicitly, all the "institutional and community decisions [that] support [the] individual batterer's ability to use abusive tactics (police, courts, media, medical, clergy, business, education, human services)."[55] Today, people who experience abuse are asked only the former. As noted by sociologist Joshua Price, the "second part of the code, *that part that seeks to*

[53] Ga. Code Ann. § 16-5-23.1; Ind. Code Ann. § 35-42-2-1.3(c)(4) states that "Domestic Battery" is a Class A misdemeanor, but the crime becomes a Level 5 felony if the person has a previous conviction for a battery offense against the same family or household member, or has a previous conviction for a similar offense in any other jurisdiction against the same family or household member; Mich. Comp. Laws Ann. § 750.81 (2016); N.M. Stat. Ann. § 30-3-17 (2008).

[54] Ellen Pence & Shamita Das Dasgupta, *Re-examining "Battering": Are All Acts of Violence against Intimate Partners the Same?* Praxis Int'l, Inc. 2, 2–3 (June 20, 2006), https://praxisinternational.org/wp-content/uploads/2016/02/ReexaminingBattering-1.pdf.

[55] *See* Joshua M. Price, Structural Violence: Hidden Brutality in the Lives of Women 21 (2012).

uncover and describe institutional and cultural collaboration with the batterer, is often eliminated."[56]

A growing consensus among feminist scholars, in addition to activists, is that too little attention has been paid to the contribution of structural conditions to the problem of intimate partner violence[57] and too much attention has been paid to fine-tuning the law.[58] How could this not be the case, when law and particularly criminal law is the primary solution we have created for addressing DV?

The potential for co-option of definition should be of even greater concern to animal rights activists. The animal rights movement has yet to come to agreement, amongst its stakeholders, about what is, and what is not, abuse and what will, and what will not, sufficiently protect nonhuman beings.[59]

8.4 REFLECTIONS FROM THE TRENCHES

Recently, I was asked to make a presentation to the staff of a local anti-DV agency. One of the members of the audience asked: "What's the biggest change, since you were a shelter worker in 1990, about how we (advocates in shelters) help people experiencing domestic violence?" In reply, I recalled that I was taught to counsel women: "Leave. Abuse *only* increases over time. If you don't leave, things *only* are going to get worse. Leaving is the *only* way to be safe." This was the training I received as a shelter worker, in the early 1990s; this was the training that many shelter workers and anti-DV advocates received at the time.[60]

Yet only twenty years earlier, at the start of the shelter movement, getting women to leave their partners was not the goal. At the start of the second wave, the idea was to help people experiencing abuse identify their own solutions while providing them a space to live that was safe. Shelter provided not merely housing in an emergency,

56 *Id.* at 25.

57 *See, e.g.*, Deborah M. Weissman, *The Community Politics of Domestic Violence*, 82 BROOK. L. REV. 1479, 1480 (2017) (characterizing the anti-IPV movement as "indifferent to the structural sources of domestic violence as a problem"); *Id.* at 1483 ("Domestic violence persists as manifestation of gender and other forms of inequality, and social norms that oppress and repress victims. But mainstream responses often accomplish little to eliminate or repair damage, and often serve to undermine alternate responses to structural problems deeply entangled in a complicated web of larger political-economic crises.").

58 *See, e.g.*, Kristin Bumiller, *The Nexus of Domestic Violence Law Reform and Social Science: From Instrument of Social Change to Institutionalized Surveillance*, 6 ANN. REV. L. & SOC. SCI. 173, 185 (2010) (demonstrating the focus on evaluating efficacy of law and arguing that a better question to address would be how domestic violence is linked to underlying conditions that create violence in the home, including the conditions that perpetuate women's subordination and gender inequality).

59 MARCEAU, *supra* note 2, at 3 (noting the divergency "almost to the point of incompatibility" of the definition of animal protections and animal abuse).

60 DONILEEN LOSEKE, THE BATTERED WOMAN AND SHELTERS: THE SOCIAL CONSTRUCTION OF WIFE ABUSE (1992).

but the support and company of other women; childcare co-ops; advocacy for benefits; job training; and a host of other supports.

Today, we (advocates for survivors) have returned to an era in which we don't dictate to women what to do. We sit down with each survivor, aspiring to partner with them to create realistic strategies given their particular context. We now understand that DV is not a problem for which a single solution can work for everyone, let alone be summed up in a sentence. We understand that "we" don't tell "them" how to live. We understand that suggesting that someone "just leave" an abusive home is about as realistic as asking teens to "just say no" to drugs.

Unfortunately, the response offered by the criminal justice system has not been recalibrated. Separation of the parties via mandatory arrest, aggressive prosecution, and automatically imposed criminal restraining orders, regardless of the individual victim's wishes, is the system's singular response to people who experience DV. The criminal justice system's separation strategy is a strategy that anti-DV activists lobbied for. Because anti-DV activists put all their eggs in the criminalization basket as a means of ending DV, rather than in community-based, or economic or restorative or therapeutic or other justice strategies, it is a strategy that we no longer have control over, and one that we therefore will not be able to undo anytime soon.

If I were able to rewind the clock, I would spend considerably more time gathering data to better understand what victims actually need, and then spend considerably more time prioritizing that need. In the case of DV, victims tell us what they need. They need housing. They need a safe space to live, and not just a safe place to "be" temporarily, for the thirty or sixty days that most shelters offer. They need a home of their own and one that is in their community. I would look less to law generally, but far less to criminal law particularly, as a means of changing a social norm – especially ones that are sticky, such as DV and the abuse of nonhuman beings. I would look more toward the community and the building of relationships and alliances and ascertaining where values across various constituencies align, to create momentum for change at a grassroots level. The anti-DV movement has alienated communities of color in its efforts. This too, I fear, will not be undone any time soon.

Perhaps the most important lesson to draw about the criminalization strategy in the anti-DV realm is one that cuts deep. Given the incontrovertible data about overincarceration generally, but overincarceration of certain groups of people more than others, it is hypocritical (to put it mildly) for social movements to on one hand fight for equality using terms like dignity, liberation, and "humane" treatment while on the other turning a blind eye to the inhumane treatment of so many people in the criminal justice system. It is my hope that animal rights activists will, if they do not already, see the writing on the wall.

9

Humanizing Animals, Dehumanizing Humans

Aya Gruber

9.1 LIBRE'S LAW

On a summer afternoon in 2017, Pennsylvania governor Tom Wolf gathered supporters and advocates to join him in an outdoor public bill-signing ceremony. The crowd assembled to watch Wolf enact "Libre's Law," a popular bipartisan piece of legislation. The mood was celebratory, as the governor had planned a festival of sorts, with the media, social media fans, and community members in attendance. Libre, the legislative namesake, was of course part of the spectacle. And due to his celebrity and the high-profile nature of his cause, Libre did something that nonlawmakers rarely get to do. He signed the bill. Libre, a Boston terrier, bore a quizzical look as his rescuer-owner, Janine Guido, guided his paw to a bowl of black ink, dipped it in, and pressed it firmly on the document. The moment elicited cheers from the crowd and barks from the dogs Wolf had invited as special "canine advocate guests."[1]

Animal rights groups and social media commentators heaped praise on Wolf for showing "compassion" and "caring" by supporting Libre's Law, a tough-on-crime bill that created a barrage of new and strengthened misdemeanors and felonies for animal abuse and neglect. Wolf characterized it as a "landmark" piece of legislation that brought "long overdue" justice to dogs.[2] After signing the bill, the Democratic governor made several appearances with the photogenic pup, including organizing an anniversary celebration where Libre "got his own puppy cake." A Wolf aide

[1] *Governor Wolf Invites Public to Attend Animal Protection Overhaul Bill Signing*, GOVERNORPA.GOV (June 27, 2017), https://www.governor.pa.gov/newsroom/governor-wolf-invites-public-to-attend-animal-protection-overhaul-bill-signing/ [https://perma.cc/7A9N-9P9T]; Mike Straub, *Gov. Wolf Signs Anti–Animal Cruelty Bill Libre's Law into Law*, WGAL8 (June 28, 2017, 5:47 PM), [https://perma.cc/GVC3-FDU9].

[2] *Governor Wolf Celebrates Landmark Animal Protection Legislation Becoming Law Today*, GOVERNORPA.GOV (Aug. 28, 2017), https://www.governor.pa.gov/newsroom/governor-wolf-celebrates-landmark-animal-protection-legislation-becoming-law-today/ [https://perma.cc/FJ6Z-YK7A].

called Libre "a beloved and valued member of our team."[3] When Wolf came up for reelection in 2018, his campaign ran an advertisement featuring Libre during peak prime-time slots on Pennsylvania channels. The "feel-good" and "smart" ad began with pictures of a sickly and starved Libre—pictures that had sparked international outrage – and moved to video of the healthy "bug-eyed miracle boy"[4] licking the smiling politician. "People say a dog is man's best friend," the actor voicing Libre proclaimed. "I say a Wolf is mine."[5]

The pictures of a near-dead Libre shocked the world and enabled his whirlwind transformation from sick puppy to social-media influencer, gubernatorial team member, and poster dog for zero tolerance of animal cruelty. One would expect the tale of his abuse would be similarly spectacular and involve horrific and malicious cruelty by his caretaker. However, Libre's caretaker's behavior was not shocking and gleefully cruel; in fact, it was questionably neglectful.

On July 4, 2016, Dextin Orme was making deliveries to an Amish farm in Lancaster county when he spied a nearly lifeless puppy in a dog cage. Orme convinced the farmer, thirty-three-year-old Benjamin Stoltzfus, to allow him to take the sixteen-week-old dog to a friend and former humane society employee. She, in turn, brought the dog to a pet hospital and contacted the Speranza Animal Rescue. Janine Guido, Speranza's director, immediately took an interest in the puppy, whom she named Libre.[6] Guido was shocked at the puppy's condition. Libre was suffering from severe mange, which left him hairless, covered in sores, and so malnourished and dehydrated that he could barely hold his head up. Normally, a dog so far gone would be euthanized, and Guido discussed that possibility with the vet. However, she decided to adopt the dog and give medical treatment a try.[7]

Guido took to social media and posted pictures of the pathetic-looking little guy under the handle "Justice for Libre."[8] The pictures provoked immediate and strong

3 Linda Fuoco, *Pet Tales: Famous Dog Comes to Gov. Wolf's Aid in Political Commercial*, PITTSBURGH POST-GAZETTE (Oct. 26, 2018, 6:00 AM), https://www.post-gazette.com/pets/pet-tales/2018/10/26/Pet-Tales-Libre-Boston-terrier-animal-abuse-law-PA-Governor-Tom-Wolf-commercial/stories/201810260016 [https://perma.cc/8PNX-94SW].

4 Jan Murphy, *Libre's Law on Its Way to Gov. Tom Wolf for Enactment*, PENNLIVE.COM: POL. (Jan. 5, 2019), https://www.pennlive.com/politics/2017/06/libres_law_on_its_way_to_gov_t.html [https://perma.cc/YDC8-UFEL]; Abby Zelko, *From the "Brink of Death," Libre the Dog Now Inspires Others*, YORK DAILY REC. (June 28, 2017, 5:32 PM), https://www.ydr.com/story/life/2017/06/28/brink-death-libre-now-inspires-others/430841001/ [https://perma.cc/6XSX-8Z2R].

5 Fuoco, *supra* note 3.

6 Tom Knapp, *Rescuer Decides to Adopt Libre, the Puppy Found Near Death on a Lancaster County Farm*, LANCASTER ONLINE (July 21, 2016), https://lancasteronline.com/news/local/rescuer-decides-to-adopt-libre-the-puppy-found-near-death-on-a-lancaster-county-farm/article_273ada82-4f69-11e6-9578-1bce449d7453.html [https://perma.cc/TM86-8SV5].

7 Liz Evans Scorforo, *Libre Likely Gets to Go Home Soon, to the Rescuer Who Saved His Life*, YORK DISPATCH (July 22, 2016, 3:40 p.m.), https://www.yorkdispatch.com/story/news/2016/07/22/libre-dog-home-puppy-mill-speranza/87438340/ [https://perma.cc/9V5W-PMKR].

8 *Justice for Libre, Groups*, FACEBOOK, https://www.facebook.com/groups/1662998610691890/ [https://perma.cc/992U-RL98].

reactions and garnered Guido and Libre tens of thousands of followers. Libre's story was featured in news outlets around the world. Throughout Libre's treatment, Guido and Justice for Libre posted photos and updates, which fans reposted to a public rapidly becoming emotionally invested in Libre's plight. As one local paper noted, "Videos of Libre went viral as his road to recovery was documented every step of the way."[9] Instagrammers and Facebookers demanded justice in the form of Stoltzfus's arrest and criminal prosecution.

Libre's legions of supporters were accordingly crestfallen when Susan Martin, the Lancaster County SPCA director and an appointed animal control officer, declined to bring criminal charges. Outraged voices on social media and in the community demanded Martin's ouster and the immediate commencement of a criminal case against the farmer. County District Attorney Craig Stedman was listening. He charged Stoltzfus with neglect – a summary offense punishable by a $750 fine and up to ninety days in jail – and commenced proceedings to strip Martin of her license to operate as a law enforcer.[10] This took Martin by surprise. She explained to the press that she made her charging decision in Stoltzfus's case as she did in all her other cases: in consultation with the prosecutor's office. Nevertheless, an exasperated Martin surrendered her policing license, noting that it would "allow more time for me to focus on the SPCA's mission of caring for animals in need."[11] Stedman, the prosecutor, subsequently transferred animal control enforcement to the police.[12] On July 25, 2017, just under a month after Governor Wolf signed Libre's Law, the Lancaster County SPCA, still under scrutiny and out of funds, announced its closing.[13]

Martin was obviously dedicated to animals. She saw that Libre was in terrible shape and must have been aware of the high-profile nature of the case. Why would she decline to charge Stoltzfus, and why would the DA's office initially agree? According to Martin, there was simply not enough proof that the farmer had neglected the puppy. Shortly after Libre's birth, Stoltzfus sold him to a buyer. The pup had been vaccinated and was healthy at the time of sale. However, two weeks

[9] David Weissman, *Libre's Law Passes Senate Committee*, York Dispatch (Mar. 22, 2017, 10:52 AM), https://www.yorkdispatch.com/story/news/politics/2017/02/09/libres-law-reintroduced-pa-senate/97686138/ [https://perma.cc/9AZK-J8UJ].

[10] Jonas Fortune, *Lancaster County DA to Seek Suspension of Animal Cruelty Officer Who Didn't Pursue Libre Case*, Lancaster Online (Aug. 11, 2016), https://lancasteronline.com/news/local/lancaster-county-da-to-seek-suspension-of-animal-cruelty-officer-who-didnt-pursue-libre-case/article_c3ac8f70-5fcf-11e6-913a-1fcf11edfe84.html [https://perma.cc/95ZL-EM7R].

[11] Lizzy Hardison, *DA Was Unwilling to File Charges Early in Dog Abuse Case, Embattled SPCA Director Says*, Penn Live (Jan. 5, 2019), https://www.pennlive.com/news/2016/08/lancaster_spca_director_respon.html [https://perma.cc/7HHZ-KAEX].

[12] Fortune, *supra* note 10.

[13] Nora Shelly, *"Devastating": SPCA Closing Leaves Lancaster with a Void to Fill*, Penn Live (Jan. 5, 2019), https://www.pennlive.com/news/2017/07/devastating_spca_closing_leave.html [https://perma.cc/R67Z-9PLV].

later, Libre started showing signs of mange, and the buyer brought him to the vet.[14] When the vet confirmed a diagnosis of demodectic mange, the buyer returned Libre to Stoltzfus. The farmer took the afflicted pooch to his own vet for treatment. Martin and the SPCA confirmed that at the time Orme discovered Libre, the puppy was in fact under veterinarian care, but he was not responding well to treatment.[15]

Advanced cases of demodectic mange or demodicosis can be deadly. The condition is caused by the mite *Demodex canis*. Demodectic mange is not contagious, and many dogs harbor the mite in small quantities. *Demodex canis* typically causes only mild symptoms, but it can cause serious illness in dogs with malfunctioning or immature immune systems. Because of their underdeveloped immune systems, puppies under eighteen weeks old are particularly vulnerable to demodicosis. Puppies with compromised immune systems are at risk of developing generalized demodectic mange,[16] a very serious condition where "the entire body may be covered with redness, infections, scaling, swelling, and crusts [and] the dog loses most, if not all, hair."[17] In addition to the hairlessness and sores that made Libre look so pitiful, dogs with the severe condition "may lose their appetite, become lethargic and develop a fever."[18] Breeders take note of puppies who contract generalized demodectic mange because it indicates genetic vulnerabilities in the parent.[19] Libre's mom in fact also had a case of demodicosis, although much milder.[20] Experts note that "Generalised demodicosis can be very difficult to treat and requires persistent intervention and dedicated owner's cooperation, since it is multifactorial and often complicated by concurrent infections."[21]

Stoltzfus pled guilty to the summary offense and paid a fine, and now he no longer keeps dogs. But the riled-up public was yet unsatisfied with what they

[14] Myles Snyder, *SPCA: No Charges against Sick Puppy's Breeder*, SENTINEL (July 8, 2016), https://cumberlink.com/news/local/capital_region/spca-no-charges-against-sick-puppy-s-breeder/article_fcb64be6-039f-5cdf-b4aa-1f902660e589.amp.html [https://perma.cc/MT3R-ETV7].

[15] *Id.* ("The Lancaster County SPCA confirmed the puppy was under veterinarian care when it was obtained by the rescue group.") Libre's supporters dispute that Stoltzfus had Libre under veterinary care, given his condition; *See* Sue Long, *The Band Libre*, LANCASTER CNTY. MAG. https://www.lancastercountymag.com/the-band-libre/ [https://perma.cc/8J8K-2XTT].

[16] Ernest Ward & Amy Panning, *Demodectic Mange in Dogs*, VCA HOSP. https://vcahospitals.com/know-your-pet/mange-demodectic-in-dogs [https://perma.cc/5ZPP-2XGR].

[17] Mara Bovsun, *Mange in Dogs: What You Need to Know*, AM. KENNEL CLUB (Jan. 23, 2019), https://www.akc.org/expert-advice/health/mange-what-you-need-to-know/#:~:text=Symptoms%20of%25.

[18] *Id.*

[19] Gemma Gaitskell, *Demodectic Mange in Dogs: A Science-Based Guide*, NEXTGEN DOG, https://nextgendog.com/demodectic-mange-in-dogs/ [https://perma.cc/AQ82-FXDM].

[20] Stoltzfus surrendered her too, and she was adopted.

[21] OLUDUNSIN ET AL., DEATH OF A FOUR-YEAR-OLD GERMAN SHEPHERD DOG DUE TO DEMODEX CANIS IN IBADAN, SOUTHWEST NIGERIA: A CASE REPORT, LABOME (June 15, 2014), http://www.labome.org/research/Death-of-a-four-year-old-German-shepherd-dog-due-to-Demodex-canis-in-Ibadan-Southwest-Nigeria-a-case.html [https://perma.cc/42YN-N5QC].

considered a "slap on the wrist."[22] They protested that Libre deserved better. Republican state senator Richard Alloway took note of the high-profile story, as did lobbyists from the Humane Society of the United States, Humane Action Pittsburgh, and Humane PA PAC.[23] Alloway, a conservative who had in the past sponsored antiabortion bills, was also pro-animal life.[24] He was moved to sponsor Libre's Law because "no living creature should have to endure that kind of abuse."[25] And thus was born the tough-on-animal-crime bill. Had Libre's Law been in effect, Stoltzfus's neglect charge would have been a serious felony.

Under the preexisting legal regime, animal abuse and neglect were summary offenses; repeat offenses were misdemeanors; and the main animal cruelty felony involved promoting animal fighting.[26] Libre's Law changed things dramatically.[27] It established a duty for people who keep animals to maintain them by, among other things, providing "necessary veterinary care" and "clean and sanitary shelter." Any failure to do so is "neglect," punishable as a summary offense. Neglect is presumed when a dog has been tethered outside and there is "excessive waste or excrement where the dog is tethered," the dog has "open sores or wounds," or the dog has worn a "choke, pinch, prong or chain collar."[28] Libre's Law also created the crime of "cruelty" for when a person "recklessly illtreats, overloads, beats, abandons or abuses an animal." Neglect or cruelty resulting in an animal's serious bodily injury or death is a felony carrying seven years in prison. The law preserved the animal fighting felony and added a crime of possession of "animal fighting paraphernalia." The legislation set forth a slew of other animal-related crimes like being the owner of an animal who attacks a service dog and transporting an animal "in a cruel or inhumane manner" and "work[ing]" an animal for more than 15 hours a day or 90 hours a week."[29] That's a lot of carceral intervention to put on the shoulders of one little terrier.

[22] Fuoco, *supra* note 3.

[23] *Id.*

[24] *See* Legislative History of Richard A. Alloway, Legis. Tracker, https://rewirenewsgroup.com/legislative-tracker/person/richard-a-alloway/ [https://perma.cc/D9B6-D5KK]; *see also Pennsylvania Senate Bill* 3, Legiscan https://legiscan.com/PA/bill/SB3/2017 [https://perma.cc/87EM-K8GU].

[25] Vicky Taylor, *Puppy Inspires Effort to Toughen Animal Abuse Law*, Great Falls Trib. (July 27, 2016, 4:10 A.M.), https://www.greatfallstribune.com/story/news/2016/07/26/puppy-inspires-effort-toughen-animal-abuse-law/87566270/ [https://perma.cc/T2MC-YR8Q].

[26] 18 Pa. Cons. Stat. §5511(m)(1), (c)(2)(ii), (h.1) (2015) (repealed 2017).

[27] 18 Pa. Cons. Stat. §§ 5531–5561 (2017).

[28] The law has also been widely characterized by criminalizing the act of tethering a dog outside for more than nine hours, or for more than thirty minutes, in temperatures over 90 degrees and below 32 degrees. However, the statutory language allows for a "rebuttable presumption that a dog has not been the subject of neglect" if it is has "not been tethered for longer than 30 minutes in temperatures above 90 or below 32 degrees," and satisfies other conditions. 18 Pa. Cons. Stat. § 5536(a)(a).

[29] *Id.* §§ 5535, 5538, 5540, 5541, 5542 (2017).

Libre's Law supporters were thoroughly convinced that Libre and pets like him unconditionally supported the bill, despite that its sole aim was to broaden the state's ability to cage human animals. Libre's Law carried no other puppy benefits – no lifetime supply of kibble or free vet care. During the Libre saga, there was a distinct absence of advocacy for providing underresourced pet owners with the financial means to keep animals in sanitary and safe shelter. No one suggested a public option for people who could not afford the costly veterinary care required by animals who contract serious medical conditions like demodecosis. Indeed, Libre is alive today only because he received $27,000 worth of veterinary treatment. But luckily for Guido, Libre's social media fame made it possible for her to cover the exorbitant medical bills by donations from supporters and online followers.

Since Libre's Law 2017 passage, the state has prosecuted thousands of human animals – 21,206 to be exact. In 2017, the number was 967 cases, which spiked to 11,836 filings in 2018, and 8,405 in 2019. The majority of the cases (52 percent) were for neglect; 41 percent were for cruelty; and 7 percent were for aggravated cruelty.[30] That was the charge leveled against Eliezer Caraballo-Ocasio in 2018. Carballo kept his dog outside in a penned area with access to a shed. However, August 2018 saw unusually high ninety-degree temperatures in Pennsylvania. A neighbor called the police to report a dead dog in Carballo's yard, and officers went to Carballo's home, where they found him digging a grave for the dog. Carballo explained that he fed and watered the seven-year-old pit bull every day, but perhaps did not provide enough water given the weather. The police did find a food dish with food in it, but the water dish was dry. The authorities noted that the dog had access to a shed but the air conditioner in it was turned off. Because the dog had perished, prosecutors charged Carballo with a felony carrying seven years in prison.[31]

Libre's Law was always meant to be tough and punitive, and it substantially broadened the reach of the Pennsylvania penal system. What is striking is that that everyone – staunch conservatives, progressive socialists, and libertarians alike – agreed that the appropriate way to address animal mistreatment was to put more human animals in cages. Press in Pennsylvania and around the world celebrated the bill's unopposed passage as justice for dogs *and* proof of possibility of functional government. Senator Alloway remarked at the signing, "It's great, because this issue brings Democrats and Republicans together. Maybe we can take the good will of today and spill it over onto the budget process."[32] Indeed, despite stark political

[30] *Animal Abuse Cases Pass 20,000 Following Passage of "Libre's Law,"* Lancaster Online (July 28, 2020), https://lancasteronline.com/news/local/animal-abuse-cases-pass-20-000-following-passage-of-libre-s-law/article_eca81a52-d0e6–11ea-a2f6-f3a7cd30b24e.html [https://perma.cc/S2PV-JJAS].

[31] *Police: Owner Faces Charges after Dog Dies from Being Left in Heat in Silver Spring Township*, Sentinel (July 31, 2018), https://cumberlink.com/news/local/crime-and-courts/police-owner-faces-charges-after-dog-dies-from-being-left/article_2e233e54-dfb8–5890-8b38–06ad2b5c1f95.html [https://perma.cc/9X5G-HA92].

[32] Katie Meyer, *With PA's Pooches Looking On, "Libre's Law" Signed*, Nat'l Pub. Radio: WSKG (June 29, 2017), https://wskg.org/news/with-pas-pooches-looking-on-libres-law-signed/ [https://perma.cc/CCT9-KUDW].

polarization in Pennsylvania and the country as a whole, not one reporter could find someone with a bad word to say about Libre's Law. One animal-rights lobbyist explained simply, "Compassion is not a political party issue. Both parties have huge supporters on animal issues."[33]

However, Democratic governor Wolf's support for this tough-on-crime bill seems more fitting of the tough-on-crime era of 1990s, when Democrats vied against Republicans for the title of strongest general in the war on crime. It feels somewhat out of sync with today's brand of incarceration-skeptical liberalism. Libre's Law was enacted in 2017, years after many liberals and a growing number of conservatives had come to see mass incarceration as one of the most pressing problems in US society. "Smart on crime" was replacing tough on crime as the popular politics du jour.[34] While Alloway and animal rights advocates were advancing the tough-on-abuse law, Republicans elsewhere were promoting "criminal justice reform" bills to reduce the number of people incarcerated and under penal supervision.[35] Even self-proclaimed "law and order" president Donald Trump boasted about signing the 2018 First Step Act, which the Brennan Center has called "the most substantial criminal justice reform legislation in a generation."[36]

By the time Governor Wolf signed Libre's Law, the country had already witnessed several shocking viral videos of horrific police killings of unarmed Black men and boys, including Michael Brown, Laquan McDonald, Eric Garner, and Tamir Rice. Black Lives Matter protesters and others had taken to the streets to protest the deeply entrenched racism of American policing, prosecution, and imprisonment.[37] In the summer and fall of 2020, another rash of high-profile police brutality cases, including the slayings of George Floyd, Ahmaud Arbery, Breonna Taylor, and Rayshard Brooks and the shooting that left Jacob Blake paralyzed, galvanized protests

33 Fuoco, *supra* note 3.

34 Benjamin Levin, *The Consensus Myth in Criminal Justice Reform*, 117 MICH. L. REV. 259 (2018)

35 *Id. See also* Osita Nwanevu, *The Improbable Success of a Criminal-Justice-Reform Bill under Trump*, NEW YORKER (Dec. 17, 2018), https://www.newyorker.com/news/news-desk/the-improbable-success-of-a-criminal-justice-reform-bill-under-trump [https://perma.cc/KLV6-EQNV]; Arthur Rizer & Lars Trautman, *The Conservative Case for Criminal Justice Reform*, GUARDIAN (Aug. 5, 2018), https://www.theguardian.com/us-news/2018/aug/05/the-conservative-case-for-criminal-justice-reform [https://perma.cc/H4A7-VDCG].

36 First Step Act, Pub. L. No. 115-391, 132 Stat. 5194 (2018), https://www.govinfo.gov/content/pkg/PLAW-115publ391/pdf/PLAW-115publ391.pdf [https://perma.cc/3TM2-Q7PM]; *see also* Tim Lau, *Historic Criminal Justice Reform Legislation Signed into Law*, BRENNAN CTR. (Dec. 21, 2018), https://www.brennancenter.org/our-work/analysis-opinion/historic-criminal-justice-reform-legislation-signed-law [https://perma.cc/2GEN-AQVR].

37 Darran Simon, *Trayvon Martin's Death Sparked a Movement That Lives on Five Years Later*, CNN (Feb. 26, 2017), https://www.cnn.com/2017/02/26/us/trayvon-martin-death-anniversary/index.html [https://perma.cc/2EU6–6FUF]; *Herstory*, BLACKLIVESMATTER.COM https://blacklivesmatter.com/herstory/ [https://perma.cc/6X99-RQC5]; Houston A. Baker, Jr., *The Black Bottom Line: Reflections on Ferguson, Black Lives Matter, and White Male Violence in America*, 28 AM. LITERARY HIST. 845 (2016).

involving millions of concerned citizens around the world.[38] Much of the public watched in horror as state officers and federal paramilitaries brazenly used weapons of war, engaged in wanton violence, utilized terroristic tactics like "disappearing" protesters, and targeted reporters.[39] These events elevated police reform to the top of the liberal political agenda.

Still, by 2017, many progressive policy makers already recognized that aggressively policing socially, racially, and economically marginalized communities and prosecuting people for crimes associated with social vulnerability and poverty perpetuated, rather than interrupted, cycles of violence and community discohesion.[40] Commentators regularly decried the US carceral system that disenfranchised and imposed onerous collateral consequences on people of color and the impoverished, operatively fomenting their "civic death."[41] Legal scholars and sociologists had produced study after study demonstrating that social services and economic empowerment are key to reducing intrafamily abuse and neglect and that interposing violent and life-ruining policing and punishment often exacerbates the underlying stressors that lead to harm.[42]

And yet here was Libre's Law entangling tens of thousands of people in the carceral web where they faced imprisonment, some like Carballo for many years.

[38] Buchanan et al., *Black Lives Matter May Be the Largest Movement in U.S. History*, N.Y. Times (July 3, 2020), https://www.nytimes.com/interactive/2020/07/03/us/george-floyd-protests-crowd-size.html [https://perma.cc/LW67-PSA8].

[39] Francine Prose, Opinion, *Watching Trump's Paramilitary Squads Descend on Portland, It's Hard Not to Feel Doomed*, Guardian (July 21, 2020), https://www.theguardian.com/commentisfree/2020/jul/20/trump-shock-troops-portland-doomed [https://perma.cc/3NRZ-BJR3]; Laurence Tribe, "*A Profoundly Un-American Attack on Civil Society*": *Why Trump's Paramilitary Force Is Unconstitutional*, WBUR: Cognoscenti (July 23, 2020), https://www.wbur.org/cognoscenti/2020/07/23/trump-federal-police-portland-laurence-tribe [https://perma.cc/CGH8-F2X5]; Jonathan Levinson & Conrad Wilson, *Federal Law Enforcement Use Unmarked Vehicles to Grab Protesters Off Portland Streets*, Or. Pub. Broad. (July 16, 2020), https://www.opb.org/news/article/federal-law-enforcement-unmarked-vehicles-portland-protesters/ [https://perma.cc/NRG8-ATAY]; Harmeet Kaur, *The Military Is Banned from Using Tear Gas on the Battlefield, but Police Can Use It on Crowds at Home. Here's Why*, CNN (June 8, 2020), https://www.cnn.com/2020/06/08/us/military-tear-gas-protesters-trnd/index.html [https://perma.cc/M9LJ-66P5].

[40] *Criminal Justice Fact Sheet*, NAACP, www.naacp.org/criminal-justice-fact-sheet/ [https://perma.cc/GX9Q-PU8A]; Ta-Nehisi Coates, *The Black Family in the Age of Mass Incarceration*, The Atl.: Pol. (Oct. 2015), https://www.theatlantic.com/magazine/archive/2015/10/the-black-family-in-the-age-of-mass-incarceration/403246/ [https://perma.cc/ZH79-LPMV]; Ashley Nellis, *The Color of Justice: Racial and Ethnic Disparity in State Prisons*, Sent'g Project (June 14, 2016), https://www.sentencingproject.org/publications/color-of-justice-racial-and-ethnic-disparity-in-state-prisons/ [https://perma.cc/K4QN-8KF2]; Dorothy E. Roberts, *The Social and Moral Cost of Mass Incarceration in African American Communities*, 56 Stan. L. Rev. 1271 (2004).

[41] Loic Wacquant, *From Salvery to Mass Incarceration: Rethinking the "Race Question" in the US*, 13 (Jan.–Feb. 2002); *see generally* Meda Chesney-Lind & Marc Mauer, Invisible Punishment: The Collateral Consequences of Mass Imprisonment (2003).

[42] *See* Aya Gruber, The Feminist War on Crime 76–78, 84–85 (2020) (discussing studies).

Under the law, *the* mechanism of ensuring that people provided "clean and sanitary shelter" and "necessary [medical] care" to pets was to imprison a subset of marginalized pet owners who drew the attention of the police. These human animals went to jails that, as the coronavirus crisis has shown, are anything but "clean and sanitary" and fall woefully short of minimum medical standards. Just across the Susquehanna River from Lancaster, where Libre was rescued, lies a large penal institution, York County Prison. On September 14, 2020, the prison was the site of a massive coronavirus outbreak.[43] Nick Lake was set to be released when he caught the virus and had to remain detained. Due to the virus ripping through the institution, the prison halted all in-person visitation, requiring inmates' loved ones to use costly telephone services. Lake's fiancée, Taylor George, explained that "she can speak to her fiancé on the phone, but . . . worried about other families who cannot afford that luxury." The overall impact on her family was severe: "George said she had been counting on her fiancé coming home and help[ing] out. His children, she said, have asked questions including, 'Is my dad going to die?'"[44]

One would think that progressives would have questioned whether ratcheting up criminal punishment, rather than using other tools of contemporary governance, really did serve the interests of animals, including the marginalized pet owners for whom animal companionship was a small raft of joy in a sea of misery. But one would be wrong. Few justified Libre's Law on the ground that criminal punishment would transform the neglectful into better future pet owners. To the contrary, advocates argued that abusive owners must surrender their pets and *never* have any again. Libre's Law supporters made it clear that punishment is the point. For the law's supporters, inflicting the pain of carceral confinement on human offenders evened the score and provided "justice" to animal victims. Jennifer Nields, cruelty officer for the Lancaster County Animal Coalition, remarked plainly, "This won't stop cruelty but it will put an emphasis on the importance of justice for their suffering. The laws are recognition of their pain and what they *deserve*."[45]

9.2 VICTIMS IN THE WAR ON CRIME

It may seem surprising that in the midst of a decarceral sea-change, liberals and libertarians alike reflexively embraced Libre's Law, a punitive bill that broadened the reach to criminal law and substantially increased prison time for conduct so

[43] Dylan Segelbaum, *"The Unknown Is Scary": York County Prison COVID-19 Outbreak Tests Prisoners, Loved Ones*, York Daily Rec. (Sept. 14, 2020), / [https://perma.cc/822C-ZCPY].

[44] *Id.*

[45] Tom Knapp, *Libre's Law Goes into Effect Today: Here's What the New Animal-Cruelty Statutes Mean for Pennsylvania*, Lancaster Online (Aug. 28, 2017), https://lancasteronline.com/news/local/libres-law-goes-into-effect-today-heres-what-the-new-animal-cruelty-statutes-mean-for/article_9feof7d4-5c0e-11e7-b014-ebfcod03542a.html (emphasis added) [https://perma.cc/8NG6-BBBJ].

readily traced to economic precarity and social marginality. But for those who study the American crime victims' movement during the tough-on-crime era of the 1980s and 1990s, the phenomenology and trajectory of Libre's Law looks like familiar territory.

Victims' rights and victim-speak have long galvanized politicians and people on both sides of the political aisle to support zero-tolerance criminal policies. The peculiarly American institution of mass incarceration was built upon a foundation of victims' rights. Spectacular narratives of suffering at the hands of monstrous offenders have repeatedly united Americans in the abandonment of reasoned analysis of how to prevent harm in favor of an unreflective, punitive, but emotionally satisfying impulse to inflict severe pain on the evil criminals who harm innocent victims. Legal sociologist Jonathan Simon remarked in 2000, "Victims' rights has emerged over the past 25 years as one of the most important social movements of our time" due "in part because of the enormous appeal of victimization to television media."[46]

Marshaled by prosecutors committed to high conviction rates and savvy politicians committed to reelection, victim narratives fomented public demands for more criminal prohibitions, weaker constitutional protections for defendants, and higher – even exorbitant – sentences. The sheer number of crimes that became life offenses during that era led to a 500 percent increase in the number of people serving life sentences between 1984 and 2016,[47] and a current prison system ill-equipped to meet the needs of its large and growing geriatric population.[48] A key principle of victims' rights is that victims' interests in justice-as-punishment should trump defendants' interests in liberty and due process. Scholar Lynne Henderson observed, "'Victims' rights' were – and are – used to counter 'defendants' rights' and to trump those rights if possible. In an argument that traces back to at least the early 20th Century, people accused of crimes are probably 'guilty as sin' and undeserving of so much legal protection."[49]

Centering the victim in advocacy and law reform is not inexorably punitive. Such is evidenced in recent times by the heartening surge of survivor-led movements calling for restorative justice, alternatives to incarceration, and even penal

46 Jonathan Simon, *Megan's Law: Crime and Democracy in Late Modern America*, 25 Law & Soc. Inquiry 1111, 1136 (2000).

47 Ashley Nellis, *Still Life: America's Increasing Use of Life and Long-Term Sentences*, Sent'g Project (May 3, 2017), https://www.sentencingproject.org/publications/still-life-americas-increasing-use-life-long-term-sentences/#III.%20Life%20by%20the%20Numbers [https://perma.cc/U6GN-PR8H] (showing an increase of from 34,000 "lifers" to 206,268, between 1985 and 2016 (including "virtual life"), a 506.7 percent increase; without "virtual life," lifers were approximately 161,957.)

48 Michael Ollove, *Elderly Inmates Burden State Prisons*, Pew Charitable Trusts: Health (Mar. 17, 2016), https://www.pewtrusts.org/en/research-and-analysis/blogs/stateline/2016/03/17/elderly-inmates-burden-state-prisons [https://perma.cc/E49K-D57H].

49 Lynne Henderson, *Co-opting Compassion: The Federal Victims' Rights Amendment*, 10 St. Thomas L. Rev. 579, 582–83 (1998).

abolition.[50] Although, in theory, victim-centered lawmaking and advocacy is not inherently carceral, the American victims' rights movement, in practice, has always been. That movement was a key driver of the shift toward tough-on-crime politics in the 1980s and proved invaluable to the policy architects of the modern American penal state. Those in the victims' rights movement and their allies insisted that "justice for victims" meant one thing, and one thing only: "meaningful," as in long, imprisonment of the offender. As such, centering the victim fueled the carceral sentiments that culminated in the United States' dishonorable distinction of most punitive nation on earth.

In the late 1970s, nascent victims' rights organizations arose around the country with a stated goal of reforming "the poor response of the criminal justice system to victims' needs."[51] Early in the movement, many victims' rights were about protecting victims from *prosecutors* who mistreated or ignored them. Not content to be cogs in a prosecutorial wheel, victims championed legal provisions to require prosecutors to give them notice of relevant dates, seek their input before making major decisions, and help them obtain monetary compensation.[52] But even in those early days, the movement had no tolerance for victims who wanted to avoid the criminal punishment system altogether.[53] Sociologist Marie Gottschalk notes that "activists in victims' organizations tended to be overwhelmingly white, female, and middle-aged – a group demographic that is hardly representative of crime victims in general."[54] They "were more supportive of the death penalty and of the police, prosecutors, and judges than were victims not active in these organizations."[55]

Ronald Reagan, who swept into office in 1981 with a pledge to take on crime, took notice of the fledgling movement. Reagan had emphasized the crime issue as part of his larger socioeconomic plan to shift the United States away from social welfare toward the "free market" by cutting taxes on the wealthy, gutting aid programs,

[50] *See, e.g.*, Impact Just., https://impactjustice.org/ [https://perma.cc/ZC8A-BUZL]; *see also* Danielle Sered, Until We Reckon: Violence, Mass Incarceration, and a Road to Repair (2019).

[51] Marlene Young & John Stein, *The History of the Crime Victims' Movement in the United States*, Off. for Victims of Crime Archive (Dec. 2004), https://www.ncjrs.gov/ovc_archives/ncvrw/2005/pg4c.html#f [https://perma.cc/RBN8-WX9F].

[52] Marie Gottschalk, The Prison and the Gallows 88–90 (2006); *see generally* Markus Dirk Dubber, Victims in the War on Crime: The Use and Abuse of Victims' Rights (2002); Aya Gruber, *Victim Wrongs: The Case for a General Criminal Defense Based on Wrongful Victim Behavior in an Era of Victims' Rights*, 76 Temp. L. Rev. 645 (Dec. 2003).

[53] Arizona's Victims' Rights Amendment confers the "right" to "refuse an interview, deposition, or other discovery request by the . . .*defendant's* attorney," a right all people *already have*. It does not confer the right to refuse to cooperate with police or prosecutors, which is far more compulsory. Az. Const., art. II, § 2.1, cl. (A)(5).

[54] Gottschalk, *supra* note 52, at 90 (quoting Katherine Beckett & Theodore Sasson, The Politics of Injustice: Crime and Punishment in America 161 (2000) (internal quotation marks omitted)).

[55] *Id.*

deregulating financial institutions, and curtailing labor protections.[56] The so-called Reagan Revolution "changed the trajectory of America," as President Obama remarked in 2008,[57] and it set the stage for today's exorbitant levels of wealth inequality.

Reagan and his allies sold a program tailor-made for the 1 percent to the other 99 in part by recasting the problems of poverty as products of criminality. Reagan observed, "Individual wrongdoing, they told us, was always caused by a lack of material goods, and underprivileged background, or poor socioeconomic conditions. And somehow ... it was society, not the individual, that was at fault when an act of violence or a crime was committed."[58] He concluded, "Is it any wonder, then, that a new privileged class emerged in America, a class of repeat offenders and career criminals who thought they had the right to victimize their fellow citizens with impunity."[59] Reagan's narrative reversed the moral order, transforming the "underprivileged" poor into a "privileged class" of criminals and society's victims of poverty into "victimizers." He strategically publicized the image of scary criminals to frighten voters into believing that crime control, rather than employment, health, or other services, was the only legitimate form of federal domestic governance.

Still, scare ads about criminals may inspire fear, but narratives and images of brutalized innocent victims inspire the loathing that drives punitivity.[60] Elayne Rapping observes that "[b]eneath the compelling emotion that informs the demands of victims, there is all too often an ugly and irrational cry for blood." Drawing on Lauren Berlant's critique of the "sentimentality" of Reagan-era conservatism,[61] Rapping asserts that the victim's rights movement, which involves "the valorization of 'surplus' or excess feeling, the tendency to substitute passion for reason in determining political and legal policy," serves as a prime example of political sentimentality.[62] The innocent victim/monstrous offender narrative in "television, in fiction, in docudrama, in tabloids, and now in trials" effectively triggers our

[56] *See* Michael Allen Meeropol, Surrender: How the Clinton Administration Completed the Reagan Revolution (2000); Melinda Cooper, Family Values: Between Neoliberalism and the New Social Conservatism (2017).

[57] *In Their Own Words: Obama on Reagan*, N.Y. Times: The Caucus (captured April 21, 2019), https://archive.nytimes.com/www.nytimes.com/ref/us/politics/21seelye-text.html?module=inline [https://perma.cc/4LJ6-GTED].

[58] Ronald W. Reagan, *Remarks at the Annual Conference of the National Sheriff's Association in Hartford, Connecticut*, Ronald Regan Presidential Libr. & Museum Archives (June 20, 1984), https://www.reaganlibrary.gov/archives/speech/remarks-annual-conference-national-sheriffs-association-hartford-connecticut [https://perma.cc/SU8G-V6A4].

[59] *Id.*

[60] Henderson, *supra* note 49, at 584.

[61] Lauren Berlant, The Queen of America Goes to Washington City (1997).

[62] Elayne Rapping, *Television, Melodrama, and the Rise of the Victims' Rights Movement*, 43 N.Y.L. Sch. L. Rev. 665, 680 (2000).

"melodramatic imagination" where we crave "moral simplification, [and] reassuring fantasies."[63]

Sentimental images of this sort are particularly effective – and dangerous – because they "seem to be superpolitical" and "beyond ideology," when they are in fact "deployed in the service of an agenda which is intensely political and ideological," Rapping observes.[64] She concludes that "a political movement based on such precepts must be viewed with grave suspicion."[65] Reagan indeed knew the power of sentimentality, and in the first week of his presidency and every April thereafter, he pronounced "Victims' Rights Week."[66] In 1982, his administration formed the President's Task Force on Victims of Crime.[67] Asserting that the criminal system had lost "essential balance,"[68] the Task Force advocated nothing less than a reversal of the due-process regime put in place by the liberal "Warren Court."[69] The Task Force's recommendations, which included abolishing parole, limiting pretrial release, and limiting judges' sentencing discretion, became the very laws that paved the path to mass incarceration.[70] Of course, the Task Force did not recommend addressing the endemic poverty and inequality that impacts the marginalized people who constitute the bulk of actual crime victims.

That's because the movement was never about the heterodox class of actual crime victims. "To maintain its fever pitch of hatred, the war on crime need[ed] ever more, and ever more sympathetic, victims," Markus Dubber remarks.[71] The victim images that drove carceral policies were very specific. First, victims were *innocent*. Within the rhetoric, victims were "'blameless,' innocent, usually attractive, middle class, and white."[72] These images stood in contrast to images of criminals, who were "subhuman … monsters" or alternatively "the ominous, if undifferentiated, poor, angry, violent, Black, or Latino male." Such imagery relieved the public of the burden of grappling with the contested ethical questions of criminality and state-imposed pain, rendering penal management akin to pest management. "The

[63] *Id.* at 678 (quoting Lynn Joyrich, *All That Television Allows*, in PRIVATE SCREENINGS: TELEVISION AND THE FEMALE CONSUMER 227, 233 [Lynn Spigel & Denise Mann eds., 1992]).

[64] Rapping, *supra* note 62, at 681 (quoting BERLANT, *supra* note 61, at 37).

[65] Rapping, *supra* note 62, at 280.

[66] Ronald W. Reagan, *Proclamation 4831 – Victims' Rights Weeks*, 1981, RONALD REAGAN PRESIDENTIAL LIBR. MUSEUM ARCHIVES (April 8, 1981), https://www.reaganlibrary.gov/archives/speech/proclamation-4831-victims-rights-weeks-1981 [https://perma.cc/YG7M-7R4J].

[67] In 1987, Reagan appointed Herrington as "Chairman" and Executive Director of the White House Conference for a Drug Free America; *see* LOIS HAIGHT HERRINGTON ET AL., PRESIDENT'S TASK FORCE ON VICTIMS OF CRIME, *Recommendations for Government Action*, NAT'L CRIM. JUST. REFERENCE SERV. at 32 (Dec. 1982), https://www.ncjrs.gov/pdffiles1/ovc/87299.pdf [https://perma.cc/FF4N-ESLQ].

[68] *Id.* at 114.

[69] The "Warren Court Era" lasted from 1953 to 1969, when Earl Warren presided as Chief Justice. The Court is remembered for rulings with a distinctly civil libertarian bent.

[70] HERRINGTON ET AL., *supra* note 67.

[71] DUBBER, *supra* note 52, at 192.

[72] Henderson, *supra* note 49.

identification with the victim at the expense of identifying with the offender provides an additional benefit to the onlooker," Dubber observes. "By denying any similarities with the offender upon which identification could be based, the onlooker transforms the essentially ethical question of punishment into one of nuisance control."

Second, victims were *devastated*. Berlant specifies that it is "traumatized subjectivity" that "replaces rational subjectivity as the essential index of value for personhood and thus for society."[73] To be sure, the victim label confines people to one identity – the harmed object of a private wrongdoer. "Any richer sense of the person undermines the claim of victimhood, because victimhood depends on a reductive view of identity," Martha Minow remarks.[74] Of course, this one-dimensional vision of a ruined victim sometimes ran up against harmed people's self-conception, and they chose instead the more empowering label of "survivor." Nevertheless, the devastated victim image tapped into "an almost religious view of suffering, empowering those who suffer with ... reverence from others," as Minow notes.[75] President Bill Clinton's attorney general Janet Reno, in a speech supporting the federal Victims' Rights Amendment, called victims "but little lower than the angels."[76] Decades later, candidate Donald Trump picked up on this theme and featured "Angel Moms," the mothers of children killed by immigrants, at his rallies.[77] Through such reverential veneration, Dubber asserts, the public can "[purge] itself of deviant elements and thereby heal itself as it salves the victim's pain."[78]

Finally, and perhaps most importantly, victims were *vengeful*. Forgiveness, when mentioned at all, was a concept appropriate for consideration only in addition to, not in lieu of, punishment. Only after the defendant accepted responsibility, apologized, and received his life sentence (or death sentence) could victims say, "I forgive you – may God forgive you too." Law professor Elizabeth Joh observes that victims' rights ideology could not "generate[ ] or tolerate[ ] narratives in which victims' families can exercise mercy, kindness, or forgiveness towards defendants."[79] These vengeful victims invariably desired *more* involvement with police, prosecutors, and the criminal process.[80] Their primary targets of disapprobation were

73 Berlant, *supra* note 61, at 35.

74 Martha Minow, *Surviving Victim Talk*, 4 UCLA L. Rev. 1433 (1993).

75 *Id.* at 1434.

76 Janet Reno, *Remarks of the Honorable Janet Reno, Attorney General of the United States, to the Child Welfare League of America*, U.S. Dept. of Just. Archives (Mar. 13, 1998), https://www.justice.gov/archive/ag/speeches/1998/0313_agcwl.htm [https://perma.cc/WR42–3BU7].

77 Michelle Goldberg, *Trump's "Angel Moms" Deserve Our Sympathy. But Their Message Is a Lie*, Slate (Sept. 1, 2016), https://slate.com/news-and-politics/2016/09/trumps-angel-moms-deserve-our-sympathy-but-not-our-vote.html [https://perma.cc/GZX2-R27D].

78 Markus Dirk Dubber, *The Victim in American Penal Law: A Systematic Overview*, 3 Buff. Crim. L. Rev. 3, 8 (1999).

79 Elizabeth E. Joh, *Narrating Pain: The Problem with Victim Impact Statements*, 10 S. Cal. Interdisc. L.J. 28 (2000).

80 Lynne Henderson, Revisiting Victims' Rights, 1999 Utah L. Rev. 383, 408 (arguing that victim participation in criminal litigation may not help their healing process).

insufficiently zealous prosecutors, defense attorneys, due process protections, and lenient judges. Victims' rights discourse thereby situated victims' interests as necessarily separate from and adverse to those of defendants. Victims' and defendants' interests were also zero-sum: the more the defendant suffered, the more the victim healed.[81]

These attributes made idealized victims formidable weapons in prosecutors' and politicians' anti-crime arsenals. First, the combination of innocence and devastation fomented a strong sentimentality, such that the public always sided with the victim. Henderson remarks, "The symbolic strength of the term 'victims' rights' overrides careful scrutiny: Who could be anti-victim?"[82] Sentimental reverence generated near-total deference to victims' purported wishes. Minow notes that "there is a strong tendency for people to couple a claim of victimhood with a claim of incorrigibility – that the victim knows better than anyone else about the victimization, and indeed, the victim cannot be wrong about it."[83] Second, with the victim now lionized and beyond challenge, the presumption of vengefulness came in to establish the victim as inalterably in opposition to the defendant. Thus, victims' interests always overlapped with prosecutors' interests, unless of course the prosecutor was lenient, in which case the victim's interest overlapped with whomever was most punitive.

This highly specific victim image, carefully curated by tough-on-crime prosecutors, profit-seeking media, and opportunistic politicians, actively excluded the marginalized men and women who disproportionately suffer from crime but view prosecution with a jaundiced eye.[84] Indeed, many crime victims, and especially victims of color, have had contacts with the criminal system as defendants, witnesses, or even pedestrians subjected to invasive stop-and-frisk policies, which make them wary of involvement with the state's penal apparatus and its functionaries. Moreover, victimhood and criminality narratives have always had distinctly racist overtones, situating innocent whiteness as the foundation of the victim image and blackness and brownness as the foundation of criminality. Stephen Carter notes that victims' rights rhetoric's "[e]motive power would be lost were one to conjure instead an image of 'innocent blackness' surrounded by 'threatening whiteness.'"[85]

In 2007, the Bureau of Justice Statistics released a telling report on Black victimization between 2001 and 2005.[86] It found that Black people were victimized at significantly higher rates than white people and were about twice as likely to be

[81] *See generally* Aya Gruber, *A Distributive Theory of Criminal Law*, 52 Wm. & Mary L. Rev. 1 (2010).

[82] Lynne N. Henderson, *The Wrongs of Victim's Rights*, 37 Stan. L. Rev. 937, 952 (1985).

[83] Minow, *supra* note 74, at 1434.

[84] Henderson, *supra* note 49, at 585 (quoting President Clinton's announcement in support of a Victims' Rights Amendment) ("[W]e sure don't want to give criminals like gang members, who may be victims of their associates [any rights].").

[85] Stephen L. Carter, *When Victims Happen to Be Black*, 97 Yale L.J. 420, 428 (1988).

[86] Erika Harrell, Bureau of Just. Stat., NCJ 214258, Black Victims of Violent Crimes (2007), https://www.bjs.gov/content/pub/pdf/bvvc.pdf [https://perma.cc/M2QU-KD8F]. This

victims of sexual assault, robbery, and aggravated assault.[87] Moreover, in 2005, African Americans made up approximately 13 percent of the US population but 49 percent of the country's homicide victims.[88] Among the Black population, victimization correlated with being male, young, low-income, and residing in an urban area.[89] However, in victims' rights parlance, the poor, young, Black, urban teen was never a victim but the ultimate criminal – a "superpredator," as some nineties Democrats infamously declared.[90] Victims' rights supporters were quite open that not all people harmed by crime merited the victim label. Supporting a federal Victims' Rights Amendment in 1996, President Bill Clinton added a seemingly obvious caveat: "[W]e sure don't want to give [rights to] criminals like gang members, who may be victims of their associates."[91]

As much as they were racialized, victimization narratives were also deeply gendered and classed. They centered on nonpoor white women, along with children, as the category of people against whom violence – especially sexual violence – was particularly intolerable and disgusting. *America's Most Wanted* was a long-running television crime series created by John Walsh, the father of a murdered child, who turned anti-crime warrior. The show aimed to deputize all Americans in catching "antisocial loners and lunatics [who] prey[ed] on women and especially children."[92] The show's producer, Michael Linder, was surprisingly honest about which victims counted: "A drug dealer who shoots another drug dealer is not as compelling as a child molester or murderer . . . If a man brutalizes innocent children, that definitely adds points."[93] The fascination with white women's and children's vulnerability to extreme violence persists even in this incarceration-skeptical era through the

appears to be the only report of its kind, although there are other victimization surveys, but those focus on general victimization. *See infra* note 87.

87 *Id.* at 3. *But see* Rachel E. Morgan & Jennifer L. Truman, U.S. Dept. of Just., NCJ 255113, Criminal Victimization, 2019 (2019), https://www.bjs.gov/content/pub/pdf/cv19.pdf [https://perma.cc/PLN5-AGKY] (showing similar rates of victimization among white people and Black people when based on survey results, but a much higher rate for Blacks when based on police reports; Black victims constitute a higher percentage of the overall Black population than white victims in the white population.).

88 Harrell, *supra* note 86, at 1.

89 *Id.*

90 Beth Caldwell & Ellen C. Caldwell, *Superpredators and Animals – Images and California's Get Tough on Crime Initiatives*, 11 J. of Inst. of Just. & Int'l Stud. 61 (2011); *see also* Anne Gearan & Abby Phillip, *Clinton Regrets 1996 Remark on "Super-Predators" after Encounter with Activist*, Wash. Post (Feb. 25, 2016), https://www.washingtonpost.com/news/post-politics/wp/2016/02/25/clinton-heckled-by-black-lives-matter-activist/ [https://perma.cc/LU2C-PFW7].

91 Online News Hour, *Clinton's Announcement in Support of a Victims' Rights Amendment*, Pub. Broad. Serv. (June 25, 1996), https://www.pbs.org/newshour/politics/law-jan-june96-victim_06-25 [https://perma.cc/GMF7-4H5G].

92 Rapping, *supra* note 62, at 675.

93 *Id.* at 675–76 (citing Van Gordon Sauter, *Rating the Reality Shows and Keeping Tabs on the Tabloids* at 18, TV Guide (May 2, 1992); Anna Williams, *Domesticity and the Aetiology of Crime in "America's Most Wanted* "at 97–98, Camera Obscura [Jan.–May 1993]).

proliferation of true-crime broadcasts that, as Monika Bauerlein notes, tell "stories largely about white victims, based on uncritical accounts of police and prosecutors."[94]

9.3 VICTIMS' RIGHTS AND POLICY WRONGS

The tough-on-crime era produced a glut of laws created in the image of – and often named after – victims. Because the laws were based on narratives of victimhood carefully curated by political actors, they often reflected a distorted picture of the problem and exceedingly narrow view of how to remedy it. For example, in the 1980s and 1990s, advocates pressed for laws to take domestic violence [DV] seriously by mandating that police arrest and prosecutors pursue cases against all alleged DV offenders. These reforms were propelled by stories, both real and fictionalized, of white women who had been abused and wanted to separate from the abuser, but were ignored and left to be brutalized (and even die) by indifferent police officers and lenient prosecutors. In the 1990s, as Laurie Levenson notes, Nicole Brown Simpson became "synonymous with the image of the battered wife – a young, beautiful woman, unable to escape her abuser, and unable to get the criminal justice system to respond to her pleas."[95]

Once these spectacular and racialized narratives established battering as a function of the absence of policing and punishment, law enforcement became the solution *in and of itself.* With leniency defined as injustice, every tough-on-crime reform became an instance of gender justice, regardless of the consequences. This rendered the questions of whether such reforms in fact deterred violence, were more beneficial than harmful, or even satisfied victims totally beside the point. And, as it turned out, the tough-on-DV program was no panacea for battered women, in large part because the marginalized women of color who made up a substantial portion of the DV victim population had been excluded from the prevailing narrative. From the beginning, Black women warned advocates of carceral DV policy that Black victims often bore a very different relationship to the criminal system from white victims and did not invariably desire more involvement with it or even for the defendant to have more involvement with it. As one activist of color put it, "I think white women talked more as if the courts belonged to us [all women] and therefore should work for us where we [women of color] always saw it as belonging to someone else and talked more about how to keep it from hurting us."[96]

[94] Monika Bauerlein, *True Crime Is Cathartic for Women. It's Also Cop Propaganda*, MOTHER JONES (May/June 2020), https://www.motherjones.com/media/2020/06/true-crime-podcasts-white-women/ [https://perma.cc/XK3S-Y2ZD].

[95] *See* Laurie L. Levenson, *Stereotypes of Women in the O.J. Simpson Case*, 1994 WL 681370 (O.J. Commentaries).

[96] Ellen L. Pence & Melanie F. Shepard, *An Introduction: Developing a Coordinated Community Response*, *in* COORDINATING COMMUNITY RESPONSES TO DOMESTIC VIOLENCE: LESSONS

Indeed, activists of color had argued that money, services, shelter, job opportunities, childcare, and the like would go a long way in aiding abused women. But such welfare and social services would not be of much use to nonpoor white victims because of their "reluctance to reduce their's [*sic*] or their children's standard of living" and the "welfare stigma" that "prevented [them] from considering AFDC payments as a potential solution," as one advocate noted frankly in 1978.[97] For such women, arrest might be the most promising avenue toward reforming her husband or creating favorable divorce conditions. Of course, arrest would do little for poor women, for whom divorce money would be like getting blood from a turnip. Indeed, DV studies in the late 1980s confirmed that arrest reduced violence among white, employed men but aggravated violence among Black, unemployed men.[98] Researchers warned, "If three times as many [Black people as white people] are arrested in a city like Milwaukee, which is a fair approximation, then an across-the-board policy of mandatory arrests prevents 2,504 acts of violence against primarily white women at the price of 5,409 acts of violence against primarily Black women."[99]

The ideal victim narrative obscured the fact that victims of DV also engaged in violence, even if mostly defensive, which made them vulnerable to arrest under strict enforcement policies. The state of California compared DV arrest data from 1988, before mandatory arrest policies, to data from 1998. It found that the arrests of men rose by 60 percent, but women's arrests rose by 400 percent.[100] Stripping police of discretion, it turned out, countered their masculinist instinct *not* to arrest women. And of course, this newfound willingness to arrest women disproportionately impacted Black women.

Moreover, the innocent yet vengeful victim narrative hid many other reasons why DV victims did not want to interact with police and prosecutors. In 2015, the ACLU published the results of a survey of more than 900 DV service providers. The survey asked them to, among other things, "identify the primary reasons survivors do not call or cooperate with law enforcement."[101] Providers responded that most victims were rightly afraid that police would call in Child Protective Services to investigate them for "failure to protect." In addition, the providers noted that some "clients were committing crimes (using illegal substances, participating in sex work, had a taser in

From Duluth and Beyond 7, Melanie F. Shepard Ellen L. Pence eds.,) (quoting a legal advocate interview from Sept. 19, 1995).

97 U.S. Comm'n on Civil Rights, Battered Women: Issues of Public Policy 30–31, 172 (1978), https://www.ncjrs.gov/pdffiles1/Digitization/53356NCJRS.pdf [https://perma.cc/EE3R-MFUW, 172].

98 Lawrence Sherman et al., *The Variable Effects of Arrest on Criminal Careers: The Milwaukee Domestic Violence Experiment*, 83 J. of Crim. L. & Criminology 137 (1992).

99 *Id.* at 160.

100 Mekha Rajan & Kathy A. McCloskey, *Victims of Intimate Partner Violence: Arrest Rates across Recent Studies*, 15 J. Aggression, Maltreatment & Trauma 37 (2007).

101 *Responses from the Field: Sexual Assault, Domestic Violence, and Policing*, Am. Civ. Liberty Union 10 (2015) https://www.aclu.org/sites/default/files/field_document/2015.10.20_report_-_responses_from_the_field.pdf [https://perma.cc/VXU2-DHCW].

their possession, etc.) while they were being abused" and were "afraid of being prosecuted."[102] Indeed, one respondent observed that in her community, "checking victims for warrants is so encouraged, it is part of institutionalized policy."[103] These were just some of the many ways that carceral policies harmed victims who had been excised from the idealized narratives that drove DV policy.

These costs to victims came on top of the costs to the defendants – disproportionately men of color – and their families and communities. The vengeful victim narrative presumed that what was bad for the abuser was necessarily good for the victim, but the ACLU survey makes clear that in the DV context, the lives of the victims and defendants are intertwined and arrest is not a zero-sum game. One provider observed:

> A lot of victims don't want to call the police because they don't want the abuser to be incarcerated or deported, and they don't want to bring DSS down on their families and lose their kids. In communities of color and immigrant communities these concerns are paramount. Victims are afraid that if they call the police, the abuser will be subjected to a racist system of "justice" that leaves black families devoid of fathers (if he's in prison that also means no child support, no help raising the kids, etc.) and Latino families [are] in fear of having loved ones deported (often back to places they left because of violence and/or economic hardship).[104]

Perhaps the clearest examples of idealized victims' rights narratives propelling terrible policy is the war on sex offenders. In the 1980s and 1990s, media relentlessly covered child kidnappings, rapes, and killings that represented "every parent's worst nightmare." The names Adam Walsh, Jacob Wetterling, Polly Klaas, and Megan Kanka were seared into public consciousness and memorialized in the titles of federal anti–sex offender legislation.[105] Legislatures capitalized on this fear and scored political points by passing sex offender punishment and management regimes that tested the limits of constitutional powers, including mandatory registration and community notification, strict residency restrictions, and for some offenders, indefinite civil commitment.[106]

In fact, however, such brutal serial child murders were exceedingly rare, and the common assaults involved lower-level sexual touching perpetrated by familiars, often by other children.[107] In 2009, "juveniles account[ed] for more than one-third

[102] *Id.* at 28.

[103] *Id.* at 29.

[104] *Id.* at 30.

[105] *See* William J. Clinton, *Remarks on Signing Megan's Law and an Exchange with Reporters* at 763, Gov. Info: Admin. of William J. Clinton (May 17, 1996), https://www.govinfo.gov/content/pkg/PPP-1996-book1/pdf/PPP-1996-book1-doc-pg763.pdf [https://perma.cc/PFD9–92L2].

[106] *See, e.g.*, S.C. Code Ann. § 23-3-430 (2018); Wash. Rev. Code § 9A.44.130 (2018); Miss. Code Ann. § 45-33-25 (2018).

[107] *See Child Sex Abuse Statistics: Perpetrators*, Darkness to Light (Dec. 22, 2015), https://www.d2l.org/wp-content/uploads/2017/01/Statistics_2_Perpetrators.pdf [https://perma.cc/MP3U-EKWD]; Sarah W. Craun & Matthew T. Theriot, *Misperceptions of Sex Offender*

(35.6 percent) of those known to police to have committed sex offenses against minors," according to a Bureau of Justice Statistics report.[108] The report further notes, "Early adolescence is the peak age for offenses against younger children."[109]

In 2006, John Walsh of *America's Most Wanted* fame successfully lobbied the US Congress to pass the "Adam Walsh Child Protection Act" on the twenty-fifth anniversary of his son's death. Federal sex offender law was already exceedingly harsh by that time, but the Walsh Act symbolically increased already exorbitant penalties and broadened eligibility for registration and civil commitment. These draconian provisions were irrelevant to nearly all sex-crime arrestees, whose cases were governed by state, not federal, law. Federal law on violent crime has limited jurisdiction, generally affecting only defendants in federalized areas, including at the time Indian territory. The federal public defender had warned that Native Americans would bear the brunt of these laws.[110] In 2006, "[n]early three-quarters of federal sex abuse defendants were American Indian or Alaska Native," according to the Department of Justice.[111] These suspects "tended to be younger … and less educated" than other offenders.[112]

The Walsh Act also required states to register juveniles as sex offenders. The irony is painful: Children, so revered as angels when used as symbols of the horrors of abuse, lost all claims to innocence when accused of sex crimes, so much so that few were troubled about subjecting them to state-sanctioned brutality and sexual abuse. A 2016 *New Yorker* article profiled child registrants' gut-wrenching tales of homelessness, inability to attend school, public shaming, violence, humiliating "medical

Perpetration: Considering the Impact of Sex Offender Registration, 24 J. OF INTERPERSONAL VIOLENCE 2057 (2009); Naomi J. Freeman & Jeffrey C. Sandler, *The Adam Walsh Act: A False Sense of Security or an Effective Public Policy Initiative?* 21 CRIM. J. POL'Y REV. 46, __ (2010) ("[S]everal recent studies … have found registration and notification laws to be ineffective methods of reducing sexual victimizations … [T]here is some evidence to suggest that these types of laws are increasing recidivism.").

[108] David Finkelhor et al., *Juveniles Who Commit Sex Offenses against Minors* 1–2, U.S. DEP'T OF JUST.: OFF. OF JUV. JUST. & DELINQ. PREVENTION (2009), https://www.ncjrs.gov/pdffiles1/ojjdp/227763.pdf [https://perma.cc/C93A-P9WR].

[109] *Id.* at 2.

[110] Jon M. Sands, *Re: Adam Walsh Child Protection and Safety Act of 2006, Pub. L.* 109-248 at 12–13, FED. PUB. DEF. DIST. OF ARIZ. (November 16, 2006), https://www.fd.org/sites/default/files/criminal_defense_topics/essential_topics/sentencing_resources/defender_recommendations/sex-offense-issues-addessed-by-letter-on-11-16-06-to-ussc.pdf [https://perma.cc/CU6M-S358]; *see also* Robert Ecoffey et. al., *Report of the Native American Advisory Group on the Organizational Sentencing Guidelines* 32, U.S. SENT'G COMM'N (2003), https://www.ussc.gov/sites/default/files/pdf/research-and-publications/research-projects-and-surveys/miscellaneous/20031104_Native_American_Advisory_Group_Report.pdf [https://perma.cc/QQY8-JV4B].

[111] Mark Motivans & Tracey Kyckelhahn, *Federal Prosecution of Child Sex Exploitation Offenders*, 2006, U.S. DEPT. OF JUST.: BUREAU OF JUST. STAT. BULLETIN (2007), https://www.bjs.gov/content/pub/ascii/fpcse06.txt [https://perma.cc/6H25-5DCB]; Sarah Stillman, *The List*, NEW YORKER (Mar. 14, 2016) https://www.newyorker.com/magazine/2016/03/14/when-kids-are-accused-of-sex-crimes [https://perma.cc/42EB-B7R2].

[112] Motivans & Kyckelhahn, *supra* note 111.

treatment," and suicide.[113] There is Charla, who was placed on the registry at ten for pulling a boy's pants down at school and whose photo still appears online under the banner "Protect Your Child from Sex Offenders." There is Anthony, convicted under "statutory rape" laws for consensual sex as a teenager. Years later, the conditions of his sex-offender status prohibited him from living with his newborn daughter, and his violations of those conditions landed him a ten-year sentence. There is Leah, who at age ten, was convicted of molesting her siblings. During college, she and her boyfriend drove out of state and stopped at the local police station so that she could fulfill her sex-offender notification requirement. The front-desk officer said, "We don't serve your kind here. You better leave before I take you out back and shoot you myself."[114]

The government intervention imposed on these children is Kafkaesque, involving "youth shaming"[115] treatments like masturbation logs and penile plethysmography—a process utilizing a machine that physically measures the subject's erection upon viewing sexual images, which was once used in the military to ferret out homosexuals. One pediatric psychologist derided them as "coercive techniques of doubtful accuracy, untested benefit, and considerable potential for harm."[116] Today, the expert consensus is that the draconian sex offender laws did not reduce, and may have increased, child sex offenses.[117]

9.4 HUMANIZED ANIMALS VS. SUBHUMAN HUMANS

When Libre's story broke on social media, a concerned citizen wrote a letter to the editor of a Lancaster newspaper stating the photos of the sickly pup "rip my heart apart."[118] The writer insisted that "the owner, *whoever he or she is*, needs to pay for this horrific, draconian crime."[119] The letter urged authorities to mete out meaningful punishment to the human to demonstrate that state authorities "are kinder, more compassionate people than to allow this cruelty to continue" and to "find[ ] justice for Libre."[120] "I have never seen such sadness on a puppy's little face," the writer lamented. Notice the contrast. The author humanized and sentimentalized Libre,

[113] Stillman, *supra* note 111; *see also* Hal Arkowitz & Scott O. Lilienfeld, *Once a Sex Offender, Always a Sex Offender? Maybe Not.*, Sci. Am.: Scis. (Apr. 1, 2008), https://www.scientificamerican.com/article/misunderstood-crimes/ [https://perma.cc/2FUM-VWU7].

[114] Stillman, *supra* note 111.

[115] *Id.*

[116] *Id.* (quoting psychologist Mark Chaffin).

[117] Puck Lo, *Sex-Offender Laws are Ineffective and Unfair, Critics Say*, Al Jazeera Am. (Oct. 17, 2004) http://america.aljazeera.com/articles/2014/10/17/challenges-to-sexoffenderregistries.html [https://perma.cc/KN7S-Y46A]; Wayne Logan, *Challenging the Punitiveness of "New-Generation" SORN Laws*, 21 New Crim. L. Rev. 426 (2018).

[118] Ann L. Carter, *Letter to the Editor*, Lancaster Newspapers (July 21, 2016), 2016 WLNR 22341505.

[119] *Id.* (emphasis added).

[120] *Id.*

describing the look on his face as one, not of pain, but of *sadness*.[121] At the same time, the person responsible was totally devoid of any description – indeed any identity or gender. The only relevant information given was that the unnamed person did something "horrific" and "draconian." The more the animal was humanized, the more subhuman the human became.

The rhetoric of advocates and policy makers who support tough-on-animal abuse reforms like Libre's Law mirrors victims' rights rhetoric. Advocates pit innocent, devastated animals against evil, monstrous human animals. One of the key features of animal rights' rhetoric is contrasting animals' inherent innocence with human animals' sinful and guilty nature. Applauding Libre's Law, the editorial board of an Erie, Pennsylvania, paper stated, "Animal cruelty is sickening in its own right because animals are so unevenly matched with human strength and capacity for evil."[122] Within the discourse, animals are innocent, by definition. They can entertain the human emotions of sadness, love, longing, loyalty and the like, but they do not have a "capacity for evil." The sex animals impose on other animals is never rape. The harms, even deaths, they cause are never assaults and murders. Within the narrative, animal-caused harm is either the fault of the bad human owner or a product of the animal's morally neutral instincts.

While animals have no capacity for guilt, human animals who offend against them have no capacity for innocence. Consider the 2019 case of Heidi Lueders, who ran "Bully Breed Rescue" and was charged with several counts of misdemeanor animal cruelty when five dogs in her care died. Photos that depicted the dogs as little more than skeletons surrounded by feces, piles of trash, and drug paraphernalia circulated on the internet. Protesters from "Desmond's Army," named after another dog who was abused and killed, rallied outside the Bridgeport, Connecticut, courthouse in the dead of winter on the day of Lueders's hearing. Holding signs supporting the "Fairfield Five" (the deceased dogs), the group demanded that Lueders be

[121] This anthropomorphic projection (puppy-dog eyes) is not an accident—it is a product of thousands of years evolution. Researchers observe:

> The evidence is compelling that dogs developed a muscle to raise the inner eyebrow after they were domesticated from wolves. We also studied dogs' and wolves' behaviour and, when exposed to a human for two minutes, dogs raised their inner eyebrows more and at higher intensities than wolves. The findings suggest that expressive eyebrows in dogs may be a result of humans' unconscious preferences that influenced selection during domestication. When dogs make the movement, it seems to elicit a strong desire in humans to look after them. This would give dogs that move their eyebrows more a selection advantage over others and reinforce the 'puppy dog eyes' trait for future generations."

Juliane Kaminski et al., *Evolution of Facial Muscle Anatomy in Dogs*, PROC. OF THE NAT'L ACAD. OF SCI. OF THE U.S.A. (June 17, 2019), https://www.pnas.org/content/116/29/14677 [https://perma.cc/LWH7-BLM3].

[122] *Our View: Pa. Finally Gives Abused Animals the Protection They Deserve*, GOERIE (June 23, 2017), https://www.goerie.com/opinion/20170623/our-view-pa-finally-gives-abused-animals-protection-they-deserve [https://perma.cc/HG6Y-DBG3].

charged with felonies. Protester Anette Matthews told the press, "This is one of the most horrendous cases of animal cruelty. Knowing that she disguised herself as an animal rescuer . . . makes her the worst kind of *monster*."[123]

The prosecutor heard Desmond's Army's clarion call and during the hearing upgraded Lueders's charges to felonies. The judge appointed the five dead dogs a victim advocate, as required under the 2016 "Desmond's Law."[124] Lueders's lawyer explained to the press that his client "is not a bad person but a victim of the opioid epidemic. And this situation is a direct result of an addiction to opiates." Protester Nicola Improta was unmoved: "I'm here for justice and to show support. This woman needs to be taken down with the fullest extent of the law . . . Drug abuse is no excuse."[125] There was no chance that Lueders' drug addiction would elicit sympathy because, within the activist narrative, the animal cruelty is just the of tip of the defendant's larger violence iceberg. Animal advocates regularly remind us that defendants charged with animal abuse are rotten to the core. If a person is cruel to animals, the argument goes, it is likely they also engage in violence against people. They may even go on to commit a mass atrocity.[126]

A critical component of Desmond's story, for example, was that the man who beat and killed Desmond did so as part of a larger pattern of abusing and harassing his ex-girlfriend. Indeed, the idea that animal cruelty correlates with domestic violence against human women frequently came up in discussions of Libre's Law, although Libre's case had nothing to do with DV. The "animal cruelty predicts DV" argument is an odd argument from a substantive criminal law standpoint. Even if there were clear evidence that animal cruelty (in all its forms) predicts violence against humans – which there isn't[127] – the law punishes people for the crimes they committed, not for uncharged acts that might correlate with future crime. The claim that we need to toughen animal abuse laws to get at batterers completely ignores that there are already a plethora of laws that criminalize – even

[123] *Animal Cruelty Charges Upgraded to Felonies for Heidi Lueders*, GREENWICH FREE PRESS (Feb. 13, 2019) (emphasis added), https://greenwichfreepress.com/dogs/charges-upgraded-to-felonies-for-heidi-lueders-118687/ [https://perma.cc/EZ8G-38QG].

[124] *History of Desmond's Law*, UNIV. OF CONN.: THOMAS J. MESKILL L. LIB., https://libguides.law.uconn.edu/c.php?g=923213&p=6653929 [https://perma.cc/AGF2-HB5J].

[125] *Animal Cruelty Charges Upgraded to Felonies for Heidi Lueders*, *supra* note 123.

[126] JUSTIN MARCEAU, BEYOND CAGES: ANIMAL LAW AND CRIMINAL PUNISHMENT 199–204 (2019); *see also* Matthew Kemeny, Column, *Libre's Law Might also Help Stop Domestic Abuse*, YORK DAILY REC. (June 28, 2017), https://www.ydr.com/story/opinion/columnists/2017/06/28/libres-law-might-also-help-stop-domestic-abuse-column/436137001/ [https://perma.cc/ET8L-V3T8]; *Our View: Pa. Finally Gives Abused Animals the Protection They Deserve*, *supra* note 123; *Cold Hard Facts about Animal Abuse Offenders*, NAT'L COAL. ON VIOLENCE AGAINST ANIMALS: ANIMAL ABUSE FACTS, https://ncovaa.org/facts/ [https://perma.cc/L3J8-W7B6].

[127] One cannot imagine a more thorough analysis than the one provided by Justin Marceau of all the major studies linking animal cruelty and violence against humans. He comes to the unsurprising conclusion that there is no clear consensus that a person who commits an act of "animal cruelty," as defined by heterogenous laws, is significantly more likely than anyone else to commit violence against humans. *See* MARCEAU, *supra* note 126, at 205–27.

overcriminalize – domestic violence against humans. And, of course, the harsh penalties in Desmond's Law and Libre's Law apply with equal force to defendants who, like Lueders and Stolzfus, have no connection to domestic abuse. In the end, the argument that animal cruelty correlates to violence against humans seems like a ploy to make the non–animal rights camp comfortable with punitive animal cruelty. They justify animal cruelty laws as getting at "real" bad guys who harm humans too.

In his groundbreaking book critiquing carceral animal law, *Beyond Cages*, Justin Marceau discusses cases similar to Lueders's where activists invoke images of innocent devastated animals and juxtapose them with perpetually culpable, monstrous offenders. He tells a tale involving a severely neglected and sick dog, Sammy, who like Libre and Desmond, drew widespread public sympathy and calls for the owners, a couple, to be prosecuted to the fullest extent of the law. At the time of Sammy's neglect, the couple was going through a terrible divorce, and the husband was dying of kidney disease. Both struggled with depression and considered suicide. Sammy had been residing with the husband when he degenerated, and the wife remarked, "I should have foreseen that Sammy wouldn't have been safe with my husband, but I didn't know [my husband] was going to get so sick ... If I had foreseen it, I would have taken Sammy with me... I'm sorry it turned out the way it did." Marceau describes the disturbing details of the couple's day in court:

> More than 250 people filed into the municipal courtroom wearing shirts demanding justice for Sammy. At one hearing a woman was removed from the courtroom for yelling "go kill yourself" at the man dying of kidney disease and suffering from depression. The prosecuting attorney explained that he was "very satisfied" with obtaining incarceration for both parties.... Indeed, the local SPCA called the maximum sentence for the ill, suicidal man "admirable" insofar as it reflected a strong stand against animal cruelty, even though the cruelty took the form of an omission rather than a set of brutalizing, malicious acts. Many other animal protection groups were involved in urging a maximum sentence, and their advocacy likely had a direct impact on the judge, who explained at sentencing that justice would not be served "[u]nless the defendants are sentenced to [maximum] imprisonment for their depraved acts toward Sammy."[128]

Animal cruelty activists and zealous prosecutors urge judges to condemn human animals to prisons – sites of domination, discrimination, and dehumanization – as an act of "compassion" and "kindness." Advocates' strategy of selectively anthropomorphizing animals as innocent victims produces the exact kind melodramatic sentimentality that Rapping and Berlant warn enables "irrational" demands for blood.[129] Jungian psychologist Marie-Louise von Franz's remarks that "where there is sentimentality there is also a certain amount of brutality" and provides this example: "Goering [a high-ranking Nazi] without a qualm ... could sign the death

[128] Marceau, *supra* note 126, at 49–50.
[129] *Id.* at 29 and accompanying text.

sentence for three hundred people, but if one of his birds died, then that fat old man would cry. He was a classic example! Cold brutality is very often covered up by sentimentality."[130]

Having sentimentalized the animal victim, advocates have no qualms about imprisoning vulnerable human animals of all kinds. To be sure, the Libre conversation left little room for thoughtful analysis of not just the costs of widespread incarceration for pet-related offenses but also the simple issue of whether Stoltzfus *deserved* to be imprisoned. Instead, the images of Libre's sad, hairless pink snout and swollen-shut eyes on his otherwise adorable floppy-eared puppy body were enough to dethrone anyone's reason in favor of the basest desire of a pound of flesh from the identity-less "monster who did that." It should thus come as no surprise that animal rights activists even support imprisoning children who run afoul of animal abuse laws and treating those children as adult offenders.[131] In animal victims' rights rhetoric, juvenile defendants are not vulnerable, troubled, and traumatized kids but "ticking time bombs" of mass violence.[132] Activists are content to be unaware of or indifferent to the suffering of vulnerable youths caged in adult facilities.[133] Marceau criticizes the "paradoxical notion . . . that the caging of children will liberate animals."[134]

Indeed, activists give no quarter to defendants who are *definitionally* innocent. Criminal law principles dictate that unintentional and accidental harm generally does not merit punishment. Nevertheless, activists have agitated for "strict liability" animal cruelty laws. Strict liability crimes are rare and disfavored because they land people in jail who are *without fault*. Strict liability animal cruelty laws dictate that if a pet is harmed, the owner can be imprisoned even if she did not intend the harm and took reasonable steps to prevent it. Prosecutors are forthright that they like strict liability because it eases their burden to prove the owner acted intentionally or unreasonably.[135] Activists similarly believe that defendants should "have no excuses" for animal harm. They are content to sacrifice well-intentioned people whose pets' deaths are tragic accidents on the altar of zero-tolerance. Marceau concludes that the strict liability issue demonstrates "how far the animal protection movement has treaded outside of mainstream thinking on fairness in criminal law."[136]

As with human victims in victims' rights discourse, animal victims are, or at least look, devastated. Many of the high-profile animal cruelty cases involve descriptions

[130] Marie-Louise von Franz, The Problem of the Puer Aeternus 13 (2000).

[131] Marceau, *supra* note 126, at 61–63.

[132] *Id.* at 62.

[133] *Id.* at 61 ("Some 10,000 children are housed in adult jails and prisons on any given day in America. Children are five times more likely to be sexually assaulted in adult prisons than in juvenile facilities and face increased risk of suicide.") (quoting Children in Adult Prison, Equal Just. Initiative, https://eji.org/children-prison [https://perma.cc/VYA4-CRZL]).

[134] *Id.* at 63.

[135] *Id.* at 56–58.

[136] *Id.* at 57.

of brutal, deviant, and intentional acts of violence. This is despite the fact that, as the Libre's Law statistics demonstrate, few animal cruelty cases involve deliberate torture. Narratives of rare but spectacular brutality have always been an essential ingredient of victims' rights, as the sex-predator panic example demonstrates.[137] In our social-media era, disturbing pictures can substitute for sadistic stories as proof of animal victims' devastation. There are a variety of ailments that cause dogs to sicken, suffer, and die, but few *appear* as horrible as generalized mange, which was Libre's affliction. Even though, "[s]urprisingly, a dog with demodectic mange usually does not itch severely," as veterinarian Ernest Ward remarks,[138] mange is tailor-made for evocative Instagram posts. The American Kennel Club notes, "If you follow news about dogs, you know what an extreme case of mange looks like. It's a common skin disease in dogs and puppies that are strays, neglected, or abused. These dogs appear to be beyond hope – hairless, with skin covered in sores or with thickened, hard, crusty patches . . . [But] as you've seen in the many 'miracle dog' stories in the news, even serious cases can be treated effectively."[139] One blogger put it succinctly, "Dog mange often looks scarier than it is."[140]

The final characteristic of the ideal victim is vengefulness. Recall the simple polar logic of the victims' rights movement that punishment is in itself justice for victims, regardless of the larger consequences. In the DV context, focusing on proprosecution victims obscured the interests of many other victims who were not eager to pursue retribution through the state penal apparatus. In the sex offender context, the laws driven by the vengeance narrative were so broad that they captured defendants (i.e., nine-year-old kids) who were nothing like the "monsters" against whom the parents of murdered children sought retribution.[141] Nevertheless, there were plenty of vocal victims who made clear that they were, in fact, out for blood. Of course, it is another question altogether whether harmed victims or grieving family members *should* dictate criminal law policy in a civilized society. One Oklahoma City bombing victim, Bud Welch, testified to the Senate committee on the Crime Victims' Rights Amendment that after the bombing, he "wanted McVeigh and Nichols killed without a trial" and warned that "victims are too emotionally involved in the case and will not make the best decisions."[142]

The carceral animal camp similarly presumes that punishment serves animals' interests in "justice." In a recent article, Mary Maerz makes an interesting "animal rights" case in favor of "pro-carceral" animal laws and policies, and in particular, the

[137] *See supra* notes 90, 105, 107, 108.

[138] Ward & Panning, *supra* note 16.

[139] Mara Bovsun, *Mange in Dogs: What You Need to Know*, Am. Kennel Club (Jan. 23, 2019), https://www.akc.org/expert-advice/health/mange-what-you-need-to-know/.

[140] Jean Marie Bauhaus, *Dealing with Dog Mange*, Hill's (Nov. 25, 2018), https://www.hillspet.com/dog-care/healthcare/what-is-dog-mange [https://perma.cc/23LU-5L24].

[141] *See supra* notes 92–93.

[142] Senate Comm. on the Judiciary, S. Rep. No. 108-191, Report on Crime Victims' Rights Amendment at 82 (2003) (quoting Bud Welch).

prosecution of slaughterhouse workers for animal cruelty.[143] Maerz concedes a lot to the anticarceral camp: First, that the "individual deterrent abilities of these prosecutions on factory farm or slaughterhouse workers remains doubtful"; second, that "criminal prosecution of anticruelty laws in factory farms and slaughterhouses ... undoubtedly forms part of the system of mass-incarceration in the United States"; and third, that prosecutors target "workers – mostly Hispanic, increasingly undocumented, and impoverished – perpetuat[ing] the criminal justice system's unbalanced targeting of minorities and those of low socioeconomic class."[144] Despite these concessions, Maerz concludes that such carceral interventions are nevertheless warranted. She argues, "While pro-carceral animal law likely cannot be justified by empirical or criminological bases, criticism of these criminal prosecutions asks the animal protection movement to place anthropocentric social movement concerns above the interests of animals." Such a demand is inconsistent with "the animal rights movement which, at its foundation, refuses to compromise the interests of animals over human interests."[145]

The idea that animals' interest in punishment necessarily trumps defendants' and society's interest in reducing ineffective, painful, and racist mass incarceration tracks victims' rights rhetoric, although most victims' rights advocates, unlike Maerz, do not openly concede that the penal system is racist and ineffective. Maerz does not explain but simply presumes that animal victims have a unique "interest" in racist and ineffective punishment of humans, so much so that to believe otherwise is "anthropocentric."[146] Human victims can speak for themselves, as conditioned and constrained as that speech may be. With animal victims, it is not just a matter of advocates choosing *which* vengeful victims speak – the advocates speak *for* a class of victims who can never speak for themselves. In the Justice for Libre movement and elsewhere, activists make the conclusory assumption that animals invariably feel like Bud Welch in the immediate aftermath of the bombing or devastated vengeful dad, John Walsh – they want justice through strict punishment.

Gayatri Spivak has famously asked, "Can the subaltern speak?"[147] And at the risk of oversimplifying a question with many components and valences, let me focus on Spivak's caution about description and historiography. Spivak asserts that when the scholar, even a sincere anti-imperialist, "subaltern studies" scholar, undertakes to represent an as-yet-unrepresented or "insurgent" consciousness of a subaltern group,

[143] Mary Maerz, *In Defense of Pro-carceral Animal Law: Understanding the Dichotomy between Empirical Criminological Perturbation and Social Movement Values and Development*, 9 Braz. J. Pub. Pol'y 173 (2019).

[144] *Id.* at 188.

[145] *Id.*

[146] *Id.* at 186–89 (raising arguments about social movements and their use of criminal law as an important step in raising awareness, although such arguments are phrased here as *incidental* to animals' presumed interest in seeing abusers punished).

[147] Gayatri Chakravorty Spivak, *Can the Subaltern Speak?*, *in* Marxism and the Interpretation of Culture 24 (Cary Nelson & Lawrence Grossberg eds., 1988).

"what the work *cannot* say becomes important."[148] Given the risks of essentializing and interposing one's own consciousness on the group, even the "texts of insurgency can only serve as a counterpossibility for the narrative sanctions granted to the colonial subject in the dominant groups."[149] If sympathetic scholars representing the consciousness of a subaltern group that *has* language and texts is "consistently troublesome," then what of representing the consciousness of a group incapable of language?[150] In other words, we might ask, "Can the subhuman speak?"[151]

I do not feign deep knowledge of the philosophical literature on animal consciousness and how it grapples with epistemological limitations, essentialism, and colonialism. And intervention into this area is well beyond the scope of this chapter and competency of its author. I invoke Spivak's work to highlight that "our thinking on [animal's] behalf is presumptuous," as Joyce Chaplin puts it.[152] If, as Spivak observes, the deep dives into histories of colonized people's texts carried out by scholars with clear-eyed views of the limitations of their disciplinary methods are consistently troublesome, then certainly claims about animal consciousness are freighted with heavy uncertainty. Chaplin opines, "We do not know whether animals are like us, and may never know, and it should not matter. Animals may think (and therefore speak) in ways we may never comprehend."[153] Anticruelty activists' claims about animal consciousness are not epistemologically privileged but just functions of the human emotions and thought patterns that have for centuries driven state-backed punishment, which is itself an essentially human endeavor.

In other words, the claim of animal rights commentators like Maertz that there is a unique animal interest in punishment is no less anthropocentric than any other claims about animals and criminalization. And, if we are to anthropomorphically invest animals with human sentiments, why not invest them with more nuanced ones?[154] Perhaps animals' thoughts about the wrongs done to them and appropriate redress are heterodox and conflicting. Perhaps some animals who have been caged are not so sanguine about policies that put human animals in cages, much in the way that formerly incarcerated victims are not often eager to participate in prosecutions. Perhaps some abused pets, like humans abused by parents or other loved ones,

[148] *Id.* at 28.

[149] *Id.*

[150] *Id.*

[151] This is not a normative judgment on the relative moral worth of humans and animals, and I ask for literary license to use the term in this sentence.

[152] Joyce E. Chaplin, *Can the Nonhuman Speak? Breaking the Chain of Being in the Anthropocene*, 78 J. OF HISTORY OF IDEAS 509, 524 (2017).

[153] *Id.* at 523.

[154] Kim A. McDonald, *Scientists Rethink Anthropomorphism*, CHRON. OF HIGHER ED. (Feb. 24, 1995), https://www.chronicle.com/article/scientists-rethink-anthropomorphism/?cid2=gen_login_refresh&cid=gen_sign_in [https://perma.cc/332T-Z2DB]; Scott Sleek, *Why Anthropomorphism Is Not a Scientific Sin*, ASS'N FOR PSYCH. SCI. (Apr. 30, 2019), https://www.psychologicalscience.org/observer/why-anthropomorphism-is-not-a-scientific-sin [https://perma.cc/E2Z4-E4FK].

want better treatment but prefer to remain with their human companions. These are of course, just "counterpossibilities" that stand in distinction to the presumption of animal-victim vengeance. And it is certainly possible that many harmed animals see criminal punishment as justice. Nevertheless, it should be evident that with so many limitations to accessing animal consciousness, the purported subjective desires of the animal victim should not be the foundation of law, especially law that contributes to inhumane racialized mass incarceration.

9.5 CONCLUSION

Over the past several years, many Americans have come to see racialized policing and mass incarceration as among the most pressing human rights issues of our time. Despite the growing radical awareness of the grave costs of addressing social problems, community dysfunction, and individual harmful behavior through state-sanctioned violence and detention, the animal victims' rights lobby continues to push for more and stronger criminal laws – ones that go to the very edge of constitutionality and long-standing criminal liability principles. Marceau observes that the animal rights movement has become a "single-issue" movement pushing for criminal law reform by "pursuing mandatory minimums, the prosecution of juveniles as adults, more felony prosecutions, offender registries, and similar crime-based [reforms]."[155]

History has shown that activist groups concerned with larger social change can find success with criminal law, especially when they tap into the simplistic, racialized, and sentimentalized victim-versus-offender narratives that provoke the public's punitive zeal. But advancing within a system that can do little more than impose inhumane treatment on human animals is a hollow success. When animals, including human animals, are subjected to brutality and rigid confinement, they do not become more pacifistic and well adjusted. They become wounded, traumatized, and even violent. History has also starkly shown that investment in the criminal apparatus often comes at the expense of noncriminal aid that prevents abuse and neglect in the first place. Consequently, when privileged human activists expand the carceral state by creating sentimentalized narratives about idealized pets who demand justice through the suffering of humans – primarily underprivileged humans – it is not an act of compassion and kindness, but one of cold brutality.

[155] Marceau, *supra* note 126, at 151.

10

Treating Humans Worse Than Animals?

Exposing a False Solitary Confinement Narrative

Delcianna J. Winders

10.1 INTRODUCTION

The "close linkages across [human] prisoner and [nonhuman] animal carcerality and captivity"[1] are especially salient in the context of solitary confinement. As social psychologist Craig Haney, who has extensively studied the impacts of solitary confinement on human prisoners, recently observed, "Some of the most dramatic demonstrations of the harmful effects of social deprivation have been found in animal research, where researchers are able to employ more intrusive scientific procedures and controls than with humans."[2] Indeed, Harry Harlow's notoriously cruel experiments socially isolating baby monkeys – as he described it, "total maternal deprivation" compounded by "no opportunity to form affectional ties with their peers"[3] – both fueled the nascent animal rights movement[4] and bolstered opposition to solitary confinement of human prisoners.[5] Yet, even as both of these movements have gained traction, solitary confinement of humans and nonhuman animals alike has dramatically increased in the United States.

Karen M. Morin notes the "developmental similarities across the agricultural-industrial complex and prison-industrial complex," both of which have rapidly

The author thanks Brittany Rowe and Miranda Groh for their invaluable research assistance.

[1] Karen M. Morin, *Carceral Space: Prisoners and Animals*, 48 ANTIPODE 1317, 1318 (2016).

[2] Craig Haney, *The Science of Solitary: Expanding the Harmfulness Narrative*, 115 NW. U. L. REV. 211, 225 (2020).

[3] Harry F. Harlow et al., *Total Isolation in Monkeys*, 54 PROC. N.A.S. 90, 90 (1965), www.ncbi.nlm.nih.gov/pmc/articles/PMC285801/pdf/pnas00159-0105.pdf.

[4] Atul Gawande, *Hellhole*, NEW YORKER (Mar. 30, 2009), https://www.newyorker.com/magazine/2009/03/30/hellhole; John P. Gluck, *Harry F. Harlow and Animal Research: Reflection on the Ethical Paradox*, 7 ETHICS & BEHAV. 149, 151 (1997).

[5] *See* Ruth Chan, *Buried Alive: The Need to Establish Clear Durational Standards for Solitary Confinement*, 53 UIC J. MARSHALL L. REV. 235, 249 (2020); Stuart Grassian, *Psychiatric Effects of Solitary Confinement*, 22 WASH. U. J.L. & POL'Y 325, 366 (2006).

expanded in recent decades.[6] As a result, tens of thousands of prisoners in the United States are in solitary confinement today (precise data is not available because, alarmingly, there is no federal mandate that this basic information be tracked or reported), while untold millions of animals are held alone in American laboratories, factory farms, roadside zoos, and other sites of exploitation, including tens of thousands of primates in laboratories.

Indeed, the United States holds the dubious distinction of being a world leader in solitary confinement of both human prisoners and nonhuman primates used for experiments. According to United Nations special rapporteur on torture, Juan E. Méndez, "the United States uses solitary confinement more extensively than any other country, for longer periods, and with fewer guarantees."[7] And, even as the United States recently became the last industrialized nation in the world to end the use of chimpanzees in invasive experiments, "the number of monkeys used in U.S. biomedical research reached an all-time high" of 74,498[8] (with an additional 35,221 held by laboratories but not actively used for experiments).[9] The number of primates held for experimentation in other countries pales in comparison.[10]

Despite these myriad linkages, there is a notable disconnect between efforts to end solitary confinement for humans and nonhumans. As Justin Marceau has detailed, incarcerating humans – which in the United States encompasses a high rate of solitary confinement – has become "a salient feature of efforts to protect non-humans."[11] Meanwhile, those working to end solitary confinement of human prisoners appear to misunderstand deeply the reality of the situation for animals in the United States today. For example, Drs. James Gilligan and Brandy Lee's influential *Report to the New York City Board of Correction* compared appalling conditions for human prisoners with those of animals in zoos, remarking that the former are kept "in physical environments in the likes of which no zoo director would be permitted to place wild animals."[12] According to Gilligan and Lee, "we now allow animals to be kept only in 'zoological parks' designed to recreate the kinds of environments that they had evolved to survive in" and we "treat[] our jail

6 Morin, *supra* note 1, at 1320.

7 Juan E. Méndez, *Afterword: Exposing Torture*, *in* Hell Is a Very Small Place: Voices from Solitary Confinement 221, 224 (Jean Casella et al., eds., 2016).

8 David Grimm, *Record Number of Monkeys Being Used in U.S. Research*, Sci. (Nov. 2, 2018), https://www.sciencemag.org/news/2018/11/record-number-monkeys-being-used-us-research.

9 U.S. Dep't of Agric., Animal & Plant Health Inspection Serv., Annual Report Animal Usage by Fiscal Year, Fiscal Year 2018, at 2 (Jan. 7, 2020), https://www.aphis.usda.gov/animal_welfare/annual-reports/Annual-Report-Summaries-State-Pain-FY18.pdf.

10 *See* Jonathan Balcombe et al., *Self-Harm in Laboratory Housed Primates: Where Is the Evidence That the Animal Welfare Act Amendment Has Worked?* 14 J. App. Animal Welfare Sci. 361 (2011).

11 Justin Marceau, Beyond Cages: Animal Law and Criminal Punishment 12 (2019).

12 James Gilligan & Brandy Lee, Report to the New York City Board of Correction 17 (Sept. 5, 2013), https://solitarywatch.org/wp-content/uploads/2013/11/Gilligan-Report.-Final.pdf.

and prison inmates worse than we treat animals."[13] This is not only a fundamentally inaccurate description of what our laws require for nonhuman animals, as discussed below; it also gives rise to headlines like "Treating Humans Worse Than Animals: Prison System Voices Decry Solitary Confinement of Mentally Ill"[14] and "'Animals Get Treated Better': Life in Solitary Confinement"[15] that pit human and nonhuman interests against one another unnecessarily.

Others working to challenge solitary confinement for human prisoners have made similarly inaccurate statements about requirements for animals. For example, a report by the Scientist Action and Advocacy Network summarizing scientific evidence against solitary confinement for human prisoners asserts, "It is federally mandated that most animals be housed with other animals of the same species. Only in extenuating circumstances is an animal to be housed in isolation, and for as little time as possible."[16] A *Scientific American* blog similarly proclaims that animals in laboratories "may only be housed alone in extenuating circumstances," adding: "These guidelines are not just for show. There are multiple layers of oversight, to ensure labs treat animals in accordance with these standards."[17] Still others have broadly asserted, "In many cases, there are more legal protections and oversights concerning the protection of captive wild animals and the care and handling of farm animals than there are for incarcerated pregnant people in the United States."[18]

Such proclamations are inaccurate at best, but more importantly, it is not a contest: depriving any social being, human or nonhuman, companionship is fundamentally cruel and torturous. Indeed, science has shown that "[s]ocial pain can elicit extreme distress, which may exceed that of physical pain."[19] And, as Lisa Guenther underscores, "there is nothing exclusively human about the need for everyday intercorporeal experience";

13 *Id.*

14 *Treating Humans Worse Than Animals: Prison System Voices Decry Solitary Confinement of Mentally Ill*, Democracy Now! (Apr. 1, 2014), https://www.democracynow.org/2014/4/1/treating_humans_worse_than_animals_prison.

15 Monique Ross & Damien Carrick, *"Animals Get Treated Better": Life in Solitary Confinement*, ABC Radio Nat'l (Sept. 10, 2018), https://www.abc.net.au/news/2018-09-11/life-in-solitary-confinement/10203686.

16 Scientist Action and Advocacy Network, Scientific Arguments against Solitary Confinement (May 2017), https://scaan.net/docs/ScAAN_Solitary_report.pdf.

17 Kristina Pinikas, *We've Forgotten the "Human" in "Humane,"* Sci. Am. (Nov. 29, 2018), https://blogs.scientificamerican.com/observations/weve-forgotten-the-human-in-humane/.

18 Crystal Hayes, Lauren Kuhlik, & Kristie Puckett-Williams, *Pregnant Women in North Carolina Prisons Are Being Kept in Solitary Confinement*, Ms. Mag. (Oct. 23, 2019), https://msmagazine.com/2019/10/23/pregnant-women-in-north-carolina-prisons-are-being-kept-in-solitary-confinement/; *accord* Rights Behind Bars, Solitary Confinement, https://www.rightsbehindbars.org/solitary-confinement.

19 Franklin D. McMillan, *The Psychobiology of Social Pain: Evidence for a Neurocognitive Overlap with Physical Pain and Welfare Implications for Social Animals with Special Attention to the Domestic Dog (Canis familiaris)*, 167 Physiology & Behav. 154 (2016), https://www.sciencedirect.com/science/article/abs/pii/S0031938416305583?via%3Dihub.

> it is not primarily as *human beings* … that we are affected by solitary confinement … but as *living beings* … with corporeal relations to other embodied beings and to an open field of overlapping experience in a shared world. It is as *animals* that we are damaged or even destroyed by the supermax or SHU [Security Housing Unit – an extreme form of prison solitary confinement], just as our fellow animals are damaged or destroyed by confinement in cages at zoos, factory farms, and scientific laboratories.[20]

Given the inherent cruelty in confining any social being alone, it is imperative to object to solitary confinement across the board, and work to effect legal and other changes to end the United States' shamefully widespread use of this tortuous practice in both human and nonhuman contexts. Notably, although the scientific literature about the impacts of social deprivation on animals has been widely used by those opposing solitary confinement in human prisons, there is not significant discourse or collaboration among advocates urging attention to the social needs of captive humans, on the one hand, and captive animals, on the other. This is a missed opportunity. While a full discussion of the potential benefits of such discourse and collaboration are beyond the scope of this chapter, they include enhanced information sharing (including scientific information and policy analysis), greater legitimacy, and heightened effectiveness.

Before such coalition building can succeed, it is important to delineate the common ground and facilitate common understanding. As an initial step in that direction, this rest of this chapter aims to articulate the current state of the law regarding solitary confinement of animals in the United States, and to correct what appear to be widespread misimpressions about the legal protections afforded to animals. Because the federal Animal Welfare Act provides the primary explicit protections against solitary confinement, the chapter focuses on those provisions, followed by a discussion of emerging possibilities under broader protections afforded by the Endangered Species Act and state anticruelty laws.

10.2 WHICH ANIMALS?

As a preliminary matter, it is important to consider how truly limited even de jure explicit protections against solitary confinement for nonhuman animals are. There are express federal mandates for any sort of social companionship for only three categories of animals: nonhuman primates, marine mammals, and, to a lesser extent, dogs. Thus, vast categories of animals known to be primarily social do not have express legal protection against solitary confinement. For example, every year more than 100 million "profoundly social" mice and rats are caged and subjected to

[20] Lisa Guenther, *Beyond Dehumanization: A Post-humanist Critique of Solitary Confinement*, 10 J. Crit. Animal Stud. 46, 56 (2012).

invasive experiments in US laboratories,[21] without any protections whatsoever under the Animal Welfare Act (AWA) because they have been deemed not to be animals for the purposes of that statute.[22] Solitary confinement of these highly social animals has been shown to cause brain damage,[23] and yet they are so lacking in legal protections that not only is solitary confinement routine, but so too is the denial of basic pain relief.[24]

Likewise, "pigs are highly social animals"[25] who suffer when deprived of companionship, yet they too have also been deemed not to be animals for the purposes of the AWA,[26] at least when used for food or fiber, and have no express legal protection against social deprivation. Consider farmer Bob Comis's chilling description of pigs' deep sociality:

> Pigs live in groups not only because they find safety and comfort in numbers, but because they are intensely, and I believe quite consciously, gregarious ... Their social bonds run deep. . .When those bonds are broken, a pig suffers a tremendous amount of psychological stress, most often expressed in repeated deep, long, doleful groans, and when the circumstances are right, pigs express that psychological suffering (stress is an inadequate term) of broken bonds by totally and completely flipping out. They run back and forth squealing. They run aimlessly, in circles, screaming. They will jump fences, or they will plow right through them. When confined in a tight space, they will smash themselves against walls and gates, repeatedly. They will spastically chew on metal bars. They will try to climb whatever can be climbed. They will jam their snouts under the bottom rung of a gate over and over again and strain and struggle to lift it off of its hinges. They will smash themselves against the walls and gates again, repeatedly.[27]

21 Alka Chandna, *Commentary: A Belmont Report for Animals: An Idea Whose Time Has Come*, 29 CAMBRIDGE Q. HEALTHCARE ETHICS 46, 50–51 (2019).

22 7 U.S.C. § 2132(g) ("The term 'animal' . . . excludes. . . rats of the genus *Rattus*, and mice of the genus *Mus*, bred for use in research.").

23 *See* Ruth Chan, *Buried Alive: The Need to Establish Clear Durational Standards for Solitary Confinement*, 53 UIC J. MARSHALL L. REV. 235, 249–50 (2020) (citation omitted); *see also* Stuart Grassian, *Psychiatric Effects of Solitary Confinement*, 22 WASH. U. J.L. & POL'Y 325, 366 (2006) ("One study produced agitation in mice and rats after a few days of isolation, a report which corroborated previous studies with rats. Others have also found isolation-induced aggressive behavior in mice [such as biting attacks]." [citations omitted]); Haney, *supra* note 2, at 255 n.49 ("Some researchers have discerned what they believe is a relationship between isolation and an animal world analogue of PTSD, noting, for example, that socially isolated mice manifest 'an exacerbation of aggressive behavior and . . . an increase in anxiety- and depressive-like behaviors, as well as . . . exaggerated contextual fear responses and impaired fear extinction.'" [citation omitted]).

24 Chandna, *supra* note 21, at 50–51.

25 Lori Marino & Christina M. Colvin, *Thinking Pigs: A Comparative Review of Cognition, Emotion, and Personality in Sus domesticus*, 28 INT'L J. COMP. PSYCH. (2015).

26 7 U.S.C. § 2132(g).

27 Bob Comis, *What Humane Slaughterhouses Don't Solve: The Last Pig Problem*, THE DODO (Mar. 10, 2014), https://perma.cc/AJ8J-SL8W.

Comis goes on to describe, in haunting detail, the consequences of this deep sociality for the "last pig" at the slaughterhouse:

> One by one as the day at the slaughterhouse passes, pigs are pulled out of pens with groups of pigs in them, until there is one last pig left in the pen. Not always, but very, very often, that last pig loses it as described above. Regardless of whether the last pig completely loses it, it begins to suffer the moment it is alone. Sometimes, in their hysterical efforts to free themselves in order to find other pigs to be with – because that's what it is all about – last pigs are so frantic and have become so mad under the strain of their psychological distress that they will hurt themselves.[28]

Despite the highly social nature of pigs and of other farmed animals – and contrary to the assertion that "[i]n many cases, there are more legal protections and oversights concerning the... care and handling of farm animals then there are for incarcerated pregnant people in the United States"[29] – no federal law regulates the on-farm treatment of animals raised for food.[30] And state-level oversight of even basic physical conditions for farmed animals is virtually unheard of.[31]

The only categories of animals with something even approximating an express federal legal entitlement to social companionship are nonhuman primates, marine mammals, and dogs. And in all three cases, these legal promises have proven largely illusory. What follows is a detailed description of how we have failed to protect even the most social nonhuman animals against solitary confinement under the AWA despite gestures purporting to do so.

10.3 PRIMATES, PLANS, AND PRIVATION

In 1985, following the damning exposure of a federally funded laboratory in Silver Springs, Maryland, that held monkeys alone in appalling conditions, Congress amended the Animal Welfare Act to require that the Secretary of Agriculture promulgate standards that include "minimum requirements" "for a physical environment adequate to promote the psychological well-being of primates."[32] The author of this language, Senator John Melcher, a veterinarian from Montana, intended this language to ensure, inter alia, social companionship for primates.[33]

To fulfill this mandate, the US Department of Agriculture (USDA) "engaged in extensive study of the environmental needs of nonhuman primates that must be met

[28] *Id.*

[29] Hayes et al., *supra* note 18.

[30] David J. Wolfson & Mariann Sullivan, *Foxes in the Hen House: Animals, Agribusiness, and the Law: A Modern American Fable* 205–33, *in* Animal Rts.: Current Debates & New Directions (Cass R. Sunstein & Martha C. Nussbaum, eds., 2004).

[31] *Id.*

[32] 7 U.S.C. § 2143(a)(2)(B).

[33] See Jodie Kulpa-Eddy et al., *USDA Perspective on Environmental Enrichment for Animals*, 46 ILAR J. 83, 84 (2005).

to promote their psychological well-being," and convened a committee of experts "to study the psychological needs of nonhuman primates" and "to make specific recommendations."[34] The "expert committee ... recommended social grouping to promote the psychological well-being of nonhuman primates," and the USDA accordingly proposed a requirement that:

> Nonhuman primates must be housed in primary enclosures with compatible members of the same species or with compatible members of other nonhuman primate species, in pairs, family groups, or other compatible social groupings, unless the attending veterinarian determines that doing so would endanger the health, safety, and well-being of the nonhuman primates.[35]

In making this proposal, the USDA underscored that "[s]ocial deprivation is regarded by the scientific community as psychologically debilitating to social animals."[36]

Following opposition from the animal experimentation industry, however, the USDA fundamentally altered its approach. Instead of a default prohibition on solitary confinement, in 1991, the agency instead finalized a rule requiring regulated entities to "develop, document, and follow an appropriate plan for environment enhancement adequate to promote the psychological well-being of nonhuman primates" that included "specific provisions to address the social needs of nonhuman primates of species known to exist in social groups in nature."[37]

Lest there were any doubt as to how fundamentally the final rule differed from what the agency had originally proposed, the USDA underscored: "The regulations ... do not specifically call for group housing of nonhuman primates" – even as it recognized that "housing in groups promotes psychological well-being more assuredly than does individual housing" and that "individual housing has been demonstrated to give rise to significantly more stereotypical behavior than does group housing."[38]

Two years after the rule went into effect, the agency polled its inspectors and found that a third of them were unable to determine whether a regulated entity was complying with the rule – and thus unable to enforce it.[39] The survey further found that at least half of all research facilities were still generally holding primates in solitary confinement, and that nearly half of inspectors believed this was done out of "convenience" rather than for legitimate reasons.[40]

[34] Proposed Rule, 54 Fed. Reg. 10987, 10913 (Mar. 15, 1989).

[35] *Id.* at 10913, 10944.

[36] *Id.* at 10913.

[37] 9 C.F.R. § 3.81(a).

[38] Final Rule, Animal Welfare; Standards, 56 Fed. Reg. 6426, 6472, 6473 (Feb. 15, 1991).

[39] Kulpa-Eddy et al., *supra* note 33, at 86.

[40] *Id.*

Another survey of inspectors after the rule had been in effect for five years made similar findings, with "[a]lmost half" of inspectors believing "that the criteria in the regulations were not adequate for facilities to understand how to meet them and for inspectors to judge if a facility was in compliance."[41] The USDA concluded that regulated entities did not understand how to develop a plan that would meet the rule's requirements and were confused about how their compliance would be judged, and that inspectors were also in need of guidance "on how to judge whether someone was meeting the requirements."[42]

Interviews with inspectors the following year similarly documented concerns about a lack of "solid criteria on which an inspector can judge the content of the plan as 'in compliance' or 'out of compliance,'" including, specifically, compliance with the social requirements.[43] "Some inspectors said they had the impression that the only legally necessary condition for compliance was the existence of the document itself, regardless of its contents."[44] Indeed, one regulated entity reportedly told an inspector:

> You know, with regard to this plan for the psychological well-being of primates, there's nothing you can do to me because there's nothing in those regulations that tell me what I have to do. So long as I have a plan, that's all that counts, and you can't take any other action against me.[45]

Not surprisingly, inspectors continued to note a high rate of primates held in solitary confinement for convenience.[46]

Underscoring that "[s]ocial interactions are considered to be one of the most important factors influencing the psychological well-being of most nonhuman primates" and that "[t]he remarkable sociality of the primate order in general is the most relevant characteristic for their humane housing,"[47] the USDA deemed further guidance "necessary."[48]

Accordingly, the agency proposed policy guidance based "on an extensive review of the available primate literature, professional journals, and reference guides," as well as consultation with "veterinarians, primatologists," and inspectors.[49] "The draft

[41] USDA, Animal & Plant Health Inspection Serv., Final Report on Environment Enhancement to Promote the Psychological Well-Being of Nonhuman Primates (July 15, 1999), https://www.nal.usda.gov/sites/default/files/environmentalenrichmentnhp_0.pdf.

[42] Animal Welfare; Draft Policy on Environment Enhancement for Nonhuman Primates, 64 Fed. Reg. 38145, 38146 (July 15, 1999).

[43] USDA, *supra* note 41.

[44] *Id.*

[45] Quoted in Valerie Stanley, Animal Welfare Act Symposium Proceedings 109 (1996), https://archive.org/stream/CAT10860535/CAT10860535_djvu.txt .

[46] USDA, *supra* note 41.

[47] *Id.*

[48] 64 Fed. Reg. at 38146.

[49] *Id.*

policy identifie[d] five general elements" deemed "critical to environments that adequately promote the psychological well-being of nonhuman primates," with "social grouping" at the top of the list.[50] The USDA elaborated:

> According to our research, primates are clearly social beings and social housing is the most appropriate way to promote normal social behavior and meet social needs. In order to address the social needs of nonhuman primates ... the plan must provide for each primate of a species known to be social in nature to be housed with other primates whenever possible.[51]

However, the USDA never finalized the guidance. Instead, in 2002, it announced its position that, contrary to all of the evidence it had gathered, the regulation was adequate on its own.[52]

In the intervening years, evidence of how inadequate the regulation is has continued to mount. As scientists Jonathan Balcombe, Hope Ferdowsian, and Debra Durham observed in a 2011 peer-reviewed publication, "Perhaps the best-known contributor to psychological distress in primates in the laboratory is nonsocial housing; yet, available analyses suggest that little progress has been made in avoiding single-caging of these animals."[53] They noted that a 2003 survey of "almost 36,000 macaques in 22 U.S. primate laboratories ... found ... that 54% of those animals (17,471) being used in research were singly caged."[54] A separate 2003 study examined 362 rhesus monkeys held in solitary confinement at a single facility – and found that more than 80 percent of them engaged in at least one abnormal behavior.[55] "Between 2004 and 2006 at the National Primate Research Center in Seattle, Washington, 63% of monkeys (numbering between 709 and 884) were singly caged."[56] A "separate analysis of detailed records ... from three U.S. laboratories involving more than 200 macaques and baboons indicates that these animals spend, on average, more than 50% of their lives caged alone."[57] And, according to a 2010 report, a survey of six research facilities holding more than 4,000 macaques found that 70 percent of the animals were held alone.[58] According to a 2015 analysis of publicly available enrichment plans from laboratories at state universities and

50 *Id.*

51 *Id.* at 38147.

52 Animal Legal Def. Fund v. Veneman, No. C-03-3400 PJH, 2004 WL 5573950, at *1 (N.D. Cal. Mar. 2, 2004), *rev'd*, 469 F.3d 826 (9th Cir. 2006), *opinion vacated on reh'g en banc*, 490 F.3d 725 (9th Cir. 2007).

53 Balcombe et al., *supra* note 10.

54 *Id.* at 2 (citation omitted).

55 C.K. Lutz et al., *Stereotypic and Self-Injurious Behavior in Rhesus Macaques: A Survey and Retrospective Analysis of Environment and Early Experience*, 6- Am. J. Primatology 1 (2003).

56 Balcombe et al., *supra* note 10.

57 *Id.* (citation omitted).

58 Caring Hands Discussions by the Laboratory Animal Refinement & Enrichment Forum Vol. II, at 121 (ed. Viktor Reinhard, 2010), https://awionline.org/sites/default/files/products/Pub-CaringHands-Part4-032912.pdf.

laboratories receiving federal funding, single-housing rates remain very high, with multiple plans conceding that convenience is a common reason for such solitary confinement.[59]

Though this chapter is focused on solitary confinement, it is worth underscoring that social housing alone is not a panacea for humans or nonhuman animals. Allowing – or forcing – incompatible animals to interact with no opportunity to retreat or escape can pose significant psychological and physical risks to primates and other animals. For example, an altercation between two chimpanzees at the Honolulu Zoo resulted in one of the animals losing half of his left middle finger,[60] while an altercation between chimpanzees through a metal mesh panel at a sanctuary resulted in a "large injury" to one of the animals.[61] Generally, however, social housing of primates has been found to be safe and to outweigh the risks, especially if done with attention to compatibility and risk mitigation.[62]

Nevertheless, decades after Congress amended the AWA to "promote the psychological well-being of primates" and the USDA underscored that "[s]ocial interactions are … one of the most important factors influencing the psychological well-being of most nonhuman primates," tens of thousands of nonhuman primates across the United States continue to languish in solitary confinement.

10.4 DESERTED MARINE MAMMALS

Congress has not specifically mandated standards to address the psychological well-being of marine mammals as it did for nonhuman primates. Nevertheless, pursuant to its general mandate to promulgate standards to ensure the humane care and treatment of animals under the AWA,[63] in 2001 the USDA promulgated a regulation providing:

> Marine mammals, whenever known to be primarily social in the wild, must be housed in their primary enclosure with at least one compatible animal of the same or biologically related species, except when the attending veterinarian, in consultation with the husbandry/training staff, determines that such housing is not in the best interest of the marine mammal's health or well-being. However, marine mammals that are not compatible must not be housed in the same enclosure. Marine mammals must not be housed near other animals that cause them unreasonable stress or discomfort or interfere with their good health. Animals housed

59 Debra Durham, Analysis of Environmental Enhancement Plans from Public Universities and Federal Institutions 25–26 (2015).

60 USDA, APHIS, Inspection Report, City and County of Honolulu 1 (July 22, 2018).

61 USDA, APHIS, Inspection Report, Save the Chimps 1 (Mar. 4, 2019).

62 *See, e.g.*, Viktor Reinhardt, *Pair-Housing Rather Than Single-Housing for Laboratory Rhesus Macaques*, 23 J. Med. Primatology 426 (1994); Louis DiVincenti, Jr. & Jeffrey D. Wyatt, *Pair Housing of Macaques in Research Facilities: A Science-Based Review of Benefits and Risks*, 50 J. Am. Assoc. Lab. Anim. Sci. 856 (2011).

63 7 U.S.C. § 2143.

> separately must have a written plan, approved by the attending veterinarian, developed in consultation with the husbandry/training staff, that includes the justification for the length of time the animal will be kept separated or isolated, information on the type and frequency of enrichment and interaction, if appropriate, and provisions for periodic review of the plan by the attending veterinarian.[64]

Although this mandate affords considerable discretion to the attending veterinarian – which raises delegation concerns given that this person is on the regulated entity's payroll and the USDA problematically has a long-standing practice of blindly deferring to the decisions of attending veterinarians – the standard appears to be more enforceable than the primate regulation. Rather than merely requiring a vague plan, it creates a presumption that social marine mammals will not be deprived of social companionship (though notably it does not require that they be held with conspecifics[65]).

However, a review of publicly available AWA inspection reports spanning more than five years reveals that the USDA has not once cited any of the many facilities that hold marine mammals for violating this standard.

This lack of citations must not be considered an indication that the standard is being met and that no marine mammals are being denied of social companionship. Consider the case of Lolita, an orca whom the Miami Seaquarium has confined for more than five decades. Orcas are famously social, remaining with their mothers for life, but Lolita has not seen another orca since 1980, when her tank mate, Hugo, died after ramming his head into the side of their tank.[66] Nevertheless, Lolita reportedly continues to use vocalizations that are known only to her pod, and seemed to recognize the calls of her pod when played a recording of them.[67] To add insult to injury, Lolita is confined with Pacific white-sided dolphins, with whom she would never interact in nature and who rake her skin with their teeth, wounding her.[68]

Such conditions appear to blatantly defy the mandates that marine mammals who are primarily social in the wild be held with "at least one compatible animal of the same or biologically related species"; that "marine mammals that are not compatible must not be housed in the same enclosure"; and that "[m]arine mammals must not be housed near other animals that cause them unreasonable stress or discomfort or interfere with their good health."[69]

64 9 C.F.R. 3.109.

65 Cathy Liss, et al., *Animal Welfare Act: Welfare Standards*, 25 Animal L. 157, 176 (2019).

66 *See* People for Ethical Treatment of Animals, Inc. v. Miami Seaquarium, 879 F.3d 1142, 1145 n.4 (11th Cir.), *adhered to on denial of reh'g sub nom.* People for the Ethical Treatment of Animals, Inc. v. Miami Seaquarium, 905 F.3d 1307 (11th Cir. 2018).

67 Christopher Frizzelle, *The Fight to Free Lolita*, Stranger (Sept. 30, 2015), https://www.thestranger./features/feature/2015/09/30/22939219/its-time-to-free-lolita-a-puget-sound-killer-whale-thats-been-trapped-in-miami-for-45-years.

68 Miami Seaquarium, 879 F.3d at 1145 n.4.

69 9 C.F.R. § 3.109.

However, the USDA has steadfastly refused to cite the Seaquarium for Lolita's social conditions; a recent assessment of Lolita and what the agency referred to as her "cetacean companions" concluded that the conditions are fully compliant with all AWA requirements.[70] Not long thereafter, the USDA renewed the Seaquarium's license to exhibit Lolita. Although Lolita is the most well-known marine mammal who is denied the social companionship ostensibly guaranteed to her by law, she is hardly the only one.

The USDA's utter failure to enforce its own standard for marine mammal social companionship highlights that although there is a dire need to render the requirements for primates' social needs legible and enforceable, that alone is insufficient.

10.5 DOLEFUL DOGS, DERELICTIONS OF DUTY

At the same time that it amended the AWA to address the psychological needs of nonhuman primates, Congress also added a mandate that the USDA promulgate minimum standards "for exercise of dogs."[71] This was a last-minute addition to the law by Senator Robert Dole, a response to the USDA's long-standing insistence that such a requirement was unnecessary. At the time, solitary confinement of dogs in laboratories was standard.[72]

To fulfill the statutory mandate, the USDA proposed a rule titled "Exercise and Socialization for Dogs" that would have required social grouping.[73] The agency reasoned:

> The scientific evidence available to us now leads us to conclude that space alone is not the key to whether a dog is provided the opportunity for sufficient exercise ... [I]t appears that additional space provided to certain dogs would be underutilized – i.e., even if released into a relatively large run, many dogs will find a corner and lie down. The evidence available to us indicates that certain dogs can receive sufficient exercise, even in cages of the minimum size mandated by the regulations, if they are given the opportunity to interact with other dogs or with humans.
>
> Intimately connected with the issue of exercise for dogs is the issue of the animals' socialization. The research data available, and in large measure simple observation, indicate that dogs given the opportunity to interact are more active than dogs housed individually. In short, social interaction among dogs is an effective means of promoting exercise.[74]

Facing backlash, the USDA stepped back its proposal, removing references to "socialization" from the final rule. The agency explained:

70 USDA, APHIS, INSPECTION REPORT, FESTIVAL FUN PARKS, LLC, MIAMI SEAQUARIUM 1 (Dec. 18, 2019).
71 7 U.S.C. § 2143(a)(2)(B).
72 Kulpa-Eddy et al., *supra* note 33, at 85 (citation omitted).
73 Animal Welfare—Standards, 54 Fed. Reg. 10897, 10904 (Mar. 15, 1989).
74 Animal Welfare; Standards, 55 Fed. Reg. 33448, 33467 (Aug. 15, 1990).

> we believe that socialization of dogs, including sensory contact, is the single most effective means of providing the opportunity for adequate exercise. Based on the evidence presented to us, however, we do not believe that it is essential for the health and well-being of dogs that they have sensory contact with other dogs, and do not believe that it is appropriate to include such a provision in the regulations as a required minimum standard.[75]

Given that the deep sociality of dogs had already been documented for decades, the USDA's suggestion that contact with other dogs was not essential for the basic well-being of the species – and thus not something it could require under the broad mandate to ensure the humane care and treatment of these animals – is remarkable.

But perhaps even more remarkable, given the agency's history of failing to protect animals, was its simultaneous conclusion "that dogs housed singly ... need regular interaction with humans," and accompanying proposal that dogs held in solitary confinement "must receive positive physical contact with humans at least daily."[76]

Despite opposition, the USDA finalized this mandate – though it did so in the context of requirement of a "plan," much like the plans required for primates discussed above. Thus, the USDA requires that regulated entities "develop, document, and follow an appropriate plan to provide dogs with the opportunity for exercise" and that "in developing their plan" they "should consider providing positive physical contact with humans that encourages exercise through play or other similar activities. If a dog is housed, held, or maintained at a facility without sensory contact with another dog, it must be provided with positive physical contact with humans at least daily."[77] "Positive physical contact" is defined by regulation as "petting, stroking, or other touching, which is beneficial to the well-being of the animal."[78]

On first glance, this might appear to be tremendously progressive law. But it has been all but ignored. It is buried within a lengthy regulation focused on the requirement that regulated entities have a plan – a requirement that, unsurprisingly, poses similar challenges to the primate plans. Thus, the 1996 survey of AWA inspectors discussed above found that "25% felt the criteria for dog exercise plans did not make clear what facilities needed to do to be in compliance," and approximately 40 percent felt that the criteria "were not adequate for enforcement purposes."[79] An analysis of USDA citations involving this regulation over a four-year period by agency officials found that the "vast majority" were for total failure to develop, document, or follow an exercise plan – and that "[o]nly rarely was a facility cited for not providing an isolated dog with positive physical contact with

[75] *Id.* at 33468.
[76] *Id.*
[77] 9 C.F.R. § 3.8(c)(2).
[78] *Id.* at § 1.1.
[79] Kulpa-Eddy et al., *supra* note 33, at 87 (citation omitted).

humans."[80] My analysis of more recent USDA citations, which span more than five years, reveals *no* citations for such violations, despite the fact that dogs are still routinely held in solitary confinement by laboratories and other regulated entities. Thus, while these animals theoretically have a legal right to "petting, stroking, or other touching" – a right that would understandably make anyone fighting to challenge solitary confinement of humans outraged – it has proven a wholly empty promise.

10.6. BEYOND THE AWA: SOLITARY CONFINEMENT UNDER THE ENDANGERED SPECIES ACT AND STATE CRUELTY LAWS

Although the AWA provisions discussed above provide the most explicit purported protections against solitary confinement for animals, emergent case law applying the Endangered Species Act's (ESA) prohibition on taking protected animals has also assured such protections for other, albeit narrow, categories of animals. In addition, state-level cruelty-to-animals laws can also be interpreted to afford such protections.

10.6.1 *Solitary Confinement and the ESA*

The ESA, which applies to both captive and wild members of protected species,[81] includes a prohibition "taking" such animals, including "harming" or "harassing" them.[82] Harm is as "an act which actually kills or injures wildlife," while harassment is "an intentional or negligent act or omission which creates the likelihood of injury to wildlife by annoying it to such an extent as to significantly disrupt normal behavioral patterns which include, but are not limited to, breeding, feeding or sheltering."[83]

Federal courts reviewing citizen suits challenging conditions of captive wildlife belonging to highly evolved species have begun to recognize that solitary confinement can amount to unlawful harm and/or harassment under the ESA.[84] For example, a federal district judge in Maryland held that "[f]orcing a lemur to live a solitary existence ... visits permanent psychological and physical injury on a species

[80] *Id.* at 88.

[81] *See* Delcianna J. Winders, Jared Goodman, & Heather Rally, *Captive Wildlife*, *in* ENDANGERED SPECIES ACT 361, 369–70 (Donald C. Baur & Ya-Wei Li eds., 3d ed. 2021).

[82] 16 U.S.C. §§ 1538(a), 1532(19).

[83] 50 C.F.R. § 17.3.

[84] *See, e.g.*, Kuehl v. Sellner, 887 F.3d 845, 852 (8th Cir. 2018) (affirming district court ruling that roadside zoo harassed lemurs "by keeping them in social isolation"); Mo. Primate Found. v. People for Ethical Treatment of Animals, Inc., No. 4:16-cv-02163-CDP, *slip op. at* 1–2 (E.D. Mo. Nov. 20, 2019) (holding that solitary chimpanzee was unlawfully taken).

born to engage in constant interaction with his kind" and thus violates the ESA.[85] The court further found that social interactions "are integral to the well-being of lions," "[s]olitude is extremely stressful for lions and disrupts their natural social behaviors," and "solitary confinement" of a lion "produce[d] a constant source of stress and negatively impact[ed] her physical and psychological health."[86] In so holding, the court credited an expert's testimony that "a lion forced to live in solitude with a single ball for company is tantamount to confining a human in a single room with a single book for years on end."[87] Notably, the court also recognized the harms that can arise from confining naturally solitary animals together, noting that "[t]igers, in contrast to . . . lions, are generally solitary animals who should not be housed together," and that "forced cohabitation ran contrary to their basic and natural instincts, which manifested in obvious signs of stress such as overt conflict and stereotypic pacing, as well as an imbalance in feeding."[88]

In addition, the United States recently filed an unprecedented civil ESA enforcement action alleging that removing ring-tailed lemurs from their social groups constitutes an unlawful take, explaining, "Removal of a ring-tailed lemur from its social group, even for a brief period of time, can cause a reshuffling of the social structure causing the briefly removed ring-tailed lemur to be ousted from or even attacked."[89]

Although these are promising developments, they mustn't be overstated. Only a small fraction of animals belong to species that are protected under the ESA. In addition, enforcement of captive conditions like solitary confinement has been almost entirely relegated to private citizen suits, which are costly and face significant standing and other procedural hurdles.

10.6.2 *Solitary Confinement and State Cruelty Laws*

State animal cruelty laws may also offer at least some limited protection against solitary confinement of nonhuman animals. Through originally focused on the infliction of physical pain,[90] some state cruelty laws could be interpreted to reach the harms inflicted by solitary confinement.

[85] People for Ethical Treatment of Animals, Inc. v. Tri-State Zoological Park of W. Maryland, Inc., 424 F. Supp. 3d 404, 414 (D. Md. 2019), *aff'd*, No. 20-1010, 2021 WL 305546 (4th Cir. Jan. 29, 2021).

[86] People for Ethical Treatment of Animals, Inc., 424 F. Supp. 3d. at 430, 416, 426.

[87] *Id.* at 417.

[88] *Id.*

[89] Compl. ¶¶ 154–57, United States v. Lowe, No. 20-cv-423-JFH (Nov. 19, 2020 E.D. Okla.).

[90] *See* Claire Priest, *Enforcing Sympathy: Animal Cruelty Doctrine after the Civil War*, 44 Law & Soc. Inquiry 136 (2019); David Favre & Vivien Tsang, *The Development of the Anti-Cruelty Laws during the 1800s*, 1 Det. C. L. Rev. 1 (1993).

According to a 2005 analysis of state cruelty laws, “none include language specifically acknowledging or addressing emotional neglect, abuse, or suffering in their definitions of cruelty. Furthermore, nine states specifically prohibit consideration of emotional suffering by specifying that any injury or suffering must be physical in nature.”[91]

Between these two extremes, however, is a wealth of possible interpretation. Cruelty prohibitions are broad. Moreover, there is a growing body of “[e]vidence that emotional pain can be more distressing than physical pain.”[92] Indeed, “[c]-urrent research leaves little room for doubt that experiences of emotional pain in general, and social pain in particular, can be associated with distress and suffering equal to experiences of physical pain.”[93] Thus, to the extent a cruelty law prohibits “pain” or “suffering,” it should not be assumed to be limited to physical harms.

Consider North Carolina’s prohibition of “every act, omission, or neglect whereby unjustifiable physical pain, suffering, or death is caused or permitted.”[94] A 2012 permanent injunction recognized that the conditions in which a bear was held violated this prohibition by causing the animal *both* “unjustifiable physical *and psychological suffering* and physical pain,” elaborating that “suffering” “encompasses physical, mental, and psychological suffering” and that “the unjustifiable suffering” inflicted on the bear “would be sufficient by itself to constitute unlawful cruelty.”[95]

Similarly, a lawsuit currently pending in federal district court in Maryland alleges that solitary confinement of a capuchin monkey, llama, New Guinea singing dog, squirrel monkey, and wolf “inflict[s] unnecessary suffering or pain on an animal” in violation of the state’s cruelty law.[96]

Here again, however, it is important not to overstate the significance of these developments. These are rare examples, and notably they arise in the context of civil suits. Typically, state cruelty laws are enforced criminally, “and in a criminal statute, an ambiguity should be resolved in favor of lenity.”[97] Thus, any ambiguity as to whether psychological harm from solitary confinement is prohibited would be interpreted in favor of the defendant and against a finding of liability.[98]

[91] F.D. McMillan, *Emotional Maltreatment in Animals* 167, *in* Mental Health and Well-Being in Animals (F.D. McMillan, ed., 2005).

[92] McMillan, *supra* note 19, at 162.

[93] *Id.* at 166.

[94] N.C. Gen. Stat. Ann. §§ 19A-1 to 19A-4.

[95] Permanent Injunction 16-17, Ray v. Jambbas, No. 12 CVD 669 (Cumberland Co, NC, District Court Aug. 27, 2012) (emphasis added).

[96] Md. Code, Crim. Law § 10-604(a)(3); Compl. ¶¶ 66, 72-76, Collins v. Tri-State Zoological Park of W. Md., No. 1:20-cv-01225 (D. Md. May 14, 2020); *see also* 514 F.Supp.3d 773 (D. Md. 2021) (denying motion to dismiss the case).

[97] Amrein v. State, 836 P.2d 862, 865 (Wyo. 1992).

[98] *See id.*; State v. Cleve, 1999-NMSC-017, ¶ 26, 127 N.M. 240, 250, 980 P.2d 23, 33; Com. v. Kneller, 2010 PA Super 122, ¶ 1, 999 A.2d 608, 609 (2010).

10.7. CONCLUSION

While it might seem on first glance that our laws provide robust protections for social animals against solitary confinement, such protections are illusory. They apply only to a small category of animals. And even for those animals who are explicitly provided some federal legal protection against solitary confinement – nonhuman primates, marine mammals, and dogs – they are not enforced in any meaningful way. Thus, suggestions that federal law "mandate[s] that most animals be housed with other animals of the same species"[99] are grossly inaccurate.

Notably, however, the federal government has at least acknowledged the fundamental importance of social contact for these animals – which, alarmingly, may be more than can be said for human prisoners. These acknowledgments – and the ever-increasing body of scientific evidence about the dire impacts that solitary confinement has on all social beings, human and nonhuman – can provide a foundation for a legal structure that meaningfully protects against these harms. But we must first acknowledge that we aren't "Treating Humans Worse Than Animals." We are subjecting both to appalling and unacceptable deprivation – and should work together to redress that.

99 Scientist Action and Advocacy Network, *supra* note 16.

11

Carceral Logics beyond Incarceration

Justin Marceau

No one claims that prosecutions and longer sentences are the exclusive focus of animal law. For many animal advocates, criminal prosecution is not a central focus of their attention or work. Yet one would be remiss to ignore the salience of carceral strategies in animating the work, and in influencing the image of animal activists. Protecting animals, many believe, is gainfully pursued through a "war on animal cruelty" such that tough-on-crime politics has been a mainstay of modern animal advocacy.[1]

In a very recent shift, however, certain pockets of the animal law movement have begun embracing what might be thought of as the logic of progressive prosecution. After years of public outreach and lobbying urging the view that incarceration is a pillar of animal protection, there is noticeable shift in recent years in the tone of the advocacy. Punishment is often now described as a necessary evil, and incarceration just one of the many responses that might be pursued against a person accused of harming animals. Indeed, many animal lawyers now oppose criminal registries, prosecuting juveniles as adults, and what might otherwise be called the most "grotesque flourishes" of carceral animal law.[2] To be sure, leading voices in animal law continue to insist that "incarceration has a valid place" in animal law, and to argue that diversions and treatment for felony charges of animal crimes generally are

[1] Jessica Rubin, *Desmond's Law: A Novel Approach to Animal Advocacy*, 24 ANIMAL L. 243, 275 (2018) (quoting *Why You Should Join the War on Animal Cruelty*, ANIMAL COALITION FOR ANIMAL JUST., accessed June 29, 2007), www.animal-justice.org/involved.html [site no longer available]).

[2] Alec Karakatsanis, *The Punishment Bureaucracy: How to Think about "Criminal Justice Reform"*, 128 YALE L.J. FORUM 848, 851 n.1 (2019) (describing progressive prosecution reforms as "making just enough tweaks to protect [the system's] perceived legitimacy" and noting that such reformers often target only changes that will not transform the system, and instead will "curb only its most grotesque flourishes.").

not tolerable.[3] But there seems to be a deliberate effort on the part of movement lawyers to distance themselves from retributivists (or even deterrence) rationales for punishment, and instead incarceration is championed as something like a last-resort when needed for incapacitation.[4] The appetite for incapacitation, however, is broader than it might seem, and underlies tough-on-crime enactments, including a recent increase in the statutory maximum sentence for animal cruelty crimes in Iowa, and a new federal felony cruelty law, the PACT Act.[5] For years animal lawyers have pursued "Bella's Law" in New York as a legislative priority, because the law promises "stronger sentences for animal cruelty." Punishment for animal abusers is still very much en vogue.

Nevertheless, there is an emerging trend among animal lawyers that downplays incarceration and appears willing to prioritize noncustodial responses to at least some cases of animal abuse and neglect. Incarceration is being billed as something like a last resort response to particularly hardened abusers. I applaud the willingness of animal lawyers to consider other-than-incarceration approaches to animal crimes. But I worry that the animal lawyers have come to believe that policing and prosecution that lead to outcomes other than incarceration are largely beyond critique. More specifically, I fear that the animal protection movement ignores the broader umbrella of carceral logics, including the literature observing that "incarceration as a logic and method of dominance is not reducible to the particular institutional form of jails, prisons, detention centers."[6] There is a sense that carceral logics detached from a singular zeal for imprisonment are tantamount to a progressive approach to animal maltreatment, and one that is liberated from the baggage of

3 *Animal Legal Defense Fund Position Statement: Sentencing for Animal Cruelty Crimes*, ANIMAL LEGAL DEFENSE FUND 3, 10 (2019), https://aldf.org/wp-content/uploads/2019/09/Position-Statement_Sentencing-2019.pdf.

4 *Id.* at 3 (noting that the "foremost" reason to incarcerate is to remove "offenders from society" so as to prevent them from harming animals and humans). This logic has been called into question by research suggesting that longer sentences may actually increase recidivism—that is to say, it is possible that the incapacitation benefit is outweighed in the long term by the criminogenic consequences of increased incarceration. JUSTIN MARCEAU, BEYOND CAGES 270–73 (2020) (compiling research on this point); *Id.* at 29 ("any decrease in crime due to incapacitating an offender is offset [and surpassed according to some studies] by the increased criminal activity that follows longer terms of incarceration."); Guyora Binder & Ben Notterman, *Penal Incapacitation: A Situationist Critique*, 54 AM. CRIM. L. REV. 1, 6 (2017) (placing significant blame for the problems of mass incarceration on the modern impulse to incapacitate dangerous persons, and noting that in fact crime may increase in the communities as the "return of traumatized and unemployable ex-prisoners to these neighborhoods creates additional risk of violent crime"); *see also Economic Perspectives on Incarceration and the Criminal Justice System*, COUNCIL OF ECON. ADVISORS 3–5 (2016), https://obamawhitehouse.archives.gov/sites/whitehouse.gov/files/documents/CEA%2BCriminal%2BJustice%2BReport.pdf.

5 Preventing Animal Cruelty and Torture Act, Pub. L. No. 116-72, 133 Stat. 1151 (2019), https://www.congress.gov/bill/116th-congress/house-bill/724/text.

6 Dylan Rodríguez, *Abolition as Praxis of Human Being: A Foreword, in Developments in the Law—Prison Abolition*, 132 HARV. L. REV. 1575, 1578 (2019).

racial disparity that infects the criminal system more generally. In reality, there is a long history of reformist discourse in other areas of the criminal system serving as a mechanism for justifying and entrenching the central features of what many regard as a fundamentally broken system, and one that does not have the best interests of animals in mind.

This chapter argues that animal law is still far too carceral in its rhetoric and approach to law reform, and the pivot toward fines, fees, and probation is not nearly as salutary as the animal protection lawyers imagine. Leaders in the animal protection world will likely regard this argument as quite radical – the idea that even nonincarceration criminal interventions might be treated as undesirably harsh. But for many who study the criminal system, it is far more radical to take on faith and intuition that animals are protected through carceral logics (or that they are harmed by critiquing carceral logics).[7] It is time to stop pretending that an uncritical acceptance of criminal responses to abuse and neglect help more than they hurt animals.

11.1 THE ANIMAL PROTECTION MOVEMENT'S SHIFT ON CARCERAL LOGICS IS MORE STYLE THAN SUBSTANCE

Many animal lawyers react to critiques of carceral animal law by contending that punishment is no longer a priority, and that there are only but a handful of anecdotes about overcharging.[8] My prior work has been criticized for emphasizing specific examples of racism within the criminal enforcement of animal law on the perverse theory that such data points are "not helpful for analyzing the current state of animal law," and for focusing on discrete examples.[9] Modern animal law, one is assured, is distancing itself from its historically punitive origins.

But the death of carceral logics among animal lawyers has been greatly exaggerated. Despite the movement's avowed distancing from carceral approaches, felonies are still the primary metric by which animal protection lawyers mechanically

[7] Recent research has shown that defendants who are not prosecuted for misdemeanor cases are almost 60 percent less likely to be charged with a crime in the next two years compared to those who were prosecuted. Michael Jonas, *Study Finds Not Prosecuting Misdemeanors Reduces Defendants' Subsequent Arrests*, CommonWealth (Mar. 29, 2021), https://commonwealthmagazine.org/criminal-justice/study-finds-not-prosecuting-misdemeanors-reduces-defendants-subsequent-arrests/.

[8] There is some irony in the movement's willingness to suggest that reforms to the carceral approach must await less anecdotal evidence. After all the movement has obtained felony laws and pursued harsher criminal responses based on nonrepresentative cases of extreme abuse and torture, and has never hesitated to link their efforts to broader efforts to combat serial killers or terrorists. I have personally seen animal protection legislation supported by reference to the need to combat violence, including terrorism, with the speaker showing a slide of the 9/11 attacks on the World Trade Center.

[9] Rubin, supra note 1, 271 n. 50 (arguing as well that there is probably not a racially disparate impact in the enforcement of crimes like cockfighting and dogfighting).

measure the importance of animals in the law, and law reform efforts in animal law continue to prioritize incarceration as a critical element in gauging whether the law is being meaningfully enforced. Scholars still seem to believe that the movement can incarcerate its way to animal rights. For example, a recent article urges harsher, more "proportionate" sentences as a vehicle for acknowledging the sentience of nonhuman animals.[10] This is consistent with the advocacy of animal protection groups that have long celebrated criminal prosecutions as first-steps in the march toward legal protections for sentient beings.

Similarly, when President Trump signed into law a federal animal cruelty statute in 2019, animal protection groups celebrated the accomplishment as long overdue and heralded it as one of the greatest legal victories in decades.[11] Likewise, Iowa amended its animal cruelty laws in 2020 so as to make criminal liability easier to prove, and the reforms were heralded by national groups as "upgrades" with lawyers for the movement taking credit for making the law as "impactful as possible."[12] But many features of the celebrated Iowa law have the trappings of a traditional tough-on-crime approach. For example, the new statute reduces the required mental state for establishing criminal liability from "intentionally" to "recklessly," which means that inadvertent abuse or neglect is now a crime in Iowa.[13] The statute also increased the penalties for animal abuse and neglect, and expanded the range of criminalized conduct.

Perhaps even more notable is the impetus behind many reforms that expand criminal penalties. The local organization urging the passage of the Iowa law explicitly claimed that the goal behind the more punitive legislation was to improve the state's ranking on the "Animal Protection Laws State Rankings."[14] As the Iowa

[10] Mirko Bagaric, A *Rational Approach to Sentencing Offenders for Animal Cruelty: A Normative and Scientific Analysis underpinning Proportional Penalties for Animal Cruelty Offenders*, 71 S.C. L. Rev. Vol. 4 (2019), https://papers.ssrn.com/sol3/papers.cfm?abstract_id=3585498 (urging reforms that would allow for harsher sentences based on animal sentience and noting that such "changes to the law would acknowledge animals' moral status and the impact of cruelty offenses on them, and harmonize this area of the law with scientific knowledge regarding the physiology and psychology of animals").

[11] *Extreme Animal Cruelty Can Now Be Prosecuted as a Federal Crime*, The Humane Society of the United States (Nov. 25, 2019), https://www.humanesociety.org/news/extreme-animal-cruelty-can-now-be-prosecuted-federal-crime.

[12] *Updating Iowa's Animal Protection Laws (Iowa)*, Animal Legal Defense Fund (2021), https://aldf.org/project/updating-iowas-animal-protection-laws-iowa/.

[13] H.J. 789, 88th Gen. Assembly (Iowa 2020), Www.Legis.Iowa.Gov/Legislation/Billbook?Ga=88&Ba=HF737. Oliver Wendell Holmes famously distinguished intended from unintended crimes by quipping that "a dog distinguishes between being stumbled over and being kicked." Holmes, The Common Law 3 (1887). It is not clear that criminal liability in Iowa does so distinguish after the new amendments. *Cf.* Bailey v. Bly, 231 N.E.2d 8 (Ill. App. Ct. 1967) (involving civil litigation based on stumbling over a dog).

[14] *The Community and Pet Protection Act (HF737): Why This Bill Is Important*, The Iowa Pet Alliance (2021), https://iowapetalliance.org/hf737/ ("Iowa is ranked 49th in the nation for our animal protection laws, according to Animal Legal Defense Fund's 2019 U.S. Animal Protection Laws State Rankings").

sponsor of the legislation emphasized, "What we're trying to solve here is Iowa being one of the lowest-ranked states in regards to animal abuse."[15]

There is an uncomfortable irony in seeing Iowa seek to improve its animal protection rankings by passing more punitive felony laws of this sort. The state with one of the highest concentrations of factory farms in the country seeks to improve its public standing with regard to animal issues, and it is able to use the animal protection movement's own ranking system to facilitate this deception and distraction.[16]

Industrial agriculture and its supporters are happy to celebrate the hierarchy of animal suffering codified through the animal law rankings. Animal advocates have explained that they "hope this [rankings] report encourages states, especially those at the lower end of the ranking, to refocus their attention"[17] to more carceral policies. Consider the movement's own reporting on another state infamous for its factory farms, Kansas. Reporting on ranking-induced progress in Kansas, the Animal Legal Defense Fund explained,

> When ALDF initially published the report, Kansas was ranked among the worst states because it did not have any statute that allowed for felony prosecution of animal abusers. In a happy update, after ALDF had been working with Kansas lawmakers for a year, a new law went into effect ... that makes severe cruelty to animals a felony. The law, known as "Scruffy's Law" after a terrier who was maliciously tortured in a gruesome 1997 killing, also includes mandatory minimum sentence.[18]

In publicizing these rankings, the lawyers framed the question underlying the rankings as "Best States to Abuse an Animal?"[19]

In this way, the rankings displace attention from systemic violence and keep the attention focused squarely on acts of individual abuse and neglect. The criteria used to rank states are one of the great symptoms of the persistence of carceral thinking within the animal protection movement. Ranking systems always present a risk of oversimplifying complicated matters. Can a list of a city's top ten restaurants capture the nuance of a dining experience? Ranking state laws across multiple legal dimensions, moreover, is infinitely more subjective and fraught. Yet, at least in the case of animal law state rankings, the criteria for evaluation are transparent. These rankings categorically reward states that take more punitive measures. Looking at the publicly

[15] Stephen Gruber-Miller, *Iowa Senate Passes Bill Increasing Penalties for Animal Abuse, Neglect*, Des Moines Register (Mar. 4, 2020), https://www.desmoinesregister.com/story/news/politics/2020/03/04/iowa-senate-passes-bill-strengthening-penalties-animal-abuse-neglect-torture/4952238002/.

[16] For a map of animal agricultural density across the country, *see* https://www.foodandwaterwatch.org/news/brand-new-see-americas-factory-farms-mapped-out.

[17] Animal Legal Defense Fund, *Best States to Abuse an Animal?* The Animals' Advocate 25 2, 2006, https://aldf.org/wp-content/uploads/2018/06/Animals-Advocate-Summer-2006.pdf.

[18] *Id.*

[19] *Id.*

available grading criteria, one can quickly see that the current rankings system incentivizes legislation on topics including: (1) mandatory arrest provisions; (2) the availability of felony penalties; (3) a broader scope of criminal liability (to include neglect and bestiality); (4) increased penalties for repeat offenders; and (5) mandatory reporting of suspected abuse to law enforcement.[20] Moreover, the rankings additionally make specific suggestions to states for improvement, including adding a felony penalty for abandonment, increasing sentences, enacting a broader felony provision, and treating animal cruelty as a predicate offense to trigger the sweeping and much-critiqued web of criminal liability under RICO.[21] It would be an interesting experiment to run to see how a state would rank under the existing methodology if it had no felony laws relating to animal neglect or abuse, but prohibited all factory farming practices,[22] all fur production, and all cruel animal exhibitions, while also providing financial support to low-income persons with pets. If the state would rank very near the bottom of all states, despite providing the best quality of life for the largest number of animals, what does this tell us about legal advocacy around animals?

I would be remiss if I failed to emphasize that among many well-intentioned animal advocates, there is a pervasive fear that critiquing the criminal focus of animal law prioritizes human interests above animal interests. We are animal lawyers, not human rights lawyers, one can almost hear them yelling. But the reality is much more complicated, and much less of a zero-sum situation. There is no data to support the proposition that harsher animal cruelty laws are reducing crime. Indeed, the movement has never commissioned research about the rates of crime before they started the tough-on-crime model, much less compared it to crime rates for animal crimes in the modern era. We assume that the harsher laws are reducing animal crimes, but what if research shows an inverse relationship, which is not unheard of in criminology?[23]

Yet, there is a sense among many thoughtful persons in the movement that these legislative reforms, along with the rankings that drive them (at least in part), should

[20] *Animal Protection U.S. State Laws Rankings Report*, ANIMAL LEGAL DEFENSE FUND (2019), https://aldf.org/wp-content/uploads/2020/02/2019-Animal-Protection-US-State-Laws-Rankings-Report.pdf.

[21] *See* Antonio Califa, *RICO Threatens Civil Liberties*, 43 VAND. L. REV. 805 (1990), https://scholarship.law.vanderbilt.edu/cgi/viewcontent.cgi?article=2524&context=vlr; Peter Henning, *RICO Lawsuits Are Tempting, but Tread Lightly*, N.Y. Times (Jan. 16, 2018), https://www.nytimes.com/2018/01/16/business/dealbook/harvey-weinstein-rico.html.

[22] Note that that under the state rankings, having an ag-gag law (generally criminalizing trespass and recording on animal agriculture facilities) warrants only an "asterisk," as opposed to an actual legislative suggestion for improvement.

[23] There are examples where conduct targeted by criminal law has increased or at least not materially decreased in the face of harsher penalties. *See, e.g.*, Dan M. Kahan, *Gentle Nudges vs. Hard Shoves: Solving the Sticky Norms Problem*, 67 U. CHI. L. R. 607–8 (2000) (explaining that enacting more severe criminal statutes does "nothing to reduce the incidence of these offenses. Indeed, they may even increase the incidence of such crimes.").

be understood as largely unrelated to incarceration. Broader felony laws, a wider net of RICO liability, and longer maximum sentences are not necessarily aimed at more incarceration on the ground, it is argued. Animal lawyers have explained that these reforms simply provide prosecutors with more options, allowing for greater discretion in individual cases. According to this logic, enacting felony offenses into law is simply "a way of acknowledging that animal abuse is a violent crime."[24]

Apart from being ahistorical, prioritizing felony laws while pretending that one does not expect them to be used (or used often)[25] is a strained form of logic: why prioritize laws without actually intending to see them enforced? Why spend money lobbying for higher maximum sentences, or incentivizing them through rankings, only to claim that you don't actually anticipate more incarceration? The suggestions of nonuse or only expressive or symbolic value are almost insulting to the intelligence of persons familiar with the criminal system. Prosecutors and the animal lawyers who seek legislation adopting new charges and longer sentences are smart people who would not waste their time pursing the changes if the law reforms did not provide them tactical advantages. Put differently, pushing for increased penalties as a way of acknowledging the violence of harming animals, without expecting that the sentences will increase in actuality, is a form of deliberate ignorance. It is almost bizarre to suggest that the movement spend its limited resources seeking *more* felony laws and *higher* felony sentences (and penalize in rankings the absence of such felony provisions) without expecting any uptick in the number of felony charges or sentences. In 2021, a prominent animal lawyer made this point clear in an interview with the *Toronto Star* about an animal abuse case, "The law allows (a prison sentence of up to five years), so why not hand down the maximum?"

Consider the relatively recent enactment of Desmond's Law in Connecticut. The law, which allows for victim advocates in animal cruelty cases, is now championed by its drafters as a reform that is not a "punitive approach."[26] But the history of the law tells a different story. Desmond was a dog who was brutally abused, and the person who inflicted the injuries was not sentenced to incarceration. The sponsor of the bill, Representative Diana Urban, was understandably heartbroken over Desmond's suffering, and was so outraged by the minimal sentence in Desmond's case that she "immediately began her battle to write legislation that would make sure that this travesty of justice would never happen again."[27] In other words, the law was

[24] *ALDF Position Statement*, *supra* note 3, at 4.

[25] It is beyond question that the tough-on-crime turn in animal law was motivated by a desire for more incarceration. As the executive director of one prominent organization explained, "our Criminal Justice Program is working with law enforcement agents and prosecutors to assure the successful prosecution of criminal animal abusers. This is the program that inspired our famous bumper sticker: '*Abuse an Animal, Go to Jail!' And we mean it.*" (emphasis added), https://aldf.org/wp-content/uploads/2018/06/Animals-Advocate-Summer-2006.pdf.

[26] Rubin, *supra* note 1, at 270.

[27] *The Origin of Desmond's Army*, Desmond's Army, https://desmondsarmy.org/the-origin-of-desmonds-army/ (last visited Aug. 5, 2020).

always about incarceration. Lamenting the failure of the legal response to the Desmond case, Professor Jessica Rubin observes that the "owner was allowed to enroll in a diversionary program" called accelerated rehabilitation.[28] Even bracketing what it means for the animal protection movement to be openly opposed to a program called "accelerated rehabilitation," it is striking that commentators now assert that the law has nothing to do with "trying to maximize incarceration."[29]

It cannot be doubted that the movement has pursued new felony laws and expanded sentencing regimes in recent years,[30] and the notion that one can pursue more felonies, longer sentencing provisions, advocate laws, and broader definitions of crimes *without* expecting longer sentences is both at war with the existing data from other fields and in tension with the movement's own ongoing advocacy. Research has consistently shown what is common sense to most: when sentencing ranges are increased for a crime, the average length and frequency of incarceration will also increase.[31]

Passing more and harsher criminal penalties can be expected to produce more incarceration. Moreover, as already noted, many of the animal protection lawyers who favor prosecution point to the importance of incapacitation. But if the goal is to

[28] Rubin, *supra* note 1 at 263. Opposing something called Accelerated Rehabilitation is a pretty trenchant example of carceral exceptionalism in animal law. A person sentenced to accelerated rehabilitation is released to the custody of the Connecticut Court Services Division for a two-year term of supervision, during which time conditions such as restitution, community service, psychiatric or psychological counseling, alcohol or drug treatment, or even an animal cruelty prevention and education program may be imposed. *See Accelerated Rehabilitation Diversionary Program*, CONN. JUD. BRANCH (2017), https://www.jud.ct.gov/Publications/CR137D.pdf.

[29] *Id.* A reader might get whiplash if she reads too quickly Rubin's argument that Desmond's Law was necessary as response to allowing an abuser to enter accelerated rehabilitation, while noting that Desmond's Law really has nothing to do with criminalization or punitiveness.

[30] Consider Bella's Bill, one of the movement's legislative priorities in recent years. As described in the movement's own summaries, the law was an effort to update the New York cruelty laws by "allowing for stronger sentences for animal cruelty." *Bella's Bill: Overhauling New York's Cruelty Laws*, ANIMAL LEGAL DEFENSE FUND (2021), https://aldf.org/project/bellas-bill/.

[31] *See, e.g.*, Rochelle Morton, Michelle Hebart & Alexandra Whittaker, *Increasing Maximum Penalties for Animal Welfare Offences in South Australia – Has It Caused Penal Change?* ANIMALS (Dec. 8, 2018), https://www.ncbi.nlm.nih.gov/pmc/articles/PMC6316723/ (analyzing animal cruelty prosecutions and convictions after enactments strengthening sentences, noting that the types of penalties have changed, moving from "less severe penalties" to "more severe penalties."); *Id.* ("Fines and prison sentences handed down have doubled in magnitude since Parliament increased the maximum penalties."); Marc Mauer, *Long-Term Sentences: Time to Reconsider the Scale of Punishment*, THE SENTENCING PROJECT (Nov. 5, 2018), https://www.sentencingproject.org/publications/long-term-sentences-time-reconsider-scale-punishment/ (linking increased federal sentencing policies with increased prison and jail populations); Consensus Study Report, *The Growth of Incarceration in the United States: Exploring Causes and Consequences*, THE NATIONAL ACADEMIES OF SCIENCES, ENGINEERING, MEDICINE 70 (2014), https://www.nap.edu/read/18613/chapter/5 (noting that a driving force behind increases in incarceration rates was "the proliferation in nearly every state and in the federal system of laws and guidelines providing for lengthy prison sentences").

create safer communities by incapacitating persons who harm animals, it would be odd to suggest that longer sentences are not an affirmatively good or necessary outcome based on that logic. If one believes in incapacitation, then five years of community safety should be better than one year, and much better than probation. And if one lobbies for a law based on the promise of "stronger sentences," only to later claim that it is surprised by or uninterested in such sentences, the entire project begins to reek of duplicity.

Moreover, as a practical matter, if incarceration were not really the goal of punitive animal cruelty felony laws, then the movement would likely care very little about actual enforcement efforts on the ground after a symbolically significant law was passed. But it is simply not true that the movement passes new or expanded felony criminal laws and then turns a blind eye to their underenforcement. As one commentator recently summarized, "[t]he biggest problem with the effectiveness of animal abuse statutes involves their enforcement."[32] Another law review article essentially parrots the logic of the movement: "The most significant issue in dealing with animal cruelty, animal abuse, and dogfighting cases is an overall lack of enforcement."[33] There is an overriding sense among the academic commentary that, "[e]ven when the abusers do face trial, many offenders are given 'slap-on-the-wrist' punishments."[34] For decades the movement has lamented what it calls the "enforcement gap," or underenforcement of animal cruelty crimes,[35] and in recent years the movement has made it a priority to respond to the alleged underenforcement of animal cruelty statutes through creative legislation, including animal advocates in criminal cases involving animal abuse and neglect.[36]

Consistent with this agenda, one of the most lauded and pursued types of animal protection legislation among local lobbyists and some national organizations is the animal-victim advocate laws mentioned above. "Desmond's Law" and others like it provide animal victims a human advocate in addition to the prosecutor to speak about the impact of the crime. The express purpose for pursuing these laws is to

[32] Kirsten E. Brimer, *Justice for Dusty: Implementing Mandatory Minimum Sentences for Animal Abusers*, 113 Penn. St. L. Rev. 649, 650–51 (2008) ("infrequent enforcement of animal cruelty laws and relatively light penalties for animal abuse create the social message that injuring animals through neglect or deliberate cruelty is marginally acceptable or a minor criminal infraction").

[33] Katie Galanes, *The Contradiction: Animal Abuse – Alive and Well*, 44 J. Marshall L. Rev. 209, 221–22 (2010).

[34] Brimer, *supra* note 32, at 650; *see also* Jennifer H. Rackstraw, *Reaching for Justice: An Analysis of Self-Help Prosecution for Animal Crimes*, 9 Animal L. 243 (2003).

[35] Penny Conly Ellison, *Time to Give Anticruelty Laws Some Teeth - Bridging the Enforcement Gap*, 3 J. Animal L. & Ethics 1 (2009); Joan E. Schaffner, An Introduction to Animals and the Law 69 (2010).

[36] Galanes, *supra* note 33, at 225 ("Thankfully, some of these criminal defendants were punished with significant jail time; more often, however, defendants receive light sentencing or find ways to escape proper sentencing."). Rubin, *supra* note 1, 275 (2018) (arguing that the enforcement gap can be narrowed through the use of victims' advocates in animal cruelty cases).

address the so-called enforcement gap. As the Animal Legal Defense Fund explained in its testimony supporting the legislation, prosecutors "lack the resources to pursue cases involving animal victims to the fullest extent possible ... [but Desmond's Law] would help to fill that enforcement gap."[37] An unused or under-enforced felony law is seen as an affront to justice, and an expanding prosecutorial bureaucracy is necessary to ensure robust enforcement. That same logic is also obvious from the legislative moves pursued in the wake of the enactment of the federal PACT Act, which created felony level liability for certain animal cruelty crimes. Leaving no doubt that they wish the new felony law to be aggressively prosecuted, just months after enactment of the PACT Act, animal protection advocates proclaimed that the new law is "only effective if enforced," and called for the creation of Animal Cruelty Prosecution Unit at the Department of Justice.[38] Federal legislation creating this new unit of prosecutors, dubbed the Animal Cruelty Enforcement Act, has already been introduced with bipartisan support, and with the promise that the law will help the nation "to step up federal action against perpetrators."[39]

The animal protection movement is anything but monolithic, but the idea that the movement as a whole has distanced itself from a strongly carceral posture is greatly exaggerated. Commentators and advocates continue to signal that the creation of new felony laws is an affirmatively positive development, and treat the underuse of such felony laws as creating a presumption of malfeasance, or representing a lack of acknowledgment that animal suffering should be taken seriously.

11.2 THE PROBLEM IS WITH ANIMAL POLICING, NOT JUST INCARCERATION

The explicit historical support for incarceration among leading scholars and advocates in animal protection is deserving of critique, as noted above. But a critique of incarceration alone would actually let the movement off too easy. As Dorothy Roberts and other scholars have recognized, a narrow focus on the problems associated with incarceration might imply that investments in more policing[40] and

[37] Letter, Animal Legal Defense Fund, *Re: Testimony of Animal Legal Defense Fund in Support of H.B. 5344, An Act Concerning Support for Animals That Are Neglected or Treated Cruelly ("Desmond's Law")*, Judiciary Comm. 810 (Mar. 22, 2016), https://ctstatelibrary.org/wp-content/lh-bills/2016_PA30_HB5344.pdf. The sponsor of the legislation explained that the legislation was in response to the light punishments for animal abuse that were commonplace. *Id.*

[38] Press Release, *Braun, Whitehouse, Kennedy, Other Senators Introduce Bill to Crack Down on Animal Cruelty*, Animal Wellness Action (Sept. 16, 2020), https://animalwellnessaction.org/2020/09/16/braun-whitehouse-kennedy-other-senators-introduce-bill-to-crack-down-on-animal-cruelty/.

[39] *Id.*

[40] The term *policing* here is used a broad sense to include all efforts to enforce animal cruelty–related crimes. In many areas of criminal law, enforcement and policing are roughly synonymous, but in the realm of animal protection there is a large cadre of unsworn animal control

prosecutions that result in punishments other than incarceration are desirable alternatives.[41] In reality, however, incarceration is just the low-hanging fruit, not the root of the problem. The incarceration obsession that treats light sentences, proverbially referred to as slaps on the wrist, as immoral is a symptom of the belief that social and moral attitudes are appropriately shaped through criminal interventions. Prosecutions that do not result in sentences of imprisonment, under this logic, are examples of the merciful progression of animal law. In the remainder of this chapter, I focus attention on the other-than-incarceration efforts that might be incorrectly conflated with leniency and just outcomes by animal advocates.

11.2.1 *General Considerations beyond Incarceration*

The United States is the world leader in incarceration, and some animal rights activists are beginning to acknowledge the harms that might flow from contributing to this system. The animal movement, however, seems unaware that incarceration is far from the only example of American exceptionalism in criminal law. In his book *The Process Is the Punishment*, Malcolm Feeley argues that for many persons facing criminal charges, the worst thing about the criminal system is the likelihood of lost wages, lost employment, ruined relationships, commissions to bondsmen, and other fees and burdens that are commonplace even if charges are ultimately *dismissed* by the prosecution or by acquittal.[42] Being charged with a crime, or even just being targeted by police efforts to intervene and educate, can manifest as punishments for many persons, particularly persons in marginalized communities.

Even for those who are ultimately convicted of crimes, a large body of work has shown that the fact of a conviction can be worse than any short custodial detention. As Alexandra Natapoff has explained in her path-marking book, "one of the great myths of our criminal system is that minor arrests and convictions are not especially terrible for the people who experience them."[43] As Natapoff shows, these myths obscure the reality that arrests, much less charges (even without any incarceration), destroy families and lives. Indeed, the US system of collateral consequences has created systemic barriers that often exclude persons convicted of crimes from fully

officers (employed by animal protection groups) who are deputized to enforce the animal cruelty laws, and whose role in policing animal abuse is relevant to the critiques raised in this chapter.

[41] *See, e.g.*, Dorothy E. Roberts, *Prison, Foster Care, and the Systemic Punishment of Black Mothers*, 59 UCLA L. Rev. 1474, 1484 (2012) (critiquing the child welfare system's willingness to prioritize policing and increased carceral interventions); *Id.* ("State intrusion is typically viewed as necessary to protect maltreated children from parental harm.").

[42] Malcolm Feeley, The Process Is the Punishment: Handling Cases in a Lower Criminal Court (1979); *see also* Nora V. Demleitner, *Collateral Sanctions and American Exceptionalism*, in American Exceptionalism in Crime and Punishment 487 (Kevin Reitz, ed., 2018).

[43] Alexandra Natapoff, Punishment without Crime: How Our Massive Misdemeanor System Traps the Innocent and Makes America More Unequal, 19 (2018).

reintegrating into society. For example, a felony conviction, even if it does not result in incarceration, will oftentimes trigger disenfranchisement, which as of 2016, resulted in more than 6 million Americans being ineligible to vote.[44] Collateral consequences can result in the loss of employment licensures, a loss of public housing, the loss of one's right to serve on a jury, deportation, and many other harms that are determined at a state or local level, in addition to the often lawful, private discrimination by employers, landlords, universities, and others reviewing applications. Even noncriminal fines and fees, including fees or fines relating to animal offenses like tethering, could result in the loss of one's driver's license in many states.[45] There are as many as 11 million people who have a suspended driver's license at any given moment in this country because of a fine or fee. As one commentator has observed, the "sheer number of collateral sanctions has become staggering, and it has been impossible to detail all the sanctions potentially befalling" any particular defendant.[46] Thus, the problem of carceral animal law defies any tidy calculations about the number of arrests or prosecutions for animal crimes.

I often hear animal lawyers remarking that probation is likely the most common punishment for animal crimes, and the assumption is that this places the carceral project beyond rebuke. But scholars outside of animal law have recognized that a myopic focus on incarceration as the sole marker of penal severity is at odds with the lived reality of supervision for the 4–5 million people on probation in the United States. In 2020, Human Rights Watch issued a report summarizing the ways that probation and parole are troubling symptoms of and contributors to the mass incarceration system in the United States.[47] The animal rights movement's working assumption that probation is the soft-on-crime approach to crimes ignores the reality that nearly 50 percent of persons enter the state prison system because of a (often technical) probation or parole violation.[48] Probation cannot be easily and cleanly cordoned off from the mass incarceration system in the United States.

44 Jean Chung, *Felony Disenfranchisement Primer*, The Sentencing Project (June 27, 2019), https://www.sentencingproject.org/publications/felony-disenfranchisement-a-primer/.

45 The failure to pay a court-imposed fine or fee is a frequent reason for the suspension of one's driver's license. Nonpayment of court costs and fees from criminal cases can result in suspension of driver's license in forty-four states. And nonpayment of civil fees or fines appears to be a basis for suspending one's driver's license in approximately a dozen states, some of which allow for the suspension even if the civil fine is not related to a traffic offense. *See, e.g.*, Ark. Code Ann. § 16-13-708 (Arkansas); Me. Rev. Stat. Tit. 14, § 3141; Me. Rev. Stat. Tit. 29-a § 2608 (Maine); Va. Code Ann. § 46.2-395 (Virginia); Wis. Stat. Wis. Stat. § 345.47, 800.095 (Wisconsin).

46 Demleitner, *supra* note 42, at 488.

47 *Revoked: How Probation and Parole Feed Mass Incarceration*, Human Rights Watch (July 31, 2020), www.hrw.org/report/2020/07/31/revoked/how-probation-and-parole-feed-mass-incarceration-united-states#.

48 *Id.* ("People under supervision, lawyers, and even some judges and former supervision officers recognize that supervision often sets people up to fail. People must comply with an array of wide-ranging, sometimes vague, and hard-to-follow rules, including rules requiring them to pay

The animal movement does not exist apart from this background of severe collateral consequences resulting from other-than-incarceration criminal sanctions. When a movement focused on humanizing the suffering of animals cannot fathom the hardship imposed on marginalized communities flowing from increased policing and prosecution, it betrays a kind of naivete or, worse, arrogance. For the persons and their families caught up in the web of policing, probation, and fines, it is the height of privilege to suggest that these movement-inspired police interventions do not impose serious hardships. The lived reality of persons impacted by increased policing and prosecution, even when incarceration does not ensue, is very different from what the animal lawyers might imagine.

I recognize that for many persons invested in animal protection, it is difficult to appreciate how police-dominated interventions that are not focused on incarceration could oftentimes actually be bad for animals.[49] To many of our readers, it will sound ridiculous to suggest that police interventions that do not lead to incarceration can ever be an *overreaction* to animal crimes. That is why the remainder of this section comprises short vignettes that describe the role of police in animal protection efforts that *do not involve incarceration*. These stories are based on events spread across the country, spanning blue and red states, and they are not meant to be exhaustive; rather, they are merely illustrative examples of the systemic problems resulting from a harsh policing approach to animal crimes, even in the absence of criminal convictions. These examples provide a foundation for thinking about how policing and prosecution that does not result in incarceration or even a conviction can be affirmatively bad for animals.

11.2.2 *When Poverty and Pets Can Mean Deportation: Texas*

A number of assumptions undergird the carceral turn in animal protection efforts. The defining and most prominent assumption is that increased policing and criminal interventions will ultimately reduce animal suffering. Implicit in this assumption is the conclusion that marginalized communities will not cease reporting or underreport animal crimes out of a fear of immigration or criminal consequences. Another animal protection assumption, and one that has historically been disconnected from the carceral turn in animal law, is the overriding belief that animal shelters and animal service agencies exist to protect animals, and should be viewed

steep fines and fees, attend frequent meetings, abstain from drugs and alcohol, and report any time they change housing or employment.").

[49] There are countless ways that the imposition of fines and fees on persons with pets can be devastating for the animals. For example, the economic pressure that fines create for persons who are already struggling financially are passed down to the animal in terms of fewer available resources for animal care. And the cost of rehoming an animal, even bracketing the emotional costs to the animal and the person, are much higher than keeping the pet in the home that they already know and love. In addition, some percentage of confiscated animals are euthanized when they cannot be adopted.

as critical resources for communities. A recent case in Dallas reveals the tension between these assumptions.[50]

In January 2020, Maria Flores brought her Maltese dog, Muffy, to a veterinarian to have a recent limp checked out. The veterinarian observed severe matting across the dog's body, which was likely the source of the limp, and prescribed a treatment plan that included sedation, shaving, and antibiotics. Maria paid the fee for the vet visit. Unfortunately, however, Maria could not afford the proposed $1,500 treatment plan. After a few weeks of monitoring the dog and hoping she would get better, Maria realized that Muffy's limp was getting worse. Maria made the difficult decision to surrender Muffy to Dallas Animal Services (DAS), so that the dog could receive treatment.

Like other animal service programs across the country, DAS promises an important service to community members; it agrees to accept "pet surrenders" from any person within the city limits.[51] Muffy was surrendered by her family because they could not afford the medical care she needed.

The veterinarian at DAS who examined Muffy discovered that the matted hair had caused a set of serious injuries, including muscle loss and the tearing of an Achilles tendon, and because of these injuries contacted the Dallas Police Department. In conjunction with the Texas Society for the Prevention of Cruelty to Animals, the Dallas Police arrested Maria in August 2020, and she was charged with felony animal cruelty, which carries a maximum of ten years in prison (based on "updates" to the law urged by animal groups). Maria was booked in the Dallas jail and remained there without bond, away from her husband and kids, until September, at which point she was taken into custody by Immigration and Customs Enforcement officers and moved to an immigration detention facility.

Maria, who is undocumented, faced years in prison and a felony record. She still faces likely deportation – all because she turned her dog over to the Dallas Animal Services after she could not afford a veterinarian's suggested treatment plan. It is true that a grand jury subsequently refused to indict her on the criminal cruelty charges, and she was eventually released on bond from the immigration detention center. But irrevocable damage had already been done: Maria was detained for more than a month, and now faces a daunting challenge in immigration court to her ability to remain in the country.

There is a growing body of research documenting the fact that persons living in marginalized communities, particularly undocumented persons, are reticent to

[50] Rebecca Lopez, *Dallas Woman Faces Deportation after Taking Sick Dog to Animal Shelter*, WFAA (Sept. 26, 2020), https://www.wfaa.com/article/news/local/dallas-woman-faces-deportation-after-taking-sick-dog-to-animal-shelter/287-99474cb1-e977-4ae1-9116-7aabba035eed.

[51] Dallas Animal Services, *Can't Keep Your Pet?* City of Dallas (2021), https://dallascityhall.com/departments/dallas-animal-services/Pages/CantKeepYourPet.aspx.

report crimes in their neighborhoods.[52] The reasons for such underreporting are varied, but an ACLU report makes clear that a fear of deportation is a leading reason that many immigrant communities might underreport crime.[53]

The animal protection movement wrongly assumes that more aggressive policing and intervention will help animals, but research suggests that the carceral turn in animal law may actually deter persons from reporting abuse in their community, impeding efforts to intervene and help animals. Police officers have reported that crimes like sexual assault, human trafficking, and domestic violence are harder to investigate because immigrant communities are less likely to use local resources out of fear it will result in harm to their community. The notion that marginalized communities might fear animal protection groups and community shelters because of the carceral turn is illustrated perfectly by a close friend of Maria, who said of her case: "They're committing many injustices and it's unfortunate that where people go seek help, they're attacked."[54] And this is precisely the point.

The involvement of police and immigration officials has become routine for many groups concerned with animal protection, rather than focusing on processes that might help the injured animals. For example, many states have "mandatory reporting" laws that require veterinarians or other professionals who suspect animal crimes to report the matters to law enforcement. Indeed, the state rankings of animal protection laws value such measures, which appear innocuous, even obvious. But this is all part of a logic that treats police intervention as an affirmatively good and necessary part of a commitment to animal protection. Stories like Maria's problematize this narrative by showing that increased policing, even in the absence of a conviction, can produce negative impacts for individuals, communities, and the animals themselves.

For many in the animal protection movement, Maria's story will be uncomfortable, and rightfully so, but there is no reason to believe it is unusual. In fact, many in the animal protection movement might react to Maria's story by lamenting that she came to the shelter too late, when the dog's condition had deteriorated badly enough to warrant police intervention. If only she had come sooner, they will say, all of these consequences could have been avoided. But for those living in marginalized communities, there is a sad futility in the suggestion that more frequent or earlier interactions with animal protection groups would ameliorate the problems resulting from circumstances such as this one. As Maria's lawyer observed, the

[52] Stefano Comino, Giovanni Mastrobuoni, and Antonio Nicolo, *Silence of the Innocents: Illegal Immigrants' Underreporting of Crime and Their Victimization*. IZA Discussion Paper No. 10306, https://ssrn.com/abstract=2861091.

[53] *Freezing Out Justice*, ACLU (2018), https://www.aclu.org/report/freezing-out-justice.

[54] Stella Chávez, *A Dog Owner Couldn't Afford Her Pet's Treatment; Now She's in an Immigration Detention Center*, KERA News (Sept. 8, 2020), https://www.keranews.org/news/2020-09-08/a-dog-owner-couldnt-afford-her-pets-treatment-now-shes-in-an-immigration-detention-center.

groups involved seem to prefer throwing her in jail instead of exploring alternatives in circumstances where a person may not be able to afford resources for their pet.[55]

Equally important, Maria's case will never end up in a database compiling the overuse or abuse of the criminal justice system in animal cases because her case was ultimately dismissed. In the eyes of many animal protection advocates who might want to track data about the system, this case will be invisible. It is a nonevent. Cases that do not result in a conviction, much less a sentence of incarceration are well beyond the universe of data that anyone is talking about when conversations about the utility of a carceral response to animal suffering are being undertaken. A suffering animal whose case brings a small punishment or no conviction is the very sort of slap on the wrist that seems to justify the need for more felonies and policing. But the reality, as Maria's case illustrates, is considerably more complicated.

Many cases that never result in incarceration or a conviction (or as in Maria's case a formal charge from, for example, a grand jury) still have devastating impacts on the accused's life, as well as on the way that communities perceive animal protection efforts. Cases like Maria's show that the harms of the propolicing agenda extend well beyond the easily counted cases and quantitative data that will emerge from FBI databases. The impacts on the safety of animals in a community from a carceral animal law posture is probably best understood by looking to qualitative accounts like those in Maria's case. Would anyone really fault Maria if she fails to report to animal protection groups or authorities a dog she thinks is being neglected in her neighborhood after her experience? Maria may not even be in the country to report the abuse, since she still faces deportation because of the chain of events triggered by her efforts to obtain costly medical care for her dog. As a result of policing and fear of prosecution, more animals may actually suffer.

11.2.3 *The Quintessential "Slap on the Wrist," a Sentence of Home Arrest: Florida*

The case of Tammy Brown from Florida is illustrative of the sort of prosecution effort that might be written off as de minimus by many in the animal movement because she was ultimately sentenced to house arrest and probation.[56] But the ultimate sentence only tells part of the story.

55 *Id.* (quoting her attorney as saying that there is a "disconnect between the agencies charged with protecting animals and the families who may need help caring for their pets.").

56 In a podcast discussing the carceral impulses in animal law, leading animal law commentator Mariann Sullivan appeared skeptical of the critique because, as she observed, it seems that relatively few persons are sentenced to incarceration for animal abuse. *Animal Law Podcast #50: Justin Marceau on Animal Law and Criminal Punishment*, Our Hen House (July 24, 2019) https://www.ourhenhouse.org/2019/07/animal-law-podcast-50-justin-marceau-on-animal-law-and-criminal-punishment/.

Tammy has a disability and lived on about $500 per month from social security, of which she spent about $300 on the mortgage and utilities for her mobile home, leaving her about $200 for food and all personal expenses.[57] In 2011, an animal control officer seized Tammy's elderly dog, Harley, and Tammy was charged with animal abuse for failing to treat a variety of medical conditions that the dog was suffering from. Explaining the need for criminal charges, the local prosecutor conceded a lack of malice but noted that "[t]he problem is that she allowed things to get to a point where the dog suffered." As a means of protecting the animals in our community, the dog was seized, and Tammy was tried and convicted of animal neglect. The dog was promptly euthanized.

No one disputed that the problem was really one occasioned by poverty, because Tammy simply could not afford to take the dog to a veterinarian. Nevertheless, Tammy became a victim of the animal policing system, and now she is also registered felon. Ultimately, she was sentenced to probation, house arrest, and a thousand dollars in fees, which on her income might take years to pay off. And based on general criminology statistics, one might surmise that Tammy will end up incarcerated because she may fall behind on her fine payments. But equally striking, because she could not afford bail, Tammy spent more than a month incarcerated before she was sentenced. A month of incarceration was far less than the one year of imprisonment sought by the prosecutor, but the combination of the loss of her dog, fees, and probationary terms that may well lead to future incarceration, and a felony record that will make future employment or housing opportunities even more limited for persons like Tammy, present challenges that are almost unimaginable to most of us who live comfortably.

The point is not to diminish the suffering of the dog, though it should be noted that it seems unlikely that this type of prosecution will meaningfully prevent persons living in poverty from perpetrating animal neglect in the future, whenever the cost of care goes beyond their financial means. Rather the point is to note that cases like this one pose a risk of increasing animal suffering across the country. What is a person living in poverty to do when she hears of cases like Tammy's? A rugged neoliberal approach might suggest that future persons should seek out better employment or not have pets when they are poor. But the reality is that persons who learn about this case might be advised by peers to abandon their pets when they realize the prohibitive cost of medical care, lest they risk prosecution either after bringing the animal to the shelter (as in Maria's case above) or a police seizure of the animal.

Maria, Tammy, and others similarly situated could not be blamed for feeling as though they were being targeted because they were poor. Indeed, incidents of

[57] *Pasco Woman Who Couldn't Afford Vet Is Convicted of Animal Cruelty*, Tampa Bay Times (Apr. 25, 2013), www.tampabay.com/news/courts/pasco-woman-who-couldnt-afford-vet-is-convicted-of-animal-cruelty/2117238/.

conduct labeled as animal neglect and cruelty are often higher in communities suffering from poverty.[58] But relying on the punitive criminal justice system to address this kind of harm results in more harm for the humans involved, often further enmeshing already marginalized people in cycles of poverty, incarceration, and societal exclusion. Moreover, such prosecutions make persons involved in animal protection seem elitist by sending a message about the incompatibility of poverty and pet companionship. Animal lawyers have previously taken appeals in criminal cases urging courts to refuse a poverty-type defense to animal neglect.[59] As the sentencing judge told Tammy, to the delight of many animal advocates, in adding a condition to her sentence, "I don't want you to own any animals. Not even a goldfish." Harley was "rescued" from Tammy and treated to a prompt death, and now an impoverished woman whose only friend may have been that dog is a registered felon saddled with fines. And before we dismiss such cases as aberrational, it is necessary to reflect on the fact that most animal crime cases are for neglect rather than affirmative abuse.

11.2.4 *Citations, Fines, and Fees, All across the United States*

For many persons who support better protection for animals in the law, a police response to animal suffering is commonsense. The focus is on high-profile cases of horrific abuse, and these cases seem to necessitate a larger and more aggressive police force dedicated to animal protection. But as in other areas of law, the incidence of increased policing is felt most acutely in low-income neighborhoods and among marginalized communities.[60] Animal well-being is ultimately not well served by an aggressive system of policing with fines and fees, even when no criminal conviction is obtained.

58 *E.g.*, David Vognar, *Animal Welfare, Human Welfare Linked*, HUFFPOST (Aug. 1, 2012), https://www.huffpost.com/entry/animal-welfare-poverty-b_1560440; *see also* Vanessa Alva, Matthew Causey, and Abbey Reddig, *High Number of Animal Cruelty Cases Linked to Poverty, Says Expert*, THE TELEGRAPH (Jan. 29, 2018), www.macon.com/latest-news/article117995063.html.

59 Scott Heiser & Niki Caferri, *Prosecuting Animal Abuse: Common Issues and Hot Topics*, YOUTUBE (Feb. 2, 2016), https://www.youtube.com/watch?v=ml1bjaQn5mk (transcript on file with the Author) ("The defense in that case was justification. The defendant claims he was justified because he didn't have any money, so he didn't feed his dog because he had no money. Laura Dunn and Virginia Coleman did a fantastic job on that brief and we were victorious and it changed the course of events for me."); *Id.* (deriding as foolish a defense argument against prosecution based on poverty, "The defendant said, 'I couldn't afford to feed him,' so he never claimed that the dog somehow was sick or there was some other underlying physical problem that made the dog so skinny").

60 Although the criminology data regarding animal-related offenses is nascent, the limited data that exists confirms that, as with other offenses, animal related offenses appear to be disproportionately enforced in low-income, vulnerable neighborhoods. For example, research has shown that pit bull bans have been enforced primarily in communities of color. Sloane M. Hawes et al., *A Quantitative Study of Denver's Breed-Specific Legislation*, 26.2 ANIMAL L. 195 (2020).

Although based on good intentions, the push to police animal crimes more aggressively fosters what a Human Rights Watch report describes as a "devastating cycle of poverty and arrest."[61] In some jurisdictions 40 percent or more of police arrests are based on warrants, a large percentage of which are issued based on an unpaid fine. Thus, the proverbial slap on the wrist – a fine or fee, perhaps for tethering one's dog in violation of an ordinance – will often be a precursor to a warrant and arrest for a low-income family. Policing actions that result in fines for vaccine violations, tethering violations, or other animal welfare violations may seem so trivial to privileged animal lawyers as to not even register as carceral interventions.[62] And yet these fines can have life-altering impacts for the impacted family, including the animal. As the American Bar Association reported in 2019, it is not uncommon for the parents of dogs or children to be unable to purchase their release from jail, leaving the animal or the family to suffer; every day across the country people "cycle in and out of jail because they can't afford to pay old fines as their debt grows from new ones."[63] This often-unseen part of animal law is the reality caused by fines and fees relating to animal crimes.

There are countless stories exemplifying an approach to everyday animal policing that produces a lose-lose situation for the humans and the animals. As one investigation revealed, animal control officers across the country are aggressively enforcing animal offenses such as registration laws, anti-tethering laws, and vaccine laws against poor and marginalized communities.[64] The resulting fines and fees often mean that a family is separated from a companion animal, and sometimes the animal is killed. For example, in 2013, Gerilynn Afleje's dog was impounded, and when Gerilynn could not come up with the money to pay the fees, her dog was euthanized.[65] A 2015 investigation of just fifteen cities and counties across the country revealed "thousands of outstanding arrest warrants for small pet-related offenses."

For those familiar with the critiques of overpolicing, these findings should not be surprising. Criminal law has been criticized for its consistent disparate impacts on poor, disadvantaged, and marginalized communities. As the punishment bureaucracy is expanded and celebrated by the animal protection movement, it is inevitable that cases other than the high-profile examples of sadistic abuse will comprise the bulk of many animal enforcement officer efforts. Thus, even setting aside the question of whether a carceral response is the best course of action in cases of

[61] John Raphline, *Interview: How Policing in One U.S. City Hurts Black and Poor Communities*, Human Rights Watch (Sept. 12, 2019), https://www.hrw.org/news/2019/09/12/interview-how-policing-one-us-city-hurts-black-and-poor-communities.

[62] Natapoff, *supra* note 43, at 25–26.

[63] John Mathews II & Felipe Curiel, *Criminal Justice Debt Problems*, American Bar Association (Nov. 30, 2019), https://www.americanbar.org/groups/crsj/publications/human_rights_magazine_home/economic-justice/criminal-justice-debt-problems/.

[64] Blake Ellis & Melanie Hicken, *Dogs Killed over Unpaid Fines*, CNN Money (Apr. 6, 2015), https://money.cnn.com/interactive/pf/pet-fines/.

[65] *Id.*

extreme violence to animal victims, framing animal police as central to animal protection efforts has resulted in an expanding enforcement system for animal offenses, and one that functions in ways that are similar to the traditional criminal system. When the policing bureaucracy is expanded, it should not be surprising that the outcomes impact certain communities more than others – in the view of leading scholars like Paul Butler, "the system is working the way it is supposed to."[66] In some low-income neighborhoods, there are documented reports of animal police going door to door and providing citations for failing to sterilize, license, vaccinate, or untether an animal.[67] Fines and fees for misconduct associated with animals, including citations for tethering a dog or failing to vaccinate the animal, are part of the carceral animal law bureaucracy.

11.3 CONCLUDING THOUGHTS ABOUT ANIMAL ENFORCEMENT

The point of this chapter is not to suggest that animal suffering should be treated as an illegitimate or trivial concern. On the contrary, the lives of animals in this country are afforded too little value and protection in the law. Animals are deserving of legal protection, and I share the same ultimate goals as the activists pursuing criminal law reform in the name of animals. The only disagreement concerns whether increased policing and prosecution is a realistic vehicle for reducing the suffering of animals. As the discussion above makes clear, in many instances animal policing causes more harm than good. Even when the focus is on animal policing that does not result in convictions, or even incarceration, the outcomes for animals and humans are often more harmful rather than helpful. It cannot be assumed that policing of animal crimes in circumstances such as those described in this chapter is actually improving animal well-being.

In this chapter, I cannot offer anything approaching a blueprint for next steps, but I think the priority should be interventions targeting the protection of animals *without* an increase in policing, fines, or prosecution. Subsidies and direct services to animals, and perhaps programs aimed at something more like restorative justice for animals, promise to protect animals better than punitive and regressive systems of police intervention. Some private organizations, for example, the Pets for Life Program at the Humane Society of the United States, invest in veterinary care and subsidies for families with pets as opposed to defaulting to a punitive response, and

66 Paul Butler, *The System Is Working the Way It Is Supposed To: The Limits of Criminal Justice Reform*, FREEDOM CENTER JOURNAL, Vol. 2019, Iss. 1, 75, 81 (2020) ("It is possible for police to selectively invoke their powers against African-American residents, and, at the same time, act consistently with the law.").

67 Ellis & Hicken, *supra* note 64.

they are already recognizing the benefits for communities and animals from this type of intervention.[68]

Unlike the stories told above, there are countless examples emerging from the program with great outcomes. Dogs that might have been euthanized have been treated and returned to their homes. Persons who might have been incarcerated, or fined and separated from their animal, continue to enjoy the companionship of a beloved animal friend, free from collateral consequences of criminal charges. Cases that very likely would have led to felony charges have been handled as issues of poverty and met with resources, resulting in the animal and the family now living out their lives together happily.

There is no silver-bullet that will end animal suffering. But it is time to think seriously about diverting the resources devoted to policing and prosecution to programs aimed at building up communities and protecting animals. Protecting animals or reducing their suffering might be costly, but in truth so is the enforcement and policing bureaucracy that has developed in support of conventional approaches to combating cruelty and neglect. We should seek opportunities to redeploy resources away from policing, so as to avoid outcomes where a dog is taken from her home and either euthanized or rehomed.

For much of the animal protection movement's history, there has been an implicit assumption that incarceration was a vehicle for vindicating the rights of animals. I reject the notion that society can ever punish or prosecute its way to animal rights. But in the interest of animal well-being and human well-being, I would go one step further.

That is to say, it is time for the movement to appreciate that increased policing and prosecution should not be celebrated as an unmitigated good simply because incarceration may not always (or even often) be obtained. Law-and-order approaches to social problems tend to ignore systemic abuse and may create more problems than they solve. We applaud those within the movement who are looking to deescalate the tough-on-crime rhetoric by seeking punishments less than incarceration, but we also caution against increased policing and enforcement even when the stated goal is not incarceration. These more subtle forms of carceral thinking warrant closer scrutiny.

[68] Animal Sheltering, *Pets for Life*, The Humane Society of the United States (2021), https://www.animalsheltering.org/programs/pets-for-life.

PART III

Implications of Carceral Spaces for Animals and for Humans

Introduction

Lori Gruen and Justin Marceau

This section explores the ways carceral logics shape carceral spaces, which in turn impact the lives and well-being of the humans and nonhumans within them. Carceral spaces raise a variety of questions, some of which are explored in the chapters here. Can zoos educate children about the lives of other animals, or is that impossible given the distorted situation in which humans are so clearly dominating and controlling the captive animals? Do conservation efforts justify holding individual wild animals captive or provide an excuse for carceral enclosure? Does bringing animals into prisons for training and care further entrench carceral logics for prisoners and captive animals? How do carceral responses to activism on behalf of animals and the environment impact the potential for social change?

Carceral logics inform the building and justification of captive enclosures that contain humans and other animals. While captive settings vary considerably, there are certain features of carceral spaces that exist across captive contexts, whether one is confined by bars, chains, ankle bracelets, cages, prisons, coops, fences, or locked doors. The most obvious feature is that captives are denied freedoms of various kinds, including freely choosing those things which will satisfy their most basic desires. Of course, none of us is free to make any choice we want; we are restricted by state, economic, and social institutions and ideologies that limit us in a range of ways – by the binary genders we are assigned, by social and psychic worlds structured by ableism, and by the thick boundaries based on class, religion, ethnicity, race, and even our species. But these constraints on liberty, that also are informed by carceral logics, are worsened by the effects of physical confinement.

Among carceral strategies, the decision to pursue or permit physical confinement is uniquely deserving of heightened attention. Those who are physically confined generally do not have the opportunity to make basic decisions about what to eat and when, when to sleep, where to go, whom to spend time with (or not spend time with). Even decisions relating to sexual autonomy, reproduction, and the care of one's offspring may be made by persons running captive facilities. Almost all choices are restricted, and activities are controlled. Animals held in concentrated animal feeding operations (CAFOs), research labs, and zoos and other carceral spaces often suffer from captivity itself, in addition to any specific forms of harm and injury they are subjected to as a result of the purpose of the confinement. They are poked, prodded, branded, injected, shocked, subject to noxious stimuli, forcibly impregnated, and they can't escape. Many have never known freedom as they are bred into commodification or specimenification. Some animals may never go outside or stand on natural surfaces. Even when they have always been captives, their inability to control their circumstances, flee their environments, or have their minds or bodies stimulated in positive ways often leads to behavioral anomalies referred to as "stereotypies," behaviors that do not occur in the wild. "Stereotypies are thought to be caused by brain dysfunction brought on by stress-induced damage to the central nervous system" (Bekoff and Pierce). And the damage and dysfunction are not exclusively a result of "bad" captive conditions, as Bekoff and Pierce say: "There is no such thing as 'good captivity' or 'good incarceration.'" Boredom, self-harm, and other aberrant behaviors emerge from captivity itself.

In prisons, humans suffer in demeaning, often violent, conditions that cause physical and psychological harms. Prisoners experience frustration, loneliness, shame, depression, humiliation, and dehumanizing, deanimalizing indignities.[1] There are long-term psychological impacts that also develop due to boredom, anxiety, lack of loving touch, and general lack of control. Some of those incarcerated had one terrible day when things went horribly wrong and a human or animal was injured or killed. Others have more of a history of harmful or socially disapproved behaviors. Some incarcerated people are activists who worked toward bringing about better conditions for other animals and the environment and their imprisonment is not just harmful to them, but also to the social justice movements they were a part of. One of the points of incarcerating those activists is "to repress the people and ideas that generate resistance to multispecies oppressions and to ensure the continued functioning of a white supremacist, heteropatriarchal, speciesist, ecocidal capitalist state" (Pellow).

Though it is not usually discussed in the context of human imprisonment, animals suffer from the existence of prisons too. Countless animals are harmed to feed those who are incarcerated; other animals are harmed when they find their way into prisons and are exterminated; some are harmed in programs that are designed to

[1] Lisa Guenther notes in her 2012 paper *Beyond Dehumanization: A Post-humanist Critique of Solitary Confinement* in the Journal for Critical Animal Studies, 10(2) that dehumanization occurs in carceral contexts when human dignity is violated and prisoners are treated "like animals." But solitary confinement, as well as conditions in maximum security and supermax prisons, often cause a type of sensory deprivation that fails to even treat humans like animals. "It is as animals that we are damaged or even destroyed by the supermax or SHU, just as our fellow animals are damaged or destroyed by confinement in cages at zoos, factory farms, and scientific laboratories" (56).

train animals to "work"; and many more animals living near prisons are harmed by the waste that is produced in the prison. Some prisons are now operating factory farms with prison labor. "The prison as structure harms surrounding waters, lands, and ecosystems, often making life impossible for the more-than-human displaced and affected by its presence" (Montford). Prisons are not good for people, not good for other animals, not good for the environment. And most forms of animal confinement harm animals and humans alike. Increasingly, researchers are showing that the health of humans and animals is interconnected, and carceral spaces for any species will likely harm others.

Carceral spaces, whether prisons, zoos, ranches, or some other system of confinement, cause a variety of direct harms to those held within them, and there are also potential harms to those who live around these spaces, as well as those who work there or visit those held captive. Too often the justification for inflicting such harms is not obvious or ultimately tenable. In the context of zoos and immigrant detention centers, for example, human children are often invoked as a way to "soften the edges" of these harmful environments (Deckha). This is particularly obvious in the justification of zoos and aquaria – it is often claimed that putting wild animals on display helps children to develop respect for nature. But in reality, children seem to gain very little from these experiences beyond momentary excitement, and instead their presence does more to justify these spaces. Children serve to create "social credibility" for the existence of these carceral spaces, and the narrative of preserving endangered species for future generations furthers the narrative. Whether captive animals in fact help with conservation efforts and whether their captivity is a necessary part of conservation programs is rarely discussed.

The chapters in Part III make vivid one of the central points of the book: carceral logics are bad for animals and for humans. Incarcerating humans invariably harms animals directly, with little downstream promise of deterring or protecting animals in the community more generally. Likewise, animal confinement often threatens the health and well-being, both physical and psychological, of human communities. The impacts of captivity are not nearly as discrete and limited as often imagined, and advocates for humans and advocates for animals will do well to consider the interconnected ways that carceral spaces enforce and support various oppressions.

12

Incarcerating Animals and Egregious Losses of Freedoms

Jessica Pierce and Marc Bekoff

Freedom is one of the values humans most cherish. We are free if we are not imprisoned or enslaved. We are free if we are not unduly coerced or constrained in our choices or actions. Freedom can be difficult to define, but surely, we know when we lose it or when it has been taken from us.

Human rights advocates are rightly concerned when certain groups of people are exploited for their labor, like migrant workers forced into virtual slavery on fishing vessels or toiling in fields for little pay. They are concerned when groups of people are exploited for their bodies, as when young girls are forced into the sex trade. And they are concerned when groups of people are not allowed to move about or speak freely or engage in cultural rituals that are important to them. We value the freedom to choose our family and friends, to bear and raise children, to think for ourselves, and to work for a decent living. Of course, there is no such thing as pure, unadulterated freedom – we are controlled by our unconscious impulses, genetics, unspoken social conventions, and by government rules that ensure public safety and order. But we are nonetheless free in important respects. Some measure of freedom is fundamental to human well-being: it provides the substrate for human flourishing.[1]

Yet although we prize our freedom above all else, we routinely deny numerous freedoms to nonhuman animals (animals) with whom we share our planet. We imprison and enslave animals, we exploit them for their labor and their skin and bodies, we constrain what they can do and with whom they can interact. We do not let them choose their family or friends, we decide for them when and if and with whom they mate and bear offspring, and often take their children away at birth. We control their movements, their behaviors, their social interactions, while bending them to our will or to our self-serving economic agenda. Animal incarceration is so pervasive and insidious that we often do not even notice that animals are being held

[1] Lori Gruen, ed., The Ethics of Captivity (2014).

prisoner. If we think about it at all, we imagine animals as creatures so different from us that they don't value the same things – and, in particular, that they don't value their freedom because they lack the cognitive awareness to know what freedom is.

But, in fact, animals are like us in the most important respects. All animals want and need food, water, air, sleep. They need shelter and safety from physical and psychological threats, and an environment they can control. And like us, they have what might be called "higher-order" needs, such as the need to exercise control over their lives, make choices, do meaningful work, form meaningful relationships with others, and engage in forms of play and creativity. Some measure of freedom is fundamental to satisfying these higher-order needs and provides a necessary substrate for individuals to thrive and to look forward to a new day. Although they might not write books about the concepts of freedom and incarceration, animals nonetheless value their freedom and suffer in captivity just as we do.

The goods that animals value stand in stark relief against the lives that we force on them. Animals are held captive in a dizzying array of venues: zoos, factory farms, research laboratories, wet markets, fur farms, breeding facilities, pet store shelves, and so on and so on. Billions of animals around the globe are subjected to a lifetime of incarceration. (Incarceration and captivity are taken to be the same, for the purposes of this chapter.)

Incarceration clearly is more complicated and far-reaching than merely being behind bars. When we put nonhumans and humans in prison, we are dealing out punishment. Being physically confined is understood as a temporary deprivation of life's higher-order goods. But with animals, the routine deprivations of prolonged incarceration are not understood by humans as a punishment, but rather as a neutral action, or even – as is the case with pets – a favor we do them.

Although there might be some reasonable conversation or debate about the appropriateness of incarceration for humans, there is no reasonable justification for incarcerating animals. Animals should not be behind bars, whether those bars are real or metaphorical. Animals don't commit crimes, they aren't violent offenders, and they don't disregard any real or imagined social contract with humankind. Any confinement of animals against their will (which would be pretty much every instance of confinement one could imagine) counts as incarceration.

12.1 THE MYRIAD HARMS OF CAPTIVITY

The fact that there is an entire literature dedicated to so-called captivity effects should leave us in no doubt that captivity causes suffering. "Captivity effects" refers to the range of physical, physiological, and even neurobiological changes induced by captive conditions. These captivity effects are similar in humans and other animals. The vast empirical database on captivity effects in nonhuman animals spans a broad range of species – from chimpanzees, dolphins, and wolves to domesticated animals such as dogs, cats, pigs, and chickens, to reptiles, amphibians, and fish – kept in a range of captive conditions, from the most obviously captive (the cows, chickens, pigs, and other animals on factory farms) to the animals caged in research and testing laboratories, to animals caged in zoos, to the animals who are captive in more ambiguous ways, such as pet dogs and cats.[2] (Because the literature uses the language of "captivity" rather than "incarceration" we will use the term *captivity* in this section – but take it to be synonymous with incarceration.)

Captivity – including physical confinement, social isolation, and chronic exposure to stress – leads to measurable physiological changes in the brain, including loss of neural plasticity, long-term activation of the hypothalamic-pituitary-adrenal axis,[3] and permanent changes in brain morphology.[4] It can lead to changes to immune function,[5] reproductive behaviors,[6] circadian rhythms, and psychological trauma.[7] The loss of freedom often manifests in observable abnormal behaviors. Since many of the people who will read this book come from the perspective of human incarceration, we offer a few specific examples of the physical and psychological sequelae of incarceration documented in animals. In particular, we give a few examples of what, in the scientific literature, are called "stereotypic behaviors or stereotypies" but which we could more loosely call "captivity-induced madness."

Stereotypic behavior is the term used to describe animal behavior which is invariant, repetitive, and serves no obvious function. Stereotypes are thought to be caused by brain dysfunction brought on by stress-induced damage to the central nervous system. It is important to note that stereotypic behaviors do not occur in the wild; they are a product of captivity, a captivity-induced psychosis.[8]

Irregular pacing behavior is often observed in captive animals who, in the wild, have large home ranges. This behavior pattern is referred to as a repetitive locomotion stereotype, or locomotory stereotypy. Polar bears, to give one example, are known to do poorly in captivity. A study published in *Nature* suggested that the reason why locomotory stereotypies may be so common in polar bears is that in the

[2] Marc Bekoff & Jessica Pierce, The Animals' Agenda: Freedom, Compassion, and Coexistence in the Human Age (2017).

[3] Xaviar Belda et al., *Critical Features of Acute Stress-Induced Cross-Sensitization Identified through the Hypothalamic-Pituitary-Adrenal-Axis Output*, 6 Sci. Rep. 1, (2016).

[4] *See. e.g.*, Bob Jacobs, *The Neural Cruelty of Captivity: Keeping Large Mammals in Zoos and Aquariums Damages Their Brains*, Conversation (2020), https://theconversation.com/the-neural-cruelty-of-captivity-keeping-large-mammals-in-zoos-and-aquariums-damages-their-brains-142240; Lori Marino et al., *The Harmful Effects of Captivity and Chronic Stress on the Well-Being of Orcas (Orcinus Orca)*, 35 J. Veterinary Behav. 69, 69–82 (2020).

[5] Clare P. Fischer & Michael L. Romero, *Chronic Captivity Stress in Wild Animals Is Highly Species-Specific*, 7 Conservation Physiology 1, 21 (2020).

[6] Katherine A. Farquharson et al., *A Meta-analysis of Birth-Origin Effects on Reproduction in Diverse Captive Environments*, 9 Nature Commc'n (2018).

[7] *See e.g.* Kathleen N. Morgan & Chris T. Tromborg, *Sources of Stress in Captivity*, 102 Applied Animal Behav. Sci., 262, 262–302 (2007).

[8] Georgia Mason and Jeffrey Rushen, eds., Stereotypic Animal Behaviour: Fundamental Applications to Welfare (2nd ed. 2008).

wild, the animals can range over tracts of land as large as 185,000 square miles each year.[9] Locomotory stereotypies are well documented in elephants, tigers, lions, wolves, and other canids.[10] The frenetic weaving of the mink back and forth within their tiny wire cages, as seen in undercover video footage of mink farms, is a disturbing example of locomotory stereotypy or captivity-induced madness.[11]

Grooming to the point of baldness, feather plucking, and other self-mutilation behaviors are sometimes called self-directed stereotypies.[12] These behaviors occur in a wide range of species including rodents and primates in research laboratories, parrots, and other birds in captivity and cats in shelter environments or other stressful situations.

Oral stereotypies, in which an animal performs repetitive and seemingly functionless oral and oronasal activities, are prevalent in captive ungulates such as cows, pigs, and horses.[13] One example is a repetitive movement of the jaw, such as the "sham-chewing" commonly seen in pigs kept in gestation crates.[14] The behavior mimics the exact movement of the jaw when food is being consumed. However, sham-chewing is performed in the absence of food. Oral stereotypies surrounding food and eating are a good place to explore why providing animals with their basic needs – food, shelter, enough space to turn around – isn't enough to ensure that they don't suffer from profound distress caused by captivity. Next to breathing, eating is the behavior most essential for survival, and different species are exquisitely adapted to meet their survival needs within the ecosystems in which they evolved. Many of the behavioral patterns of a given animal are directed at finding food, and animals are highly motivated to perform these food-acquiring behaviors, because they are basic to survival. Providing a cow with a trough of grain may satiate the cow's physical hunger but will not allow the cow to use any of the behavioral skills she

[9] Ros Clubb & Georgia Mason, *Animal Welfare: Captivity Effects on Wide-Ranging Carnivores*, 425 Nature 473, 473–74 (2003).

[10] Brian J. Greco et al., *Why Pace? The Influence of Social, Housing, Management, Life History, and Demographic Characteristics on Locomotor Stereotypy in Zoo Elephants*, 194 Applied Animal Behav. Sci. 104, 104–111 (2017); *see also* David Shepherdson et al., *Individual and Environmental Factors Associate with Sterotypic Behavior and Fecal Glucocorticoid Metabolite Levels in Zoo Housed Polar Bears*, 147 Applied Animal Behav. Sci. 268, 268–277 (2013).

[11] Georgia J. Mason, Age and Context Affect the Stereotypies of Caged Mink, 127 Behav. 191, 191–229 (1993).

[12] For example, Colin M. Brand & Linda F. Marchant, *Hair Plucking in Captive Bonobos (Pan Pansicus)*, 171 Applied Animal Behav. Sci. 192, 192–96 (2015); Lori A. Gaskins & Laura Hungerford, *Nonmedical Factors Associated with Feather Picking in Ptet Psittacine Birds* 28 J. Avian Med. & Surgery 109, 109–17(2014); Yvonne R.A. Van Zeeland et al., *Feather Damaging Behavior in Parrots: A Review with Consideration of Comparative Aspects*, 121 Applied Animal Behav. Sci. 75, 75–95 (2009).

[13] R. Bergeron, A.J. Badnell-Waters, S. Lambton & G. Mason, "Stereotypic Oral Behaviour in Captive Ungulates: Foraging, Diet and Gastrointestinal Function," in Mason & Rushen, *supra* note 8, 19–57.

[14] *An HSUS Report: Welfare Issues with Gestation Crates for Pregnant Sows* (2013), https://www.humanesociety.org/sites/default/files/docs/hsus-report-gestation-crates-for-pregnant-sows.pdf.

has evolved to acquire food for herself. The behavioral urge to forage is present, even when cows are fed ad libitum. And a strong behavioral urge or motivation that goes unsatisfied leads to welfare problems. Other commonly seen oral stereotypies include tongue-rolling, object licking, chewing on cage bars or chains, and polydipsia or excessive drinking.

Often, and unfortunately for animals, the behavioral sequalae resulting from captivity are described as "problem behaviors" – this is to say, they are problematic *for us*, the animals' keepers. This is perhaps most obvious in relation to animals caught in the wheels of the food industry, where the sequalae of incarceration pose a challenge to productivity. For example, agonistic behaviors among chickens or tail-biting behaviors among piglets kept in unnaturally crowded conditions can lead to injury and death – and loss of revenue. The human response to these manifestations of suffering is indecent: instead of addressing the source of suffering, we go for a Band-Aid solution, and one that simply piles one cruelty on top of another. Chickens have their beaks cut off with a hot knife and piglets have their tails cut off with clippers. A less obvious example – but closer to home for many of us – are the perceived behavioral problems of dogs who are confined to a home or crate or backyard for long periods of time: excessive barking, obsessive compulsive behaviors such as self-grooming to the point of developing lick granulomas. Many people who live with dogs fail to connect their animals' "problem behaviors" with psychological distress, boredom, or frustration, and, as with the chickens and piglets, simply compound cruelty with more cruelty: excessive barking is "fixed" with a shock collar or a one-way trip to the shelter.

It can be difficult to untangle the threads of harm arising from animal incarceration: which aspects of animal suffering are attributed to the specific conditions of their captivity and which are the result of captivity itself? This distinction is critically important because the focus of attention in discussions of animal welfare and animal ethics is often on reducing specific harms suffered by captive animals, and never questions the broader harms of captivity itself. The physical, psychological, social harms to animals caused by the captive state are *not* or at least not always the result of poorly executed captivity, but of captivity itself. Take, for example, the problems of captive snakes, which have been highlighted by the work of Clifford Warwick. Most snakes in captivity as kept in enclosures that are too small to allow full extension of the snake's body, and snakes are harmed physically and psychologically by not having enough space to spread out.[15] But they are also harmed by captivity itself, no matter whether their enclosure is adequately large relative to their body size.

Suffice it to say that alleviating some of the suffering caused by "bad captivity" may be a good short-term goal, as we move beyond cultural and economic structures that institutionalize violence toward animals. But improving the lot of captive

[15] Clifford Warwick, Phillip Arena, & Catrina Steedman, *Spatial Consideration for Captive Snakes*, 30 J. Veterinary Behav. 37, 37–48 (2019).

animals is not enough. There is no such thing as "good captivity" or "good incarceration" for animals, and we need to stop pretending that there is. A well-appointed prison is still a prison.

12.2 FAKE FREEDOMS: THE APPROPRIATION OF "FREEDOM" DISCOURSES

Many people who have taken an interest in issues of animal protection are familiar with the "Five Freedoms." The Five Freedoms have become a popular cornerstone of animal welfare around the world and in various contexts of animal incarceration.

The Five Freedoms originated in the early 1960s in an eighty-five-page "Report of the Technical Committee to Enquire into the Welfare of Animals Kept under Intensive Livestock Husbandry Systems."[16] This document, informally and widely known as The Brambell Report, was a response to public outcry over the abusive treatment of animals within agricultural settings. Ruth Harrison's 1964 book *Animal Machines* brought readers inside the walls of the newly developing industrialized farming systems in the United Kingdom, what we have come to know as "factory farms." Harrison, a Quaker and conscientious objector during World War II, described appalling practices like battery cage systems for egg-laying hens and gestation crates for sows, and consumers were shocked by what was hidden behind closed doors.

To mollify the public, the UK government commissioned an investigation into livestock husbandry, led by Bangor University zoology professor Roger Brambell. The commission concluded that there were, indeed, grave ethical concerns with the treatment of animals in the food industry and that something must be done. In its initial report, the commission specified that animals should have the freedom to "stand up, lie down, turn around, groom themselves and stretch their limbs." These minimal requirements became known as the "freedoms," and represented the conditions the Brambell Commission felt were essential to animal welfare.

The Commission also requested the formation of the Farm Animal Welfare Advisory Committee to monitor the UK farming industry. In 1979, the name of this organization was changed to the Farm Animal Welfare Council, and the "freedoms" were subsequently expanded into their current form. The Five Freedoms state that all animals under human care should have:

1. *Freedom from hunger and thirst, by ready access to water and a diet to maintain health and vigor.*
2. *Freedom from discomfort, by providing an appropriate environment.*

[16] Animal Humane Society, *The Five Freedoms for Animals*, Animal Humane. Soc. (2022), www.animalhumanesociety.org/health/five-freedoms-animals.

3. *Freedom from pain, injury and disease, by prevention or rapid diagnosis and treatment.*
4. *Freedom to express normal behavior, by providing sufficient space, proper facilities and appropriate company of the animal's own kind.*
5. *Freedom from fear and distress, by ensuring conditions and treatment, which avoid mental suffering.*

The Freedoms are now invoked not only in relationship to farmed animals, but also to animals in research laboratories, zoos. and aquaria, and even to companion animals in shelters and breeding facilities. The Freedoms appear in nearly every book about animal welfare, can be found on nearly every website dedicated to food animal or lab animal welfare, form the basis of many animal welfare auditing programs, and are taught to many of those working in fields of animal husbandry.

It is worth stopping for a moment to acknowledge how forward thinking the Brambell Report on animal freedoms was. The report was crafted at a time when the notion that animals might experience pain was still just a superstition for many researchers and others working with animals. The Brambell Report not only acknowledged that animals experience pain but went a giant step further by also providing evidence that they experience mental states and have rich emotional lives. The report (the full text of which very few people who ascribe to the Five Freedoms actually read) said plainly that making animals happy involves more than simply reducing sources of pain and suffering, but also involves providing them with positive, pleasurable experiences.

Yet although widely hailed as a huge step forward, the Brambell Report was arguably the worst thing that has happened to animals in the past century. The Five Freedoms became the cornerstone of an academic discipline called "animal welfare science" and provided a justificatory framework – a logic of incarceration which we call "welfarism" – for thinking about and justifying the widespread confinement and exploitation of animals. The Five Freedoms have become shorthand for "ethical treatment of animals." They provide, according to a current statement by the Farm Animal Welfare Council, a "logical and comprehensive framework for analysis of animal welfare" and are typically the end of the conversation about what animals need and want. Welfarism delivers a scientific and moral buttressing for incarceration, under the auspices of caring for animals and giving them Freedoms. Under the welfarist regime, the number of animals under incarceration around the globe has been steadily climbing.

Why the Brambell Commission fixed upon the word "freedom" in their formulation of welfare guidelines remains unclear – no record exists of how this language came to be adopted. It is hard to imagine that the crafters of the Freedoms failed to recognize the fundamental paradox: how can an animal in an abattoir or battery cage be free? Being fed and housed by your captor is not freedom; it is simply what your caregiver does to keep you alive. Indeed, the Five Freedoms are not concerned with freedom but rather define the outer limits of incarceration; they provide guidance for keeping animals under conditions of profound deprivation.

Welfare concerns generally focus on preventing or relieving suffering, and making sure animals are being well-fed and cared for, without questioning the underlying conditions of incarceration that shape the very nature of their lives. We offer lip service to freedom, in talking about "cage-free chickens" and "naturalistic zoo enclosures" and in producing a steady stream of academic papers offering incremental improvements to animal prisons. But real freedom for animals is the one value we don't want to acknowledge because it would require a deep examination of our own behavior. It might mean we should change the way we treat and relate to animals, not just to make cages bigger or provide new enrichment activities to blunt the sharp edges of boredom and frustration, but to allow animals much more freedom in a wide array of venues.

12.3 WORKING TOWARD ABOLITION

A great deal of advocacy on behalf of animals focuses on "improving welfare" by paying attention to the Five Freedoms. This amounts to making animal prisons somewhat nicer, somewhat kinder and gentler. But the fundamental violence against animals remains intact. Welfarism and "the Freedoms" do considerable damage to animals by reinforcing and even providing improved moral padding for the logic of incarceration. This explains why some of the most vocal advocates for animal welfare work for zoos, slaughterhouses, and animal research laboratories, and sit on the boards of organizations who support the industrialized incarceration of animals.

Even the literature on captivity effects has been entwined into the logic of animal incarceration, using what we are learning about animal cognition and emotions – the very research that confirms how much animals have to lose in captivity – to make their incarceration incrementally less torturous while simultaneously reinforcing the structures of violence that keep them imprisoned.

The typical justification for holding animals captive is that although captivity may impose some harms, these harms are justified by the benefits that accrue from these practices. But one of the golden rules of ethics is that in a balancing of harms and benefits, it is unjust for the harms to befall one group and the benefits another. In the case of incarcerated animals, all the harms fall on animals while all the benefits fall to us. The animals have everything to lose and nothing to gain. This is a serious justice issue and a blatant abuse of power.

It is hard not to see a profound moral problem in our unjust incarceration of billions of animals. Making incremental welfare improvements and giving lip service to Five Freedoms is a face-saving maneuver: let's admit that holding animals captive is not ideal and causes some harm, so let's make the prison experience less unpleasant by decreasing the harms of captivity. The audaciousness of the workaround is remarkable: incarcerating animals is morally wrong, so let's give them "freedoms." The Five Freedoms are really designed to liberate *us*, allowing us to slip quietly past the prison gates, ensuring our peace of mind in the face of animal suffering.

The incarceration of animals, in all its myriad forms, should stop. But it cannot and will not suddenly tomorrow. A phase out is key. The animals who are currently in captivity will need to remain so, because it is unlikely that they could survive on their own and offering them "freedom" without the requisite skills to survive and without a home or family will only compound their suffering. But starting tomorrow there should be no more captive breeding of animals in captivity, for captivity. No animals should be captured from the wild and made captive, even for experiments that are aimed at saving the species from extinction since it is not fair to ask an individual to suffer for the sake of a group. (We wouldn't justify this with humans, so shouldn't with animals either.)

Abundant scientific research supports the idea that animals suffer physically and psychologically when held captive. It is not only the "aversive" experiences felt *within* captivity – the too-small cages, the boredom of eating the same food every day for your whole life, or the lack of sensory stimulation – but the captivity experience itself, the loss of self-determination, bodily integrity, the sense of experiencing life as the kind of animal that hundreds of thousands, perhaps millions, of years of evolution have prepared you to be. Captivity is a harm because it robs animals of their own lives.

13

Juvenile Smokescreens

Softening the Harm of Zoos, Aquaria, and Prisons through (Human) Children

Maneesha Deckha

13.1 INTRODUCTION

This chapter explores how human children soften the abusive edge of carceral spaces. Prisons, immigration detention centres, and zoos and aquaria are institutions that attract sustained public scrutiny from prisoner rights, migrant rights, anti-racist, and animal rights movements. Critics and scholars note the entwined nature of race, gender, and species logics that shape and unite these spaces and object to the short- and long-term incarceration these institutions make possible as well as the conditions residents confined within experience.[1] Prisoner rights, migrant rights, and animal rights critics also contest the messaging that these institutions and their proponents use to assure the public of the need for confinement and the ethical acceptability of the conditions captive animals and humans experience.[2] These

[1] *See, e.g.*, RALPH R. ACAMPORA, CORPORAL COMPASSION: ANIMAL ETHICS AND PHILOSOPHY OF BODY 3-6 (2006). *See also* Michelle Brown & Judah Schept, *New Abolition, Criminology and a Critical Carceral Studies*, 19 PUNISHMENT & SOC'Y 440, 441 (2017); Bree Carlton, *Penal Reform, Anti-carceral Feminist Campaigns and the Politics of Change in Women's Prisons, Victoria, Australia*, 20 PUNISHMENT & SOC'Y 283, 285–90 (2018); Kathryn Gillespie, *Placing "Angola": Racialization, Settler Colonialism, and Anthropocentrism at the Louisiana State Penitentiary's Angola Rodeo*, 50 ANTIPODE 1267, 1268–71 (2018); Rachel Kronick et al., *Refugee Children's Sandplay Narratives in Immigration Detention in Canada*, 27 EUR. CHILD & ADOLESCENT PSYCHIATRY 423, 423–24 (2018); Karen M. Morin, *Carceral Space: Prisoners and Animals*, 48 ANTIPODE 1317, 1318–20 (2016); AMY NETHERY & STEPHANIE J. SILVERMAN, IMMIGRATION DETENTION: THE MIGRATION OF A POLICY AND ITS HUMAN IMPACT 1–9 (2015); AFFRICA TAYLOR & VERONICA PACINI-KETCHABAW, THE COMMON WORLDS OF CHILDREN AND ANIMALS: RELATIONAL ETHICS FOR ENTANGLED LIVES 1–5 (2018).

[2] Eva Boodman, *An Immanent Critique of the Prison Nation: The Contradictions of Carceral "Anti-violence"*, 44 PHIL. & SOC. CRITICISM 571, 574–76 (2018); Bronwyn Dobchuk-Land, *Resisting "Progressive" Carceral Expansion: Lessons for Abolitionists from Anti-colonial Resistance* 20 CONTEMP. J. REV. 404, 405 (2017); Rachel Kronick et al., *International Solidarity to End Immigration Detention*, 389 LANCET 501, 501 (2017); Alexandra Palmer et al., *Caregiver/Orangutan Relationships at Auckland Zoo*, 24 SOC'Y & ANIMALS 230, 232, 239–45 (2016).

discourses, depending on the specific institution, highlight the larger public "law and order" interests of safety and border control, but also "progressive" interests of rehabilitation, conservation, and education.[3]

In highlighting these latter "progressive" interests, carceral institutions seek to *humanize* themselves and their work to bolster their social credibility. This "humane-washing" occurs through long-standing rationales about rehabilitation for offenders in the prison context, and more recent rationales about the conservation of nature and conservation education in the zoo and aquarium context. It also, I will argue, occurs through a specific type of marshaling of the human child. I seek to add to the literature on "humane-washing"[4] as well as contestations and uses of "childhood" and "family" narratives[5] in general in this analysis. I apply a multispecies lens to consider how the real and imagined human child in the zoo and aquaria context, and narratives about what is in the best interests of human children in the immigration and prison context, figure into characterizing such carceral institutions as legally and socially legitimate spaces.[6] The argument acknowledges that these carceral spaces can yield positive benefits for some, such as rehabilitation or rescue of a specific individual or even conservation of a specific species. However, it accepts the existing critical scholarly literature against such spaces overall to focus on the question of how carceral spaces mask their problematic and oppressive nature by integrating the presence of human children.

13.2 THE USE OF "CHILDREN" TO HUMANIZE CARCERAL SPACES

To be sure, prisons, detention centres, and zoos and aquaria are not primarily or simply spaces for children. But this makes the question of when and where children

[3] E.g., Siena Anstis et al., *Separate but Unequal: Immigration Detention in Canada and the Great Writ of Liberty*, 63 McGill L.J. 1, 12–14 (2017); Debra Parkes, *Solitary Confinement, Prisoner Litigation, and the Possibility of a Prison Abolitionist Lawyering Ethic*, 32 Canadian J. L. & Soc'y 165, 166–69 (2017).

[4] Saskia Stucki, *(Certified) Humane Violence? Animal Welfare Labels, the Ambivalence of Humanizing the Inhumane, and What International Humanitarian Law Has to Do with It*, 111 Am. J. Int'l L. 277, 279 (2017); Delcianna J. Winders, *Captive Wildlife at a Crossroads – Sanctuaries, Accreditation, and Humane-Washing*, 6 Animal Stud. J. 161, 167 (2017).

[5] Barbara Baird, *Child Politics, Feminist Analyses*, 23 Austl. Feminist Stud. 291, 291–92 (2008); Nancy Scheper-Hughes & Carolyn Sargent, Small Wars: The Cultural Politics of Childhood 1 (1998).

[6] Carceral institutions also benefit from public inaccessibility or engage in visibility management to conceal more objectionable practices. The general public has no right to enter prisons, and zoos and aquaria use almost invisible enclosures that shield the public from the barriers incarcerated animals experience and the hidden close bodily management of captive populations across species including the slaughter of healthy animals. See Braverman 2011. This discussion, however, will focus on the public messaging and experience-shaping strategies they employ, namely those involving children.

do acquire importance in these "paradigm institutions of domination"[7] all the more pressing. This part of the analysis takes up this question.

13.2.1 *How Children's Need for Conservation Education Legitimates Zoos and Aquaria*

If there is one carceral place where children are encouraged to attend for educational and recreational purposes, it is the zoo and aquarium. A zoo is a place of childhood[8] and family.[9] As one travel writer put it: "Spending a night at the zoo is a perennial childhood fantasy: many a popular children's book features a lock-in with exotic animals as its plot."[10] As one example of this fantasy turning into reality, consider the Edmonton Valley Zoo, where Lucy, an Asian elephant languishes on her own with chronic health conditions, and has been the subject of two high-profile lawsuits by animal rights advocates to move her to a sanctuary.[11] Annually, the Edmonton Valley Zoo hosts such a "magical evening" for children with disabilities that they call "Dreamnight."[12] Edmonton Valley Zoo is not alone in this child-centered initiative. Its website indicates that "Dreamnight now spans over 300 zoos internationally, with more zoos joining each year."[13] In Canada and the United States, industry statistics also confirm the tight correlation between zoos and children, with well over half of visitors comprising children under eleven years of age.[14]

7 Lori Gruen, The Ethics of Captivity 243 (2014).

8 Kathryn Denning, *Regarding the Zoo: On the Deployment of a Metaphor*, 14 Int'l J. Heritage Stud. 60, 65 (2008).

9 Jane Desmond, Staging Tourism: Bodies on Display from Waikiki to Sea World 217–18 (1999).

10 Sally Peck, *British Safaris: A Night at the Zoo*, The Tel. (July 4, 2015), https://www.telegraph.co.uk/travel/destinations/europe/united-kingdom/articles/British-safaris-a-night-at-the-zoo.

11 Tyler Dawson, *Advocates for Lucy the Elephant Fail to Convince Courts to Review Her Confinement Conditions at Edmonton Zoo*, Nat'l Post (May 28, 2019), https://nationalpost.com/news/canada/lucy-the-elephant; *see also* Zoocheck Can. Inc. v. Alberta (Agriculture and Forestry), 2017 ABQB 764; Reece v Edmonton, 2011 ABCA 238.

12 Edmonton Valley Zoo, *Dreamnight at the Zoo*, Edmonton Valley Zoo (2020), https://www.edmonton.ca/attractions_events/edmonton_valley_zoo/dreamnight-at-the-zoo.aspx.

13 Edmonton Valley Zoo, https://www.edmonton.ca/attractions_events/edmonton_valley_zoo/dreamnight-at-the-zoo.aspx.

14 Visitor demographics recorded by the American Association of Zoos and Aquariums (AZA) indicate that out of the roughly 12 million visitors to member-accredited zoos, 57 percent were children under 11 and that "two out of three adults visit a zoo with a child and 50% of adults visit an aquarium with a child." Am. Zoo Ass'n, *Visitor Demographics*, Am. Zoo Ass'n (2020), https://www.aza.org/partnerships-visitor-demographics?locale=en#:~:text=Visitors%20are%3A,54%25%20women%2F46%25men. Demographics from Canada may even be higher, as a report from the Toronto Zoo on the 2016 statistics showed that 78.1 percent of respondents had at least one child in the group and 51.9 percent had two children in the group. Robin D. Hale, *Staff Report*, Toronto Zoo 2 (Feb. 22, 2017), https://www.toronto.ca/legdocs/mmis/2017/zb/bgrd/backgroundfile-101510.pdf.

With young children's lives generally being immersed in animal narratives through picture books, television shows, films, apps, and toys and stuffed animals,[15] it is not surprising that children want to go to zoos and aquaria or that their families wish to take them to these places to see the animals. Yet, with increased protest against animal captivity in zoos as well as the acculturation of accredited zoos to the science of conservation biology, such places have had to reposition themselves to maintain respectable public stature. They have dissociated themselves from their traditional but now increasingly-discredited reasons for why animals have to be in captivity related to imperial history, exotica, leisure, and recreation[16] to re-branding themselves as conservation and educational centres.[17] Moreover, when zoos and aquaria are critiqued for keeping wild animals captive or for running captive breeding programs, many point to educational and conservation mandates of their institutions and the social value of wild animal captivity for these purposes.[18] As Irus Braverman has documented in her comprehensive study of American zoos, zoos emphasize the boost that captive breeding in zoos plays for conservation efforts of wild populations (whether such populations are characterized as in situ, ex situ, or intersitu) in response to animal rights opponents seeking zoos' abolition.[19] As well, zoos and aquaria point to their rescue and rehabilitation of injured wild animals and claim to serve a leading role in teaching the public about the need for conservation given the ongoing phenomenon of species extinction.[20]

Although it is not a point that Braverman herself unpacks, we can observe that such justificatory mandates for the continued purported need for zoos and aquaria revolve around the human child. The presence of children in zoos and aquaria as visitors on family outings and school trips is routine and critical to the continued viability of zoos and aquaria.[21] Some scholars have noted how children are the target audiences for conservation messaging from zoos and aquaria, making them the principal human cohort that is said to benefit from the conservation work zoos and

[15] Sandra R. Waxman et al., *Humans (Really) Are Animals: Picture-Book Reading Influences 5-Year-Old Urban Children's Construal of the Relation between Humans and Non-human Animals*, 5 FRONTIERS PSYCH. Article 172, 1, 1–2 (2014).

[16] JOHN BERGER, *Why Look at Animals? in* ABOUT LOOKING 3, 19-21 (1st ed. 1980); DESMOND, *supra* note 9, at 149, 157.

[17] Irus Braverman, *Conservation without Nature: The Trouble with* In Situ *Versus* Ex Situ *Conservation*, 51 GEOFORUM 47, 49 (2014); Tema Milstein, *Somethin' Tells Me It's All Happening at the Zoo: Discourse, Power, and Conservationism*, 3 ENV'T COMMC'N: J. NATURE & CULTURE 25, 29–32 (2009).

[18] IRUS BRAVERMAN, ZOOLAND: THE INSTITUTION OF CAPTIVITY (2012); Milstein, *supra* note 17, at 17, 25, 27, 40–46.

[19] BRAVERMAN, *supra* note 19, at 18.

[20] *Id.*; IRUS BRAVERMAN, ZOO VETERINARIANS: GOVERNING CARE ON A DISEASED PLANET 1 (2020).

[21] Milstein, *supra* note 17, at 42; Gail F. Melson, Why the Wild Things Are: Animals in the Lives of Children 75 (2001).

aquaria do.[22] Conservation discourses are aimed at preserving species for *future* human generations. We see that above in the Canadian context of the Edmonton Valley Zoo. But a quick look at zoo and aquarium websites worldwide reveal that such messaging is not anomalous; conservation educational efforts are disproportionately directed at children with school visits, overnight stays, birthday parties, and camps as regular parts of the zoo and aquarium offerings and overall experience.

Consider the mission statement for the global industry-leading San Diego Zoo. In the rotating banner on their website's home page, it says their mission is to end species extinction.[23] When a visitor clicks on the banner to learn more, they are taken to a painting of various animals that looks like it is from a children's picture book, with the caption underneath indicating that the "San Diego Zoo global is a conservation organization committed to saving species around the world."[24] After depictions of children along with their parents happily gazing at the animals swimming in a tank, the page goes on to discuss "The Human-Animal Connection":

> For more than a century, people have flocked to the San Diego Zoo to discover animals. The Zoo connects people with wildlife to inspire a passion for nature. *Picture the wide-eyed wonder on a child's face upon meeting a living, breathing giraffe, something she's only seen on a digital screen before*. Or the wonder of encountering a penguin that is looking at you with the same curiosity you have about him. These are the moments that tell the story of the San Diego Zoo and San Diego Zoo Safari Park. It is these connections that spark the desire to protect and save species.[25]

Messaging on the website of other world-famous top-ranked zoos,[26] such as at Taronga Zoo Sydney[27] and Singapore Zoo (as part of Wildlife Reserves Singapore[28]), is similar. For example, under the heading "Our Animals" across from an image of a baby chimpanzee latched onto her mother, Taronga Zoo Sydney states: "Taronga cares for over 4000 animals from over 350 species, many of which are threatened. Find out which fascinating animals you might meet on your visit, and how we're contributing to global efforts to save species from the brink of

[22] Anette Therkelsen & Maria Lottrup, *Being Together at the Zoo: Zoo Experiences among Families with Children*, 34 Leisure Stud. 354, 356–57 (2015); Aaron J.C. Wijeratne et al., *Rules of Engagement: The Role of Emotional Display Rules in Delivering Conservation Interpretation in a Zoo-Based Tourism Context*, 42 Tourism Mgmt. 149, 149, 150, 153 (2014).

[23] San Diego Zoo (2020), https://zoo.sandiegozoo.org.

[24] San Diego Zoo, *Our Mission*, *San Diego Zoo* (2020), https://zoo.sandiegozoo.org/our-mission.

[25] *Id.* (emphasis added).

[26] Oishimaya Sen Nag, *The Top Zoos in the World*, WorldAtlas (Sept. 28, 2018), https://www.worldatlas.com/articles/best-rated-zoos-in-the-world.html.

[27] Taronga Zoo, *Our Actions*, Taronga Zoo (2020), https://taronga.org.au/conservation-and-science/our-actions.

[28] Wildlife Reserves Singapore, *About Us*, Wildlife Rsrv. Sing. (2020), https://www.wrs.com.sg/en/about-us.html.

extinction."[29] Virtual visitors are then invited to click on animals by species to learn more and are taken to new webpages with photos and a short description of the animal species along with how the zoo is saving the species through breeding programs, participation in rehabilitation and release programs, or other initiatives.[30] Virtual visitors can also watch the animals on Taronga TV.[31] School excursions are offered, and the website assures parents that there are many "kid-friendly" activities at the zoo.

The offering of "educational" programming for children allows the zoos to present themselves as an essential provider of an important public service: teaching and inspiring the next human generation about the wonders of "nature" and the importance of wildlife conservation. How can a space that children flock to with their families to see cute animal babies and learn about the "natural world" possibly be objectionable? It is challenging to look past the family-friendly veneer of these spaces, especially given the other measures zoos have adopted to erase visible signs of captivity,[32] to expose the conditions of captivity and the harms they produce. The marshalling of children and families as principal implicit stakeholders for zoos contributes to the humane-washing that zoo critics have already pointed to regarding zoos' efforts to improve animal welfare[33] which "make the intrinsic violence of custody and display more palatable, more subtle, and less visible."[34]

And even when such violence is on display, as it was on February 9, 2014, when the Copenhagen zoo chose to kill a healthy eighteen-month old giraffe they had named Marius because he was seen as a "surplus" animal that threatened the carefully cultivated genetic pool of giraffes in European zoos should he mature and reproduce, children are deployed to rationalize it.[35] A zoo veterinarian shot Marius in the head outside of the public eye, but the feeding of his carcass to three zoo lions (who were killed a month later to be replaced by a young male lion unrelated to the females in the den) was made public as a children's "educational" event.[36] The zoo sought to quell the storm of international controversy that erupted through multiple justifications: (1) the breeding program's genetic parameters, (2) using Marius' flesh as food for zoo lions, and (3) conducting a three-hour dismemberment and dissection of Marius' body in front of a public audience as an educa-

[29] Taronga Zoo, *Our Animals*, TARONGA ZOO (2020), https://taronga.org.au/sydney-zoo/animals.

[30] Taronga Zoo, https://taronga.org.au/sydney-zoo/animals.

[31] Taronga Zoo, *Taronga TV*, TARONGA ZOO (2020), https://taronga.org.au/taronga-tv.

[32] Denning, *supra* note 8, at 69; BRAVERMAN, *supra* note 19, at 71-72, 80-86.

[33] Jessica Pierce & Marc Bekoff, *A Postzoo Future: Why Welfare Fails Animals in Zoos*, 21 J. APPLIED ANIMAL WELFARE SCI. 43, 43 (2018).

[34] Denning, *supra* note 8, at 61.

[35] BRAVERMAN, *supra* note 20, at 17.

[36] LORI GRUEN, DISPOSABLE CAPTIVES, Oxford University Press: Blog (Apr. 10, 2014), https://blog.oup.com/2014/04/disposable-captives-zoo-animals-philosophy/.

tional experience for children in anatomy and the realities of life.[37] All of these justifications can be impugned. Lori Gruen has noted that the disposable treatment of Marius spurred by reigning genetic logic was also then later applied to kill the lions (a mother and her two cubs) to whom Marius was fed a mere month later.[38] Despite the reining narrative of conservation, Gruen pointedly observes that "[c]-ausing death is what zoos do" not simply due to genetic management concerns but also due to the effects of captivity.[39]

It is instructive that the Copenhagen zoo did not merely rest on the first two justifications about why Marius had to be killed, perhaps aware that its rationalizations about genetic control of animals for conservation purposes and that Marius' carcass was not "wasted" because three lions benefitted are not sufficient to convince the public about the ethics of killing a very young giraffe. It is likely not fortuitous that the zoo chose to market the killing as an educational opportunity – not generically, but for schoolchildren. Pointing to the absurdity of this particular invocation of the educational value of Marius' death, Craig Gingrich-Philbrook observes: "It seems never to occur to the zoo officials offering this pedagogical alibi that, if a culture does indeed wish to educate children about the relationships between animals and death, one could easily bus them to a nearby slaughterhouse."[40] As Gingrich-Philbrook goes on to note, of course, this does not occur, as the slaughterhouse is not perceived to be suitable viewing material for children or a family-friendly place. Children are not present at slaughterhouses, and industrialized societies take enormous discursive and material efforts to hide the way in which animals are produced from our sensibilities[41] and even from slaughterhouse employees themselves.[42] Gingrich-Philbrook exposes the not-so-subtle ways in which the presence of children at the zoo is critical to its organizing genetic conservationist logic justifying the zoos and aquaria's continued need for existence. When the lethal nature of zoo decisions and activities are put (exceptionally) on public display, children are made visible to attenuate negative perception and restore confidence of zoos as ethical spaces that the public should support.

Doubtless, death of megafauna is never on display at a for-profit aquarium like SeaWorld, whose family brand – iconized through the ageless killer whale

[37] Craig Gingrich-Philbrook, *On the Execution of the Young Giraffe, Marius, by the Copenhagen Zoo: Conquergood's "Lethal Theatre" and Posthumanism*, 36 TEXT & PERFORMANCE Q. 200, 206 (2016); *Disposable Captives*, https://blog.oup.com/2014/04/disposable-captives-zoo-animals-philosophy/.

[38] *Disposable Captives*, https://blog.oup.com/2014/04/disposable-captives-zoo-animals-philosophy/.

[39] *Id.*

[40] Gingrich-Philbrook, *supra* note 36, at 206.

[41] ELLEN K. SILBERGELD, CHICKENIZING FARMS AND FOOD: NEW PERILS FOR PUBLIC HEALTH 2, 62 (2016).

[42] TIMOTHY PACHIRAT, EVERY TWELVE SECONDS: INDUSTRIALIZED SLAUGHTER AND THE POLITICS OF SIGHT 8-9, 43–52 (2013).

Shamu – and messaging to children is powered by relentless marketing that suggests to (the largely white or middle class families that visit), that SeaWorld is family-friendly entertainment at its best. In her incisive account of spectacle and performance on display at SeaWorld, Jane Desmond calls attention to the conservation and family-oriented discourses and practices SeaWorld marshals to validate its entertainment and reduce the chance that its adult visitors might question the captivity of orcas for the fun and thrill of watching the ocean's top predators perform elaborate tricks at the behest of human trainers.[43] Marketing to families and even children directly is central to SeaWorld's commercial success – gift shops that sell stuffed animals and toys to children are strategically placed throughout the theme park,[44] and SeaWorld has launched three SeaWorld Kids apps to target this key demographic.[45]

But more so than marketing to ensure top profits, it is the *presence and figure* of human children that is critical to the validating messaging of the "good work" that SeaWorld and other animal-display venues (whether for-profit or not) are doing as "family-friendly" places to visit. Without children, the emphasis on "family" is unintelligible given the dominant heteronormative futurist logics through which most of us understand the term "family."[46] Further, SeaWorld makes it clear that its educational and conservation messaging is directed at children.[47] Children are also invoked in legal battles that question captivity. The documentary *BlackFish* and memoirs by former lead trainers have affected SeaWorld's bottom line[48] as well as its

[43] DESMOND, *supra* note 9, at 234–36, 243.

[44] *Id.* at 221–23.

[45] *See* SeaWorld Ent., Inc., *SeaWorld Kids Explores Nature with Five New, Fun Mobile Apps*, CISION PR NEWSWIRE (Dec. 16, 2014), https://www.prnewswire.com/news-releases/seaworld-kids-explores-nature-with-five-new-fun-mobile-apps-300010207.html; *see aslo* https://seaworld.com/orlando/shopping/ and https://seaworld.com/san-diego/shopping/.

[46] Cassie Peterson, *The Lies That Bind: Heteronormative Constructions of "Family" in Social Work Discourse*, 25 J. GAY & LESBIAN SOC. SERV. 486, 494–95 (2013).

[47] SeaWorld provides a variety of educational e-learning resources on their website which they describe as "ideal for students in grades K–8". SeaWorld Parks & Ent., *@ Home*, SEAWORLD PARKS & ENT. (2020), https://seaworld.com/at-home/. They promote day camps and sleepaway camps for children from grade 2 to grade 8 as part of their educational programming in addition to field trips and behind-the-scenes tours. *See* SeaWorld Parks & Ent. (2020), https://seaworld.org. In describing their rescue and rehabilitation efforts, the website includes a quote from their senior veterinarian indicating her intention to inspire children: "I hope to inspire others, particularly bright young minds who want to know more about ocean life and what they can do to help." SeaWorld also portrays teaching children about the world around them as a component of their conservation efforts: "Today, we cared for an injured animal. Today, we taught a child about the world around them. Today, we celebrated life, in all of its magnificent and powerful forms. Tomorrow we'll do the same. This is our commitment." SeaWorld Parks & Ent., *Our Commitment*, SEAWORLD PARKS & ENT. (2020), https://seaworld.org/conservation/our-commitment/.

[48] Maya Rhodan, *Seaworld's Profits Drop 84% after Blackfish Documentary*, TIME (Aug. 6, 2015), https://time.com/3987998/seaworlds-profits-drop-84-after-blackfish-documentary.

ability to breed any more cetaceans.[49] *BlackFish* has also had a similar, if less direct, effect on Canada's Vancouver Aquarium,[50] despite the fact it did not then house orcas.[51] Both have resisted the efforts of legislative bans on future breeding or captivity and animal rights campaigns against them through careful reiteration of their conservation mandate and benefit to human children.[52]

13.2.2 *The Use of Children to Humanize Immigration Detention and Human Prisons*

In marked contrast to zoos and aquaria, immigration detention facilities and human prisons are not promoted as educational sites for children to visit. Those confined in these facilities attest to their extensive adverse effects.[53] The scholarly literature documenting the negative effects in general on humans who are kept captive is well established and will not be repeated here. What is lesser known is how children also inhabit these spaces, not only during visiting hours or as teenagers in juvenile detention facilities, but as young children who reside inside alongside their parents, overwhelmingly mothers. In this section, I discuss this phenomenon in the Canadian context and its underlying rationale as something "progressive" meant to improve the conditions of and reduce the family separation and, specifically mother-child attachment, harms that prisons and immigration detention occasion in the first place. I show how human children are marshalled to humanize these captive spaces with known disruptive and often devastating family harms.

[49] E.C.M. Parsons & Naomi A. Rose, *The Blackfish Effect: Corporate and Policy Change in the Face of Shifting Public Opinion on Captive Cetaceans*, 13 Tourism Marine Env't 73, 78 (2018).

[50] Blackfish was a catalyst for a cetacean anti-captivity bill that eventually became law in Canada, namely, the *Ending the Captivity of Whales and Dolphins Act*, SC 2019, c 11. Katie Sykes, *The Whale, Inside: Ending Cetacean Captivity in Canada*, 5 Canadian J. Compar. & Contemp. L. 349, 354 (2019).

[51] The COVID-19 global pandemic and the severe downturn in public attendance caused the Vancouver Aquarium to close in summer of 2020. Although it has since re-opened, its chances of regaining financial viability despite continued provincial and federal government support may still be bleak. Hina Alam, *Vancouver Aquarium Will Reopen, Operator's CEO Vows, as It Searches for Solution to Financial Struggles*, CBC News (Sept. 17, 2020), https://www.cbc.ca/news/canada/british-columbia/vancouver-aquarium-covid-19-financial-solution-pandemic-1.5727870.

[52] Associated Press, *SeaWorld Sues over Orca Breeding Ban*, Wall St. J. (Dec. 30, 2015), https://www.wsj.com/articles/seaworld-sues-over-orca-breeding-ban-1451493595; Canadian Broad. Corp. News, *Vancouver Aquarium Files Legal Challenge to Whale, Dolphin Breeding Ban*, CBC News (Aug. 27, 2014), https://www.cbc.ca/news/canada/british-columbia/vancouver-aquarium-files-legal-challenge-to-whale-dolphin-breeding-ban-1.2748326.

[53] Gruen, *supra* note 7, at 240-44.

13.2.2.1 Immigration Detention

In immigration detention centres, while some countries enforce the devastating measure of separating children from their caregivers, other countries house parents in immigration detention with their children; and others still take the further step of housing children legally entitled to be in a country (usually because they are born there after their mother entered illegally) with their "illegal" parent in detention centres. As I discuss below with respect to the Canadian context, this practice arises out of a concern for the welfare of the children as well as of the parents who wish to avoid separation from their children while detained. As recent practices at the US-Mexican border have showcased, the forced separation of children from their parents upon detention has attracted overwhelming public outcry.[54] Family maintenance during immigration processing and detention can thus be a positive measure that softens the harsh edges of immigration detention.[55]

In Canada, however, separating children from their parents is supposed to be a last resort under the Immigration and Refugee Protection Act.[56] Minor children are not supposed to be detained except according to their best interests.[57] In 2017–18, advocacy organizations reported that 155 children were detained, an increase by their count of 4 children from 2016–17, but also a decrease from 232 in 2014–15.[58] Compared to the militarized and neoliberal border confinement practices in the United States since the 1980s,[59] Canada's "last resort" policy appears responsive to

[54] Camilo Montayo-Galvez, *U.S. Planned to Separate 26,000 Migrant Families before Outcry over "Zero Tolerance" Policy*, CBS NEWS (Nov. 27, 2019), Www.Cbsnews.Com/News/Family-Separations-Zero-Tolerance-Policy-Us-Planned-To-Separate-More-Than-26000-Migrant-Families-2019-11-27.

[55] Rachel Kronick et al., *Asylum-Seeking Children's Experiences of Detention in Canada: A Qualitative Study*, 85 AM. J. ORTHOPSYCHIATRY 287, 290-91, 293 (2015); Rachel Kronick et al., *Refugee Children's Sandplay Narratives in Immigration Detention in Canada*, 27 EUR. CHILD & ADOLESCENT PSYCHIATRY 423, 434-435 (2018); Lauren Vogel, *Health Professionals Decry Detention of Migrant Children in Canada*, 190 CANADIAN MED. ASS'N J. E867, E867 (2018).

[56] Immigration and Refugee Protection Act, S.C. 2001, cl. 27, § 6 (2001) (Can.).

[57] *Id.*

[58] HUM. RTS. WATCH & U. TORONTO INT'L HUM. RTS. PROGRAM, JOINT SUBMISSION BY HUMAN RIGHTS WATCH AND THE UNIVERSITY OF TORONTO'S INTERNATIONAL HUMAN RIGHTS PROGRAM TO THE COMMITTEE ON THE RIGHTS OF THE CHILD'S CONSIDERATION OF CANADA'S FIFTH AND SIXTH PERIODIC REPORTS 2 (2020), https://www.hrw.org/sites/default/files/supporting_resources/hrw_crc_submission_canada_final_1.pdf. There is some discrepancy between the numbers reported by Human Rights Watch and the University of Toronto's International Human Rights Program and those reported by Canada Border Services Agency. According to Canada Border Services Agency: in 2017–18, 151 children were detained, representing a decrease of 11 children from 2016–17, and a decrease from 232 in 2014–05. *See* Can. Border Serv. Agency, Annual Detention Statistics – 2012–18 (2018), https://www.cbsa-asfc.gc.ca/security-securite/detent/stat-2012-2018-eng.html.

[59] Linda Alvarez, *No Safe Space: Neoliberalism and the Production of Violence in the Lives of Central American Migrants*, 5 J. RACE, ETHNICITY, & POL. 4, 9 (2020).

the needs of parents and children. Yet, as a recent report prepared by the University of Toronto's Faculty of Law entitled *No Life for a Child* explains, the situation is anything but.[60] Parents and children face conditions and resulting harm and trauma even when together. For one, where the children themselves are Canadian citizens, parents must confront the decision of permitting their child to enter the foster care system or having them detained with them to avoid losing their children.[61] Tracking children defined as seventeen and under, the *No Life for a Child* report notes that "between 2010 and 2014, an average of 242 children were detained each year" with numbers declining in the last two years.[62] The authors are careful to clarify that these numbers represent children under formal detention orders, arguing that the figures are higher given that many children also live with their mothers on a de facto basis in Immigration Holding Centres.[63]

Although the children are called "guests" and not "detainees,"[64] this change in language does not materially erase the violation of their rights or those of children who are also considered illegal under the United Nations Convention on the Rights of the Child (CRC), a convention to which Canada is a signatory and has ratified.[65] The CRC stipulates in Article 3 that "the best interests of the child" should be paramount in any state decision (CRC). The authors of *No Life for a Child* and the UN Special Rapporteur on the Special Rights of Migrants, who wrote the Foreword to the report, both emphasized that the detention of children, even when rationalized as a last resort option, does not comply with the best interests principle.[66] Children stand to suffer psychologically and have traumatized caregivers even post-release.[67] The *No Life for a Child* report, the United Nations Commissioner for Children, and other child rights organizations have called for children to be able to stay with their families *outside* of detention even while undergoing refugee, asylum, and immigration processing.[68] Such critiques of "living in" help us recognize the brutalities for children in detention while also recognizing "progressive" policies for

[60] Hanna Gros & Yolanda Song, "No Life for a Child": A Roadmap to End Immigration Detention of Children and Family Separation 1 (Samer Muscati ed., 2016), https://ihrp.law.utoronto.ca/news/no-life-child-roadmap-end-immigration-detention-children-and-family-separation.

[61] *Id.* at 41.

[62] *Id.* at 9.

[63] *Id.* at 9–10. The authors note that some family separation occurs because "children must live separately from their fathers because the family rooms are restricted to mothers and children." *Id.* at 9.

[64] *Id.* at 55–56.

[65] G.A. Res. 44/25, United Nations Convention on the Rights of the Child (Nov. 20, 1989), https://treaties.un.org/doc/Publication/MTDSG/Volume%20I/Chapter%20IV/IV-11.en.pdf.

[66] Gros & Song, *supra* note 59, at 2.

[67] *Id.* at 10.

[68] *Id.* at 2, 56; Hum. Rts. Watch & U. Toronto Int'l Hum. Rts. Program, *supra* note 57, at 8–9.

families as a welfarist measure that permits the underlying and problematic detention to continue.

13.2.2.2 Prisons

In order to contend with the growing number of female prisoners who give birth while in prison – a phenomenon related to the fast-rising rate at which women are being incarcerated – and to respect the mutual benefits of maternal care and bonding for both the mother and child, prisons worldwide have housed young children with their mothers.[69] The realization by some governments that separating children from their incarcerated parents, particularly their mothers, even for short custodial sentences, entails long-lasting adverse effects on the child[70] is to be welcomed. It is a significant achievement when contrasted with jurisdictions such as the United States, which incarcerates roughly one-third of the world's female prisoner population estimated at 625,000 in 2018,[71] and where the opportunities for children to stay with their mothers are scant.[72] In such situations of forced parental-child separation, a parental prison sentence is still effectively shared by the child, particularly when incarceration removes a *mother* from the child(ren) she was caring for,[73] and not only during the period of incarceration.[74] Having an incarcerated parent is a prominent "adverse childhood experience" (ACE) that predisposes children to additional ACEs for the child's future adult years across many measures

69 E.g., Jane R. Walker et al., *Residential Programmes for Mothers and Children in Prison: Key Themes and Concepts*, 21 Criminology & Crim. Just. 21, 22 (2021). *See also* Carlton, *supra* note 1, at 290; Aron Shlonsky et al., Literature Review of Prison-based Mothers and Children Programs: Final Report, 1 (Soc. Work Melbourne Sch. Health Sci. et al. 2016); Helen Namondo Linonge-Fontebo & Marlize Rabe, *Mothers in Cameroonian Prisons: Pregnancy, Childbearing and Caring for Young Children*, 74 Afr. Stud. 290, 290-91 (2015); Sylvia I. Mignon & Paige Ransford, *Mothers in Prison: Maintaining Connections with Children*, 27 Soc. Work Pub. Health 69, 70-73 (2012); Pat Carlen, Women and Punishment: The Struggle for Justice XX (Routledge ltd. ed. 2013); Patricia J. Thompson & Nancy J. Harm, *Parenting from Prison: Helping Children and Mothers*, 23 Issues Comprehensive Pediatric Nursing 61, 61-62 (2000).

70 Natalie Booth, *Disconnected: Exploring Provisions for Mother-Child Telephone Contact in Female Prisons Serving England and Wales*, 20 Criminology & Crim. Just. 150, 151-52, 162 (2020).

71 Helen Myers et al., *Impact of Family-Friendly Prison Policies on Health, Justice and Child Protection Outcomes for Incarcerated Mothers and Their Dependent Children: A Cohort Study Protocol*, 7 BMJ Open e016302 1, 1 (2017).

72 Lynne Haney, *Motherhood as Punishment: The Case of Parenting in Prison*, 39 Signs: J. Women Culture & Soc'y 105, 108-9 (2013).

73 John Hagan & Holly Foster, *Children of the American Prison Generation: Student and School Spillover Effects of Incarcerating Mothers*, 46 Law & Soc'y Rev. 37, 38-44 (2012); Myers et al., *supra* note 70, at 2.

74 Dan Levin, *As More Mothers Fill Prisons, Children Suffer "a Primal Wound,"* N.Y. Times (Dec. 29, 2019), https://www.nytimes.com/2019/12/28/us/prison-mothers-children.html; Anais Ogrizek et al., *Mother-Child Attachment Challenged by Prison*, Eur. Child & Adolescent Psychiatry (2020), https://doi.org/10.1007/s00787-020-01585-6.

of success and well-being.[75] Such effects are heightened further when the incarcerated parent is the mother and contribute to the intergenerational compounding of gender, race, and class inequities given the disproportionate rate at which racialized and poor mothers are incarcerated in the United States and elsewhere[76] and that the bulk of caring for children left behind falls on related female kin rather than non-incarcerated fathers.[77]

Still, it would be erroneous to assume that programs that allow children to accompany their mothers to prison or stay once they are born for their early formative years are a categorical improvement for children or their mothers. Taking a closer look at the Canadian program helps understand why. In Canada, a woman who is federally sentenced has had the right to apply to live with her child since 2001 when Correctional Services Canada implemented the federal Mother-Child Program (MCP),[78] following recommendations by the Task Force on Federally Sentenced Women in its report entitled *Creating Choices.*[79] The Task Force was established after intense media coverage of deaths in the then-existing Kingston Penitentiary for Women in Kingston, Ontario, and widespread reporting of the inhumane conditions therein.[80] The Task Force was established to change prison conditions for women.

The Task Force's Report emphasized a "constant touchstone" for its plan to reform Canadian prisons for women, comprising the following factors: the need to "create choices" and for prison programming and operation to "mirror caring responses for women" that they would find "in the community, including Aboriginal and other ethnic communities";[81] as in other jurisdictions where colonialism, poverty, and other forms of structural violence form the bedrock for vulner-

75 Kristin Turney, *Adverse Childhood Experiences among Children of Incarcerated Parents*, 89 Child. & Youth Serv. Rev. 218, 218 (2018).

76 Hagan & Foster, *supra* note 72, at 41; Myers et al., *supra* note 70, at 1-2.

77 Haney, *supra* note 71, at 109.

78 Sarah Brennan, *Canada's Mother-Child Program: Examining Its Emergence, Usage and Current State*, 3 Canadian Graduate J. Socio. & Criminology 11, 11 (2014).

79 *Id.*; Task Force on Federally Sentenced Women, Creating Choices: The Report on the Task Force on Federally Sentenced Women 1 (1990), https://www.publicsafety.gc.ca/lbrr/archives/hv%209507%20t3%201990-eng.pdf. The MCP is overseen by the Office of the Correctional Investigator. The program underwent considerable shifts in 2008 and in 2016. Brennan, *supra* note 77, at 28.

80 Sherri Barron, *Life and Death in the Cage*, Ottawa Citizen Mar. 9, 1991 at XX; Canadian Press, *First "Dangerous Offender," Woman, 30, Dies in Prison*, Globe & Mail, Dec. 5, 1988, at A15; Mary Lasovich, *Vigil Tomorrow for Dead Prison for Women Inmate*, Whig, Dec. 17, 1988, at X; Whig, *Critical Judge Agrees to Visit Kingston Prison for Women*, Whig Mar. 25, 1987 at XX.

81 Task Force on Federally Sentenced Women, *supra* note 78, at 138–39. https://www.publicsafety.gc.ca/lbrr/archives/hv%209507%20t3%201990-eng.pdf.

abilities that place some more than others on a "pipeline" to prison, the incarcerated population in Canada is disproportionately poor and Indigenous.[82] In stressing the need to "empower women to take responsibility of their lives,"[83] the report asked that prison initiatives "ensure that women are treated with respect and dignity" and be driven from the ground up by listening to the voices of women who are incarcerated as to their needs.[84] In sum, the report "envisioned an idealized prison environment that emphasized serenity and tranquility, plenty of space and privacy, was rehabilitative rather than security-focused and recognized women's particular needs."[85] As part of the changes that were then recommended, the report stressed the important need for inmates' living choices to include "the opportunity for mothers and children to live together based on the rights and needs of the children, mothers and significant others in each individual case" by directing that each prison facility construct "an appropriate environment to enable a child or children to live with the mother" in a cottage-like setting.[86]

As of 2014, MCPs were operational in five of the six federal facilities for women inmates across Canada.[87] Full-time residency for children under five, part-time residency for children under six (originally available to children five to twelve), and regular visiting for other children are all components of the program.[88] Despite these options, overall participation is extremely low;[89] across the country a mere fourteen children lived with their mothers between 2008 and 2014 in federal prisons and only eight lived full-time.[90] Numerous academic critiques have pointed to systemic gendered, colonial, ability, and class barriers to explain the non-optimal functioning of the program leading to very low rates of participation.[91] Significantly,

[82] Lynsey Race & Lorna Stefanick, *Mother-Child Programs in Prison: Disciplining the Unworthy Mother*, in MOTHERING AND WELFARE: DEPRIVING, SURVIVING, THRIVING 43, 44, 49 (Karine Levasseur et al. eds., 2020).

[83] TASK FORCE ON FEDERALLY SENTENCED WOMEN, *supra* note 78, at 111.

[84] *Id.* at 137.

[85] Brennan, *supra* note 77, at 28.

[86] TASK FORCE ON FEDERALLY SENTENCED WOMEN, *supra* note 78, at 144, https://www.publicsafety.gc.ca/lbrr/archives/hv%209507%20t3%201990-eng.pdf.

[87] Brennan, *supra* note 77, at 15. Nova Institution for Women (Truro, Nova Scotia), Edmonton Institute for Women (Edmonton, Alberta), Grand Valley Institute for Women (Kitchener, Ontario), Jolliette Institute (Joliette, Quebec), Fraser Valley Institution (Abbotsford, British Columbia), Okimaw Ohci Healing Lodge (Maple Creek, Saskatchewan). *Id.* at 15. Sections 76 and 77 of the Corrections and Conditional Release Act provide the principal legal authority for the creation of the MCP program, providing that the Service should design programs that "contribute to [inmates'] successful reintegration into the community" and requiring the Service shall provide programs tailored to women, respectively. Corrections and Conditional Release Act, S.C. 1992, cl. 20, §§ 76-77. (Can.). *Commissioner's Directive* 768, developed by the Women Offender Sector and Strategic Policy, sets out the details of the program.

[88] Kayliah Miller, *Canada's Mother-Child program and Incarcerated Aboriginal Mothers*, 37 CANADIAN FAM. L.Q. 1, 6 (2017).

[89] *Id.* at 8; Brennan, *supra* note 77, at 16.

[90] Race & Stefanick, *supra* note 81, at 56.

[91] Brennan, *supra* note 77, at 11, 21, 28; Miller, *supra* note 87, at 11, 16–17; Jane M. Paynter & Erna Snelgrove-Clarke, *"Breastfeeding in Public" for Incarcerated Women: The Baby-Friendly Steps*,

however, as Sarah Brennan highlights, despite the program's minimal uptake, "[i]t is noteworthy that not a single respondent identified a lack of interest on the part of incarcerated women as a possible reason for the low participation rate in the program."[92] We can understand that the MCP is of utmost value to women who are mothers who wish to be with their children,[93] a valuation that is common to imprisoned mothers across the globe.[94] We can also understand that the presence of such a program in a prison context is one important way prison policies can become compliant with the "constant touchstone" of the *Creating Choices* Report,[95] namely, to treat women with respect, dignity, and care and empower them and help generate a more compassionate prison environment. Allowing mothers to stay with their children prevents trauma and other psychological and social ills to both.[96] Correctional Service Canada (CSC) itself has stated that the program "aims to provide a supportive environment that fosters and promotes stability and continuity for the mother-child relationship."[97] In other words, the MCP can be understood as making the prison better and thus a more humane and socially defensible place to live.

But if the CSC's goal is "to provide a supportive environment that fosters and promotes stability and continuity for the mother-child relationship," it is necessary to ask whether the impetus for the program should not focus on how children can best *enter* the prison to be with their mothers but, instead, how mothers can *exit* the prison environment altogether to be with their children outside of captivity and in the community context. Thus far, acknowledging the harms of mother-child separation and benefits of keeping mothers with their children has not persuaded legislatures to stop the practice of incarcerating women who are mothers with children or otherwise have had caregiving responsibility for children disrupted by their imprisonment. Neither has awareness of Canada's international law obligations as a signatory to the CRC, where all decisions regarding children must conform to the best interests of children. If the "best interests of children" is the ultimate benchmark for state decisions where children are involved, including whether a child can stay with her mother, and it is in the case of the MCP,[98] surely doing what is in the best interests means incarcerating neither the child nor her mother.

14 INT'L BREASTFEEDING J. 1, 4 (2019); Martha J. *Paynter, Policy and Legal Protection for Breastfeeding and Incarcerated Women in Canada*, 34 J. HUM. LACTATION 276, 276 (2018).

92 Brennan, *supra* note 77, at 19.

93 *Id.* at 12; Miller, *supra* note 77, at 4.

94 Booth, *supra* note 69, at 151-53.

95 TASK FORCE ON FEDERALLY SENTENCED WOMEN, *supra* note 78, at 138, https://www.publicsafety.gc.ca/lbrr/archives/hv%209507%20t3%201990-eng.pdf.

96 Miller, *supra* note 77, at 2–4, 21–22; Brennan, *supra* note 77, at 11–13.

97 CORR. SERV. CAN., COMMISSIONER'S DIRECTIVE 768 INSTITUTIONAL MOTHER-CHILD PROGRAM ¶ 1 (Gov't Can. 2020), https://www.csc-scc.gc.ca/politiques-et-lois/768-cd-en.shtml.

98 Miller, *supra* note 77, at 2–4, 21–22; *see* Inglis v. B.C. (Minister of Public Safety), 2013 B.C.S.C. 2309 (2013).

This option has not yet emerged as a priority, let alone a solution, in public government discourse in the year since *Inglis* was argued and decided. Canada is also a signatory to the United Nations Rules for the Treatment of Women Prisoners and Non-custodial Measures for Women Offenders ("the Bangkok Rules"), which emphasize maximizing leave opportunities for mothers where safe to do so and in children's best interests.[99] The Canadian government has cited these rules as part of the legal framework underlying a "gender responsive" and "trauma-centred" approach to corrections outlined in a report entitled *Gender Responsive Corrections for Women in Canada: The Road to Successful Reintegration.*[100] Despite referencing the Bangkok Rules, and identifying the high proportion of women who are mothers/active caregivers as a key gendered reality of the female prison population, *and* prioritizing for future work "(o)pportunities that promote stability and continuity for the mother-child relationship," this "trauma-informed" report makes no mention of non-custodial sentences.[101]

Judicial review of the MCP's operation has also not led to a questioning of the carceral model for mothers despite the child-centered constitutional and international law obligations constraining government action in Canada. In *Inglis v. British Columbia*, the only constitutional challenge brought by mothers and their babies in relation to the program, here in relation to the closing of the MCP at the Alouette Correctional Centre for Women, the defendants Minister of Public Safety and Solicitor for British Columbia, the Attorney General of British Columbia, and the warden of the prison denied that the decision to cancel the program had to take into account the best interests of the children. The court rejected this argument, citing the CRC as well as the provincial child protection statute's emphasis on the best interests of children as relevant context for the federal closure decision.[102] In addition, the court noted other child- and family-related international law principles that were applicable given Conventions that Canada had ratified. These regarded state protection for families in general, state protection for pregnant women and to mothers and newborns, and a mandate against separating children from their families unless necessary according to the best interests principle.[103] Madam Justice Ross found that the MCP was a program guided by the individualized best interests of each child, as decided by the ministry's child protective administrative arm pursuant to the *Child and Family Community Services Act.*[104] She further observed that given the vulnerability and disadvantage experienced by incarcerated

[99] G. A. Res. 65/229. United Nations Rules for the Treatment of Women Prisoners and Non-custodial Measures for Women Offenders (the Bangkok Rules), Rule 43 (Mar. 16, 2011).

[100] Corr. Serv. Can., Gender-Responsive Corrections for Women in Canada: The Road to Successful Reintegration (2021), https://www.csc-scc.gc.ca/women/002002-0005-en.shtml#t3.

[101] *Id.*

[102] Inglis, 2013 B.C.S.C. at ¶ 9.

[103] *Id.* at ¶ 7.

[104] *Id.* at ¶ 14.

mothers and their babies, and noting in particular the "overrepresentation of Aboriginal women in the incarcerated population and the history of dislocation of Aboriginal families caused by state action," that the MCP "represented a significant step forward in the amelioration of the circumstances of the mothers and their babies."[105]

The court went on to find that the closure violated section 7 of Canada's Charter of Rights and Freedoms, the country's constitutional rights-protecting document vis-à-vis state action. It did so by denying both mothers and their infants their security of the person and liberty interests in remaining attached to each other and enjoying numerous benefits that attachment to mothers and breastfeeding bring for both parties now and later in life.[106] The court also held that the closure violated the equality rights of the mothers.[107] These violations could not be justified per the rationale and effects of the decision. The judicial remedy, in the end, however, was only to set aside the Corrections decision to close the program and the policy underlying it and to order the prison decision-makers to retake their decision. The mothers remained incarcerated.[108]

The *Inglis* outcome is a "victory" for its plaintiffs in terms of the parameters of the constitutional challenged launched. Against the larger socio-legal landscape of the adverse effects of prisons on adults, but particularly children,[109] and the possibility that the MCP itself, similar to programs elsewhere,[110] is operationalized to judge women for their mothering in prison and thereby serves as "another mode of social control,"[111] the "victory" quickly loses its sheen. The option to remove mothers into the community to be with their babies or other children is not considered despite the strong rights vindication the court provides. As in the zoo context, the interests of human children, even the "best" interests of human children informed by national and international legal recognition of children's rights, are not sufficient to question the need for incarceration of their mothers in the first place. With zoos and aquaria, animals' incarceration is seen to be necessary to the conservation and education mandate. And in human prisons, the ongoing incarceration of mothers is presumed to be necessary presumably for reasons of public safety and deterrence. The presence of children in these carceral spaces helps to soften or gloss over the wide-ranging violence and vulnerability these spaces promote to make the captivity they embody less contentious.

[105] *Id.* at ¶ 15.
[106] *Id.* at ¶ 11.
[107] *Id.* at ¶ 13.
[108] *Id.* at ¶ 656.
[109] Barry Holman & Jason Ziedenberg, The Dangers of Detention: The Impact of Incarcerating Youth in Detention and Other Secure Facilities 1 (2006).
[110] Haney, *supra* note 71, at 112-18.
[111] Race & Stefanick, *supra* note 81, at 57.

13.3 HUMAN CHILD–ANIMAL NEXUS: UNDERSTANDING CHILD-INVOKING CARCERAL DISCOURSES AS PERVERSE DEPLOYMENTS AND BETRAYALS OF CHILDHOOD

It is well established that certain human bodies are associated with nature and animals more than others. As Western societies were industrializing, human children were posited as closer to nature and surrounded with animal figures (through the rise of stuffed animals, companion animal keeping, and jungle gyms) even as societies and families transitioned from rural to urban landscapes.[112] In contemporary times, the association of children as closer to nature and animals is still intact through the continuation of stuffed animals and companion animals as normative in middle-class households,[113] coveted outdoor early childhood educational curriculums,[114] children's picture books, readers, and other literature that is highly mediated by animal figures,[115] and, as we saw above, zoos and aquaria that pitch themselves as the ideal place for family-friendly outings where children can see "wild" animals. With this nexus in mind, this Part illuminates how this human child-animal nexus is marshaled to harm both animals and human children.

13.3.1 *Children, Nature, and Innocence: Policy Drivers*

The naturalization of children with an idea of pristine nature also marks their ostensible innocence and need for protection from those who would prey upon them.[116] For many non-white children in the United States, Canada, and elsewhere, the narrative of childhood innocence does not reliably apply as they (and their families) are animalized to the extent of being dehumanized.[117]

What can we make of the fact that human children are naturalized and animalized more so than adults, which helps to mark them out as innocent and in need of protection, and yet certain human children are animalized to such an extent that they lose the "innocence" marking and may be rendered (like animals) dispensable if not disposable? First, the partiality and instability of the childhood innocence

[112] Jane Desmond, *Staging Privilege, Proximity, and "Extreme Animal Tourism,"* in OXFORD HANDBOOK ANIMAL STUD. XX (Linda Kalof ed., 2017); MEGAN H. GLICK, INFRAHUMANISMS SCIENCE, CULTURE, AND THE MAKING OF MODERN NON/PERSONHOOD 1, 34-42 (2018).

[113] MATTHEW COLE & KATE STEWART, OUR CHILDREN AND OTHER ANIMALS: THE CULTURAL CONSTRUCTION OF HUMAN-ANIMAL RELATIONS IN CHILDHOOD 3, 53-54, 65-67 (2014).

[114] Conor Williams, *The Perks of a Play-in-the-Mud Educational Philosophy*, THE ATL. (Apr. 26, 2018), www.theatlantic.com/education/archive/2018/04/early-childhood-outdoor-education/558959.

[115] COLE & STEWART, *supra* note 112, at 55, 70; Waxman et al, supra note 16 at 1-2.

[116] *Id.*

[117] Toby Rollo, *The Color of Childhood: The Role of the Child/Human Binary in the Production of Anti-Black Racism*, 49 J. BLACK STUD. 307, 309-10 (2018); Phillip A. Goff et al., *The Essence of Innocence: Consequences of Dehumanizing Black Children*, 106 J. PERSONALITY & SOC. PSYCH. 526, 526-27 (2014).

frame confirms that although all human children are vulnerable to exploitation because of their developmental stage, this vulnerability is differentiated according to the social location of a child. But the juxtaposition also highlights how "childhood" is a socially constructed category, a reality brought into sharp relief not only through the prism of race- and class-based concepts of innocence, but also through the implicit human qualifier that delineates the concept of "children" and denies that status to animals, often leading human exceptionalists to protest any attempt to draw analogies between human children and animals.[118]

This type of "boundary maintenance"[119] to shore up the fiction of humans as not-animal alerts us to how the figure of the child can be deployed in contested social arenas to validate certain policies or laws, and dismiss or otherwise marginalize alternative possibilities, a correlation others have established.[120] I have been arguing that with respect to the ongoing socially contested nature of zoos, prisons, and detention centres, the human child helps to validate the social acceptability of zoos, prisons, and detention centres by ostensibly humanizing these carceral spaces. This dynamic ensues even as vulnerable, disproportionately poor, and racialized human children within prisons and detention centres suffer inside them and even as ideologies about improving human children's education and futures through exposure to zoos and aquaria violate the bodies and terminate the lives of animals and their children.

13.3.2 *Inculcating Human Exceptionalism through Childhood Familiars*

It is important to point out the particularly perverse dimensions of this deployment of the human child in these spaces. With respect to sites of animal captivity, it seems perverse that human children, whose social worlds are immersed and entwined with those of animals,[121] who closely identify with animals,[122] and who come to them for acceptance, resilience building, and to learn social-emotional skills,[123] learn through zoos to objectify, commodify, and dominate them instead.[124] The magnitude of this perversion is amplified particularly in zones of zoo and aquarium captivity. In these sites, both for growing insurance populations to buffer possible extinction in situ and for attracting visitors and revenue, captive breeding is practiced and thus the deliberate practice of bringing *animal* children into this world to grow up in

[118] Taimie Bryant, *Denying Animals Childhood and Its Implications for Animal-Protective Law Reform*, 6 Law, Culture & Human. 56, 57 (2010).
[119] *Id.*
[120] *Id.*; Baird, *supra* note 5, at 291, 294.
[121] Taylor & Pacini-Ketchabaw, *supra* note 1, 2-5.
[122] Cole & Stewart, *supra* note 112, at 84-85.
[123] Louise Chawla, *Children's Engagement with the Natural World as a Ground for Healing*, in Greening in the Red Zone 111 (Keith G. Tidball & Marianne E. Krasny eds., 2013).
[124] *Disposable Captives*, https://blog.oup.com/2014/04/disposable-captives-zoo-animals-philosophy/.

conditions of captivity if they are permitted – unlike Marius and the two lion cubs to whom his body parts were fed – to grow up at all.

What is also deeply troubling is that we misrepresent to children what they are seeing or otherwise apprehending when we take them to the zoo to see newborn animal babies or otherwise. These visits idealized as family-friendly educational outings are excursions to enjoy a particular type of spectacle and performance, one that expresses human domination and entails torture and misery for the captive animals that is hidden or explained away.[125] Early work on learned helplessness in animals has shown that animals suffer from "behavioural despair" when repeated attempts to escape aversive conditions are unsuccessful.[126] They also experience neuroplasticity loss and long-term activation of parts of the brain that are adverse. The problem is not just solitary confinement, but massive overcrowding and under-stimulation or over-stimulation that leads to repetitive pacing, swaying, and other signs of captivity-induced madness.[127] The observation of animals in captivity, in the end, does not inculcate a conservationist mindset; the claim has no substantiation though it is oft repeated.[128] To the contrary, studies have demonstrated that people leave zoos with a human "superiority" mindset intact[129] even if they learn something about biodiversity.[130] The zoo is clearly a site where animal childhoods are always already compromised and the almost boundless level of control that humans legally exert over animals to instrumentalize them for human purposes is on display. What the typical zoo and aquaria-going human child and animals experience in this setting (and generally) is incommensurable.[131] But we also betray human children when we present the zoo as an innocuous space rather than expose it as one that teaches them that the ideal human subject denies their kinship with animals and learns to dominate them.

13.3.3 *Incarcerating Children for Their Own Good*

It also seems perverse to rationalize the incarceration of human children so that they can stay with their mothers (or other primary caregivers). How can being incarcerated be in their *best* interests when it is demonstrable that it is better for children and

[125] *Id.*; DESMOND, *supra* note 9, at 226–30, 234–36.

[126] ROGER D. PORSOLT, *Behavioral Despair: Past and Future*, in NEW DIRECTIONS IN AFFECTIVE DISORDERS 17, 17 (Bernard Lerer & Samuel Gershon eds., 1989); Martin E.P. Seligman, *Learned Helplessness*, 23 ANN. REV. MED. 407, 407–08 (1972). It bears highlighting that these results came from deadly and highly injurious forms of animal experimentation as described in these studies themselves.

[127] NEVILLE G. GREGORY, PHYSIOLOGY AND BEHAVIOUR OF ANIMAL SUFFERING 1, 39 (2004); Andrew Flack, *"In Sight, Insane": Animal Agency, Captivity and the Frozen Wilderness in the Late-Twentieth Century*, 22 ENV'T & HIST. 629, 637–38, 644, 646 (2016).

[128] Lori Marino, *Cetacean Captivity*, in THE ETHICS OF CAPTIVITY 22 (Lori Gruen ed., 2014).

[129] GRUEN, *supra* note 7, at 232–34.

[130] *Disposable Captives*, https://blog.oup.com/2014/04/disposable-captives-zoo-animals-philosophy/.

[131] Bryant, *supra* note 118, at 56–58.

their mothers to be out of a carceral environment, however socioeconomically compromised their home living situation might be?[132] Attachment theory tells us that human children suffer on multiple levels when separated from their primary caregivers.[133] But to imagine that attachment theorists would accept prison as an acceptable way to maintain family bonds, rather than return human children with their families to their communities where the family poses no risk to the child and can be supported with proper services, is a disingenuous and deeply flawed deployment of attachment theory.

13.4 CONCLUSION

The COVID-19 pandemic and the bans on public gatherings it has entailed gave many humans worldwide their first experience of lockdown, shelter in place, and of generally not being able to leave their homes for many weeks if not months. Even if they could leave, the closure of familiar places of learning, recreation, and business did not allow them much choice as to where to go and what to do. Although the privileged among us had our many digital devices as per usual, many media stories appeared, presumably meant for those securely resourced and at home but now without their regular range of mobility, as how not to get bored,[134] how to keep children entertained and stimulated,[135] and how generally to keep a positive mood and get through the experience.[136] Although doubtless a stressful experience for even those privileged by class, geographic location, and species, the reality is that we place captive animals and humans in something markedly worse and vulnerability-inducing than a COVID-19 lockdown every single day of their captive existence. What this chapter has shown is how the presence of the human child helps to obscure the chronic harms of the permanent lockdown sites our societies normalize as well as justifies their continued existence.

The social and legal remedy for zoos seems straightforward (which is not to say it will be easy to implement or that other social supports will not be needed for transitions to sanctuaries or other models of living for the former captive animals).

[132] Race & Stefanick, *supra* note 81, at 58.

[133] Richard A. Bryant et al., *Separation from Parents during Childhood Trauma Predicts Adult Attachment Security and Post-traumatic Stress Disorder*, 47 PSYCH. MED. 2028, 2028-29 (2017); VIVIEN PRIOR & DANYA GLASER, UNDERSTANDING ATTACHMENT AND ATTACHMENT DISORDERS: THEORY, EVIDENCE AND PRACTICE 15-18, 81 (2006).

[134] Heather R. Morgan, *15 Ways to Fight Boredom and Anxiety amidst the Coronavirus Pandemic*, FORBES (Mar. 17, 2020), https://www.forbes.com/sites/heathermorgan/2020/03/17/15-ways-to-fight-boredom-and-anxiety-amidst-the-coronavirus-pandemic/#47749d9615ef.

[135] Meg Roberts, *Here Are 8 Ways to Keep Your Kids Learning … and Entertained*, CBC NEWS (Apr. 24, 2020), https://www.cbc.ca/news/canada/newfoundland-labrador/8-ways-kids-learning-1.5537254.

[136] Sara Spary, *Feeling Overwhelmed? Top Tips for Staying Positive Online during the Coronavirus Crisis*, CNN (Mar. 19, 2020), https://www.cnn.com/2020/03/19/world/coronavirus-stay-positive-online-scli-intl-wellness/index.html.

As Pierce and Bekoff argue, the vast majority of the world's zoos should be shut down and technological exhibits should replace live animal ones in the remaining zoos that remain open and are well managed. They write: "If zoos are mainly for children (and, as the paying addendum, the parents), these interactive exhibits have the potential to be more fun and more educational than traditional zoo animal exhibits without the collateral damage of real animal lives . . . Zoos with live animals would become a thing of the past."[137] As for the captive breeding argument, zoo administrators themselves admit the limits of this argument given the increasing difficulty of introducing animals back into the wild and the loss of their natural habitat in any case.[138]

The answer to the harms that prison and detention centers occasion for children also behooves us to seek out alternative justice models and community-based alternatives to prison and detention while processing immigration claims.[139] If countries, like Canada, have signed and ratified the CRC, then they have committed themselves to upholding the CRC's championing of the best-interests-of-the-child test as the primary consideration involving all state decisions regarding children and their parents.[140] Given the literature showing both the harms to children in prison or detention as well as the harms if they are separated from their parents, particularly mothers, the answer here also seems straightforward: children and their mothers or other caregivers should not be incarcerated or detained.[141] Instead of bringing children into captivity to avoid separation, the mother or caregiver and child should remain together outside of captivity (where there is no safety risk to the child and older children able to decide for themselves wish to do so). The rights and present and future interests of the child in remaining with a loving mother or other caregiver must take priority over incarceration rationales. The funds used to support

[137] Pierce & Bekoff, *supra* note 33, at 46.

[138] The loss of natural habitat for wild animals, and the increasing human-animal contact that has occasioned through wildlife trade, consumption, and general living proximity, is itself a reason for the age of pandemics in which the whole world is now ensconced. Grant Lingel, *How to Prevent Future Pandemics: Fix the Broken Food System*, SENTIENT MEDIA (Apr. 27, 2020), https://sentientmedia.org/how-to-prevent-future-pandemics-fix-the-broken-food-system; Phoebe Weston, *"We Did It to Ourselves": Scientist Says Intrusion into Nature Led to Pandemic*, GUARDIAN (Apr. 25, 2020), https://www.theguardian.com/world/2020/apr/25/ourselves-scientist-says-human-intrusion-nature-pandemic-aoe.

[139] On the harms of incarceration for Race & Stefanick, *supra* note 81, at 58; JUSTIN MARCEAU, BEYOND CAGES: ANIMAL LAW AND CRIMINAL PUNISHMENT 35-37 (2019).

[140] GROS & SONG, *supra* note 59, at 37-38.

[141] Although not the focus of this present chapter, I would also argue that it is important to centre children's rights in remaining with their mothers and other parents in deportation proceedings that threaten to separate them. For a groundbreaking Supreme Court of Canada decision recognizing as much in 1999, *see* Baker v. Canada, 2 SCR 817 (1992). For a valuable critical contextualization of the judgment *see* CONSTANCE BACKHOUSE, *Fairness in Immigration: Baker, 1999*, *in* CLAIRE L'HEUREUX-DUBÉ: A LIFE 470 (2017).

incarceration and detention can now be redirected to the social services that will be required to implement alternative justice models and housing arrangements. These funds can also support the mother and her child(ren) in the community and mitigate vulnerabilities in communities in general which shape most adults',[142] particularly women's, pathways to prison.[143]

[142] MARCEAU, *supra* note 137, at 39-41.
[143] Race & Stefanick, *supra* note 81, at 45-50; Haney, *supra* note 71, at 121.

14

Bovine Lives and the Making of a Nineteenth-Century American Carceral Archipelago

Karen M. Morin

14.1 INTRODUCTION

Thousands of scholarly books and articles, films and documentaries, memoirs, biographies, illustrated weeklies, paintings and other artistic works, and museum artifacts and displays have depicted the history and geography of the nineteenth-century western American "cattle trails" and the small rural towns that sprang up at their termini.[1] This outsized body of American West literature and culture has collectively depicted bovine animals as an instrument, albeit an integral one, of cowboys, ranchers, cattle barons, and a multitude of other enterprising entrepreneurs who economically, politically, and culturally maneuvered control over the emerging livestock (beef) industry in the United States. From the classic John Hawkes 1948 Western film *Red River* to the more recent 2018 Coen brothers' *The Ballad of Buster Scruggs*, key sites of this emergent industry such as Abilene and Dodge City, Kansas, figure prominently, while the animals themselves appear only as figures on the landscape, without lives, experiences, or agency. In such Western films the animals are typically portrayed as either peacefully grazing in beautiful pastoral landscapes or wholly out of control and wildly stampeding in clouds of dust. Once captured within the Abilene or Dodge City "cow town" we find them obediently if anxiously being herded into stock pens or other controlling devices,

[1] For a couple of well-trod examples, *see, e.g.*, Robert R. Dykstra, The Cattle Towns (1968); Jimmy Skaggs, The Cattle-Trailing Industry (1973). Kathryn Gillespie, The Cow with Ear Tag #1389 (2018), offers an apt explanation about why referring to the animals under study here as "cattle" is problematical, as the term has etymological roots in the word chattel, meaning property, and these animals were more than mere property. While I cannot avoid use of the term "cattle" when referring to the many actors, practices, and processes that indeed treated and named them as property, I opt for the terms "bovine animals" or the more colloquial "cow" whenever possible (and regardless of gender and breeding history of the animals under discussion, which in many cases will not be known).

being made ready for shipment by railroad to slaughterhouses in Chicago and beyond.

My assessment of this body of work is that real animal lives and stories are nearly totally absent and remain to be studied and documented. My ultimate aim in this chapter is to begin to center these animals' experiences within the "carceral archipelago" of the cattle trails and towns into which they were forced, identifying some of the material, social, and psychological experiences and trauma of becoming an animalized commodity within the carceral practices and infrastructures of the emergent cattle industry. Studying these animal lives fundamentally involves understanding their gradual commodification – these formerly free-roaming lives were literally turned into money, "free for the taking," with virtually no official regulatory apparatus at the time guiding their capture, enclosure, movement, exploitation, and eventual death.

Animals had not heretofore figured in my field of carceral geography until my attempt to conceptualize a "trans-species carceral geography" in *Carceral Space, Prisoners and Animals* (2018), a book which considered factory farms, slaughterhouses, research labs, and zoos as prisons or prisonlike spaces, with those incarcerated within them as animalized prisoners. In the book I placed into parallel conversation the connected and entangled spatial, structural, operational, and embodied carceral practices and processes of a number of industrial sites and institutions in the present-day United States. I aimed to uncover the epistemic violence that pervades spaces of both human and nonhuman animal captivity, confinement, exploitation, and death, a violence that is normalized and neutralized in countless ways in everyday life. Naming spaces of animal captivity and confinement as prisonlike allowed insights into the way that "carceral logics"[2] extend throughout the prison-, agricultural-, and medical-industrial complexes in similar ways. These logics impact both human and nonhuman animals in consistent and detrimental ways via processes of animalization, racialization (particularly via anti-blackness), and criminalization.

My conceptual intervention in this chapter occurs at the interface of carceral geography, critical animal histories, and material culture. Such an intervention requires a new understanding or remapping of the historical and empirical context of the Texas-Oklahoma-Kansas cattle trails and towns as a "rural carceral archipelago" – an archipelago with a very specific rural spatiality.[3] Unlike the scores of works that have focused on these trails and towns from cultural, economic, political,

[2] On carceral logics from different disciplinary perspectives, see, for example, LORI GRUEN, THE ETHICS OF CAPTIVITY (2014); D. Moran, J. Turner & A. Schliehe, *Conceptualizing the Carceral in Carceral Geography*, 42 PROGRESS IN HUM. GEOGRAPHY 666, 666–86 (2018); JUSTIN MARCEAU, BEYOND CAGES: ANIMAL LAW AND CRIMINAL PUNISHMENT (2019).

[3] For a discussion of this archipelago as a specifically rural one, *see* Karen M. *Morin, Cattle Towns, Prison Towns: Historical Geographies of Rural Carceral Archipelagoes*, 47 HIST. GEOGRAPHY AT 141 (2019).

agricultural, or social lenses, I chart new ground by thinking about historical animal lives as those lived within carceral practices, operations, structures, and logics. Framing the carceral as a lived experience for bovine animals, as well as how this space developed as a specifically carceral archipelago, structures what follows in this chapter.

The illegal enclosure of the land by the emergent "cattle baron" class in the nineteenth century, enabled with new technologies such as barbed wire and governments lacking the interest, will, or ability to challenge it, offers important insights into how carceral logic works in place, and the impact of these practices and institutions on animals. Fencing became a primary mode of seizure of public land and resources for the benefit of individual ranching enterprises in the West. Despite the fact that land laws prohibited taking public lands, there were usually no repercussions for doing so. What then does it mean to think of the enclosure of public lands as illegal? The evolution of land law, with its ostensible legal remedies to resolve conflict among big-enterprise cattlemen and between smaller-scale farmers and ranchers, is an important component of carceral logics, particularly when considering who is helped by such legal remedies and who is not. Certain legal as well as extragovernment actions mediated human relations at the time, for example the "fence-cutting wars" emerged as one human resistance to carceral enclosure. But an equally important part of the story is about carceral practices mediating relations among humans (mostly men) and animals.

So rather than thinking of cattle trails and towns as sites of adventure, work, endurance, and romance for some humans, then, we can also focus on these places as sites of violence enacted upon animals – the capturing, transporting, fencing, corralling, branding, ear-marking, whipping, and shipping of animals as commodities for distant markets. What was it like for the animals to be "driven" quickly by workers (cowboys) who were themselves laboring under difficult circumstances? How did the cattle experience the new technologies such as wire fencing? What forms of bodily modification and appropriation were the animals subjected to – for example, the brutality of branding, whipping, and harnessing that marked them as property? What were the physical, emotional, and psychological implications of existing as beings with no legal standing, outside of the informal claims made by cattle barons and others? Any "laws" with oversight to the emergent cattle industry related only to access and control over land and water, not treatment of animals. No ostensible "protections" for farmed or ranched animals would appear in the United States until well into the twentieth century, and these to an extremely restricted degree. Even today, the only law that governs treatment of farm animals is the Humane Slaughter Act of 1958.

In this work I focus on the period prior to extensive railroad advancement onto the Great Plains and West and shipment via train of live animals or carcasses to slaughterhouses beyond – a period with practices that have received much needed and important scholarly attention.[4] This project requires a creative methodological engagement with historical sources that offer insights into animals' lived experiences and thus the foundational, violent building blocks of the beef industry.[5]

14.2 THE COLONIAL CARCERAL ARCHIPELAGO: LAND AND LAW

In her *Creatures of Empire* (2004), Virginia Anderson details the important, agenic role of farm animals – especially cows and horses – in the North American colonial project. Anderson argues that animals were one of two "immigrant groups," human and nonhuman, who were "central to the plot" of colonization. Though highly mobile under a free-range style of animal husbandry – the animals foraged and fed themselves, found their own shelter, transported themselves to new areas, and cared for their young – they not only altered whole ecosystems but were key to English colonists' land claims and the "cause of permanence."[6] Though they required little human labor, these animals required vast acreages for foraging – five-to-twenty acres per animal[7] – which quickly led to overgrazing, moving on to new lands, and ultimately complete appropriation and displacement of indigenous land and peoples (the carceral effect writ large). As such the animals functioned as what Specht calls a "technology" or "biotechnology" of conquest.[8] While authors such as Anderson focus primarily on the eastern colonies, similar colonial processes and increasing land acquisitions were in play in western cattle enterprises as well, if on a remarkably larger scale than the small-scale farming enterprises in the East.

Southern Texas as the epicenter of US cattle ranching and origin point of the cattle trails dates to the Spanish colonial period. The first bovine animals were shipped to North America by Spanish explorers and conquistadors in the fifteenth and sixteenth centuries. Fast forward to the last quarter of the eighteenth century, and Franciscan clergy had established more than fifty missions in what is now Texas, each with their own small herds. After Mexican independence in 1821 most clergymen refused loyalty to the Mexican government and abandoned their missions, with their animals free to run loose, allowing wild herds to flourish. Estimates are that

[4] Among many examples, *see, e.g.*, JEREMY RIFKIN, BEYOND BEEF: THE RISE AND FALL OF THE CATTLE CULTURE (1992); JEREMY D.A. PACYGA, SLAUGHTERHOUSE: CHICAGO'S UNION STOCK YARD AND THE WORLD IT MADE (2015).

[5] Among those scholars who offer models, *see* Erica Fudge, *What Was It Like to Be a Cow: History and Animal Studies*, in THE OXFORD HANDBOOK OF ANIMAL STUDIES 258, 258–78 (Linda Kalof ed., 2017); GILLESPIE, *supra* note 1; SHARON WILCOX & STEPHANIE RUTHERFORD, EDS., HIST. ANIMAL GEOGRAPHIES (2018).

[6] VIRGINIA ANDERSON, CREATURES OF EMPIRE 3–10 (2004).

[7] MAUREEN OGLE, IN MEAT WE TRUST: AN UNEXPECTED HISTORY OF CARNIVORE AMERICA 4–5 (2013).

[8] Joshua Specht, *The Rise, Fall, and Rebirth of the Texas Longhorn: An Evolutionary History*, 21 ENV. HIST. 343, 343–63 (2016).

100,000 bovine animals roamed Texas by 1830. Three decades later, on the eve of the Civil War, that number had increased to an estimated 3.5–5 million.[9]

The history of grazing "rights" on western land tells us a great deal about the evolution of the carceral landscape under study here, and can also tell us a great deal about the experiences of animals ensnared within it. In the boom years of the 1870s and 1880s, the cattle barons enjoyed "near hegemony" over western public lands by declaring a simple right of sovereignty. An informal code of entitlement, range rights if you will, was established if a rancher could claim to be the first to appropriate a local stream. The aspiring cattle grazer could, by claiming the water supply, control the surrounding terrain. Thus, the first step in consolidating power over the herds was in gaining control over grazing land – grass for food – and water. Richard White describes cattlemen as "the most prone to violence of any economic interest group in the West," with their predilection for violence "largely result[ing] from the tenuousness of their own legal claims to the land."[10] Legal ownership of the land was secondary to simply gaining access to it, and ranchers employed various means to graze animals on land to which they had no legal title. Most conflicts over land and grazing rights related to attempts to maintain an illegal monopoly on public-domain lands, and the ranchers' preference was to physically drive out the competition rather than fight them in courts.

A number of scholars have shown how the "Wild West" get-rich schemes of turning public land and other resources into private ownership was largely unregulated, and cattlemen sought control over vast acreages mostly by simply claiming them, as well as through manipulation of federal law such as the Homestead Act of 1862. Land fraud of various flavors was used to create large blocks of real estate under a single title, and involved an intersection of war widows, children, and family members working together with land agents and local politicians. In the mid-nineteenth century, Texas was particularly ripe for land schemes due to overlapping and contested Mexican, Texan, and US sovereignty claims, but so were numerous other locations throughout the Plains and West. On such illegally acquired land, animals could be fed for free, guaranteeing an enormous profit margin at the point of sale north. Thus, part and parcel of the American colonial project was this type of land acquisition – the process of turning the public domain into private property – yet the General Land Office, a Bureau under the Secretary of the Treasury, was inefficient and ill-equipped to handle the highly complex machinations of surveying, selling, and registering of public lands. This was particularly the case when prior appropriation or "getting there first" bumped up against the complexity and overlapping nature of the 375 land laws passed by Congress from

9 *See* Rifkin, *supra* note 4, at 68–70; Richard White, "It's Your Misfortune and None of My Own": A History of the American West 220–25 (1991); Paul F. Starrs, Let the Cowboy Ride: Cattle Ranching in the American West (1998).

10 White, *supra* note 9, at 344–45.

1789 to 1834 – laws adjusting the size of lots for sale, shifting the price per acre, altering the requirements for payment, and granting rights of preemption in specific regions.[11] As Limerick argued, "first arrival" made the distinction between legitimate acquisition and theft a fine one. In both cases, the act was similar – one simply appropriated something for one's own use – but, by a sometimes-subtle difference of timing, one act was honored and protected by law, and the other was punished. This would provide a basis for the carceral logic of the time and place.

As the railroads began to extend and connect to rural outposts in the Plains states, entrepreneurs in the new cow towns such as Abilene, Kansas, sought out Texas livestock trails to reach them, benefiting greatly from the new trade. The most-well-known of the western cattle trails ran from Texas northward to the state of Kansas, as herders drove millions of cows north from the mid-nineteenth century through the 1880s. From 1867 until 1871, the 1,000-mile-long Chisholm Trail was the main livestock trail from Texas, a trail that ran from San Antonio to Fort Worth, Texas, through Oklahoma and ended at Abilene.[12] An individual cowboy would oversee the movement of 245–350 animals, and they collectively drove 600,000–700,000 of them north from Texas during 1871 alone, all eventually bound for abattoirs in St. Louis and Chicago. These animals generally covered between ten and twelve miles per day on their three-month trek north to the rail link, becoming more "trail broke" as days and weeks wore on and thus becoming "easier to handle" – or to put another way, less able to resist their circumstances. Stock breeding and domestication always have the effect of "breaking" animals and thus reducing their potential for resisting their conditions, even if they also then appear to be colluding with or somehow collaborating with their oppressors.[13] In the case of the cattle trails, as cowboys needed to minimize the weight loss of their herds, they moved them slowly, pasturing them along the way.

They arrived at sites such as Abilene that were still relatively unpeopled, well watered, and offered plentiful grass for the incoming herds. The geography and carceral infrastructures that developed in Abilene and other towns would reflect their central nodal function in the developing cattle beef industry. These also collectively constituted what I call a colonial "carceral archipelago" of cattle trails and cattle towns. In using that term I am borrowing from Foucault's *Discipline and Punish* (1978), wherein he argued that this island concept can be applied to a set of institutions, surveillance systems, and technologies that "discipline" and exert power

[11] Patricia Nelson Limerick, Legacy of Conquest: The Unbroken Past of the American West 59–72 (1987); White, *supra* note 9, at 223.

[12] Wayne Ludwig, The Old Chisholm Trail: From Cow Path to Tourist Stop (2018).

[13] David Lambert, *Runaways and Strays: Rethinking (Non)human Agency in Caribbean Slave Societies*, *in* Hist. Animal Geographies 185, 185–89 (Sharon Wilcox & Stephanie Rutherford eds., 2018); Fudge, *supra* note 5; William Cronon, Nature's Metropolis: Chicago and the Great West 217–24 (1991).

and control over populations and indeed whole societies in a spatially ordered and universalizing way.[14]

Importantly again, though, the Texas longhorns of the emergent beef industry were nearly wild, and thus their capture, movement, and enclosure, by fencing and other means, was an important piece of this historical carceral logic. At the time, acquiring physical control over herds was more efficacious for the cattlemen and cattle barons than seeking legal control over them. Those who were most successful at turning these animal lives into personal property simply rounded them up, claimed them, branded them, and enclosed them. Sometimes whole herds would be collected through rustling or "mavericking" (hunting and branding wild calves).[15] As the herds were gradually declared property of individual humans and commodities for capital accumulation, not only their status but their lives and experiences dramatically changed. While the animals' status as property, much discussed among animal scholars, had a violent impact on their lives, it does not explain all the violence.[16] Violence toward animals occurs whether they are "owned" or not. Having particular status within the law would not have likely changed much about their treatment; despite certain protections for certain animals within the law, then and now, the lack of bovine animals' legal "standing" simply made it easier to claim, buy, sell, and kill them.

14.3 THE CARCERAL INFRASTRUCTURE AND TECHNOLOGICAL DEVELOPMENTS

Infrastructural and technological developments at towns such as Abilene where bovine animals were corralled and then loaded onto railroad cars at the termini of the cattle trails also represent a singularly important carceral phenomenon of the nineteenth-century United States Innovations in transportation, specifically, the "cattle car" (and by 1869, the refrigerated car that hauled dead animal carcasses) was one of the most important technological developments that impacted and

[14] Michel Foucault, Discipline and Punish: The Birth of the Prison (1978). As I discuss in Karen M. Morin, Carceral Space, Prisoners and Animals 11–12 (2018), Foucault's theorizing of this universality of the carceral can and has been challenged. If everything and everywhere is carceral, then the concept becomes evacuated of meaning and loses its potential for helping us understand how a very specific carceral logic extends only or mainly to certain bodies and certain populations – and not to others – incapacitating and disposing of them in particular kinds of ways and in particular kinds of spaces. Carceral sites and institutions do share a particular spatiality encompassing animalized bodies – creating, in the case argued here, one particular carceral archipelago of cattle trails and cattle towns that diffused in specific ways throughout the rural American landscape in the nineteenth century.

[15] Reviel Netz, Barbed Wire: An Ecology of Modernity 12, 20 (2004).

[16] For example, *see* Gary L. Francione, *Animals – Property or Persons?* in Animal Rights: Current Debates and New Directions 108–42 (Cass R. Sunstein & Martha C. Nussbaum eds., 2004); *see, e.g.*, Steven M Wise, Rattling the Cage: Toward Legal Rights for Animals (2000); Dinesh J. Wadiwel, The War against Animals (2015).

increased the trade in bovine animals, and indeed, that structured so much of their lived experience. It was primarily British companies that played a major role in developing the transcontinental railroad in the 1870s and 1880s – the foreign "cattle barons" – and who eventually also shipped refrigerated cow carcasses to Britain in ocean steamers. Railroad development actually included an array of ancillary infrastructural developments in the cow towns that impacted animal lives – railroad stations with telegraph facilities, supervisory personnel, and company-owned cow pens and stockyards.

One of the earliest and most successful Kansas entrepreneurs to link the cattle trails with the railroad, the dealer and town promotor Joseph McCoy built stock pens near the rail depot on 250 acres of land in Abilene, Kansas, to hold cows awaiting shipment north on the Kansas Pacific Railroad. The first twenty-car shipment of cows from Abilene to Chicago was in September of 1867. McCoy convinced the railroad to construct a rail siding for a cow pen at the Abilene depot, and then pay him a commission on every carload of animals shipped. This north-south cattle complex expanded in the 1870s, as the demand for beef, tallow, and hides greatly expanded amid postwar prosperity.[17]

Concomitantly, one of the most significant instruments of violence and spatial control within the emergent bovine and other livestock industry of the time was the revolutionary invention of wire fencing, which facilitated the enclosure of public pasture land for private use. The traditional wooden fence of the East or Europe would not be feasible in a landscape lacking trees for lumber; large-scale fencing only became possible in this region with the invention of barbed wire. Netz argues for the critical importance of examination of this technology across species lines – and in the case of barbed wire, the violent enclosure and control of bovine animals during colonization of the American West.[18]

Joseph Glidden patented barbed wire in 1874 and opened a small manufacturing plant in DeKalb, Illinois, for its production, with large-scale production and sale eventually located to Washburn and Moen Manufacturing in Worcester, Massachusetts. More than 350 barbed wire patents were issued between 1875 and

[17] Ogle, *supra* note 7, at 18–19; Skaggs, *supra* note 1, at 73–77; Claire Strom, Making Catfish Bait out of Government Boys: The Fight against Cattle Ticks and the Transformation of the Yeoman South (2010); Joshua Specht, Red Meat Republic: A Hoof-to-Table History of How Beef Changed America 153–60 (2019). J. Specht also provides a detailed portrait of another of the five main Kansas cow towns, Ellsworth, Kansas, in his article, Joshua Specht, *For the Future in the Distance: Cattle Trailing, Social Conflict, and the Development of Ellsworth, Kansas*, 40 Kan. Hist.: J. Central Plains 104, 104–19.

[18] Netz, *supra* note 15, at 29, after Cronon, *supra* note 13, argues that because wooden posts were required to hold the barbed wire in place, the new fences actually increased demand for timber from the North. Many books have been written about the history and uses of barbed wire; for example *see also*, *e.g.*, Lyn Ellen Bennett & Scott Abbot, The Perfect Fence: Untangling the Meanings of Barbed Wire (2017); Olivier Razac, Barbed Wire: A Political History (2002); Joanne S. Liu, Barbed Wire: The Fence That Changed the West (2009).

1890, although it was the Glidden patent that came to monopolize the market (and indeed, is the fence still in use today). The ideal barbed wire purportedly prevented injury to animals – or at least purportedly did not cause open wounds that would become infected – and aimed to increase a wire's visibility to humans and animals alike (including horses). Marketing of the wire fence was an important piece of advancing this carceral technology, as were improvements in iron and steel production. Glidden's patent (no. 157,124) is an interesting document of torture unto itself,[19] declaring that unlike other wires that seriously harmed animals, "the double, machine-twisted stand of galvanized steel wire, carrying four-pointed steel barbs … prick[s] smartly on contact and warning, but not wounding the animal." This "perfect fence … borrowed from nature the principle of the sharp pricking thorn thus appealing to the sense of pain and danger that resides in the skin of the farm animal." Many of the proposed wires caused too much injury and loss of animals; competition among wire makers thus focused on loss of one's property value rather than concern for animal welfare or suffering. The barbs were intended to domesticate or "retame" by shock an entire breed of animals through such immediate painful impact,[20] but also ultimately served as an efficient biotechnology through which enclosed animals could be more easily bred, fed, and controlled.

One rather infamous early adopter in the Texas Panhandle, Charles Goodnight, fenced in over 3 million acres of public range with illegal fences while others followed suit, fencing land over which they had no legal claim.[21] Also in the Texas Panhandle, the Scottish-backed XIT ranch pursued its own 3 million acre fencing project, operating on a grant from the state with an estimated 6,000 miles of fence. Fencing provided greater control over animals for ranchers who had possession, if not the title, to large sections of land.

Such fraudulent or at best questionable fencing activities led to what has been called the "Fence Cutting Wars" in the early 1880s, which pitted such large cattle companies that had illegally fenced thousands of acres of public lands against the smaller scale "open range" ranchers – many of whom were former cowboys trying to eke a living from ranching – as well as pitting farmers against ranchers, the latter of whom argued that farmers should fence their crops to protect them from free-grazing animals. Widespread fence cutting ensued by the small-scale ranchers and farmers in 1883–84, with more than half of Texas counties reporting fence cutting and pasture burning, and episodes of violence including gunfights and deaths in places like Dodge City, Kansas. Local, state, and federal governments attempted to legislatively prevent fencing of public land. Many small farmers and ranchers wrote

[19] Pamphlet of Washburn and Moen Manufacturing Glidden Patent, *in* NAT'L COWBOY HALL OF FAME & W. HERITAGE MUSEUM, DONALD C. & ELIZABETH M. DICKINSON RESEARCH CENTER.

[20] NETZ, *supra* note 15, at 38.

[21] RIFKIN, *supra* note 4, at 101–13; WHITE, *supra* note 9, at 222, 345; SPECHT, *supra* note 17, at 68, 76.

to the Secretary of the Interior angered by "unauthorized fencing" by cattlemen, with their letters presented to Congress in 1884. The letters explicate the extent of large-scale and fraudulent inclosures [*sic*] of public lands by stockmen, including entire counties in Kansas. As the then–Secretary of the Interior H. M. Teller wrote to Congress,

> The cases mentioned in the reports and correspondence herewith submitted are to be regarded merely as indicative of the situation. I am satisfied from the information received that the practice of illegally inclosing the public lands is extensive throughout the grazing regions, and that many millions of acres are thus inclosed and are now being so inclosed to the exclusion of the stock of all others than the fence owners, and to the prevention of settlements and the obstruction of public travel and intercourse.[22]

The US Congress finally passed a law in 1885 designed to prosecute anyone who attempted to fence public land for private use. The large British and American cattle companies suffered little repercussion from such legislation, however, and continued large-scale fencing unabated through manipulation of the Homestead Act (1862), the Timber Culture Act (1873), and the Desert Land Act (1887) throughout the Great Plains and West, which awarded land based ostensibly on building construction, planting trees, or installing irrigation (respectively), or they purchased land abutting the railroads and preempted the public lands next to them. Estimates are that up to 7.3 million acres of public land was fraudulently expropriated by cattle companies in this way in the 1870s and 1880s. The endgame of this system of "imprisonment" of cows via fences, of course, legally or illegally, was their eventual death in the northern slaughterhouses.[23]

14.4 CENTERING ANIMAL EXPERIENCES IN THE AMERICAN CARCERAL ARCHIPELAGO

Bovine animal experiences that began with their forced migration to North America in slings on Spanish sailing ships in the fifteenth and sixteenth centuries and ended with their boarding railroad cars bound for Chicago abattoirs in the nineteenth represent a singularly poignant historical example of how violence toward nonhuman animals with attendant pain and suffering is a basic ingredient – and

[22] Letter from the Secretary of the Interior, H.M. Teller, to the General Land Office, *in* NAT'L COWBOY HALL OF FAME & W. HERITAGE MUSEUM, DONALD C. & ELIZABETH M. DICKINSON RESEARCH CENTER.

[23] RIFKIN, *supra* note 4, at 104; NETZ, *supra* note 15, at 33 compares the "cow business" driving out the "bison business," writing that the "comparison is meaningful: in a sense, cows were driven off the land just as surely as the bison had been. The only difference was that whereas the bison were killed, the cows were imprisoned, in an Archipelago Ranch, so to speak, strewn across the plains." Allow me to add that these cows, too, were killed, after their imprisonment.

outcome – of industries whose design is based on carceral logic.[24] Recent scholarship in critical animal studies offers helpful understandings of the lived experiences of captive animals on farms, in zoos, in research labs, and in other carceral spaces within which they undergo harmful processes and practices. Gillespie's *The Cow with Ear Tag #1389* (2018) offers an example of "witnessing" bovine social, emotional, and psychological responses to a number of carceral settings such as auction yards and dairy farms, as well as sites of refuge. But how might one engage such affective, visceral knowing in a historical context? A different or more expansive approach is needed to understand the experiences of historical animals, those long dead and no longer able to be directly "witnessed." If we consider bovine animals as shapers of histories and geographies as Anderson suggests, we must entertain the notion of them as historical agents with lives, kinship relations, emotions, preferences, interests, and agency along with those of their human captors. Thus, an important question revolves around how to access animal experiences to try to understand the worlds – albeit colonial carceral worlds – that they cocreated with their human captors and for themselves. Many scholars of animal histories and historical geographies have demonstrated that this can be done and have modeled useful approaches.[25]

Colonial and postcolonial scholars have taught us that the experiences of those heretofore silenced in the historical record or archive can be made accessible – indeed must be made accessible – and in much the same way that we understand the historical experience of any other "other" whose lives and stories were represented in archival, textual, photographic, and so forth, sources by someone else. Erica Fudge reminds us that past subjectivities, human and nonhuman, have always been difficult to access – that the archive is always already fraught as a representational tool. Both humans and nonhumans have been shaped by an archive not of their own making. As Fudge observes, humans can write anything about animals, whether "true" or "false," but this applies to *all history* and any being written about: "these are problems of history in general and not specifically about the history of animals."[26] It is important to keep in mind meanwhile that animal cultures, identities, experiences, and so on are not simply a function of species habits and characteristics: the spaces and places of their experiences, in the case here, within carceral contexts, is equally important. Different environments or communities will

[24] Of course, this applies to human animals as well, particularly those ensnared within the Prison Industrial Complex, numbering 6–7 million people in the United States today (including those on probation or parole).

[25] *See* Martha Few & Zeb Tortorici, eds., Centering Animals in Latin American History (2013); Erica Fudge, A *Left-Handed Blow: Writing the History of Animals*, *in* Representing Animals 1, 1–18 (Nigel Rothfels ed., 2002); Fudge, *supra* note 5; Susan Nance, ed., Hist. Animal 99, 101–5, 110 (2015).

[26] Fudge, *supra* note 25; Fudge, *supra* note 5, at 261.

produce different kinds of animals and animal experiences and behaviors.[27] As always though, decentering our human, anthropocentric interpretations of animal perspectives and experience, of carceral or any other spaces, remains our collective challenge.[28]

Obviously, animals express themselves. But as Buller argues, though we may not "share language with non-humans we do share embodied life and movement and, in doing so, different – yet both biologically and socially related – ways of inhabiting the world."[29] But can we even imagine bovine animals creating life-worlds for themselves in nineteenth century western trails and towns? Royle[30] argues that such animals have been so thoroughly objectified that to think of them as having any sort of *life* at all is almost unthinkable. What would it mean to discover historical bovine subjectivity – that of beings under intense external human control accompanied nonetheless by the everyday experiences of walking or running across pastures and streams, eating, resting, playing, fighting, caring for one another, procreating, and so on. The Finnish authors and editors of *History according to Cattle* (2015) offer a most provocative attempt to try to capture this embodied way of inhabiting the world for bovine animals, via the Museum of the History of Cattle exhibitions. To these authors, for example, the "cattle tongue is not a written language. In cattle culture, the tongue is a means of touching others." Installations feature partial, blurry, shadowy images of light, objects, and landscape as well as intensely vibrant magnified images of other objects within close range such as "companion species" dress patterns and the veins on a leaf, all imaginings of bovine perspective.[31]

Historians have typically relied on narrative mechanisms to understand animal pasts. Many refer to animals in historical narratives as "absent presences" – presences in the archive albeit ones who do not speak or control the narrative. Archival documentary sources and narratives produced by humans provide one access point to these lives – films, paintings, photographs, memoirs – even if they offer only traces of historical animals' lived experiences. A poignant example we might easily return to is one seemingly innocuous but unforgettable scene in the Western film *Red River*, whose depiction of branding restrained animals – searing hot irons onto sizzling animal flesh – is gruesome in its realistic detail. And yet, the overall effect of this filming is wholly artificial and sanitized for a meat-eating postwar American

[27] Fudge, *supra* note 5; SUSAN NANCE, ENTERTAINING ELEPHANTS: ANIMAL AGENCY AND THE BUSINESS OF THE AMERICAN CIRCUS 12–13 (2013).

[28] Fiona Probyn-Rapsey, *Anthropocentrism*, *in* CRITICAL TERMS FOR ANIMAL STUDIES 47, 47–63 (Lori Gruen ed., 2018).

[29] Henry Buller, *Animal Geographies II: Methods*, 39 PROGRESS HUM. GEOGRAPHY 374, 378 (2015).

[30] Camilla Royle, *Shaking the Ground: Histories of Earthworms from Darwin to Niche Construction*, *in* HIST. ANIMAL GEOGRAPHIES 37, 37–50 (Sharon Wilcox & Stephanie Rutherford eds., 2018); *see also* ANIMAL SPACES, BEASTLY PLACES: NEW GEOGRAPHIES OF HUMAN-ANIMAL RELATIONS 6–14 (Chris Philo & Chris Wilbert eds., 2000).

[31] LAURA GUSTAFSSON & TERIKE HAAPOJA, EDS., HISTORY ACCORDING TO CATTLE 7 (2015).

audience; the real, live animals undergoing an undoubtedly painful procedure lie still and are portrayed as eliciting no reaction at all. When examining such representations we must think seriously about the extent to which human ideas about bovine animals were "invented" by certain actors whose purpose was to produce certain kinds of bodies and behaviors upon which to profit.

The second access point to past animal lives are historical-material artifacts that can speak to the kinds of bodily management practices and tools that cowboys and ranchers employed to capture and commodify animal lives – for example carceral apparatuses and practices such as barbed wire, stock pens, branding irons, and dehorning tools. Wilcox and Rutherford[32] observe that histories and memories are passed down through generations of animals in ways that humans cannot fathom. For scholars attempting to materially reconstruct past animal lives, though, little remains that testifies to these prior existences. Individual lives are erased by chemical, biological, and physical processes acting upon the landscape that wipe away identifiable traces, tracks, and remains. Cox illustrates how material objects in the archive, in her case, veterinary archives, are useful in writing the history of animals.[33] Cox interestingly found that such objects and instruments contained traces of fur, skin, and blood of real, deceased animals that can help formulate theories about emotional and psychological stress. These insights should prompt us to recategorize objects such as fences, branding irons, ropes, whips, and a myriad of restraining devices as important and relevant archival evidence, to human-animal interaction as well as animal-to-animal experience.

Examining samples of such instruments and artefacts of torture at museums such as at the National Cowboy Hall of Fame and Western Heritage Museum in Oklahoma City, alongside "cinematographical" tricks of film production such as that of *Red River* against other photographic and artistic images of carceral practices, can help us begin to triangulate important understandings of animals' lived experiences. As Fudge writes, "material and rhetorical are linked in their context, and the history that recognizes this can, in turn, force a reassessment of the material through its analysis of the rhetorical strategies of the written record."[34]

The Barbed Wire Study Collection located at the National Cowboy Hall of Fame museum offers a useful entreé into instruments of animal control and dominance – by the sheer volume of variously pointed and strung iron and steel devices – as well as evidence of how an individual might experience their use. As Netz writes, the "history of barbed wire took place precisely at the level of the flesh ... the tool was created to control animals by inflicting pain on them ... the simple and unchanging equation of flesh and iron."[35] On display are 1,300 strands of barbed wire, among a

[32] WILCOX & RUTHERFORD, *supra* note 5, at 2.

[33] *See* Lisa Cox, *Finding Animals in History: Veterinary Artifacts and the Use of Material History*, *in* HIST. ANIMAL 99, 101–5, 110 (Susan Nance ed., 2015).

[34] Fudge, *supra* note 25, at 11.

[35] NETZ, *supra* note 15, at xiii–xiv.

collection of 8,000 strands, claimed to be the largest such collection in the world. The text accompanying this well-maintained and catalogued collection primarily emphasizes "advancements" in wire technology, belying the pain and trauma inflicted by its samples. Entanglements in wires, suffering open wounds derived from them (which led to insect infestation), and becoming stopped and trapped by fencing have been well documented by human observers. White details eyewitness accounts of impacts of wire fencing during dangerous weather events such as droughts and blizzards. One poignant example involved animals encountering and being stuck by the "drift fences" that the Texas Panhandle Cattlemen's Association, working with large cattle companies in northern Texas, erected in the 1880s, intended to control the number of animals traveling south. Winter blizzards drove tens of thousands of animals south but the "drift fences" became "death traps" for perhaps two-thirds, who ran into them, piled up against them, and died by freezing or starving.[36]

The National Cowboy Hall of Fame museum also features a Branding Exhibition, a special collection of branding irons and instruments used (and still used) to differentiate property claims made by various cattlemen by marking cow flesh with a hot, heavy iron poker, typically a symbol about four inches in height. While the collection primarily is focused on the historical evolution of brands and the various "styles" and symbols used by cattlemen, these instruments and accompanying wall text also offer a unique and indispensable insight into the painful procedure of burning a mark onto cow flesh. The "stamp irons," some now corroded with age, were used to apply a mark in one impression. Wall text accompanying the irons recounts the branding process:

> After calves were rounded up they were branded with the same brands and ear marks as their mothers … One man sat behind the calf and pulled the upper hind leg back onto his lap as he shoved the lower hind leg forward with his foot, hooking the calf's leg with his boot heel. Another man placed his knee on the calf's head and held the upper foreleg while removing the rope from its neck… The hot iron burned the hair and seared the hide deep enough to form a scab, which later peeled off to leave a scar where no hair would grow back … [Eventually] branding cattle in corrals and chutes reduced the number of men needed for the job. The modern use of squeeze chutes made branding and doctoring chores even easier … While calves are held for branding, other chores like castration, vaccination, and worming are usually done at the same time.

As human witnesses have recounted,[37] during this gruesome process "there is an acrid odor, strong, repulsive … [the animal] will go BAWR-R-R-R, its eyes will bulge alarmingly, its mouth will slaver, and its nose will snort."

[36] White, *supra* note 9, at 223–24.

[37] Netz, *supra* note 15, at 19 (quoting Arnold and Hale, western authors writing in 1940); Anderson, *supra* note 6, at 128–29, discusses related process of making earmarks or simply cutting off a branded animal's ears.

Both the barbed wire and branding iron museum artifacts force us to consider more nonrepresentational, emotional, affective approaches to the historical study of animal suffering: "visceral knowing."

14.5 CONCLUDING COMMENT

The nineteenth-century American cattle trails and cattle towns remain an integral piece of American legend and mythology, and though many scholars have made valuable interventions into the "reality" of the political, economic, environmental, and cultural factors that constituted the emergent cattle beef industry, much remains to be studied about animal experience in this story. It is a story of lived animal experiences of carceral spaces, developed within and facilitated by a range of legal or extralegal, technological, and political-economic carceral apparatuses. Certainly use of instruments of torture such as wire fencing and branding have not abated – although perhaps today's cows are tattooed with identification numbers on their ears or lips or have computer chips inserted under their skin, and owners of the mass production of meat processing have become the twenty-first-century version of the cattle baron. But through study of available historical, especially material cultural, sources and evidence these lives ensnared within an American carceral archipelago can be understood and appreciated anew.

15

Animals in Prison

Collateral Damage and Commodities of "Rehabilitation"

Kelly Struthers Montford

15.1 INTRODUCTION

On November 25, 2019, the president of the United States signed the bipartisan Preventing Animal Cruelty and Torture Act (PACT). Given the bill was unanimously supported by both the House of Representatives and the Senate, it would seem incarceration is becoming the preferred solution to specific forms of abuse against certain animals. Prior to PACT, there was no US federal *felony* law prohibiting animal cruelty. PACT does "not apply to people who slaughter animals for food or to those who hunt, trap and fish," nor does it apply to non-human animals threatening human life or property, subject to scientific experimentation, or under veterinary care.[1] Instead, it makes a federal crime the "crushing, burning, drowning, suffocating, impaling or sexual exploitation" of animals that would fall outside of state legal jurisdiction.[2] This broadens previous federal legislation prohibiting the sale of "crush videos" by criminalizing not just the sale but the actions these videos capture. It has been celebrated by animal protectionists as a reflection of "American values" and as a mechanism that will enhance the investigatory power of animal protection groups to "truly bring justice for the animals . . . by ensur[ing] some of the most horrific acts of animal cruelty are prosecuted to the fullest extent of the law."[3]

If convicted under PACT, offenders can be fined or sentenced to a maximum of seven years in prison. Animal cruelty legislation in all fifty US states includes felony provisions. While what constitutes a "felony" varies across states, it often refers to

1 Laura M. Holson, *Animal Cruelty Moves One Step Closer to Being a Federal Crime*, N.Y. Times (Nov. 6, 2019), https://www.nytimes.com/2019/11/06/us/politics/animal-cruelty-pact-bill.html.

2 Federal jurisdiction is applicable in instances of interstate commerce and/or events occurring in locations under US territorial jurisdiction. *See also Laws that Protect Animals*, Animal Legal Defense Fund (2021), https://aldf.org/article/laws-that-protect-animals/.

3 Mihir Zaveri, *President Trump Signs Federal Animal Cruelty Bill into Law*, N.Y. Times (Nov. 25, 2019), https://www.nytimes.com/2019/11/25/us/politics/trump-animal-cruelty-bill.html.

sentences of incarceration that are more than twelve months and that can be served at either state or federal institutions. PACT is meant to allow for the prosecution of cases not captured by state law, such as those involving multiple state jurisdictions or occurring on federal grounds. The establishment of PACT could also result in more resources for the investigation and prosecution of violence against animals, thereby adding to available laws that drive incarceration. Animal protection groups have been instrumental in lobbying for the institution of new animal cruelty legislation and the strengthening of extant law.[4] Like the laws themselves, the supposed "justice"/"benefit" achieved would be almost explicitly limited to companion animals. As I argue in this chapter, these laws will not benefit animals writ large. Instead, such laws will bolster the intertwined logics of race and species that underpin the caging and incarceration of those categorized as sub-/non-humans.

In the Americas, race and species are inseparable. Indigenous theorists, Black studies scholars, and political theorists have argued that the making of race and animality have been integral to colonialism and the transatlantic slave trade.[5] This does not mean that we ought to analogize between the experiences of racialized individuals and non-human animals, but to instead "focus on interspecies connectedness" as "the history of the animal and the Black in the black Atlantic is connected, rather than simply comparable."[6] In this sense, race is "a permanent presence inextricably part of the animal question."[7] In her work on race and animality, Claire Jean Kim shows that taxonomies of life rely on the subjugation of animality and blackness.[8] It is upon this mutual subjugation that "the human" is established. For Kim, "blackness is a species construct (meaning 'in proximity to the animal'), and animalness is a racial construct (meaning 'in proximity to the Black'), and the two are dynamically interconstituted *all the way down*."[9] A clean separation between race and species is, according to Kim, impossible because their mutual constitution is foundational to how "the human" is ontologized: "the anti-black social order that props up the 'human' is also a zoological order, or what we might call *a zoologo-racial order*."[10]

[4] *See* Tené Johnson, *House and Senate Pass Bill Making Animal Cruelty a Federal Offense*, Journal of Law and Social Problems (Nov. 20, 2019), http://jlsp.law.columbia.edu/2019/11/20/house-unanimously-passes-bill-making-animal-cruelty-a-federal-offense/; Animal Legal Defense Fund, *supra* note 2.

[5] *See* Aph Ko, Racism as Zoological Witchcraft: A Guide to Getting Out (2019); Bénédicte Boisseron, Afro-Dog: Blackness and the Animal Question (2018); Claire Jean Kim, Dangerous Crossings: Race, Species, and Nature in a Multicultural Age (2015); Colin Dayan, The Law Is a White Dog: How Legal Rituals Make and Unmake Persons (2013).

[6] Boisseron, *supra* note 5, at xx.

[7] *Id.* at 2.

[8] *See* Kim, *supra* note 5; Claire Jean Kim, *Murder and Mattering in Harambe's House*, 3 Pol'y & Animals 1 (2017).

[9] Kim, *supra* note 5, at 10.

[10] *Id.* at 10; *see also* Ko, *supra* note 5.

In the Americas the prison is a colonial and racial project. Prior to colonization of what are now called the Americas, responses to harm did not include confinement or incarceration. Lisa Monchlin demonstrates that specific to "the Indigenous cultures of the northern hemisphere, no First Nations practiced methods of incarceration and no communities used holding cells for punishment."[11] For Katherine McKittrick, the prison "twins" and continues the placelessness constituted by plantation slavery as it is a location of racialized spatial violence premised on "displacement, surveillance, and enforced slow death."[12] Projects of colonialism also entail the intentional placelessness of nonhuman animals who remain targeted by violent and racialized geographies.[13] The prison remains a place of racialized and animalized encounters[14] that maintains the singularity of colonial rule.[15]

Nonhuman animals are part of prison life in various manners: as food, as "pests," as therapy and/or companion animals, as commodities in penal agricultural programs, and as those liminal to the grounds. Some examples include those used in prison rodeos,[16] in penitentiary agriculture,[17] and those who live with and amongst prisoners as "pests."[18] Prison-animal programs (such as "puppy programs") have also become popular in the United States and Canada since the late 1990s.[19]

[11] Lisa Monchalin, The Colonial Problem: An Indigenous Perspective on Crime and Injustice in Canada 39 (2016).

[12] Katherine McKittrick, *On Planatations, Prisons, and a Black Sense of Place*, 12 Soc. & Cultural Geography 947, 956 (2011).

[13] Heather Davis & Zoe Todd, *On the Importance of a Date, or Decolonizing the Anthropocene*, 16 ACME: An Int'l J. of Critical Geographies 761–80 (2017); Billy-Ray Belcourt, *Animal Bodies, Colonial Subjects: (Re)Locating Animality in Decolonial Thought*, 5 Societies 1–11 (2014); Virgina Anderson, Creatures of Empire: How Domestic Animals Transformed Early America (2004).

[14] *See* Kathryn Gillespie, *Placing Angola: Racialization, Anthropocentrism, and Settler Colonialism at the Louisiana State Penitentiary's Angola Rodeo*, *in* Colonialism and Animality: Anti-colonial Perspectives in Critical Animal Studies 250 (Kelly Struthers Montford & Chloë Taylor eds., 2020); Karen M. Morin, Carceral Space, Prisoners and Animals (2018).

[15] *See, e.g.*, Kelly Struthers Montford & Dawn Moore, *The Prison as Reserve: Governmentality, Phenomenology, and Indigenizing the Prison (Studies)*, 21 New Crim. L. Rev. 640 (2018); Heidi Kiiwetinepinesiik Stark, *Criminal Empire: The Making of the Savage in a Lawless Land*, 19 Theory & Event (2016); Robert Nichols, *The Colonialism of Incarceration*, 17 Radical Philosophy Rev., 435–55 (2014).

[16] *See* Gillespie, *supra* note 14.

[17] *See* Kelly Struthers Montford, *Land, Agriculture, and the Carceral: The Territorializing Function of Penitentiary Farms*, 22 Radical Philosophy Rev. 113 (2019); Amy J. Fitzgerald, *Doing Time in Slaughterhouses: A Green Criminological Commentary on Slaughterhouse Work Programs for Prison Inmates*, 10 J. for Critical Animal Studies 12 (2012).

[18] *See* Yvonne Jewkes & Dominique Moran, *The Paradox of the "Green" Prison: Sustaining the Environment or Sustaining the Penal Complex?*, 19 Theoretical Criminology 451 (2015).

[19] For Canadian context: Colleen Dell et al., Accessing Relational Connections in Prison: An Evaluation of the St. John Ambulance Therapy Dog Program at Stony Mountain Institution 17 (2019). For American context: Gennifer Furst, *Prison-Based Animal Programs: A National Survey*, 86 The Prison J. 407–30 (2006).

Animals who live on or near prison grounds have often had their habitats destroyed or irreparably altered by building the prison in the first place, and prisons are a source of ongoing environmental harm associated with their operation.[20]

While animal cruelty laws are promoted on the basis that they "protect" animals, I argue that they, rather unwittingly, participate in and further promote harm to animals – harms that are enacted by the prison through its racialized logic of caging those deemed subhuman.[21] I do so by examining the prominent human-animal relationships produced in the context of incarceration: liminal animals, farmed animals who are prison property and industry, and animals used in rehabilitative/therapeutic programs. The examples that follow are by no means exhaustive, but they provide a précis of specific human-animal relationships occurring in Canadian and US prisons. It is then the case that in the bid to denounce animal cruelty, PACT and other legal mechanisms that drive incarceration also drive the forms of animal cruelty that remain culturally acceptable. Criminalization measures such as these find their footing in flawed notions of rehabilitation and justice. As this chapter shows, it is not possible for a prison to rehabilitate animal cruelty when it itself requires and practices animal cruelty.

15.2 ANIMALS IN PRISON

15.2.1 *Liminal Animals*

The prison, like other human activities, can be a form of human encroachment into animal environments, destroying their habitats and/or polluting their sources of sustenance such that life is untenable.[22] While life becomes impossible for some animals because of the prison, others come to inhabit and/or access the prison.

[20] *See Prison Ecology Project: Facts*, NATION INSIDE (2021), https://nationinside.org/campaign/prison-ecology/facts/; *Government Announces Plans to Build Four More Mega-prisons*, CORPORATE WATCH (July 1, 2020), https://corporatewatch.org/newprisons/; *Prison Island: A New Report on Prison Expansion in England, Wales and Scotland—Download Now*, CORPORATE WATCH (Aug. 15, 2018), https://corporatewatch.org/prisonisland/; Keith 'Malik' Washington, *Horrific Conditions for Live-Stock Animals in Texas Prisons Exposed*, COMRADE MALIK (June 8, 2017), https://comrademalik.com/2017/06/08/horrific-conditions-for-live-stock-animals-in-texas-prisons-exposed/; Jewkes & Moran, *supra* note 18.

[21] Andrew Dilts, *Carceral Enjoyments and Killjoying the Social Life of Social Death, in* BUILDING ABOLITION DECARCERATION AND SOCIAL JUSTICE 196–224 (Kelly Struthers Montford & Chloë Taylor eds., 1st ed. 2021); Kelly Struthers Montford & Eva Kasprzycka, *The "Carceral Enjoyments"' of Animal Protection in* BUILDING ABOLITION DECARCERATION AND SOCIAL JUSTICE 227–47 (Kelly Struthers Montford & Chloë Taylor eds., 1st ed. 2021); Claire Jean Kim, *Abolition in* CRITICAL TERMS FOR ANIMAL STUDIES (Lori Gruen ed., 2018); *Cf.* JUSTIN MARCEAU, BEYOND CAGES: ANIMAL LAW AND CRIMINAL PUNISHMENT (2018).

[22] *See, e.g.*, Prison Ecology Project, *Facts: Background on Mass Incarceration and the Environment*, NATION INSIDE (2021), https://nationinside.org/campaign/prison-ecology/facts/; Elizabeth A. Bradshaw, *Tombstone Towns and Toxic Prisons: Prison Ecology and the Necessity of an Anti-Prison Environmental Movement*, 26 CRITICAL CRIMINOLOGY 407–22

Examples include feral cats, pigeons, gulls, rabbits, rats, prairie dogs, and coyotes.[23] For these animals, it is a matter of opportunity and peril, with some targeted for eradication by the prison administration, whereas others are "adopted" and provided for by prisoners. Donaldson and Kymlicka define liminal animals as those who border divisions between the "domesticated" and "wild."[24] While they live near or amongst humans, humans do not enforce ongoing and direct control over them as they do "farmed" animals or those who are "members" of our society such as companion animals. Liminal animals are better understood as ferals:

> opportunistic animals and niche specialists ... [who] may have adapted to urban and suburban environments when humans encroached on their wild territories, or they may have migrated opportunistically to cities and suburbs when they realized that these spaces offered steady means of sustenance and fewer predators.[25]

While not domesticated, these animals and their future generations become dependent on human-made environments for their survival. Perhaps, it is then most apt to consider prison "pests" as liminal animals who enter the prison not because they are brought in by the administration, but who enter on their own volition to some degree, with a context of prison-building leaving them little other choice.

Calvin Smiley shows that in real life and as depicted in films, animals such as birds, mice, and rats feature as those with whom prisoners are in relationships of mutual care. Prisoners at Rikers Island have also identified and expressed solidarity with liminal canines in or around the prison grounds whom they indicate as similarly situated carceral subjects. Reflecting on his volunteer work, Smiley writes:

> In the spring of 2019, while volunteering at Riker's Island, I spotted a creature in the wooded-area next to the bridge onto the island. At first, I thought it was a dog, but quickly noticed this canine was not a household pet. Its grey markings, wolf-like face, big ears, and large paws indicated she was a wolf, coyote, or hybrid. I began to exclaim about what I was seeing but quickly muffled my voice when a correctional officer walked by. Yet, the officer had already seen my expressive face and remarked, "They are all around here." When I got to the classroom, I told the participants what I witnessed. After class, a student told me that he knew which "wolf-dog" I was describing as his work detail brought him outside the jail to clean

(2018); CORPORATE WATCH, PRISON ISLAND: PRISON EXPANSION IN ENGLAND, WALES & SCOTLAND (2018).

23 *See* Calvin Smiley, *Coexistence as Resistance: Human and Non-human Animals in Carceral Settings*, *in* BUILDING ABOLITION DECARCERATION AND SOCIAL JUSTICE 294–95 (Kelly Struthers Montford & Chloë Taylor eds., 1st ed. 2021); Dominique Moran, *Budgie Smuggling or Doing Bird? Human-Animal Interactions in Carceral Space: Prison(er) Animals as Abject and Subject*, 16 SOC. & CULTURAL GEOGRAPHY 634, 645 (2015); Alan Mobley, *Killing Time on the Prairie*, 10 J. FOR CRITICAL ANIMAL STUDIES 114, 116 (2012).

24 SUE DONALDSON & WILL KYMLICKA, ZOOPOLIS: A POLITICAL THEORY OF ANIMAL RIGHTS 210–50 (2011).

25 Kelly Struthers Montford & Chloë Taylor, *Feral Theory: Editors' Introduction*, 6 FERAL FEMINISMS 5, 5 (2016).

up trash in the area. He told me that he would occasionally smuggle small pieces of bread to leave behind for her and her pups. When I asked if he was ever afraid, he shook his head and said, "Nah that's the homie."[26]

Contra to Smiley's positive reflections on liminal animals in prison settings, Moran writes that those often categorized "pests," such as insects, rats, and mice, remain both abject – categorized as undesirable to share space with. While abject they are still revered as "formidable adversaries" against whom prisoners go to great lengths to prevent from entering their cells.[27] Because of this orchestrated antagonism, prisoners attribute some degree of subjectivity to pests such as cockroaches.[28] The presence of these abject animals, especially when their presence is categorized as an "infestation," is used to demarcate inhumane conditions of confinement, with some courts finding this to constitute cruel and unusual punishment as prohibited by the US Constitution.[29] With their habitats destroyed or altered by the presence of the prison, the prison then provides a stable supply of sustenance for liminal animals, bringing them into relationships of survival, danger, and/or companionship with the prison and prisoners. Liminal animals, while certainly effected and/or targeted for extermination by the prison to various extents, are not subject to the same constraints, targeted transformations, or disavowal of subjectivity as those whose legal status is property. It is to non-human animals specifically brought in for prison industry – animals that are intentionally targeted and transformed by the prison – that this chapter now turns.

15.2.2 *Animals as Prison Industry and Property: Deaded Life*

As a carceral institution in and of itself, animal agriculture requires and reproduces the property status of farmed animals. This property status leads to farmed animals being conceptually positioned as "deaded life": as those who in life are imagined only as the products they will be become in death. Often this takes the form of their being reduced to input-output machines. As deaded life they exist as "living meat," "egg machines," "milk machines," and the like.[30] In agribusiness modes of production, nonhuman animals are "both *producing* or *being produced as* commodities."[31] Morin argues that the prison exacts a specific form of property relationship over humans, too. Drawing on the fact that plantation grounds are now prison grounds, as well as the fact that slavery remains legal as a form of punishment under the Thirteenth Amendment, Morin claims that "if the prison is more or less tantamount

26 Smiley, *supra* note 23, at 295.
27 Moran, *supra* note 23, at 649.
28 *Id.*
29 *Id.* at 648.
30 James Stanescu, *Beyond Biopolitics: Animal Studies, Factory Farms, and the Advent of Deading Life*, 8 PHAENEX 135, 155 (2013).
31 MORIN, *supra* note 14, at 101.

to the plantation, and the prisoner is tantamount to the slave, the prisoner also can be thought of as the de facto property of the state."[32] What then does it mean to have prisoners working in animal agriculture as mandated by the state? How can we understand the overlapping yet divergent forms of carcerality and property at work in these interstices? I suggest that prison-based animal agriculture is best understood as a location that produces ontologies of life, such as the human and the animal, to serve the ends of profit and settler colonial territorialization. It does so by continually using land and animals in a way that perpetuates the colonial project of settling the new world in the image of the old.[33] Prison-based animal agribusiness is rendered possible due to its capacity for trafficking in a pastoral idealism. These enterprises purport that access to "nature" will reform the offender and train individuals for the market economy. These claims lack empirical evidence.[34] Instead, penal agribusinesses continue settler-colonial and plantation-slavery projects, in which the subjugation of blackness, indigeneity, and animality have been integral and mutually produced.

Morin argues that these subjugations remain integral to the exploitation of prisoner and animal labour, especially in the location of the prison animal farm:

> The carceral logic of prisoners as animal – or prisoners as "Blackened" which itself begets animalization – further enables their enslavement within the prison. Exploitation of labour (and killing itself) within the prison is enabled by animalizing the human and "isolating the nonhuman within the human," since animal bodies can be exploited and killed without the commission of a crime. Humanness, then, is made a political, conceptual category rather than a biological fact.[35]

15.2.3 *Prison Agribusiness in Canada*

Canadian penitentiary agribusiness predates confederation in 1867 and was present in all institutions for men until 2010. These programs closed after ceasing to be profitable. There was also a dearth of evidence suggesting this "vocational training" resulted in commensurable employment once prisoners were released.[36] Their operations entailed meat, dairying, and egg industries, including having prisoners work in abattoirs. While carceral agribusiness programs in Canada stopped in 2010, the Joyceville Institution in the Kingston, Ontario, area kept their abattoir. Named Wallace Beef, this abattoir is part of a "co-venture" in that it is privately owned by an individual and staffed by CORCAN. CORCAN is the federal prison industry "rehabilitation" program. Following the announcement that penal agribusiness

[32] *Id.* at 109.
[33] *See, e.g.*, Montford, *supra* note 17, at 117–19.
[34] *Id.* at 130.
[35] Morin, *supra* note 14, at 110.
[36] Montford, *supra* note 17, at 113.

would cease to operate, community members – especially farmers – campaigned for their continuation. They were immediately successful in having the slaughterhouse remain operational, claiming the Correctional Service of Canada had "recognized the importance of the abattoir to the local community and the local food system and in terms of what they needed to satisfy public safety and inmate training."[37] The local community to which they refer includes the "150 local farmers, [and] 300 local businesses including the prisons" who contract their slaughter to Wallace Beef via CORCAN.[38] As of 2017, prisoners employed by CORCAN were paid approximately $1.95 per day after deductions. Between the years of 1993 and 2017, CORCAN operated at a loss of 66% during these fiscal years. Its programming/"training" has been found to have no impact on recidivism rates.[39]

A collective of community members in favour of animal-based prison agriculture, "Save Our Prison Farms," continues to campaign for the re-opening of animal farms on penitentiary grounds, which have begun to re-open in two penitentiaries for men in the Kingston, Ontario, area. Smaller-scale cow dairy operations have resumed, with planning ongoing for large-scale goat dairies to supply a growing demand in China.[40] Again, these farms are a CORCAN venture and will also include the slaughtering and butchering of male animals not "useful" to dairying.[41] These organizers repeatedly mobilized a rhetoric of community safety and that prisoners would build empathy. Their campaigns included improperly cited academic research in an effort to boast purported benefits to prisoners who are given the opportunity to work in animal agriculture. The literature cited was in fact about the benefits of prison-animal programs such as puppy and dog training and was explicit that these findings not be applied to animal agriculture given the very different dynamics and outcomes occurring in these relationships.[42] The majority of prisoners surveyed by another community-based group – Evolve Our Prison Farms, who advocate for plant-based agriculture and animal sanctuaries rather than animal agriculture – reported a preference (75%) for the former.[43] Prisoners have described that working in animal-agriculture is re-traumatizing, involves dangerous working

37 Jeff Green, *Abattoir*, Frontenac News (May 28, 2009), https://www.frontenacnews.ca/2009-archives/item/4713-abattoir (quoting Peter Dowling).

38 *Id.*

39 Claire Brownell, *Prisoners Making $1.95 a Day Want a Raise. Taxpayers Want a Break*, Financial Post (Sept. 1, 2017), https://financialpost.com/news/court-challenge-to-inmate-pay-places-prison-labour-program-in-the-crosshairs.

40 The goat dairies are currently on hold due to the COVID-19 pandemic. *See, e.g.*, Ian MacAlpine, *CSC Suspends Plans for Goat Farm at Joyceville Institution*, Kingston Whig Standard (Mar. 5, 2021), https://www.thewhig.com/news/csc-temporarily-suspends-plans-for-goat-farm-at-joyceville-institution.

41 Montford, *supra* note 17, at 115.

42 Gennifer Furst, *Prison-Based Animal Programs: A National Survey*, 86 Prison J. 407, 425 (2006).

43 *Prisoner Perspectives*, Evolve Our Prison Farms (2021), https://evolveourprisonfarms.ca/prisoner/.

conditions, and that animal abuse is ubiquitous.[44] Prisoners have also reported that they cannot meaningfully refuse to work as this is often met with threats to be sent to solitary confinement because such a refusal would represent disobeying their correctional plan. In obeying the prison's demand for performing agricultural labour, prisoners are more likely to be seen as engaging their "rehabilitation" plan and are more likely to cascade down to lower-security facilities and/or be granted parole.[45]

15.2.4 *Prison Agribusiness in the United States*

Based on available data, US penal agribusiness appears to be ubiquitous and is likely increasing.[46] US agriculture relies on migrant and undocumented labour, and it is likely that, of the 1.2 million agriculture workers in the United States, 70% are undocumented.[47] Recent anti-immigration policies have decreased the available labour supply, meaning that another pool of vulnerable individuals will be used to support this industry: prisoners. Doing so remains the latest iteration of using prisoner labour to support dominant interests. During US Reconstruction – and especially in the South – convict leasing was instituted to bolster economies that were built on slave labour and to maintain Black subjugation. Ultimately, convict labour was a mechanism to maintain white supremacy; laws were instituted to ensure Black persons were criminalized and therefore legally available to be commercially exploited by the state and the white capitalists who leased these prisoners for their companies. By the late 1800s, convict leasing was so profitable that some states garnered revenues that were 400% of the operational cost of the prison system. Unsurprisingly, convict labour was deeply racialized. During a period of mass incarceration between 1870 and 1910, close to 90% of those leased in Georgia were Black individuals.[48]

Concerns of convict leasing undercutting the open market, coupled with the economic depression of the 1930s, led to the passing of laws prohibiting leasing programs as well as the sale of prison-manufactured goods. This did not stop prison systems from requiring prisoners to labour in agriculture. Instead, it meant that the food produced by prisoners could only be used by the prison or state workers. This would last until the late 1970s, when foreign manufacturing threatened US domestic markets and agricultural industries again sought cheap domestic labour. Again, lobbyists campaigned for legal changes which, yet again, allowed private companies to hire prisoners. Prisoners were mostly used in manufacturing and service sectors.

[44] *Id.*

[45] Brownell, *supra* note 40.

[46] Stian Rice, *Convicts Are Returning to Farming—Anti-immigrant Policies Are the Reason*, The Conversation (June 7, 2019), https://theconversation.com/convicts-are-returning-to-farming-anti-immigrant-policies-are-the-reason-117152; Morin, *supra* note 14, at 94.

[47] Rice, *supra* note 47.

[48] *Id.*

At this time, agriculture continued to rely on migrant workers. During the fifty years following the re-establishment of convict leasing, the imprisonment of Black persons has quadrupled.[49]

Comprehensive accounts of penal agribusiness are not available. The following discussion includes examples reported by investigative journalists, correctional administrations, non-profit organizations, and academic researchers. Some reports estimate that approximately 30,000 prisoners in the United States work in the food system. Heal Food Alliance, for example, reports that forty-six states have prison-based agriculture, with 20% of states having large-scale agricultural operations.[50] The majority of prison agricultural labour is state administered (~76%), with industry-run operations representing approximately 21%.[51] State-run examples include the sale of prison-produced products at market prices. At the Louisiana State Penitentiary, which is built on the grounds of the Angola Plantation, prisoners perform agricultural labor, which entails the hand-cultivation of plant crops and the raising of 2,000 steers who will be consumed as beef. They are paid between four and twenty cents per hour.[52] Industry-run examples include the Arizona Corrections Industry having a labour contract worth $5 million with Hickman's Family Farms, the United States' fourth-largest egg producer.[53]

At present, convict leasing remains very lucrative and increasingly relied on by agricultural industries. During their 2015–16 fiscal year, for example, the California prison industry state system's agriculture and food sector posted a $2 million profit.[54] Courts have ruled that prisoners are not employees and therefore cannot organize for better pay or working conditions. Nor are prisoners protected by various labour laws, including minimum wage requirements, making them "leasable" at very low rates. To compare, note that, in Arizona, the minimum wage for farm workers is $11 per hour. Meanwhile, Arizona Correctional Industries pays prisoner agricultural labourers $3–4 per hour. Most prisoners' wages are subject to deductions that "offset" the costs of incarceration or go toward victim restitution. Others receive no remuneration.[55] Research has shown that across all US states, "Black men represented the highest percentage of men participating in agriculture and facility service assignments, while a higher percentage of White men worked in public

[49] *Id.*

[50] *Food, Race and Labor: A Brief Explainer*, HEAL FOOD ALLIANCE (2021), https://healfoodalliance.org/a-brief-explainer-on-food-and-labor/.

[51] HEAL FOOD ALLIANCE, THE PRISON INDUSTRIAL COMPLEX AND AGRICULTURAL LABOUR (2021), *available at* https://drive.google.com/file/d/1ZWdBH5zlKbV6K6subbGMm4nUMY3_ZZgJ/view.

[52] Gillespie, *supra* note 16.

[53] *Id.*

[54] HEAL FOOD ALLIANCE, *supra* note 51.

[55] Rice, *supra* note 47.

works and prison industries."[56] Men imprisoned in the southern states are also more likely to be assigned to agricultural labour than other sectors, and are less likely to be paid. Not only does prison agriculture generate profits for the prison, it also is a cost-saving measure as it produces food for the prison itself – a practice that in effect sustains and makes the prison viable.[57] This broader context of convict leasing, anti-immigration policies, and the ongoing use of penal labour as a mechanism of racial organization then situates and informs prison-based animal agriculture. Because I was unable to find a comprehensive account of federal- and state-based penitentiary agribusiness programs, I focus on a few state prison systems as examples of the scale and breadth of prison-based animal agriculture.

The Colorado Department of Corrections currently runs a diverse agribusiness program as part of sixty programs run by Colorado Correctional Industries (CCi).[58] The agribusiness program began in 1874, and CCi claims "farming [continues to] help. . .address inmate idleness, provided food products for the prison and was a means of generating revenue from surplus crops sold to outside markets."[59] Agribusiness now spans three areas – farming, fisheries, and vineyards – that comprise twenty programs that depend on the labour of approximately 800 prisoners. Framed as honouring the department's "heritage," farming programs occupy 560 acres across eight Colorado state prisons. Of this, 30 acres are used to grow vegetables for state prisons, whereas the remaining 530 acres grow corn used by CCi dairying operations. This breakdown of land use demonstrates the staggering inefficiency of growing plant-based foods to supply animal-based food markets. Information on CCi dairying, however, is not provided on the website. They do not indicate whether dairy products supply prison and/or external markets, nor do they mention what happens to the male cows not useful to dairying. Despite limited information on their website, journalists in 2015, for example, reported that some prisoners in Colorado were working for agricultural companies that supplied Whole Foods with buffalo mozzarella, goat cheese, and tilapia. Prisoners were paid $1.50 per hour.[60] Following media attention, Whole Foods announced that it would cease selling products made using prisoner labour.[61]

[56] Courtney A. Crittenden et al., *Being Assigned Work in Prison: Do Gender and Race Matter?*, 13 Feminist Criminology 359, 374 (2018).

[57] Montford, *supra* note 17, at 129.

[58] *General Information*, CCi (2021), https://www.coloradoci.com/bin-htm/generalinfo.html?intro.

[59] *Agribuisiness*, CCi (2021), https://www.coloradoci.com/manufacturers/agriculture/index.html?intro.

[60] Graeme Wood, *From Our Prison to Your Dinner Table*, Pacific Standard (June 14, 2017), https://psmag.com/economics/from-our-prison-to-your-dinner-table.

[61] Allison Aubrey, *Whole Foods Says It Will Stop Selling Foods Made with Prison Labor*, NPR (Sept. 30, 2015), https://www.npr.org/sections/thesalt/2015/09/30/444797169/whole-foods-says-it-will-stop-selling-foods-made-by-prisoners.

CCi has industrially farmed fish for decades, with their brochure promoting this as "netting marketable skills."[62] CCi advertises that "Fish Rearing continues to be one of our most successful programs."[63] This program supplies pond industries with live koi and goldfish. They also rear trout, tilapia, catfish, and freshwater red claw lobster for the food industry. For example, their trout production process "holds an average of 135,000 gallons of pure Rocky Mountain spring water...with a maximum of 115,000–130,000 fish swimming in a rearing unit."[64] CCi claims that this constitutes a "stress free existence" for the fish and is an environmentally responsible approach as they "recycle fish waste and repurpose the water throughout our numerous agricultural programs."[65] Fish are referred to in much the same way as farmed land animals – desubjectified property imagined as the commodity they will become when killed. References to "fish husbandry and processing," "humane handling," and "meat retaining its natural colour" demonstrate that these aquatic animals are subject to the carcerality of agriculture and property law in which they are deemed prison property.[66]

In Pennsylvania, animal agriculture occurs in both federal and state institutions. At the federal USP-Lewisburg, prisoners farm "poultry, dairy cattle, hay, corn, clover, soybeans, alfalfa, sorghum and potatoes."[67] While federal prison industries claim to "provide meaningful work for inmates,"[68] merely 10% of those able to work did so and were paid between $0.23 and $1.15 per hour. The state correctional industry – PCI – branded as "Big House Products," also entails slaughterhouse labour. Morin analyzed a 2005 audit of PCI operations and found that during that year approximately 1,600 prisoners (3.9%) of its 41,000-person prison population were assigned to this program while being paid $0.59 per hour.[69] PCI industries include the manufacturing of licence plates, workboots, laundry services, and the "process[ing of] 4.1 million pounds of beef, pork, turkey, and fish."[70] While prison labour is ubiquitously marketed as a way to decrease idleness, provide income, and aid in re-entry, the 2005 audit concluded that this program was "a phenomenal waste of taxpayer dollars, and [contained] evidence that the programs had no impact whatsoever on prison recidivism despite aims to instill skills and a work ethic in prisoners."[71]

[62] Colorado Correctional Industries, Netting Marketable Skills (2021), https://www.coloradoci.com/bin-pdf/Off_agriculture/Fishery_Brochure.pdf.
[63] *Id.*
[64] *Id.*
[65] *Id.*
[66] *Id.*
[67] Morin, *supra* note 14, at 94.
[68] *Id.* at 112.
[69] *Id.*
[70] *Id.*
[71] *Id.* at 113.

The state of Texas too has a robust and profitable agribusiness program.[72] The Texas Department of Public Safety reported:

> About 10,000 inmates work in the system's agriculture jobs which last year produced almost $50 million worth of edible crops, livestock and cotton for the prison system on 139,000 acres of farm and ranch land. Prison units that don't have enough land to be in the agricultural program still produce several million pounds of fresh vegetables each year to donate to local food banks for the needy.[73]

The kinds of foods produced by prison labour shape prison diets. The Texas Department of Public Safety further described:

> Most meals consist of ground beef dishes, chicken, or pork. The ground beef is bought with proceeds from the sale of prison-raised cattle. Although the prisons have more than 250,000 hens, they are used only for egg production. It is less expensive to buy chicken meat at market. The system raises and serves its own pork products.[74]

Farmed animal products are the commodities produced and sold by the prison, *and* it is this profit that the prison then uses to purchase more animal-based foods. Prison industries and diets can be understood as largely prescribing specific relationships between humans and other animals. Quite literally, the prison sustains itself on the backs of prisoners and nonhuman animals.

Currently incarcerated activist and investigative journalist Keith "Malik" Washington has described the abuse suffered by farmed animals in Texan prisons and its attendant detrimental impact. He writes that the Texas Department of Criminal Justice (TDCJ) has consistently refused to allow or institute the independent oversight of "these prison plantations" as it is to their benefit to remain "immune to any oversight of any regulatory agency."[75] Washington recounts having a visceral reaction to how farmed animals are treated and to the scale of the operations:

> I smelled the large hen warehouse before we actually got right up on it . . . Hens were packed like sardines. Underneath the cages were virtual mountains of bird feces. . . The cages are so small, hens cannot turn around or spread their wings. Our job was to remove the fecal matter. The smell of ammonia was very strong. Some birds I noticed had burns on their feet and legs, this from being housed in filth.[76]

[72] *See* Washington, *supra* note 20; Fight Toxic Prisons, *Horrific Conditions for Live-Stock Animals in Texas Prisons Exposed and Other Updates from Malik Washington*, FIGHT TOXIC PRISONS (Feb. 12, 2018), https://fight-toxic-prisons.org/2018/02/12/horrific-conditions-for-live-stock-animals-in-texas-prisons-exposed-and-other-updates-from-malik-washington/; LOÏC WACQUANT, PUNISHING THE POOR: THE NEOLIBERAL GOVERNMENT OF SOCIAL INSECURITY (2009).

[73] WACQUANT, *supra* note 74, at 180.

[74] *Id.* at 180–81.

[75] Washington, *supra* note 20.

[76] *Id.*

The TDCJ does not even meet the minimal spatial requirements that exist for chickens: half a square foot per bird. Washington reports that the prison puts two to three birds in spaces prescribed for one. Like animal agriculture operations outside of prison walls, prison agriculture also considers it more efficient to have its animals routinely die than it is to improve conditions and treatment. Washington confirms this by writing that "many birds at Wynne die of asphyxiation and dehydration. Decomposing corpses are found in cages with live birds every day."[77]

At another Texan institution in which Washington was imprisoned, the Coffield Unit, a prison for men in Tennessee Colony, there are three large units where hog and cattle rearing take place alongside slaughterhouse labour. Washington reports that the scale of these operations has affected the surrounding environment, with runoff polluting nearby rivers and lakes and contaminating the prison's water supply. In one of the units in particular, Washington reports that significant levels of coliform bacteria were regularly present in water that prisoners had to drink because there were no alternative sources. At Eastham, a prison for men in Lovelady, Texas, Washington describes a massive egg-laying operation where hens lay "80,000 eggs per week. It is a 24-hour-a-day operation, the lights never go out."[78] This operation generates approximately $100,000 a week for the TDCJ. Another unit at Eastham routinely houses 3,000 hogs and 600 sows, in addition to selling 21 piglets a week. Washington aptly highlights the prison's financial interest in its "livestock." Whereas air-conditioning is rare in Texas prisons and where heat-related prisoner deaths are not uncommon, the TDCJ has invested "$175,000 for a cooling system for the pigs. The pigs are being preserved for slaughter so TDCJ can benefit. TDCJ does not have any concern for animal rights or human rights. Its main focus is profits by any means."[79]

Inasmuch as Washington describes deplorable and dangerous working conditions in prison animal agriculture, the state has been explicit that prisoner refusal in labour will be met with "cell confinement," the conditions of which exceed international legal definitions of solitary confinement. The Department writes:

> Offenders who refuse to work lose their privileges and are placed on "cell restriction." Cell restriction means remaining in the cell 24 hours a day, with no trips to the day room, commissary, or recreation yard. Meals are also eaten in the cell. Personal property is taken away.[80]

Generally, solitary confinement entails being in-cell for twenty-two hours or more a day and without meaningful interaction. Solitary confinement can meet the threshold for torture if mitigation efforts – such as personal belongings, access to current

77 *Id.*
78 *Id.*
79 *Id.*
80 Wacquant, *supra* note 74, at 180.

events, the ability to exercise, and the like – are not provided.[81] To refuse to labour for the prison is then to face conditions of confinement that can cause irreversible psychological and physical impacts. Effects (aka "SHU syndrome") include the development of mental illness, uncontrollable anger, pacing, dissociation, violence to the self and others, anxiety when in the presence of others, back pain, and the decreased effectiveness of psychotropic medications.[82] A Canadian court has accepted the effects of solitary as a matter of judicial notice. In other words, expert witnesses should no longer have to testify as to the harms of segregation; it being a matter of judicial notice means that it is so widely known to be true that a court does not need to adduce evidence on the matter.[83]

We might then say that prison labour is irrevocably transformative regardless of whether prisoners "participate" or not. Prisoners are required to act upon animals in a manner that transforms the animals, but which also subjects prisoners to the detrimental psychological effects of violent work.[84] If they refuse to work, they are in turn subjected to extremely repressive conditions of confinement.

The transformation of carceral subjects is perhaps the core tenet of human-animal relations in these spaces. As Morin writes:

> What happens in the space can never be undone, the subject can never be transformed back ... [I]f the carceral space does not kill – e.g., transforming a sentient being to a commodity such as a piece of meat or lab specimen – the action performed within carceral space will nonetheless change the subject, transforming a wild creature to a domesticated or rescued animal.[85]

Specific to prison farm animals, their entire lives will be spent in prison for them to be transformed into food. There are other animals, however, such as those brought in for training purposes who will spend only part of their lives in the prison. It is to the latter mechanics of transformation to which I turn next.

15.2.5 *Rehabilitated Animals as Lively Communities*

Many animals are temporary "guests" of the prison.[86] Those brought into the prison for spectacle, such as prison rodeos, are selected *because* of their "liveliness." Morin

[81] *See* Kelly Struthers Montford et al., *The Use of Solitary Confinement and Prisoner Rights, in* CANADIAN PRISONS: UNDERSTANDING THE CANADIAN CORRECTIONAL SYSTEM 271, 274–75 (Carla Cesaroni ed., 2021).

[82] *Id.*

[83] Montford et al., *supra* note 83, at 283 (citing R. v. Roberts [Richard], No. 2018/04159 A1, 2018 WL 06345027, at *34 [Ct. App. Dec. 6, 2018]).

[84] *Cf.* Amy J. Fitzgerald et al., *Slaughterhouses and Increased Crime Rates: An Empirical Analysis of the Spillover from "The Jungle" into the Surrounding Community*, 22 ORGANIZATION & ENV'T 158, 158 (2009).

[85] MORIN, *supra* note 14, at 116.

[86] *See* Moran, *supra* note 23, at 642.

argues that Collard's concept of "lively commodities" describes the "value" of prison rodeo animals.[87] It is their liveliness that at once presents a physical threat to participating prisoners and it is this liveliness that is to be dominated as the very point of the rodeo. In this case, their "active demonstrations of being full of life – their labor – is more important to their value than even their sentience."[88] Other temporary "guest" animals include those brought into the prison for Prison Animal Programs (PAPs). To make claims about the possibility of rehabilitation, the prison requires the undisciplined "liveliness" of "untrained" dogs and "wild" horses in order to intervene and transform them into acceptable workers and companions. It is this aspect of their liveliness that makes them valuable to the prison. I suggest that animals subjected to "rehabilitation" in prisons be thought of as "lively commodities" who, with prisoners, are to be transformed into pro-social creatures. The commodity relationship is also important as their transformation ("training") by prisoners and eventual adoption or sale generates income for the prison. Moreover, prisoners are ideal and cheap trainers given prison schedules provide long periods of unstructured time.[89]

Beginning in the 1980s, PAPs have become increasingly widespread in prison settings. The majority are dog training programs, but PAPs also include cat care and wild horse training. Dog programs now exist across the United States, Canada, Australia, New Zealand, and Italy.[90] Overwhelmingly, the literature on PAPs does not question the ethics of animal captivity or instrumentalization. Instead, through discourses of mutual saviour/rehabilitation, administrations position these as benevolent endeavours for all parties. At the same time, PAPs operate within a broader context in which nations have used non-human animals in various projects of social control. The use of bloodhounds in slave patrols for tracking fugitive slaves has transmuted into the continued use of police dogs as tools of racial subjugation.[91] Some police dogs are trained by prisoners. For example, the Pelican Bay State Prison in California – an institution notorious for its extremely repressive supermax unit where prisoners are held in solitary confinement for years with zero human contact, no phone calls, and in windowless cells – also has a prison dog training program. This program trains canines to become police attack dogs.[92] Dogs "working" for the prison are also used to track and hunt escaped prisoners, many of whom attempt to flee prisons located on former plantation grounds. On the basis of rehabilitation, dogs, who are themselves incarcerated, are trained and deployed to

[87] Morin, *supra* note 14, at 103.

[88] *Id.*

[89] *See* Furst, *supra* note 43, at 413.

[90] *Id.*; Dana M. Britton & Andrea Button, *Prison Pups: Assessing the Effects of Dog Training Programs in Correctional Facilities*, 9 J. of Family Social Work 79, 79 (2005).

[91] *See* Morin, *supra* note 14, at 97–98; Larry H. Spruill, *Slave Patrols, "Packs of Negro Dogs" and Policing Black Communities*, 53 Phylon 42, 42 (2016).

[92] Morin, *supra* note 14, at 97.

keep those who are legally enslaved on former plantation grounds. The use of dogs in PAPs then carries a particular historical significance that remains unaddressed by those in favour of such programs.[93] For the purposes of this chapter, I focus on Colorado's dog training and wild horse programs, which I supplement with research from other jurisdictions.

The Colorado Department of Corrections began their "Prison Trained K-9 Companion Program" in 2002. Their website describes it "as a perfect marriage of ideas – saving humans through saving dogs."[94] As a result of participating, prisoners are meant to acquire skills, self-esteem, compassion, caregiving, and a salary. Prisoners can also become certified in Canine Behaviour Modification, thereby expanding their vocational opportunities once released. The puppies and dogs come from shelters, rescues, and individual surrenders. The dogs subject to such programs are said to "get a new 'leash on life'" as they are transformed into "wonderfully trained family pets and many move on to become very sophisticated assistance dogs which perform a variety of tasks for their human partners."[95] Services provided through this canine program include in-prison boarding, adoption and alumni training should dogs need re-correction. The CCi is explicit that this program is self-sustaining based on its fees and does not rely on taxpayer monies. Photos of adoptable dogs on the program's website feature a blue backdrop speckled with pawprints; the dog's name is followed by "CI: [number]." The staging and composition of the photos reference mugshots, and "CI" presumably refers to "Colorado Inmate." One can infer that these dogs too are Colorado Inmates, reformed by the prison and ready for pro-social re-entry into the broader community.

CCi's description is consistent with most of the literature that frames prison dog programs as a form of "co-rehabilitation." The purported benefits of PAPs – which are largely anecdotal – include improved institutional behaviour and engagement in therapeutic programs, lower rates of depression and aggression amongst prisoners, increased morale amongst prisoners and staff, improved self-reported social skills, and lower rates of re-offending upon release.[96] Prisoner participants have also reported that their participation is a way for them to contribute to society.[97] Others have suggested that interacting with animals in programs such as these provides support and validation that prisoners require to transform themselves into law-abiding citizens.[98] I would caution, however, that this presumes that offending is merely the result of individual behaviour rather than broader structures of inequality

[93] *See id.*

[94] *About Our Dog Program*, CCi (2021), https://www.coloradoci.com/serviceproviders/puppy/index.html?p=aboutDogsDiv.

[95] *Id.*

[96] Laura Wheaton, Prison-Based Animal Programs: A Critical Review of the Literature and Future Recommendations 79 & 83 (July 26, 2013) (Ph.D. dissertation, Pacific University).

[97] *Id.*

[98] *See, e.g.*, Furst, *supra* note 43, at 425.

and marginalization. Moran observes that like animal assisted therapy programs (AATs), in PAPs "the animal is present purely for the therapeutic benefit of the human involved, and which draw on the observed physical and emotional benefits for humans of interactions with animals."[99] In this sense, animals function as "devices through which to enable positive change in the inmates."[100] Unlike AATs, however, PAPs are framed as having distinct community benefits, whether these be the training of service dogs for drug and explosives detection, or to assist those experiencing disability.

Some argue that, because humans and canines domesticated one another, prison dogs might not experience incarceration negatively. Moran, for example, suggests that dogs in PAPs "may experience prison programming in much the same way as domestic dogs experience being family pets, benefitting from human company and engaging in the kind of kinesthetic empathy widely observed amongst companion dogs."[101] Does this then mean that these programs constitute ethical human-animal relationships? Alexandra Horowitz argues that domestication is foundational to the species of *canis familiaris.* Put simply, there are no true "wild" dogs because the evolution of their species has meant that humans and other dogs are part of their social groups. According to Horowitz, freedom for dogs does not simply equate to freedom from humans.[102] Instead, Horowitz suggests that our obligation to this species is to provide the conditions in which they can be the freest and flourish. In practice, this may ask that humans respect their "dogness,"[103] rather than trying to train it out of them due to its transgression of our human expectations around "civility." Allowing dogs to be entirely themselves would require an ethical approach that has as its goal that humans impose their cultures onto dogs as little as possible. It is then worth asking to what extent training programs such as these are the imposition of human culture. Do such programs support the flourishing of dogs or represent their ongoing subordination to human norms? Do these programs – designed to transform wayward dogs into perfect family pets, service dogs, and "carceral canines"[104] – not then represent the epitome of the application of human culture to nonhuman others? PAPs also raise the question about the trauma that is experienced when dogs are separated from their prisoner handlers as the dogs are adopted. Within a foundationally speciesist society, it is also the case that these are

[99] Moran, *supra* note 23, at 643.

[100] *Id.*

[101] *Id.* at 644.

[102] Alexandra Horowitz, Canis familiaris: *Companion and Captive, in* The Ethics of Captivity 7, 11–12 (Lori Gruen ed., 2014).

[103] *See* Colin Dayan, With Dogs at the Edge of Life 162 (2015).

[104] "Carceral canines" is a term used by Paula Cepeda Gallo and Chloë Taylor to describe those put to work by the criminal punishment system, such as police dogs and prison dogs. *See* Paula Cepeda Gallo & Chloë Taylor, *Carceral Canines: Racial Terror and Animal Abuse from Slave Hounds to Police Dogs, in* Building Abolition: Decarceration and Social Justice 248–68 (Kelly Montford & Chloë Taylor eds., 2021).

dogs who might otherwise be destroyed if not part of these programs. This is a tension and reality upon which these programs are founded and highlight to promote and sustain themselves.

Both New Mexico and Colorado state Departments of Corrections began "wild horse" programs in the late 1980s. New Mexico's program ran from 1988 to 1992. While prisoners and staff reported this program to be successful in decreasing recidivism and institutional misconduct, especially amongst prisoners deemed to be violent offenders and/or those who were simultaneously participating in substance abuse programming, empirical evidence does not support all of these claims. Specifically, the relationship between the program and recidivism is inconclusive.[105] Colorado's Wild Horse Inmate Program (WHIP) was established in 1986 as a partnership between CCi and the Bureau of Land Management.[106] Up to 3,000 horses can be housed at a time at the facility located in Canon City, Colorado,[107] an isolated town that is also home to thirteen prisons. In true colonial fashion, the promotion of this program adopts iconic symbols of pastoral life and a toughened frontier spirit of cowboys. The marketing of WHIP uses a narrative trifecta dependent on the relationship between mustang horses, frontier masculinity, and settler colonialism. CCi writes:

> Mustangs played a vital role in the settling of our American West. These noble creatures carried cowboys up the Chisholm Trail, mountain men through the Tetons, trappers into Oregon, native Americans into buffalo hunts and settlers from the east coast to the west. Today these mustangs are helping troubled men make a new beginning with an old craft – horse training.[108]

In his description of WHIP, former commissioner of the Colorado Department of Corrections Rick Raemish gestures to their "new" role in sustaining the prison:[109] "today these intelligent, loyal creatures *continue* to forge new beginnings, playing an important role in inmate rehabilitation."[110] Despite the prison's explicit failure to rehabilitate,[111] the institution continues to traffic in rehabilitative rhetoric to justify its existence. Wild horses are then captured and transformed by prisons in the name

[105] *See* Judy L. Cushing & James D. Williams, *The Wild Mustang Program: A Case Study in Facilitated Inmate Therapy*, 22 J. of Offender Rehabilitation 95, 95 (1995).

[106] CCi, *Wild Horse Inmate Program*, Colorado Correctional Industries (2021), https://www.coloradoci.com/serviceproviders/whip/.

[107] *Cañon City Wild Horse Inmate Program*, Bureau of Land Management (2021), https://www.blm.gov/programs/wild-horse-and-burro/adoption-and-sales/adoption-centers/canon-city-inmate-program.

[108] Colorado Correctional Industries, *supra* note 108.

[109] Andrew Dilts argues that the prison, through disenfranchisement, applies racial categories, and is an act of racialization.

[110] Rick Raemisch, *Insight Inside: WHIP—Taking the Reins*, International Corrections & Prisons Association (2021), https://icpa.org/insight-inside-whip-taking-the-reins/ (emphasis added).

[111] *See* Angela Davis, Are Prisons Obsolete? (Greg Ruggiero ed., 2003).

of rehabilitation, a practice that occurs within a broader context of ideologically and economically sustaining the prison and the racial relations it produces.

More than 5,000 horses have been adopted to "qualified applicants" through this program. Like the canine programs, both prisoners and horses are positioned as those given "second chances" through these programs. The horses are trained over a period of 90 days[112] and prisoners receive 200 hours of "on-the-job training" that allows them to "develop a good work ethic, animal husbandry skills, and respect – creating a better future for themselves and the mustangs."[113] Seven to ten horses are trained on a monthly basis. The rationale as to *why* "wild" horses require second chances and training is not explained. Mustangs, the quintessential symbol of free-living horses, become carceral subjects and are then "rehabilitated" and adopted out for personal and state use. Some horses are trained and adopted to trail riders, while a proportion of younger horses are reserved and trained for the US Border Patrol,[114] again, highlighting the link between the prison, prison animals, and state repression. Whereas dogs might not experience their time in prison as such, previously free-living horses "may be subject to a kind of double or two-fold carcerality."[115] In the case of free-living horses, it is likely the case that "'multispecies justice' might be found in distance rather than proximity and intimacy."[116]

15.3 CONCLUSION

It is a gruesome irony that incarceration is positioned both by lawmakers and the animal protection movement as a mechanism to achieve justice for non-human animals. The prison as structure harms surrounding waters, lands, and ecosystems, often making life impossible for the more-than-human displaced and affected by its presence. More directly, as this chapter has shown, the prison also structures human-animal relationships: between prisoners and liminal animals, in animal agriculture, and in community service training programs. Liminal animals are not targeted for transformation in the way that those in animal agriculture and PAPs are. While they might, to some degree, enter and exit prison grounds on their own accord, some are targetted for extermination, while others are in relationships of mutual care with human prisoners. Farmed animals in prisons are produced as deaded life, whereas

[112] "Training" a free living horse cannot be done in ninety days without "shortcuts." "Shortcuts" include increasing the severity of training tools/aids and harsh equipment such as leverage bits, spurs, whips, tie-downs, martingales, etc. *See, e.g.*, Andrew N. McLean & Paul D. McGreevy, *Horse*-Training Techniques That May Defy the Principles of Learning Theory, 5 J. OF VETERINARY BEHAVIOR 187–95 (2010).

[113] Raemisch, *supra* note 112.

[114] Raemish, *supra* note 112.

[115] Moran, *supra* note 23, at 644.

[116] Rosemary-Claire Collard & Kathryn Gillespie, *Introduction*, *in* CRITICAL ANIMAL GEOGRAPHIES: POLITICS, INTERSECTIONS AND HIERARCHIES IN A MULTISPECIES WORLD 1, 9 (Kathryn Gillespie & Rosemary-Claire Collard eds., 2015).

those present in training programs are valuable as lively commodities. Both are used as props from which the prison sustains itself materially and makes (empirically unfounded) claims about its ability to rehabilitate. Because the prison always entails multi-species relationships, it is not the case that criminalizing animal abuse will protect animals. At best, it will protect some animals while redirecting violence to farmed animals in prisons. At worst, it will bolster the prison's colonial and anti-black function and perpetuate harm to communities.

The prison also serves an ideological function; it animalizes captives who are often constructed as extra-bodily in their dangerousness – as animals who cannot be controlled otherwise and thus require caging.[117] Yet, ontology and power are not unidirectional. It is not just that we understand the human and the animal in a way that authorizes various treatments, but that these ontological orderings are justified and remade through our witnessing of caged prisoners and other animals.[118] The prison's continued existence, in part, relies on our racialized and speciesized acceptance of cages and the evisceration of life – purposefully and collaterally – that the prison requires and produces. Animal cruelty will only be meaningfully addressed through anti- and de-carceral strategies that take a multi-species approach – strategies which are are better positioned to decrease harm while protecting and benefiting humans, animals, and the environment.

[117] On extra-bodiliness, *see* Kim *supra* note 8, at 39.

[118] *See* Montford, *supra* note 57, at 80; Chloë Taylor, *Foucault and the Ethics of Eating*, 9 FOUCAULT STUDIES 71, 75 (2010).

16

Political Prisoners and the Repression of Animal Liberation and Intersectional Environmental Justice Movements

David N. Pellow

16.1 INTRODUCTION

Josh Harper is a long-time animal liberation activist and former political prisoner who became a national figure in the movement when he was sentenced to prison for three years on "animal enterprise terrorism" charges related to his support of a direct-action campaign focused on the notorious Huntingdon Life Sciences (HLS) animal testing lab. The organization he worked with was called Stop Huntingdon Life Sciences or SHAC, and Harper was one of several activists – known as the SHAC7 – sent to prison for their involvement in this effort. The campaign was ambitious, bold, creative, and highly impactful. The aim was to shut down HLS, which was one of the largest animal testing contract services in the world and had been accused of animal cruelty and multiple violations of animal welfare laws in the United States and Britain. In addition to directly targeting HLS, the SHAC campaign also focused on businesses that supplied HLS with key resources, and further singled out those businesses that contracted with HLS's suppliers in what activists refer to as primary, secondary, and tertiary targeting. Specifically, any business in HLS's network of clients was pressured to cancel those contracts or face relentless public protests, including actions outside the homes of directors and employees. This series of tactics supported a strategy of starving HLS of the resources it needed to survive, and SHAC successfully persuaded scores of companies to cut ties with the laboratory. When the campaign's victory seemed imminent, UK and US governmental authorities stepped in to to provide emergency financial support for HLS and to bring the full power of state repression down on the advocacy campaign. Josh Harper paid for his activism with a three-year prison term. Harper's time on the inside was difficult, beginning with dietary concerns:

> When I was sentenced to prison, one of the things that was very, very important to me was that I didn't want to let it change who I was to the degree that I was able. I definitely wanted to be in the sort of position where I wasn't going to let the state

> force me to consume the products of the animals who I was trying to defend to begin with. I'd heard that when I was first sent down that all federal prisons offer a vegetarian option, so I was very excited by that, and thought maybe it'd be vegan, but very quickly I realized that that wasn't the case. All of the vegetarian options at FCI Sheridan contained animal lactation or they had eggs, it wasn't easy to stay vegan in there.[1]

Harper described his time in prison as a "monstrous. . .thirty-two-month nightmare."[2] He has been quite open about the mental health impacts associated with serving time and has advocated that activists providing support for political prisoners do a better job of addressing those needs more directly and effectively. He stated, "Prison is something that's horribly traumatizing, I can't imagine most people being incarcerated for very long at all without having some sort of long-term effect on their lives."[3]

In this chapter I examine prisons and imprisonment to explore how these institutions, policies, and practices constitute a form of multispecies repression and a set of structural forces that are directly harmful to animal liberation movements and intersectional environmental justice movements (those grassroots efforts focused on defending marginalized communities and their land bases). I argue that by imprisoning animal liberation activists and intersectional environmental justice movement leaders, the criminal legal system hampers or removes critical resources for addressing the harm to nonhumans and that prisons themselves are sites of routine violence against more-than-human populations. Drawing on a range of sources of evidence and literatures, I find there are two reasons explaining this wide-ranging series of impacts by carceral institutions on both human and more-than-human communities:

First, some of the most effective leaders in the animal, earth liberation, and intersectional environmental justice movements are locked behind bars. Removing them from society and daily engagements with social movements significantly diminishes their ability to foment social change. Key activists from groups like SHAC, the Animal Liberation Front, the Earth Liberation Front, as well as "lone wolves" have spent many years behind bars, making it difficult for them to intervene materially and discursively in service to the cause of defending and protecting nonhuman populations and ecosystems. Frequently, when such activists speak out from behind bars during their time in prison, they are severely punished. For example, while he was in prison, SHAC7 activist Kevin Kjonaas wrote a statement about animal liberation that a musical artist read over the public address system at a concert, and Kjonaas was punished by prison officials. Similarly, his colleague Josh Harper was placed into solitary confinement for one hundred days for speaking out

1 Interview by *It's Going Down with Josh Harper*, Animal Liberation Activist (May 28, 2017).
2 Interview with Josh Harper, Animal Liberation Activist (Nov. 9, 2009).
3 *Id.*

from prison. And when they are released from prison and return to their communities, these activists frequently carry the burdens of their disabling time in prison and feel less efficacious and less willing to engage in the level of activism they pursued prior to incarceration.

While many committed animal liberation activists have spent time in America's penal system, activists from revolutionary movements in communities of color and Indigenous communities (such as the Black Liberation Army, MOVE, Puerto Rican Independence, and American Indian Movement) have tended to face much harsher sentences as well as more violent repression by agents of the state (compounding the more general, daily repression those entire communities face). While the latter set of movements is not usually thought of in the vein of animal liberation causes, I include them here because I consider them to be a part of intersectional environmental justice movements. By that, I mean they are concerned with defending and improving the well-being of marginalized populations and their land bases, which are necessarily multispecies territories. What also makes these movements relevant to intersectional environmental justice is that among their primary concerns are combating state and corporate power, racism, colonialism, and militarism and their effects on vulnerable peoples and ecosystems, in favor of community-based solutions that would result in peoples exercising democratic control over land, territory, and space. The American Indian Movement continues to fight for Native American treaty rights and sovereignty. The Puerto Rican Independentistas seek nothing short of the removal of the US occupying government from that island, while the Black Panther Party and the Black Liberation Army have fought for the same with respect to African American communities. And the MOVE organization in particular is explicitly anti-racist, anti-capitalist, anarchist, and pro–animal liberation. More recently, the rise of the Black Lives Matter movement (or the Movement for Black Lives) has continued to build on these earlier efforts, promoting a vision of justice that is intersectional and deeply critical of racist state violence. In sum, these revolutionary movements offer an opportunity to articulate and achieve a broader aim, which is to develop a more robust way of linking movements for animal liberation and environmental and social justice, with efforts to abolish prisons in particular and the caging of living beings of any species more broadly.

The second reason for the wide-ranging spectrum of impacts of carceral institutions on multispecies communities is that prisons and jails produce a range of direct and indirect harms to nonhuman species and ecosystems. In many cases, carceral facilities are constructed on or adjacent to lands and bodies of water that are critical habitats for vulnerable and/or endangered species. Prisons and jails regularly pollute waterways through waste discharges, both routine and accidental, which place many aquatic species at risk. Furthermore, the day to day functioning of a prison or jail is made possible by the mass consumption of nonhuman animals for food, clothing, and other "goods" and "services," reflecting the general trends we see outside of prisons. Finally, the carceral system contributes significantly to global anthropogenic climate change by producing considerable greenhouse gas emissions,[4] a socioecological phenomenon that, in turn, contributes to the devastation of nonhuman habitats, well-being, and lives.

Below I elaborate on these two arguments above by considering cases that support these claims.

16.2 PRISONS AS SITES OF POLITICAL REPRESSION

Many activists from animal liberation, earth liberation, and social justice movements have served time in carceral facilities, making it difficult for them to promote and support transformative social change. This is a major aim of the prison industrial complex – to repress the people and ideas that generate resistance to multispecies oppressions and to ensure the continued functioning of a white supremacist, heteropatriarchal, speciesist, ecocidal capitalist state.

16.2.1 *Spaces of State Repression*

Marius Mason is currently serving time in prison for his actions in the name of earth and animal liberation. He is a longtime supporter of the radical environmental movement group Earth First!, has worked as a gardener and a volunteer for a free herbal health care collective, and made great strides to unite labor and environmental activists through volunteering for the Industrial Workers of the World (IWW) and building alliances alongside famed radical labor-environmental leader Judi Bari. Mason was involved in an arson at Michigan State University intended to destroy data and equipment that he believed were used to further the production of genetically modified crops. This action was intended as a material demonstration of solidarity with global South nations struggling under the weight of free trade agreements that favor the transition from natural crops to genetically engineered agriculture. The day after the arson action at Michigan State, Mason and his partner set fire to commercial logging equipment at a timber camp in Mesick, Michigan, as a direct action and protest against deforestation. Mason later acknowledged that he also burned boats owned by a mink farmer as a protest action directed at the fur industry. Mason said his actions were "individual acts of conscience," and that the property damage he committed was intended "to protect my community and the Earth, to respond in defense of the living systems of animals, land and water."[5] In alignment with the published guidelines of the Earth Liberation Front and Animal Liberation Front (both of which are underground radical movements that

[4] Julius Alexander McGee et al., *Locked into Emissions: How Mass Incarceration Contributes to Climate Change*, Soc. Currents 1, 3–5 (2020).

[5] Transcript of Sentencing Hearing at 91, United States v. Mason, No. 08-CR-47, http://freemarius.mayfirst.org/wp-content/uploads/2016/08/mason-sentencing-transcript.pdf (W.D. Mich. Feb. 5, 2009).

deliberately refuse mainstream, reformist tactics and strategies), no people or animals were physically harmed as a result of these arsons.

Drawing on legislation prohibiting "terrorism" in defense of nonhuman animals, a judge sentenced Mason to twenty-one years and ten months in prison – the longest sentence that any animal or earth liberation activist has faced. Mason was instantly and widely regarded as a political prisoner, given this extraordinary punishment for what amounted to arson and property damage (actions that are already illegal under the law and for which the typical sentence is far less harsh). He is an outspoken transgender man who advocates for the rights of marginalized populations, both human and nonhuman. And while imprisonment has clearly made his activism more difficult, like many political prisoners, Marius Mason continues to seek out ways to make a difference from behind bars. For example, Mason is a prolific artist who has produced numerous paintings that are featured in publications and zines within activist communities around the nation and the world. Mason's paintings include a wide range of subjects, speaking to a radical intersectional politics that I have elsewhere called a "total liberation" framework,[6] which seeks to confront all forms of hierarchy, inequality, and domination. A sampling of Mason's many paintings features the following:

> *Nonhuman animals facing oppression in: "tigers for sale" – concerning tigers left in limbo after the closure of the Ringling Bros. circus; chimpanzees facing threats from a large hydroelectric dam in Guinea; a painting decrying laboratory experimentation on mice titled "The Toxicity Test" or "Welcome to Hell, Exhibit A"; and a painting highlighting the plight of the endangered vaquita porpoise in the Gulf of California titled "Netting Vaquitas";
>
> *A series on transgender luminaries titled "Trans Hero/Heroine Series." This series includes: "Sylvia Rivera: Trans Action Revolutionary"; "Chris Mosier – transathlete and activist"; a painting of African American writer, social activist, and trans woman imprisoned for fighting back against transphobic, racist violent vigilantes, titled: "Cece McDonald"; a painting of an imprisoned African American transgender woman who was refused hormone therapy and wrongfully placed in a male prison facility, titled "Ashley Diamond";
>
> *A number of paintings celebrating Indigenous environmental justice activists. This series includes: "Tara Houska of Honor the Earth" and "For Naelyn Pike [San Carlos Apache] standing with Standing Rock";
>
> *Paintings honoring a number of political prisoners, including Puerto Rican *independentista* Oscar Lopez Rivera while he was incarcerated, titled "Free Oscar Lopez," and "Pine Ridge Sundance Tree for Leonard Peltier";

Mason has also produced artwork focused on the struggle against environmental racism in America's cities ("The Trouble in Flint") and much more. In addition to

[6] David Pellow, Total Liberation: The Power and Promise of Animal Rights and the Radical Earth Movement (2014).

his paintings, Mason writes poetry and offers words of inspiration in letters to supporters and activists worldwide. And while Mason's intersectional environmental justice activism has inspired many supporters and admirers, the prison system severely limits his capacity to engage in that work. For example, he has had to fight for his right to vegan meals while being placed in solitary confinement.

American Indian Movement political prisoner Leonard Peltier was a dedicated AIM activist during the early 1970s, during which time he actively supported Native sovereignty and opposed predatory federal and corporate activities designed to extract mineral and ecological wealth from Native lands. He was sentenced to two consecutive life terms for the alleged murder of two FBI agents during a government assault on the Pine Ridge reservation. Peltier's writings from prison also articulate a critique of US colonialism and empire as environmental racism directed at Indigenous peoples:

> White society would now like to terminate us as peoples and push us off our reservations so they can steal our remaining mineral and oil resources. It's nothing new for them to steal from nonwhite peoples. When the oppressors succeed with their illegal thefts and depredations, it's called colonialism. When their efforts to colonize indigenous peoples are met with resistance or anything but abject surrender, it's called war. When the colonized peoples attempt to resist their oppression and defend themselves, we're called criminals.[7]

Peltier's argument reflects the widely held view among AIM supporters and human rights attorneys that his imprisonment was based on scant evidence and rooted in the US state's desire to punish an Indigenous man and movement for resisting conquest.

MOVE is a Black revolutionary group founded in Philadelphia in the early 1970s. The group organized around a determination to improve community health and to challenge the racist-capitalist state, and the dispossession, police brutality, and industrial pollution it routinely metes out. A clear illustration of a movement committed to intersectional environmental justice, many MOVE members were vegetarians and staunch animal rights advocates. Not surprisingly, MOVE was targeted with massive police repression and militarized violence, and numerous members were killed while others were imprisoned, including Ramona Africa. Years after her release, MOVE activist and former political prisoner Ramona Africa describes how she and other prisoners pushed back against their jailers by embracing multispecies ecological awareness and interdependence:

> [I]t was really something to be [imprisoned] with MOVE women. . .One thing we did was we fed the birds leftover food. . .Leftover food. . .if it wasn't used, [the jail] couldn't save it according to their health codes, they had to toss it. The county jail is right along the river and there are a lot of seagulls there and the river is so polluted there is virtually no edible food for the seagulls, so we used to take leftover fish

[7] Leonard Peltier, Prison Writings: My Life IS My Sundance 44 (1999).

sticks, eggs or bread, different things that we figured the birds would eat – we had these plastic buckets and we would take the leftovers out [during yard time]. We would dump [the food] and walk away and the birds would swoop down and eat it. This one particular day, a Sunday, we had gotten the birds some food at breakfast and we were waiting for [yard time] so we could take the food out. This one sergeant, a Black woman, was in a very nasty mood, she told us that we could not take those buckets of food out. Well, we went off. We told her, "What are you talking about? You were gonna throw this food away. Can you substantiate to us why this food should go in the trash when those birds could eat it? If you feel that life should not eat then apply it to your own self and stop eating. It's not the birds' fault they can't feed themselves, they don't wanna eat this slop, but man has poisoned their source of food…You're not gonna tell us that we aren't gonna feed life."

We went off. Well, she got all mad, she got pissed off, she called the riot squad over, said we were disturbing the institution, they didn't lock us in our cells then but that night at lock-in time they locked us in [and] when we got up the next morning our cell doors were locked…They had locked us in and gave us write-ups, misconducts…We got found guilty…[and] we each got a fifty-thousand-dollar bail, all for taking a stand on feeding the birds. We didn't threaten anybody, you know, but that is the attitude of the prisons. But these are the things I learned from MOVE, about taking a stand for life, taking care of life.[8]

Ramona Africa's story powerfully reflects the ways that incarceration is predicated on anti-ecological principles that subject caged beings to a living death, that seek to impose immobility on a world where mobility is a constant, and that seek separation and dependence in a world of interconnection and interdependence. Africa and her colleagues resisted based on the fundamental principles of intersectional environmental and multispecies justice.

16.2.2 *Chemical Warfare*

Another terrain of intersectional environmental struggle inside the carceral system concerns the use of chemicals. For example, the considerable volumes of pepper spray used to pacify and punish imprisoned persons for noncompliant behavior is quite concerning, which includes a range of people, particularly those suffering from mental illness.[9] Corrections officers routinely apply pepper spray to imprisoned persons in order to force them to follow orders and/or to subdue them during moments of conflict. The results of exposure to pepper spray can range from eye irritation and temporary blindness, burning sensations, second- and third-degree

8 Interview by Sormeh Ayari with Ramona Africa, in Riverside, Cal. (Apr. 16, 2004).

9 Hum. Rts. Watch, Callous and Cruel: Use of Force against Inmates with Mental Disabilities in U.S. Jails and Prisons (May 12, 2015), www.hrw.org/report/2015/05/12/callous-and-cruel/use-force-against-inmates-mental-disabilities-us-jails-and.

burns, positional asphyxia, psychotic episodes, and possibly death.[10] I refer to such practices as *chemical warfare* because they are actions intended to harm, subdue, and incapacitate an individual and/or group for the purpose of controlling that population and their associated territory. The Merriam-Webster Dictionary defines chemical warfare as "tactical warfare using incendiary mixtures, smokes, or irritant, burning, poisonous, or asphyxiating gases" and, according to that same source, a chemical weapon is defined simply as "a weapon used in chemical warfare."[11] I believe these definitions accurately and appropriately describe many of the practices of using chemicals on the bodies and communities of incarcerated persons *as well as* the broader realities of environmental injustice that affect communities beyond the prison walls around the world. In many ways, the prison is the ideal space for the use of chemical warfare and the practice of environmental injustice because the target population is so severely limited in its mobility and the space that is the terrain of conflict is so well defined.

From a multispecies justice and animal liberation perspective, we can also point to the ways in which chemical warfare directed at *nonhumans* generally precedes and facilitates chemical warfare used against humans. Studies of pepper spray's primary active ingredient – oleoresin capsicum (OC) – have been used to determine its efficacy and safety on humans by first using it on nonhumans, particularly mice. One recent study notes that OC causes numerous physiological reactions: "Cardiopulmonary functions such as respiratory depression, severe irritation, inflamed respiratory tract, hyperventilation and, tachycardia are the most affected ones when it comes to the riot control agent oleoresin capsicum (OC) exposure."[12] It is noteworthy that the authors of that study explicitly name OC as a method of "riot control," which is an open acknowledgment of its use as a weapon of state violence.

European American activist Ray Luc Levasseur was deeply involved in anti-war and anti-racist organizing in the 1960s and 1970s. In 1986, he was indicted and charged with taking part in paramilitary actions in support of a range of anti-imperialist and social justice struggles (including support for Puerto Rican Independence, the Anti-Apartheid movement in South Africa, and opposition to US military involvement in Central America) as part of the United Freedom Front. All of these movements – anti-war, anti-imperialist, anti-racist – are, in my view, clearly and comfortably within the ambit of environmental justice, as they are organized in support of democracy, self-determination, public health, and the reclamation of territories by colonized peoples. While he was acquitted of seditious conspiracy, Levasseur still had to serve his original sentence. During his time

[10] *Id.*

[11] *Chemical warfare*, Merriam-Webster.com, www.merriam-webster.com/dictionary/chemical%20warfare.

[12] Pompy Patowary et al., *Cardiopulmonary Function and Dysregulated Cardiopulmonary Reflexes Following Acute Oleoresin Capsicum Exposure in Rats*, 405 Toxicol. & Appl. Pharmac. (Oct. 15, 2020), https://doi.org/10.1016/j.taap.2020.115188.

incarcerated at ADX – Administrative Maximum, in Florence, Colorado, the nation's highest security prison – Levasseur noted the presence and power of pepper spray and rightly called it an instrument of chemical warfare:

> I'm deeply cornered in their prison. My sight is diminished, but I maintain my vision. I see their hand in the use of four point "restraints" to spread-eagle prisoners, something inherently abusive regardless of the excuse. I see forced feedings, cell extractions, mind medications, and *chemical weapons* used to incapacitate.[13]

Other forms of chemical warfare in carceral facilities are quite widespread. Recent reports have surfaced that immigrant children apprehended by federal authorities and placed in prisons ("detention centers") have been forcibly injected with psychotropic drugs, rendering them lethargic, dizzy, listless, incapacitated, afraid, and obese.[14] And while these chemicals are not strictly "incendiary," they are indeed *weapons* used to neutralize and pacify populations deemed enemies. Author, professor, and former Black liberation political prisoner Angela Davis served time in a jail in New York state in a section where all or most of the female imprisoned persons were mentally ill. While serving time, Davis's capacities to work as an activist were severely hampered – one of the key aims of state repression. But she also noticed that many of the women in the prison were being given Thorazine (now called chlorpromazine) – a drug intended to control the moods of mentally ill persons, and one that is reportedly overused in many prison settings:

> After they took their seats, they became completely absorbed in themselves, blank stares telling me that no matter how much I wanted to talk, it would be futile to approach any of them. Later I learned that these women received Thorazine with their meals each day and, even if they were completely sane, the tranquilizers would always make them uncommunicative and detached from their surroundings. After a few hours of watching them gaze silently into space, I felt as though I had been thrown into a nightmare.[15]

There was resistance to this practice as well, Davis reported:

> One morning in the day room, Barbara, the young Black woman from the cell directly across from mine, broke her habitual silence to tell me she had refused her daily dose of Thorazine. It was very simple: she was tired of feeling like a vegetable all the time. She was going to resist the Thorazine and was going to get out of 4b [a special section of the jail where mentally ill prisoners were held].[16]

[13] Raymond Luc Levasseur, *Trouble Coming Every Day: ADX – The First Year, in* The New Abolitionists: (Neo)Slave Narratives and Contemporary Prison Writings 45, 48 (Joy James ed., 2005) (emphasis added).

[14] Matt Smith & Aura Bogado, *Immigrant Children Forcibly Injected with Drugs at Texas Shelter, Lawsuit Claims*, Tex. Trib. (June 20, 2018) www.texastribune.org/2018/06/20/immigrant-children-forcibly-injected-drugs-lawsuit-claims/.

[15] Angela Davis, Angela Davis: an Autobiography 39–40 (1998).

[16] *Id.* at 42–43.

Thorazine/chlorpromazine is prescribed as an anti-psychotic treatment for people with schizophrenia and other mental disorders. It was the first widely prescribed anti-psychotic drug. And while Davis herself may not have been forced to ingest this drug while incarcerated, the impacts of witnessing its effects on her fellow incarcerated peers clearly left an imprint and affected her for decades. Moreover, chlorpromazine was and remains widely used in experiments on nonhuman animals.[17]

The relevance of chlorpromazine and oleoresin capsicum here is twofold: (1) there is evidence that these substances have been used to sedate, harm, and control human beings in carceral settings, thus reducing their capacity to think clearly and resist their conditions of confinement; and (2) like virtually any other drug on the market and like many other industrial chemicals in use, chlorpromazine and oleo capsaicin were first tested on nonhumans, reflecting the medical industry's long-standing use of "animal models" as a way of ensuring that a treatment is "safe" and acceptable for humans.[18] In other words, these chemicals were and are simultaneously being used on nonhumans and humans to officially advance medically and politically desirable outcomes for the capitalist, carceral state, but are also integral to maintaining the speciesist and racist brutality of the medical-industrial complex and the prison-industrial complex, which means sacrificing the lives of nonhumans in experiments and harming imprisoned persons who are force-fed or sprayed with these substances. Moreover, the use of these harmful chemicals in prisons and jails is directly linked to the broader trend of medical experimentation on incarcerated human populations, a phenomenon occurring in many prison systems around the world.[19]

Carceral institutions are of significance to scholars and advocates of animal liberation, earth liberation, and intersectional environmental justice movements because leaders in these movements have been routinely incarcerated, which, in addition to reflecting state-based punishment for their resistance activities, often severely limits their ability to continue the work of social change. Furthermore, the use of chemical warfare in carceral facilities is frequently used to pacify and punish imprisoned persons deemed a threat, which directly harms those populations and indirectly harms those who witness such abuses (including political prisoners), a practice that is made possible by experimentation on nonhuman animals. Even so,

[17] Mark A. Geyer et al., *From Antipsychotic to Anti-schizophrenia Drugs: Role of Animal Models*, 33 TRENDS PHARMAC. SCIS. 515–21 (July 16, 2012), https://doi.org/10.1016/j.tips.2012.06.006.

[18] Anne-Noël Samaha et al., *"Breakthrough" Dopamine Supersensitivity during Ongoing Antipsychotic Treatment Leads to Treatment Failure over Time*, 17 J. NEUROSCI. 2979–86 (Mar. 14, 2007), https://doi.org/10.1523/JNEUROSCI.5416-06.2007.

[19] *See* Keramet Reiter, *Experimentation on Prisoners: Persistent Dilemmas in Rights and Regulations*, 97 CALIF. L. REV. 501–66 (2009); Silja J.A. Talvi, The Prison as Laboratory, 26 THESE TIMES (Dec. 7, 2001) https://inthesetimes.com/article/the-prison-as-laboratory; Mike Ward & Bill Bishop, *Becoming Guinea Pigs to Avoid Poor Prison Care: Ill Inmates Urge Each Other to Join Experiments*, AUSTIN AM.-STATESMAN, Dec. 17, 2001, at A1.

many such activists find ways of pursuing some level of movement support and leadership, even under exceedingly harsh conditions.

16.3 PRISONS AS HARMFUL TO NONHUMAN SPECIES AND ECOSYSTEMS

Prisons, jails, and other carceral facilities are also sites of direct harm to nonhuman animals and ecosystems. These impacts include the use of nonhumans for food and profit, the effects of prison construction and daily operations on sensitive ecological habits where endangered species live, and the significant contributions to global climate gas emissions associated with prison systems.

16.3.1 *Food*

As noted earlier, Josh Harper found it difficult to maintain a vegan diet in prison because meals served in US carceral facilities in many ways reflect the general diets and eating habits embraced by much of the American public, which is heavily centered on animal products. For example, a menu from the infamous federal prison on Alcatraz Island, dated 1946, listed the following dishes: "roast pork shoulder, beef pot pie Anglaise, baked meat croquettes with Bechamel sauce, potato chowder, fried eggs and spinach with bacon."[20] A 2015 analysis of prison menus from around the United States bears out this observation as well, with the following items appearing on meal trays regularly: boiled or scrambled eggs, milk, margarine, gravy, chicken livers, meat patties, hot dogs, chicken, turkey, bologna sandwiches.[21] In a study of a twenty-eight-day cycle menu at a large county jail in the state of Georgia, researchers found that the following items containing animal products were regularly served: sausage links or sausage patties, chicken patties, beef chili, macaroni and cheese, mayonnaise, cheese slices, lemon cake, buttered rice, cookies, chocolate cake, yellow cake, devil's food cake, cornbread, pancakes, buttered grits, ham, charbroiled beef, and breaded fish. Not only is this menu heavy on animal products, the study's authors concluded that it is nutritionally unhealthy in that it exceeds national recommendations (e.g., the Institute of Medicine and the National Academies' Dietary Reference Intakes) on sodium, saturated fat, and cholesterol,

[20] David Reutter, *Prison Food and Commissary Services: A Recipe for Disaster*, Prison Legal News (Aug. 4, 2018), www.prisonlegalnews.org/news/2018/aug/4/prison-food-and-commissary-services-recipe-disaster/.

[21] Alysia Santo & Lisa Iaboni, *What's in a Prison Meal?* Life Inside (July 7, 2015), www.themarshallproject.org/2015/07/07/what-s-in-a-prison-meal.

and because it provides less than two-thirds of the recommended daily allowance for magnesium, potassium, and vitamins A, D, and E.[22]

The largest single utilizer of the California state Department of General Services contracts is the California state prison system. Specifically, the California Department of Corrections and Rehabilitation (CDCR) feeds some 118,000 incarcerated persons each day. The California Prison Industry Authority (CALPIA) is the state agency that oversees the work assignments for thousands of imprisoned persons in the state's prison system, managing some 57 manufacturing and service operations. CALPIA produces these goods and services for federal, state, county, and city governments as well as tribal governments, and each year the agency makes and sells some $65 million worth of agricultural and food products, including meat, eggs, milk, and chicken. By far the largest purchaser of these goods from CALPIA is the CDCR, revealing that the prison system is a both a massive producer and consumer of animal products. Moreover, the CDCR is the largest state of California food purchaser and service provider, delivering 130 million meals each year across the state's thirty-five carceral facilities at a cost of $150 million.[23] And while there are vegetarian options available to a small subset of incarcerated persons, the vast majority of meals feature animal products, making the prison system a site and source of significant nonhuman suffering and violence. Thus, within the carceral system, massive volumes of nonhumans are conscripted and consumed.

During his time in Texas prisons, environmental justice activist Keith "Malik" Washington regularly narrated the multispecies injustices occurring in that state's prisons. In an article he wrote (that was published in the radical environmental publication *Earth First! Journal*), Washington explains that the Eastham Unit (where he served time for many years) produces approximately 80,000 eggs per week and that the Texas Department of Criminal Justice (TDCJ) nets around $100,000 in revenue each week from that operation alone.[24] He also noted that Eastham places 3,000 hogs, 600 sows, and ships 21 piglets out for sale each week.[25] Washington draws links between the struggle for nonhuman animal and human rights, and urges his readers to act:

> Many prisoners have died on account of the deadly extreme heat in Texas prisons. Young pigs are vulnerable to extreme heat. Young piglets generate profits for TDCJ.

[22] Emma A. Cook et al., *The Diet of Inmates: An Analysis of a 28-Day Cycle Menu Used in a Large County Jail in the State of Georgia*, 21 J. CORR. HEALTH. (Aug. 14, 2015), https://doi.org/10.1177/1078345815600160.

[23] CALIFORNIA HEALTH IN ALL POLICIES TASK FORCE, CALIFORNIA STATE GOVERNMENT FOOD PROCUREMENT POLICIES AND PRACTICES, 18 (2016), https://sdcoi.org/wp-content/uploads/2017/12/ca-state-government-food-procurement-policies-and-practices_2016.pdf.

[24] Keith "Malik" Washington, *Horrific Conditions for Live-Stock Animals in Texas Prisons Exposed*, FIGHT TOXIC PRISONS (Feb. 12, 2018), https://fighttoxicprisons.wordpress.com/2018/02/12/horrific-conditions-for-live-stock-animals-in-texas-prisons-exposed-and-other-updates-from-malik-washington/.

[25] *Id.*

> A couple years ago, TDCJ invested $175,000 for a cooling system for the pigs. The pigs are being preserved for slaughter so TDCJ can benefit. TDCJ does not have any concern for animal rights or human rights. Its main focus is profits by any means. It is time we take a closer look at what is really going on inside Texas prisons. As activists who are on the "front lines," we have a duty to confront those entities who abuse and mistreat animals as well as pollute our precious water supplies.[26]

And while the consumption of nonhuman animals in jails and prisons should be a major concern for any animal liberationist, it must also be noted that the general quality and quantity of prison food in the United States and in most countries is deplorable, frequently contributing to malnutrition, illness, and even starvation.[27] One legal complaint on behalf of imprisoned persons held in Gordon County, Georgia's jail reported that "inmates have told us they are so hungry they eat toothpaste and toilet paper. Most reported losing a significant amount of weight."[28] These long-standing practices have only been exacerbated during this era of the privatization of food services in carceral facilities.[29] Imprisoned people in prisons around the U.S. and the world regularly engage in hunger strikes, riots, and other forms of resistance in response to unhealthy, unappetizing, and insufficient food.[30]

16.3.2 *Impacts on Sensitive Ecological Habitats*

There are additional reasons to be concerned about the impacts of prisons on nonhuman populations, and examining the relationship between prisons and broader ecosystems reveals some troubling trends. The Monroe Correctional Complex (North of Seattle) is the site of two interrelated problems that are increasingly common in carceral facilities: overcrowding and excessive strain on waste management systems. As a result of punitive criminal legal system policies (such as "three strikes"), many prisons and jails have incarcerated populations that are far greater than the number of people such facilities were built and designed to house. The frequent result is that sewage systems are overtaxed and break down, producing spills both inside and outside of these institutions. In the Monroe Correctional Complex case, several hundreds of thousands of gallons of sewage spilled from this prison into the nearby Skykomish river, where chinook, coho, and pink salmon populations live, and where steelhead and bull trout thrive as well. This river is also a

26 *Id.*

27 *See* Reutter, *supra* note 20; Santo & Iaboni, *supra* note 21.

28 Southern Center for Human Rights, Letter to Gordon County Sheriff's Office Re: Failure to Provide Adequate Nutrition to People in the Gordon County Jail 1 (2014), www.schr.org/files/post/files/SCHR%20to%20Sheriff%20Ralston%2010%2028%2014.pdf.

29 *See* Reutter, *supra* note 20.

30 Doug McMurdo, *Last Riot at Kingman Prison Could Have Been Prevented by Water, Lunch*, Miner (Sept. 6, 2015), https://kdminer.com/news/2015/sep/06/last-riot-at-kingman-prison-could-have-been-preve/.

popular site for human recreation, fishing, kayaking, and swimming, so when the prison's sewage system overflows, both human and nonhuman communities are placed at risk.[31]

In another example, a proposed federal prison to be located in Letcher County, Kentucky, would have caged hundreds of human beings and also negatively impacted critical habitat for the endangered grey bat and the Indiana bat. Both species continue to suffer extensive damage related to a deadly disease called White Nose Syndrome.[32] In addition to these vulnerable nonhuman populations, some seventy-one different species of fauna were potentially threatened by the construction of what would be the most expensive federal prison in US history. Furthermore, the prison would have been located atop a site where coal mining via mountaintop removal occurred for years, adding insult to injury. A coalition of incarcerated persons, prisoners' rights organizations, and environmental justice activists mobilized for years to oppose the construction of USP Letcher because it would threaten the health of imprisoned people, nonhuman species, and local ecosystems, and because the environmental impact report the government commissioned did an insufficient job of addressing those anticipated effects. In June of 2019, a group of twenty-one incarcerated people and several allied organizations succeeded in stopping this project when the federal Bureau of Prisons withdrew its proposal[33] – a major victory for carceral, environmental, climate, and multispecies justice.

In June of 2000, the abolitionist organization Critical Resistance filed a lawsuit to challenge the proposed construction of the Kern Valley State Prison in central California. One of the many reasons for this intervention by Critical Resistance and its coalition partners was that not only would this prison be inherently harmful for the humans caged within it; it also threatened the habitats and well-being of vulnerable nonhuman species like the Tipton kangaroo rat and the San Joaquin Valley kit fox. The unlikely coalition of partners in this struggle included the Rainforest Action Network, the NAACP, and a group called Friends of the Kangaroo Rat. While the movement lost that particular battle and the prison was built despite their efforts, the struggle underscored the many ways in which the fates of humans and more-than-human species are entangled and threatened by the prison system.[34]

[31] Rick Anderson, *Greenwashing Washington State's Prison System in a River of Sewage*, Prison Legal News (July 31, 2015), www.prisonlegalnews.org/news/2015/jul/31/greenwashing-washington-states-prison-system-river-sewage/.

[32] Human Rights Defense Center, Letter to Bureau of Prisons Re: Proposed USP/FPC Letcher County Draft Environmental Impact Statement 14 (2015).

[33] *Inmates and Activists Stop New Prison on Strip Mine Site in Kentucky*, PR Newswire (June 13, 2019), www.prnewswire.com/news-releases/inmates-and-activists-stop-new-prison-on-strip-mine-site-in-kentucky-300867324.html.

[34] Rose Braz & Craig Gilmore, Joining Forces: *Prisons and Environmental Justice in Recent California Organizing*, 95 Radical Hist. Rev., 95, 95–111 (2006); Mark Martin, *Critics Say*

16.3.3 *Prisons as Engines of Climate Injustice*

In a groundbreaking study, McGee, Greiner, and Appleton (2020) find that increases in the number of people incarcerated in a given state are significantly associated with growth in greenhouse gas emissions. These climate-disrupting emissions occur as a result of construction for new prison facilities, the delivery of goods and services to feed and clothe incarcerated persons, and because imprisoned people constitute a cheap labor force that provides a major economic boost to corporations that, in turn, produce additional emissions. In other words, prisons play an important role in contributing to global anthropogenic climate change and are a key component of what scholars have called the Treadmill of Production[35] – a theory that explains how the global economy relies on the continuous extraction of material wealth from ecosystems, which is then used to fuel capital investment, resulting in rising pollution levels and social inequalities. In the context of the prison industrial complex, these dynamics reinforce a Treadmill of Mass Incarceration, wherein the existing tensions between labor and capital are further amplified by the monopolization of low-cost, nonunionized, coerced, imprisoned workers, which feeds the process of capital accumulation.[36]

These linkages are (or at least should be) of great concern because climate change's effects on nonhuman populations is extensive. However, it must be noted that climate change's documented impacts on nonhuman animals are rarely centered in major scientific reports and generally ignored.[37] Despite that fact, the effects are grave and include: the widely documented harm to polar bears associated with the multiplier effects of Arctic sea ice loss; the widespread extinction of harlequin frogs in Central and South America due to the growth of a lethal fungus that attacks their skin and teeth;[38] and significant declines in the British ring ouzel population, a songbird.[39]. More broadly, there is a general scientific consensus that we are in the midst of the sixth mass extinction, and one study quantified potential losses of species by concluding that between 15 and 37 percent of all nonhumans could be extinct by the year 2050, as a consequence of human-caused climate

New State Prison Defies Logic, S.F. GATE (Jan. 5, 2004), www.sfgate.com/news/article/Critics-say-new-state-prison-defies-logic-They-2816998.php.

35 *See* KENNETH A. GOULD ET AL., THE TREADMILL OF PRODUCTION: INJUSTICE AND UNSUSTAINABILITY IN THE GLOBAL ECONOMY (2015).

36 McGee, *supra* note 4, at 11–12.

37 Wayne Hsiung & Cass R. Sunstein, *Climate Change and Animals*, 155 U. PA. L. REV., 1695, 1695–1740 (2007).

38 Alan J. Pounds et al., *Widespread Amphibian Extinctions from Epidemic Disease Driven by Global Warming*, 439 NATURE 161–63 (2006),www.nature.com/articles/nature04246.

39 Colin M. Beale et al., *Climate Change May Account for the Decline in British Ring Ouzels Turdus Torquatus*, 75 J. ANIMAL ECOL. 826-28 (2006), https://doi.org/10.1111/j.1365-2656.2006.01102.x.

disruption.[40] It should also be noted that the vast majority of scholarly and activist narratives around *climate justice* focus almost entirely on the uneven and disproportionate impacts of anthropogenic climate change on vulnerable and marginalized *human* populations.[41] Given the clear and undeniable effects of climate disruption on nonhuman communities, it would behoove scholars and activists to consider expanding the ambit of their concerns to include a multispecies climate justice framework.

Carceral institutions present major threats to the well-being and futures of nonhuman populations because of (1) the common construction and location of prisons in critical animal habitat and fragile ecosystems; (2) the routine, daily operations of prisons that extract life from millions of nonhumans for food (among other goods and services); and (3) prisons' production of substantial greenhouse gas emissions, contributing both to anthropogenic climate change and mass extinction.

16.4 CONCLUSION

Prisons and jails represent a form of multispecies violence and repression directed at nonhuman animals and their defenders. Carceral institutions are literally built on and rely upon the bodies and territories of nonhumans and vulnerable human populations, producing massive harm across species and space. Furthermore, activists from animal liberation, earth liberation, and intersectional environmental justice movements have been frequently imprisoned as punishment for their resistance efforts and as a way to neutralize their efficacy, which means they have fewer means to promote justice for nonhumans and humans alike. Since this book volume is aimed at confronting the logic of criminalization and incarceration as a pathway toward justice for nonhumans, this chapter offers a critical perspective on this matter. The evidence presented here suggests quite clearly that the criminal legal system and the prison-industrial complex operate in ways that are deeply detrimental to the present and future life chances of nonhumans for a myriad of reasons.

My inclusion and consideration of intersectional environmental justice movements (such as the American Indian Movement, the Black Liberation struggles, the Puerto Rican Independence movement, and the Movement for Black Lives) stems from my view that these political formations present scholars and activists with an opportunity to articulate substantive linkages between animal liberation and environmental/social justice efforts, with a specific focus on prison abolition and the abolition of caging across species. Here I draw on the wisdom and vision of the Black Liberation struggle to make this case. Mumia Abu-Jamal is a former member of the

[40] Chris D. Thomas et al., *Extinction Risk from Climate Change*, 427 NATURE 145 (2004), www.nature.com/articles/nature02121.

[41] *See* KUM-KUM BHAVNANI ET AL., CLIMATE FUTURES: REIMAGINING GLOBAL CLIMATE JUSTICE (2019); NAOMI KLEIN, THIS CHANGES EVERYTHING: CAPITALISM VS. THE CLIMATE (2014).

Black Panther Party, a supporter of the MOVE organization, an internationally renowned journalist and activist on death row in Pennsylvania. Widely viewed as a political prisoner, Abu-Jamal is serving time at SCI Frackville, Pennsylvania, for the alleged murder of a police officer, another case based on highly questionable and suspect "evidence." During the 1980s, Mumia Abu-Jamal served time at SCI Huntingdon in Pennsylvania, and, in 1989, wrote about contaminated water in that facility:

> It appears that this water problem is more than prison wide; civilian communities, sharing the same water source, are also affected...The heavy gaseous odor still lingers, and a dark oily ring stains cups. It makes me wonder about a saying my wife and I share, that bars and steel can't stop the power of love. The dark side of that also is true: bars, steel, and court orders can't stop the seepage of pollution that afflicts both the caged and the "free." Despite the legal illusions erected by the system to divide and separate life, we the caged share air, water, and hope with you, the not-yet-caged. We share your same breath. As John Africa teaches, "All life is connected."[42]

In the passage above, Abu-Jamal quotes MOVE founder, the charismatic John Africa, who once declared, "Go as far as you want in the forest, and you won't find no jails. Because the animals of the forest don't believe in jail. But come to civilization, that's all you see."[43]

These two quotations underscore my view that carceral systems are harmful and destructive of everyone and everything they touch because caging – whether of humans or nonhuman animals – is inherently violent and environmentally unjust. Abu-Jamal and Africa both insist that all life is connected, so whether one is among the caged or the "not-yet-caged," the overwhelming majority of us are impacted by the prison industrial complex's widescale impacts on our bodies, climate, land, food sources, and water, and therefore have a vested interest in seeking its abolition.

[42] Mumia Abu-Jamal, Live from Death Row 50–52 (1995).

[43] Craig R. McCoy, *Unsettled Legacy of MOVE*, Phila. Inquir. (May 9, 2010), www.inquirer.com/philly/news/homepage/20100509_Unsettled_legacy_of_MOVE.html.

PART IV

Challenging Captivity and Changing Carceral Thinking

Introduction

Lori Gruen and Justin Marceau

Carceral logics are so woven into contemporary social institutions, it is often hard to imagine approaches to solving social problems that do not rely heavily on punitiveness. The chapters in this section suggest ways to think differently about captivity, its harms, its justifications, and carceral logics more broadly. One way to do that is by exploring philosophical and legal arguments that are used to justify holding prisoners captive and assessing how and when these arguments fail. Comparing these arguments to arguments that are used to justify holding animals captive is another way we can begin to think beyond the carceral. These sorts of comparisons, for example, between prisoners' rights and animal rights, are not intended to conflate two distinct forms of cause lawyering, but rather, as Amar and Chen suggest, to highlight parallels that can help identify strategies for reaching each movement's respective goals.

One of the central goals of challenging carceral thinking is to make visible the hold it has on our political imagination, the ways it negatively impacts humans and nonhumans who are trapped in the institutions it justifies, and to elevate social justice causes that condemn it. Too often, however, the causes that condemn carceral logics in the human case, like prison abolition, are dismissed because they are too radical. Attempting not to appear "too radical" has led many social justice lawyers and groups to operate within accepted legal norms, rather than challenging those norms, working instead to reform some of the more egregious practices, like solitary confinement and the death penalty. In the realm of animal law, there is a long-standing effort to avoid looking radical and to appear "mainstream"[1] by embracing, and "naturalizing" carceral thinking. The punitive impulse in animal law has

[1] Joyce Tischler, *A Brief History of Animal Law*, Part II (1985–2011), 5 STAN. J. ANIMAL L. & POL'Y 27, 59 (2012) ("Supporting the enforcement of state anticruelty laws has enabled animal law practitioners to work in a collegial manner with prosecutors, judges, and law enforcement, and has helped in the move to mainstream animal law in the legal community.").

become so strong that one could confuse a defense of the death penalty by the Supreme Court with calls for more policing and prosecution in the animal law realm: "The instinct for retribution is part of the nature of man, and channeling that instinct in the administration of criminal justice serves an important purpose."[2]

This section reminds us of the long history of human confinement, and the efforts by civil rights lawyers to push back against the trend of treating social problems with ever more punitive approaches. It asks us to think about what confinement means, and how, for example, our understanding of human confinement and false imprisonment might have implications for how we think about the animals living among and with us (Kysar). Equally important, the chapters in this section seek to reimagine the animal rights movement as the civil rights movement and to position the struggle of animal advocates alongside the history of great civil rights efforts (Potter). For some, the current efforts to reimagine and challenge carceral approaches through habeas corpus litigation or other rights litigation is valuable insofar as it spotlights the autonomy and dignity harms suffered by animals (Eisen). Yet some raise a concern that an uncritical celebration of rights, including habeas corpus, tends to entrench the very systems and the oppressions that are inherent to them, that ought to be challenged.

In sum, social justice activists, including animal activists, and cause lawyers, including those who work to elevate the status of animals, have often worked within the logic of the law and legal system to try to gain more expansive and inclusive results. But there is always a danger that tinkering within the system creates a sort of release valve that diffuses pressure to fundamentally reimagine the system. In the realm of animal confinement and human imprisonment, there is a risk that litigation efforts aimed at celebrating the potential of the legal system to serve as a check on itself will legitimize and confirm the very hierarchies and problematic systems in question. It does not mean that short-term litigation to address the immediate problems faced by suffering humans or animals should be abandoned. After all, our idealism is surely lost on the prisoners living in squalor or the animals being marched to slaughter at this very moment. Still, long-term thinking is a necessary part of anti-oppression efforts. Thus, research and discourse have to be focused on the project of "abolition" and what it means to think beyond carceral logics (Gruen). This section and the book end by calling for us to tap into a deep imagination about how things could be otherwise, to allow for the possibility of establishing new conceptions of justice that might provide freer ways for us to be in relationships with other animals and each other. Abolition, after all, is no more utopian than the view that through more prisons we will create less crime, or the view that animal

[2] Gregg v. Georgia, 428 U.S. 153, 183 (1976).

confinement is a necessary feature of human thriving. There is no reason to accept on faith that our punitive impulses are protecting animals better than a new, more imaginative framework yet to be fully fleshed out. We call on scholars to imagine beyond carceral logics, and to take the next step of developing a research agenda to make concrete what that might look like.

17

Cause Lawyering for the Caged

Invisibility, Moral Suasion, and Disenfranchisement in the Prisoners' Rights and Animal Protection Movements

Alan K. Chen & Vikram David Amar

17.1 INTRODUCTION

An important aspect of reexamining carceral logics is the careful consideration of approaches for reforming the law and social practices surrounding confinement more generally. Toward that end, this chapter undertakes a comparative examination of cause lawyering[1] in the prisoners' rights and animal protection movements. Drawing on the rich literature on cause lawyering and social movements, and on our backgrounds in American constitutional law, we discuss the similarities and differences in the possibilities for legal advocacy concerning the rights of incarcerated persons and the treatment of nonhuman animals. In the limited space available for our discussion, we aim primarily to offer a descriptive comparison rather than a normative prescription. We hope that, to the extent possible, viewing these movements through a comparative lens might lead to a collaboration and dialogue among public interest lawyers working in these respective spaces to share ideas about strategic approaches and potential similarities that might be employed to overcome common barriers to progress.[2] Furthermore, by pursuing such a typological approach, we suggest that these same points of comparison might be useful in assessing similar connections between or among other social movements.

The authors thank John Bliss for helpful comments on an earlier draft of this chapter and Richard Barahona and Michelle Penn for their excellent research support.

[1] By cause lawyering, we mean "using legal skills to pursue ends and ideals that transcend client service – be those ideals social, cultural, political, economic, or, indeed, legal." STUART SCHEINGOLD & AUSTIN SARAT, SOMETHING TO BELIEVE IN: POLITICS, PROFESSIONALISM, AND CAUSE LAWYERING 3 (2004).

[2] Cause lawyers sometimes study other social movements to learn about different strategic approaches. Michael McCann & Helena Silverstein, *Rethinking Law's "Allurements": A Relational Analysis of Social Movement Lawyers in the United States, in* CAUSE LAWYERING: POLITICAL COMMITMENTS AND PROFESSIONAL RESPONSIBILITIES 286 (Austin Sarat and Stuart Scheingold eds., 2004) (describing animal rights movement attorneys' awareness and knowledge of strategies undertaken by other social movements).

We begin the chapter with a brief discussion of the missions of each movement and observe that within each there are both long-term structural goals and narrower, concrete objectives. Though we could discuss a wide range of factors in comparing the movements, we narrow our focus to just three. First, we examine the important role that attorneys who work in these movements play in overcoming the *invisibility* of the populations they represent. Second, we explore ways in which lawyers advocating for these groups can facilitate *moral suasion* that could have a potentially more extensive real-world impact than might formal legal reforms. Third and lastly, we discuss the role of cause lawyering in addressing *disenfranchisement* of the relevant communities. Of course, these three categories are overlapping and coconstitutive, and by organizing the discussion in this way, we do not mean to suggest otherwise. For example, addressing the disenfranchisement problem may lead to more vocal advocacy and less invisibility. Similarly, great visibility can result in more public engagement in relevant moral debates. For the purposes of our discussion, however, we deem it valuable to address them as distinct points of comparison.

17.2 MOVEMENT GOALS AND OBJECTIVES AND THE GENERAL ROLE OF CAUSE LAWYERS

An important element in measuring the success of any social movement is identifying its precise goals. We acknowledge, of course, that movements are not monolithic and are constantly in flux, and that divisions, even sharp ones, commonly arise within any movement about its goals. For our purposes, we identify what might be considered the aspirational or long-term goals of each movement and then home in on each movement's more discrete objectives (though by discrete, we mean separable from the aspirational goals; many of the discrete objectives are themselves quite substantial). But we also note that within each movement, given limited resources, there may well be a divide between those who wish to seek broader, structural reforms and those who prioritize improving the conditions and quality of life for each individual involved.[3] Moreover, as in other social movements, there will be disputes about incrementalism versus more immediate, radical transformation of the law. These goals can be debated at the margins, but we view them as creating a helpful organizing frame for the discussion.

A starting point is considering how to characterize each movement and identifying what might be described as aspirational or ultimate goals for each of them. As in other realms of public interest law, it is tempting to center discussions about a movement around major victories in the judicial or legislative arenas. Indeed, in the early years of the prisoners' rights movement, the nation witnessed pathbreaking Supreme Court decisions solidifying previously unrecognized rights for incarcerated

[3] Alan K. Chen & Scott L. Cummings, Public Interest Lawyering: A Contemporary Perspective 224 (2013).

persons, including basic due process rights in disciplinary proceedings,[4] the right that prison living conditions not be so severe as to violate the Eighth Amendment's prohibition of "cruel and unusual punishment,"[5] and prisoners' entitlement to "the minimal civilized measure of life's necessities," including food, clothing, and medical care,[6] to name a few. A number of later decisions, however, would make it much more difficult for incarcerated persons to successfully press these claims. For example, in *Wilson v. Seiter*, the Court erected a deliberate indifference standard, substantially reducing the likelihood of a prisoner's success on a claim challenging "inhumane conditions of confinement."[7] And in *Sandin v. Conner*, the Court cut back on procedural due process protections for prison disciplinary proceedings, finding that they apply only when the resulting sanction imposes an "atypical and significant hardship on the inmate in relation to the ordinary incidents of prison life."[8]

Focusing on bold judicial proclamations risks essentializing a social movement around law only, which might result in the neglect or marginalization of other critical political and social factors. Scholars whose work focuses on the prisoners' rights movement thus approach the definitional question in a more nuanced manner. Marie Gottschalk defined the prisoners' rights movement as "the broader effort by a variety of groups and organizations from roughly the 1950s to the early 1980s to redefine the moral, political, economic, and legal status of defendants and offenders in democratic societies through a range of activities, including lawsuits, legislation, demonstrations, strikes, riots, and calls for revolution."[9] Similarly, an older characterization of the prisoners' rights movement that still resonates today sees it as "a broadscale effort to redefine the status (moral, political, economic, as well as legal) of prisoners in a democratic society."[10]

But toward what end? In the context of prison reform, the ultimate aspirational goal for many may be prison abolition, though that phrase itself is fraught with contested and diverse meanings.[11] To some, abolition is an umbrella term for broad,

[4] Wolff v. McDonnell, 418 U.S. 539, 555–56 (1974).

[5] Estelle v. Gamble, 429 U.S. 97, 102–5 (1976).

[6] Rhodes v. Chapman, 452 U.S. 337, 347 (1981).

[7] 501 U.S. 294, 303 (1991).

[8] 515 U.S. 472, 484 (1995). The judicial decisions on prison conditions have not all limited rights in more recent years. *See, e.g.*, Brown v. Plata, 563 U.S. 493, 545 (2011) (holding that California's prisons provided medical and mental health care to prisoners that "falls below the standard of decency that inheres in the Eighth Amendment" and that the necessary remedy was court-ordered reduction in prison population to reduce overcrowding).

[9] Marie Gottschalk, The Prison and the Gallows: The Politics of Mass Incarceration in America 165–66 (2006).

[10] James B. Jacobs, *The Prisoners' Rights Movement and Its Impacts, 1960–80*, 2 Crime and Justice 429, 431 (1980).

[11] For an excellent discussion of the theories of prison abolition in the context of thoughts about integrating the movement into a theory of constitutional law, see Dorothy E. Roberts, *Foreword: Abolition Constitutionalism*, 133 Harv. L. Rev. 1, 4–10 (2019).

structural reform that includes not only eradication of mass incarceration, but also the transition toward alternatives that address more embedded social problems, including poverty, drug dependency, and racism, that lead to crime. Such reform is also integrally related to reexamining other crucial aspects of the criminal justice system, most notably policing. Importantly, abolition is a perspective that has thus far gained more traction in academic circles than it has on the ground in social-movement lawyering.[12] For example, the ACLU's National Prison Project describes its work in this, more limited, way: "Through litigation, advocacy, and public education, we work to ensure that conditions of confinement are consistent with health, safety, and human dignity, and that prisoners retain all rights of free persons that are not inconsistent with incarceration,"[13] which implicitly does not embrace abolition insofar as it assumes at least some imprisonment will be ongoing in our society. That does not diminish the centrality of prison abolition, however, because intellectual and political movements that broadly reframe social goals, even in radical (and perhaps impractical) ways, can strongly influence how public interest lawyers view their tactical approaches.

In terms of relatively more discrete reform efforts, those in the prisoners' rights movement have worked tirelessly to end capital punishment; to abolish or severely limit solitary confinement; to promote basic rights of dignity, safety, and security for prisoners; to seek material improvement of conditions for those who remain incarcerated, by, for example, eliminating overcrowding and improving medical and mental health care; ending forced labor of convicted persons; promoting the free exercise of religion, especially among incarcerated persons who are Muslim; ensuring rights of access to reading materials, law libraries, and the courts; and, as has been much in the news of late, restoring voting rights to persons who have completed their terms of incarceration. Of course, cases can raise important constitutional issues on behalf of individual prisoners as well.

Like prison abolition, the big-picture concept of animal protection embraces a variety of positions that are not always in harmony.[14] The emergence of an animal protection movement is a story built around two separate campaigns, one to change law and society to promote substantial improvements in animal welfare and another, bolder one that seeks to expand the legal recognition of rights for animals and to end

[12] *Introduction*, 132 Harv. L. Rev. 1568, 1571 (2019) (noting activist lawyer and writer Derecka Purnell's observation that "lawyers have, for the most part, yet to contemplate prison abolition in any serious way").

[13] ACLU National Prison Project, https://www.aclu.org/other/aclu-national-prison-project.

[14] Cass R. Sunstein, *Introduction*, *in* Animal Rights: Current Debates and New Directions 5 (Cass R. Sunstein & Martha C. Nussbaum eds., 2004) (explaining different strands of the animal protection movement); *see generally* Steven M. Wise, Rattling the Cage: Toward Legal Rights for Animals (2000) (suggesting that animals should have rights commensurate with their cognitive capacities).

all human exploitation of animals.[15] At first glance, these goals do not appear to be mutually exclusive, but they do reflect serious divisions over the ultimate end goals of the movement. Animal welfare advocates seek greater protection for animals from inhumane or cruel treatment, enforcement of laws against animal cruelty, and limits on, or the end of, the exploitation of animals across all contexts, but do not assert that the law should recognize nonhuman animals as having independent rights. It could be argued that animal welfare proponents are concerned less with global or structural change, and instead care more about incremental reform and stronger enforcement of existing laws protecting animals. Animal rights proponents, by contrast, pursue the more ambitious, aspirational objective of legal recognition of rights for nonhuman animals, equivalent or functionally comparable to those of humans, though there are disagreements within the movement about the scope of that recognition. As with prison abolition, the more expansive vision of animal rights has led to a greater degree of philosophical and academic discourse than it has lawyering on the ground, at least to date.[16]

In the near term, the goals of animal welfare and animal rights advocates often converge. Well shy of, along an aspirational spectrum, something approximating a rights-based approach to animal welfare, one can observe common goals in enhancing legal protection and enforcement of laws against animal cruelty, defined broadly to include the exploitation and mistreatment of animals in the industrial agriculture and entertainment industries. Animal welfare proponents seek the enforcement and enactment of stronger legal protection for animals from cruel treatment, tougher regulation of businesses that use animals for commercial gain, such as the agriculture, entertainment, cosmetics, and fashion industries, and action to address cruelty in the commercial breeding of pets.[17] But even groups more closely associated with rights-recognition describe their objectives in ways that do not differ significantly from those of animal welfare groups. For example, while People for the Ethical Treatment of Animals (PETA) proclaims that "[a]nimals are not ours to experiment on, eat, wear, use for entertainment, or abuse in any other way,"[18] which connotes a rights orientation, it focuses much of its work on discrete projects designed to reduce or minimize animal suffering. Similarly, the Animal Legal Defense Fund states that its mission is to "protect the lives and advance the

[15] Gary L. Francione, Rain without Thunder: The Ideology of the Animal Rights Movement 1–2 (1996); Helena Silverstein, Unleashing Rights: Law, Meaning, and the Animal Rights Movement 18–19 (1996) (describing tensions between "the traditional animal welfare movement and the newer, more radical, animal rights movement").

[16] Silverstein, *supra* note 15, at 19 (observing that "lawyers in the movement rarely speak of animal rights in the courtroom").

[17] *See, e.g.*, American Society for the Prevention of Cruelty to Animals, https://www.aspca.org/; The Humane Society of the United States, https://www.humanesociety.org//.

[18] *What PETA REALLY Stands For*, PETA, https://www.peta.org/features/what-peta-really-stands-for/.

interests of animals through the legal system."[19] Yet ALDF seeks to accomplish this mission principally "by filing high-impact lawsuits to protect animals from harm, providing free legal assistance and training to prosecutors to assure that animal abusers are held accountable for their crimes, supporting tough animal protection legislation and fighting legislation harmful to animals, and providing resources and opportunities to law students and professionals to advance the emerging field of animal law."[20]

One thing that distinguishes the two strands of animal advocacy is that animal-rights groups also engage in strategies that will directly or indirectly lead to the recognition of greater rights for animals. For example, those who focus on animal rights have promoted efforts to establish legal standing for animals to pursue their rights in the courts. In some cases, animal rights organizations have sought to stand in as the legal representative of specific animals as a "next friend" or legal surrogate pursuant to the Federal Rules of Civil Procedure,[21] even though several courts have rejected those arguments because the rules refer to representing an incompetent "person."[22] Interestingly and perhaps importantly, a couple of decisions from the US Court of Appeals for the Ninth Circuit have stated that animals can have standing, even without a next friend, under Article III of the US Constitution.[23] In both of those cases, however, the court went on to hold that the animals could not establish standing under the relevant federal statutes they invoked as the substantive bases for their lawsuits. Surely, the right of an animal to sue in federal court could be acknowledged as one step toward legal rights recognition.

Another noteworthy observation about divisions within each movement is how much they parallel each other. In a sense, in both the prisoners' rights and animal protection movements, one might see the differences in vision as "no cages" versus "bigger and better cages." Prison abolitionists and animal rights advocates argue for the end to incarceration and all human exploitation of animals, respectively. Prison conditions advocates and animal welfare proponents argue for reforms that improve the lives of the caged, but do not liberate them. These parallels are not only interesting, but also may inform how reform advocates set their priorities. To some extent, some abolitionists may look at the "bigger and better cages" group as a counterproductive force, believing that small-bore reforms in some way perpetuate the status quo or create the illusion that such reforms have addressed the main problems, thus perhaps reducing the urgency of more ambitious abolitionist goals.[24]

[19] Animal Legal Defense Fund, https://aldf.org/about-us/.

[20] *Id.*

[21] Fed. R. Civ. P. 17(c).

[22] *See, e.g.*, Citizens to End Animal Suffering & Exploitation, Inc. v. New England Aquarium, 836 F. Supp. 45 (D. Mass. 1993); Hawaiian Crow ('Alala) v. Lujan, 906 F. Supp. 549 (D. Haw. 1991).

[23] Naruto v. Slater, 888 F.3d 418, 421 (9th Cir. 2018); Cetacean Cmty. v. Bush, 386 F.3d 1169, 1176 (9th Cir. 2004).

[24] *See, e.g.*, Francione, *supra* note 15, at 190–219.

In contrast, the bigger-and-better-cages proponents may charge the abolitionists as unrealistic idealists whose work might ignore the value of incremental progress.[25] This may create fissures within the movements that may be inescapable. An introspective understanding of these dynamics may be valuable in assessing the movements' strategic futures.

Before moving on to the rest of the discussion, we make two observations that are widely recognized in the cause-lawyering literature. First, we acknowledge that litigation, which we identify and analyze as one strategic option for lawyers in these two movements, has been the subject of widespread criticism as a social movement tool. In short, such critics

> suggest that rights litigation is a waste of time, both because it is not actually successful in achieving social change and because it detracts attention and resources from more meaningful and sustainable forms of work such as mobilization, political lobbying, and community organizing. In this sense, the critics claim that rights lawyers offer nothing but "hollow hope" and create false expectations of sustainable social transformation.[26]

For purposes of our discussion, we assume these critiques to have some validity, even as we seek to identify a broader understanding about the contributions attorneys can make to advance social movements.

Second, we recognize the concern that cause lawyers in these fields might not be fully sensitive to the power imbalance between clients or constituents, on the one hand, and their attorneys, on the other.

> Although clients have the ultimate authority to define the goals of representation, as many commentators have noted, the line between 'ends' and 'means' is not so neat, and lawyers may (even sometimes unknowingly) use their position of relative power to advance agendas that may diverge from the clients', thus undercutting client autonomy. . . . [T]he problem arises [especially] when the client is relatively weak, which permits the lawyer to make crucial case decisions, often persuading the client to go along.[27]

While these challenges are ever-present in most areas of public interest law, they may be particularly acute in the context of prisoners and animals, making both groups subject to replication of the disempowerment that exists because of the laws, structures, and carceral logics that shape their treatment. Public interest lawyers addressing the three areas discussed below must be sensitive to these power dynamics in working on behalf of their clients and the causes they represent.

[25] *Id.* at 147–89 (describing, but disputing, this critique). Of course, these divisions have existed in numerous social movements and are not indigenous to these groups.

[26] Alan K. Chen, *Rights Lawyer Essentialism and the Next Generation of Rights Critics*, 111 MICH. L. REV. 903, 922 (2013) (citing, inter alia, GERALD N. ROSENBERG, THE HOLLOW HOPE: CAN COURTS BRING ABOUT SOCIAL CHANGE? [2d ed. 2008]).

[27] CHEN & CUMMINGS, *supra* note 3, at 369.

17.3 COUNTERING INVISIBILITY

In any given generation, there are multiple worthy social causes vying for public attention. Advocates for such causes compete for scarce resources, including charitable donations, legal and policy advocates, and level of public concern. For some causes, even ones that present existential threats such as climate change, constituents are diffused and unorganized, which makes for difficulties in gaining attention and also creates collective action problems. For example, in the 1960s and 1970s this was the case for environmental and consumer protection interests.[28]

In other contexts, the challenges to commanding public attention might be driven primarily by the fact that constituencies are not as readily visible; for many groups, it is "out of sight, out of mind." There are numerous reasons why a particular group may be invisible to the broad spectrum of the public eye. First, all invisibility problems may be partly a function of lack of power. This factor is one that likely affects most communities seeking greater legal protection in our society. Second, invisibility may be the product of a subjective sense of public discomfort predicated on biases and stereotypes. Thus, the general public may look at members of powerless groups, such as persons experiencing homelessness, people with disabilities, and transgendered persons, without really seeing them in a way that acknowledges their humanity and dignity. These causes of invisibility likely affect both incarcerated persons and many animals. But a third cause of group invisibility is as elementary as actual physical segregation. Prisoners and many categories of animals, including farmed animals and animals used for experimentation and testing, are literally behind walls.[29] As Justice Kennedy once observed in a speech to the American Bar Association, "When the door is locked against the prisoner, we do not think about what is behind it."[30] However, he went on, "As a profession, and as a people, we should know what happens after the prisoner is taken away." Indeed, this is one of the central challenges in dismantling carceral logics. Here invisibility is not just a metaphor, but a product of social and physical isolation through incarceration.

To invoke a comparison from constitutional doctrine, there is a strong relationship between invisibility and insularity. In the widely referenced footnote 4 in *United States v. Carolene Products Company*,[31] the Supreme Court observed that heightened judicial scrutiny might be necessary to protect "discrete and insular minorities" from the majority-driven political process. The concept of insularity connotes a separateness from the general public that results in unfamiliarity with

[28] *Id.* at 14.

[29] There are, of course, many other groups that are similarly made invisible by physical barriers, including persons being held in migrant detention centers, people institutionalized in mental health facilities, and others.

[30] Justice Anthony Kennedy, Speech at the American Bar Association Annual Meeting 3 (Aug. 9, 2003), https://www.supremecourt.gov/publicinfo/speeches/sp_08-09-03.html.

[31] 304 U.S. 144, 152 n.4 (1938).

such groups, causing voters and lawmakers to be, at best, insensitive to, and at worst, actively prejudiced toward, members of such groups.[32] And insularity surely begets invisibility.

A challenge, then, for social movement lawyers in these fields is to make their clients and their clients' experiences visible to the world. Enhanced transparency can lead to public recognition of the plights of prisoners and animals; public recognition, in turn, can lead to increased understanding, attitudinal shifts, and ultimately law reform. Being visible means garnering public attention, sympathy, and support.

Sometimes visibility arises spontaneously on account of discrete, high-profile events or series of events. In the summer of 2020, for instance, the nation watched in shock as cell phone videos of horrifying police violence toward and killing of Black men and women went viral, calling focused public attention to the Black Lives Matter movement. These victims included Ahmaud Arbery, Breonna Taylor, George Floyd, Rayshard Brooks, and Jacob Blake. And those were just the violent incidents that became public. At the Democratic National Convention, George Floyd's brother called on Americans not only to mourn those whose names were already widely known, but also those who were unknown "'because their murders didn't go viral.'"[33] But this attention can be fleeting. Despite what seems like an endless string of tragic school shootings, the public's interest in comprehensive gun regulation seems to quickly wane over time.[34] And 2020 is hardly the first time the country's focus has been drawn to what seem like obvious incidents of unjustified police shootings of young Black men. The attention generated by the numerous other police killings of Black people a few years ago and the ensuing protests were, sadly, short-lived.[35]

But more often than not, making clients and their causes visible requires a conscious, affirmative, and sustained effort. Cause lawyers may promote their clients' visibility through a combination of advocacy tactics such as public education and media campaigns.[36] Sometimes litigation can serve not only the primary objective of vindicating and enforcing legal rights, but also as a mechanism to educate the broader public about the underlying conditions that caused a particular

[32] John Hart Ely, Democracy and Distrust: A Theory of Judicial Review 164 (1980).

[33] Tyrone Beason & Melissa Gomez, *"'George should be alive today': Floyd's brother, Eric Garner's Mother Speaks at Democratic Convention*, L.A. Times, Aug. 18, 2020.

[34] Eric Bradner & Jennifer Agiesta, *Americans Want Strict Gun Laws after Mass Shootings. Then Their Interest Fades*, CNN (Oct. 2, 2017), https://www.cnn.com/2017/10/02/politics/gun-control-polling-las-vegas-shooting/index.html.

[35] There were some efforts to address systemic racism and structural police reform, though they have as yet to be widely implemented. *See* President's Task Force on 21st Century Policing, Final Report of the President's Task Force on 21st Century Policing (May 2015), https://cops.usdoj.gov/pdf/taskforce/taskforce_finalreport.pdf.

[36] For an extended discussion of such campaigns, see Chen & Cummings, *supra* note 3, at 267–72.

conflict. Indeed, even when the litigation is unsuccessful, it can promote learning and call attention to an otherwise overlooked social problem.[37]

In the early stages of the prisoners' rights movement, litigation was often used as a tool not only to reveal problems with the treatment of prisoners to the courts, but also to establish sustained oversight of prison systems by federal judges.[38] This had an important transparency dimension because it contemplated an ongoing role for the judges to be informed about prisons' compliance with injunctive orders or consent decrees. Not surprisingly, over time these orders were met with increasing resistance by state officials and judicial conservatives, who argued that this exceeded the proper role of the federal judiciary, which was accused of micromanaging day-to-day prison operations.[39] Eventually, those criticisms took hold, and the courts mostly abandoned such efforts to oversee prisons. Moreover, federal legislation such as the Prison Litigation Reform Act made it much harder for prisoners to file civil rights claims by limiting the types of damages that could be recovered and capping attorneys' fees.[40]

Other transparency mechanisms are limited as well. As one commentator has noted:

> Currently, prisons and jails are shrouded in secrecy. Media access to prisoners and prisons is extremely limited and completely discretionary. Moreover, investigative reporting is generally in decline given the changing nature of media, news, and reporting. In combination with the high barriers to obtaining prison related information, media coverage is less able to fill the prison transparency gap.[41]

Indeed, the Supreme Court has directly rejected the idea that the media should have a special First Amendment right to gain access to prisons in the interest of

[37] Silverstein, *supra* note 15, at 162 (noting that without regard to outcomes, litigation can achieve "the advancement of education through publicity and consciousness-raising," "movement building and mobilization," and "the creation of political pressure and leverage against the opposition"). *See also* Catherine Albiston, *The Rule of Law and the Litigation Process: The Paradox of Losing by Winning*, 33 LAW & SOC'Y REV. 869 (1999); Jules Lobel, *Courts as Forums for Protest*, 52 UCLA L. REV. 477 (2004); Doug NeJaime, *Winning through Losing*, 96 IOWA L. REV. 941 (2001).

[38] Margo Schlanger & Giovanna Shay, *Preserving the Rule of Law in America's Jails and Prisons: The Case for Amending the Prison Litigation Reform Act*, 11 U. PA. J. CONST. L. 139, 140 (2008) (noting that because of barriers to transparency in prisons, "lawsuits, which bring judicial scrutiny behind bars, and which promote or even compel constitutional compliance, accordingly take on an outsize importance").

[39] *See, e.g.*, Brown v. Plata, 563 U.S. 493, 555 (2011) (Scalia, J., dissenting) ("Structural injunctions depart from that historical practice, turning judges into long-term administrators of complex social institutions such as schools, prisons, and police departments. Indeed, they require judges to play a role essentially indistinguishable from the role ordinarily played by executive officials.").

[40] *See* 42 U.S.C.A. § 1997e.

[41] Andrea C. Armstrong, *No Prisoner Left Behind? Enhancing Public Transparency of Penal Institutions*, 25 STAN. L. & POL'Y REV. 435, 462 (2014).

transparency.[42] But perhaps prisoners' rights advocates might pursue federal legislation that requires or incentivizes correctional institutions to report data in important categories, such as statistics on medical care, violence in prisons, and the administration of prison disciplinary policies as one mechanism to increase transparency.[43]

Addressing invisibility has similarly been an emphasis of some aspects of the animal protection movement. As McCann and Silverstein observed, there are constraints on traditional litigation tools in the animal rights context that do not limit other movements.[44] This helps explain why cause lawyers in the movement often focus on more conventional rights claims that will indirectly yet still importantly promote the interests of animals. "For animal rights advocacy, this mean[s] creatively using resources like free speech laws and open meetings laws to heighten awareness about hunting, dissection, and animal experimentation."[45]

Another example of this is in sustained efforts to promote transparency about animals farmed for food production. These animals are exempt from the Animal Welfare Act's protections,[46] and the conditions in which they live and are killed are decidedly nonpublic. To address this lack of transparency, undercover investigators in several states have gained access to slaughterhouses and other animal facilities and made secret video recordings of severe mistreatment of farmed animals that were then made widely available over the internet.[47] Dismayed at the negative publicity, the industry lobbied state legislatures to bar such investigations, which many states have done by making it a crime to misrepresent one's identity to gain access to an animal agriculture facility or to take photographs or make a video recording without the owner's consent.[48] These so-called "Ag-Gag" laws were soon enacted in a number of states where animal agriculture is a prominent part of the local economy. ALDF, PETA, and other animal rights groups have mounted a nationwide litigation campaign to challenge these laws as violating their First Amendment free speech rights. While the campaign is ongoing, many of these suits have been successful, with federal courts in several jurisdictions declaring the laws to

[42] Houchins v. KQED, Inc., 438 U.S. 1, 15–16 (1978).

[43] Armstrong, *supra* note 41, at 470–73 (proposing reforms of prison transparency in several specified areas).

[44] McCann & Silverstein, *supra* note 2, at 282–84.

[45] *Id.* at 283.

[46] Justin Marceau, *How the Animal Welfare Act Harms Animals*, 69 Hastings L.J. 925, 930 (2018).

[47] *See, e.g.*, Matthew L. Wald, *Meat Packer Admits Slaughter of Sick Cows*, N.Y. Times (Mar. 13, 2008), http://www.nytimes.com/2008/03/13/business/13meat.html. Professor Jed Purdy, who once conducted an undercover investigation of a slaughterhouse as a journalist, has proposed an alternative, transparency-promoting policy: a legal requirement that animal facilities install video cameras and make a link to the live video feeds available to the general public. Jedediah Purdy, *Open the Slaughterhouses*, N.Y. Times (Apr. 8, 2013), https://www.nytimes.com/2013/04/09/opinion/open-the-slaughterhouses.html.

[48] *See, e.g.*, Utah Code Ann. § 76-6-112.

be invalid.[49] The central point of Ag-Gag challenges it that transparency is an essential component of animal law reform. If a larger percentage of the public was aware of how the mass production of animals for food creates an environment of cruelty and raises substantial concerns about food safety, efforts to seek legislative reforms would be much more likely to gain traction. Moreover, the information disclosed through these investigations may sway public opinion in ways that will enhance the possibility of greater recognition of animals' rights.

Notably, some progress on the public-opinion front has already been made in recent years. A 2015 Gallup Poll found increasing support for animal rights in the United states, with 32 percent of respondents believing that animals should have the same rights to be free from harm and exploitation as humans, and 62 percent believing that animals deserve "some" protection from such harm but that animals may still be used for the benefit of humans.[50] These figures both represented a notable increase in affirmative responses to the same questions asked in 2008 and 2003.[51]

Conversations across the prisoners' rights and animal protection movements might promote the sharing of meaningful and thoughtful suggestions for law reform and tactical approaches to overcoming the invisibility of their constituencies. Moreover, recognition of the parallels between the two movements could lead to conscious strategic collaborations through reform efforts – for example, a joint campaign to promote greater transparency for all those who are caged. This could also lead to public education efforts that might lead to a broader understanding of the harms that can result when misconduct occurs but is obscured from the public eye. Similarly, lawyers from one movement might submit amicus briefs in support of court cases brought by advocates in the other movement, calling judicial attention to the parallels between concerns about prisoner and animal welfare. These types of partnerships might also reduce the incidence of the potentially problematic public rhetoric used by movement leaders that we discuss below.

17.4 FACILITATING MORAL SUASION

Historically, moral suasion has been one of many tactical approaches social movements have employed to achieve their objectives, although the degree of its effectiveness has been debated. A major segment of the slavery abolition movement rested

49 Animal Legal Def. Fund v. Wasden, 878 F.3d 1184, 1199 (9th Cir. 2018); Animal Legal Def. Fund v. Kelly, 9 F.4th 1219, 1246 (10th Cir. 2021); Petition for Certiorari filed, Nov. 22, 2021, S.Ct. No. 21–760.; Animal Legal Def. Fund v. Reynolds, 8 F.4th 781, 787 (8th Cir. 2021); Animal Legal Def. Fund v. Herbert, 263 F. Supp. 3d 1193, 1213 (D. Utah 2017). Professor Chen discloses that he has served as plaintiffs' counsel in all of these cases.

50 Rebecca Riffkin, *In U.S., More Say Animals Should Have Same Rights as People*, GALLUP (May 18, 2015), https://news.gallup.com/poll/183275/say-animals-rights-people.aspx.

51 *Id.*

on moral suasion, whether on the legislative or judicial battlefronts.[52] Moral leadership, from Gandhi to the Reverend Martin Luther King, Jr., has often been coupled with social movements. Moral commitment to causes can also be one of the driving forces of public interest lawyers working within these movements.[53] What is distinct about moral suasion as a social reform tactic is that there is nothing uniquely connecting lawyering to moral claims. Indeed, the standard conception of the role of the lawyer suggests that an attorney's moral views are not to be confused with those of her clients.[54] As with other social movements, both the prisoners' rights and animal protection movements engage in moral suasion to help transform public opinion, and ultimately influence public policy, another feature that connects these movements.

Although moral argumentation is not a skill unique to lawyering, it frequently occurs in the context of advocacy in the courtroom and before legislative bodies, two arenas where more traditional legal arguments are commonly employed and where lawyers tend to be heavily utilized. Litigation is not merely a tactic to win rights in specific disputes, but can also be integrated into a broader strategic approach that is designed to facilitate public education, which correlates strongly with movement building.[55]

Within the context of the prisoners' rights movement, moral claims have probably been most commonly employed in arguments against capital punishment.[56] Moreover, the contemporary debates over mass incarceration are frequently based on moral claims.[57] But more broadly, beyond dealing with these more discrete issues, prisoners' rights advocates can seek to employ moral rhetoric more generally to reexamine basic theories of punishment and the carceral state. This is all the more important because of the connection between social attitudes toward prisoners and incarceration rates. Studies of the effects of the expanding movement against

[52] *See* Robert M. Cover, Justice Accused: Antislavery and the Judicial Process 160–63 (1975).

[53] Scheingold & Sarat, *supra* note 1, 3 (2004) ("[P]olitical or moral commitment [is] an essential and distinguishing feature of cause lawyering.").

[54] This is embodied in the Model Rules of Professional Conduct, which disassociate an attorney's moral position from that of her client. ("A lawyer's representation of a client . . . does not constitute an endorsement of the client's political, economic, social, or moral views or activities."). Model Rules of Prof'l Conduct 1.2(b).

[55] McCann & Silverstein, *supra* note 2, at 269.

[56] ACLU, *The Case against the Death Penalty* ("Because life is precious and death irrevocable, murder is abhorrent, and a policy of state-authorized killings is immoral. It epitomizes the tragic inefficacy and brutality of violence, rather than reason, as the solution to difficult social problems."), https://www.aclu.org/other/case-against-death-penalty.

[57] Vincent Southerland, *Private: The Immorality of Mass Incarceration*, ACS Blogs: Expert Forum ("At bottom, criminal justice reforms need to be driven by the moral imperative of repairing all that is wrong with the current system. As advocates for change, we must make sure that the reform narrative includes the human costs of mass incarceration and a broken criminal justice system, not just the concern over dollars and cents."), https://www.acslaw.org/expert forum/the-immorality-of-mass-incarceration/.

mass incarceration have captured some elements of public sympathy in moving public opinion. One study shows a direct correlation between public views on punitiveness toward convicted persons and incarceration rates.[58] But public opinion seems to be shifting to a more sympathetic view of prisoners and in favor of major criminal justice reform efforts. And though these results cannot be directly linked to moral arguments, a 2017 poll by the ACLU's Campaign for Smart Justice found that 91 percent of Americans support criminal justice reform.[59]

However, there may be important limits on the ability of advocates to influence attitudes about prisoners through moral arguments because views about mass incarceration may differ significantly with regard to prisoners who have been convicted only of minor drug crimes than concerning persons who have committed violent offenses. The reform efforts that have been successful thus far have focused on nonviolent offenders.[60] Meaningful efforts to end mass incarceration must reach beyond those offenders, however, as 80 percent of incarcerated persons are imprisoned on non-drug-related offenses.[61] In some sense, then, moral arguments could end up being counterproductive if people feel righteous only about deincarcerating a small segment of the prison population.

Although these may be framed publicly as moral debates, they can also be mapped onto legal ones. Indeed, the Eighth Amendment's very text invites moral debate through its focus on what counts as unconstitutionally "cruel and unusual."[62] Moral values even make it into the Supreme Court's opinions from time to time. In *Roper v. Simmons*, for example, in the course of declaring that the application of the death penalty to persons who were minors at the time of their crimes is unconstitutional, the Court observed that "[f]rom a moral standpoint it would be misguided to equate the failings of a minor with those of an adult, for a greater possibility exists that a minor's character deficiencies will be reformed."[63]

Moral claims for animal rights might meet somewhat less resistance, perhaps because at least some animals may be inherently more sympathetic to a broader spectrum of the public than are people convicted of capital crimes. In evaluating

[58] Peter K. Enns, *The Importance of Shifting Public Opinion about Criminal Justice and America's Prison Boom*, Scholars Strategy Network (Sept. 20, 2017), https://scholars.org/brief/importance-shifting-public-opinion-about-criminal-justice-and-americas-prison-boom.

[59] *91 Percent of Americans Support Criminal Justice Reform, ACLU Polling Finds*, ACLU (Nov. 16, 2017), https://www.aclu.org/press-releases/91-percent-americans-support-criminal-justice-reform-aclu-polling-finds.

[60] For example, the primary focus of the First Step Act of 2018 was on nonviolent offenders who are incarcerated. Pub. L. No. 115-291, 132 Stat. 5194.

[61] Wendy Sawyer & Peter Wagner, *Mass Incarceration: The Whole Pie 2020*, Prison Pol'y Initiative (March 24, 2020), https://www.prisonpolicy.org/reports/pie2020.html.

[62] U.S. Const. amend VIII; *see also* Margo Schlanger, *Beyond the Hero Judge: Institutional Reform Litigation as* Litigation, 97 Mich. L. Rev. 1994, 1999 (1999) ("'Cruel,' after all, is a word with moral content, and 'unusual' is best read in a national charter of rights to direct a national comparison.").

[63] 543 U.S. 551, 570 (2005).

moral claims here, we must tread carefully, however, as many in the animal protection movement have pointed out that while people may be sympathetic toward their own pets, they are simultaneously not as likely to feel the same way about farmed animals, animals used for products other than food, and animals exploited for human entertainment.[64] Indeed, studies have demonstrated that people engage in motivated cognition that causes them to block out relevant information, such as a farmed animal's intelligence, to avoid the moral dilemma that they would face with such a recognition.[65] Just as moral claims in the prison reform context may reach a limit that confines the scope of meaningful reforms, these distinctions between domesticated pets and farmed animals may act as a ceiling on more ambitious animal rights claims. Thus, moral claims for animals based in public sentiment may meet more resistance than one might first imagine. If this is the case, then movement leaders must reflect on how to use moral suasion in the face of this type of barrier. Further, the parallels with the limits of moral claims in the mass incarceration context might be worth discussing strategically across movements.

The founding of the animal rights movement has been strongly linked to the writings of moral philosophers such as Tom Regan[66] and Peter Singer.[67] In the advocacy movement, moral arguments are presented on a range of issues to oppose keeping animals in captivity for human entertainment, wearing fur, eating meat, using animal products, and medical experimentation on animals, to name just a few.[68] Moreover, animal rights lawyers use moral claims as a building block for legal rights. As Helena Silverstein has noted:

> Animal advocates have increasingly defined their cause in terms of rights. In doing so, movement activists have relied partly on philosophical grounding in rights theory to appropriate rights language and to attribute meaning to rights. This philosophical foundation attempts to extend the meaning of rights, calling for the application of moral rights to animals. It further translates this demand for moral rights into a demand that legal rights be extended to animals.[69]

[64] Sunstein, *supra* note 14, at 3 ("[T]hrough their daily behavior, people who love those pets, and greatly care about their welfare, help ensure short and painful lives for millions, even billions of animals that cannot easily be distinguished from dogs and cats.").

[65] *See, e.g.*, Jared Piazza & Steve Loughnan, *When Meat Gets Personal, Animals' Minds Matter Less: Motivated Use of Intelligence Information in Judgments of Moral Standing*, 7(8) Soc. Psych. & Personality Sci. 867 (2016); Steve Loughnan, Brock Bastian, & Nick Haslam, *The Psychology of Eating Animals*, 23(2) Current Directions Psych. Sci. 104 (2014) (describing the "meat paradox," the conclusion that "[m]ost people care about animals and do not want to see them harmed but engage in a diet that requires them to be killed and, usually, to suffer").

[66] Tom Regan, The Case for Animal Rights (1983).

[67] Peter Singer, Animal Liberation: A New Ethics for Our Treatment of Animals (1975).

[68] Sunstein, *supra* note 14, at 11–12.

[69] Silverstein, *supra* note 15, at 17. Ironically, some in the animal rights movement sought to embrace rights rhetoric to pull the movement from the margins into the mainstream, while

However, although public sympathy toward animals is strong, the same cannot be said for their human advocates.[70] Opponents of animal rights activists have attempted to derail the movement by branding all who advocate of animal rights as "terrorists."[71]

Ironically, however, the prisoners' rights and animal protection movements sometimes unwittingly engage in moral arguments that are at cross-purposes to the other. One of the largest and most prominent animal rights organizations, the Animal Legal Defense Fund, is frequently associated with the slogan "All Our Clients Are Innocent."[72] This offers tremendous appeal from a moral standpoint because non-human animals lack agency, so all human exploitation of animals is thrust upon them. Another public relations campaign involves raising the consciousness of pet owners to recognize the moral equivalency of mistreatment of pets with the abominable treatment of animals who are hunted, used for human entertainment, and mass-produced for food and products through our commercial agricultural industry.[73] As morally persuasive as these approaches to public education can be, they may inadvertently promote a form of "othering," in that the converse of the ALDF slogan is that perhaps we needn't care as much about humans who are not "innocent" (using that in the legal as well as colloquial sense).

And at the same time, the morality switch can be flipped in the prisoners' rights movement, which frequently employs moral rhetoric to raise issues with prison conditions by complaining that the basic rights of incarcerated persons are illustrated by the fact that they are frequently treated "like animals."[74] Indeed, sometimes prisoners point out that they are being treated *worse* than animals. In one reported instance, a man incarcerated at a California prison complained about conditions in overcrowded cells with temperatures of 114 degrees and little ventilation, while pointing out that the prison's dog kennels were air conditioned.[75] In another

others resisted the use of rights language out of fear that it branded the movement as too radical. *Id.* at 18.

[70] Pat Andriola, *Equal Protection for Animals*, 6 Barry U. Envtl. & Earth L.J. 50, 69 (2016) ("In a recent study, 30% of respondents thought unfavorably of vegans and 22% thought unfavorably of vegetarians.").

[71] *See generally* Will Potter, Green is the New Red: An Insider's Account of a Social Movement inder Siege 55 (2011); Kimberly E. McCoy, *Subverting Justice: An Indictment of the Animal Enterprise Terrorism Act*, 14 Animal L. 53 (2007).

[72] *See* Animal Legal Def. Fund, 2018 Annual Report, 52, https://aldf.org/wp-content/uploads/2019/09/2018-Animal-Legal-Defense-Fund-Annual-Report.pdf.

[73] For a description of some of these comparative moral attitudes, see *Why Some Animals Are More Equal Than Others . . .*, Independent (Oct. 23, 2011), https://www.independent.co.uk/news/science/why-some-animals-are-more-equal-than-others-2103074.html.

[74] *See, e.g.*, Kitty Calavita & Valerie Jenneses, Appealing to Justice: Prisoner Grievances, Rights, and Carceral Logic 209 (2014) (reporting incarcerated person's request that he "'be treated like other inmates and not locked away like a dog.'"); *id.* at 115 (quoting another incarcerated person's complaint that one prison officer "'talks to people like they're animals.'").

[75] *Id.* at 16.

complaint from a Texas prison that reportedly registered 130-degree temperatures and where fourteen prisoners had died from the heat in recent years, it was noted that the prison has recently constructed a $750,000 climate-controlled, swine-production facility on site to produce food for the prisoners.

What is problematic with these characterizations is that, like the claim that all animals are innocent, it pits groups that are oppressed by carceral logics against each other, creating a hierarchy of moral worthiness. Saying prisoners shouldn't be treated like animals sends an implicit message to the public that not only should humans not be treated like animals, but also that animals are lesser beings and that it may even be acceptable to treat animals "like animals." And saying that all animals are innocent implies that people who are not innocent may deserve punishment or incarceration. This conflicting moral discourse could ultimately lead to undermining both claims, thereby diluting, if not erasing, the moral message. Indeed, it is potentially troubling messages like that this that can perpetuate the carceral logics that plague our society and undermine important social movements. Thus, conversing across movements and engaging in introspection about moral claims can be a productive way of getting us outside of these types of rhetorical traps.

We note one other area in which there are tensions between these two movements relating to moral suasion claims. Some animal protection groups have included as part of their mission the stricter enforcement of criminal sanctions against persons who engage in unlawful acts of animal cruelty.[76] That is, such advocates have pursued a carceral strategy against humans to advance the welfare, safety, and dignity of nonhuman animals. To some degree, such campaigns reflect moral claims on behalf of animals while simultaneously making moral arguments for punitive sanctions against those who abuse them. While we point to this as another example where the prisoners' rights and animal protection movements could be at odds, others have argued more strenuously that not only are such measures ineffective, but also are counterproductive to the larger cause of animal rights. As Professor Justin Marceau has observed, "the logic of increased attention to crimes and penalties for individual animal abusers actually reinforces hierarchies and perpetuates larger-scale animal abuse and exploitation caused by corporations."[77] While we acknowledge this patent tension, we see this as yet another area where cross-movement collaboration and discourse could lead to revisitation of such reflexive carceral approaches to animal cruelty.

[76] Animal Legal Def. Fund, *Criminal Justice: Collaborating with Prosecutors and Law Enforcement on Animal Cruelty Cases*, https://aldf.org/how_we_work/criminal-justice/.

[77] Justin Marceau, *Palliative Animal Law: The War on Animal Cruelty*, 134 Harv. L. Rev. F. 250 (March 20, 2021), https://harvardlawreview.org/2021/03/palliative-animal-law-the-war-on-animal-cruelty/. *See also* Justin Marceau, Beyond Cages: Animal Law and Criminal Punishment (2019).

17.5 OVERCOMING DISENFRANCHISEMENT

A major element of social justice is redressing imbalances in political power. Frequently, public interest lawyers focus their work on reviving power for their clients where it has been lost and enabling power where it never existed. This is consistent with the ultimate objective of client empowerment, which decentralizes power to individuals to advocate for themselves. Ironically, client disenfranchisement frequently steers advocates toward the courts, which are somewhat independent of the political system and are, by some measures, already designed to account for protection of those without political power.[78] However, for a variety of reasons, advocates sometimes overlook the limits of litigation as a tool for social change.[79]

With regard to incarcerated or formerly incarcerated persons, disenfranchisement is both formal and sweeping. Many states' laws deprive people who have been convicted of a felony of their right to vote, not only while they are incarcerated but even after they have completed the terms of their sentence.[80] In some states, even those convicted of misdemeanors may lose their voting rights.[81] Although some of those states have established mechanisms to allow people to regain their voting rights, such systems have been widely criticized for long delays, for cumbersome or arbitrary administrative processes, and extremely low success rates.[82]

No fair discussion of prisoners' rights can ignore the deep connection between incarceration and race. Indeed, the prisoners' rights movement began as an outgrowth of the activism of Black Muslims, who organized incarcerated persons and asserted their rights through activism and litigation.[83] In the US prison system as of 2018, Black men were incarcerated at a rate 5.8 times that of white males.[84] Not surprisingly, then, the disenfranchisement of formerly incarcerated persons has had and continues to have a substantially disproportionate impact on people of color.[85]

78 Ely, *supra* note 32, at 4–9.

79 Chen & Cummings, *supra* note 3, at 204–72.

80 For a summary of the various state law approaches to felon disenfranchisement, see *Felon Voting Rights*, Nat'l Conf. State Legis. (Sept. 3, 2020), https://www.ncsl.org/research/elections-and-campaigns/felon-voting-rights.aspx. The exceptions are Maine and Vermont, which do not remove the right to vote from incarcerated persons even while they are serving their sentences. *Id.*

81 Gabriel J. Chin, *The New Civil Death: Rethinking Punishment in the Era of Mass Conviction*, 160 U. Pa. L. Rev. 1789, 1799 n.49 (2012).

82 *See* Dexter Filkins, *Who Gets to Vote in Florida?*, New Yorker (Sept. 7, 2020), www.newyorker.com/magazine/2020/09/07/who-gets-to-vote-in-florida.

83 Gottschalk, *supra* note 9, at 174–76. For a discussion of the strong connections between prisons and the legacy of slavery, see Roberts, *supra* note 11, at 37–38.

84 *Prisoners in 2018*, U.S Dep't of Just., Bureau of Just. Stat. (April 2020), https://www.bjs.gov/content/pub/pdf/p18_sum.pdf.

85 Erin Kelley, *Racism & Felony Disenfranchisement: An Intertwined History*, Brennan Ctr. for Just. (May 9, 2017), https://www.brennancenter.org/our-work/research-reports/racism-felony-disenfranchisement-intertwined-history.

But support for reenfranchisement of formerly incarcerated persons seems to be increasing. According to a 2018 Huff Post/YouGov poll, 63 percent of Americans support the restoration of voting rights for persons incarcerated for felony convictions after they have completed their sentences.[86] In that same year, nearly 65 percent of Florida voters approved a ballot measure to amend the state constitution to restore voting rights to most persons convicted of a felony after completion of their sentences.[87] Some 85,000 persons filed formal requests to have their voting rights restored pursuant to the amendment. The Florida legislature soon pushed back, enacting a statute that interpreted the amendment's phrase "completion of all terms of sentence" to include not only a prison sentence and terms of parole, but also the payment of any amount of restitution, fines, and fees ordered by a court to be paid as part of a sentence.[88] Those provisions were immediately challenged in federal court. As of now, the law has been upheld by an *en banc* decision of the Eleventh Circuit Court of Appeals, meaning that a substantial number of otherwise qualified persons were probably unable to vote in the 2020 election.[89]

Through executive action, New York and Iowa have taken steps to narrow the impact of disenfranchisement. Under New York law, the Democratic governor issued an executive order in 2018 to restore voting rights to persons who had completed their prisons sentences, but were still on parole.[90] And in Iowa, which previously had permanently barred voting for anyone convicted of an "infamous crime,"[91] the Republican governor issued an executive order restoring voting rights for most convicted persons who have completed their sentence, probation, and

[86] Sam Levine & Ariel Edwards-Levy, *Most Americans Favor Restoring Felons' Voting Rights, but Disagree on How*, HuffPost (March 21, 2018), https://www.huffpost.com/entry/felons-voting-rights-poll_n_5ab2c153e4b008c9e5f3c88a.

[87] The provision stated that with the exception of those convicted of murder or felony sexual assault, "any disqualification from voting arising from a felony conviction shall terminate and voting rights shall be restored upon completion of all terms of sentence including parole or probation." Fla. Const. art. VI, § 4.

[88] Fla. Stat. Ann. § 98.0751. In addition, the Florida Supreme Court issued an advisory opinion interpreting the amendment, independent of the statute, to require formerly incarcerated persons to fulfill all legal financial obligations before having their rights restored. Advisory Opinion to Governor re Implementation of Amendment 4, The Voting Restoration Amendment, 288 So. 3d 1070, 1084 (Fla. 2020).

[89] Jones v. Governor of Fla., 975 F.3d 1016 (11th Cir. 2020). Notably, two of the judges voting to uphold the law were previously Justices on the Florida Supreme Court that issued the aforementioned advisory opinion but did not recuse themselves. Filkins, *supra* note 82. Professor Chen discloses that he was a signatory to an amicus curiae brief filed on behalf of those challenging the constitutionality of the Florida statute in the *Jones* case.

[90] Governor Andrew Cuomo, *Governor Cuomo Signs Executive Order to Restore Voting Rights to New Yorkers on Parole* (Apr. 18, 2018), https://www.governor.ny.gov/news/governor-cuomo-signs-executive-order-restore-voting-rights-new-yorkers-parole.

[91] Iowa Const. Art. 2, § 5.

parole.[92] Unlike Florida, Iowa does not require such persons to pay any restitution to their victims before regaining the right to vote.[93]

Turning to the animal movement, nonhuman animals, of course, have no recognized legal rights, much less the right to vote in elections, and it is difficult, of course, to understand how it would work if they did.[94] But we might think of disenfranchisement for these purposes not only as the denial of formal voting rights, but also as the exclusion from all forms of participation and representation in the political system. And political advocacy for the interests of animals is surely imaginable, even as it must necessarily be undertaken through surrogates, such as animal rights groups that engage in lobbying and policy reform, or official ombudspersons. But query whether the current framework for permitting or encouraging such advocacy is sufficient. As one commentator has noted, animals are a politically powerless constituency, one of the factors the Supreme Court considers in evaluating whether heightened judicial scrutiny should apply to laws that discriminatorily burden such groups under the Equal Protection Clause. "The political powerlessness of animals [is] more than evident. . . . [T]hey are completely disenfranchised due to linguistic barriers. Some may argue that they are derivatively represented by animal rights proponents, but this seems a lackluster form of democratic participation without real bite."[95] And yet, even in countries that have legally recognized animals as sentient beings, such status does not confer full political rights.[96]

Cause lawyers in the prisoners' rights and animal protection movements might consider mechanisms of reenfranchisement as a point of comparison across movements. Some states, for example, have ombudspersons for prisoners to serve as a representative voice to advocate for their interests. Similarly, some countries have established ombudspersons to represent the interests of animals.[97] The effectiveness of such measures depends to a large degree on the scope of ombudspersons' powers

92 Stephen Gruber-Miller & Ian Richardson, *Gov. Kim Reynolds Signs Executive Order Restoring Felon Voting Rights, Removing Iowa's Last-in-the Nation Status*, Des Moines Reg. (Aug. 5, 2020), https://www.desmoinesregister.com/story/news/politics/2020/08/05/iowa-governor-kim-reynolds-signs-felon-voting-rights-executive-order-before-november-election/5573994002/.

93 *Id.*

94 Richard A. Posner, *Animal Rights: Legal, Philosophical, and Pragmatic Perspectives*, *in* Animal Rights: Current Debates and New Directions 51, 57–58 (Cass R. Sunstein & Martha C. Nussbaum eds., 2004) ("conventional rights bearers are with minor exceptions actual and potential voters and economic actors. Animals do not fit this description."); *but see* Will Kymlicka & Sue Donaldson, *Animals and the Frontiers of Citizenship*, 34 Oxford J. Legal Stud. 201 (2014) (exploring the case for citizenship for domesticated animals, which involves recognition of rights and participation in communities even though such animals "cannot vote, or engage in rational debate, or collectively mobilize or rebel.").

95 Andriola, *supra* note 70, at 69.

96 *See generally* Treaty Establishing a Constitution for Europe, Part III, Art. III-121 (Oct. 29, 2004).

97 *See* Regina Binder, *A Large Step – but Still a Long Way to Go: Austrian Animal Welfare Legislation: An Overview*, 8 J. Animal & Nat. Res. L. 91, 111–12 (2012) (discussing the powers and limits on the position of Animal Ombudsman, established by the Austrian Animal Welfare Act).

and the degree to which they may participate in different types of government proceedings, from judicial to administrative to political. Movements could identify what features are essential to an effective ombudsperson and what types of limitations hamper their ability to adequately assert the interests of the powerless.

Another important point of comparison could be the relative merits of different advocacy tactics to combat disenfranchisement. As in other areas of public interest law, there are serious questions about which tactical approaches to advocacy are most effective, and there is ample room for a full investigation of the limits of such tactics. A conventional approach to social movements over the past half century might at least first look to rights litigation in the federal courts, which earlier movements have counted on to achieve progress for politically powerless constituencies. Setting aside for a moment the substantive question about the source and scope of rights for incarcerated persons and nonhuman animals, the idea of a litigation-centric, rights-based approach to protecting these groups fits within what we might characterize as traditional or "old school" models of social reform. Turning again to *Carolene Products*,[98] the Supreme Court observed in its famous footnote 4 that courts might have to be more vigilant about safeguarding the rights of underrepresented minorities. The Court recognized that it did not need to decide "whether prejudice against discrete and insular minorities may be a special condition, which tends seriously to curtail the operation of . . . political processes ordinarily to be relied upon to protect minorities, and which may call for a correspondingly more searching judicial inquiry."[99] But this footnote has been understood by subsequent cases to imply just that point – that groups that are politically unpopular, disenfranchised, or both may be structurally unable to redress their grievances through ordinary political processes, and therefore are more deserving of more aggressive judicial interventions.

Both incarcerated persons and nonhuman animals can certainly be described as discrete and insular minorities who are unlikely to be able to achieve meaningful policy change through ordinary political processes. In the case of prisoners, the "special condition" that impedes their ability to pursue ordinary political processes is, as we have seen, formal disenfranchisement and resistance to reinstatement of voting rights. (The same is true for noncitizens, and one arguable justification for treating both groups as outsiders is that their status is, for the most part at least, not thought to be based on immutable characteristics. But whether justified or not, the exclusion from political participation is stark.) For animals, there has never, of course, been any formal political power, so they are situated similarly to other groups that have always been excluded from the political process. For these reasons, both groups might seek to employ impact litigation to achieve meaningful law reform, and in the case of animals, there is no possible rejoinder of them having

[98] 304 U.S. 144 (1938).
[99] *Id.* at 153 n.4.

been guilty of misconduct that might be true for some convicted felons or loyalty to another government that might be true for some noncitizens. On the other hand, as many commentators have observed, reliance on litigation as a long-term tactic for achieving social reform has perhaps not been as successful as we might imagine. Pathbreaking cases such as *Brown v. Board of Education*[100] and *Roe v. Wade*[101] are quite rare, and rather than effectively embedding rights in our constitutional firmament permanently, frequently instead lead to resistance in their implementation and substantial, and often quite effective, backlash.[102] These responses reflect the potential instability of a litigation-centered approach to reform.

And litigation approaches to reenfranchisement are subject to additional substantial barriers in both movements. In the context of persons who have been convicted of felonies, in addition to the complexity of footnote 4 theory as applied to a class of people defined not by who they are or what they were born with but rather what they did, the text of the Fourteenth Amendment implicitly contemplates the removal of voting rights by States. Section 2 provides that states will not be penalized regarding their proportional representation in Congress if they deny the right to vote to persons engaged in "rebellion, or other crime."[103] And the history of the Reconstruction Amendments is in line with this understanding. It would therefore be difficult, if not impossible, to argue for a federally required constitutional right to vote for formerly incarcerated persons. In theory, it would be possible to win a constitutional challenge recognizing the legal rights of nonhuman animals, but that would require that they be deemed "persons" within the meaning of the Constitution's text, which is also highly unlikely.

Thus, despite the arguments that might be drawn from footnote 4 of *Carolene Products*, it would seem that, at least with regard to voting and other participatory rights, other social change tactics would be more effective and sustainable. One might look at recent democratically driven successes in prison reform and view them as reason for hope that mobilization, community organizing, and policy advocacy are among those effective options. The initial success of the Florida movement to restore voting rights to the formerly incarcerated, as well as a more receptive public, at first blush suggests that there are realistic tactical options to address reenfranchisement for prisoners. Of course, because this movement suffered almost immediate backlash from the Florida legislature, advocates turned to the state and federal courts to block efforts to dilute the amendment. But this type of litigation is reactive and serves a more complementary role to the underlying mobilization strategy, as opposed to the litigation model, where the courts are the primary venue in which advocates seek change. Other signs of political mobilization in the prisoners' rights

[100] 347 U.S. 483 (1954).
[101] 410 U.S. 113 (1973).
[102] Chen & Cummings, *supra* note 3, at 59.
[103] U.S. Const. amend XIV, § 2.

movement may be seen in the surprisingly bipartisan cooperation that led to enactment of the First Step Act of 2018, which reformed federal criminal justice system by, among other things, reducing mandatory minimum sentences for nonviolent crimes, softening the federal "three strikes" sentencing requirements, and instituting some measures to improve prison conditions.[104] Though these do not directly relate to enfranchisement, they represent the possibility of political and policy reforms advancing other related rights for prisoners and former prisoners.

What about nonlitigation efforts to improve the welfare of animals? Here, we have witnessed only mixed success, and none of the reforms has come close to addressing animal disenfranchisement. The most prominent piece of federal legislation regarding animals is the federal Animal Welfare Act (AWA), which establishes some legal standards for the protection of animals used for research and exhibition.[105] Enacted in 1966, the AWA has been praised as an important foundation setting minimum standards for human treatment of nonhuman animals. At the same time, it has been widely criticized on the ground that the definition of "animal" is so narrow that it does not cover treatment of farmed animals or many animals commonly used in animal experimentation, provides those who work in the animal industry with cover that makes their activities less transparent, precludes efforts at stronger animal welfare legislation, and diminishes meaningful public discourse about animal rights and welfare.[106] Legislative reform also occurs, of course, at the state and local level, and here groups such as ALDF have accomplished some success addressing discrete animal welfare issues in a number of jurisdictions.[107] If some of this success can be directed toward legal recognition of surrogates such as ombudspersons to represent animals' interests in the political and judicial process, it could promote at least some enfranchisement for animals.

17.6 CONCLUSION

In this chapter, we have attempted to establish a typological model for comparing cause lawyering across different social movements that share a common goal of challenging carceral logics in the United States. This is a very limited snapshot, but we hope to promote further discussion, not only about comparisons between the prisoners' rights and animal protection movements, but also between and among other social movements. Moreover, we do not mean to suggest invisibility, moral suasion, and disenfranchisement are the only important factors to compare. Indeed,

[104] Pub. L. No. 115-291, 132 Stat. 5194. "First Step" is an acronym for Formerly Incarcerated Reenter Society Transformed Safely Transitioning Every Person.

[105] 7 U.S.C. § 2131 *et seq.*

[106] *See, e.g.*, Marceau, *supra* note 46; Jessica Eisen, *Beyond Rights and Welfare: Democracy, Dialogue, and the Animal Welfare Act*, 51 U. Mich. J.L. Reform 469 (2018).

[107] *See Legislation – Victories: Strengthening Laws that Protect Animals and Striking Down Laws Hurting Animals*, Animal Legal Def. Fund, https://aldf.org/project/legislation-victories/.

other researchers could address a range of other considerations that might yield rich and interesting comparisons across movements, including availability of resources, reliance on rights-oriented approaches to reform, and the comparative life stage of different movements, to name a few. We hope that this chapter will prompt further academic discussions and that such comparisons may, in turn, promote open and candid dialogue among cause lawyers associated with different movements to generate an appreciation for the value that can be drawn from such a comparative approach.

18

Litigating Animal Captivity

Habeas Corpus in the Carceral State

Jessica Eisen

18.1 INTRODUCTION

On April 27, 2014, the *New York Times Magazine* ran a cover depicting a chimpanzee in a witness box, wearing a blue suit, with a microphone and glass of water before him.[1] The well-dressed chimpanzee sat in a grand courtroom – dark wood, marble, an American flag – with a headline reading "His Day in Court." The teaser reports that "A chimpanzee is making legal history by suing his captor – and raising profound questions about how we define personhood." In terms of the burgeoning field of "animal law," the iconography and messaging seem to be decidedly more about *the law* than about *the animal*.[2] In terms of media representations, the costuming and juxtaposition is more evocative of comedies featuring nonhuman apes doing "human things"[3] than of the few cinematic works that have endeavored to depict nonhuman apes as subjects, as members of communities, or as victims of human violence.[4]

[1] Charles Siebert, *Should a Chimp Be Able to Sue Its Owner?* N.Y. TIMES MAGAZINE (April 27, 2014), https://www.nytimes.com/2014/04/27/magazine/the-rights-of-man-and-beast.html. Within the magazine, the cover photo is reproduced, along with another courtroom scene featuring the besuited chimpanzee-as-witness, with the following credits: "Alex Prager for The New York Times. Animatronic chimpanzee: AnimatedFX. Location: Diane Markoff's DC Stages, Los Angeles. Props: Colin Roddick. Stylist: Callan Stokes."

[2] For descriptions of "animal law" as a field of study, *see* PAUL WALDAU, ANIMAL STUDIES: AN INTRODUCTION 114–20 (2013); Megan A. Senatori & Pamela D. Frasch, *The Future of Animal Law: Moving Beyond Preaching to the Choir*, 60 J. LEGAL ED. 209 (2010).

[3] *See, e.g., Dunstin Checks In* (Fox Family Films 1993); *MVP: Most Valuable Primate* (Keystone Family Pictures 2001). For an argument that representations of animals as "laughable spectacles" violates their "dignity" through acts of "visual and physical control," *see* Lori Gruen, *Dignity, Captivity and an Ethics of Sight, in* THE ETHICS OF CAPTIVITY 231, 231–32, 235–36 (Lori Gruen ed., 2014).

[4] *See, e.g., Gorillas in the Mist* (Universal Pictures 1988); *Project Nim* (Red Box Films 2011).

The accompanying article describes the efforts of the Nonhuman Rights Project (NhRP) and its founding president, Steven M. Wise, to achieve judicial recognition of animals as legal rights-holders. The juridical form of this advocacy is most often a *habeas corpus* claim brought on behalf of a particular animal.[5] The writ of habeas corpus, dating back to at least the early-thirteenth century, originally represented a bare "command. . .to have the defendant to an action brought physically before the court."[6] In its contemporary role, the writ entails a command to "produce the body" of a detained individual so that the courts may review the legality of their detention.[7] Where a reviewing court finds that an individual is being deprived of their liberty without lawful authority, the writ of habeas corpus will issue, and the individual may be released.

The writ's ancient pedigree and its association with bodily liberty have made it a legal tool with a complex relationship to carceral practices. The writ has functioned both to liberate illegally detained individuals and to affirm the validity of underlying systems of legally authorized incarceration.[8] The so-called Great Writ of Liberty[9] has thus survived and even thrived in a number of contexts where liberty interests have been systematically denied.[10] Advocacy surrounding the use of the writ on behalf of nonhuman animals in US courts has, however, tended toward aspirational, sometimes bordering on fantastical, accounts of the writ's achievements in human justice contexts. These accounts rarely attend to the writ's historical and contemporary role in *sustaining* rather than *disrupting* entrenched practices of human confinement, ranging from American racial slavery, mass incarceration, immigration detention, and the so-called war on terror. Instead, the writ, and the common law tradition

5 *See, e.g.*, People ex rel. Nonhuman Rights Project v. Lavery, 124 A.D.3d 148 (3d Dept. 2014); Matter of Nonhuman Rights Project v. Lavery, 152 A.D.3d 73 (1st Dept. 2017); Nonhuman Rights Project, Inc. ex rel. Happy v. Breheny, 2020 N.Y. Slip Op. 73074 (N.Y. App. Div. 2020); *Client: Tommy*, NonHuman Rights Project, https://www.nonhumanrights.org/client-tommy/ (last visited May 21, 2021); *Client: Kiko*, NonHuman Rights Project, https://www.nonhumanrights.org/client-kiko/ (last visited May 21, 2021); *Client: Beulah, Karen, and Minnie*, NonHuman Rights Project, https://www.nonhumanrights.org/clients-beulah-karen-minnie/ (last visited May 21, 2021).

6 Judith Farbey & R. J. Sharpe (with Simon Atrill), The Law of Habeas Corpus 2 (3rd ed. 2011).

7 *Id.*

8 See *infra* notes 41–58 and accompanying text. My thanks to Benjamin Levin for helping to sharpen my thinking on this point.

9 *See* Paul D. Halliday, Habeas Corpus: From England to Empire 2, 2 n.3 (2010) (noting that habeas corpus has been called "the Great Writ of Liberty" for "three hundred years," and reporting the earliest use of the phrase uncovered in his own research to be reference to the "great writ of English Liberty" in Giles Jacob, A New Law-Dictionary (1729), s.v. habeas corpus).

10 *Cf.* Halliday, *supra* note 9, at 309–13 (citing instances of legislative and executive efforts in the 1800s and 1900s, across commonwealth jurisdictions, to engage in large-scale carceral practices despite the existence of the common law writ: "now the work of detention had been put into the hands of bureaucrats: keepers of registers who enrolled the names and shipped their bearers off. Habeas corpus, bound by the logic of detention, could do little to slow their work.").

more broadly, are portrayed by these advocates as manifesting a just and morally appropriate legal order that needs only to correct the "mistake" of omitting animals from its purview.[11]

This chapter will introduce a corrective to this superlative vision of habeas corpus, its achievements in human justice contexts, and its potential for animal liberation. This study will begin by elaborating a critique of Wise and the NhRP's approach to habeas corpus, arguing that this advocacy tradition overstates the writ's accomplishments, often relying on an incomplete account of the writ's history to do so. In particular, these accounts of the writ's successes tend to paint struggles against racial violence and inequality as complete, thus minimizing the import of urgent ongoing justice projects. Next, a historical corrective is offered, demonstrating how closer attention to the writ's actual role in human carceral systems can enrich our understanding of the writ's limits and potential. This account will emphasize that the writ of habeas corpus operates only to challenge illegal (rather than unjust) detention; that it operates only at the margins of legal confinement systems to contain rather than to eliminate carceral practices; and that it therefore serves a role not only in challenging individual instances of confinement, but also in sustaining and validating ongoing carceral practices.

This more critical picture of habeas corpus, however, does not strip the writ of its potential as an advocacy tool for the interests of nonhuman animals. Instead, this chapter will argue, animal advocates might join other social justice movements in adopting a more ambivalent embrace of rights litigation. It is possible, often necessary, for advocates to turn to legal tools without adopting an uncritical posture toward law. Indeed, as with other ambivalent embraces of rights – including historical uses of habeas corpus – litigation is often a critical tool in bringing political attention to social injustices. In the case of habeas corpus litigation, this is best achieved through legal analyses that focus on the harms of confinement. Such efforts do not depend on a sanguine account of law. In fact, an excessive fealty to the underlying justice of carceral systems can thwart efforts to publicize their harms through litigation. Successful transformation of animals' circumstances under law have almost always been driven by public attention to the suffering of animals at human hands. This chapter will propose that the greatest potential offered by the writ of habeas corpus is a focus on liberty that invites advocacy spotlighting the experiences of animals living within human systems of violence and confinement. It is this prospect of exposing and exploring the harms of human domination of other species – not any fantastical account of the writ's human achievements – that gives habeas corpus its most meaningful transformative potential.

[11] *Cf.* Jessica Eisen, *Feminist Jurisprudence for Farmed Animals*, 5 Canadian J. Comp. & Contemporary L. 1, 21–22 (2019).

18.2 THE "GREAT WRIT": FROM FANTASY TO REALITY

Wise's discussions of habeas corpus vacillate between acknowledgment of the writ as a strategic or imperfect vehicle and description of the writ in lofty, idealistic terms. The focus of my criticism is on Wise's more grandiloquent celebrations of the writ and the common law tradition more broadly. Wise's honorific treatment of "the Great Writ"[12] is grounded in a similarly admiring approach to the common law tradition from which the writ emerged.[13] Wise describes the common law tradition as including an "objective" component that "thoroughly permeates Western law at every level and creates the near absolute barriers to the domination of one person by another that is the outstanding characteristic of western liberal democratic justice."[14] This claim that law has created an effective bulwark against domination "seems to misstate the achievements of rights within human communities," making sense only if we "look away from the facts and conditions of mass incarceration, immigration detention, police violence, and private violence indirectly supported by the state."[15] This general mischaracterization of Anglo-American legal traditions is illustrated and made concrete in the context of Wise's particular treatment of the writ of habeas corpus.

Wise's description of the writ's history is heavily focused on a general account of the writ's development in the English medieval and Renaissance periods,[16] together with a discussion of the writ's use in the context of American racial slavery.[17] Wise's account of the writ's emancipatory potential relies in significant part on his most developed case study, the 1772 case of *Somerset v. Stewart*, in which the writ of habeas corpus was successfully deployed to challenge the legality of the detention of an enslaved person.[18] In this historic decision, a British court found that slavery was contrary to the common law of England, and so refused to return an escaped, formerly enslaved person in England to a man claiming to be his "owner" under Virginia law.[19] The case is now widely regarded as establishing that slavery (which

[12] *See supra* note 9. For Wise's use of this phrase, see, e.g., Steven M. Wise, *The Entitlement of Chimpanzees to the Common Law Writs of Habeas Corpus and de Homine Replegiando*, 37 GOLDEN GATE U. L. REV. 219, 277 (2007).

[13] *But see* FARBEY, ET AL., *supra* note 6, at 5 (discussing the writ's use in the English Court of Chancery as well as common law courts).

[14] Steven M. Wise, *Hardly a Revolution - The Eligibility of Nonhuman Animals for Dignity-Rights in a Liberal Democracy*, 22 VT. L. REV. 793, 797–98 (1998). For an argument that this formulation draws a dubious distinction between "objective" and "subjective" elements of law, *see* JESSICA EISEN, *Beyond Rights and Welfare: Democracy, Dialogue, and the Animal Welfare Act*, 51 U. MICH. J. L. REFORM 469, 522 (2018).

[15] Eisen, *supra* note 14, at 522–23.

[16] Wise, *supra* note 12, at 255–63.

[17] *Id.* at 263–76.

[18] Somerset v. Stewart, 98 ER 499 (1772). *See* Wise, *supra* note 12, at 263–72.

[19] Somerset v. Stewart, *supra* note 18.

was not as widely practiced on English soil as in the Americas[20]) was illegal under English common law.[21]

Wise's treatment of this case tends to overstate both its practical achievements and its usefulness in illuminating the ordinary functioning of the writ of habeas corpus. Wise's book examining this case is titled "Though the Heavens May Fall: The Landmark Trial that Led to the End of Human Slavery."[22] The title "Though the Heavens May Fall" comes from the Latin maxim *Fiat justicia, ruat coelumi* ("Let justice be done, though the heavens may fall"), invoked by the presiding judge in the trial.[23] The subtitular reference to this as the trial that "led to the end of human slavery" exaggerates the role of this English decision in ending the American system of racialized chattel slavery, which drew to its formal close over one hundred years later,[24] within a different legal jurisdiction, and in the wake of economic transformation, a civil war, and the rebellion and advocacy of enslaved and formerly enslaved people themselves.[25] The titular reference to "the end of human slavery" erases the persistence of slavery as an economic and social practice around the world.[26] This description also obscures the fact that even within the United States, "involuntary servitude. . .as punishment for a crime" remains a legally permissible and highly raced carceral practice.[27]

Wise describes the writ's use in *Somerset v. Stewart* as "[p]aradigmatic," suggesting that this was a typical example of the writ's operation.[28] In fact, this was quite an exceptional case.[29] The availability of habeas corpus and other legal mechanisms for reviewing the legality of the detention of enslaved people generally posed little or no disruption to the institutions of American racial slavery.[30] The court's conclusion

[20] *But see* Aamna Mohdin, *Researchers Discovered Hundreds of Ads for Runaway Slaves in 18th-Century Britain*, QUARTZ (June 12, 2018), https://qz.com/1301918/researchers-discovered-hundreds-of-ads-for-runaway-slaves-in-18th-century-britain/.

[21] *But see* ALAN WATSON, *Lord Mansfield; Judicial Integrity or Its Lack; Somerset's Case*, 1 J. OF COMP. L. 225, (2006).

[22] STEVEN M. WISE, THOUGH THE HEAVENS MAY FALL: THE LANDMARK TRIAL THAT LED TO THE END OF HUMAN SLAVERY (2005).

[23] *Id.* at 173–74.

[24] *But see* DOUGLAS BLACKMON, SLAVERY BY ANOTHER NAME: THE RE-ENSLAVEMENT OF BLACK AMERICANS FROM THE CIVIL WAR TO WORLD WAR II (2008).

[25] *See, e.g.*, STEVEN HAHN, A NATION UNDER OUR FEET: BLACK POLITICAL STRUGGLES IN THE RURAL SOUTH FROM SLAVERY TO THE GREAT MIGRATION (2003)

[26] Kate Hodal, *One in 200 People Is a Slave. Why?*, THE GUARDIAN (Feb. 25, 2019), https://www.theguardian.com/news/2019/feb/25/modern-slavery-trafficking-persons-one-in-200.

[27] U.S. CONST. amend. XIII; MICHELLE ALEXANDER, THE NEW JIM CROW: MASS INCARCERATION IN THE AGE OF COLORBLINDNESS 39–40 (2010).

[28] Wise, *supra* note 12, at 263.

[29] The writ was likely resorted to by more than 11,000 individuals before the English courts between 1500 and 1800, many of which remain "unread in the archives." HALLIDAY, *supra* note 9, at 3, 28.

[30] *See* JUSTIN J. WERT, HABEAS CORPUS IN AMERICA: THE POLITICS OF INDIVIDUAL RIGHTS 199 (2011) (explaining that the writ was, in fact, used "to enforce the institutions of chattel slavery," including through enforcement of "slave law" and "the property rights of slave owners").

that Somerset could not lawfully be held as a slave depended on a finding that his common law liberty rights had not been displaced by statute: "The state of slavery is of such a nature, that it is incapable of being introduced on any reasons, moral or political; but *only by positive law*. . . : it's so odious, that nothing can be suffered to support it, *but positive law*."[31] In other words, if English legislation had authorized Somerset's enslavement, the writ would not have issued. Even within England, the *Somerset* judgment was confined to the individual case before the court, and was not followed by a "rush for writs" on behalf of other enslaved people within England.[32] The impact of the decision was even slighter within American states, where slavery was authorized and regulated by statute. As legal historian Paul Halliday has observed in connection with this case, "[h]abeas corpus, by its nature, could not enable a judge to declare illegal an entire system of bondage created by colonial legislatures."[33] The writ of habeas corpus is available to review the *legality* of detention; insofar as slavery or other kinds of detention were *lawful*, the writ posed no threat to associated systems of confinement. The availability of the writ of habeas corpus is entirely consistent with ongoing, systemic, legalized confinement.

Exaggeration of the writ's role in bringing slavery to an "end" is part of a broader, damaging rhetorical strategy that has often been deployed by animal advocates. Analytic links (implicit and explicit) between contemporary animal use and American racial slavery have been pervasive in the animal advocacy movement,[34] despite persistent objections. Animal advocates have been criticized for taking an interest in chattel slavery not to attend to its complexity and ongoing impacts, but with the aim of "pronouncing it dead and naming animal slavery as its successor."[35] As Angela Harris has observed, these analogies often depend on an "implicit assumption that the African American struggle for rights is over, and that it was successful" – an implication that is both inaccurate and potentially harmful to the ongoing justice struggles of Black Americans.[36] Claire Jean Kim elaborates that such

[31] Somerset v. Stewart, *supra* note 18, at 510 [*sic*].

[32] HALLIDAY, *supra* note 9, at 175. *See also* George van Cleve, *"Somerset's Case" and Its Antecedents in Imperial Perspective*, 24 L. & HIST. REV. 601, 635–37 (2006) (offering evidence that the presiding judge in *Somerset v. Stewart*, Lord Mansfield, did not intend his judgment to emancipate slaves in England more generally).

[33] *Id.* (observing further that "slavery's foes would be disappointed that habeas corpus had not, with one fell swoop, ended an infamous regime of oppression.")

[34] *See, e.g.*, STEVEN BEST, THE POLITICS OF TOTAL LIBERATION: REVOLUTION FOR THE 21ST CENTURY 21–49 (2014); GARY L. FRANCIONE, RAIN WITHOUT THUNDER: THE IDEOLOGY OF THE ANIMAL RIGHTS MOVEMENT 222 (1996); MARJORIE SPIEGEL, THE DREADED COMPARISON: HUMAN AND ANIMAL SLAVERY (1988).

[35] Claire Jean Kim, *Abolition*, *in* CRITICAL TERMS FOR ANIMAL STUDIES 15, 21 (Lori Gruen ed., 2018) (critiquing GARY FRANCIONE & ANNA CHARLTON, ANIMAL RIGHTS: THE ABOLITIONIST APPROACH [2015]). A further concern with these analogies is that they assume a comfort with human-animal comparisons that is particularly fraught for Black Americans given the history of animal comparisons as a tool of their contemporary and historical subjugation. *See, e.g.*, Kim, *supra* note 37, at 17; Harris, *supra* note 36, at 27.

[36] Angela P. Harris, *Should People of Color Support Animal Rights?*, 5 J. ANIMAL L. 15 (2009).

an approach "relentlessly displaces the issue of black oppression, deflecting attention from the specificity of the slave's status then and mystifying the question of the Black person's status now."[37]

The retelling of the human history of habeas corpus as one of triumph – especially triumph over legalized forms of race-based violence and confinement in the United States – is both misleading and dangerous. Black Americans continue to experience disproportionate levels of state violence, including through policing, surveillance, and mass incarceration.[38] The availability of habeas corpus has not dismantled these systems, nor has it eliminated their disparate impacts along racial lines. Habeas corpus – the Great Writ of Liberty – thus continues to operate within racially ordered carceral systems that confine and kill human beings. The writ has not been a wrecking ball of justice, boldly demolishing systems of confinement, "though the heavens may fall."[39] Instead, the writ has served as a more modest legal tool – one that has curbed the excesses of those carceral practices that are *illegal* even within systems that generally authorize violence and detention.

18.3 RETHINKING HABEAS CORPUS AND ITS LIMITS

Habeas corpus is best understood as operating to contain specific carceral *practices* at the margins while also working to authorize or confirm the legal legitimacy of carceral *systems* as a whole. The writ functions only to stop or restrain detentions that are *unlawful*, meaning that the underlying legal order must disapprove of the carceral practice in order for the writ to work as a restraint on that practice. Moreover, the writ serves as an effective check only where one part of government is thought to be disobeying the law, and the judiciary can be expected to intervene to correct this disobedience. Habeas corpus is not a legal mechanism for dismantling systems of confinement – it is a mechanism for holding those systems of confinement to their own rules. Its effectiveness depends on the strength of underlying substantive rights (i.e., legal limits on detention) and on institutional considerations (i.e., whether reviewing courts are likely to safeguard those limits more effectively than other legal decision-makers). This characterization of the writ is supported by two well-studied contexts of US habeas corpus litigation: federal judicial oversight of state criminal procedure and judicial review of executive detentions at Guantánamo Bay.

Consider, first, the role that the writ of habeas corpus has played in facilitating the oversight of state criminal procedure by federal courts. During the 1960s, the

[37] Kim, *supra* note 35, at 18.

[38] For explorations of mass incarceration as a structural descendent of slavery and other historical forms of racialized social control in the United States, see ALEXANDER, *supra* note 27; Loïc Wacquant, *From Slavery to Mass Incarceration: Rethinking the "Race Question" in the US*, 13 NEW LEFT REVIEW 41 (Jan./Feb. 2002).

[39] *See supra* note 23 and accompanying text.

Supreme Court of the United States substantially increased the application of federal constitutional protections to state criminal process, including prohibiting the use of evidence obtained through illegal searches[40] and requiring that accused persons be advised of their rights in interrogation.[41] State courts adjudicating criminal proceedings, however, were often hostile and resistant to the introduction of these federal constitutional requirements.[42] The writ of habeas corpus came to play a critical role in subjecting state criminal convictions to review before federal courts, assuring the protection of federal constitutional protections in the face of state court recalcitrance.[43] Historians and legal scholars have debated the extent to which this represented a major expansion of habeas corpus or simply a modest continuation of the writ's historic office.[44] In either case, it is undisputed that any waxing in the availability of habeas corpus certainly waned in subsequent years of legislative and judicial restrictions on the writ's availability.[45] Nonetheless, the writ continues to play a role in assuring the legality of detention in state criminal proceedings through review by federal courts.

The availability of habeas corpus as a mechanism for bringing constitutional violations before federal courts is, of course, deeply significant to individual defendants and incarcerated persons who would have otherwise had little meaningful hope for protecting their rights.[46] However, if we hope to understand the role of habeas review within the broader context of criminal carceral practice, another reality becomes equally important: that the availability of habeas corpus in individual cases has not worked to end or reduce the scale of state carceral systems. Instead, rates of incarceration have ballooned since habeas review of state courts' compliance with

[40] Mapp v. Ohio, 367 U.S. 643, (1961).

[41] Miranda v. Arizona, 384 U.S. 436, (1966). *See* WERT, *supra* note 30, at 156–61(summarizing the expansion of federal constitutional protections enforced through *habeas corpus* in this period, and political backlash).

[42] Vicki C. Jackson, *World Habeas Corpus*, 91 CORNELL L. REV. 303, 334–38 (2006). This hostility and resistance reflected a broader rejection of federal constitutional restrictions on state lawmaking, including in the context of racial desegregation. *See* MICHAEL J. KLARMAN, FROM JIM CROW TO CIVIL RIGHTS 320–24, 334–35 (2004); Robert Jerome Glennon, *The Jurisdictional Legacy of the Civil Rights Movement*, 61 TENN. L. REV. 869, 870 (1994).

[43] Jackson, *supra* note 42, at 347 (explaining that federal courts came to serve something like an "appellate review" function respecting federal constitutional questions arising in state criminal proceedings)

[44] *See generally* ERIC M. FREEDMAN, HABEAS CORPUS: RETHINKING THE GREAT WRIT OF LIBERTY (2001), refuting PAUL M. BATOR, *Finality in Criminal Law and Federal Habeas Corpus for State Prisoners*, 76 HARV. L. REV. 441 (1963).

[45] Jackson, *supra* note 42, at 347–48. *See also* John H. Blume & David P. Voisin, *An Introduction to Federal Habeas Corpus Practice and Procedure*, 47 S.C.L. REV. 271, 273 (1996) (noting that "despite the expansive tone of much of the language describing habeas corpus, its effective reach has been curtailed, especially in recent years.")

[46] *See* FREEDMAN, *supra* note 44, at 158–59.

federal constitutional requirements was affirmed.[47] Moreover, in all cases, the writ's function remains the supervision of the *legality* of the particular detention under review, rather than the underlying justice of criminal carceral systems more broadly.

Perhaps the most striking and intuitive example of the split between habeas review (focused on legality) and interrogation of the underlying justice of detention is the Supreme Court of the United States' judgment in *Herrera v. Collins*.[48] In that case, the Court effectively established that actual innocence of the crime for which a person has been convicted is insufficient as a basis for postconviction relief: "federal habeas courts sit to ensure that individuals are not imprisoned in violation of the Constitution – not to correct errors of fact."[49] Habeas corpus was thus found to offer a veneer of judicial oversight, expressly foreclosing attention to the justice or injustice of the underlying carceral system.[50] Because of the writ's focus on legality and procedural oversight, the enforcement of rights through habeas corpus proceedings has played a role not only in challenging specific instances of illegality, but also in confirming and legitimizing underlying carceral systems.[51]

We can observe similar limits on the transformative potential of habeas corpus in the writ's application to persons detained at the Guantánamo Bay detention camp. In a series of cases before the Supreme Court of the United States, advocates successfully argued that the writ must be formally available to those detained at the camp,[52] and that statutes limiting access to the federal courts to adjudicate such habeas claims amount to an unconstitutional suspension of the writ.[53] The

47 *See* National Research Council, The Growth of Incarceration in the United States: Exploring Causes and Consequences (2014) (observing massive growth in rates of incarceration in the United States after the early 1970s).

48 506 U.S. 390 (1993).

49 *Id.* at 400–1. *See also* Brandon L. Garrett, *Habeas Corpus and Due Process*, 98 Cornell L. Rev. 47, 122 (2012) (elaborating that the *Herrera* Court did leave open the possibility of relief based on actual innocence in a "truly persuasive" case, but that, thus far, even persons exonerated by DNA evidence have been unsuccessful in convincing courts that their cases fall into this category).

50 *Cf.* Freedman, *supra* note 44, at 159 (observing that persistent findings of systemic discrimination and injustice in capital and noncapital cases has led to restrictions of habeas proceedings rather than dismantling of carceral systems: "both the courts and Congress over the past fifteen years or so have shown a consistent inclination to shoot the messenger: to respond to the unfairness revealed in capital habeas proceedings by devising mechanisms to restrict such proceedings, rather than ones to remedy the unfairness").

51 *C.f.* Keramet Reiter, *The Most Restrictive Alternative: A Litigation History of Solitary Confinement in U.S. Prisons, 1960–2006*, 57 Studies in L., Politics and Soc'y 71, 117–18 (2012) (arguing that, although litigation of constitutional rights may have created some substantive and procedural limits around the use of solitary confinement in US prisons, it may also have worked to legally confirm and legitimize solitary confinement as a carceral practice more generally); Debra Parkes, *Solitary Confinement, Prisoner Litigation, and the Possibility of a Prison Abolitionist Lawyering Ethic*, 32 Can. J.L. & Soc'y 165, 180 (2017) (arguing that "prisoner rights advocacy may. . .have the effect of entrenching correctional logics in constitutionalized form, thereby undermining broader critiques of the carceral state and efforts to dismantle it").

52 Rasul v. Bush, 542 U.S. 466 (2004); Hamdi v. Rumsfeld, 542 U.S. 507 (2004).

53 Boumediene v. Bush, 553 U.S. 723 (2008).

imperative to achieve meaningful access to the writ derived largely from these advocates' assumptions that federal judges would recognize and apply the legal rights of detainees more effectively than the military commissions established to adjudicate these cases.[54] In practice, however, the appellate court to which most of these cases flowed turned out to be remarkably resistant to these habeas claims, even where they had been successful before lower courts.[55] Notably, the Supreme Court's affirmation of the availability of habeas review respecting detentions at Guantánamo Bay left open the essential question of which legal rules might actually constrain executive authority to detain in these cases. A recent federal court judgment answered this question with a remarkably restrained account of the substantive legal rights that might apply in these cases. The court held that the Due Process Clause of the federal constitution's Fifth Amendment could not be invoked by "an alien detained outside the sovereign territory of the United States," effectively limiting constraints on detention at Guantánamo Bay to those created by statute.[56] Limited to these minimal statutory protections, prosecutors are permitted, for example, to rely on evidence obtained from another detainee through torture or coercion.[57]

It is difficult to pin down the precise impact of this habeas litigation on the carceral project at Guantánamo Bay. The total number of detainees at Guantánamo Bay has dropped significantly as a result of policy choices by the Obama administration. It is at least arguable that years of habeas litigation played a role in keeping the spotlight of public opinion on the plight of Guantánamo Bay prisoners, provoking this policy shift. There may be, moreover, some symbolic significance to the Court's extension of the writ to Guantánamo Bay detainees, emphasizing in the public psyche the principle that the demands of justice must extend even to the most detested prisoners, and even to a space seemed designed to operate outside the confines of law. In terms of direct legal effect, however, the Supreme Court's confirmation that the writ of habeas corpus may be used to challenge detentions at Guantánamo Bay has had starkly limited consequences. The limited scope of legal rights constraining detentions has meant that prisoners have not

[54] James Oldham, *The DeLloyd Guth Visiting Lecture in Legal History: Habeas Corpus, Legal History, and Guantánamo Bay*, 36 Manitoba L.J. 361 (2012).

[55] Harvey Gee, *Habeas Corpus, Civil Liberties, and Indefinite Detention during Wartime: From Ex Parte Endo and the Japanese American Internment to the War on Terrorism and Beyond*, 47 The U. of Pac. L. Rev. 791, 822–25 (2016). *See also* Oldham, *supra* note 54, at 364 (observing that "[o]f the cases heard by the DC Circuit on the merits, the total number in which the prisoner prevailed is zero").

[56] Al Hela v. Trump, No. 19-5079, slip op. at 46 (D.C. Cir. 2020). For a critique of this holding in light of Supreme Court precedent, and suggestion that the decision would nonetheless likely be upheld by the Supreme Court as currently constituted, *see* Linda Greenhouse, *A Court Just Slammed the Guantánamo Gate Shut*, N.Y. Times (Sept. 10, 2020), https://www.nytimes.com/2020/09/10/opinion/Guantánamo-due-process.html.

[57] Carol Rosenberg, *Court Rules Guantánamo Detainees Are Not Entitled to Due Process*, N.Y. Times (Sept. 10, 2020), https://www.nytimes.com/2020/09/02/us/politics/Guantánamo-detainees-due-process.html.

actually been released as a result of judicial pronouncements in habeas corpus proceedings. In fact, the D.C. Circuit Court has sided with the executive in every single case where it has challenged a habeas claim asserted by a person detained at Guantánamo Bay.[58] The D.C. Circuit Court's caselaw in these matters underlines the reality that the writ's effectiveness in challenging detentions will always depend on both institutional realities (here, respecting whether the judiciary might serve as a check on executive power) and on the definition of underlying substantive rights. In the case of Guantánamo Bay, a finding that few substantive rights constrain government authority has gutted the practical impact of habeas corpus review: individual prisoners are simply not being set free on judge's orders pursuant to the writ. Moreover, despite the decrease in the number of prisoners held at Guantánamo Bay, the writ's availability has not ended the basic underlying carceral system in issue. The detention center remains open and legally authorized, holding prisoners who are unprotected by federal constitutional rights.[59]

The writ, then, has not proven itself to be an effective device for reliably dismantling systems of legalized confinement. As a legal tool, it is best understood as a procedural mechanism designed to ferret out instances of illegal detention within systems that, more broadly, continue to authorize carceral practices. The significance of the writ derives not from its capacity to unearth new substantive protections, but from its particular function within systems where some part of the government is disobeying or overstepping the established confines of its legal authority. It is for this reason that the writ is so strongly associated not only with the "liberty" of individuals but also with structural features of the American legal system. In the Guantánamo Bay cases, the relevant structural feature is "'separation of powers," balancing the roles of executive, judicial, and legislative authority.[60] In cases respecting federal courts' oversight of state courts, the relevant structural feature is "federalism," balancing the roles of state and federal governments.[61] The writ of habeas corpus serves to restrain illegal confinement, allowing one part of government to supervise the legality of another authority's particular actions within contexts of legalized violence and incarceration. The writ operates within, and lends legitimacy to, the broader carceral systems and logics of which it forms a part, even

58 Greenhouse, *supra* note 56.

59 Brian Bouffard & Aaron Shepard, *There's No Justice in Guantanamo Bay. For America's Sake, That Must Change*, WASH. POST (Jan. 12, 2021), https://www.washingtonpost.com/opinions/2021/01/12/theres-no-justice-guantanamo-bay-americas-sake-that-must-change/.

60 *See, e.g.*, Robert Bejesky, *Closing Gitmo due to the Epiphany Approach to Habeas Corpus during the Military Commission Circus*, 50 WILLAMETTE L. REV. 43, 47 (2013) (referring to the role of habeas corpus proceedings respecting Guantánamo Bay as "a separation of powers case study").

61 *See, e.g.*, FREEDMAN, *supra* note 44, at 11 (noting that "federal habeas corpus is closely linked to federalism"); John H. Blume & David P. Voisin, *An Introduction to Federal Habeas Corpus Practice and Procedure*, 47 S.C.L. REV. 271, 273–74 (1996) (referencing federalism concerns and finality of litigation as the two core rationales for restraints on the application of the writ of habeas corpus).

as it works to invalidate some individual instances of confinement. In short, the writ is better described as confining carceral systems to "business as usual" than to mandating transformation "though the heavens may fall."[62]

18.4 SPECIAL CHALLENGES FOR HABEAS CORPUS CLAIMS ON BEHALF OF ANIMALS

This understanding of habeas corpus – as a tool within, rather than a threat to, carceral systems – is of particular significance in the animal protection context. On what basis might we claim that it is not only wrong but *unlawful* to confine an animal? In the case of federal court supervision of state criminal procedure, the limits of lawful detention are defined by federal constitutional rights. In the case of Guantánamo Bay prisoners, it is breach of statutory protections that might render detention unlawful. In the case of *Somerset v. Stewart*, it was the common law that was held to prohibit the detention in issue, a protection that the court explicitly noted would extend only as long as no positive law permitted slavery in England.

A hard reality for animal advocates is that most practices of contemporary animal confinement are clearly authorized – and often affirmatively encouraged or practically required – by legislation and regulation.[63] This statutory context poses special challenges for *habeas corpus* claims on behalf of animals. The presence of statutes governing the conditions in which animals may be confined stands to frustrate claims rooted in the common law. Wise and the NhRP have been clear that it is not their intention to seek enforcement of animal protection legislation; they instead assert that there is an underlying illegality to animal confinement (at least in some cases) that is defined by common law principles.[64] Given the thicket of statutory law governing animal captivity,[65] it is difficult to imagine a court accepting an argument of this kind, even if they were to find the writ to be available in respect of animals. Recall that even in *Somerset*, the court acknowledged that positive law could

[62] *See supra* notes 22–23 and accompanying text.

[63] *See e.g.* The Animal Welfare Act, 7 U.S.C. § 2131 (positing that one of the act's objectives is "to prevent and eliminate burdens upon" prescribed commercial uses of animals); *see also* Jessica Eisen, *Milked: Nature, Necessity, and American Law*, 34 BERKELEY J. GENDER L. & JUST. 71, 73 (2019) (arguing, in the dairy context, that harms to animals flow not only from a lack of legal protection, but also from "a complex of legal and cultural practices that affirmatively support the intensification and industrialization of milk production").

[64] *See, e.g.*, NonHuman Rights Project v. Breheny, No. 260441/2019, 4 (Feb. 18, 2020) ("The NhRP argues that whether Respondents are in violation of any federal, state or local animal welfare laws in their detention of Happy is irrelevant as to whether or not the detention is lawful... The Petition does not allege that Happy is illegally confined because she is kept in unsuitable conditions, nor does it seek improved welfare for Happy. Rather, this Petition seeks that this Court recognize Happy's alleged common law right to bodily liberty, and order her immediate release.").

[65] *See supra* note 63 and accompanying text.

authorize slavery in England even if the common law prohibited it.[66] Consequently, even if the NhRP were to succeed in arguing that the common law included liberty rights for animals, it would be an additional hurdle to prove that animal confinement is the sort of unregulated space in which a meaningful common law claim might grow unencumbered by statutory interventions.[67]

One approach to these statutes might be to incorporate them into habeas claims: to argue that the detention of some animals is unlawful precisely because these animals are held in contravention of animal protection legislation.[68] There is longstanding debate and contradictory jurisprudence respecting whether human prisoners may use the writ of habeas corpus to challenge conditions of confinement as opposed to the fact of confinement itself. At the federal level, the Supreme Court of the United States has left open the possibility that habeas corpus may be available to challenge conditions of confinement,[69] and circuit courts are presently split on the question.[70] In New York State, where the NhRP has brought its habeas corpus claims, the case law has generally rejected the application of the writ to challenge conditions of confinement, but has allowed that such claims may succeed where a prisoner seeks to be removed to "an institution separate and different in nature" from the correctional setting specified by their sentence.[71] As the NhRP has argued, seeking a chimpanzee or elephant's removal to a sanctuary might fall within this

66 The statutory context surrounding habeas corpus has also transformed significantly since *Somerset*. In addition to substantive hurdles to successful habeas claims arising from animal protection statutes, a further set of procedural challenges may arise from the statutes that now shape access to the common law writ. My thanks to Justin Marceau for raising this point.

67 For example, federal regulations detail the requirements for the "primary enclosure" of "nonhuman primates," including specification that the enclosure must "contain" the primates "securely and prevent accidental opening of the enclosure, including opening by the animal." 9 C.F.R. § 3.80. This is plainly a regulatory scheme that contemplates lawfully caging animals against their will.

68 Notably, habeas corpus claims advanced in other jurisdictions have taken this approach. *See* Argentina Sandra Case before FCCCC (wherein petitioners sought a writ of habeas corpus in connection with alleged violation of the National Animal Protection Law No. 14,346 and the Wildlife Conservation Law No. 22,421); Colombian Constitutional Court Chucho Case (in which a *habeas corpus* petition alleged violation of Law 1774 of 2016, setting animal protection standards, and Law 71 of 1981, protecting endangered species).

69 *See* Preiser v. Rodriguez, 411 U.S. 475, 499 (1973) ("This is not to say that habeas corpus may not also be available to challenge. . .prison conditions."); Bell v. Wolfish, 441 U.S. 520, 527 n.6 (1979) (leaving "to another day the question of the propriety of using a writ of habeas corpus to obtain review of the conditions of confinement, as distinct from the fact or length of confinement itself"); Boumediene v. Bush, 553 U.S. 723, 792 (2008) (choosing not to "discuss the reach of the writ with respect to claims of unlawful conditions of treatment or confinement").

70 Allison Wexler Weiss, *Habeas Corpus, Conditions of Confinement, and COVID-19*, 27 WASH. & LEE J. CIV. RTS. & SOC. JUST. 131, 149 (2020).

71 People ex rel. Dawson v. Smith, 69 N.Y.2d 689, 691, (1986), citing People ex rel Brown v. Johnston, 9 N.Y.2d 482, 485 (2017).

ambit.[72] This certainly seems more plausible[73] than the claim that an underlying common law liberty right for animals has survived the thorough legislative and regulatory codification of animal captivity.

The NhRP, however, has spurned the route of advancing claims that animal detentions are unlawful due to contraventions of statutes and regulations.[74] To be sure, the thin legal protections that are afforded to animals respecting their autonomy and bodily integrity (i.e., animal "welfare" laws)[75] are often woefully under-enforced.[76] Access to the writ of habeas corpus to cure these defaults would represent a victory for animals, especially considering the obstacles animal advocates have faced in arguing that they have standing to compel agency enforcement action.[77] Nonetheless, the NhRP has chosen the more difficult path of grounding their claims in common law liberty rights. This decision is likely informed by the organization's commitment to an "animal rights" philosophy,[78] pursuant to which animals (at least great apes, elephants, dolphins and whales) should have legally protected rights to "bodily liberty" and "bodily integrity."[79]

A legal order that respected animals' rights to bodily liberty or bodily integrity would not allow the routine injury, capture, or killing of animals – all practices that are currently commonplace and legally authorized. Recognition of such animal rights would require revolutionary transformations in our practical relationships with other animals, notwithstanding Wise's insistence that it would be an incremental

72 *See* NhRP Happy COA Motion at 35–36 (noting that one concurring judgment has expressed agreement with the NhRP position on this point: Matter of Nonhuman Rights Project, Inc. v. Lavery, 31 N.Y.3d at 1058 (Fahey, J. concurring); *but see* Nonhuman Rights Project, Inc., ex rel. Kiko v. Presti, 999 N.Y.S.2d 652 (4th Dept. 2015), *lv. denied* 26 N.Y.3d 901 (2015) (denying an NhRP habeas corpus petition on behalf of a chimpanzee because the remedy sought was transfer to a different facility rather than release); Nonhuman Rights Project, Inc. ex rel. Tommy v. Lavery, 54 N.Y.S.3d 392 (1st Dept. 2017), *lv. denied* 31 N.Y.3d 1054 (2018) (finding that habeas corpus is not available to chimpanzees, but, even if it were, an NhRP claim seeking transfer to another facility would not amount to a challenge to detention cognizable in habeas corpus).

73 *But see supra* note 72.

74 *See supra* note 64 and accompanying text.

75 On the distinction between animal "rights" and animal "welfare," see Eisen, *supra* note 14, at 488–93.

76 *See* Cass Sunstein, *Can Animals Sue? in* Animal Rights: Current Debates and New Directions 251, 252 (Cass R. Sunstein & Martha C. Nussbaum eds., 2004); Laurence H. Tribe, *Ten Lessons our Constitutional Experience Can Teach Us about the Puzzle of Animal Rights: The Work of Steven M. Wise*, 7 Animal L. 1, 3 (2001).

77 *See* Eisen, *supra* note 14, at 485–87.

78 *See Who We Are*, NonHuman Rights Project, https://www.nonhumanrights.org/who-we-are/ (last visited May 20, 2021) ("We work to secure fundamental rights for nonhuman animals through litigation, legislation, and education."). *See supra* note 73 (distinguishing animal "rights" from animal "welfare").

79 *Who We Are*, NonHuman Rights Project, https://www.nonhumanrights.org/who-we-are/ (last visited May 20, 2021).

change within the logic and jurisprudence of the common law.[80] But, as we have seen, habeas corpus is not a revolutionary tool. The writ, instead, provides remedies for individual cases of confinement that fall outside of the legally sanctioned norms of entrenched carceral systems. The NhRP's litigation briefs take this individualistic form, emphasizing in each case that the court need not – must not – consider the policy implications of animal liberation.[81] Instead, the NhRP urges, each case concerns only the one animal before the court.[82] In the case of Happy the elephant, the NhRP argues, the court must consider only Happy, not the other (metaphorical) elephant in the room: if Happy may not be legally detained, what does this mean for a sociolegal order that has long treated the injury, captivity, and death of animals to be routine, even foundational?[83]

It is perhaps this tension between revolutionary ambitions and the limits of quotidian legal tools that has contributed to Wise's overly celebratory accounts of the common law and the writ of habeas corpus. Suggestions that the writ requires justice be done "though the heavens may fall"[84] may be thought to give hope for the claims of animals despite significant doctrinal obstacles and entrenched practices of legalized animal confinement. But, as we have seen, such lavish praise for the "Great Writ" and its achievements is both misleading and harmful. In reality, the writ has served comfortably within and alongside systems of confinement, curbing only those marginal practices that are unlawful within the terms of those systems themselves. To suggest otherwise minimizes or erases the ongoing realities of state-sanctioned violence and carcerality.

18.5 HABEAS CORPUS AND THE CRITIQUE OF RIGHTS: THE AMBIVALENT EMBRACE OF LEGAL TOOLS

Other justice movements have struggled with this tension between their own revolutionary ambitions and the conservative nature of legal tools. Social justice advocates have often found it necessary to rely on legal languages and logics, even

80 Wise, *supra* note 14. *Cf.* Happy First Department Decision at 2–3 ("A judicial determination that species other than homo sapiens are 'persons' for some juridical purposes, and therefore have certain rights, would lead to a labyrinth of questions that common-law processes are ill-equipped to answer."); Richard Posner, *Animal Rights* (Reviewing *Steven M. Wise, Rattling the Cage: Toward Legal Rights for Animals* [2000]), 110 YALE L.J. 527, 532 (2000) ("[J]udges asked to step onto a new path of doctrinal growth want to have some idea of where the path leads, even if it would be unreasonable to insist that the destination be clearly seen. Wise gives them no idea.").

81 *See, e.g.*, NhRP Happy COA Brief at 22–23 (dismissing judicial concerns about the policy implications of recognizing animal personhood in a habeas corpus case, averring that "this case seeks judicial recognition of just one right...on behalf of just one nonhuman animal: Happy.").

82 *Id.*

83 DINESH WADIWEL, THE WAR AGAINST ANIMALS 28–29 (2015) (arguing that we might conceive of human "war" against animals as "the war from which our conceptualization of the political sphere may be said to have originated").

84 *See supra* notes 22–23 and accompanying text.

while acknowledging their limits. Legal tools can be, and have been, picked up by advocates who maintain a critical posture toward the systems with which they engage. As Mari Matsuda explains in describing the use of rights strategies in human and civil rights contexts:

> [I]t would be absurd to reject the use of an elitist legal system or the use of the concept of rights when such use is necessary to meet the immediate needs of [a] client. There are times to stand outside the courtroom door and say, "This procedure is a farce, the legal system is corrupt, justice will never prevail in this land as long as privilege rules in the courtroom." There are times to stand inside the courtroom and say, "This is a nation of laws, laws recognizing fundamental values of rights, equality and personhood." Sometimes, as Angela Davis did, there is a need to make both speeches in one day.[85]

It is possible to appeal to entrenched legal tools and values while keeping in view the reality that these tools and values may be elements of unjust carceral orders. The choice to resort to habeas corpus advocacy does not require animal advocates to claim that the writ has ended injustice wherever it has applied, or that urgent, ongoing justice struggles are complete or resolved.

The embrace of rights litigation by feminist and critical race theorists offers a model for a more ambivalent relationship to legal tools. As telegraphed in Matsuda's quotation above, the language of "rights" has long been criticized by feminist and critical race theorists, who nonetheless conclude that rights can be an important device for advancing substantive justice projects.[86] These scholars have largely accepted a body of arguments referred to collectively as "the critique of rights."[87] One element of this critique is that rights are less transformative than many people assume, and may in fact play a critical role in sustaining existing hierarchies and power relationships.[88] Another element of this critique is that rights language is "mystifying," obscuring how law functions in practice, and directing an inordinate focus on individual cases at the expense of structural dynamics.[89] These critiques – of mystification, individual rather than systemic focus, and participation in sustaining the status quo – are echoed in the preceding critique of grandiose habeas rhetoric. Yet, despite general agreement that legal rights advocacy has these shortcomings, feminist and critical race theorists have largely settled on an uneasy

85 Mari Matsuda, *When the First Quail Calls: Multiple Consciousness as Jurisprudential Method* (1988), *in* WHERE IS YOUR BODY? 7 (Mari Matsuda, ed., 1996).

86 My thanks to Alan Chen for drawing my attention to this connection.

87 *See, e.g.*, Mark Tushnet, *The Critique of Rights*, 47 S.M.U.L. REV. 23, 23–25 (1994).

88 *See, e.g.*, *Id.*; Robert Gordon, *Some Critical Theories of Law and Their Critics*, *in* THE POLITICS OF LAW 647 (David Kairys, ed., 3d ed. 1998) (arguing that "The labor movement secured the vitally important legal right to organize and strike, at the cost of fitting into a framework of legal regulation that certified the legitimacy of management's making most of the important decisions about the conditions of work.").

89 *See, e.g.*, Peter Gabel & Jay Fineman, *Contract Law as Ideology*, *in* THE POLITICS OF LAW 496 (David Kairys, ed., 3d ed. 1998).

embrace of rights-based litigation strategies.[90] The ambivalent embrace of rights is grounded in strategic imperatives that hold true for habeas corpus advocacy as well.

First, rights are critical sites of power and contest within existing legal systems.[91] This is also true of habeas corpus, a procedural mechanism with deep roots in the Anglo-American legal system, and which has served as a focal point for social and legal battles ranging from racial slavery to civil rights to the "war on terror," as we have already seen.[92] Second, rights carry distinctive social and legal force as a means of expressing need, constraining power, or, at the very least, demanding official response.[93] This, too, is a feature of habeas corpus advocacy. At a minimum, claims brought in habeas corpus on behalf of animals have required those holding animals captive to offer legal justifications, and have required courts to offer reasons for their conclusions as to why these justifications are legally sufficient.[94]

Those pursuing habeas corpus claims on behalf of animals may benefit from the writ's deep roots in American legal thought and practice, and its capacity for demanding official response, without advancing grand, misleading claims about the writ's achievements for human beings and the law's "objective" tendency to end domination.[95] In fact, once we strip away Wise's sanguine account of the writ's achievements in human justice contexts, the writ offers a different kind of promise for animal advocates.

18.6 HABEAS CORPUS AND THE HARMS OF CAPTIVITY

Habeas corpus claims offer more than an entrée into existing American legal praxis, capable of forcing engagement with the claims of animals. The writ also invites substantive engagement with some of the most grievous harms facing animals: harms of captivity.[96] Animals are so routinely caged, and this caging so widely

[90] In addition to the rationales set out below, feminist and critical race theorists defend recourse to rights on the basis that rights language can serve to build community and power amongst oppressed constituencies, and provides a common language as between rights-seekers and those in power. The strengths of rights as rhetorical and community-building devices for rights-holders does not hold the same force for animals who do not share in human language communities. For a related discussion, see Jessica Eisen, *Animals in the Constitutional State*, 15 INT'L J. CONST. L. 909, 935–37 (2017).

[91] *See e.g.* JENNIFER NEDELSKY, LAW'S RELATIONS: A RELATIONAL THEORY OF SELF, AUTONOMY, AND LAW 73 (2011).

[92] *See supra* notes 39–61 and accompanying text.

[93] *See, e.g.*, MARTHA MINOW, MAKING ALL THE DIFFERENCE: INCLUSION, EXCLUSION, AND AMERICAN LAW 207 (1990); Patricia J. Williams, *Alchemical Notes: Reconstructing Ideals from Deconstructed Rights*, 22 HARV. CIVIL RIGHTS CIVIL LIBERTIES L. REV. 401 (1987).

[94] *See, e.g.*, Matter of Nonhuman Rights Project, Inc. v. Lavery, 152 A.D.3d 73, 78, 54 N.Y.S.3d 392 (1st Dept. 2017), lv denied 31 N.Y.3d 1054, 100 N.E.3d 846 (2018); *see also* People ex rel. Nonhuman Rights Project, Inc. v. Lavery, 124 A.D.3d 148, 152, 998 N.Y.S.2d 248 (3d Dept. 2014), lv denied 26 N.Y.3d 902 (2015).

[95] *See supra* notes 14–15 and accompanying text.

[96] *See generally* LORI GRUEN, ED.,THE ETHICS OF CAPTIVITY (2014).

understood as harmful, that the idiom "like a caged animal" has become a central metaphor for the pains of liberty deprived.[97] To the extent that the harms of confinement, and the corollary value of liberty, are core justice concerns of animals, habeas corpus presents a particularly apt legal framework for elaborating claims. Wise and the NhRP are correct in identifying the writ of habeas corpus as being intimately connected to "liberty" as a legal value both historically and in contemporary practice.[98] The demands of "liberty" are, however, famously contested in human justice contexts.[99] The strongest forms of habeas corpus advocacy are those that recognize that the common law, and the writ of habeas corpus, do not represent an inexorable march toward a predefined and objective liberty, but rather a partial and fraught inroad into debates about carceral practices and the value of autonomy.

Wise's view of habeas corpus as part of an inherently just common law order, grounded in part in "objective" principles,[100] has at times manifested in advocacy strategies that attend to supposedly objective facts about animals. The attendant evidentiary focus is on the intrinsic qualities of animals, rather than on the subjective and relational experiences of animal lives in captivity. Such lines of argumentation seek to prove, for example, that nonhuman great apes have legally relevant "autonomy" because they are logical, able to use tools, are self-aware, or have the capacity for language.[101] In response, scholars have charged that Wise and the NhRP focus excessively on arguments that animals are "like" people on a series of measurable metrics.[102] This focus on animals' similarities to humans has been criticized for replicating underlying logics of domination and hierarchy and for wrongly accepting

[97] *See also* Mark Feldman, *The Physics and Metaphysics of Caging: The Animal in Late-Nineteenth-Century American Culture*, 4 Mosaic: An Interdisciplinary Critical Journal 161 (2006).

[98] *See e.g.*, Fay v. Noia, 372 U.S. 391, 401 (1963) ("Although in form the Great Writ is simply a mode of procedure, its history is inextricably intertwined with the growth of fundamental rights of personal liberty.").

[99] Feminist theorists have argued that Anglo-American legal traditions often rely on an overly individualistic account of liberty. Relational feminists have developed, as an alternative, "relational autonomy," a value that is denied, sought or realized through relationships with others. *See* Nedelsky, *supra* note 91. For a criticism that Wise's conception of "liberty" might be enriched by a more relational conception of autonomy, see Eisen, *supra* note 14, at 523–24. *See also* Maneesha Deckha, *Humanizing the Nonhuman: A Legitimate Way for Animals to Escape Juridical Property Status? in* Critical Animal Studies: Towards Trans-species Social Justice 209, 216 (Atsuko Matsuoka & John Sorenson eds., 2018), (advocating for a focus on "care" rather than "rights-oriented personhood claims," citing Julietta Hua & Neel Ahuja, *Chimpanzee Sanctuary: "Surplus" Life and the Politics of Transspecies Care*, 65 American Quarterly 619 (2013)).

[100] *See supra* notes 14–15 and accompanying text.

[101] *See, e.g.*, Steven Wise, Rattling the Cage: Toward Legal Rights for Animals 179–237 (2000).

[102] *See* Eisen, *supra* note 11, at 21–28; Lori Gruen, *Should Animals Have Rights?*, The Dodo (Jan. 20, 2014), https://www.thedodo.com/should-animals-have-rights-396292655.html; Will Kymlicka and Sue Donaldson, *Rights*, *in* Critical Terms for Animal Studies 320, 327

the premise that "facts about difference. . .explain why powerful groups exploit and harm less powerful groups."[103]

Significantly, this strategy is not a capitulation to some clear, existing legal standard. There is no accepted judicial or statutory framework for assessing which entities are eligible for habeas corpus under the relevant statute[104] or who counts as a rights-bearing legal "person" more generally.[105] Instead, Wise and the NhRP have chosen to foreground this scientistic approach, echoing the supposed objectivity that Wise has attributed to just common law reasoning.[106] *Habeas* advocacy might just as easily pursue a different track. Instead of seeking to prove as a matter of "science" or "logic" that animals fall into the category of rights-holders, advocates might seek to prove as a matter of relationship and recognition that animals live, love, and hurt in ways that should matter to law.[107] Rather than focusing on animals' ability to meet sterile scientific tests of capacity (mirror self-recognition, for example), habeas corpus advocacy might focus instead on what animals value in their own lives.

I have proposed a simple standard for assessing whether an animal ought to qualify as a holder of rights in habeas corpus: whether the animal in question has a substantial interest in their own liberty.[108] Rather than focus on an animal's provable skills or talents, this inquiry directs us to consider the animal's subjective experience: "Does this animal *feel* the burdens of captivity? Does this animal yearn to be free?"[109] If so, their confinement gives rise to "the underlying harm at which habeas corpus aims: that the burdens of captivity should not be imposed without lawful cause."[110] Juridically speaking, this standard does not resolve all of the

(Lori Gruen ed., 2018) (observing this critique, and noting that it may apply with greater force to the Nonhuman Rights Project than to other animal rights efforts).

[103] Eisen, *supra* note 11, at 22–23.

[104] ART 70 CPLR (providing that any unlawfully detained "person" or their representative may seek habeas corpus, but without offering guidance as to the definition of "person"). For conflicting approaches to how personhood should be assessed under this statute, see Verified Petition at ¶ 19, NonHuman Rights Project v. Breheny (Oct. 2, 2018), https://www.nonhumanrights.org/content/uploads/Happy-Petition-10.1.18.pdf; Memorandum of Law In Support of Petition for Habeas Corpus at 11–14, NonHuman Rights Project v. Breheny (Oct. 2, 2018), https://www.nonhumanrights.org/content/uploads/Memo-of-Law-in-Support.pdf (proposing that the inquiry should focus on "autonomy"); BREHENY COA at 23-25 (arguing that "humanity" is the relevant standard); People ex rel. Nonhuman Rights Project, Inc. v. Lavery, 124 A.D.3d 148, 150-151 (3d Dep't 2014), *lv. denied* 26 N.Y.3d 902 (2015) (suggesting that the ability to bear duties is the fundamental criteria for personhood).

[105] *Cf.* NGAIRE NAFFINE, LAW'S MEANING OF LIFE: PHILOSOPHY, RELIGION, DARWIN, AND THE LEGAL PERSON 9–10 (2009).

[106] *See supra* note 14 and accompanying text.

[107] Eisen, *supra* note 14; Eisen, *supra* note 11.

[108] *See* Transcript of Video Submission of Professor Jessica Eisen, Auto 381 De 2019, *Audiencia Pública sobre la Acción de Tutela Instaurada por la Fundación Botánica y Zoológica de Barranquilla – Fundazoo- Contra la Corte Suprema de Justicia*, Re. Oficio No. A-1075/2019 (on file with the author).

[109] *Id.*

[110] *Id.*

challenges that habeas corpus actions on behalf of animals face. The significant obstacles to proving animal confinement unlawful remain. But the threshold inquiry to which we are directed is reshaped. Instead of a prodding assessment of the animal's intrinsic qualities, the analysis would begin with an exploration of the harms of confinement.

Scientific evidence may still play a role in evaluating habeas corpus claims on this standard, but the focus would be on what research reveals respecting the value of freedom to animals, for example in their lives as friends, as mothers, and as kin.[111] Rather than arguing that chimpanzees, for example, ought to have access to habeas corpus because they are objectively "like us," it might be argued that chimpanzees value their own relational autonomy,[112] that they suffer in isolation or when their kinship bonds are broken, and that law can and should serve as a vehicle for those interests. Under such an approach, ethological evidence respecting how chimpanzees form relationships, care for their young, grieve their dead – and how these relationships are frustrated by confinement – tells us more about the validity of claims for chimpanzees' liberty than facts about, for example, whether chimpanzees can learn to use sign language in a laboratory.[113]

Elements of this proposed approach already exist in the NhRP's filings. Their petition on behalf of Happy the elephant, for example, explains that "elephants are a social species who suffer immensely when confined in small spaces and deprived of social contact with other members of their species," citing expert evidence that elephants held in isolation experience boredom, depression, and other emotional and physical harm.[114] The petition further notes that elephants recognize and respond to the voices of their family members,[115] and that separation from their families in human captivity causes trauma so severe that their cognitive capacities are impaired for years following the separation.[116] The framework within which this evidence is advanced, however, does not emphasize the harms of captivity. Instead, the NhRP marshals this evidence to prove that Happy "possesses complex cognitive abilities" that should qualify her for liberty rights – appearing alongside detailed evidence of elephant brain size, complexity of communication patterns, and memory.[117] This focus on proving Happy's intrinsic qualities – that she is *like*

[111] *Cf.* Eisen, *supra* note 63, at 102–03 (setting out a role for scientific research on animal experience in legal analyses that reject a focus on how animals are "like" human beings).

[112] *See supra* note 97 and accompanying text (on "relational autonomy").

[113] For a foundational exploration of chimpanzee communities and relationships, see JANE GOODALL, IN THE SHADOW OF MAN (1971).

[114] Verified Petition at ¶ 19, NonHuman Rights Project v. Breheny (Oct. 2, 2018).

[115] *Id.* at ¶ 79.

[116] *Id.* at ¶ 83.

[117] *Id.* at ¶ 70 (elaborating that these complex cognitive capacities. . .include: autonomy; empathy; self-awareness; self-determination; theory of mind (awareness others have minds); insight; working memory, and an extensive long-term memory that allows them to accumulate social knowledge; the ability to act intentionally and in a goal-oriented manner, and to detect animacy and goal directedness in others; to understand the physical competence and

humans in her skills and capacities[118] – comes at the expense of an inquiry into her experience of captivity. Pages of submissions are dedicated to proving these "abilities,"[119] while a single paragraph attends to the fact that "elephants are a social species who suffer immensely when confined in small spaces and deprived of social contact with other members of their species."[120] This is not for want of evidence on the point.[121] In addition to the well-documented "social and psychological deprivation, physical deterioration, suffering and premature death" suffered by captive elephants, experts report that captivity leaves elephants "unable to fully engage in the seminal activities that define individual identities, relationships and cultural experiences – activities that may be among the most important components of elephants' lives, providing purpose, depth and meaning."[122]

A legal standard focused on animals' experiences of their own liberty and its deprivation would reverse this emphasis, calling attention not to animals' abstract capacities, but to their values, relationships, and experiences – including the realities and details of their suffering in captivity. The underlying portrait of law need not be one of an intrinsically fair system, embodied in a Great Writ that will aid liberty in any just case. Instead, the legal order may be accepted as a complex field of power and persuasion, littered with battles that have been hard-fought and half-won. Instead of proceeding as though logic and objective proof are the driving force of habeas argumentation, it is possible to proceed as though the writ's availability should be anchored in the tedium, frustration, and sorrow of life in a cage.

emotional state of others; imitate, including vocal imitation; point and understand pointing; engage in true teaching (taking the pupil's lack of knowledge into account and actively showing them what to do); cooperate and build coalitions; cooperative problem-solving, innovative problem-solving, and behavioral flexibility; understand causation; intentional communication, including vocalizations to share knowledge and information with others in a manner similar to humans; ostensive behavior that emphasizes the importance of a particular communication; wide variety of gestures, signals, and postures; use of specific calls and gestures to plan and discuss a course of action, adjust their plan according to their assessment of risk, and execute the plan in a coordinated manner; complex learning and categorization abilities; and, an awareness of and response to death, including grieving behaviors.

[118] *Cf.* Memorandum of Law In Support of Petition for Habeas Corpus at 13–16, NonHuman Rights Project v. Breheny (Oct. 2, 2018) (elaborating that the principle of "equality" demands that habeas corpus be available to elephants because their cognitive capacities and associated autonomy interest is similar to those of human beings).

[119] Verified Petition at ¶ 69–117, NonHuman Rights Project v. Breheny (Oct. 2, 2018).

[120] *Id.* at ¶ 19.

[121] *Id.*

[122] Catherine Doyle, *Elephants in Captivity*, *in* THE PALGRAVE HANDBOOK OF ANIMAL ETHICS 181, 181 (A. Linzey & C. Linzey eds., 2018); *See also* Jessica Pierce, in this volume (reviewing the harmful effects of captivity on animals).

18.7 REPRESENTING ANIMAL LAW: BEYOND A CHIMP IN A SUIT

Courts are not the only audience for *habeas corpus* litigation. Halliday sums up his historical survey of the writ's use in England and its colonial empire by noting that the "idea of *habeas corpus*" has often been "more powerful outside of courtrooms than inside them."[123] He reports that advocates – including Somerset's lawyer, Granville Sharp – were "often disappointed in the liberating ambitions they pursued at law," but that, crucially, "[i]n cases like theirs. . .the idea of habeas corpus has continued to influence public debate."[124]

Wise and the NhRP have not limited their battles to the courtroom. Litigation stands as just one pillar of their three-pronged mission, alongside legislative advocacy and a broad "education" mandate.[125] The NhRP's petitions must be assessed in this context: as part of a broader strategy for transforming the legal status of animals.[126] Whatever difficulties we may identify in their strategies and tactics, it is undeniable that the NhRP has been wildly successful in attracting media attention to their cause.[127] Might the shortcomings of the NhRP's framings be justified by the public attention they have drawn to the claims of captive animals?

I have argued elsewhere that the law reform efforts that have most effectively achieved transformation for animals have been those that have illuminated and publicized the particular facts of animal experience in compelling emotional appeals.[128] Wise's emphasis on the significance of the writ can lead to media stories that feature the grandeur of law: the Greatness of the Great Writ, or the weight and meaning of "personhood" as a legal status. This focus draws attention to animals as a legal curiosity – a chimp in a suit – rather than animals as victims of violence and confinement. The media coverage often emphasizes the *law* rather than the *animal*.[129] As the *New York Times Magazine* cover suggests,[130] the media image projected may focus on the oddity of an ape in a courtroom rather than on the tragedy of an ape in a cage.

[123] Halliday, *supra* note 9, at 316; *Cf.* Wert, *supra* note 30, at 198 ("The salient cases that legal academics identify as important markers in the development of the writ's jurisprudence are almost always only the final steps in a larger ongoing political process.").

[124] *Id.*

[125] NonHuman Rights Project, www.nonhumanrights.org/ (last visited May 21, 2021).

[126] *Who We Are*, NonHuman Rights Project, https://www.nonhumanrights.org/who-we-are/ (last visited May 20, 2021) (including, among their stated objectives, "[t]o develop. . .campaigns to promote recognition of nonhuman animals as beings worthy of. . .legal consideration and with their own inherent interests in freedom from captivity, participation in a community of other members of their species, and the protection of their natural habitats").

[127] *See* Happy COA Brief (reporting that "[s]ince 2018 alone. . .there have been hundreds of items of media coverage in diverse local, state, national and international media outlets about Happy and the NhRP's efforts to free her" [citation omitted]); *see, e.g.*, Siebert, *supra* note 1.

[128] Eisen, *supra* note 14.

[129] *See supra* note 2 and accompanying text.

[130] *See supra* notes 1-4 and accompanying text.

Habeas corpus advocacy, however, need not advance a triumphalist vision of law. Strategies that emphasize the harms of captivity, rather than the supposed greatness of legal traditions, have greater potential to persuade courts and publics that animals need and deserve legal protection. Litigation focused on animals' own lives, values, and relationships might dovetail with public education and advocacy approaches that recognize the value of animal experiences on their own terms – not as near-humans, but as beings whose experiences matter in their own right.[131] The NhRP's legal strategy has invited the image of an awkwardly styled chimpanzee in a suit – a misfit in a system designed with others in mind. Habeas corpus claims grounded in a threshold concern with the harms of captivity might instead invite images of animals as mothers, brothers, or friends – beings whose realities our legal system should strive to recognize.

[131] *See* Eisen, *supra* note 11.

19

"True" Imprisonment

Douglas A. Kysar

19.1 INTRODUCTION

In 2018, the Animal Legal Defense Fund and an equine rescue organization filed suit on behalf of a neglected horse against its past owner seeking monetary damages to cover the costs of the animal's rehabilitation and care, as well as compensation for the animal's pain and suffering. Departing from the ordinary practice of bringing suit in their own right as animal protection organizations, the two groups sought to name the horse directly as a plaintiff with standing to assert its own legal rights. The animal, an American quarter horse previously known as Shadow but renamed Justice following its rescue, had been badly neglected by its prior owner, Gwendolyn Vercher. At the urging of a neighbor, Vercher surrendered the emaciated horse to a rescue organization. She later pled guilty to criminal animal neglect under Oregon's anticruelty statute. Justice's civil lawsuit sought monetary damages to establish a trust fund in hopes that the financial support might enable the horse to be adopted by a new owner.

After a trial judge dismissed Justice's complaint, the animal organizations appealed. An amicus brief authored by leading animal law experts supported Justice's quest for legal standing, arguing that "he has a right to sue in civil court in order to recover damages in Oregon."[1] The brief detailed a variety of ways in which nonhuman animals already hold special status under the law as living beings entitled to be treated as more than mere property. In particular, because Oregon's criminal anticruelty statute expressly recognizes animals as the recipients of legal protection, the scholars argued that allowing an animal victim to sue its abuser directly for civil remedies would be a "straightforward" proposition:

[1] Brief for Randall S. Abate, et al., at 1, as Amici Curiae Supporting Petitioners, Justice v. Gwendolyn Vercher, A169933 (Or. Ct. App. 2020).

> There is no real dispute that Justice has met the requirements for civil liability. The only question is whether this panel will close the courthouse doors on a being whose rights of judicial access have been recognized by statute and common law developments in this state and across the country. Oregon is a national leader in recognizing the status of animals as more than property, and this case presents a modest application of that principle.[2]

As of this writing, the appeal in Justice's case was still pending, and the possibility that nonhuman animals might bring their own civil lawsuits in the United States remains an imaginative exercise only.

This chapter takes up the imaginative exercise by asking what it would look like if nonhuman animals were allowed to bring false imprisonment claims to challenge their captivity. The Anglo-American legal tradition includes a civil tort of "false" imprisonment, whereby one who acts intending to confine another without justification within fixed boundaries may be held liable, so long as the other is conscious of or harmed by the confinement. This cause of action is distinct from the criminal and constitutional law framework that governs the authority of the state to detain, investigate, or imprison. At the heart of that framework in the Anglo-American legal tradition lies the writ of habeas corpus—the so-called Great Writ that was considered by Jessica Eisen in the previous chapter along with the legal campaign to extend its protection to nonhuman animals. Like habeas corpus, the false imprisonment tort encompasses concerns regarding government overreach,[3] but also extends to confinement that is wrongfully – that is, "falsely" – imposed by nongovernmental actors. Victims of such conduct are afforded a right of civil redress against their captors, with remedies available including compensatory, nominal, and punitive damages. Thus, while the habeas corpus writ stands as a constitutional check on the state's infringement of bodily autonomy, the tort of false imprisonment offers a common law cause of action against wrongful detention by any actor, public or private.

This chapter considers how a false imprisonment action might unfold if it were pursued by a nonhuman animal held in captivity. The exercise has the dual purpose of (1) learning how existing false imprisonment doctrine might apply to nonhuman animals if they were given standing to bring civil actions; and (2) exploring what might be learned about the current application of false imprisonment law to human plaintiffs when we engage in such an effort to "think with animals."[4] As will be argued, envisioning the false imprisonment claim of nonhuman animals reveals

[2] Animal Law Professors *Amicus Curiae* Brief, Justice v. Vercher, at 17.

[3] *See, e.g.*, Zok v. State, 903 P.2d 574, 577 (Alaska 1995) ("False arrest is one way of committing the tort of false imprisonment.").

[4] *Cf.* Claude Lévi-Strauss, Totemism 89 (1962). Despite the apparent felicity of this phrase from Lévi-Strauss, it bears noting that its translation and significance are not without controversy. *See* James K. Stanescu, *Animals Are More than Good to Think With, Part 1*, Critical Animal (July 6, 2012), http://www.criticalanimal.com/2012/07/animals-are-more-than-good-to-think.html.

fissures and tensions within the doctrine that go to the very foundation of legal and political organization.

19.2 THE TORT OF FALSE IMPRISONMENT

The false imprisonment tort offers a civil remedy to individuals who have been intentionally and wrongfully confined by another actor. The rationale behind the tort of false imprisonment is to recognize the plaintiff's right to be free from unwanted, intentional interference with freedom of movement, which in the liberal legal tradition is taken to be bound up with a person's fundamental interest in autonomy. Like other intentional torts such as battery and assault, the false imprisonment tort has deep historical roots in the common law and is considered one of the basic legal measures of protection for the plaintiff's bodily integrity, peace of mind, and essential dignity.[5] As two leading American tort theorists note, "[i]f battery promises to shield individuals from being wrongfully targeted for contact by others, false imprisonment promises to free them from others' efforts to keep them located in a particular space."[6]

The basic doctrinal elements of the false imprisonment tort in the United States are summarized in the American Law Institute's *Restatement (Third) of Torts*:

> An actor is subject to liability for the tort of false imprisonment when (1) the actor intends to confine the plaintiff within a limited area; (2) the actor's conduct causes the plaintiff's confinement or the actor breaches a duty to release the plaintiff from such confinement; (3) the plaintiff is aware of the confinement or suffers bodily harm as a result; and (4) the plaintiff does not consent to the confinement.[7]

The most interesting aspect of the false imprisonment tort for purposes of this chapter is the requirement that the plaintiff must either be conscious of the confinement or physically harmed by it. That requirement appears to set up both a subjective and an objective path to recovery for the complainant.

On the subjective path, courts are quite clear that a false imprisonment claim may be pursued even though the confinement does not cause bodily injury, pain and

[5] Demonstrating that legal tradition:

> The false imprisonment tort protects the interest of persons to go freely through the world, subject to legal restrictions on their entry into particular places. This interest in physical freedom has a corresponding foundation in personal dignity, an interest that receives protection from all of the intentional tort categories.

See MARSHALL S. SHAPO, PRINCIPLES OF TORT LAW, ¶ 10.07, at 61 (4th ed. 2016).

[6] JOHN C.P. GOLDBERG & BENJAMIN C. ZIPURSKY, THE OXFORD INTRODUCTIONS TO U.S. LAW: TORTS 211 (2010).

[7] RESTATEMENT (THIRD) OF TORTS: INTENTIONAL TORTS TO PERSONS § 7 (AM. LAW INST., Tentative Draft No. 3, 2018) [hereinafter RESTATEMENT (THIRD) OF TORTS].

suffering, emotional harm, or loss of opportunity.[8] Indeed, a plaintiff need not prove that she would have chosen to leave the area of confinement had she not been confined. Nor does the plaintiff need to show that she understood the confinement to be wrongful.[9] The nonconsequentialist underpinnings of this path to liability are strong. Even if a defendant believes that the confinement is in the best interests of the plaintiff or that the plaintiff will or should welcome the confinement, the actor is subject to liability if the confinement is not consented to or does not fall within a recognized defense. The essence of the wrong from this perspective seems to be the plaintiff's cognitive experience of the sensation of being trapped, much as the essence of the wrong for an assault is the plaintiff's visceral feeling of nearly being physically struck.[10]

When a plaintiff is not conscious of being confined, they may still recover if they are "harmed" by the confinement. American tort law owes this path of false imprisonment liability to the influential scholar William Prosser, who authored a short article in 1955 arguing that even unaware plaintiffs ought to recover when a defendant confines them without permission. In Prosser's view, through their confinement alone, "a tort of real gravity has occurred" against such plaintiffs.[11] Some prior authorities had declined to recognize liability in these circumstances, apparently believing that relaxing the consciousness requirement altogether would lead to situations in which the strong medicine of intentional tort liability would be invoked for relatively trivial invasions. Yet, as Prosser noted, cases also could be found in which infants or adults with mental disability recovered for false imprisonment despite being arguably unaware of their detainment.[12] The line, therefore, did not appear insuperable.

The *Restatement (Second) of Torts*, for which Prosser served as the chief architect, balanced these various positions by expanding liability beyond cases of conscious confinement but only if the plaintiff suffers actual harm from the restriction,[13] a

[8] Supporting the point that false imprisonment does not require proof of physical or emotional injury when the plaintiff is conscious of the confinement, *see* John C.P. Goldberg & Benjamin C. Zipursky, *Torts as Wrongs*, 88 TEX. L. REV. 917, 955 (2010).

[9] RESTATEMENT (THIRD) OF TORTS § 7 cmt. g; *see also* RESTATEMENT (SECOND) OF TORTS § 42 cmt. c (AM. LAW INST. 1979) ("If the plaintiff is conscious of the confinement at the time, it is not necessary that he know by whom or how it is imposed.").

[10] *But see* text accompanying notes 16–17 (reviewing commentators who would deem the essence of the false imprisonment wrong to be confinement itself, rather than the victim's perception of confinement).

[11] William L. Prosser, *False Imprisonment: Consciousness of Confinement*, 55 COLUM. L. REV. 847, 850 (1955).

[12] *Id.* at 848.

[13] The *Restatement (Second) of Torts* states:

> Where. . .no harm results from a confinement and the plaintiff is not even subjected to the mental disturbance of being made aware of it at the time, his mere dignitary interest in being free from an interference with his personal liberty which he has only discovered later is not of sufficient importance to justify the recovery of the nominal damages

compromise approach that, as noted above, continues in the more recent *Restatement (Third) of Torts*. Courts have not been entirely clear in specifying what kinds of "harm" qualify for liability under this alternative doctrinal path to recovery. The obvious cases for liability include physical harms such as malnutrition or medical deterioration during a period of unaware confinement.[14] Conversely, many authorities contend that an unaware plaintiff cannot recover if they suffer only emotional, economic, relationship, or dignitary harm as a result of the confinement.[15] As the *Restatement (Third) of Torts* puts it, the policy considerations in favor of recovery are weaker in the case of "someone who does not subjectively experience the loss of freedom at the time when she might have exercised it,"[16] and who does not otherwise suffer physical harm. The relative weakness of the deprivation in such circumstances becomes outweighed by tort law's general interest in avoiding adjudication of what are deemed to be minor social disputes that could be resolved outside the courtroom.

Commentators have long questioned whether Prosser's more liberal approach of abandoning the consciousness requirement altogether should have been adopted, with the answer hinging in part on how one conceives of the interest being protected by the tort. The essential question seems to be whether, in the words of three leading torts scholars, "false imprisonment is a tort protecting a *psychological* perception of autonomy and not simply the denial of personal autonomy."[17] Writing in 1957, a New York state judge reasoned that:

> [m]uch can be said for the proposition that an imprisonment brought about by barriers or physical force ought to be actionable without regard to consciousness of restraint on the part of the victim. If the tort is designed to protect one's actual freedom of movement against impairment, the tort is committed when one is confined whether he knows of it at the time or not. Upon this view, the tort of false imprisonment is like battery. One may be held liable in battery for offensively touching another, even though the victim is not aware of the touching at the time. On, the other hand, if. . .the tort is designed to protect one's *sense* of freedom of movement against impairment, just as the tort of assault is designed to protect one's interest in freedom from *apprehension* of attack, there is no tort if there is no consciousness of the restraint because in that case there is no interference with one's sense of freedom.[18]

involved. Accordingly, no action for false imprisonment can be maintained in such a case.

See Restatement (Second) of Torts § 42 cmt. a.

[14] Restatement (Third) of Torts § 7 cmt. h.

[15] *Id.*

[16] *Id.*

[17] John L. Diamond, Lawrence C. Levine & Anita Bernstein, Understanding Torts 18 (5th ed. 2013) (emphasis added).

[18] Philip Halpern, *Intentional Torts and the Restatement: A Petition for Rehearing*, 7 Buff. L. Rev. 7, 23–24 (1957); *see also* John Fleming, The Law of Torts 38 (Carolyn Sappideen & Prue Vines eds., 10th ed. 2011) ("[F]alse imprisonment affects not only liberty but also dignity

This basic distinction – between a tort designed to protect one's actual freedom from confinement and a tort designed to protect one's *sense* of being free from confinement – has rarely been broached in case law. Only very unusual factual circumstances or limited categories of plaintiff victims are likely to present the case of a confinee who is both unaware and unharmed.

In the case of *Scofield v. Critical Air Medicine*, California courts faced a near example when presented with a false imprisonment claim brought on behalf of minor children who were seriously injured in an automobile accident in Baja, Mexico, that also killed their mother.[19] Upon learning of the accident and the extent of their injuries, which were too significant to be handled by the local Mexican medical facility, the children's father directed that they be transported to a US hospital by a specific emergency medical air transport carrier. Instead, an opportunistic third-party carrier swept in and took off with the children by representing that they were the authorized company. Although the plaintiffs were unable to demonstrate any actual physical harm to the children or awareness by the children that they were traveling in an unauthorized emergency vehicle, the court nonetheless accepted testimony by the plaintiffs' experts that the event was actually harmful to the children because their trust in authority was irrevocably shaken upon later learning that they had been airlifted illicitly. With respect to consciousness of confinement, the court concluded that false imprisonment requires only "knowledge of the restraint or confinement at some time, whether contemporaneous or subsequent, and resulting harm or damage,"[20] a holding that departed from other authorities.[21] It appears significant to the court's holding that the plaintiffs' status as injured minors rendered the simultaneous consciousness of confinement requirement inapposite, given that they lacked the information or capacity to know at the time of being airlifted that they were being wrongfully transported. What should stand in place of that requirement, however, remains unclear given that courts do

and reputation, a position reflected in the calculation of damages. The plaintiff's humiliation is not lessened by only hearing about it afterwards and the plaintiff's lack of awareness at the time does not prevent others observing the plaintiff's predicament.") (footnotes omitted); Sheldon H. Nahmod, *Awareness of Confinement for False Imprisonment: A Brief Critical Comment*, 15 Duq. L. Rev. 31, 35 (1976) (advocating abandonment of the consciousness requirement because confining another person is "a serious matter and should be discouraged").

19 *See* Scofield v. Critical Air Med., Inc., 52 Cal. Rptr. 2d 915 (Ct. App. 1996).

20 *Id.* at 917; *see also* Ware v. Gower, No. 2:13-cv-0979, 2016 WL 1734750 (E.D. Cal. May 2, 2016), at *3 (stating in dicta that "[w]e do not hold that California law requires the person physically restrained to know of the confinement or be harmed by it").

21 *See, e.g.*, Cruz v. Cent. Iowa Hospital Corp., 826 N.W.2d 516 (Iowa Ct. App. 2012) (denying liability in the absence of harm or contemporaneous awareness); Restatement (Third) of Torts § 7 cmt. h (same). A little-noticed illustration in the *Restatement (Second) of Torts* comes close to supporting the *Scofield* result, although it requires the subsequent emotional upset to result in physical injury. *See* Restatement (Second) of Torts § 42 cmt. b, illus. 5 (noting that actual harm may include contexts where a plaintiff suffers "serious illness" resulting from "emotional distress" after being "greatly humiliated" upon learning of a prior confinement).

not appear ready to accept Prosser's recommendation of fully abandoning the consciousness test. The *Third Restatement of Torts*, despite disapproving of the *Scofield* result and retaining the "sensible bright-line rule" of "either contemporaneous awareness or consequent bodily harm," nevertheless equivocates while doing so: "if compelling cases arise in the future in which the cautious approach of this Restatement proves to be inadequate, courts have the ability to develop a more expansive liability rule."[22] The remaining sections of this chapter explore one such compelling case.

19.3 ANIMALS IMPRISONED

To shed further light on the false imprisonment tort and the particular case of the involuntary but unaware prisoner, one might look to the case of nonhuman animal confinement. Billions of animals are held captive throughout the world in farms, zoos, aquaria, research labs, and other facilities,[23] often in conditions that "cause inescapable physical or psychological suffering."[24] Except perhaps in the case of companion animals,[25] no claim could plausibly be made that the animals have consented to their confinement, whether because they are deemed to lack capacity to consent or because their behavior reveals a rather strong objection to confinement.[26] Nor is there doubt that the animals' captors have confined them intentionally. Thus, if nonhuman animals were given standing to assert civil law claims on

22 Restatement (Third) of Torts § 7 cmt.

23 Indeed, through the impacts of climate change, habitat destruction, and habitat fragmentation, the amount of wilderness remaining for noncaptive species may increasingly be viewed as confining in relation to their survival needs. Thus, we might envision a continuum of confinement that extends from labs to zoos to sanctuaries to wildlife refuges to the degraded and splintered habitats that count as today as "wilderness." Such a conception of universal confinement and domination by humans of the nonhuman world would hold dramatic implications for our political economy. *See generally* Jedediah Purdy, After Nature: A Politics for the Anthropocene (2017).

24 Lori Gruen, Ethics and Animals: An Introduction 134 (2011).

25 Whether companion animals should be classified as captive animals is an important and underexplored topic. *See* Marc Bekoff & Jessica Pierce, The Animals' Agenda: Freedom, Compassion, and Coexistence in the Human Age 117–38 (2017). The dog or cat that returns home after being let out for the day in some respects appears to be revealing a preference for confinement. But the animal has been conditioned for confinement through domestication and its range of possible actions may not be rich enough to deem its behavior one of preference or choice in a meaningful sense.

26 Consider these observations from the animal research veterinarian Larry Carbone:

> By most philosophers' and behaviorists' accounts, nonhuman animals lack the mental capacity for full autonomy and for informed consent as we know it, and I will not argue with the philosophers on autonomy. But informed consent? In one sense I have indeed asked animals almost every day for their consent as research subjects. Their resounding "no" would quickly put me out of a job as a laboratory animal veterinarian, as so much of my work has been helping researchers to overlook the animals' dissent. . .If voluntary consent were our standard for animal research, the whole business would end – not because we cannot understand what the animals are telling us, but because we can.

their own behalf in accord with the legal scholars' brief in support of Justice the horse, the only potential barrier to false imprisonment recovery for captive animals would be whether they can demonstrate either consciousness of confinement or bodily harm.

The question of whether nonhuman animals have consciousness has been given extensive scientific and philosophical inquiry. In 2012, a group of international scientific experts sought to settle that question once and for all by issuing the Cambridge Declaration on Consciousness, which stated:

> Convergent evidence indicates that non-human animals have the neuroanatomical, neurochemical, and neurophysiological substrates of conscious states along with the capacity to exhibit intentional behaviors. Consequently, the weight of evidence indicates that humans are not unique in possessing the neurological substrates that generate consciousness. Non-human animals, including all mammals and birds, and many other creatures, including octopuses, also possess these neurological substrates.[27]

Other scientists and philosophers remain unconvinced,[28] in part because the nature of consciousness itself – in human or nonhuman animals – remains imperfectly understood.[29] Does consciousness merely indicate the status of being awake as opposed to being asleep or in a coma? Does it indicate the sensation of having mental states like pain or pleasure, fear or hunger, desire or disgust? Does it require a thicker phenomenological experience of being subjectively aware of one's inner mental life? Does it require coupling that awareness with an even thicker

LARRY CARBONE, WHAT ANIMALS WANT: EXPERTISE AND ADVOCACY IN LABORATORY ANIMAL WELFARE POLICY 178–79 (2004). I am grateful to Joel Marks for highlighting this passage to me.

27 Philip Low, The Cambridge Declaration on Consciousness, Francis Crick Mem'l Conference on Consciousness in Human & Non-human Animals 1, 2, July 7, 2012, http://fcmconference.org/img/CambridgeDeclarationOnConsciousness.pdf. Philosophers also have made the case for animal consciousness. *See, e.g.*, JOEL MARKS, HARD ATHEISM AND THE ETHICS OF DESIRE: AN ALTERNATIVE TO MORALITY 97–109 (2016) (contending that animals "act[ ] on the basis of a rich mental life, and in fact one similar to ours"); Dale Jamieson, *Science, Knowledge, and Animal Minds*, 98 PROC. ARISTOTELIAN SOC. 79, 79 (1998) ("The reluctance of contemporary philosophers and scientists to embrace the view that animals have minds is primarily a fact about their philosophy and science rather than a fact about animals."); John R. Searle, *Animal Minds*, 19 MIDWEST STUD. PHIL. XIX 206 (1994) (arguing that intuitive, commonsense attribution of emotions and intentionality to companion animals carries greater weight than philosophically motivated skepticism).

28 *See, e.g.*, MARIAN STAMP DAWKINS, WHY ANIMALS MATTER: ANIMAL CONSCIOUSNESS, ANIMAL WELFARE, AND HUMAN WELL-BEING 171–72 (2012) ("The mystery of consciousness remains. The explanatory gap is as wide as ever and all the wanting in the world will not take us across it."); Peter Carruthers, *Brute Experience*, 86 J. PHIL. 258–69 (1989) (contending that nonhuman animals lack consciousness and our intuitive sentiments to the contrary should be rejected).

29 *See* Colin Allen & Michael Trestman, *Animal Consciousness*, STAN. ENCYCLOPEDIA OF PHIL. (Oct. 24, 2016), https://plato.stanford.edu/entries/consciousness-animal ("The term 'consciousness' is notoriously ambiguous and difficult to define. Having origins in folk psychology, 'consciousness' has a multitude of uses that may not be resolvable into a single, coherent concept").

conception of one's *self* as the entity holding the awareness? It is one thing to debate whether studies on animal perception, memory, categorization, communication, self-recognition, and so on constitute evidence of animal cognition.[30] It is quite another to grapple with the problem of other minds in other beings, as speculation about animal consciousness requires.[31]

Perhaps the basic question of whether nonhuman animals have consciousness can be bracketed for the false imprisonment thought exercise: even if they can have consciousness, they may not be capable of having consciousness *of their confinement*. That is, they may not have subjective awareness of confinement in the sense of possessing a concept of confinement and an ability to fit their perception and experience of being restricted in movement with that concept. This line of questioning requires one first to be clear on what would constitute an adequate concept of confinement. Philosophers have helpfully distinguished between (1) a comparative conception of confinement which is "focuse[d] on the size relations between the area left accessible to the individual and the area rendered inaccessible to the individual," and (2) an agential conception of confinement which "incorporates the purposes of the agent doing the confining."[32] By focusing on the "additional exercise of dominion over the individual" which distinguishes captivity from confinement,[33] one might helpfully isolate what is especially psychologically troubling about the subjective awareness of being imprisoned. The essence of the wrong from this perspective is the confined individual's awareness of the denial of her status as a coequal being with rights of self-determination, including the freedom of movement.

Showing consciousness of confinement in this sense – that is, awareness of being intentionally detained by the will of a dominating power – would require first

[30] *See* Kristin Andrews, *Animal Cognition*, STAN. ENCYCLOPEDIA OF PHIL. (May 6, 2016), https://plato.stanford.edu/entries/cognition-animal ("Philosophers have asked whether animals are minded or rational, and whether they have concepts or beliefs, but they have also struggled with the issue of how to answer such questions given the inherent limitations of the investigation.").

[31] For an extraordinary and engaging effort to do just that, see PETER GODFREY-SMITH, OTHER MINDS: THE OCTOPUS, THE SEA, AND THE DEEP ORIGINS OF CONSCIOUSNESS (2016). Godfrey-Smith argues persuasively that octopuses evince consciousness, despite their radical alterity when considered from the perspective of human minds.

[32] Robert Streiffer & David Killoren, *Animal Confinement and Use*, 49 CANADIAN J. PHIL. 1, 4 (2019); *see also* Robert Streiffer, *The Confinement of Animals Used in Laboratory Research*, *in* THE ETHICS OF CAPTIVITY 174, 179 (Lori Gruen ed., 2014) (distinguishing between confinement and captivity, which both "involve external limits on an individual's freedom of movement," but in which only captivity entails "the additional exercise of dominion over the individual").

[33] Nicolas Delon, *Animal Agency, Captivity, and Meaning*, 25 HARV. REV. PHIL. 127, 134 (2018) (quoting Streiffer, *supra* note 32, at 179). Lisa Rivera offers an additional distinguishing feature of captivity worth bearing in mind: an "extreme lack of reciprocity of benefit" flowing from the captivity as between the captor and the captive. *See* Lisa Rivera, *Coercion and Captivity*, in THE ETHICS OF CAPTIVITY 248, 249 (Lori Gruen ed., 2014).

showing that nonhuman animals have a theory of mind with which they can attribute mental states such as intentionality to other individuals. A long line of research has attempted to address this question, with debate continuing over whether the findings demonstrate that animals make actual inferences about others' mental states or simply respond to observed behaviors.[34] Again, though, the debate can be put aside for purposes of the false imprisonment tort analysis because the tort only requires consciousness of confinement in the weaker, comparative sense. That is, as noted above, the false imprisonment plaintiff does not need to demonstrate awareness of the wrongfulness of her confinement. While knowingly being confined by a dominating agent (i.e., held captive) may be more psychologically troubling than merely being confined, tort law regards the latter awareness as adequate to state a false imprisonment claim.[35]

Can nonhuman animals have consciousness of their confinement in this weaker sense? Undoubtedly, confinement causes behavioral and physiological responses in nonhuman animals. Whether those responses also indicate conscious awareness of confinement seems less certain and may collapse back onto the more fundamental question of whether nonhuman animals have consciousness. That question in turn depends on how demanding one makes the definition of consciousness and the standard of proof required for demonstrating it. In the extreme, even the consciousness of other humans remains an unknowable phenomenon that enters our mental life in ways that are indistinguishable from dreams. Yet most of us do not embrace solipsism; instead, we live with the working assumption that others *do* have consciousness. That working assumption enables us to regard those others as beings with "values, preferences, aims, principles, autonomy, and personal beliefs."[36] That regard in turn enables us to see them as subjects who matter, who hold interests, and who can make a claim on us to treat them accordingly. It is curious that this working assumption is not generally extended to nonhuman animals, as evidenced both by the philosophical tradition of mechanism that extends from Descartes to today's laboratories and industrial farms, and in the Anglo-American legal tradition that generally regards nonhuman animals as mere objects of possession, rather than as subjects with interests and entitlements. This is not to suggest that nonhuman animals lack consciousness as an actual fact, but rather that – for purposes of legal analysis – the deck is stacked against that conclusion.

[34] *See* GRUEN, *supra* note 25, at 13–17.

[35] An illustration in the *Restatement (Third) of Torts* makes this plain:

> Dahlia locks the only door in her store, not realizing that customer Pedro is still browsing in the back of the store. When Dahlia later drives by the store, she sees that Pedro is at the front door, trying to get out. Instead of stopping, Dahlia drives to another location to perform an errand, then returns to the store and lets Pedro out. Dahlia is subject to liability to Pedro for false imprisonment.

RESTATEMENT (THIRD) OF TORTS § 7 cmt. f, illus. 5.

[36] Angela K. Martin, *On Respecting Animals, or Can Animals Be Wronged without Being Harmed?*, 25 RES PUBLICA 83, 89 (2019).

One area in which the law *has* evolved to offer greater protection for nonhuman animals is in the area of anticruelty statutes, such as the Oregon laws that were used to prosecute Gwendolyn Vercher.[37] Whether these laws unequivocally recognize nonhuman animals as subjects with their own entitlements is historically debatable and still varies from jurisdiction to jurisdiction.[38] In many cases, the laws seem animated by a concern over how animal cruelty impacts humans and the manner in which humans treat one another, rather than with interests of the nonhuman animals for their own sake.[39] Nevertheless, the focus of such laws is on the treatment and well-being of nonhuman animals, which suggests that a more sure route to recovery for the nonhuman false imprisonment claimant may be to focus on physical harm, rather than on consciousness of confinement. After all, ample scientific evidence establishes that negative welfare effects occur in animals from being confined depending on the species involved and the conditions of confinement. Even without overtly inflicted pain such as through vivisection or animal husbandry practices, harm may still result through confinement alone in the form of weight loss, chronic stress, lethargy, aggression, compulsive pacing, self-mutilation, and so on. Such harms typically do not suffice to establish an animal-cruelty violation in the case of animals confined for agriculture, research, or entertainment, either because the relevant statute exempts such animals entirely from coverage or because the harms would not be considered "unnecessary" in light of the benefits to humans generated from the confinement and use.[40] For the false imprisonment

37 *See* Or. Rev. Stat. §§ 167.305(1)-(2) (2020) (finding and declaring that "[a]nimals are sentient beings capable of experiencing pain, stress and fear," and that "[a]nimals should be cared for in ways that minimize pain, stress, fear and suffering").

38 For a fascinating overview of the history of animal law and an argument that "there has been a historical progression in the primary motives underlying animal laws" over time, see Thomas G. Kelch, *A Short History of (Mostly) Western Animal Law: Part I*, 19 Animal L. 23, 23 (2012); Thomas G. Kelch, *A Short History of (Mostly) Western Animal Law: Part II*, 19 Animal L. 347, 347 (2013).

39 According to Gary Francione, "close examination of. . .[anticruelty] statutes indicates quite clearly that they have an exclusively humanocentric focus, and the duties they impose give no corresponding rights for animals." Gary L. Francione, *Animals, Property and Legal Welfarism: "Unnecessary" Suffering and the "Humane" Treatment of Animals*, 46 Rutgers L. Rev. 721, 737, 753, 756 (1994); *see also* Ani B. Satz, *Animals as Vulnerable Subjects: Beyond Interest-Convergence, Hierarchy, and Property*, 16 Animal L. 65 (2009) (deploying Derrick Bell's interest-convergence theory to explain the limited circumstances in which animal protection receives legal support). For an argument that animal laws have been misunderstood by critics such as Francione, see Jerrold Tannenbaum, *Animals and the Law: Property, Cruelty, Rights*, 62 Soc. Res. 539 (1995). The Oregon statutory scheme under which Justice the horse's former owner was prosecuted appears to endorse both views, with legislative findings declaring both that "[a]nimals are sentient beings capable of experiencing pain, stress and fear" and that "there is a direct link between the problems of animal abuse and human abuse." Or. Rev. Stat. §§ 167.305(1), 686.442 (2020).

40 *See* Gruen, *supra* note 24, at 117 (analyzing 1985 animal experimentation amendments to the U.S. Animal Welfare Act and concluding that the act "still represents minimal standards for animal welfare, [and] does not even cover the vast majority of animals used in research"); Luis E. Chiesa, *Why Is It a Crime to Stomp on a Goldfish? – Harm, Victimhood, and the Structure of*

tort – assuming it was made available to nonhuman animals – no such exemptions would be available to the defendant. Intentional confinement that results in bodily harm alone would suffice to establish liability and no amount of offsetting benefit could excuse the violation. Because "keeping animals in actual captive conditions often causes them to suffer injuries and other physical harms,"[41] it would seem initially that a great many captive animals could successfully press their false imprisonment claims. For instance, consider the case of a cetacean stolen from the wild and forced into a decades-long life of isolation and confinement for the amusement of aquarium visitors. That scientists may advise against releasing her into the wild following her lengthy incarceration[42] should not detract from the fact that her particular life course has been irreparably altered and harmed due to her confinement.

A potential problem for some classes of nonhuman claimants may be that the harm-based branch of false imprisonment liability is amenable to different accounts of the relevant baseline of well-being.[43] On many of these accounts, despite suffering harm through captivity, the animal may still appear to be better off overall, giving rise to what Lori Gruen aptly terms "dilemmas of captivity:"

> Given that most conditions of captivity cause inescapable physical or psychological suffering, we might think that unless there is a very good reason for holding animals captive we should release them. However, in the case of many, perhaps most, captive animals, release would be a death sentence. [M]any of the wild counterparts of animals living in captivity exist precariously because their habitats are being destroyed at alarming rates. In many cases, there may be no wild left into which the captive animals can be released. More importantly, even if there are environments into which captive animals may be returned, most captives have lost the ability to survive on their own in their native habitats.[44]

Although some criticize this "wilderness baseline view" as setting "an implausibly low standard,"[45] it is not hard to imagine a court finding refuge in its logic when faced with a false imprisonment claim on behalf of zoo, sanctuary, or companion animals. For instance, an analysis of more than fifty mammal species found that 84 percent lived longer in zoos than in the wild, a disparity the researchers attributed to protection against disease, competition, and predation afforded by zoos.[46] A court

Anti-cruelty Offenses, 78 MISS. L.J. 1, 11, 40, 65 (2008) ("[A]nti-cruelty statutes are riddled with exceptions allowing people to harm animals.").

[41] GRUEN, *supra* note 24, at 143.

[42] *See* Chabeli Herrera, *Lolita May Never Go Free. And That Could Be What's Best for Her, Scientists Say*, MIAMI HERALD, November 29, 2017.

[43] *See* David DeGrazia, *The Ethics of Confining Animals: From Farms to Zoos to Human Homes*, in OXFORD HANDBOOK OF ANIMAL ETHICS 738 (Tom L. Beauchamp and R.G. Frey, eds., 2011).

[44] GRUEN, *supra* note 24, at 134.

[45] Streiffer & Killoren, *supra* note 32, at 15.

[46] *See* Morgane Tidière et al., *Comparative Analyses of Longevity and Senescence Reveal Variable Survival Benefits of Living in Zoos across Mammals*, 6 SCI. REP. 36361 (2016).

might easily cite such research as evidence that confinement, at least in certain facilities such as zoos, does not lead to a welfare detriment over existence in the wild. Even for those species that would have lived longer or more fulsome lives had they been born outside of captivity, there remains the problem of adaptation: for captive-bred animals, release into the wild may not be beneficial to their particular life courses, even if a wild existence would have been preferable in the abstract.[47] Unlike the cetacean referenced above who was caught from the wild, the captive-bred animal does not have ready recourse to a counterfactual life of nonconfinement. Their counterfactual instead is one of nonexistence. Similarly, when presented with the claims of domesticated farm animals, it is hard not to see a court cabining the harm analysis by noting that the animals would not exist at all but for their domestication, confinement, and use by humans. From that perspective, it would seem that – so long as their lives are minimally worth living – such animals have not been harmed in a causal sense by being bred into a confined existence. Confinement *is* their existence.

Are the lives of captive-bred animals minimally worth living – not for us, but for them? The question throws us back into the vagaries of consciousness and the dilemma of whether we can ever know what it is like to be a Milking Shorthorn.[48] When we regard the lives of animals on industrial farms as miserable and perhaps not worth living, we do so inevitably through our subjective viewpoint and without direct access to theirs. To be sure, the practices of industrial animal agriculture are sufficiently brutal as to make compelling the thought that many livestock animals would be better off dead, whether or not we can inhabit their consciousness when facing the question. But in the analogous context of "wrongful life" claims brought by human plaintiffs, where a physician's negligence is alleged to have caused a parent to lose the opportunity to terminate a pregnancy that results in a severely disabled child being born, courts have shown great reluctance to engage the question of whether the child is worse off for having been born. Such claims, which are brought in the name of an infant for its own alleged damages, require courts to "compare the value of nonexistence – the state that [a child] would have been in but for defendants' alleged negligence – and the value of his life with [a condition or disability]."[49] Courts routinely decline to engage in such searching philosophical analysis: "[s]imply put, as a matter of law, that comparison is impossible to make."[50] Given such reticence in

[47] *See* Richard Frankham, *Genetic Adaptation to Captivity in Species Conservation Programs*, 17 Molecular Ecology 325, 325 (2008) ("In captivity, species adapt genetically to the captive environment and these genetic adaptations are overwhelmingly deleterious when populations are returned to wild environments.").

[48] *See* Thomas Nagel, *What Is It Like to Be a Bat?*, 83 Phil. Rev. 435 (1974).

[49] Tomlinson v. Metro. Pediatrics, LLC, 366 P.3d 370, 389 (Or. Ct. App. 2015).

[50] *Id. See also* Clark v. Children's Meml. Hosp., 955 N.E.2d 1065, 1084 (Ill. 2011) ("In the wrongful-life context, there is no cause of action because the child, while burdened, cannot be said to have suffered a legal wrong."); Turpin v. Sortini, 643 P.2d 954, 964 (Cal. 1982) ("In a wrongful life action…what the plaintiff has 'lost' is not life without pain and suffering but rather the unknowable status of never having been born. In this context, a rational,

the human "wrongful life" context, one suspects that courts would likewise balk in the nonhuman context and instead simply hold that captive-bred animals have not been harmed so long as their captors comply with minimum applicable animal protection statutes and regulations. Especially considering the vast economic and political stakes involved in deeming industrial animal agriculture tortious, the tendency of courts to outsource decision-making responsibility to the other branches of government in such a manner would be great.[51]

Harm in the sense of being better off not existing at all is harm of a philosophical rather than a physical character. As noted above, in all but the rarest of cases, courts have been reluctant to extend the concept of harm beyond tangible bodily injury in the false imprisonment context. Returning to the case of *Scofield v. Critical Air Medicine* is instructive. In that case, the court credited expert testimony that the children suffered subsequent psychological harm upon learning that their emergency medical transport was unauthorized. But this ground felt somewhat speculative,[52] and the court went on to note that, in California, the minor plaintiffs could recover for nominal damages even without a showing of actual harm. False imprisonment, the court stressed, is a "dignitary tort," and the "purely nominal" harm of being denied one's "personal interest in freedom from restraint of movement" suffices to support liability.[53] Although the court did not go this far, its reasoning would seem to support recovery for the unharmed plaintiff who *never* becomes conscious of her confinement, whether contemporaneously or subsequently. As argued in the next section, the dignity impairment in such a case would take on a new structure, one that might be of relevance to confined nonhuman animals.

19.4 THE INDIGNITY OF CONFINEMENT

The false-imprisonment tort remains inchoate and confused because it rests on a dichotomy of freedom and confinement that is inadequate to the normative task it is being invoked to resolve. The *Restatement (Third) of Torts* discounts the unaware

nonspeculative determination of a specific monetary award in accordance with normal tort principles appears to be outside the realm of human competence."); Gleitman v. Cosgrove, 227 A.2d 689, 711 (N.J. 1967) (Weintraub, C.J., dissenting) ("Ultimately, the infant's complaint is that he would be better off not to have been born. Man, who knows nothing of death or nothingness, cannot possibly know whether that is so. . .To recognize a right not to be born is to enter an area in which no one can find his way.").

51 *See generally* R. Henry Weaver & Douglas A. Kysar, *Courting Disaster: Climate Change and the Adjudication of Catastrophe*, 93 Notre Dame L. Rev. 295 (2017) (describing such tendencies in the context of tort and environmental disputes).

52 The entirety of the court's discussion on the matter was contained in a footnote to the opinion: "The jury apparently based its damage award largely on the uncontroverted testimony of Dr. James Long, a psychiatrist. Dr. Long opined the girls' relationship with authority figures had been undermined by Critical Air's deception, and it was reasonably probable the incident would affect their development during adolescence." Scofield, 52 Cal. Rptr. 2d at 919 n.8.

53 *Id.* at 1008 (citation omitted).

victim of false imprisonment as "someone who does not subjectively experience the loss of freedom at the time when she might have exercised it."[54] But whether she holds a freedom of movement to exercise in the first place depends in substantial part on what forms of restraint the law will recognize as wrongful. Her lack of subjective awareness of the deprivation is made to seem more significant – and damning to her claim – because tort law has defined her experience from the outset as not being one of real deprivation. This circularity becomes unsettling when the false imprisonment doctrine is applied to those individuals who cannot be imagined ever to meet the standards of the doctrine, whether because of age, impairment, or innate characteristics. In such cases, the alterity of the other living being – and the possibility that they might flourish in ways other than standard humanistic ideals of autonomy and self-determination[55] – is not seriously considered. They appear to us as mere "moral patients" rather than moral agents, worthy of some "moral attention and concern"[56] but not as fully agentic equals.

The fact that power and domination exist in the world and are used to confine living beings is unsettling, whether or not those others are aware of their treatment or are tangibly harmed by it. In his *Essay Concerning Human Understanding*, John Locke posed the case of someone who was carried, while deep asleep, into a room where they woke to find a person who they had longed to see and speak with, which they immediately did upon waking. Unbeknownst to the individual, the room the two were in was locked and their freedom of movement curtailed. Locke asked whether their liberty has been violated, despite their lack of awareness. His answer is telling as it focuses attention unequivocally on power and control by the confiner, rather than on the capacity and psychological awareness of the confined:

> I ask, is not this stay voluntary? I think nobody will doubt it: and yet, being locked fast in, it is evident he is not at liberty not to stay, he has not freedom to be gone. So that liberty is not an idea belonging to volition, or preferring; but to the person having the power of doing, or forbearing to do, according as the mind shall choose or direct.[57]

Here we learn much from thinking with animals. Even if we grant the deflationary case that animals do not have consciousness or preferences such that they can be aware of or object to confinement, and even if we accept the skeptical view that many captive animals are not harmed physically in comparison to their most likely alternative existences, we might still accept the argument made by leading animal

[54] Restatement (Third) of Torts § 7 cmt. h.

[55] *See* Delon, *supra* note 33, at 132 ("[M]eaning doesn't presuppose autonomy understood as the rational capacity to determine one's own goals and principles, or to shape one's life in accordance with an overall plan.").

[56] Gruen, *supra* note 24, at 60.

[57] John Locke, Essay Concerning Human Understanding bk. II, 134 (Mary Whiton Calkins ed., The Open Court Publishing Co. rev. ed. 1920) (1690).

ethics theorists that the dignity of animals is impaired when they are confined in ways that are inconsistent with their essential being.[58] Confinement forecloses full realization of "the unique capacities that other animals possess,"[59] depriving both the animal and the world of the fullness of their existence. The elephant born and reared in captivity may not know that her wild counterparts live a different reality, roaming many miles a day in complexly interrelated and communicative herds. But the counterfactual seems to demean her existence, whether or not she knows. The fact that she might not have lived at all but for the confinement does not forgive the insult.

The philosopher Angela Martin argues that nonhuman animals are not the kinds of beings that can be wronged in the manner just described. In order to be disrespected, she argues, someone must act toward another in a way that is inconsistent with their preferences. Because most animals are not capable of forming preferences, she asserts, they cannot be humiliated or disrespected.[60] From this perspective, the harm that arises when nonhuman animals are placed in conditions of *un-freedom* might not be a harm that is personal to the individuals confined. Instead, it might be a harm that accrues to all of us from witnessing their condition of indignity. Lori Gruen's notion of relational dignity is useful here: "Rather than focusing on the worth of individual rational agents making autonomous choices, a relational conception of dignity brings into focus both the being who is dignified and the individual or community who value the dignified in the right ways."[61] As Gruen further observes, "[d]ignity, understood relationally, can be compromised or undermined even when the individual whose dignity is at stake does not object or complain"[62] – or, one might add, even when the individual does not have awareness of the treatment or condition that insults their dignity. From this perspective, the locus of concern in the case of the unaware victims of confinement may be less the harm that inures to them and more the harm that visits those of us who bear witness

58 *See, e.g.*, GRUEN, *supra* note 24, at 151–55 (introducing a notion of "Wild dignity" that is denied to nonhuman animals "[w]hen we project our needs and tastes onto them, try to alter or change what they do, and when we prevent them from controlling their own lives," all of which occurs in captivity); Martha Nussbaum, *The Moral Status of Animals*, CHRON. HIGHER EDUC. B6 (Feb. 3, 2006) ("Each form of life is worthy of respect, and it is a problem of justice when a creature does not have the opportunity to unfold its [valuable] power, to flourish in its own way, and to lead a life with dignity.").

59 LORI GRUEN, ENTANGLED EMPATHY: AN ALTERNATIVE ETHIC FOR OUR RELATIONSHIPS WITH ANIMALS 25 (2015).

60 Martin, *supra* note 36, at 93 ("One feels ashamed and humiliated only if one is treated in a way which is incompatible with one's preferences regarding one's social standing and which impugns one's self-respect. Most animals lack the prerequisite cognitive capacities for this."). *See also* Alasdair Cochrane, *Do Animals Have an Interest in Liberty?*, 57 POL. STUD. 660, 669 (2009) (suggesting that "for non-autonomous animals, their interest in liberty is only instrumental, whereas for autonomous humans it is intrinsic").

61 Lori Gruen, *Dignity, Captivity, and an Ethics of Sight*, in THE ETHICS OF CAPTIVITY 231, 234 (Lori Gruen ed., 2014).

62 *Id.* at 240.

to their deprivation and who shoulder the responsibility of deciding their fate without recourse to familiar liberal concepts like autonomy, preference, and choice.[63]

In the liberal individualist tradition of the Anglo-American legal system, such relational or collective sentiments find little purchase. To illustrate how far removed mainstream legal thought is from the philosophical tributaries explored in this chapter, two closing examples from the *Restatement (Third) of Torts* are offered. First, in acknowledging the worrisome gap created by the false imprisonment doctrine's requirement of either bodily injury or consciousness of confinement, the volume notes:

> [I]t is troubling to accept the notion that a very young child or a mentally disabled adult who is incapable of understanding that he or she has been confined is therefore "free prey" for those who would deliberately confine him or her, so long as such actors do not cause bodily harm.[64]

The use of the term "free prey" was likely innocent. But it is hard not to extend that language to, say, industrial farm animals who are indeed deemed "free prey" by the legal system so long as minimal standards of harm-prevention are maintained prior to their slaughter.[65] Such denial of agency and personhood may be more troubling in the case of differently abled human subjects, but it does not eliminate entirely the trouble with respect to nonhuman animals. Whenever a legal system denotes living beings as "free prey," a profound exercise of power has occurred.

Second, a hypothetical illustration from the *Restatement (Third) of Torts* is particularly revealing:

> Edward, a visitor at a zoo, notices that Peter, a zoo employee, is locked inside one of the cages. Peter yells to Edward that he dropped his keys just outside the cage door before entering to clean the cage and asks Edward to pick them up and unlock the door. Edward selfishly ignores Peter's request. Because Edward owes no duty to aid Peter, Edward is not liable to Peter for false imprisonment.[66]

Edward and Peter are both human subjects. Peter may well be in danger; we do not know from the facts of the hypothetical because we are not told what other animals share the cage with Peter. But these missing facts do not matter because the law sees Edward as a complete stranger who bears no responsibility for Peter's confinement and therefore holds no duty to assist Peter toward safety and liberation.

63 *See id.* at 237 ("[N]onhuman dignity may only come into question when animals are part of a human social world in which questions of dignity arise.").
64 Restatement (Third) of Torts § 7 cmt. h.
65 *See* David J. Wolfson & Mariann Sullivan, *Foxes in the Hen House: Animals, Agribusiness, and the Law: A Modern American Fable*, *in* Animal Rights: Current Debates and New Directions 205–6 (Cass R. Sunstein & Martha C. Nussbaum eds., 2004).
66 Restatement (Third) of Torts § 7 cmt. f, illus. 6.

Putting aside the dissonance in the illustration's failure to acknowledge the layers of human and nonhuman confinement, the hypothetical even on its own terms shows how far humans are willing to pursue the fantasy of self-determination. The maximal freedom afforded to Edward to pursue his life course without being interrupted by the needs of others apparently includes the freedom to become a moral monster, if he so chooses. Unlike the inarticulate pleas issued by encaged nonhuman animals, Peter's call for help is unmistakable and directed personally at Edward. Still, an accommodating legal system helps exonerate Edward from responsibility by defining Peter a priori as a stranger and by viewing Peter's act of dropping the keys as the proximate cause of his just deserts.

This airtight system of right and responsibility – a system "so perfect that no one will need to be good"[67] – is haunted by those living beings who fail its criteria for full membership, yet whose existence still makes an undeniable claim on our concern. To identify "false" imprisonment, one might instead begin by asking what constitutes "true" or lawful imprisonment. To ask that question, though, is to raise fundamental issues regarding the state's membership and legitimate scope of authority, including how it came to be that nonhuman animal confinement is presumed to constitute "true" imprisonment absent some extraordinary showing to the contrary. The case in favor of the existence of animal consciousness and the grave welfarist and dignitary impairments caused by animal confinement is strong, yet the legal system has ample intellectual reserves with which to parry such conclusions and to construct nonhuman animals instead as "free prey." Whether or not they are conscious of their confinement or physically harmed by it, however, nonhuman animals *are* confined, and their lives are accordingly limited and directed by human power. The more pressing consideration should therefore be *our* consciousness of their confinement and how we choose to respond to it.

19.5 CONCLUSION

A central puzzle of Anglo-American false imprisonment law is how to explain why no legal recourse exists for an individual whose dignity is denied through confinement but who is neither conscious of the confinement nor harmed by it. A possible answer to that puzzle can be found in the experience of nonhuman animals and the indignity that we all experience when we contemplate seriously their lot. The fact that we cannot at present identify a legally eligible individual within which to locate the harm suffered by confined nonhuman animals should not be taken to mean that the harm is not real. Instead, it should cause us to question the reality of our framework for identifying and locating harm.

[67] T.S. ELIOT, *Choruses from "The Rock," in* T.S. ELIOT: THE COMPLETE POEMS AND PLAYS, 1909–1950 106 (1958).

20

Imagining Animal Rights as a Civil Rights Movement

Will Potter

A big march can be tolerated. But there is no form of protest, expressing real rage and demanding real change, that will not be smeared and dismissed. For being too disruptive or too destructive; too incoherent or too orchestrated. It's a power struggle and power fights back.

– Naomi Klein[1]

Robert Meeropol has dedicated his life to supporting political activists who have been targeted by the government. It is a calling one might say was inevitable; as a child his parents, Julius and Ethel Rosenberg, were convicted of spying for the Soviet Union and executed by the United States at the height of McCarthyism and the Red Scare.[2]

In 1990, Meeropol created the Rosenberg Fund for Children to aid the families of progressive activists who have faced political repression related to their advocacy. The group has provided more than $7.5 million in small grants to help families pay for expenses such as school tuition, therapy, and travel costs related to visiting family members in prison.[3]

His organization functions much like a nondenominational church shelter for social justice struggles, opening its doors wide to those under attack, regardless of the social movement from which they come. "When people turn their backs on those they feel have been imprisoned for being too militant, it reminds me of my parents' case," Meeropol says.[4]

[1] Naomi Klein (@NaomiAKlein), Twitter (June 1, 2020 7:23 AM), https://twitter.com/naomiaklein/status/1267446792888692737.

[2] Robert D. McFadden, *David Greenglass, the Brother Who Doomed Ethel Rosenberg, Dies at 92*, N.Y. Times (Oct. 14, 2014), https://www.nytimes.com/2014/10/15/us/david-greenglass-spy-who-helped-seal-the-rosenbergs-doom-dies-at-92.html.

[3] Rosenberg Fund for Children, Inc., *Granting*, Rosenberg Fund for Child., Inc. (2015), https://www.rfc.org/granting.

[4] Robert Meeropol, *Green Is the New Red?*, Rosenberg Fund for Child., Inc.: Exec. Dir.'s Blog (Dec. 1, 2011), www.rfc.org/blog/article/1067.

In the early 2000s, Meeropol went to his members as he had so many times before, to enlist their support for a new wave of activists under attack. "They are attempting to intimidate this movement just as they attacked the communists, anti-war, civil rights. . .and other movements before them," he argued. "This is part of a larger corporate strategy to have law enforcement treat all progressive activism as a form of terrorism."[5] If we allow these activists to be treated as terrorists, he argued, then any other cause could be next. When Meeropol told his members *who* he wanted to support – animal rights and environmental activists – he says he was often met with a "blank look."[6]

Some of his members said they were afraid to align the organization, and Meeropol's parents, with those labeled "eco-terrorists." "Others on the Left, although not necessarily members of the RFC community, have characterized environmental and animal rights activists as self-indulgent, well-off white kids who seem more concerned with trees, birds, and puppies than they are with worldwide human suffering."

Whether it was because of their tactics or their beliefs, many longtime progressive activists felt these animal rights and environmental activists just did not belong. "I've had difficulty convincing left-wing friends to support targeted animal rights activists," Meeropol says. "One friend responded, 'aren't they the people who think animals are more important than people?'"[7]

20.1 CARCERAL LOGIC AND SOCIAL MOVEMENTS

For more than 50 years, the animal rights and environmental movements have been targeted with increasingly draconian campaign of political repression. As I documented in my book *Green Is the New Red: An Insider's Account of a Social Movement under Siege*, the term "eco-terrorism" was itself created by anti-environmental groups to smear their opponents in the 1980s, and over subsequent decades a coalition of corporations and trade associations successfully lobbied both lawmakers and the FBI to criminalize animal rights and environmental activists as "domestic terrorists." In the wake of the attacks of September 11, 2001, these anti-activist campaigns intensified dramatically. By 2005, the FBI was publicly declaring that animal rights and environmental activists were their "number one" domestic terrorism priority.[8]

[5] Robert Meeropol, *Freeing Mink not Terrorism; Corporate Contributions Not Speech*, Robert Meeropol: Still Out on a Limb (July 24, 2014), http://www.robertmeeropol.com/blog/archives/2014-07.

[6] Meeropol, *supra* note 5

[7] *Id.*

[8] Henry Schuster, *Domestic Terror: Who's Most Dangerous? Eco-Terrorists Are Now above Ultra-right Extremists on the FBI Charts*, CNN (Aug. 24, 2005), https://www.cnn.com/2005/US/08/24/schuster.column/.

No other contemporary social struggle has been as targeted by state and corporate power as "terrorists," as we will explore further in this article. And yet for decades, these precedent-setting expansions of police, surveillance, and prison powers have gone largely unnoticed, ignored, and even *approved* by civil rights and civil liberties organizations.

Alongside colleagues in this volume who are exploring connections between what might loosely be described as the caging of humans and animals, I am interested in similar questions in relation to the study of political repression – the caging of social movements.

20.1.1 *Imagine a Movement*

Imagine a civil rights movement. Any civil rights movement. It can be centered on the struggles of women, people of color, children, immigrants, refugees, the LGBTQ community, workers. Imagine protests, marches, and civil disobedience. Like all social movements, activists employ a variety of tactics, both lawful and unlawful, and that is the case in this one too. Finally, as part of this imaginary David versus Goliath struggle for justice, do not forget to imagine the Goliaths. Even in a hypothetical struggle for justice, remember that power, as Naomi Klein said, fights back.

Now imagine this movement in the crosshairs of the FBI, lawmakers, and multiple industries:

- The FBI has classified this movement, which has never harmed a human being, as the "number one domestic terrorism threat."[9]
- Prosecutors have applied "terrorism enhancement" penalties,[10] which were approved by Congress in the wake of the Oklahoma City bombing, to members of this movement who have burned vehicles and empty buildings, torn open cages, and spray-painted slogans like "liberation is love."[11]
- Corporations have lobbied for sweeping new laws against these protesters locally, nationally, and internationally.[12] States have passed new laws

[9] Kristen Philipkoski, *Eco-Terror Cited as Top Threat*, Wired (June 16, 2004), www.wired.com/2004/06/eco-terror-cited-as-top-threat/.

[10] Shane Harris, *The Terrorism Enhancement: An Obscure Law Stretches the Definition of Terrorism, and Metes Out Severe Punishments*, Nat'l J. (July 13, 2007), http://shaneharris.com/magazinestories/terrorism-enhancement-obscure-law-stretches-the-definition-of-terrorism-and-metes-out-severe-punishments/.

[11] F.B.I., *Animal Rights Extremists: Pair Took Law into Their Own Hands*, F.B.I.: News (June 10, 2016), https://www.fbi.gov/news/stories/animal-rights-extremists.

[12] Will Potter, *Australia Risks Copying US 'Ag-Gag' Laws to Turn Animal Activists into Terrorists*, Sydney Morning Herald (May 1, 2014 4.19 PM), https://www.smh.com.au/environment/conservation/australia-risks-copying-us-aggag-laws-to-turn-animal-activists-into-terrorists-20140501-37k8i.html.

against making it illegal for activists to photograph or video-record workplace abuses.[13] Activists have been charged under this legislation for filming a business from the public street.[14]

- Imprisoned activists have been confined to experimental Communications Management Units, radically restricting their contact with their family, supporters, and social movement.[15] The US Bureau of Prisons said it is because of these activists' "inspirational significance."[16] Internal government documents say it is due to their "anti-government and anti-corporate" beliefs.[17]
- The repression of these movements in the United States has already become a model for corporations criminalizing advocacy against other social movements and in other countries. EUROPOL has issued terrorism warnings to law enforcement throughout Europe about activists documenting abuse to use with the media and in campaigns.

If this were taking place against the social movement you imagined, or seemingly *any* progressive cause, one would not only expect for the diehard Leftist groups like the Rosenberg Fund for Children to be enraged, but for wide swaths of civil society to be as well. Would we not expect, at minimum, civil rights groups to assist in criminal defense, and to oppose any new laws that could be used against other progressive social movements?

It would be unconscionable for any credible free speech or civil rights organization in the world to ignore.

20.1.2 *Not Worth Defending*

Yet for decades, civil rights and civil liberties organization have repeatedly declined to assist targeted animal rights and environmental activists. The American Civil Liberties Union has famously defended even the rights of the white supremacists to

[13] Ctr. for Const. Rts. & Def. Rts. & Dissent, *Ag-Gag across America: Corporate-Backed Attacks on Activists and Whistleblowers*, Ctr. for Const. Rts. (Sept. 6, 2017), https://ccrjustice.org/AgGagAcrossAmericaReport.

[14] Amy Meyer, *'Ag-Gag' Laws Will Deter Reporting on Animal Abuse*, Wash. Post: Opinions (June 7, 2013), www.washingtonpost.com/opinions/ag-gag-laws-will-deter-reporting-on-animal-abuse/2013/06/07/f93e8876-ca42-11e2-9245-773c0123c027_story.html.

[15] Ctr. for Const. Rts., *CMUs: The Federal Prison System's Experiment in Social Isolation*, Ctr. for Const. Rts. (Mar. 31, 2010), https://ccrjustice.org/home/get-involved/tools-resources/fact-sheets-and-faqs/cmus-federal-prison-system-s-experiment.

[16] Dep't of Just., Bureau of Prisons, *Communications Management Units*, Fed. Reg. (Jan. 22, 2015), https://www.federalregister.gov/documents/2015/01/22/2015-01024/communications-management-units.

[17] A Counter terrorism Unit memorandum about Andy Stepanian's transfer to the CMU, dated March 27, 2008, noted his protest activity, advocacy of "direct action" and civil disobedience, and espoused antigovernment belief. http://willpotter.com/wp-content/uploads/2015/08/2008.03.27-stepanian-designation.pdf

speak and protest.[18] However, the national organization seems to have drawn a line at defending speech by animal rights activists.

For example, Lauren Gazzola, an aspiring civil rights lawyer, repeatedly begged for their assistance as she and other animal rights activists with Stop Huntingdon Animal Cruelty faced federal terrorism prosecutions for their campaigns to shut down a notorious animal testing lab in New Jersey.[19] Gazzola doggedly pursued the ACLU at their national conference, and via phone, email, and letters for years "without even the courtesy of a return phone call."[20]

In a 2005 letter to ACLU leaders, Gazzola noted that the government's case against Stop Huntingdon Animal Cruelty was "the FBI's largest investigation of 2003."

The government collected more than 600 90-minute audio tapes from wiretaps of Gazzola and codefendants, along with more than 100 videotapes, and 24,000 pages of discovery materials. The four-year investigation involved more than 100 FBI agents and 12 US attorneys.[21] "After all this we are not accused of hurting anyone, attempting to hurt anyone, vandalizing anything, trying to vandalizing anything, stealing anything, attempting to steal anything, trespassing, or any other physical act," she wrote. "We are accused only of posting words on a website (by and large, words composed by other individuals, who are not defendants). Yet we are 'terrorists,' facing 23 years in Federal prison."[22]

Gazzola warned that the ACLU and others were ignoring not just her case, but an entire movement under attack. "In just the past two months, 17 activists have been subpoenaed to grand juries in California, three homes have been raided, and one activist was detained by the FBI threatening to take DNA samples, right there, on the street corner," Gazzola said.

> I know of no activist who can travel internationally without being interrogated upon reentering the U.S. The FBI even contacted our landlord, just to inform her who her tenants were. This is just a fraction of the harassment this movement has endured. How the ACLU can ignore it is beyond me.[23]

It's not just the ACLU. Civil rights groups have said "no" so often and so loudly to such pleas that animal rights and environmental activists have created new civil rights groups to fill the void. For example, the Civil Liberties Defense Center in

[18] David Cole, *The ACLU's Longstanding Commitment to Defending Speech We Hate*, Am. Civ. Liberties Union: Speak Freely (June 23, 2018), https://www.aclu.org/blog/free-speech/aclus-longstanding-commitment-defending-speech-we-hate.

[19] Lauren Gazzola, *Bad Things Happened: Metaphorical Fingerprints, Constellations of Evidence, and "Guilt* for *Association"*, 40 Vt. L. Rev. 813, (2016), https://lawreview.vermontlaw.edu/wp-content/uploads/2016/08/40VtLRev813-Gazzola.pdf.

[20] Personal letter, copy given to author.

[21] *Id.*

[22] Gazzola Letter, *supra* note 20.

[23] *Id.*

Eugene, Oregon, was created by Lauren Regan, longtime environmentalist and criminal defense lawyer, to defend prosecuted tree-sitters and Earth Firsters.[24] In the animal rights movement, the Equal Justice Alliance was created to oppose sweeping new laws targeting animal rights activists. The founder, Odette Wilkins, was dismayed that the New York City Bar Association and the broader legal community had not already facilitated such a defense.[25]

Civil rights groups have even cheered on the FBI,[26] and created lengthy dossiers on the the animal rights and environmental movements, marked "for law enforcement," to aid in the prosecution and imprisonment of these activists.[27]

The Southern Poverty Law Center created a listing of "Eco-violence" as a resource for media and lawmakers.[28] The page begins with an acknowledgment that "these extremists have yet to kill anyone in America." Yet SPLC has gone so far as to compare animal rights activists with the Army of God[29] – an anti-abortion group that used a website to coordinate assassinations of doctors – and environmentalists to "the radical right, with its racist and fascist appeals."[30]

Respected civil rights leaders have actually been champions of anti-terrorism legislation criminalizing a wide range of protest activity. US Representative Bobby Scott, for example, led the campaign for the Animal Enterprise Terrorism Act in the House alongside Republican Representative Tom Petri.[31]

In response to criticism from animal activists that the law was vague and overly broad, Scott acknowledged on the House floor that yes, the legislation could be used

24 Artin Kaste, *Critics Say Federal Prosecutors Are Pushing the Envelope with Protest Charges*, WXXI News (Sept. 27, 2020), https://www.wxxinews.org/post/critics-say-federal-prosecutors-are-pushing-envelope-protest-charges.

25 Comm.on Legal Issues Pertaining to Animals & Comm. on Civ. Rts., Re: The Animal Enterprise Terrorism Act, 18 U.S.C. § 43 (N.Y.C. Bar Ass'n 2009), https://www.nycbar.org/pdf/report/AETA_Animal&CivilRights_Letter072109.pdf.

26 S. Poverty L. Ctr., *Feds across Country Move to Smash "Eco-terrorists"*, Intelligence Rep. (Apr. 19, 2006), https://www.splcenter.org/fighting-hate/intelligence-report/2006/feds-across-country-move-smash-eco-terrorists.

27 Anti-Defamation League, Ecoterrorism: Extremism in the Animal Rights and Environmentalist Movements (Anti-Defamation League), https://www.adl.org/education/resources/reports/ecoterrorism?gclid=CjwKCAiAxeX_BRASEiwAc1QdkSrPtpeVRUZ5qLL53_oUicXAaRKbWTnqFkcs9k5m4SourNv5s1-t6hoCnj4QAvD_BwE.

28 S. Poverty L. Ctr., *Ecoterrorism: Extremism in the Animal Rights and Environmentalist Movements*, Intelligence Rep. (2002?), https://www.splcenter.org/fighting-hate/intelligence-report/2015/eco-violence-record.

29 S. Poverty L. Ctr., *Stop Huntingdon Animal Cruelty Threatens Terrorist-Style Attack*, Intelligence Rep. (Sept. 20, 2002), https://www.splcenter.org/fighting-hate/intelligence-report/2002/stop-huntingdon-animal-cruelty-threatens-terrorist-style-attack.

30 S. Poverty L. Ctr., *Left Wing Earth Liberation Front Advocates Extremist Agenda*, Intelligence Rep. (May 8, 2001), www.splcenter.org/fighting-hate/intelligence-report/2001/left-wing-earth-liberation-front-advocates-extremist-agenda.

31 Adam Klasfeld, *Freeing Minks Triggers Anti-terror Statute*, Courthouse News Serv. (Mar. 6, 2015), https://www.courthousenews.com/freeing-minks-triggers-anti-terror-statute/.

to prosecute nonviolent civil disobedience as terrorism, but only if it intended to cause a loss of profits to the "animal enterprise."[32]

As the legislation was being fast-tracked through Congress, with bipartisan support, civil liberties and privacy groups remained silent. The ACLU, which had been vocal of its opposition to expansion of domestic terrorism powers post-9/11, sent a letter to Congress saying, "the ACLU does not oppose this bill."[33]

If this were any other social movement, Scott and fellow Democrats would have likely opposed this legislation. Civil liberties and privacy groups would have been up in arms.

Instead, they did not even show up for the vote in the House; most lawmakers were absent because they attended a groundbreaking ceremony for the new memorial honoring Dr. Martin Luther King.[34] They were honoring the legacy of Dr. King as they approved legislation that would classify King's tactics as "terrorism," if directed against an "animal enterprise."

20.1.3 *Exceptionalism*

To be clear, there have been many inspiring exceptions to this dynamic. The Center for Constitutional Rights and the National Lawyers Guild are established progressive organizations – going back to the Red Scare – and they have spoken up early, and often, in defense of these activists. Robert Meeropol and the Rosenberg Fund for Children have come to the defense of animal rights and environmental groups, despite any initial hesitations, and they still do. Lauren Gazzola's phone calls were not returned by the ACLU national office, but ACLU affiliates have assisted her and other activists under attack.

But how are we to explain that for decades now, a white nationalist has had an inarguably greater chance of being defended by leading civil liberties groups than an animal rights activist or environmentalist? Why have some of the most sweeping expansions of counterterrorism policy post-9/11 been not just ignored, not just permitted, but actively championed and institutionalized by segments of the civil rights and civil liberties community?

How have we arrived at such a dystopian moment?

There have been plenty of offensive animal rights campaigns, and offensive animal rights activists. Groups like PETA have been called racist, sexist, and

[32] Congressional Record House Articles (2006), https://www.congress.gov/congressional-record/2006/11/13/house-section/article/H8590-1.

[33] Caroline Fredrickson & Marvin J. Johnson, *Re: ACLU Urges Needed Minor Changes to AETA, but Does Not Oppose Bill (S. 3880, the "Animal Enterprise Terrorism Act")* American Civil Liberties Union 2006, https://www.aclu.org/sites/default/files/images/general/asset_upload_file809_27356.pdf.

[34] W. Koch, *Memorial Groundbreaking Honors MLK's Legacy*, USA Today (Nov. 13, 2006) (last visited Apr. 11, 2007), http://www.usatoday.com.

anti-human for media campaigns that compare the mistreatment of animals to human slavery, rape, the beheading of journalists, and the Holocaust.

It's a mistake to assume that the intentionally controversial campaigns of a polarizing, media-savvy organization are the beliefs of entire communities of activists. But even if we assume the absolute *worst* intentions about every animal rights and environmental activist, though – that they all hate humans and only mention human struggles to "bootstrap" their cause – it still doesn't explain such an extreme disconnect. After all, the most important free speech and civil liberties cases have often come from the most offensive, even vile speech.

Moreover, these animal rights and environmental activists have been vocal that *they* view *themselves* as connected to broader progressive struggles. For example, when Robert Meeropol first learned about Daniel McGowan and other "eco-terrorists," it wasn't because they came knocking on his door for support. McGowan had approached the organization to enlist their support for another (nonanimal or environmental) activist.[35] For years, the animal rights movement has resisted discussing the repression it faced, because activists felt it was not as important as what civil rights activists have endured.

The members of Stop Huntingdon Animal Cruelty repeatedly noted their inspiration – publicly, and in their trial – was anti-apartheid struggles in South Africa. When SHAC activists in the Oakland, California area began receiving grand jury subpoenas – used to force them to testify about their political beliefs and political affiliations or face jail time – they turned to activists they respected for advice: the Black Panther Party. The only reason they even knew what a grand jury was was because of the Panthers, they said. This wasn't bootstrapping; if anything, it was hero worship.

If animal rights and environmental activists abandon these beliefs, and veer to the far right, there is no tolerance or sympathy from others in the movement. For example, the Animal Liberation Front and Earth Liberation Front are uncompromising in their policies of supporting political prisoners: If any activist aligns themselves with white supremacists in prison, even if it is a misguided attempt at self-preservation, they are removed from prisoner support groups entirely.[36] Cut off from letters, commissary money, they are no longer mentioned in interviews or publications, and there are no support concerts or benefits. They are gone. For a radical

[35] Robert Meeropol, *Daniel McGowan*, Rosenberg Fund for Children, Inc.: Exec. Dir.'s Blog (Apr. 5, 2010), https://www.rfc.org/blog/article/478.

[36] Break the Chains, *ELP Public Statement on Christopher 'Dirt' McIntosh*, Break the Chains: ELP Info. Bull. (Feb. 18, 2008), https://breakallchains.blogspot.com/2008/02/elp-public-statement-on-christopher.html; Edelweiss Pirates, *A Field Guide to Straw Men: Sadie and Exile, Esoteric Fascism, and Olympia's Little White Lies*, Puget Sound Anarchists (DATE), https://pugetsoundanarchists.org/a-field-guide-to-straw-men-sadie-and-exile-esoteric-fascism-and-olympias-little-white-lies/.

social movement, this is the equivalent of sending your comrade into the desert with no boots and no water.

And it's not just the most radical elements that are making connections between these movements. Indeed, there appears to be positive correlation between advocacy for human rights and advocacy for animal rights. That was the conclusion of researchers at Harvard University and Dartmouth College after conducting a study of individual attitudes regarding the suffering of animals and humans.

As researchers Yon Soo Park and Benjamin Valentino discussed in *Human Rights Quarterly*: "Our results demonstrate that support for animal rights strongly links to support for disadvantaged or marginalized human populations, including LGBT groups, racial minorities, undocumented immigrants, and the poor."[37]

For example, Americans who were more politically conservative and more religious were much less likely to support animal rights. And Americans who said they strongly support governmental programs to aid the sick were significantly *more* likely, by 80 percent, to support animal rights than those who strongly opposed it.

"In other words, people who supported an expansive conception of human rights and welfare were also more likely to support animal rights," Park and Valentino wrote in the *Washington Post*.[38]

So what is it that prevents us from imagining animal rights as a civil rights movement? How do we explain that, for decades, the animal rights and environmental movements have been the top target of an increasingly dystopian campaign of political repression that has gone virtually untouched and unnoticed by the broader left, the legal community, and scholars of authoritarianism and political repression globally?

20.1.4 *The Animal*

There is only one factor distinguishing the animal rights movement and environmental movements from the loose constellation of causes we point to and declare "social justice." It's the idea of the movement itself. Unlike every other contemporary social justice movement, these are the only activists who have placed nonhumans (animals and the natural world) at their center.

This absence of the human marks animal rights as an outsider in the history of social movements. Our ever-expanding conception of morality, and legal systems ostensibly designed to reflect those norms, is rooted in a shared humanity. The animal rights and environmental movements challenge this by making the nonhuman the focus of their inquiry and activism.

[37] Yon Soo Park & Benjamin Valentino, *Animals Are People Too: Explaining Variation in Respect for Animal Rights*, 41 Animal Rts. Q. 39, XX (2019), https://cpb-us-e1.wpmucdn.com/sites.dartmouth.edu/dist/b/1324/files/2019/06/Park-and-Valentino-HRQ-Animals-are-People-Too.pdf.

[38] *Id.*

At best, this has been viewed as an anomaly, a strange new creature in the world of social movements. The movement isn't right-wing, but it's not left-wing either. The term most frequently used by the FBI and national security think tanks to describe animal rights and environmental activists are "single issue extremism" and "special interest terrorism."[39] The language is replicated in databases of terrorism crimes, congressional reports, and legislation. These movements are something different, according to leftists and the FBI alike, and we as a culture haven't figure out how to categorize them yet.

At worst, the very existence of the animal rights movement has been viewed as antagonistic to the merit of civil rights struggles. "We have human problems to deal with" is a line that every animal rights activist has heard at some point in their efforts, as Meeropol's experiences reflect. A focus on nonhuman animals equates, in this framework, to a devaluation of humans.

Theoretically, I think there is a connection between the concept of human exceptionalism[40] – which argues animals are so different from us that they are not worthy of ethical consideration – with what has occurred at the social movement level. These movements have been excluded from the broader progressive movement, and shared defenses of civil liberties, because the subject of these movements is viewed, as we discussed, as either removed from or standing in opposition to human struggles.

If animals are not worthy of our consideration, then these activists, by extension, aren't worthy of defense; their focus on animals delegitimizes them as social activists. And if these aren't legitimate activists, then what they are experiencing is not treated as "state repression," or a threat to shared civil liberties, at all.

In this way "animal" functions as a social marker. It is used to separate animals, and their advocates, from human-oriented considerations. The effects of this animal marker are dangerous in our culture; they delegitimize the subject and remove it from the moral framework.

"Animal" is *such* a powerful social marker, such a delegitimizing presence, that it can actually transform the identities of people who would otherwise unquestionably be regarded as civil rights activists. We see this clearly with those discussions between Meeropol and members of the Rosenberg Fund for Children, and we see it in the decades of silence from the civil rights community.

To illustrate this further, let us look at two examples of what happens when "civil rights" activists disrupt the paradigm, and connect their struggles to animals.

39 James F. Jarboe, *Testimony: The Threat of Eco-terrorism*, F.B.I. (Feb. 12. 2002), https://archives.fbi.gov/archives/news/testimony/the-threat-of-eco-terrorism.

40 Gregg Henriques, *On Human Exceptionalism*, Psych. Today (Jan. 2, 2013), https://www.psychologytoday.com/us/blog/theory-knowledge/201301/human-exceptionalism (*responding to* Marc Beckoff, *Animal Minds and the Foible of Human Exceptionalism*, Psych. Today (July 30, 2011), https://www.psychologytoday.com/us/blog/animal-emotions/201107/animal-minds-and-the-foible-human-exceptionalism.).

20.1.5 *MOVE*

First, consider MOVE, a Black-liberation collective founded in Philadelphia in the 1970s.[41] The group was created by John Africa, whose teachings combined the revolutionary ideology of groups like the Black Panther Party with protests for animal rights at zoos and a raw food vegetarian diet.

The group believes, "Each individual life is dependent on every other life, and all life has a purpose, so all living beings, things that move, are equally important, whether they are human beings, dogs, birds, fish, trees, ants, weeds, rivers, wind or rain."[42] Or as *The Guardian* said: "Black liberation, animal liberation – the two are as one with MOVE."[43]

MOVE lived as a commune, grew their own food, wore their hair in dreadlocks, and lived like hippies. They were social outcasts, and their neighbors wanted them evicted. The police department loathed them. Philadelphia Mayor Frank Rizzo said: "You are dealing with criminals, barbarians, you are safer in the jungle!"[44] There had been several violent encounters with the police, culminating in an eviction siege.

On May 14, 1985, the police department dropped a bomb from a helicopter on the group's home, killing eleven people in the MOVE commune, four of them children.[45] "You could see the flames, 20, 30 feet above the rooftops, reaching over like blazing fingers, igniting houses first on Osage, then adjacent houses on Pine. Soon a solid wave of flame was sweeping down the street," a neighbor told *Time Magazine*.[46]

A US police department dropped a bomb on a dissident group, killing children and setting an entire neighborhood ablaze, and yet this remains largely unknown and undiscussed.[47] It is one of the most vile, egregious abuses of police power against social movements in US history. In 2000, the Philadelphia City Council

[41] John Africa, *Timeline of the MOVE Organization Leading to May 13, 1985*, Phila. Trib. (May 9, 2015), https://www.phillytrib.com/news/timeline-of-the-move-organization-leading-to-may-13-1985/article_91170189-7446-5a6b-97cc-db04660d69a6.html.

[42] MOVE Org., *About MOVE*, MOVE Org. (2021), http://onamove.com/about/.

[43] Ed Pilkington, *A Siege. A Bomb. 48 Dogs. And the Black Commune That Would Not Surrender*, Guardian (July 31, 2018), https://www.theguardian.com/world/2018/jul/31/a-siege-a-bomb-48-dogs-and-the-black-commune-that-would-not-surrender.

[44] *Id.*

[45] William K. Stevens, *Police Drop Bombs on Radicals' Home in Philadelphia*, N.Y. Times (May 14, 1985), https://www.nytimes.com/1985/05/14/us/police-drop-bomb-on-radicals-home-in-philadelphia.html.

[46] Frank Trippett, *"It Looks Just Like a War Zone,"* TIME (June 24, 2001), http://content.time.com/time/magazine/article/0,9171,141842,00.html.

[47] Gene Demby, *Why Have So Many People Never Heard of the MOVE Bombing?*, NPR: Code Sw!tch (May 18, 2015), https://www.npr.org/sections/codeswitch/2015/05/18/407665820/why-did-we-forget-the-move-bombing.

formally apologized for the bombing.[48] But outside of the West Philadelphia neighborhood where it occurred, the bombing remains largely omitted from discussions of political repression and police violence.

"You got to think about how they were portrayed in the '70s," said Tommy Oliver, the creator of a documentary about the fallout of the MOVE attack. "They were dehumanized. And when you dehumanize a people, it becomes really easy to justify whatever happens to them. And so, of course, whatever happened to them was their fault."[49]

20.1.6 *Dick Gregory*

This dehumanization seems to occur whenever the animal is invoked, even when the speaker has long established themselves as a civil rights leader. Consider comedian and social justice advocate Dick Gregory, for example. Gregory, a long-time civil rights activist, grew increasingly vocal about the connections he felt between civil rights and animal rights.

> I had been a participant in all of the "major" and most of the "minor" civil rights demonstrations of the early sixties. Under the leadership of Dr. King, I became convinced that nonviolence meant opposition to killing in any form. I felt the commandment "Thou Shalt Not Kill" applied to human beings not only in their dealings with each other – war, lynching, assassination, murder, and the like – but in their practice of killing animals for food and sport. Animals and humans suffer and die alike. Violence causes the same pain, the same spilling of blood, the same stench of death, the same arrogant, cruel, and brutal taking of life.[50]

This was not a fleeting concept for Gregory. It guided his life, into old age. He created a health empire around his vegetarianism, and created cookbooks like *Dick Gregory's Natural Diet for Folks Who Eat: Cookin' with Mother Nature*.[51] He remained a tireless advocate of both human and animal rights till his death.[52]

48 Laura McCrystal, *Philly City Council Has Formally Apologized for the Deadly 1985 MOVE Bombing*, PHILA. INQUIRER (Nov. 16, 2020), https://www.inquirer.com/news/philadelphia/move-bombing-apology-philadelphia-walter-wallace-20201112.html.

49 All Things Considered, *Tommy Oliver on His Documentary about 1978 MOVE Standoff in Philadelphia*, NAT'L PUB. RADIO (Dec. 21, 2020, 3:44 PM), https://www.npr.org/2020/12/21/948873778/tommy-oliver-on-his-documentary-about-1978-move-standoff-in-philadelphia.

50 Tracye McQuirter, *This Civil Rights Activist Is the Reason I've Been Vegan for 30 Years*, BON APPETIT: HEALTHYISH (Sept. 1, 2017), https://www.bonappetit.com/story/dick-gregory-vegan-civil-rights.

51 Studs Terkel Radio, *Dick Gregory Discusses His Book "Dick Gregory's Natural Diet for Folks Who Eat: Cookin' with Mother Nature,"* WFMT RADIO NETWORK (May 30, 1973), https://studsterkel.wfmt.com/programs/dick-gregory-discusses-his-book-dick-gregorys-natural-diet-folks-who-eat-cookin-mother.

52 Dennis McLellan, *Dick Gregory, Groundbreaking Comedian and Activist Who Ran for Chicago Mayor, Dies at 84*, CHI. TRIB. (Aug. 19, 2017, 10:52 PM), https://www.chicagotribune.com/news/obituaries/ct-dick-gregory-dead-20170819-story.html.

His public eulogies by the civil rights community and Hollywood made no mention of this, though. A glowing obituary in the *New York Times* said Gregory developed an interest in "fasting" and "health-food," and omitted his ethical concerns.[53] The *Chicago Sun-Times* said he was "fried chicken for the soul."[54]

When Dick Gregory urged Black civil rights activists to go vegetarian, he did so as both a civil rights activist and an animal rights activist; Gregory integrated the "health, politics, economics, and culture of what we ate."[55] Our present vocabulary of intersectionality didn't exist at the time, but Gregory was a living example of it.[56]

When he is praised, though, anything about Gregory related to animals must be either omitted entirely or reframed as an interest in health. The animal marker is so delegitimizing that it would presumably tarnish the reputation of someone otherwise seen as a civil rights hero.

20.2 SOLITARY CONFINEMENT

Humans are a social species. When placed in isolation, we suffer in extreme ways both physically and psychologically.

In prison, placing someone in solitary confinement is often described with a variety of euphemisms to mask its cruelty: "segregation," "the hole," "lockdown," "social exclusion." The practice is rampant in US prisons. The UN Special Rapporteur on torture noted in alarm that US prisons "routinely resort to repressive measures, such as prolonged or indefinite isolation."[57]

A 2020 report from UN Human Rights said that the use of solitary confinement is so pervasive in prisons that it could amount to torture. Being placed in solitary confinement for long periods of time, its authors noted, can have "severe and often irreparable psychological and physical consequences."[58]

When we are removed from each other, we lose our ability to make sense of the world, process information, and function. Isolation can sicken social movements in similar ways.

[53] Clyde Harberman, *Dick Gregory Dies at 84, Found Humor in the Civil Rights Struggle*, N.Y. Times (Aug. 19, 2017), https://www.nytimes.com/2017/08/19/arts/dick-gregory-dies-at-84.html.

[54] Laura Washington, *Dick Gregory Was Fried Chicken for the Soul*, Chi. Sun Times (Aug. 28, 2017), https://chicago.suntimes.com/2017/8/28/18341857/washington-dick-gregory-was-fried-chicken-for-the-soul.

[55] McQuirter, *supra* note 50.

[56] Arica L. Coleman, *What's Intersectionality? Let These Scholars Explain the Theory and Its History*, TIME (Mar. 29, 2019), https://time.com/5560575/intersectionality-theory/.

[57] Nils Melzer, *United States: Prolonged Solitary Confinement Amounts to Psychological Torture, Says UN Expert*, U.N. Comm'n on Hum. Rts. (Feb. 28, 2020), https://www.ohchr.org/EN/NewsEvents/Pages/DisplayNews.aspx?NewsID=25633&LangID=E.

[58] United Nations Commission on Human Rights, *Special Rapporteur on Torture and Other Cruel, Inhuman or Degrading Treatment or Punishment*, U.N. Comm'n on Hum. Rts. (2021), https://ohchr.org/EN/Issues/Torture/SRTorture/Pages/SRTortureIndex.aspx.

The separation of the animal rights and environmental movements from the broader civil rights and civil liberties community has facilitated government repression, and left generations of new political activists unaware of post-9/11 mechanisms used by corporations and law enforcement to silence protest.

The rapid emergence of Black Lives Matter as an international movement, for example, was met with an equally swift clampdown on the movement. The militarizations of police, restrictions on protest, counterterrorism rhetoric, civil lawsuits, and other repressive measures framing these activists as "domestic extremists" and "terrorists" was shocking for many activists. However, none of this should have been a surprise. It should have been expected.

The suite of repressive measures used against animal rights and environmental activists have become the new playbook for the criminalization of dissent. Activists of all social movements, globally, need to understand these counterattacks, and be prepared to face them.

What would it look like, then, to end this "social exclusion"? The collaboration involved in creating this volume is one example of what that process might entail. Human rights and animal rights advocates discussing their fields in tandem find common ground not only in their research findings and cruelty inflicted upon their clients, but in the institutional opposition they face.

A trove of leaked documents from Amazon's Global Security Operations Center, for instance, revealed widespread spying and disinformation campaigns against both labor and environmental groups.[59] FBI training materials and PowerPoint presentations have been updated to routinely describe "eco-terrorists" alongside a more recent threat: "black identity extremists."[60]

Whether or not we view animal rights activists as civil rights activists, and regardless of how we characterize the divisions within and between social justice movements, at minimum we must acknowledge that our opponents rarely make such distinctions.

Historically speaking, when social movements emphasize their differences and disagreements, rather than shared values, it has repeatedly been used as a tool to accelerate state repression.

As Robert Meeropol of the Rosenberg Fund for Children noted:

> Few alive today remember that A.J. Muste, the pacifist mainstay of the War Resisters' League, refused to get involved in the effort to save my parents' lives because they had been accused of aiding the Soviet military. Fellow pacifist, Dave

[59] Lauren K. Gurley, *Secret Amazon Reports Expose the Company's Surveillance of Labor and Environmental Groups*, VICE (Nov. 23, 2020, 10:16 AM), https://www.vice.com/en/article/5dp3yn/amazon-leaked-reports-expose-spying-warehouse-workers-labor-union-environmental-groups-social-movements.

[60] Michael German, *The FBI Targets a New Generation of Black Activists*, BRENNAN CTR. FOR JUST. (June 26, 2020), https://www.brennancenter.org/our-work/analysis-opinion/fbi-targets-new-generation-black-activists.

Dellinger, disagreed. He argued that regardless of what my parents might have done, all progressives should stand in solidarity with them because they were being subjected to violent, right-wing political repression.

20.3 "STEROIDS FOR FASCISM"

This is a conversation we can no longer afford to ignore. Two global crises will soon force us to confront this disconnect, whether we agree or not. Authoritarianism is on the rise, globally, and the increasing threat of climate change and ecological collapse is already being used to close borders and accelerate concentrations of power. As Gizmodo noted, the "climate crisis will be steroids for fascism."[61] Meanwhile, far-right groups have begun using environmentalism and "eco-fascism" to promote white nationalism.[62]

As I write this, fascists – including well-documented white supremacists and Neo-Nazis – have stormed the US Capitol. In the wake of this failed coup attempt, the incoming Democratic administration has vowed to make "domestic terrorism" a priority. Biden's pick to lead the Justice Department, Merrick Garland, has pledged to fight "violent extremism" as US attorney general.[63]

"Don't dare call them protesters," incoming president Joe Biden said. "They were a riotous mob. Insurrectionists. Domestic terrorists. It's that basic. It's that simple."[64]

The Biden administration has vowed to create a new "domestic terrorism" law and is considering a new White House post to oversee the fight against "overseeing the fight against ideologically inspired violent extremists and increasing funding to combat them," according to the *Wall Street Journal*.[65]

Incredibly, the widespread failures of law enforcement to prevent a white nationalist mob – which had been promising to do exactly this for months – are being attributed to miscommunication and inadequate resources. The FBI has told the

[61] Brian Kahn, *The Climate Crisis Will Be Steroids for Fascism*, G/O MEDIA INC. (Jan. 7, 2021, 2:05 PM), https://earther.gizmodo.com/the-climate-crisis-will-be-steroids-for-fascism-1846009446.

[62] Stateside Staff, *How "Eco-fascists" Are Using Environmentalism to Promote White Nationalism*, MICH. RADIO (Sept. 12, 2019), https://www.michiganradio.org/post/how-eco-fascists-are-using-environmentalism-promote-white-nationalism.

[63] Harper Neidig, *Garland Vows to Fight "Violent Extremism" as Attorney General*, HILL (Jan. 7, 2021), https://thehill.com/homenews/administration/533200-garland-vows-to-fight-violent-extremism-as-attorney-general.

[64] Ken Thomas & Sabrina Siddiqui, *Biden Says Rioters Who Stormed Capitol Were Domestic Terrorists*, WALL ST. J. (Jan. 7, 2021, 8:40 PM), https://www.wsj.com/articles/biden-says-mob-that-stormed-capitol-were-domestic-terrorists-11610046962?redirect=amp.

[65] *Id.*

incoming administration that it needs more FBI and Homeland Security officers, and more domestic terrorism authority.[66]

It may be tempting for progressives to support an expansion of domestic terrorism policy in response to the far right. However, we must remember that the FBI has had these powers and abused them for decades. It has repeatedly ignored warnings about right-wing violence and instead defended its focus on nonviolent social protesters, namely, animal rights and environmental activists.

Historically, the FBI was founded as an institution to target the left and has been at the forefront of efforts to oppose every major progressive social movement of our time.

More broadly we need to understand that the very nature of political repression, "counterterrorism," or any coordinated campaign by the state and industry will *always* be used disproportionately against the left.

Carceral logic will never be used by the state to advance social justice, and it certainly will not be used to target the far right. A carceral civil rights movement – one that calls for more police, more prisons, more terrorism powers, all the while trusting the state to *only* use its powers to target *others*, whether it is the animal rights movement or the far right – is only building its own gallows.

Imagining animal and environmental activists as a civil rights movement is not just a theoretical discussion of the nature of social change, and it is not a plea for assistance or ideological cohesion. This is a warning.

If we continue to ignore the precedent-setting draconian attacks on the animal rights and environment movements, and how they are sentinel species for other social movements challenging state and corporate power, then it will be at the shared peril of human and animal rights alike.

[66] Mike Levine, *Domestic Terrorism and Hate Exploded in 2020. Here's What the Biden Administration Must Do*, ABC News (Dec. 29, 2020, 4:00 AM), https://abcnews.go.com/US/domestic-terrorism-hate-exploded-2020-biden-administration/story?id=74604589.

21

Abolition

Thinking beyond Carceral Logics

Lori Gruen

During the afternoon of April 20, 2021, people across the United States were tensely waiting to learn what the Minneapolis jury would decide in the murder trial of former police officer Derek Chauvin. Chauvin was being tried for killing George Floyd after pressing his knee into the back of Floyd's neck for nine minutes and twenty-nine seconds while he was facedown on the pavement. Due to the COVID-19 pandemic, a trial that would only have been witnessed by family and other locals was televised nationally and reported on every night in great detail. After millions watched Chauvin kill George Floyd on video, taken by teenage witness Darnella Frazier, Black Lives Matter protests and calls to abolish and defund the police occurred across the country, sometimes met with police and vigilante violence.

As the judge read out the verdicts on the three charges against Chauvin, second-degree murder – guilty; third-degree murder – guilty; and second-degree manslaughter – guilty, there was a collective national sigh of relief. But the reaction was also more emotional. Television news cut away from regularly scheduled programming to broadcast some of the reactions. The Congressional Black Caucus members were shown huddled together looking at their phones and other devices, nodding and hugging as they listened to the verdicts. Citizens outside the courthouse, also watching on their phones, cheered. Fists were raised high, many people looked up to the heavens in gratitude, people held each other, and some broke down in tears.

It is undeniable that many people felt deeply gratified by the carceral response to Chauvin's callous cruelty. There is a long list of police officers who have not been arrested, tried, and convicted of horrible crimes against Black people, and this history certainly contributed to the anxiety that people felt about whether "justice would be served" in the killing of George Floyd. Interestingly, almost immediately after the verdict was announced, many argued that this did not amount to "justice" but rather "accountability." Minnesota's attorney-general, Keith Ellison, who led the prosecution of Chauvin, said "I would not call today's verdict 'justice' because justice implies true restoration."[1] President Joe Biden, noted that:

> such a verdict is also much too rare. . .[I]t seems like it took a unique and extraordinary convergence of factors: a brave young woman with a smartphone camera; a crowd that was traumatized – traumatized witnesses; a murder that lasted almost 10 minutes in broad daylight for, ultimately, the whole world to see; officers standing up and testifying against a fellow officer instead of just closing ranks, which should be commended; a jury who heard the evidence, carried out their civic duty in the midst of an extraordinary moment, under extraordinary pressure. For so many, it feels like it took all of that for the judicial system to deliver. . .basic accountability.[2]

While the jury returned a guilty verdict, holding Chauvin legally accountable, genuine accountability doesn't seem to capture what resulted from convicting Chauvin. As abolitionist Danielle Sered has argued,

> Accountability requires five key elements: (1) acknowledging responsibility for one's actions; (2) acknowledging the impact of one's actions on others; (3) expressing genuine remorse; (4) taking actions to repair the harm to the degree possible, and guided when feasible by the people harmed; and (5) no longer committing similar harm.[3]

Connie Burk has suggested that, "Accountability is not something that happens to bad people. Accountability is a human skill. It is a skill that each of us must commit to developing as an internal resource for recognizing and redressing the harms we have caused to ourselves and others."[4] In this more robust sense, Chauvin's verdict is not accountability, it is not justice, it is a legal judgment of wrongdoing that will lead to his incapacitation.[5]

The desire to punish wrongdoers through courts and prisons motivates "tough on crime" policies. Citizens often feel that the violence they have suffered needs to be publicly recognized, and the courts become the place for that recognition. This

[1] Vanessa Romo, *Minnesota Attorney General Calls Chauvin Guilty Verdict "First Step" toward Justice*, NPR (Apr. 20, 2021, 6:31 PM), https://www.npr.org/sections/trial-over-killing-of-george-floyd/2021/04/20/989284035/minnesota-attorney-general-calls-chauvin-guilty-verdict-first-step-in-justice.

[2] *Remarks by President Biden on the Verdict in the Derek Chauvin Trial for the Death of George Floyd*, The White House (Apr. 20, 2021, 7:11 PM), https://www.whitehouse.gov/briefing-room/speeches-remarks/2021/04/20/remarks-by-president-biden-on-the-verdict-in-the-derek-chauvin-trial-for-the-death-of-george-floyd/.

[3] Danielle Sered, Until We Reckon, 96 (2019).

[4] Connie Burk, *Think. Re-think. Accountable Communities*, in The Revolution Starts at Home: Confronting Intimate Violence within Activist Communities, 267 (Ching-In Chan, Jai Dulani, & Leah Lakshmi Piepsna-Samarasinha, eds., 2016).

[5] Indeed, it is quite likely that Chauvin doesn't see himself as accountable, and as of this writing it seems that he is appealing the conviction.

desire for court recognition of violence done to animals is becoming more prominent in the realm of animal law.[6]

One example is from the state I live in, Connecticut. In 2012, a twenty-two-year-old man, Alex Wullaert, strangled his dog, Desmond, after Desmond peed on him and bit him. He then dumped Desmond's body, which was later found and reported. Desmond was microchipped, and that is how Wullaert was located. There were a number of hearings and continuances, and at each one, animal activists protested outside the court seeking the maximum sentence, which could have been five years in prison. Wullaert was ultimately sentenced to a rehabilitation program and the activists were furious. Some yelled, some cried. They began organizing for harsher penalties, and in 2016, then-Governor Malloy enacted "Desmond's Law," the first law in the country that allows animal advocates to testify in animal cruelty cases. Proponents of the law have suggested that they don't see the law as promoting increased carceral responses to animal abuse,[7] but the motivation for the law was to punish wrongdoers that harm animals like Desmond, and state punishment is carceral. Representative Diana Urban who sponsored the law, makes this carceral response explicit – the reason she sponsored the animal advocates law was to see higher sentences.[8] Two years after the law was passed, Robin Cannamela, the president of the group that rallied around Desmond's Law, known as "Desmond's Army" said that the law is making an impact. "Since Desmond's Law, we have seen a significant increase in jail time."[9]

The heinousness of the murder of George Floyd, the horrible cruelty of Desmond's demise, and the tragedies that have befallen so many others due to senseless violence and death generate visceral, often understandable, demands for strong punitive state action. But as the Chauvin and Wullaert verdicts show, *justice* is rarely, if ever, what the legal system can produce. The idea of "justice" has deep philosophical roots, and while an easy way to understand justice is to reduce it to whatever it is that the "justice system" metes out, it is a more nuanced notion. There are many different ways to understand justice – as a virtue, as a feature of institutions or whole societies, as an ideal. Justice can be applied to the distribution of goods in a society, justice can be applied to policies that impact disadvantaged groups, justice can be thought of as a way of addressing systematic discrimination. I don't have space in this chapter to argue about what the best conception of justice is,[10] but for present purposes, I will understand justice as a type of empathetic fairness; justice is

6 See Justin Marceau for a careful, in-depth discussion. Justin Marceau, Beyond Cages (2019).

7 Jessica Rubin, *Desmond's Law: Early Impressions of Connecticut's Court Advocate Program for Animal Cruelty Cases*, 134 Harvard Law Review.

8 Marceau, *supra* note 6, at 79.

9 Michelle Tuccitto Sullo, *Animal Advocates Help to Bring Justice for Abused Cats & Dogs*, New Haven Register (Jan. 27, 2019, 1:23 PM) https://www.nhregister.com/news/article/Animal-advocates-help-to-bring-justice-for-abused-13565197.php.

10 Two good resources: John Rawls, Justice as Fairness: A restatement (2001); and David Miller, *Justice*, The Stanford Encyclopedia of Philosophy (2017).

sensitive to the ways in which inequality of resources and opportunities limit what is fair to demand of others. Justice, in the variety of ways it is understood, tends to provide one with what they are due, and I agree, if this is understood in the actual contexts in which people live.[11] In most instances, the criminal "justice" system isn't addressing justice at all, rather as we see in the judgment against Chauvin, it is punishment, even vengeance, that, perhaps unwittingly, motivates the ongoing commitment to an imperfect, undemocratic carceral system that has caused so many men, women, and children to suffer and die in prison.

In this chapter I will discuss prison abolition as presenting both a critique of and an alternative to the criminal legal system. I will first present a brief history of the idea and practice of abolition in its various forms. I will then address two criticisms that have been made against prison abolition – that it doesn't adequately acknowledge the "victims" of harm and that it is naïve or utopian. I will end by discussing how recent trends in animal law that increase carceral responses to cruelty to animals are wrongheaded and urge those who care about animals, equity, and freedom for all to work toward alternatives to the violence of mass incarceration through a care ethics of abolition.

21.1 FORMS OF ABOLITION

The term "abolition" is best known in the context of opposition to the Atlantic slave trade in which Africans and those of African descent were denied personhood. Early abolitionists were opposed to the violent accumulation of wealth due to forced labor. According to Manisha Sinha, abolitionists, though primarily focused on resisting slavery, had wide reaching concerns. Many early abolitionists

> joined such international radical movements as utopian socialism, feminism, and pacifism and championed Native American, immigrant, and workingmen's rights. Some even anticipated contemporary American scourges, criticizing the criminalization of blackness and the use of capital punishment and force by the state. Abolitionists were the intellectual and political precursors of twentieth-century anticolonial and civil rights activists, debating the nature of society and politics, the relationship between racial inequality and democracy, nation and empire, labor and capital, gender and citizenship.[12]

Abolitionists included those who were enslaved and those recently freed, as well as members of communities that were implicated in the slave trade, including African people, British and Spanish people, and religious people, most notably Quakers. Quaker abolitionists in the United States, including John Woolman and Joshua

[11] In this sense I am speaking of "non-ideal" justice. See: Marcus Arvan, *Nonideal Justice as Nonideal Fairness*, J. Am. Phil. Ass'n 5 (Apr. 30, 2019).

[12] Manisha Sinha, The Slave's Cause: A History of Abolition, 3 (2016).

Evans, traveled the country to speak out against slavery and express "concern for Native Americans, animal abuse, violence and war."[13]

With the abolition of slavery, after the Civil War, many abolitionists were actively reimagining how to bring the ideals of democracy into fuller practice. W.E.B. Dubois, in *Black Reconstruction*, noted that "abolition-democracy" demanded the structural reform of labor, education, and opportunities.[14] It wasn't enough to emancipate Black people from slavery; many envisioned building a free and equal society in which the disadvantages that emerged from the system of slavery were not permanent. But this wasn't to be. The end of Reconstruction and the reimplementation of Black Codes, further perpetuated forms of unfreedom for Black people. For example, they could be prosecuted for not carrying proof of employment, leading to incarceration and with it, forced labor. In the South, "convict leasing" put the growing population of Black prisoners to work. Dubois, quoting from a "Southern white woman" notes:

> In some states where convict labor is sold to the highest bidder the cruel treatment of the helpless human chattel in the hands of guards is such as no tongue can tell nor pen picture. Prison inspectors find convicts herded together, irrespective of age; confined at night in shackles; housed sometimes, as has been found, in old box cars; packed almost as closely as sardines in a box. During the day all are worked under armed guards, who stand ready to shoot down any who may attempt to escape from this hell upon earth-the modern American Bastille. Should one escape, the bloodhounds, trained for the purpose, are put upon his track, and the chances are that he will be brought back, severely flogged and put in double shackles, or worse.[15]

As the shocking conditions of convict leasing became widely known, pressure built to end the practice and one by one Southern states didn't renew or initiate leases. Alabama was the final state to end convict leasing in 1928. The "abolition" of convict leasing, like the "abolition" of slavery, didn't end the extraction of uncompensated labor from Black people. As has been popularized in Ava DuVernay's 2016 film *13th*, the exploitation of prisoners as laborers, legally written into the US Constitution, continues to this day; incarcerated workers receive, on average, fourteen cents/hour at the low end and one dollar and forty-one cents/hour at the high end.[16]

Not long after the publication of George Jackson's *Soledad Brother*, and his death trying to escape prison, Quaker prison abolitionists, led by Fay Honey Knopp, published *Instead of Prisons* in 1976. The first chapter in the book lists quotations from lawyers, judges, prisoners, those employed or formerly employed by prisons,

[13] *Id.* at 20.

[14] W.E.B. Dubois, Black Reconstruction in America (First published in 1935; Free Press Ed. 1998).

[15] *Id.* at 698.

[16] Wendy Sawyer, *How Much Do Incarcerated People Earn in Each State?*, Prison Policy Initiative (Apr. 10, 2017)https://www.prisonpolicy.org/blog/2017/04/10/wages/.

authors, activists, and others who all condemn prisons. For example, in the minutes for the 1870 Congress of the American Prison Association, it is reported that "Judge Carter, of Ohio, avowed himself a radical on prison discipline. He favored the abolishment of prisons, and the use of greater efforts for the prevention of crime."[17] In 1938, Columbia University professor Frank Tannenbaum, in his book *Crime and the Community* wrote: "We must destroy the prison, root and branch. That will not solve our problem, but it will be a good beginning. . .Let us substitute something. Almost anything will be an improvement. It cannot be worse. It cannot be more brutal and more useless." Writing in the *New York Times Magazine* on January 30, 1955, the former head of the psychiatric clinic at Sing Sing prison wrote: "We profess to rely upon the prison for our safety; yet it is directly responsible for much of the damage that society suffers at the hands of offenders. On the basis of my own experience, I am convinced that prisons must be abolished."[18] In some ways calls for abolition, of slavery, of convict leasing, and of prisons are continuous.

Between 1990 and 2005, the number of state and federal prisons rose 43 percent. As the prison boom was growing in California, Ruthie Gilmore, Angela Davis, and others formed the abolitionist organization Critical Resistance to oppose what they called the prison-industrial complex (PIC).[19] But calls for prison abolition began before the era of mass incarceration.[20]

"Abolition" has also been invoked in the animal protection/liberation movement. Activists have demanded that we "abolish zoos" or "abolish fur." Animal law professor and activist Gary Francione has developed a perspective on animal rights that he calls "the abolitionist approach."[21] This approach calls for the abolition of all animal exploitation. In particular, the abolitionist approach acknowledges that other animals have one right: the basic right not to be treated as the property of others. And it is on the basis of recognition of this right "that we must abolish, and not merely regulate, institutionalized animal exploitation – because it assumes that animals are the property of humans." In calling themselves abolitionists, and demanding the right not to see animals as property, the abolitionists in the animal

[17] From the Minutes of the 1870 Congress of theAmerican Prison Association/ American Correctional Association as quoted FAY KNOPP & JON REGIER, EDS, INSTEAD OF PRISONS: A HANDBOOK FOR ABOLITIONISTS, (eds.), 1976.

[18] Ralph S. Banay, *Should Prisons Be Abolished? An Expert Says They Do Not Cure Crime, and Argues That the Real Problem Is Not One of Keeping Criminals In, but of Keeping Them Out.*, N.Y. TIMES, 13 (Jan. 30, 1955).

[19] http://criticalresistance.org/about/history/. See also ANGELA DAVIS, ARE PRISONS OBSOLETE (2003) and RUTH WILSON GILMORE, GOLDEN GULAG (2007).

[20] Though there isn't a specific "start date" for mass incarceration, the prison population doubled during the Reagan years, from 1981 to 1989 and grew exponentially after the 1994 Crime Bill was passed. Between 1972 and 2009, there was an estimated 700 percent growth in the prison population.

[21] See Gary L. Francione, *The Six Principles of the Abolitionist Approach to Animal Rights*, ANIMAL RIGHTS: THE ABOLITIONIST APPROACH https:/www.abolitionistapproach.com/about/the-six-principles-of-the-abolitionist-approach-to-animal-rights/.

movement are drawing a parallel between the treatment of animals and the institution of racial slavery.

But, unlike the seeming continuities between the abolition of slavery and the abolition of prisons, there are dangers associated with using abolitionist language in the animal context. Any project that makes comparisons between people and animals that fails, as Claire Jean Kim writes, to question "the difference between slave and animal…how recognition of this difference was built into law and practice…and how this shaped the forms of violence and coercion inflicted upon slaves and animals, respectively"[22] is flawed. Animal abolitionist projects (and this goes beyond just Francione's abolitionist approach, including some of PETA's campaigns and centrally, in the legal arena, the work of the Nonhuman Rights Project) tend to erase the specific harms of slavery on the enslaved people, perhaps unwittingly, recasting the slave as an animal or property, as a way of challenging property status.

> To keep animals center stage, animal abolition relentlessly displaces the issue of black oppression, deflecting attention from the specificity of the slave's status then, and mystifying the question of the Black person's status now. According to animal abolition's narrative of racial temporality, Black people at some point (variously, Emancipation, Reconstruction, the civil rights movement) moved demonstrably from slavery to freedom, from the outside in, from abjection to inclusion.[23]

The animal abolitionists seem to suggest that with the end of slavery, that is, no longer categorizing Black people as property, the institutions of anti-blackness and the afterlives of slavery cease to be as problematic, making animal freedom the next frontier.[24] Put differently, legally changing the status of Black people from property to persons did not accomplish for Black people the imagined freedom that animal abolitionists hope to bring about for animals.

There is a way of imagining animal abolitionism that does not succumb to the dangers of false comparisons, erasure, and imagined teleological successes toward Black freedom. The way to do this is to see the work against anti-blackness and against animal exploitation as part of the same abolitionist project. Black liberation and animal liberation can better see the structures of power they are independently resisting and better imagine a more just world by critically engaging with the white "humanist" assumptions at the heart of hierarchies of worth. Abolition in the prison

[22] Claire Jean Kim, *Abolition* 23 in Critical Terms for Animal Studies, (Lori Gruen ed., 2018).

[23] *Id.* at 18.

[24] Kim cites Steven Best,who makes this point quite vivid, "Having recognized the illogical and unjustifiable rationales used to oppress [Black people], women, and other disadvantages groups, society is beginning to grasp that speciesism is another unsubstantiated form of oppression and discrimination." *Id.* at 23. Of course, the oppression of Black people, including Black women, is rationalized in quite distinct ways from the oppression of other groups, given that Black people have a unique history and, some would argue, distinct ontological status.

context is a particularly apt place to locate the critical links between dehumanization and deanimalization. As Lisa Guenther writes: "intercorporeal relations are vital for both human and nonhuman animals…The problem with intensive confinement is not just that it treats human prisoners like animals, but that it fails to treat them like animals, where animals are understood as living beings whose corporeal and intercorporeal relations with other living beings"[25] are crucial for having a meaningful life.

21.2 REACTIONS TO PRISON ABOLITION

Abolition evokes a variety of reactions ranging from incredulity and disdain to curiosity and excitement. These reactions also vary depending on audience and the context in which the topic of prison abolition is being raised. When questions about alternatives to prisons are posed that don't mention the word "abolition" there appears to be tremendous support among the public. For example, the ACLU conducted a survey in 2017 that found that 61 percent of Americans believe that people who suffer from drug addiction and commit serious crimes don't belong in prison but should receive treatment.[26] And 87 percent believe that when people with mental health disabilities commit crimes that involve violence, they should be sent to mental health programs where they can receive treatment from professionals.[27] Such strong public support for noncarceral responses to violent crimes are welcome in a country like the United States that, as of this writing, locks up over 2 million people. And as Joy James has noted, abolitionist alternatives to prison are already available for "those with wealth and power: existential whiteness, money or capital and connections to governing elites. Elite 'offenders,' *if* prosecuted and convicted, are largely redirected to therapy, counseling, drug treatment and expensive residential treatment centers."[28]

Though some abolitionist alternatives to incarceration are generally accepted and already in practice for a privileged few, more often than not, people have the mistaken view that abolitionists would like to see the immediate closing of all prisons. Perhaps that is what some abolitionists imagine, like the immediate end to slavery and the immediate end to killing animals for fur, but for the most part what abolitionists want is to immediately end our acceptance of punitive responses to crime and begin imagining alternatives. In a society like ours, organized by profound inequality, releasing people who have nothing into a world in which

[25] Lisa Guenther, Solitary Confinement: Social Death and Its Afterlives (2013).

[26] *91 Percent of Americans Support Criminal Justice Reform, ACLU Polling Finds*, ACLU (Nov. 16, 2017) https://www.aclu.org/press-releases/91-percent-americans-support-criminal-justice-reform-aclu-polling-finds.

[27] *Id.*

[28] Joy James, *The Alchemy of Abolitionisms*, Foreword in The Routledge International Handbook of Penal Abolition (Michael J. Coyle & David Scott eds., 2021).

resources for reentry are absent, has the likelihood to create more harm. This is one of the reasons why abolitionists work to develop more just and meaningful social policy that will help support community needs and build alternative, humane institutions. These efforts involve promoting "nonreformist reforms" that allow for the development of policies and practices that minimize harms, while not contributing to or reinforcing the harmful prison system.[29]

There are a number of examples of reform efforts that are consistent with the ultimate goal of prison abolition; these include ending solitary confinement and the death penalty, working to stop the construction of new prisons and the creation of more beds to fill, fighting the expansion of surveillance, providing educational opportunities for incarcerated people, mutual aid for communities, and more. As Mariame Kaba suggests, nonreformist reforms are "those measures that reduce the power of an oppressive system while illuminating the system's inability to solve the crises it creates."[30] Calls for more humane treatment, better training for police, and releasing "nonviolent" offenders are reforms that don't challenge the system and would be rejected by most abolitionists as they will simply make the current cruel system a bit more tolerable. Abolitionists, while working to improve everyone's health and safety, ultimately hope to eliminate not just prisons that have "come to seem natural and inevitable,"[31] but to expand our imaginations to allow us to envision a more caring, just society.

21.2.1 *What about "victims"?*

One of the challenging questions that abolitionists are often asked is, "Why focus on freeing the perpetrators of harm rather on supporting the victims who were harmed?" This is an important question, but it is best not to think of the focus of abolitionist concern as either/or – many of those who commit crimes are themselves victims. The question is also probably better posed to the current criminal system.

[29] There are a of myriad harms that prisons cause, but here is a brief indication of some of them written by five incarcerated men sentenced to a combination of 225 years in a maximum-security prison:

> After our initial humiliation upon being strip searched when we enter prison, we lose all control of our lives. We will eat, bathe, and shave when told. We will be expected to follow direct orders, no matter how absurd or unfair. Noncompliance will be met with force...the depressive environment tends to stifle intellectual curiosity. We simply become too tired and sullen to engage in intellectual pursuits. Simply put, we dwell in our cells, we are not actively using our minds, and in a very real sense, we are thus losing our minds. The loneliness caused by prisons in general and prison cells in particular is exacerbated by the loss of intimacy and the loving touch of friends and family"

John Bryant, James Davis, David Haywood, Clyde Meikle, Andre Pierce, *Life Behind Bars* in Ethics of Captivity 105 (Lori Gruen ed., 2014).

[30] Mariame Kaba, et al., *What Abolitionists Do*, Jacobin Magazine, Aug. 24, 2017 https://www.jacobinmag.com/2017/08/prison-abolition-reform-mass-incarceration.

[31] Allegra McLeod, *Prison Abolition and Grounded Justice*, 62 UCLA L. Rev. 1156, 1219 (2015).

Many are led to believe that the system of punishment that now exists is designed to elevate the status and claims of victims and that guilty verdicts achieve justice for victims of crime. But as was made glaringly clear in trial of Derek Chauvin, justice for George Floyd and his family was not what the guilty verdicts provided. The carceral system does not and cannot achieve justice for the victims.

I recently witnessed two separate sentence-modification hearings, just a few months apart, for incarcerated men who were students in the prison education program I work with. In both cases, the victims of the crimes, committed over twenty-five years ago, testified and their poignant, painful testimony suggested that they hadn't gotten any relief from the lengthy incarceration of these two men. In fact, these victims seemed to be responding as if the crimes had happened recently, rather than decades ago, and it looked to me that the fact that these two men have spent a combined fifty years in prison had not amounted to "paying a debt" to the victims at all. Indeed, I was struck by how unjust it was not to provide these victims with some form of direct support or care to help them to deal with their pain and loss.

Abolitionists do care about those who are harmed and, through restorative justice work, provide support for those victims. Kaba suggests that in her experiences with restorative justice work, many victims want the harm to be addressed in "a real way" – acknowledgment that they have been hurt, that there was someone who caused their pain, and they want to know that the person took responsibility for the harm, has remorse for doing it, and won't do it again.[32] When, at their sentence modification hearings, the incarcerated men I know took responsibility for the pain they caused, apologized deeply for it, and expressed sincere remorse, it seemed that the adversarial context of the criminal court did not allow the victims to hear or believe what was being said. The system has done very little, if anything at all, to help victims, materially, epistemically, or psychologically even though punishment is often justified by appeals to giving victims what they are due.

Given that human victims are not supported, or even treated well by the carceral system, and that their pain is a cover for the further infliction of pain in the form of imprisonment of those who committed harm, there is something quite perverse about animal lawyers' efforts to elevate the status of harmed animals to "victims" in the criminal legal system. As Justin Marceau highlights "Just as claims about victims' rights in the human context have been used as a political ploy to promote mass incarceration, the claimed interest in protecting animal victims that runs through animal protection discourse is essentially a farce, or more charitably, a misdirection."[33] The state, through the criminal legal system, justifies the infliction of harm on others that would be impermissible if citizens did it to one another, by suggesting that victims deserve punitive responses to crime. But not all victims want to

[32] Kaba, *supra* note 30.

[33] Justin Marceau, *Animals as Victims*, Ariz. L. Rev. (2021)

participate or be complicit in harming others. Many family members of victims protest against the death penalty or sentences that amount to death in prison in favor of mercy, and often they are ridiculed for their nonpunitive beliefs. The victims who do believe long prison sentences for the perpetrators will somehow provide them with peace or relief don't usually find it, and they too suffer without care or support. Elevating animals to "victims" by seeking tough sentences for animal cruelty is likely to lead to equally disappointing results.[34]

That many victims believe that they will get some sort of peace from locking people up for long periods of time, even when they realize that peace never comes, reveals a central problem with the carceral logics of our current punishment system. It perpetuates a myth that punishment is an answer to one's pain and loss. Similarly, when animal lawyers believe that it will be helpful for animals to achieve the status of victim by pushing for tougher sentences for the small percentage of people who can be charged with animal cruelty, they too are caught in a trap of carceral logics that promises something it cannot deliver. Our criminal system is not designed to provide victims with elevated status, peace, satisfaction, or basic respect. It is a system of punishment, not a system that is designed to meet the needs of victims or their advocates. Yet the justification of the criminal punishment system requires that victims believe the myth that they will be protected and have their needs satisfied. In this way, oddly, the criminal system is utopian, that is, the system requires that people imagine that society will be better and that they will be safe when citizens who commit harms are punished.

21.2.2 *Is Abolition "Utopian"?*

While the prison-industrial complex seems to rely on a utopian idea of "justice," critics often focus their anti-utopian critique on abolitionists. Utopian thinking needn't always be "optimistic" or "hopeful" but rather can be thought of as a conceptual vocabulary that sets the ways we think about that which is not right in front of us, that which is yet to come. William Paris writes,

> [U]topias have been attempts to carve an alternate space of life that was sufficiently disconnected from the dominant social order…[U]topia need not concern itself with designing the perfect life. Instead, utopia may take up the task of creating social spaces that allow for deliberation over different ideas about how we might organize our social relations. Utopia is the creation of an alternative public sphere for testing out ideas and disagreements over novel forms of social life.[35]

[34] "Victim" also reduces the complexity of a person or animals' experiences to the harms they have endured, not their relationships, their achievements, their fun, their play, etc.

[35] William Paris (forthcoming in HA: The Journal 2021).

We might think all social theorizing is utopian. And some have argued that the punishment system is indeed utopian.[36] Michael Coyle notes, for example, that "Though undoubtedly to the vast majority of 'criminal justice' scholars the notion of their work as fundamentally utopian would strike them as absurd, there are those who have pointedly recognized how 'criminal justice' is comprehensively utopian." He cites one scholar who argues that we can understand the utopian nature of the criminal system by imagining it as a place where we are delivered to safety from "crime."[37]

Cages, confinement, and captivity are so central to our social imagination that it is challenging to think beyond them, and utopian thinking may help unsettle our imaginations so we can start to expand the horizons of possibility. It's remarkable to me that most of the incarcerated people whom I have worked with think it's easier to imagine being in solidarity with other animals than it is thinking beyond prisons. This shows how ingrained the ideas of prisons and punishment are in our culture. They are, as Angela Davis notes, anchors of our social order.[38] To move beyond carceral logics and their punitive manifestations in practice, we need what Erica Meiner calls for – "a jailbreak of the imagination in order to make the impossible possible."[39]

Utopian thinking can free the imagination from the constraints of the violent, oppressive, and limiting social conditions that currently exist in the United States, but such thinking is aimed not only at some hope for a peaceful future. By imagining otherwise, imagining a world without cells for humans and cages for nonhumans, we are being asked to think in fundamentally different, new ways in response to harm. Abolitionism, as James Foreman, Jr., notes "is the idea that you imagine a world without prisons, and then you work to try to build that world."[40] And abolitionists work around the country trying to build that world, starting in communities, posing very practical demands. Abolitionists are providing mutual aid; working to redirect city budgets to allocate funds in caring, healthful ways; providing support for those who are food-insecure, housing-insecure, and vulnerable to substance use; developing opportunities to support youth; creating community-based harm-reduction programs; working on supporting victims of harm through restorative justice practices and holding those who caused harm accountable; as well as other practical efforts to build a more caring world. And these sorts of community

36 Michael J. Coyle, 2018. *Who Is Mired in Utopia? The Logics of Criminal Justice and Penal Abolition*, 45 Social Justice, 79, 79–116 (2018).

37 *Id.* at 86–87.

38 Angela Davis, *supra* note 19.

39 Mariama Kaba, A *Jailbreak of the Imagination: Seeing Prisons for What They Are and Demanding Transformation*, Truthout (May 3, 2018), https://truthout.org/articles/a-jailbreak-of-the-imagination-seeing-prisons-for-what-they-are-and-demanding-transformation/.

40 Rachel Kushner, *Is Prison Necessary? Ruth Wilson Gilmore Might Change Your Mind*, N.Y. Times, (Apr. 17, 2019), https://www.nytimes.com/2019/04/17/magazine/prison-abolition-ruth-wilson-gilmore.html.

programs cost money, so abolitionists organize and protest to demand that the money pouring into policing and prisons be redirected to some of these efforts building community accountability as a condition for expressions of meaningful, entangled agency.

Abolition in the prison context, like abolition in the context of slavery and animal use, provides a framework for reimagining our own agency, for reenvisioning community, and for reframing justice. There are many people who are currently unable to think beyond the fixed carceral features of modern life. And, of course, there are some who think that it is genuinely a utopian fantasy to think we can do without prisons when there are those who are incorrigibly, irredeemably criminal in our midst. They think we need prisons, if nothing else, for those who are often referred to as the "dangerous few." But, as Kaba writes, "the carceral system has always used sensationalized cases and the specter of unthinkable harm to create new mechanisms of disposability."[41] If there are irredeemably violent people out there, chances are slight that they will be apprehended, given historical records. Perhaps they are among us, but it is utopian to imagine our system will be able to find all of them. Second, and more importantly, there are very few institutions, particularly expensive and inhumane institutions like prison, that can be justified by appeal to the handful of people that it might make us happier imagining are not among us. The vast suffering that is not just caused but perpetuated by prisons can't possibly be justified by fears of the "dangerous few." They become blocks or diversions from imagining genuinely just social arrangements.

21.3 A CARE ETHICS OF ABOLITION

Allegra McCleod, in her discussion of developing a prison abolitionist ethic, writes:

> an abolitionist ethic recognizes that even if a person is so awful in her violence that the threat she poses must be forcibly contained, this course of action ought to be undertaken with moral conflict, circumspection, and even shame, as a choice of the lesser of two evils, rather than as an achievement of justice...Even when confronting the dangerous few, on an abolitionist account, justice is not meaningfully achieved by caging, degrading, or even more humanely confining, the person who assaulted the vulnerable among us.[42]

Protecting the vulnerable in communities, particularly those who are not in any way a part of potentially dangerous or violent activities, is a very real ethical concern that abolitionists must address. In the ethics literature, there is a division made between "an ethics of justice" and "an ethics of care," where the former focuses on the application of abstract principles and the latter is concerned with making our social

[41] Kaba, *supra* note 39.
[42] McCleod, *supra* note 31, at 1171.

as well as personal relationships better. Unfortunately, this distinction, like so many others, has led many theorists to think that care is opposed to justice, when in fact, an ethics of care is very much concerned about justice, but has a different way of framing the contexts and conditions under which justice is to be achieved. An ethics of care focuses on the particularities of caring relationships, informed by differences in context, as well as the racial, economic, ethnic, cultural, and differently gendered experiences of individuals and those they care for in community. An ethics of care, rather than an ethics of justice, is better suited to be the basis for an abolitionist ethics.

I've written elsewhere about the ways that the different focus of these ethical orientations matter not just for actions and policies but also for understanding ethical problems.[43] An ethics of justice does not attend to the specifics of each individual situation, much like the legal system has to abstract from contexts and particularity in its deployment of impartial reason. An ethics of justice springs from a picture of individuals that exist outside of their relationships and seeks to ignore the community connections that individuals have, unless, for example, it is to the others who were part of criminal activity.

We turn to ethical theories in conditions of conflict, to gain insights into how we might find solutions to hard social and political problems. An ethic of care has to address situations of conflict, of course, but also is concerned with how people come to see a moral problem as a problem in the first place and works to develop moral imagination not only as a way to reframe problems, but also as a way to move toward more just and sustainable solutions. In the exercise of moral imagination, care ethics is attentive to differences in power and works to provide analyses of the economic, political, racial, gendered, as well as the cultural underpinnings of systems of exploitation, commodification, and cruelty. By analyzing the specific contexts in which systems of power operate, care ethics is concerned about the larger structures that allow or contribute to injustice. Care ethics also directs our attention to the specific beings that are involved in the conflicts, and in so doing has helped reframe concerns about other animals. Care ethics encourages the development of empathy and compassion for all, no matter what species they belong to or what mistakes they have made.

One of the incarcerated students in an ethics class in the maximum-security men's prison where I teach wrote his final paper about an ethics of care and its value in helping us rethink mass incarceration. I was struck by the example he used in opening his paper:

> I was in the prison recreational yard with about ten other prisoners when a bird landed in the yard some distance away from us. One of the prisoners walked over to the bird (that turned out to be a baby bird) who tried to fly away but could not.

[43] Lori Gruen, Entangled Empathy (2015).

> Upon noticing the bird's trouble the prisoner picked the bird up and tried to give it the lift it might have needed. The bird flapped its wings to no avail and crashed into a wall. Before long we had to leave and when we did the bird was still stuck in the yard.
>
> The next morning the baby bird was still in the yard. This time no one tried to help the bird because we did not want to see it smash the wall again. So we went about our normal activities until someone pointed out that another bird had just entered the yard. The prisoner who tried to help the baby bird the day before walked toward the two birds and realized that the other bird had brought a worm for the baby bird. An enthused conversation ensued about the mother bird bringing the worm for her child. I concluded that the mother was acting because she cared for her child.[44]

Animals, including human animals, have deep capacities for care. Of course, those incarcerated share those capacities and may engage in care for other animals that may have entered the prison, and of course, they care for each other when they are able to admit it.[45] Care is a capacity that has to be nurtured, or cared for, and the criminal punishment system not only is detached from care, but promotes that sort of detachment. An abolition ethic would involve reimagining our caring relations and encourage and deepen them. It also requires an analysis of the impacts of failures of care, both before carceral solutions are sought when harms are committed and in critiquing the dehumanizing and deanimalizing conditions that exist in prisons.

An abolitionist ethic of care would have us rethink key ethical concepts like responsibility and deservingness. A care ethic can serve as a normative framework for seeing one way that state punishment is unethical because it treats some people as deserving less care. Although David Boonin doesn't identify as a care ethicist, his argument against punishment is compatible with it. He argues that "punishment involves the state's intentionally harming some of its citizens, and it involves treating the line between those who break the law and those who do not as justifying treating people on one side in ways that it would not treat those on the other."[46] One can hear echoes of childhood admonishments here – "two wrongs don't make a right." Of course, there are important considerations of context that need to be attended to here, and care ethics attempts to consider a variety of particularities about situations when making a determination of what is the right thing to do. In addition, when

[44] Final Paper by Matt Abraham, Spring 2017.

[45] Reginald Dwayne Betts writes powerfully about this.

> We are taught not to admit this, but I realize that when I met Keese, for first time in a long while I found someone that cared about me. Call it naive, but Keese and I decided that we might trust each other, even in that strange unsettling place where we met, razor wire surrounding us, circumscribing our freedom.

Reginald D. Betts and Lori Gruen, *Are Prisons Permissible? Increasing Social Visibility of the Experiences of Incarcerated People*, Philosophical Topics (forthcoming 2022).

[46] David Boonin, The Problem of Punishment (2008).

someone who has "done wrong" and committed harm is seen through a caring lens, and that person responds to being seen in this way, many possibilities are opened.

As I mentioned earlier, often those who commit crimes are victims themselves. They probably don't care for those they harmed when they harmed them, but they also may not care for themselves. An abolitionist ethic of care can help both victims and those who caused harm reframe their experiences. Part of the solution to seemingly intractable conflicts is to care for oneself, in relations of respect and self-respect with others. As Sarah Ahmed notes, the "work [of] self-care is about the creation of community, fragile communities, assembled out of the experiences of being shattered. We reassemble ourselves through the ordinary, everyday and often painstaking work of looking after ourselves; looking after each other."[47] An ethics of care is not meant to be a paternalistic intervention, where care covers over pity or some equally contemptuous attitude, but rather it is an ethics that works to create the conditions in which caring for oneself and for others are developed and practiced. It is restorative and transformative work.

An abolition ethic of care for other animals would not endorse carceral solutions to animal cruelty. Animal lawyers decry the failure of the courts to take seriously violations of animal cruelty laws, given that such crimes are often not prosecuted and when they are, sentencing usually doesn't involve incarceration. Developing an abolitionists ethics of care may have more positive impact for animals. Often, when people are exposed to caring, empathetic ways of perceiving other animals, when they come to understand animals as sensitive, complex, relational beings who feel physical pain but also suffer when they are kept in cages or when their psychological well-being isn't promoted,[48] they change their attitudes. Accelerated rehabilitation, the sentence that Alex Wullaert received after killing Desmond, rather than being rejected, could be a place to start. One can imagine requiring participation in an animal cruelty prevention and education program as a "nonreformist" reform, if the program involves serious community work, rather that just filling in online forms after watching videos about animals. Animal lawyers who seek to promote greater awareness of the plight of animals may wish to direct their attention to the content of such programs, helping to develop a required curriculum that is grounded in an ethics of care. Someone who was fatally cruel to an animal may not do such a thing again, but they may not have changed their attitudes about their relationships to other animals (and it isn't at all clear that going to prison would do that either). Developing empathetic, caring attitudes toward other animals, other people, and oneself may very well go a long way toward elevating the status of animals and preventing crimes against them.

[47] Sarah Ahmed, *Selfcare as Warfare*, Feminist Killjoys (Aug. 25, 2014), https://feministkilljoys.com/2014/08/25/selfcare-as-warfare/.

[48] Marc Beckoff & Jessica Pierce, Wild Justice: The Moral Lives of Animals (2010).

Carceral responses to cruel assaults on others, whether human or nonhuman, are understandable yet misguided attempts to try to bring about some sort of justice. As I've argued here, there are alternatives to this system that inflict more harm and do very little to fundamentally change people's attitudes toward causing harm. Abolitionists have been working to develop ways of reimagining our relationships and our responses to harm that don't involve punitive action by the state. An abolitionist ethic of care is a promising area for revaluing those who are harmed, those who cause harm, and the broader community who are impacted not just by the pain of harms that have been committed, but by the harms that are inflicted by the state in their names. Empathetic reimagining our carceral institutions and our anthropocentric attitudes is crucially needed to promote freedom and flourishing.[49]

[49] I'd like to thank Jay Bernstein, Reginald Dwayne Betts, Alice Crary, David Haywood, Justin Marceau, Andre Pierce, and Sitar Terrass-Shah for stimulating comments/conversations. They don't share my views, but they informed them directly or indirectly.

Index

For EU product safety concerns, contact us at Calle de José Abascal, 56–1°,
28003 Madrid, Spain or eugpsr@cambridge.org.

www.ingramcontent.com/pod-product-compliance
Ingram Content Group UK Ltd.
Pitfield, Milton Keynes, MK11 3LW, UK
UKHW022301171225
466163UK00008B/426
9781108843584